About
the
Author

Bell Gale Chevigny believes,
"Nineteenth-century literature
can shed light on the
origins of contemporary problems
and on efforts made then and
now to analyze and resolve them.
But it will do so only
when approaches to established
writers are altered and
when significant other figures
become well-known."
Her brilliant study of Margaret
Fuller will strengthen the
case for the inclusion of Fuller
in American literature courses.

Chevigny teaches literature
at the State University of New
York, College at Purchase,
and has previously taught at
Sarah Lawrence College, Queens
College, and the Mount Vernon
Cooperative College Center.
She edited a volume of criticism
on Beckett's *Endgame* and published
an essay on Hopkins for
Victorian Literature. She is
the author of numerous articles
and book reviews that have
appeared in the *Village Voice,*
Commentary, Book Week, the *New*
Republic, University Review, Signs,
and *Women's Studies*. She lives
in Manhattan with her husband
and two daughters.

In the chamber
of death, I prayed
in very early years,
"Give me truth;
cheat me by no illusion."
O, the granting of
this prayer is
sometimes terrible to me!
I walk over the
burning ploughshares,
and they sear
my feet. Yet nothing but
the truth will do.

—*Margaret Fuller,*
Memoirs, I, 303

Bell Gale Chevigny

The Woman and the Myth

Margaret Fuller's Life and Writings

THE FEMINIST
PRESS

Library of Congress Cataloging in Publication Data:

Chevigny, Bell Gale.
    The woman and the myth: Margaret Fuller's life and writings.

    Includes a selection of writings by M. Fuller.
    Includes bibliographical references.

    1. Ossoli, Sarah Margaret Fuller, marchesa d', 1810-1850.
2. Woman—Social and moral questions. I. Ossoli, Sarah
Margaret Fuller, marchesa d', 1810-1850. The woman and the
myth. 1976. II. Title.

PS2506.C48   818'.3'09[B]   76-19030   ISBN 0-912670-43-6

Art Director/Designer: Susan Trowbridge
Assistants: Barbara Gore, Mary Mulrooney

This book was typeset in Press Roman by O.B.U., New York,
New York, with Caslon and Palatino heads supplied by
Automated Composition Service, Inc., Lancaster, Pennsylvania.
It was printed on 60# offset by R.R. Donnelley & Sons Company,
Chicago, Illinois.

The Feminist Press gratefully acknowledges the Schlesinger
Library, Radcliffe College, for permission to reproduce
the photo of Margaret Fuller used on the cover.

First edition

For
my
parents,

and
Paul,
Katy,
and
Blue

TABLE OF CONTENTS

Part II

The Friend   65

CONTEMPORARIES ON FULLER

FULLER'S WRITINGS

Part III

Part IV

The Feminist

CONTEMPORARIES ON FULLER

FULLER'S WRITINGS

Part V

Part VI

The Woman and the Myth

*Margaret Fuller's
Life and Writings*

INTRODUCTION

In the hundred and twenty-six years since her death Margaret Fuller has been neither forgotten nor understood. In American Studies she is generally recalled as a handmaiden to major talents, a sole female figure in the frieze of minor Transcendentalists, necessarily blue-stockinged because she edited *The Dial*, their literary magazine. There is something quaintly outrageous too in her remembrance, coming from the uses Hawthorne and James made of her in some of their colorful, pretentious, or daring female characters. More recently Fuller is recalled in women's-history surveys as author of one of the first book-length tracts on the condition of American women or inventor of consciousness-raising groups in her Conversations for women.

But whether our point of departure is the American Renaissance or feminism, the most cursory study of her life and work is surprising and provocative. Looking at her as a Transcendentalist, we find that her extraordinary erudition and articulate originality were widely recognized and honored by publication of her work and her inclusion in virtually any intellectual circle she chose. Yet we learn that this privilege did not fully satisfy her. Indeed, as Emerson wrote, with penetrating candor, she caused them all "some uneasiness, as if this athletic soul craved an atmosphere larger than it found." [1] For Margaret Fuller had a driving and adventurous temperament which led her to travel west to write about the Indians and the frontier settlements and later to become the *New York Tribune*'s first female reporter. Finally, this centrifugal restlessness carried her to Europe, where, in the last four years of her life, she became a close friend of controversial figures (George Sand, Adam Mickiewicz, and Giuseppe Mazzini among them), a skillful analyst and propagandist of the Italian revolution of 1848, a director of a hospital for the wounded in Rome, the lover of a partisan, and a mother. Returning with this family, she died

1

at forty in a shipwreck only fifty yards from American shore. Our interest deepens if we are able to see, beneath these almost melodramatic events, how her writing and her life itself in Europe offered a far-reaching criticism of the Transcendentalism from which she had sprung.

As a feminist too she may surprise us. For Fuller experienced feminism as a part of her growth, not as an end in itself. She engaged in her most concentrated feminist activity—conducting the Conversations and writing *Woman in the Nineteenth Century*—at the time that she was liberating herself from the circumscribed intellectual life of New England. Psychologically, Fuller's feminist activity supported her as she claimed for herself greater freedom than probably any woman of her class and generation in America enjoyed. Intellectually, her feminism was a way station, an early exercise in social criticism which led her to live out a much more comprehensive critique of American values. While her concern for women and their rights remained alive in her last years, it engrossed her less than it had, for it was translated into other terms. On the one hand it expanded to a concern for all oppressed people, on the other it contracted into the need—directly, without theory, and alone—to complete her own freedom.

Today we can understand Margaret Fuller's life and work as a paradigm both of the problems Americans had in developing political or social ideas and of the problematic position of middle-class American women. One object of this book is to attend more than others have done to the evolution of Fuller's political and social thought, exploring the dynamics that moved her through idealism to a critical or radical realism. [2] As an idealist, Fuller concentrated on the perfection of herself and those around her and on living in terms of universal and timeless values. Idealism made her interest in society incidental, discontinuous, and always abstract. As a realist, Fuller concentrated on specific historical and material conditions as they shaped society; her realism became radical or critical when she identified social facts and forces concealed by national institutions and ideology and called for responsive action and policy. Radical realism indirectly fed her personal development as no direct self-culture had done, but self-culture was no longer a primary objective. The seeds of a radical realism were always there, but they did not grow until she left New England and, eventually, America. In part, they grew because of differences in the kinds of experience and thought available to her in America and in Europe.

A second object requires that we reverse the usual practice of seeing Margaret Fuller as a fascinating exception to the condition of American women of her time. Much made Fuller unusual: the complexity of her personality (at once flamboyant and tormented), her driving energy, the versatility of her talents, the range of her opportunities, the many stages of her development, and, above all, her skill and courage in naming her feelings, speaking her mind. But these qualities are most interesting for what they reveal about the feelings of ordinary American women of her class: their restlessness, ambitions, and frustrations. What *was* extraordinary about Fuller was the relative success she had in resolving these feelings. From this perspective her life has the mythic quality of a woman who lived two lives or who died and returned a few generations later to complete her life with a distinctly modernized sensibility. But it was space, not time, that made the difference. For in Italy she acted out her character, in her words—taking a lover and joining the revolution—as she had not been able to do, either politically or privately, in America.

In the first half of the nineteenth century the problem of an American woman who wanted to develop all her faculties and turn them to active use was so great that Fuller could not really identify it as long as she stayed in her own country. But Alexis de Tocqueville and Harriet Martineau were among the foreign analysts who saw acutely the circumstances of American women in the 1830s when Fuller, in her early twenties, was living a problem the more oppressive and insidious because she could not name it. At first sight, the experience of the British Martineau who found Americans' treatment of women beneath their own democratic theory and the practice of parts of Europe, seems to have nothing in common with that of the Gallic Tocqueville who attributed the singular prosperity and strength of Americans to "the superiority of their women." [3] But then we discover remarkable similarity in their actual findings, which the differences in their sex and political complexion led them to evaluate differently.

Tocqueville's argument is the subtler one. As a "puritanical people and a commercial nation," Americans had a double motive for binding women in conventional marriages: the needs to ensure the purity of their morals and to secure order and prosperity in the home. But as a democratic nation, placing high value on individual independence, they believed "they had little chance of repressing in women the most vehement passions of the human heart." The only sure way to bring up a proper woman, then, "was to teach her the art of combating those passions for herself," by placing "more reliance . . . on the free vigor of her will than on safeguards which have been shaken or overthrown," by arming her reason as well as her virtue. So reared, the young unmarried woman revealed a freedom of mind and action unmatched in Europe. But as a wife she was more submissive, dependent, dutiful, and conformist than her European counterpart. How was this change effected? By the young woman herself, who, in the culminating exercise of her virtue, reason, and free will, chose such marriage. Tocqueville found that, far from seeming to feel degraded by this choice of unfreedom, American women "attach a sort of pride to the voluntary surrender of their own will, and make it their boast to bend themselves to the yoke, not to shake it off." Although Tocqueville observed that this system might produce in young women alarming forwardness and in wives a cold virtue, he admired what he took to be their freedom of choice. [4]

To modern readers, Tocqueville seems to be seduced by the very sophistry he so precisely describes. He seems indifferent to the fact that he is anatomizing a gigantic cultural con, in which half the population is persuaded to believe that conditioning, however moral and thoughtful, is freedom. We have here an early and extreme expression of

America's repressive tolerance, where the very ideology of freedom functions to limit it; it is extreme because in this case woman herself assures the inefficacy of her freedom.

Martineau's analysis is more straightforward because she never saw the American woman's choice of marriage as a free one. While she agreed with Tocqueville that it was the single role women prepare themselves for, she did not believe it was freely chosen; there were virtually no viable alternatives, and women were denied the moral and intellectual training necessary to choose freely. With Tocqueville, she recognized Americans' pride in the achievement of their women, but she saw it as springing from their willful unconsciousness of the real situation. "While woman's intellect is confined, her morals crushed, her health ruined, her weaknesses encouraged, and her strength punished, she is told that her lot is cast in the paradise of women." [5] Needless to say, Martineau remarked on no significant difference between the freedom of young women and that of wives.

While Fuller would ultimately arrive at a position closer to Martineau's, at twenty-one she would probably have agreed with Tocqueville's assessment of the moral and intellectual independence of unmarried women. Her training and early associates so fed her independent spirit and strong will that one can well imagine her boldness intimidating Tocqueville, had they met. But beyond this point, she and Tocqueville parted company. For Fuller, the goal of the *girl*'s independence was not proud womanly surrender of the will but simply the *woman*'s independence—the pursuit of an open destiny and the discovery of a life expressive, not repressive, of the self. Margaret Fuller's problem was the problem of all American women who wanted to *realize* in their adult life an ideology of freedom which was intended simply to be a plaything of their youth. It was a problem because of the cultural law Tocqueville pointed to: the religious and economic objectives which defined the American nation necessarily defined woman as well—as a creature destined for marriage and fulfilled and useful only in the family circle. To conceive of women differently was tantamount therefore to challenging the assumptions on which the nation was built. Ultimately Fuller did this, implicitly challenging the religious assumptions by her sexual behavior, explicitly questioning the economic assumptions, and especially their social and political corollaries, in her writing from Italy.

The struggle that preceded Fuller's challenge to the American conception of woman is as interesting as the challenge itself. For the woman who dreamed of an adult freedom not embodied in the wife or her attendants, the governess and the teacher, more was involved than nonconformity. She had to create a way of life not yet possible and a self whose nature was without local example. Moving, often unconsciously, toward a life that did not yet exist in America, such women lived in effect with the unreal, and often they turned the sense of unreality against themselves. American women who did not capitulate to the marital yoke often compensated by bending their necks to other family yokes, offering their services to the brothers or sisters who would support them. Some passed through emotional crises, or suffered from ill-defined sicknesses—often while contradictorily burning with energy—or turned their religious impulse destructively on themselves or on persons near them. In various seasons of her life, Fuller took each of these routes, which became the life-stories of many women.

In the years immediately following Fuller's departure from America, women like her met together to form a movement precisely to create a basis in American life for freedom for women. What made this possible was the shared recognition of their problem by women, who thus filled each other with a nascent sense of reality which was the beginning of power. Just preceding this movement, Fuller missed its stabilizing and affirming benefits. Because her life was more marked by extremes, perhaps it is more revealing than those of the organized feminists.

Her prayer, "Give me truth, cheat me by no illusion," at once humble and boastful, conveys what Fuller knew she needed most, for vying with her passion for truth was her susceptibility to illusion. Sometimes the illusion was that jewel held out to all American women—the idea that by accepting limitations defined for them by others they were indeed fulfilling themselves; at other times the illusion was of her own devising. Historical opportunity combined with her drive for clarity to very nearly free her from both sorts of illusion.

This collection of writings is designed to trace the struggle to conceive and act out of free womanhood, by showing how Margaret Fuller construed her problem and by examining, one at a time, the various identities she assumed in an effort to resolve the struggle. Though Fuller did not enter these created roles as separate rooms, but always explored her opportunities for freedom on many levels at once, it seems useful, despite overlaps, to examine each singly. And she did pursue a free vocation in roughly chronological experiments, trying first friendship, elevated nearly into art; second, Transcendentalism with its attendant opportunities of teaching, writing literary criticism, and editing the journal of that group; third, the invention of an American feminism; fourth, the practice of social criticism, mostly as a journalist; and finally, commitment to radicalism, to liberation, both political and sexual, in Italy. In this progression we see her moving gradually and erratically from virtually complete compliance with the accepted roles for women to a life which challenged the very basis of the culture and began to make the conception of different roles possible.

This anthology is divided into six parts corresponding to Fuller's sense of the problem of identity and vocation and her five approaches to resolving it. Further, in each part her writing is prefaced by a sample of relevant writings about her by her contemporaries. Each part includes a wide variety of materials—reminiscences, journal entries, letters, fragments of fiction, essays, reportage—which illuminate her interpretation of each role and her contemporaries' judgment of her performance. A number of considerations urge this approach. During her life and after her death, Fuller was for people who knew her an unsolved riddle, inspiring and alienating. She remained a thorn in the side of the American imagination—

one focus, for example, of Hawthorne's ambivalence to women and a major source for both the girl idealists and the female cranks of the early James. The complex and powerful effect Fuller had on thinking men and women is probably more revealing of American attitudes than the effect of any other woman in her century, and it cannot be deduced from her writings alone. Studying her effect also helps us understand Fuller's circumstances, feel the range of social values and pressures which Fuller sometimes accepted, sometimes rejected. By seeing with what difficulty privileged and gifted Americans in one of this country's most fertile and innovative periods greeted the violations of convention by a woman, we understand better how difficult it was to be Margaret Fuller. Finally, this juxtaposition of her work with materials on the effect she generated gives us a richer sense of what she was like than her works alone provide. Virtually all her contemporaries assert that she was in her living presence greatly more impressive and influential than in her writing. Her enduring effect, I believe, came from the combination of her living presence and her work, and the form of this anthology is designed to capture, as much as possible, that combination.

The introductions to each part are intended to flesh out the biographical background and to help the modern reader interpret both Fuller and her contemporaries. Given the distorting intensity of the response to Fuller, the unusually poor condition of her papers, and the ambiguity of much of her writing, all interpretations must be partly speculative. Most of the materials about her were written, quite naturally, after her death. But because that death was so shockingly dramatic and because it followed on a chapter of Fuller's life that was tragically heroic (in her risk of life for the people of Rome) and reeking of ill-concealed scandal (in her risk of reputation for love), her friends were confronted with a writing problem of no small dimension. In their exaltation of Fuller we sometimes feel the strain of their efforts to cover their guilt for the resentment they felt when she was with them. But the resentment they felt for the vividness of her freedom after she left America took the different form of a massive conspiracy to suppress what still menaced them. Her family appears to have concentrated on preventing publication of the love letters she wrote to James Nathan in New York (II:32, II:33). [6] They also censored what was entrusted to the editors of the two-volume *Memoirs of Margaret Fuller Ossoli* (1852), a work which blended her informal writings with the recollections of her friends. In this labor of love and gratitude the editors, James Freeman Clarke, Emerson, and W. H. Channing, came to praise but also, perhaps unconsciously, to bury her. For however rebellious they had been as clergymen, the duty of protecting a lady's reputation revitalized all their orthodoxy. Tacitly assuming that they should be the last to take interest in her papers, they freely applied pen and even scissors in preparing them for the printer. Whole letters and journal entries were "copied" and in most cases the originals destroyed. But enough scraps in her hand survive to give us some idea of the nature of the damage done. Sometimes her wordiness is abridged, but as often the vitality is converted into sonorous periods more appropriate to the pulpit. Channing, who prepared the section on the last phase of her life, was probably the worst offender: as Emerson shrewdly predicted, Channing was perhaps "too much her friend to leave him quite free enough." [7] In his hands, Fuller's adjective in "It will be terrible for me to leave Italy" becomes "sad," and "I . . . am happy, yes I *am* happy here" becomes the sedate "I am contented." He and his associates deleted the name of Jesus Christ (or diluted it to "a saint") when Fuller used it without due reverence, and supplied "O Father" when her awe was judged too freewheeling or pagan by the editors. In strikingly parallel fashion, the word "husband" is provided when Ossoli is named—and often when he is not but should have been lest Fuller seem to have thought too autonomously. (For instance, in publishing Emelyn Story's account of Fuller's confession at the time she feared she might not survive the siege of Rome, Channing added the words here placed in brackets: "Then she told me [of her marriage;] where her child was . . . and, in the event of her [and her husband's] death, I was to take the boy to her

mother . . ." [8]) With a gallantry that may break records in
the history of scholarship, these gentlemen quelled their
doubts (but forgot to destroy all the records of them) to
announce to the world that Fuller was safely married before
she conceived her child.

Consequently, I have used the *Memoirs* only when other
resources failed. The *Memoirs* is especially useful for
interpretations of Fuller, for the editors solicited diverse
opinions; but they were deficient in enlisting the
recollections of many women Fuller influenced. As women's
writings were much less frequently published or preserved
than men's, these materials have proved more difficult to
find. Moreover, the solicited reminiscences of the Brownings
and Mazzini were mysteriously lost; and, either indifferent or
fearful of what they might learn, the editors apparently did
not seek accounts of Fuller from Adam Mickiewicz, Costanza
Arconati, or many other close European friends.

As for Fuller's writings, whenever I have found an
original manuscript that differs from the record in the
Memoirs, I have used the original.

Finally, it is appropriate to remark on the quality of
Fuller's writing. While it can be argued that certain social
prejudices blocked her contemporaries from perceiving some
of its virtues, still many modern readers have difficulty with
it. At the worst, they find the style overblown, the form
rambling and repetitious, the tone self-indulgent or arrogant,
and the whole effect unremittingly intense. Although such
difficulties cannot be explained away, it is important to try
to understand them. An occasionally purple style and a form
that follows where whimsical thought may lead characterize
much of the writing of an age which placed a premium on
spontaneity and feeling. In Fuller's case, her need to feel
(and/or convince others) that she was a woman while
engaging in the intellectual pursuits of men may unconsciously have dictated a vehement and impulsive style rather than
one more logical, cool, spare, and cerebral. The same instinct
may have fed her tendency to digression; we often feel the
insistent personal presence of the woman in these intimate
asides. In a defense of the excesses of her life style, Fuller

herself implies a related explanation of her writing style: "In an environment like mine what may have seemed too lofty or ambitious in my character was absolutely needed to keep the heart from breaking and enthusiasm from extinction." [9] Her argument is that a woman seeking free action in nineteenth-century America must overdo to do at all. Applied to her writing, it may be her best defense. The rhetorical extravagance of the sentence quoted diminishes in proportion to the credence we lend to her thought. She appears to have similarly associated the strictures of literary forms with the confining social forms and to have resented what both cost her in vitality. She wrote that no old form suited her, and in writing as in life experimented and invented. Fuller was anything but vain about her writing, and her own dissatisfaction or modesty about it was so explicit and so often excessive that she herself has contributed to the low esteem in which it has been held.

Though Fuller's writing has passages of great force and beauty, my chief interest is in what it reveals of her remarkable development. In her stylistic excesses one can read the struggle she had to create the appropriate tone, or rather to generate an authentic self who could command an attentive audience. Until experience completed that self, she was obliged to try on, like many costumes, the rhetorics to which she had access. Only after much thought, and with some trepidation, I have omitted passages where digression or repetition seemed not essential to her meaning. And it has been gratifying and deeply supportive to my central understanding of Fuller to discover that the problems in her style and tone diminished as she made her progress out of New England to the self-realization of exile.

My initial study of Fuller was made possible by a grant from the National Endowment for the Humanities. I began by looking at Fuller as one of the underground figures in American letters, hoping I would be able to invite her—like John Brown, the fugitive slave writers, and the literary mill girls—into the same classroom with Thoreau, Emerson, Melville, and Hawthorne to see how these giants might fare in her company. I found in Fuller much more than I had bargained for—a woman who can speak to us still on the problems of reconciling productive independence with emotional needs, desire for singular achievement with sister-hood, feminism with other social issues, the strain of struggle with the desire for peace and acceptance, and intellectual idealism with an imperative need to act on material reality. When, in addition to all this, I saw how persistently her writing has been distorted and her real seriousness rendered sentimental or quaint, my interest in Fuller became all-consuming.

In preparing this book I have been richly helped by friends. Two who became friends in the course of the work are David Edgell, who made me fight for my view of Transcendentalism, and Liana Borghi, a Fuller scholar herself, whose help with Italian history, translation, and research (especially on the vexed question of Fuller's marriage) was invaluable. Faith Williams gave me special help with Emerson, Barbara Welter with women's history, Rik Booraem with American history, and Geoffrey Field and Norman Rush with European history. Lewis Cole, Helene Moglen, Al Fried, and Howard Waskow made useful suggestions on parts of the manuscript, and Myra Jehlen, Sara Blackburn, Danny Kaiser, and Paul Chevigny offered thoughtful and stimulating criticism of the whole. The librarians both at Sarah Lawrence College and at Purchase (especially Paula Hane) provided generous assistance, and Isabel Murray, great good humor in typing the manuscript. Nancy Woolcott offered research assistance, and Robyn Levine, Eileen Redmond, and Tim Hill acted as my first undergraduate critics. Ann Congleton provided emergency research aid and, with Frank Hutchins, extraordinary hospitality in Boston. Joel Myerson helped me date a *Tribune* article. Sue Davidson, Florence Howe, and Paul Lauter were helpful and encouraging editors. None of this work would have been possible without the help at home of Virginia Gale, Claire Chevigny, Rever Williams, and Maura Hammer, the patience and imagination of my young daughters, and the support of my husband (who can now again play records at night).

Fuller's manuscripts are here published by courtesy of Willard P. Fuller, family custodian of Margaret Fuller's literary estate, the Trustees of the Boston Public Library, and the Houghton Library of Harvard University. The Tappan, Clarke, and Samuel Gray Ward papers are here used by permission of the Houghton Library. For permission to use materials by Emerson, I am grateful to Columbia University Press, the Houghton Library, and the Ralph Waldo Emerson Memorial Association. The excerpt from Hawthorne's *American Notebooks* appears by courtesy of the Ohio State University Press.

Textual Note

In his preparation of personal papers for *Woman in the Nineteenth Century and Kindred Papers*, Fuller's brother Arthur, another clergyman, made adjustments similar to those of the editors of the *Memoirs*. He showed more editorial restraint with her *Tribune* reviews and more still with her *Tribune* social commentary in reprinting them in that book and in *Life Without and Life Within*. He barely touched her European dispatches in his *At Home and Abroad* and brought out her *Woman in the Nineteenth Century* and *Summer in the Lakes* with no alteration. I have used original manuscripts when they have differed from the record, even as to punctuation, in the *Memoirs, Kindred Papers*, or Thomas Wentworth Higginson's much more accurate biography. I have used reprinted versions of the *Tribune* pieces when I have noted that they were essentially altered only in returning to lower-case the initials of words like "man," "future," and "reform," whose capitals in the *Tribune* were more likely the work of Greeley than of Fuller. (Arthur Fuller also makes rare attempts in these dispatches to regularize Fuller's tense, and rare excisions, as of a Sicilian political manifesto or Fuller's advice about posting letters abroad.)

In transcribing original manuscripts I have retained the idiosyncratic punctuation of Fuller and her friends. I have

also retained variant spellings (e.g., of Bettina Brentano) and
errors (especially in Italian proper nouns and grammar) and
made sparing use of the intrusive "sic." In the interests of
simplicity and readability, I have not copied errors canceled
by the writers themselves (with the interesting exception of
VI:7) and have without remark included the authors' own
insertions or additions. Editorial insertions are placed in
square brackets, and editorial surmises about half-legible or
incomplete words in the manuscript are placed within angle
brackets, thus: ⟨   ⟩. When a manuscript listed as Fuller's is
written in a hand not hers, it is here called a "copy." In using
printed materials I have also retained idiosyncratic
punctuation and errors in Italian spellings though I have
eliminated quotation marks around long quotations in the
Memoirs. Asterisks, used to indicate ellipses in the *Memoirs*,
are here retained to distinguish those ellipses from my own.

The anthology entries are numbered for convenient
parenthetical reference in my text. Whenever possible, the
date the piece was written is offered in a short title. When the
date is presented in brackets, it means either that the piece
was published at that time or that internal evidence suggests
it was written at that time. Dispatches from Europe are dated
by time of writing, not publication. In the headnotes themselves, a simple form of annotation is used parenthetically
(author, title, page) whenever a source exists in a single
edition. In the citations following anthologized pieces, Fuller
papers at the Houghton Library are designated simply as
"Houghton MS" and at the Boston Public Library as "BPL
MS." Published materials that are frequently used are
abbreviated as follows:

Emerson, Notebook on MFO: Emerson, Ralph Waldo. Manuscript
    Notebook on Margaret Fuller Ossoli. Houghton Library.
Higginson: Higginson, Thomas Wentworth. *Margaret Fuller Ossoli*.
    Boston: Houghton Mifflin Co., 1885.
Rusk, *Letters: The Letters of Ralph 'Waldo Emerson*, ed. Ralph L.
    Rusk, 6 vols. New York: Columbia University Press, 1939.
At Home and Abroad: Margaret Fuller Ossoli. *At Home and Abroad, or
    Things and Thoughts in America and Europe*, ed. Arthur B. Fuller.
    1856; rpt. Port Washington, New York: Kennikat Press, 1971.

Life Without and Life Within: Margaret Fuller Ossoli. *Life Without and Life Within*, ed. Arthur B. Fuller. Boston: Roberts Bros., 1874.

Memoirs: Memoirs of Margaret Fuller Ossoli. Eds. R. W. Emerson, W. H. Channing, and J. F. Clarke. 1884; rpt. New York: Burt Franklin, 1972.

Papers on Literature: S. Margaret Fuller. *Papers on Literature and Art*. New York: Wiley & Putnam, 1846.

Kindred Papers: Margaret Fuller Ossoli. *Woman in the Nineteenth Century and Kindred Papers Relating to the Sphere, Condition and Duties of Woman*, ed. Arthur B. Fuller. 1874; rpt. New York: Greenwood Press, 1968.

Notes

1. *Memoirs*, I, 232.

2. In focusing on Fuller's radical activism, Joseph Jay Deiss, in *The Roman Years of Margaret Fuller* (New York: T.Y. Crowell, 1969), greatly advanced Fuller scholarship. This was the first book I read on Fuller, and it has remained for me one of the most richly provocative.

3. Alexis de Tocqueville, *Democracy in America*, trans. Henry Reeve (New York: Vintage, 1945), II, 225.

4. Tocqueville, II, 212, 210, 223.

5. Harriet Martineau, *Society in America* (New York: Saunders and Otley, 1837), II, 226.

6. Fugitive scraps of correspondence in the Fuller Papers at the Houghton Library hint that Thomas Hicks, to whom she wrote the indiscreet letter first published here (VI:11), cooperated with Ellen Channing in 1851 in an attempt to recapture and destroy some letters in London. I could not ascertain whether these were her letters to Nathan or to someone else.

7. September 23, 1850, Rusk, *Letters*, IV, 231.

8. For this last example, see *Memoirs*, II, 289 and VI:2e of this work.

9. *Memoirs*, II, 111-12.

PART

I

The Problem of Identity and Vocation

The problem of being Margaret Fuller was that of any woman who sought free self-development and an active life in a culture which could neither countenance nor even conceive such goals. But the illusion that they were free agents inculcated in many American girls made people locate the problem not in the culture but in the women themselves. One expression of this tendency was then, as it is today, to find uncomfortably "masculine" qualities in women seeking such freedom. Both Tocqueville and Martineau were struck by an American emphasis on sexual stereotyping unknown in Europe. "In no country has such constant care been taken as in America to trace two clearly distinct lines of action for the two sexes, and to make them keep pace one with the other, but in two pathways which are always different," Tocqueville observed, and "hence it is that the women of America, who often exhibit a masculine strength of understanding and a manly energy, generally preserve great delicacy of personal appearance and always retain the manners of women, although they sometimes show that they have the hearts and minds of men." And Martineau judged sharply that "the prevalent persuasion that there are virtues which are peculiarly masculine, and others which are peculiarly feminine" effectively crushed the morals of both men and women. [1]

Among the causes for such polarization of human qualities in the first half of the nineteenth century was the anxiety about family cohesiveness caused by the migration from the coast into the interior. The development of a market economy beginning in the eighteenth century also had the effect of breaking down the natural and relatively egalitarian division of labor within the home; as men were drawn away from the home to sell commodities or their labor, women were thrust more decisively into it. Where both had, in differing ways, been "bread makers," men alone became "breadwinners," engaged in the all-important affairs of wresting a "living" from the world. For women, a different and narrower world emerged. Family relations became more private, especially in the increasingly distinct middle class, and as the home lost its productive function in the economy, its "moral" functions took on added weight.

For as men learned to scant moral, religious, and emotional values in an increasingly competitive industrial society, women were expected to embody and enact these values for their men; hence the helpmeet was transformed into the "better"—and wholly other—half. Barbara Welter has located the years between 1820 and 1860 as those in which the "cult of True Womanhood," the conviction that piety, purity, submissiveness, and domesticity were women's essential virtues, held its potent sway. [2]

Given this atmosphere, it is not surprising that when the men who knew her best as a young woman tried to capture Fuller's essence, they resorted to one of the following related strategies: they said she was indescribable or called her a "force," ambiguously making her more or other than human; they said she was anomalous, as when Poe said that humanity is divided into three classes: men, women, and Margaret Fuller; [3] they saw her as a hybrid, a union—sometimes happy, sometimes not—of two usually exclusive tendencies. Implicitly or explicitly, they identified these tendencies as "masculine" or "feminine."

When, as a young woman, Fuller wrote about herself, she fell into all these strategies, especially the last. Since the notions of "masculine" and "feminine" were bound to cultural norms, it is clear that as long as she cast her problem in these terms, she was unwittingly conspiring to delay her progress toward freedom. Insofar as she brooded over the conventional formulations, she held herself back from acting as a whole free self; Fuller was not unlike the women in whose lives de Beauvoir later found "an inextricable confusion of revolt and complicity." [4] But it was virtually impossible for her to think beyond these formulations. By their natures, her parents reinforced the sexual stereotypes and by their method of rearing her they contributed to her sense of being hopelessly divided between these stereotypes.

If her mother, Margaret Crane, deviated in any way from the model of "true woman" (these words adorn her tombstone), no record of it survives. Although as a teen-aged schoolmistress she could keep rough boys in line, she seems to have submitted serenely as a wife to her husband's domination, to illness, to the bearing of nine children and the loss of two of them in infancy. "Duty was her daily food," her son Richard recalled, "self-sacrifice was as natural to her as self-gratification in many others." Perhaps her passionate delight in flowers, which she said "had power to bring me into harmony with the Creator, and to soothe any irritation," sustained her and helped her to infect her children with their "ideal sentiment." [5] (It is tempting to read between the lines the mother's conditioned passivity and disengagement from her children's lives in the world beyond home.)

Individuality, even idiosyncratic behavior, and strong opinion seem to have been all on the father's side. Margaret's grandfather was driven out of town for preaching against the Revolution to his congregation of Minutemen; returning as a farmer, he fought his way back into favor and represented the town at a constitutional convention, where he voted against the document because it recognized slavery. Inheriting this feisty independence, Timothy Fuller worked his way through Harvard, where he was demoted to second place in his class because of his participation in a student rebellion. Serving two terms in Congress before becoming Speaker of the Massachusetts house, he opposed the Missouri Compromise in 1820; first in his Jacobin reading and his Jeffersonian principles and later in his loyal and unpolitic support of John Quincy Adams as late as 1832, he showed his political independence. His political stances, his Unitarian faith, and his abrasive personality made him something of a renegade, and he raised his family on the social and political outskirts of Cambridge and Boston, until political discouragement drove him to the country to pursue farming as his father had finally done.

When in 1840, at the introspective age of thirty, Fuller came to write an autobiographical romance, she gave an ideal and generalized account of her parents which connects the woman with physical nature, emotionality, spirituality, and idealism, and the man with the social world, intellectual discipline, and practicality. The natural tendency of the daughter to learn to follow the mother was distorted in Fuller's case by the unusually great influence of her father and the unusually retiring role of her mother. According to Higginson, after the death of his second child, Timothy took even more responsibility for Margaret, his first-born, than she related, supervising her dress, society, correspondence. Though her mother moved closer to Margaret after Timothy's death, she appears to have been a shadowy, if loving, presence during Margaret's childhood. A scholar himself who "grudged the hours nature demands for sleep," Timothy imposed an adult regimen on Margaret, quizzing the six-year-old in Latin and English grammar till long past her bedtime. [6] In his insistence on rigorous classical training, he flew in the face of the fashionable light and sentimental education then offered girls; in his rejection of apology, hesitation, qualification, or circumlocution in her performance, he sought virtually to cut her off from prevalent female speech patterns. But Fuller herself believed the physical and mental strain of these nocturnal drills caused her to suffer as a child from nightmares of trampling horses or of her mother's funeral, and all her life from "continual headache, weakness, and nervous affections, of all kinds" (I:5).

In her psychological biography of Margaret Fuller, Katharine Anthony argues that both sets of symptoms sprang from an intense oedipal love which was also the "mainspring of her whole career." [7] While tempting and doubtless true in part, the Oedipus (or Electra) complex alone cannot account for Fuller's distress or for her dream of her mother's death. Fuller's lifelong suffering from migraine, nervous prostration, and ill-defined pain, following the widespread pattern for "nervous" difficulty in ambitious women of the century, calls also for sociological and historical analysis. [8] The dream of her mother's death, which recurred at least as long as Fuller lived in New England, surely suggests feelings of guilt, [9] but a remarkable fragmentary manuscript, never published, suggests additional interpretations. Full of autobiographical elements—the early death of a sister, the narrator's wild grief, the presence of aunts in the house—it also takes a stunning liberty with the facts. Following the sister's death, the mother *dies* from a combination of grief and the subtle neglect by a good husband ("a genuine though superficial character") of her inner needs (leaving her with "feelings that early drank the oil from her lamp"). [10] Fleshing out Fuller's nightmare, this fiction hints that the unfulfillment of her mother's life made it a slow death in the daughter's imagination and effectively robbed her of both companion and exemplar. Possibly Fuller's fear of such a life for herself, should she model herself on her mother, spurred a violent rejection she could not, in her waking moments, have reconciled with her love for her mother.

Finally, Fuller's feeling for her father and his training was probably more ambivalent than the sort of oedipal love that Anthony paints, and this ambivalence dominates her autobiographical romance. On the positive side, the paternal influence whetted Fuller's appetite for heroic action and realism, for meeting the challenges of the actual world with disciplined will—all the values she associated with the Romans, whose literature and culture Timothy, as a true son of the American Revolution, chiefly stressed. But his influence also confused her, for he failed to show her what she, as a female, could do with these powerful hungers. And it was negative—as she charged explicitly—in imposing without compromise the values of intellect, will, and action completely at the expense of others related to feeling—imagination, passion, and receptivity to nature. [11]

The constraining aspects of the Romans and Timothy's nurture were later counterbalanced in some measure by Margaret's discovery of the Greeks with their love of beauty and openness, of Shakespeare's generosity and the profundity of his doubting Hamlet. But her earliest recourse was the most telling: it was to leave the father's study altogether for the seclusion of the garden, which was significantly her mother's cherished workplace. There she would indulge all afternoon in childish and passionate dreaminess. Quite naturally, then, she came to feel herself divided into separate selves. As the side nurtured by her father came to seem public, that associated with her mother became private, even invisible:

> His influence on me was great, and opposed to the natural unfolding of my character, which was fervent, of strong grasp and disposed to infatuation, and self-forgetfulness. He made the common prose world so present to me, that my natural

bias was controlled. . . . My own world sank deep within. . . .
But my true life was only the dearer that it was secluded and
veiled over by a thick curtain of available intellect, and that
coarse but wearable stuff woven by the ages,—Common Sense
(I:5).

Probably this self-anatomy—the "female" nature repressed and blocked by the "male"—tells us less about the
real quality of her childhood than about her problems at
thirty. But she was deeply and consistently faithful to this
vision in those later years. Thus her prose becomes
sentimental and inflated when she describes how her first
friend, a visiting British woman, touched those hidden
reserves of feeling: "regions" of her being "which would else
have laid in cold obstruction burst into leaf and bloom and
song." The point about Ellen Kilshaw, who captivated the
parents as well as the eight-year-old Margaret,[12] is not
simply that she broke through barriers to the self the parents
had not nourished. More important, this intelligent,
charming, and seemingly independent woman broke down
the alienation the young girl felt from others and even from
herself by showing her a possible way to be a woman: "It was
my first real interest in my kind, and it engrossed me wholly"
(I:5), Fuller wrote. It is hardly relevant that Fuller later
found her charm and cultivation artificial (and Kilshaw's
letters in the Houghton Library are conventionally coquettish
to father, conventionally girlish and confidential to mother,
and conventionally affectionate and admonitory to child).
Kilshaw was desperately welcomed by the child because she
could both strengthen the child's confused ego and serve—for
a while—as a model.

From early adolescence Fuller was preoccupied with the
question of which of her drives, intellectual or emotional,
was more fundamental to her identity. And she was
temperamentally incapable of humor about the question or
indifference to it, partly because of a third quality: a restless
energy which even in childhood drove her to join with her
peers only for "violent bodily exercise which relieved the
nerves" (I:5) and which (as she and others remarked) often

gave the quality of action to her study and thought. While it sustained her, this energy also drove her to try to settle the question or to find some means for combining her drives.

In trying to handle the problems of female adolescence, Fuller kept revising her strategies. At twelve, taking stock of her poor complexion and tendency to overweight, this lonely and strong-willed child made up her mind to be "bright and ugly." But at fifteen, she confided to her teacher Susan Prescott her desire for womanly grace and polish to complement the intellectual genius she took for granted. Then again, she later reported that study filled her with "a gladiatorial disposition" that kept her from enjoying casual society. [13]

This vacillation did not end with adolescence. All her life Fuller's confidence in her intellectual ability was a much-needed resource. "Soon I must retire into the Intellect," she wrote in middle life, after an outburst of "childish feeling," "for *there*, in sight at least, I am a man, and could write the words very calmly and in steadfast flow." But calmness and steadfastness were not Fuller's chief virtues, and she would have appreciated and affirmed the tribute of a woman who said of her, as had been said of Goethe, "Her heart, which few knew, was as great as her mind, which all knew," adding that in character Fuller was of all she had seen "the largest woman, and not a woman who wished to be a man." [14] Again and again she affirmed her pleasure in being a woman; what she objected to was the narrowness society assigned womanhood, especially with regard to intellectual performance and activity in the world.

As she entered her twenties with the question of identity unresolved, the problem of finding a suitable vocation, the need to exercise all sides of herself, became increasingly pressing, and she looked about for a model. Many older women had stepped into the shoes of Ellen Kilshaw and had helped Fuller develop her retarded capacity for friendship. But they had not shown her what to do with her need for intellectual achievement and action. While there were in the 1830s several American women remarkable for knowledge and activism, Fuller was not able to take them as models.

Learned women preceded her in Boston circles, but their styles of life did not challenge the reigning sexual stereotypes. For instance, Sarah Alden Bradford Ripley, Emerson's relative and early mentor, was his model intellectual woman because "she was absolutely without pedantry" and her "delight in books was not tainted by any wish to shine or any appetite for praise or influence." [15] The enduring image of this woman—rocking the cradle, shelling peas, reading a treatise on optics, and helping her husband tutor young scholars for Harvard—was not calculated to satisfy Fuller's romantic intensity. And Elizabeth Peabody, despite her prodigious learning and broad influence on education, fundamentally preferred supporting and disseminating the creativity of others to developing her own; Fuller found no guide for her unfocused independence and unconventionality in her. Not these women but Aspasia, the courtesan of Pericles, noted for bold wit and intellect, inspired Fuller. She described a picture of the head of Aspasia as marked by "the voluptuousness of intellect," a locution which surely jarred on the New England imagination. [16] When female activists, like the Grimké sisters, began to become prominent as abolitionists, Fuller was already in her late twenties, and her literary pursuits and Transcendentalist bias at that time prevented her knowing them; her avid self-preoccupation might also have made their dedication unappealing to her. As for those many abolitionists who became active feminists, like Elizabeth Cady Stanton and Susan B. Anthony, they did so after Fuller left New England.

Thus, in her search for a vocation and a model, Fuller turned to women in Europe. There the institution of the salon in particular had long given women of intelligence, wit, and sympathy an influential role with men of letters and politics, a role unknown in America. For some *salonières*, like Madame de Staël, the salon had been a setting which helped women fashion their own political careers and develop their gifts as writers. As early as her sixteenth year, Fuller was attracted to de Staël not by her political audacity but by her large spirit; the brilliance of her conversation, her intense friendships, and the writing which captured the imagination of a generation amply compensated for her plain appearance. Fuller wrote Susan Prescott that she preferred de Staël to the "useful" moralistic novelist, Maria Edgeworth, "though de Stael is useful too, but it is on the grand scale, on liberalizing, regenerating principles, and has not the immediate practical success that Edgeworth has." [17] Later, Fuller's contemporaries compared her with de Staël and also with the heroine of the Frenchwoman's popular romance, *Corinne, or Italy*, usually because Fuller too was given to rushes of magnetic, extemporaneous speech. The comparison must have pleased and supported Fuller, though she often disclaimed it. Actually, Corinne's rejection of England for Italy—that is, for genius, self-expression freed of convention—provides a stronger, if prophetic, link to Fuller. The eventual defeat of Corinne's independence must have disappointed Fuller, for she outgrew de Staël and eventually disparaged her for her vanity and sentimentality.

By contrast, she was long engaged by Mme. de Dudevant, the novelist who, despite social censure, took the name of George Sand and many lovers. Fuller's letters plainly reveal her hope to find in Sand a synthesis of all her own qualities and her sharp disappointment when Sand cannot manage it, or when she too betrays "womanish" self-pity. Though she would later write warmly of Sand's courage, Fuller's anxiety about female weakness was too great in her younger years to let her choose Sand as a model. The "heroic common sense" instilled by her father was doing its work, making her disparage in women artists the emotionality she had come to cherish in her friends and leading her to discern egoism or natural inability when they sought to transcend the emotional sphere.

Her feelings about herself as a writer, especially during her years in New England, reflect these conflicts. Writing was a struggle, because in it she felt she committed herself to one part of herself while betraying another. The disparities that tormented other romantic writers—the battles between the willed and passive life, thought and action, intellect and feeling—were accentuated by her acute sense of the polar division of her own qualities. Yet her overriding energy drove her to write incessantly and in most of the available forms—poems, journals, reading notes, stories, letters, essays—hoping perhaps that the unrelenting pursuit of her dilemma or the finally accurate expression of it would produce its solution.

Meanwhile, she lived her life as richly as she could and bided her time. It is remarkable that among all Fuller's writings there is no record that she expected to marry. No doubt Fuller's combination of erudition and personal boldness drove off suitors as it tested the mettle even of friends. Then too she was not beautiful. Once in 1840 she lamented, "Of a disposition that requires the most refined, the most exalted tenderness, without charms to inspire it. Poor Mignon!" But more often she saw that beauty could become another trap. "I hear you are 'lovely' now," she teased a young friend; "Heaven help you!" She cared greatly about beauty but thought women should learn to love it in all its manifestations, not simply to mirror it. (Later in her Conversations, she laughed at "all the young ladies of Boston sighing like furnace after being beautiful" and carefully distinguished beauty from prettiness.) [18]

But Fuller may also have not wished to marry. [19] For she had a keen sense of the limitations of the married state that amounted almost at times to fear, as we saw in the fiction of her mother's death. Elsewhere she wrote of the "fetters" of marriage and thought the curse of loneliness "nothing compared with that of those who have entered into those relations but not made them real." [20] Gradually her criticism of marriage was linked to her sense of society's general restrictiveness. Thus, from Italy, she repeatedly warned her young brother Richard and his fiancée against a hasty marriage, for "in the present arrangements of society a choice of a companion for life acts as a Fate on the whole of life." [21] Increasingly her description of ideal marriage became a metaphor for the socially impossible—the discovery of one's perfect complement or the total fulfillment of the self.

Sometimes the very absoluteness of these needs made her despair. Near the end of her life she looked less to ideal marriage than to death for these marvelous transformations:

"by and by comes Death to reorganize perhaps for a fuller, freer life," she wrote gnomically. [22] But before that time she sought fulfillment characteristically in neither ideal marriage nor death but in herself, in an identity and vocation that would make her her own perfect mate by bringing all her "feminine" and "masculine" qualities together into powerful use.

Notes

1. *Democracy in America*, trans. Henry Reeve (New York: Vintage, 1945), II, 223; *Society in America* (New York: Saunders and Otley, 1837), II, 233.

2. Ann D. Gordon, Mari Jo Buhle, and Nancy E. Schram, *Women in American Society* (Cambridge, Mass.: Radical America, 1972), pp. 25-28; "The Cult of True Womanhood," *The American Sisterhood*, ed. Wendy Martin (New York: Harper & Row, 1972), pp. 243-56.

3. *Margaret Fuller: American Romantic*, ed. Perry Miller (Ithaca, N.Y.: Cornell University Press, 1963), p. 192.

4. Simone de Beauvoir, *The Second Sex* (New York: Alfred A. Knopf, 1968), p. 356.

5. *Memoirs*, I, 381; Higginson, p. 19; *Memoirs*, I, 376.

6. Higginson, p. 28; *Memoirs*, I, 361.

7. *Margaret Fuller: A Psychological Biography* (New York: Harcourt, Brace and Co., 1921), p. 25.

8. The most striking examples occur later in the nineteenth and early in the twentieth century, when ambitious women were more abundant. In *The New Radicalism in America, 1889-1963: The Intellectual as a Social Type* (New York: Alfred A. Knopf, 1965), Christopher Lasch cites Jane Addams' prolonged nervous depression before fixing on a life of active reform, and the breakdowns of Charlotte Perkins Gilman and Margaret Sanger when they abandoned careers for marriage.

9. In an 1833 journal, she wrote that she "used to fancy these dreams sent by divine direction to make me treat her with a peculiar tenderness" (Houghton MS).

10. Houghton MS.

11. Such charges recur throughout her letters and journals. From Italy she wrote that, despite her large endowments, before she was twenty she had squandered more vital energy "in inward conflict" than others in three score years and ten. Faith Chipperfield, *In Quest of Love: The Life and Death of Margaret Fuller* (New York: Coward-McCann, 1957), p. 267.

12. Failure to identify Ellen Kilshaw as the British visitor has led most biographers to accept an early guess that Fuller was thirteen when she met this woman. Letters to and from Kilshaw are in the Fuller collection in the Houghton Library.

13. *Memoirs*, I, 229, 56.

14. *Memoirs*, II, 95; I, 300.

15. F. B. Sanborn, *Recollections of Seventy Years* (Boston: Badger, 1909), II, 368.

16. August 1838 journal, Houghton MS; in her journal for December 1836, Fuller reflected, "Woman might be of use in this society by explaining the speculative man to the practical. But where could an Aspasia take her stand?" (Houghton MS copy.)

17. May 4, 1826, *Memoirs*, I, 55.

18. Emerson, Notebook on MFO; to Caroline Sturgis, April 17, 1845, Tappan Papers, Houghton; *Memoirs*, I, 343.

19. I reject the reductiveness of Emerson's private judgment: "The unlooked for trait in all these journals to me is the Woman, Poor Woman: they are all hysterical. She is bewailing her virginity and languishing for a husband" (Emerson, Notebook on MFO).

20. Emerson, Notebook on MFO. In her story "Aglauron and Laurie" (*Kindred Papers*, pp. 183-216), Fuller criticizes not only marriages in effect forced on unreflective girls but also romantic marriages because they cannot satisfy the spirit's longing for ideal fulfillment.

21. Venice [1847], Houghton MS.

22. January 8, 1848, Houghton MS; still later she wrote in an undated fragment, "Eternity is ours, beloved William—we will be true and full living beings yet" (BPL MS).

CONTEMPORARIES ON FULLER

1. At thirteen, Frederic Henry Hedge [1852]

An ardent student of German idealistic philosophy and a
charter Transcendentalist, Hedge (1805-1890) was one of
Fuller's first intellectual companions. He met her during his
student days at Harvard. For the *Memoirs*, published in 1852,
he wrote that his first impression was of excessive tight-lacing
and irrepressible vitality.

... Margaret was then about thirteen, – a child in years, but so precocious in her mental and physical developments, that she passed for
eighteen or twenty. Agreeably to this estimate, she had her place in
society, as a lady full-grown.

When I recall her personal appearance, as it was then and for ten or
twelve years subsequent to this, I have the idea of a blooming girl of a
florid complexion and vigorous health, with a tendency to robustness,
of which she was painfully conscious, and which, with little regard to
hygienic principles, she endeavored to suppress or conceal, thereby preparing for herself much future suffering. With no pretensions to beauty
then, or at any time, her face was one that attracted, that awakened a
lively interest, that made one desirous of a nearer acquaintance. It was a
face that fascinated, without satisfying. Never seen in repose, never
allowing a steady perusal of its features, it baffled every attempt to
judge the character by physiognomical induction. You saw the evidence
of a mighty force, but what direction that force would assume, –
whether it would determine itself to social triumphs, or to triumphs of
art, – it was impossible to divine. Her moral tendencies, her sentiments,
her true and prevailing character, did not appear in the lines of her face.
She seemed equal to anything, but might not choose to put forth her
strength. You felt that a great possibility lay behind that brow but you
felt, also, that the talent that was in her might miscarry through indifference or caprice. ...

Here let me say a word respecting the character of Margaret's mind.
It was what in woman is generally called a masculine mind; that is, its

action was determined by ideas rather than by sentiments. And yet, with this masculine trait, she combined a woman's appreciation of the beautiful in sentiment and the beautiful in action. Her intellect was rather solid than graceful, yet no one was more alive to grace. She was no artist, – she would never have written an epic, or romance, or drama, – yet no one knew better the qualities which go to the making of these; and though catholic as to kind, no one was more rigorously exacting as to quality. Nothing short of the best in each kind would content her. . . . [Memoirs, I, 91-95]

2. In the Transcendental Club, William Henry Channing [1852]

Channing (1810-1884), the Christian Socialist minister, also first knew Fuller when he studied at Harvard and the Divinity School. For the Memoirs, he described the style of her behavior at the meetings of reformers and intellectuals known forever by the name their mockers gave them—Transcendentalists.

. . . In conversations like these, one saw that the richness of Margaret's genius resulted from a rare combination of opposite qualities. To her might have been well applied the words first used in describing George Sand: "Thou large-brained Woman, and large-hearted Man." She blended in closest union and swift interplay feminine receptiveness with masculine energy. She was at once impressible and creative, impulsive and deliberate, pliant in sympathy yet firmly self-centred, confidingly responsive while commanding in originality. By the vivid intensity of her conceptions, she brought out in those around their own consciousness, and, by the glowing vigor of her intellect, roused into action their torpid powers. [Memoirs, II, 21]

3. Her temperament, Ralph Waldo Emerson [1852]

Emerson (1803-1882) did not come to know Fuller until 1836. Her nature seems to have caused him deeper perplexity and more lasting discomfort than it did her other biographers. After he had known her for two weeks he wrote, "It is always a great refreshment to see a very intelligent person. It is like being set in a large place. You stretch your limbs & dilate to your utmost size" (Rusk, *Letters*, II, 32). But later he wrote, "Woman should not be expected to write, or fight, or build, or compose scores; she does all by inspiring man to do all" (*Journals of Ralph Waldo Emerson*, eds. E. W. Emerson and W. H. Forbes, VI, 134). It is difficult to be enlarged by a member of a group whose activities one believes should be limited. Emerson's section in the *Memoirs* is his apology in both senses of the word for his response to Fuller; in it he admits and justifies his failure to understand her.

I said that Margaret had a broad good sense, which brought her near to all people. I am to say that she had also a strong temperament, which is that counter force which makes individuality, by driving all the powers in the direction of the ruling thought or feeling, and, when it is allowed full sway, isolating them. These two tendencies were always invading each other, and now one and now the other carried the day. This alternation perplexes the biographer, as it did the observer. We contradict on the second page what we affirm on the first: and I remember how often I was compelled to correct my impressions of her character when living; for after I had settled it once for all that she wanted this or that perception, at our next interview she would say with emphasis the very word.

I think, in her case, there was something abnormal in those obscure habits and necessities which we denote by the word Temperament. In the first days of our acquaintance, I felt her to be a foreigner, – that, with her, one would always be sensible of some barrier, as if in making up a friendship with a cultivated Spaniard or Turk. She had a strong constitution, and of course its reactions were strong; and this is the reason why in all her life she has so much to say of her *fate*. She was in jubilant spirits in the morning, and ended the day with nervous headache, whose spasms, my wife told me, produced total prostration. She had great energy of speech and action, and seemed formed for high emergencies. . . .

When I found she lived at a rate so much faster than mine, and which was violent compared with mine, I foreboded rash and painful crises, and had a feeling as if a voice cried, *Stand from under!* – as if, a little further on, this destiny was threatened with jars and reverses, which no friendship could avert or console. This feeling partly wore off, on better acquaintance, but remained latent; and I had always an impression that her energy was too much a force of blood, and therefore never felt the security for her peace which belongs to more purely intellectual natures. She seemed more vulnerable. For the same reason, she remained inscrutable to me; her strength was not my strength, — her powers were a surprise. She passed into new states of great advance, but I understood these no better. It were long to tell her peculiarities. Her childhood was full of presentiments. She was then a somnambulist. She was subject to attacks of delirium, and, later, perceived that she had spectral illusions. When she was twelve, she had a determination of blood to the head. "My parents," she said, "were much mortified to see the fineness of my complexion destroyed. My own vanity was for a time severely wounded; but I recovered, and made up my mind to be bright and ugly." . . .

She had a feeling that she ought to have been a man, and said of herself, "A man's ambition with a woman's heart, is an evil lot." In some verses which she wrote "To the Moon," occur these lines: —

"But if I steadfast gaze upon thy face,
 A human secret, like my own, I trace;
 For, through the woman's smile looks the male eye.". . .

Margaret at first astonished and repelled us by a complacency that seemed the most assured since the days of Scaliger. She spoke, in the quietest manner, of the girls she had formed, the young men who owed everything to her, the fine companions she had long ago exhausted. In the coolest way, she said to her friends, "I now know all the people worth knowing in America, and I find no intellect comparable to my own." . . . [Memoirs, I, 227-29, 336]

It is certain that Margaret occasionally let slip, with all the innocence imaginable, some phrase betraying the presence of a rather mountainous *me*, in a way to surprise those who knew her good sense. She could say, as if she were stating a scientific fact, in enumerating the merits of somebody, "He appreciates *me*." There was something of hereditary organization in this, and something of unfavorable circumstance in the fact, that she had in early life no companion, and few afterwards, in her finer studies; but there was also an ebullient sense of power, which she felt to be in her, which as yet had found no right channels. I remember she once said to me, what I heard as a mere statement of fact, and nowise as unbecoming, that "no man gave such invitation to her mind as to tempt her to a full expression: that she felt a power to enrich her thought with such wealth and variety of embellishment as would, no doubt, be tedious to such as she conversed with."

Her impatience she expressed as she could. "I feel within myself," she said, "an immense force, but I cannot bring it out. It may sound like a joke, but I do feel something corresponding to that tale of the Destinies falling in love with Hermes." [*Memoirs*, I, 227-29, 234, 236]

4. As a force, Samuel Gray Ward [1850-51]

Romantically involved with Fuller when she was in her twenties and a friend for the rest of her life, Ward (1817-1907) agreed originally to collaborate on the *Memoirs*. Later he withdrew, posing these questions to Emerson.

How can you describe a Force? How can you write the life of Margaret? [*Emerson, Notebook on MFO*]

FULLER'S WRITINGS

5. On her childhood [1840]

When she was thirty, Fuller wrote an autobiographical romance which centered on her interpretation of her parents, her early learning, her isolation, and her powerful need for a supportive friend. No original survives, but a fragment from her 1838 journal (Houghton MS), treating her mother's garden in a similar way, was somewhat more self-critical. Though the autobiographical romance may have been heavily doctored by the editors of the *Memoirs*, it is the only extensive record of her girlhood we have, as she destroyed her early diaries.

Parents. My father was a lawyer and a politician. He was a man largely endowed with that sagacious energy, which the state of New England society, for the last half century, has been so well fitted to develop. His father was a clergyman, settled as pastor in Princeton, Massachusetts, within the bounds of whose parish-farm was Wachuset. His means were small, and the great object of his ambition was to send his sons to college. As a boy, my father was taught to think only of preparing himself for Harvard University, and when there of preparing himself for the profession of Law. As a Lawyer, again, the ends constantly presented were to work for distinction in the community, and for the means of supporting a family. To be an honored citizen, and to have a home on earth, were made the great aims of existence. To open the deeper fountains of the soul, to regard life here as the prophetic entrance to immortality, to develop his spirit to perfection, — motives like these had never been suggested to him, either by fellow-beings or by outward circumstances. The result was a character, in its social aspect, of quite the common sort. A good son and brother, a kind neighbor, an active man of business — in all these outward relations he was but one of a class, which surrounding conditions have made the majority among us. In the more delicate and individual relations, he never approached but two mortals, my mother and myself.

His love for my mother was the green spot on which he stood apart from the common-places of a mere bread-winning, bread-bestowing existence. She was one of those fair and flower-like natures, which sometimes spring up even beside the most dusty highways of life – a creature not to be shaped into a merely useful instrument, but bound by one law with the blue sky, the dew, and the frolic birds. Of all persons whom I have known, she had in her most of the angelic, – of that spontaneous love for every living thing, for man, and beast, and tree, which restores the golden age.

Death in the house. My earliest recollection is of a death, – the death of a sister, two years younger than myself. Probably there is a sense of childish endearments, such as belong to this tie, mingled with that of loss, of wonder, and mystery: but these last are prominent in memory. I remember coming home and meeting our nursery-maid, her face streaming with tears. That strange sight of tears made an indelible impression. I realize how little I was of stature, in that I looked up to this weeping face; – and it has often seemed since, that – full-grown for the life of this earth, I have looked up just so, at times of threatening, of doubt, and distress, and that just so has some being of the next higher order of existences looked down, aware of a law unknown to me, and tenderly commiserating the pain I must endure in emerging from my ignorance.

She took me by the hand and led me into a still and dark chamber, – then drew aside the curtain and showed me my sister. I see yet that beauty of death! The highest achievements of sculpture are only the reminder of its severe sweetness. Then I remember the house all still and dark, – the people in their black clothes and dreary faces, – the scent of the newly-made coffin, – my being set up in a chair and detained by a gentle hand to hear the clergyman, – the carriages slowly going, the procession slowly doling out their steps to the grave. But I have no remembrance of what I have since been told I did, – insisting, with loud cries, that they should not put the body in the ground. I suppose that my emotion was spent at the time, and so there was nothing to fix that moment in my memory.

I did not then, nor do I now, find any beauty in these ceremonies. What had they to do with the sweet playful child? Her life and death were alike beautiful, but all this sad parade was not. Thus my first experience of life was one of death. She who would have been the companion of my life was severed from me, and I was left alone. This has made a vast difference in my lot. Her character, if that fair face promised right, would have been soft, graceful and lively; it would have tempered mine to a gentler and more gradual course.

Overwork. My father, — all whose feelings were now concentred on me, — instructed me himself. The effect of this was so far good that, not passing through the hands of many ignorant and weak persons as so many do at preparatory schools, I was put at once under discipline of considerable severity, and, at the same time, had a more than ordinarily high standard presented to me. My father was a man of business, even in literature; he had been a high scholar at college, and was warmly attached to all he had learned there, both from the pleasure he had derived in the exercise of his faculties and the associated memories of success and good repute. He was, beside, well read in French literature, and in English, a Queen Anne's man. He hoped to make me the heir of all he knew, and of as much more as the income of his profession enabled him to give me means of acquiring. At the very beginning, he made one great mistake, more common, it is to be hoped, in the last generation, than the warnings of physiologists will permit it to be with the next. He thought to gain time, by bringing forward the intellect as early as possible. Thus I had tasks given me, as many and various as the hours would allow, and on subjects beyond my age; with the additional disadvantage of reciting to him in the evening, after he returned from his office. As he was subject to many interruptions, I was often kept up till very late; and as he was a severe teacher, both from his habits of mind and his ambition for me, my feelings were kept on the stretch till the recitations were over. Thus frequently, I was sent to bed several hours too late, with nerves unnaturally stimulated. The consequence was a premature development of the brain, that made me a "youthful prodigy" by day, and by night a victim of spectral illusions, nightmare, and somnambulism, which at the time prevented the harmonious development of my bodily powers and checked my growth, while, later, they induced continual headache, weakness and nervous affections, of all kinds. As these again re-acted on the brain, giving undue force to every thought and every feeling, there was finally produced a state of being both too active and too intense, which wasted my constitution, and will bring me, — even although I have learned to understand and regulate my now morbid temperament, — to a premature grave.

No one understood this subject of health then. No one knew why
this child, already kept up so late, was still unwilling to retire. My aunts
cried out upon the "spoiled child, the most unreasonable child that ever
was, — if brother could but open his eyes to see it, — who was never
willing to go to bed." They did not know that, so soon as the light was
taken away, she seemed to see colossal faces advancing slowly towards
her, the eyes dilating, and each feature swelling loathsomely as they
came, till at last, when they were about to close upon her, she started
up with a shriek which drove them away, but only to return when she
lay down again. They did not know that, when at last she went to sleep,
it was to dream of horses trampling over her, and to awake once more
in fright; or, as she had just read in her Virgil, of being among trees that
dripped with blood, where she walked and walked and could not get
out, while the blood became a pool and plashed over her feet, and rose
higher and higher, till soon she dreamed it would reach her lips. No
wonder the child arose and walked in her sleep, moaning all over the
house, till once, when they heard her, and came and waked her, and she
told what she had dreamed, her father sharply bid her "leave off thinking of such nonsense, or she would be crazy," — never knowing that he
was himself the cause of all these horrors of the night. Often she
dreamed of following to the grave the body of her mother, as she had
done that of her sister, and woke to find the pillow drenched in tears.
These dreams softened her heart too much, and cast a deep shadow
over her young days; for then, and later, the life of dreams, — probably
because there was in it less to distract the mind from its own earnestness, — has often seemed to her more real, and been remembered with
more interest, than that of waking hours.

Poor child! Far remote in time, in thought, from that period, I
look back on these glooms and terrors, wherein I was enveloped, and
perceive that I had no natural childhood.

Books. Thus passed my first years. My mother was in delicate health,
and much absorbed in the care of her younger children. In the house
was neither dog nor bird, nor any graceful animated form of existence.
I saw no persons who took my fancy, and real life offered no attraction. Thus my already over-excited mind found no relief from without,
and was driven for refuge from itself to the world of books. I was
taught Latin and English grammar at the same time, and began to read
Latin at six years old, after which, for some years, I read it daily. In this

branch of study, first by my father, and afterwards by a tutor, I was trained to quite a high degree of precision. I was expected to understand the mechanism of the language thoroughly, and in translating to give the thoughts in as few well-arranged words as possible, and without breaks or hesitation, – for with these my father had absolutely no patience.

Indeed, he demanded accuracy and clearness in everything: you must not speak, unless you can make your meaning perfectly intelligible to the person addressed; must not express a thought, unless you can give a reason for it, if required; must not make a statement, unless sure of all particulars – such were his rules. "But," "if," "unless," "I am mistaken," and "it may be so," were words and phrases excluded from the province where he held sway. Trained to great dexterity in artificial methods, accurate, ready, with entire command of his resources, he had no belief in minds that listen, wait, and receive. He had no conception of the subtle and indirect motions of imagination and feeling. His influence on me was great, and opposed to the natural unfolding of my character, which was fervent, of strong grasp, and disposed to infatuation, and self-forgetfulness. He made the common prose world so present to me, that my natural bias was controlled. I did not go mad, as many would do, at being continually roused from my dreams. I had too much strength to be crushed, – and since I must put on the fetters, could not submit to let them impede my motions. My own world sank deep within, away from the surface of my life; in what I did and said I learned to have reference to other minds. But my true life was only the dearer that it was secluded and veiled over by a thick curtain of available intellect, and that coarse, but wearable stuff woven by the ages, – Common Sense.

In accordance with this discipline in heroic common sense, was the influence of those great Romans, whose thoughts and lives were my daily food during those plastic years. The genius of Rome displayed itself in Character, and scarcely needed an occasional wave of the torch of thought to show its lineaments, so marble strong they gleamed in every light. Who, that has lived with those men, but admires the plain force of fact, of thought passed into action? They take up things with their naked hands. There is just the man, and the block he casts before you, – no divinity, no demon, no unfulfilled aim, but just the man and Rome, and what he did for Rome. Everything turns your attention to what a man can become, not by yielding himself freely to impressions, not by letting nature play freely through him, but by a single thought, an earnest purpose, an indomitable will, by hardihood, self-command, and force of expression. Architecture was the art in which Rome excelled, and this corresponds with the feeling these men of Rome excite. They did not grow, – they built themselves up, or were built up by the fate of Rome, as a temple for Jupiter Stator. The ruined Roman sits among the ruins; he flies to no green garden; he does not look to heaven; if his intent is defeated, if he is less than he meant to be, he lives no more. The names which end in "*us*," seem to speak with lyric cadence. That measured cadence, – that tramp and march, – which are not stilted, because they indicate real force, yet which seem so when compared with any other language, – make Latin a study in itself of mighty influence. The language alone, without the literature, would give one the *thought* of Rome. Man present in nature, commanding nature too sternly to be inspired by it, standing like the rock amid the sea, or moving like the fire over the land, either impassive, or irresistible; knowing not the soft mediums or fine flights of life, but by the force which he expresses, piercing to the centre. . . .

The history of Rome abides in mind, of course, more than the literature. It was degeneracy for a Roman to use the pen; his life was in the day. The "vaunting" of Rome, like that of the North American Indians, is her proper literature. A man rises; he tells who he is, and what he has done; he speaks of his country and her brave men; he knows that a conquering god is there, whose agent is his own right hand; and he should end like the Indian, "I have no more to say."

It never shocks us that the Roman is self-conscious. One wants no universal truths from him, no philosophy, no creation, but only his life, his Roman life felt in every pulse, realized in every gesture. The universal heaven takes in the Roman only to make us feel his individuality the more. The Will, the Resolve of Man! – it has been expressed, – fully expressed!

I steadily loved this ideal in my childhood, and this is the cause, probably, why I have always felt that man must know how to stand firm on the ground, before he can fly. In vain for me are men more, if they are less, than Romans. Dante was far greater than any Roman, yet I feel he was right to take the Mantuan as his guide through hell, and to heaven. . . .

Ovid gave me not Rome, nor himself, but a view into the enchanted gardens of the Greek mythology. This path I followed, have been following ever since; and now, life half over, it seems to me, as in my childhood, that every thought of which man is susceptible, is intimated there. In those young years, indeed, I did not see what I now see, but loved to creep from amid the Roman pikes to lie beneath this great vine, and see the smiling and serene shapes go by, woven from the finest fibres of all the elements. I knew not why, at that time, – but I loved to get away from the hum of the forum, and the mailed clang of Roman speech, to these shifting shows of nature, these Gods and Nymphs born of the sunbeam, the wave, the shadows on the hill.

As with Rome I antedated the world of deeds, so I lived in those Greek forms the true faith of a refined and intense childhood. So great was the force of reality with which these forms impressed me, that I prayed earnestly for a sign, – that it would lighten in some particular region of the heavens, or that I might find a bunch of grapes in the path, when I went forth in the morning. But no sign was given, and I was left a waif stranded upon the shores of modern life!

Of the Greek language, I knew only enough to feel that the sounds told the same story as the mythology; – that the law of life in that land was beauty, as in Rome it was a stern composure. I wish I had learned as much of Greece as of Rome, – so freely does the mind play in her sunny waters, where there is no chill, and the restraint is from within out; for these Greeks, in an atmosphere of ample grace, could not be impetuous, or stern, but loved moderation as equable life always must, for it is the law of beauty.

With these books I passed my days. The great amount of study exacted of me soon ceased to be a burden, and reading became a habit and a passion. The force of feeling, which, under other circumstances, might have ripened thought, was turned to learn the thoughts of others. This was not a tame state, for the energies brought out by rapid acquisition gave glow enough. I thought with rapture of the all-accomplished man, him of the many talents, wide resources, clear sight, and omnipotent will. A Caesar seemed great enough. I did not then know that such men impoverish the treasury to build the palace. I kept their statues as belonging to the hall of my ancestors, and loved to conquer obstacles, and fed my youth and strength for their sake.

Still, though this bias was so great that in earliest years I learned, in these ways, how the world takes hold of a powerful nature, I had yet other experiences. None of these were deeper than what I found in the happiest haunt of my childish years, – our little garden. Our house,

though comfortable, was very ugly, and in a neighborhood which I
detested, — every dwelling and its appurtenances having a *mesquin* and
huddled look. I liked nothing about us except the tall graceful elms
before the house, and the dear little garden behind. Our back door
opened on a high flight of steps, by which I went down to a green plot,
much injured in my ambitious eyes by the presence of the pump and
tool-house. This opened into a little garden, full of choice flowers and
fruit-trees, which was my mother's delight, and was carefully kept. Here
I felt at home. A gate opened thence into the fields, — a wooden gate
made of boards, in a high, unpainted board wall, and embowered in the
clematis creeper. This gate I used to open to see the sunset heaven;
beyond this black frame I did not step, for I liked to look at the deep
gold behind it. How exquisitely happy I was in its beauty, and how I
loved the silvery wreaths of my protecting vine! I never would pluck
one of its flowers at that time, I was so jealous of its beauty, but often
since I carry off wreaths of it from the wild-wood, and it stands in
nature to my mind as the emblem of domestic love.

Of late I have thankfully felt what I owe to that garden, where the
best hours of my lonely childhood were spent. Within the house everything was socially utilitarian; my books told of a proud world, but in
another temper were the teachings of the little garden. There my
thoughts could lie callow in the nest, and only be fed and kept warm,
not called to fly or sing before the time. I loved to gaze on the roses,
the violets, the lilies, the pinks; my mother's hand had planted them,
and they bloomed for me. I culled the most beautiful. I looked at them
on every side. I kissed them, I pressed them to my bosom with passionate emotions, such as I have never dared express to any human
being. An ambition swelled my heart to be as beautiful, as perfect as
they. I have not kept my vow. Yet, forgive, ye wild asters, which gleam
so sadly amid the fading grass; forgive me, ye golden autumn flowers,
which so strive to reflect the glories of the departing distant sun; and ye
silvery flowers, whose moonlight eyes I knew so well, forgive! Living
and blooming in your unchecked law, ye know nothing of the blights,
the distortions, which beset the human being; and which at such hours
it would seem that no glories of free agency could ever repay!

There was, in the house, no apartment appropriated to the purpose
of a library, but there was in my father's room a large closet filled with
books, and to these I had free access when the task-work of the day was
done. . . .

Ever memorable is the day on which I first took a volume of Shakespeare in my hand to read. It was on a Sunday.

– This day was punctiliously set apart in our house. We had family prayers, for which there was no time on other days. Our dinners were different, and our clothes. We went to church. My father put some limitations on my reading, but – bless him for the gentleness which has left me a pleasant feeling for the day! – he did not prescribe what was, but only what was *not*, to be done. And the liberty this left was a large one. "You must not read a novel, or a play;" but all other books, the worst, or the best, were open to me. The distinction was merely technical. The day was pleasing to me, as relieving me from the routine of tasks and recitations; it gave me freer play than usual, and there were fewer things occurred in its course, which reminded me of the divisions of time; still the churchgoing, where I heard nothing that had any connection with my inward life, and these rules, gave me associations with the day of empty formalities, and arbitrary restrictions; but though the forbidden book or walk always seemed more charming then, I was seldom tempted to disobey. –

This Sunday – I was only eight years old – I took from the bookshelf a volume lettered Shakespeare. It was not the first time I had looked at it, but before I had been deterred from attempting to read, by the broken appearance along the page, and preferred smooth narrative. But this time I held in my hand "Romeo and Juliet" long enough to get my eye fastened to the page. It was a cold winter afternoon. I took the book to the parlor fire, and had there been seated an hour or two, when my father looked up and asked what I was reading so intently. "Shakespeare," replied the child, merely raising her eye from the page. "Shakespeare, – that won't do; that's no book for Sunday; go put it away and take another." I went as I was bid, but took no other. Returning to my seat, the unfinished story, the personages to whom I was but just introduced, thronged and burnt my brain. I could not bear it long; such a lure was impossible to resist. I went and brought the book again. There were several guests present, and I had got half through the play before I again attracted attention. "What is that child about that she don't hear a word that's said to her?" quoth my aunt. "What are you reading?" said my father. "Shakespeare," was again the reply, in a clear, though somewhat impatient, tone. "How?" said my father angrily, – then, restraining himself before his guests, – "Give me the book and go directly to bed."

Into my little room no care of his anger followed me. Alone, in the dark, I thought only of the scene placed by the poet before my eye, where the free flow of life, sudden and graceful dialogue, and forms, whether grotesque or fair, seen in the broad lustre of his imagination, gave just what I wanted, and brought home the life I seemed born to live. My fancies swarmed like bees, as I contrived the rest of the story; — what all would do, what say, where go. My confinement tortured me. I could not go forth from this prison to ask after these friends; I could not make my pillow of the dreams about them which yet I could not forbear to frame. Thus was I absorbed when my father entered. He felt it right, before going to rest, to reason with me about my disobedience, shown in a way, as he considered, so insolent. I listened, but could not feel interested in what he said, nor turn my mind from what engaged it. He went away really grieved at my impenitence, and quite at a loss to understand conduct in me so unusual.

— Often since I have seen the same misunderstanding between parent and child, — the parent thrusting the morale, the discipline, of life upon the child, when just engrossed by some game of real importance and great leadings to it. That is only a wooden horse to the father, — the child was careering to distant scenes of conquest and crusade, through a country of elsewhere unimagined beauty. None but poets remember their youth; but the father who does not retain poetical apprehension of the world, free and splendid as it stretches out before the child, who cannot read his natural history, and follow out its intimations with reverence, must be a tyrant in his home, and the purest intentions will not prevent his doing much to cramp him. Each new child is a new Thought, and has bearings and discernings, which the Thoughts older in date know not yet, but must learn. —

My attention thus fixed on Shakespeare, I returned to him at every hour I could command. Here was a counterpoise to my Romans, still more forcible than the little garden. My author could read the Roman nature too, — read it in the sternness of Coriolanus, and in the varied wealth of Caesar. But he viewed these men of will as only one kind of men; he kept them in their place, and I found that he, who could understand the Roman, yet expressed in Hamlet a deeper thought. . . .

These men [Shakespeare, Cervantes, and Molière] were all alike in this, — they loved the *natural history* of man. Not what he should be, but what he is, was the favorite subject of their thought. Whenever a noble leading opened to the eye new paths of light, they rejoiced; but it was never fancy, but always fact, that inspired them. They loved a thorough penetration of the murkiest dens, and most tangled paths of nature; they did not spin from the desires of their own special natures, but reconstructed the world from materials which they collected on every side. Thus their influence upon me was not to prompt me to follow out thought in myself so much as to detect it everywhere, for each of these men is not only a nature, but a happy interpreter of many natures. They taught me to distrust all invention which is not based on a wide experience. Perhaps, too, they taught me to overvalue an outward experience at the expense of inward growth; but all this I did not appreciate till later.

It will be seen that my youth was not unfriended, since those great minds came to me in kindness. A moment of action in one's self, however, is worth an age of apprehension through others; not that our deeds are better, but that they produce a renewal of our being. I have had more productive moments and of deeper joy, but never hours of more tranquil pleasure than those in which these demi-gods visited me, — and with a smile so familiar, that I imagined the world to be full of such. They did me good, for by them a standard was early given of sight and thought, from which I could never go back, and beneath which I cannot suffer patiently my own life or that of any friend to fall. They did me harm, too, for the child fed with meat instead of milk becomes too soon mature. Expectations and desires were thus early raised, after which I must long toil before they can be realized. How poor the scene around, how tame one's own existence, how meagre and faint every power, with these beings in my mind! Often I must cast them quite aside in order to grow in my small way, and not sink into despair. Certainly I do not wish that instead of these masters I had read baby books, written down to children, and with such ignorant dulness that they blunt the senses and corrupt the tastes of the still plastic human being. But I do wish that I had read no books at all till later, — that I had lived with toys, and played in the open air. Children should not cull the fruits of reflection and observation early, but expand in the sun, and let thoughts come to them. They should not through books antedate their actual experiences, but should take them gradually, as sympathy and interpretation are needed. With me, much of life was devoured in the bud.

First friend. For a few months, this bookish and solitary life was invaded by interest in a living, breathing figure. At church, I used to look around with a feeling of coldness and disdain, which, though I now well understand its causes, seems to my wiser mind as odious as it was unnatural. The puny child sought everywhere for the Roman or Shakespeare figures, and she was met by the shrewd, honest eye, the homely decency, or the smartness of a New England village on Sunday. There was beauty, but I could not see it then; it was not of the kind I longed for. In the next pew sat a family who were my especial aversion. There were five daughters, the eldest not above four-and-twenty, – yet they had the old fairy, knowing look, hard, dry, dwarfed, strangers to the All-Fair, – were working-day residents in this beautiful planet. They looked as if their thoughts had never strayed beyond the jobs of the day, and they were glad of it. Their mother was one of those shrunken, faded patterns of woman who have never done anything to keep smooth the cheek and dignify the brow. The father had a Scotch look of shrewd narrowness, and entire self-complacency. I could not endure this family, whose existence contradicted all my visions; yet I could not forbear looking at them.

As my eye one day was ranging about with its accustomed coldness, and the proudly foolish sense of being in a shroud of thoughts that were not their thoughts, it was arrested by a face most fair, and well-known as it seemed at first glance, – for surely I had met her before and waited for her long. But soon I saw that she was a new apparition foreign to that scene, if not to me. Her dress, – the arrangement of her hair, which had the graceful pliancy of races highly cultivated for long, – the intelligent and full picture of her eye, whose reserve was in its self-possession, not in timidity, – all combined to make up a whole impression, which, though too young to understand, I was well prepared to feel.

How wearisome now appears that thorough-bred *millefleur* beauty, the distilled result of ages of European culture! Give me rather the wild heath on the lonely hill-side, than such a rose-tree from the daintily clipped garden. But, then, I had but tasted the cup, and knew not how little it could satisfy; more, more, was all my cry; continued through years, till I had been at the very fountain. Indeed, it was a ruby-red, a perfumed draught, and I need not abuse the wine because I prefer water, but merely say I have had enough of it. Then, the first sight, the first knowledge of such a person was intoxication.

She was an English lady, who, by a singular chance, was cast upon this region for a few months. Elegant and captivating, her every look and gesture was tuned to a different pitch from anything I had ever known. She was in various ways "accomplished," as it is called, though to what degree I cannot now judge. She painted in oils; — I had never before seen any one use the brush, and days would not have been too long for me to watch the pictures growing beneath her hand. She played the harp; and its tones are still to me the heralds of the promised land I saw before me then. She rose, she looked, she spoke; and the gentle swaying motion she made all through life has gladdened memory, as the stream does the woods and meadows.

As she was often at the house of one of our neighbors, and afterwards at our own, my thoughts were fixed on her with all the force of my nature. It was my first real interest in my kind, and it engrossed me wholly. . . .

One time I had been passing the afternoon with her. She had been playing to me on the harp, and I sat listening in happiness almost unbearable. Some guests were announced. She went into another room to receive them, and I took up her book. It was Guy Mannering, then lately published, and the first of Scott's novels I had ever seen. I opened where her mark lay, and read merely with the feeling of continuing our mutual existence by passing my eyes over the same page where hers had been. It was the description of the rocks on the sea-coast where the little Harry Bertram was lost. I had never seen such places, and my mind was vividly stirred to imagine them. The scene rose before me, very unlike reality, doubtless, but majestic and wild. I was the little Harry Bertram, and had lost her, — all I had to lose, — and sought her vainly in long dark caves that had no end, plashing through the water; while the crags beetled above, threatening to fall and crush the poor child. Absorbed in the painful vision, tears rolled down my cheeks. Just then she entered with light step, and full-beaming eye. When she saw me thus, a soft cloud stole over her face, and clothed every feature with a lovelier tenderness than I had seen there before. She did not question, but fixed on me inquiring looks of beautiful love. I laid my head against her shoulder and wept, — dimly feeling that I must lose her and all, — all who spoke to me of the same things, — that the cold wave must rush over me. She waited till my tears were spent, then rising, took from a little box a bunch of golden amaranths or everlasting flowers, and gave them to me. They were very fragrant. "They came," she said, "from Madeira." These flowers stayed with me seventeen years. "Madeira" seemed to me the fortunate isle, apart in the blue ocean from all of ill or dread. Whenever I saw a sail passing in the distance, — if it bore itself with fulness of beautiful certainty, − I felt that it was going to Madeira. Those thoughts are all gone now. No Madeira exists for me now, − no fortunate purple isle, − and all these hopes and fancies are lifted from the sea into the sky. Yet I thank the charms that fixed them here so long, − fixed them till perfumes like those of the golden flowers were drawn from the earth, teaching me to know my birth-place.

I can tell little else of this time, − indeed, I remember little, except the state of feeling in which I lived. For I *lived*, and when this is the case, there is little to tell in the form of thought. We meet − at least those who are true to their instincts meet − a succession of persons through our lives, all of whom have some peculiar errand to us. There is an outer circle, whose existence we perceive, but with whom we stand in no real relation. They tell us the news, they act on us in the offices of society, they show us kindness and aversion; but their influence does not penetrate; we are nothing to them, nor they to us, except as a part of the world's furniture. Another circle, within this, are dear and near to us. We know them and of what kind they are. They are to us not mere facts, but intelligible thoughts of the divine mind. We like to see how they are unfolded; we like to meet them and part from them; we like their action upon us and the pause that succeeds and enables us to appreciate its quality. Often we leave them on our path, and return no more, but we bear them in our memory, tales which have been told, and whose meaning has been felt.

But yet a nearer group there are, beings born under the same star, and bound with us in a common destiny. These are not mere acquaintances, mere friends, but, when we meet, are sharers of our very existence. There is no separation; the same thought is given at the same moment to both, − indeed, it is born of the meeting, and would not otherwise have been called into existence at all. These not only know themselves more, but *are* more for having met, and regions of their being, which would else have laid sealed in cold obstruction, burst into leaf and bloom and song. . . .

My English friend went across the sea. She passed into her former life, and into ties that engrossed her days. But she has never ceased to think of me. Her thoughts turn forcibly back to the child who was to her all she saw of the really New World. On the promised coasts she had found only cities, careful men and women, the aims and habits of ordinary life in her own land, without that elegant culture which she, probably, overestimated, because it was her home. But in the mind of the child she found the fresh prairie, the untrodden forests for which

she had longed. I saw in her the storied castles, the fair stately parks
and the wind laden with tones from the past, which I desired to know.
We wrote to one another for many years; — her shallow and delicate
epistles did not disenchant me, nor did she fail to see something of the
old poetry in my rude characters and stammering speech. But we must
never meet again.

When this friend was withdrawn I fell into a profound depression. I
knew not how to exert myself, but lay bound hand and foot. Melancholy enfolded me in an atmosphere, as joy had done. This suffering,
too, was out of the gradual and natural course. Those who are really
children could not know such love, or feel such sorrow. "I am to
blame," said my father, "in keeping her at home so long merely to
please myself. She needs to be with other girls, needs play and variety.
She does not seem to me really sick, but dull rather. She eats nothing,
you say. I see she grows thin. She ought to change the scene."

I was indeed *dull*. The books, the garden, had lost all charm. I had
the excuse of headache, constantly, for not attending to my lessons.
The light of life was set, and every leaf was withered. At such an early
age there are no back or side scenes where the mind, weary and sorrowful, may retreat. Older, we realize the width of the world more, and it is
not easy to despair on any point. The effort at thought to which we are
compelled relieves and affords a dreary retreat, like hiding in a brick-
kiln till the shower be over. But then all joy seemed to have departed
with my friend, and the emptiness of our house stood revealed. This I
had not felt while I every day expected to see or had seen her, or
annoyance and dulness were unnoticed or swallowed up in the one
thought that clothed my days with beauty. But now she was gone, and
I was roused from habits of reading or reverie to feel the fiery temper
of the soul, and to learn that it must have vent, that it would not be
pacified by shadows, neither meet without consuming what lay around
it. I avoided the table as much as possible, took long walks and lay in
bed, or on the floor of my room. I complained of my head, and it was
not wrong to do so, for a sense of dulness and suffocation, if not pain,
was there constantly.

But when it was proposed that I should go to school, that was a
remedy I could not listen to with patience for a moment. The peculiar-
ity of my education had separated me entirely from the girls around,
except that when they were playing at active games, I would sometimes
go out and join them. I liked violent bodily exercise, which always
relieved my nerves. But I had no success in associating with them be-

yond the mere play. Not only I was not their school-mate, but my book-life and lonely habits had given a cold aloofness to my whole expression, and veiled my manner with a hauteur which turned all hearts away. Yet, as this reserve was superficial, and rather ignorance than arrogance, it produced no deep dislike. Besides, the girls supposed me really superior to themselves, and did not hate me for feeling it, but neither did they like me, nor wish to have me with them. Indeed, I had gradually given up all such wishes myself; for they seemed to me rude, tiresome, and childish, as I did to them dull and strange. This experience had been earlier, before I was admitted to any real friendship; but now that I had been lifted into the life of mature years, and into just that atmosphere of European life to which I had before been tending, the thought of sending me to school filled me with disgust.

Yet what could I tell my father of such feelings? I resisted all I could, but in vain. He had no faith in medical aid generally, and justly saw that this was no occasion for its use. He thought I needed change of scene, and to be roused to activity by other children. "I have kept you at home," he said, "because I took such pleasure in teaching you myself, and besides I knew that you would learn faster with one who is so desirous to aid you. But you will learn fast enough wherever you are, and you ought to be more with others of your own age. I shall soon hear that you are better, I trust." [*Memoirs, I, 11-24, 26-28, 30-37, 39-42*]

6. On her mother's imagined death, no date

While the manuscript for the autobiographical romance above has not survived, six undated pages of a more strictly fictional autobiography, buried in the midst of Fuller's copious reading notes and never published, have. In this narrative, Fuller is apparently a boy and the mother dies just at the time in Fuller's real life when her father began to control her development. The fragment begins with the death of Fuller's sister, two years younger.

... My mother never recovered from the death of this child. She had watched her too anxiously through her illness, and her life was a slender stem that would not bear more than one blow from the axe. Beside, her whole life was in her children, for her marriage was the not uncommon one of a lovely young girl, ignorant of herself, and of her capacities for feeling, to a man of suitable age and position because he chose her. He was an honorable, kind-hearted, well-educated (as it is called) and of good sense, but a mere man of business who had never dreamed of what such a woman as she needs in domestic life. He kept her in a good house, with a good wardrobe, was even in his temper, and indulgent to her wishes, but he did not know what it was to be companionable, the friend, much less the lover, and if he had he would not have had time, for his was the swift crowded course of an American business life. So she pined and grew dull, she knew not why, something was wanting she could not tell what, but there was a dreariness, a blank, she tormented herself that she was so ungrateful to a kind Providence, which had given her so much for want of which the many suffer; she tried to employ herself for the poor, she gave her heart to her children. Still she languished and the first blow found so little life to resist it, that she fell a speedy victim.

Perhaps it was well so, and yet I know not. Beside my own feeling of infinite loss there has been a bitter sense that had she lived there was enough in me corresponding with her unconscious wants to have aroused her intellect and occupied her affections. Perhaps her son might have made up to her for want of that full development of feeling which youth demands from love. . . . 'Twere too bitter to feel that all her lovely young life was wasted in the sand, but that all around I see such mutilation of lives, that I must transfer my hope for the rest to future spheres. . . . [Houghton MS]

7. To her father, January 16, 1820

It is worth comparing Fuller's recollection of childhood with letters written in childhood to her father, though it is especially difficult to interpret the tone of children's letters. Although many refer in passing to Ellen Kilshaw, the "first friend" of the autobiography, there is no indication in these letters of the paralyzing depression described there after her departure. In a letter written in Cambridge when she was nine, however, we find an outburst of devotion for Kilshaw (whose father's business had recently failed), as well as an equally romantic charitable impulse and an early sample of self-scrutiny. Fuller appears to have been translating "The Deserted Village," probably into Latin, and to have been reading for relaxation the popular moral novel, *Hesitation, or To Marry or Not To Marry?* by Mrs. Ross, and Dr. John Moore's Gothic horror tale, *Zeluco.*

My dear father,

 ... I attend a school which is kept by Aunt Abigail for *Eugene* and *myself* and my *cousins* which with writing and singing schools & my lessons to Uncle Elisha take up *most* of my time - - -

I *have* not written to Miss *Kilshaw yet as* there is no opportunity of sending our letters. *Deep rooted* indeed is my affection for her. May it flourish an *ever* blooming flower till our kindred spirits absolved from earthly clay mount together to these blissful regions where never again we shall be seperated [sic]. I am not romantic, I am not making professions when I say I love Ellen better than my life. I love her better and reverence her more for her misfortunes. Why should I not she is as lovely as sweet tempered as before. These were what I loved before and as she possesses all these now why should my love diminish. Ought it not rather to increase as she has more need of it. It is for herself alone I grieve for the loss of fortune. She will be exposed to many a trial a temptation she would otherwise have escaped. Not but I know she will go through them all? No But I shall feel *all* her sorrow - - - - - -

You will let me read Zeluco? will you not and no conditions. Have you been to the theatre this winter? Have they any oratorios at Washington? - - I am writing a new tale called The young satirist. You must expect the remainder of this page to be filled with a series of unconnected intelligence My beautiful pen now makes a large mark I will write no farther.   *17 January 1820*

Yesterday I threw by my pen for the reason mentioned above. Have you read Hesitation yet I knew you would (though you are no novel reader) to see if they were rightly delineated for I am possessed of the greatest blessing of life a good and kind father. Oh I can never repay you for all the love you have shown me. But I will do all I can We have had a dreadful snowstorm today. I never look around the room and behold all the comforts with which Heaven has blessed me without thinking of those *wretched* creatures who are wandering in all the snow without food or shelter. I am too young No I am not. In nine years a great part of my life I can remember but two good actions done those more out of selfishness than charity. There is a poor woman of the name of Wentworth in Boston who would willingly procure a subsistence but has not the means. My dear father a dollar would be a great sum to this poor woman. You remember the handsome dollar that I know your generosity would have bestowed on [me] when I had finished my Deserted Village I shall finish it well and desire nothing but the pleasure of giving it to her. My dear father send it to me immediately I am going into town this week I have a thousand things to say but neither time or paper to say them in.

> Farewel my dear Father I am
> your affectionate daughter Margaret Fuller

PS I do not like Sarah, call me Margaret alone, pray do!
[Houghton MS]

8. To her father, January 5, 1821

In a letter written in the next year, we can see the range of activities she enjoyed and swift fluctuations in tone—respectful, teasing, morally earnest, and erudite.

Dear Father,

And it is January, my dear sir; How the winter has flown. You have been gone two months. It seems as if there were neither nights or days the hours fly so quickly. We have no reason to complain of the slow foot of time. We had a ball here the other night and nearly three days were absorbed in preparations and reparations. However it was delightful and I danced as much as I wished. But mamma doubtless has given you a full description of it. I wish you would mend some pens and send them me. You would very much oblige me if you would do it.

I expect sir that when you come home you will bring me home a complete case of jewels or something equal to it and if you cant do that I will be satisfied with a gold ring plain or twisted or even with one made of tortoise shell. Aunt Fuller has taught me to play "Bounding billows" and sing it. I am sorry my dear sir you write to me so seldom. Has your affection decreased? I fear it has; I have often pained you but I hope you still love me. I should be most happy to be Dr Parks scholar. I will endeavor to gratify all your wishes. Dr Park has increased the number of his scholars if you write to him soon you may with ease get me a place Susan Williams said half in jest half in earnest she would take me to board and in earnest she said she wished I could come and live there that we might study together. I will tell you something highly to Susans honor. She has refused all invitations to go out that she may give all her time to study. This you know is really a considerable exertion of fortitude in a young lady who has such an extensive acquaintance as Susan has I think I should do so too, but I should not have nearly so many temptations to break my resolution as Susan has therefore it would not be so honorable in me as in her. . . .

> Your affectionate daughter
> S.M. Fuller *[Houghton MS]*

9. On schooling and growth, no date

This undated fragment from later years applies either to Dr. Park's school in Boston or the Prescotts' seminary in Groton, which she entered in the spring of 1824, for her drive and independence must have made her impatient with formal education in both places. (Curiously enough, the only school she repeatedly asked her father to send her to [see Houghton MS letters, winter 1823-24] was William Emerson's School for Young Ladies which had just passed into the reluctant hands of young Ralph Waldo Emerson.)

I was now in the hands of teachers, who had not, since they came on the earth, put to themselves one intelligent question as to their business here. Good dispositions and employment for the heart gave a tone to all they said, which was pleasing, and not perverting. They, no doubt, injured those who accepted the husks they proffered for bread, and believed that exercise of memory was study, and to know what others knew, was the object of study. But to me this was all penetrable. I had known great living minds, — I had seen how they took their food and did their exercise, and what their objects were. *Very early I knew that the only object in life was to grow.* I was often false to this knowledge, in idolatries of particular objects, or impatient longings for happiness, but I have never lost sight of it, have always been controlled by it, and this first gift of thought has never been superseded by a later love. *[Memoirs, I, 132-33]*

10. To Susan Prescott, July 11, 1825

When she returned from school in Groton to study at home in Cambridge, she wrote to her teacher about her intellectual regimen and the goals she cherished at fifteen.

You keep me to my promise of giving you some sketch of my pursuits. I rise a little before five, walk an hour, and then practise on the piano, till seven, when we breakfast. Next I read French, — Sismondi's Literature of the South of Europe — till eight, then two or three lectures in Brown's Philosophy. About half-past nine I go to Mr. Perkin's school and study Greek till twelve, when, the school being dismissed, I recite, go home, and practise again till dinner, at two. Sometimes, if the conversation is very agreeable, I lounge for half an hour over the desert, though rarely so lavish of time. Then, when I can, I read two hours in Italian, but I am often interrupted. At six, I walk, or take a drive. Before going to bed, I play or sing, for half an hour or so, to make all sleepy, and about eleven, retire to write a little while in my journal, exercises on what I have read, or a series of characteristics which I am filling up according to advice. Thus, you see, I am learning Greek, and making acquaintance with metaphysics, and French and Italian literature.

"How," you will say, "can I believe that my indolent, fanciful, pleasure-loving pupil, perseveres in such a course?" I feel the power of industry growing every day, and, besides the all-powerful motive of ambition, and a new stimulus lately given through a friend. I have learned to believe that nothing, no! not perfection, is unattainable. I am determined on distinction, which formerly I thought to win at an easy rate; but now I see that long years of labor must be given to secure even the "*succès de societé*," – which, however, shall never content me. I see multitudes of examples of persons of genius, utterly deficient in grace and the power of pleasurable excitement. I wish to combine both. I know the obstacles in my way. I am wanting in that intuitive tact and polish, which nature has bestowed upon some, but which I must acquire. And, on the other hand, my powers of intellect, though sufficient, I suppose, are not well disciplined. Yet all such hindrances may be overcome by an ardent spirit. If I fail, my consolation shall be found in active employment. *[Memoirs, I, 52-54]*

11. On Harriet Martineau [1835]

During her travels in America in 1835, Martineau (1802-1876), the celebrated British author, took a friendly interest in Fuller. In the older woman Fuller admired especially "the noble courage with which she stepped forward into life, and the accurate judgment with which she has become acquainted with its practical details, without letting her fine imagination become tamed" (*Memoirs*, I, 153). In an 1835 journal entry concerning Martineau, Fuller appears to have virtually equated being understood with finding a vocation, and to have highly valued strong differences in a relationship.

I sigh for an intellectual guide. Nothing but the sense of what God has done for me, in bringing me nearer to himself, saves me from depair. With what envy I looked at Flaxman's picture of Hesiod sitting at the feet of the Muse! How blest would it be to be thus instructed in one's vocation! Anything would I do and suffer, to be sure that, when leaving earth, I should not be haunted with recollections of "aims unreached, occasions lost." I have hoped some friend would do, – what none has ever yet done, – comprehend me wholly, mentally, and morally, and enable me better to comprehend myself. I have had some hope that Miss Martineau might be this friend, but cannot yet tell. She has what I want, – vigorous reasoning powers, invention, clear views of her objects, – and she has been trained to the best means of execution. Add to this, that there are no strong intellectual sympathies between us, such as would blind her to my defects. *[Memoirs, I, 153]*

12. On writing fiction, November 1835

More influential than de Staël or Martineau, George Sand's writing briefly tempted Fuller in Groton to try her hand at fiction—not a successful venture. We note the assumption in her journal that the self is divided into feminine and masculine compartments.

These books have made me for the first time think I might write into such shapes what I know of human nature. I have always thought that I would not, that I would keep all that behind the curtain, that I would not write, like a woman, of love and hope and disappointment, but like a man, of the world of intellect and action. But now I am tempted, and if I can but do well my present work and show that I can write like a man, and if but the wild gnomes will keep from me with their shackles of care for bread in all its shapes of factitious life, I think I will try whether I have the hand to paint, as well as the eye to see. But I cannot but feel that I have seen, from the mouth of my damp cave, stars as fair, almost as many, as this person from the "Flèche of the Cathedral," where she has ascended at such peril. But I dare boast no more; only, please fate, be just and send me an angel out of this golden cloud that comes after the pelting showers I have borne so long. [Higginson, p. 188]

13. On George Sand, no date and 1839

Fuller kept notes on her reactions to her reading, often sending them off as letters to friends. In two notes on Sand, the second postdated 1839, her eagerness to find a mentor is borne out by her quick criticism of Sand's failings. Though she finds Sand's freedom richer that that of Bettina Brentano, Goethe's correspondent, Sand's philosophy is as incomplete or derivative as Fuller's own, and her courage unequal to Fuller's ideal. "No self-ruling Aspasia, she," Fuller concludes at this time, "yet her style,—with what a deeply smouldering fire it burns!"

a. . . . The question of Free Will, – how to reconcile its workings with necessity and compensation, – how to reconcile the life of the heart with that of the intellect, – how to listen to the whispering breeze of Spirit, while breasting, as a man should, the surges of the world, – these enigmas Sand and her friends seem to have solved no better that M.F. and her friends.

The practical optimism is much the same as ours, except that there is more hope for the masses – soon. . . .

I am astonished at her insight into the life of thought. She must know it through some man. Women, under any circumstances, can scarce do more than dip the foot in this broad and deep river; they have not strength to contend with the current. Brave, if they do not delicately shrink from the cold water. No Sibyls have existed like those of Michel Angelo; those of Raphael are the true brides of a God, but not themselves divine. It is easy for women to be heroic in action, but when it comes to interrogating God, the universe, the soul, and, above all, trying to live above their own hearts, they dart down to their nests like so many larks, and, if they cannot find them, fret like the French Corinne. Goethe's Makaria was born of the stars. Mr. Flint's Platonic old lady a *lusus naturæ*, and the Dudevant has loved a philosopher. [*Memoirs, I, 246-47*]

b. When I first knew G. Sand, I thought I found tried the experiment I wanted. I did not value Bettine so much she had not pride enough for me, only now when I am sure of myself would I pour out my soul at the feet of another. In the assured soul it is kingly prodigality: in one which cannot forbear, it is mere babyhood. I love abandon only when natures are capable of the extreme reverse. I knew Bettine would end in nothing, when I read her book – I knew she could not outlive her love.

But in Les Sept Cordes de la Lyre, which I read first, I saw the knowledge of the passions and of social institutions, with the celestial choice which rose above them. . . .

But here (in the Lettres d'un Voyageur) what do I see? An unfortunate woman wailing her loneliness, wailing her mistakes, writing for money? She has genius, and a manly grasp of mind, but not a manly heart! Will there never be a being to combine a man's mind and woman's heart, and who yet finds life too rich to weep over? Never? . . . [*Houghton MS*]

14. On doubts about writing [circa 1839]

Her own attempts to write were often paralyzed. Besides suffering from nearsightedness and eyestrain, Fuller was dogged by chronic migraine. ("It is but a bad head," she wrote, adding mockingly, "as bad as if I were a great man!" [*Memoirs*, I, 172-73]) Sometimes she believed illness had "judiciously tempered" her spirit; sometimes pain gave her illusions of a disembodied synthesis: "I dreamt that my body was a dungeon and a beautiful angel escaped at the head" (Houghton MS). Usually illness blocked working; and in health she was often troubled by lack of conviction and a fear that art betrayed life. She voiced her doubts about writing in a letter to a friend in 1839 (first selection below) and in her journals around that time.

a. Since you went away, . . . I have thought of many things I might have told you, but I could not bear to be eloquent and poetical. It is a mockery thus to play the artist with life, and dip the brush in one's own heart's blood. One would fain be no more artist, or philosopher, or lover, or critic, but a soul ever rushing forth in tides of genial life.

b. My verses, – I am ashamed when I think there is scarce a line of poetry in them, – all rhetorical and impassioned, as Goethe said of De Stael. However, such as they are, they have been overflowing drops from the somewhat bitter cup of my existence.

c. How can I ever write with this impatience of detail? I shall never be an artist; I have no patient love of execution; I am delighted with my sketch, but if I try to finish it, I am chilled. Never was there a great sculptor who did not love to chip the marble.

d. Then a woman of tact and brilliancy, like me, has an undue advantage in conversation with men. They are astonished at our instincts. They do not see where we got our knowledge; and, while they tramp on in their clumsy way, we wheel, and fly, and dart hither and thither, and seize with ready eye all the weak points, like Saladin in the desert. It is quite another thing when we come to write, and, without suggestion from another mind, to declare the positive amount of thought that is in us. Because we seemed to know all, they think we can tell all; and, finding we can tell so little, lose faith in their first opinion of us, *which, nathless, was true. [Memoirs, I, 294-96]*

15. On Bettina Brentano and Karoline von Günderode [circa 1842]

In 1842, Fuller translated part of the correspondence between these two romantic German women. Even in their different characters she saw mirrored her difficulty in containing in one self, one life, the fullness and meaning she craved.

. . . The two girls are equal natures, and both in earnest. Goethe made a puppet-show, for his private entertainment, of Bettine's life, and we wonder she did not feel he was not worthy of her homage. Gunderode is to me dear and admirable, Bettine only interesting. Gunderode is of religious grace, Bettine the fulness of instinctive impulse; Gunderode is the ideal, Bettine nature; Gunderode throws herself into the river because the world is all too narrow, Bettine lives and follows out every freakish fancy, till the enchanting child degenerates into an eccentric and undignified old woman. There is a medium somewhere. Philip Sidney found it; others had it found for them by fate. *[Memoirs, II, 58]*

16. To Beethoven, November 25, 1843

Sometimes loneliness or despair made her dream of telling the dying Goethe her state of mind: "He would support and guide me. He would be able to understand; he would show me how to rule circumstances, instead of being ruled by them. . . . he would have wished to see me what Nature intended" (*Memoirs*, I, 122). But accounts of his impassivity to friends chilled her. In another fantasy—poured out in her journal after a concert—she addressed Beethoven. But far from releasing her to her own sphere of action, admiration of Beethoven rendered her passive and without identity of her own. In the *Memoirs* (I, 232-34), the editors provide a drastically altered version; they demurely render "cherish thee" where she wrote "receive thee wholly," and piously substitute "saint or martyr" for her disparaged "Jesus." (The ellipsis in the fourth paragraph is Fuller's own.)

My only friend,

How shall I thank thee for again tonight breaking the chains of my sorrowful slumber. I did not expect it. For months now I have been in a low state of existence. Nothing profited me; nothing budded or blossomed in my garden. I was not sad; the arrow did not rankle in my heart as sometimes it does, but it lay there a cold dull substance whose foreign pressure seemed to prevent pulsation from its harmony, life from its abundance.

My eyes are always clear, dear friend. I always see that the universe is rich, if I am poor. I see the insignificance of my sorrows. In my will, I am not a captive, in my intellect, not a slave. It is not my fault that the palsy of my affections benumbs my whole life. I would disregard it if I could.

And here indeed, my lot is accursed, yes, my friend, let me curse it. The curse like the ill is but for the time. I know what the Eternal justice promises. But on this one sphere it is sad. Thou didst say thou hadst no friend but thy art. But that one is enough. I have no art, in which to vent the swell of a soul as deep as thine, Beethoven, and of a kindred frame. Thou wilt not think me presumptuous in this saying as another might. I have always known that thou wouldst welcome, wouldst know me, as no other who ever lived upon the earth since its first creation would.

Thou wouldst forgive me, Master, that I have not been true to my eventual destiny, and therefore have suffered on every side "the pangs of despised love." Thou didst the same . . . but thou didst borrow from those errors the inspiration of thy genius. Why is it not thus with me? Is it because, as a woman, I am bound by a physical law, which prevents the soul from manifesting itself? Sometimes the moon seems mockingly to say so, – to say that I, too, shall not shine, unless I can find a sun. O cold and barren moon; tell a different tale, and give me a son of my own.

But thou, oh blessed master! dost answer all my questions, and make it my privilege to be. Like a humble wife to the sage or poet, it is my triumph that I can understand, can receive thee wholly, like a mistress I arm thee for the fight, like a young daughter, I tenderly bind thy wounds. Thou art to me beyond compare, for thou art all I want. No heavenly sweetness of Jesus, no many-leaved Raphael, no golden Plato, is anything to me, compared with thee. The infinite Shakespeare, the stern Angelo, Dante bittersweet like thee, are no longer dear in thy presence. And besides these names, there are none others that could vibrate in thy crystal sphere. – Thou hast all of them, and that ample surge of life beside that great winged being which they only dreamed of.

There is none greater than Shakespeare for he is a god, but his creations are successive, thy Fiat comprehends them all.

Beethoven, my heart beats. I live again, for I feel that I am worthy audience for thee, and that my being would be reason enough for thine.

I met thy mood and mine last summer in nature on those wide impassioned plains flower and crag-bestrown. There the tide of emotion had rolled over and left the vision of its smiles and sobs as I saw to-night from thee.

Oh, if thou wouldst take me wholly to thyself. I am lost in this world where I sometimes meet angels, but of a different star from mine. Forgive me that I love them who cannot love me. Even so does thy spirit call upon, plead with all spirits. But thou dost triumph and bring them all in.

Master! I have this summer envied the oriole which had even a swinging nest in the high bough. I have envied the least flower that came to seed, though that seed were strown to the wind. But I envy none when I am with thee. Tonight I had no wish for thee: it was long since we had met. I did not expect to feel again. I was so very cold; tears had fallen; but they were Hamlet tears of speculation. Thy touch made me again all human. O save and give me to myself and thee. *[Houghton MS]*

17. On her dilemma *[early 1840s]*

The problem of being Margaret Fuller was kept alive—as these journal entries, probably from the early 1840s, disclose—by her refusal to adopt even a rich role if some of her talent, feeling, or aspiration was sacrificed in it.

For all the tides of life that flow within me, I am dumb and ineffectual, when it comes to casting my thought into a form. No old one suits me. If I could invent one, it seems to me the pleasure of creation would make it possible for me to write. What shall I do, dear friend? I want force to be either a genius or a character. One should be either private or public. I love best to be a woman; but womanhood is at present too straitly-bounded to give me scope. At hours, I live truly as a woman; at others, I should stifle; as, on the other hand, I should palsy, when I would play the artist. *[Memoirs, I, 297]*

With the intellect I always have, always shall, overcome; but that is not the half of the work. The life, the life! O, my God! shall the life never be sweet? *[Memoirs, I, 237]*

As we shall see in the autobiographical sketch, "Mariana" (II:7), friendship came late and as a crisis into Fuller's life. In her letters and in reminiscences about her from her New England years, a sense of life dramatically heightened usually informs her contact with others. At that time, friendship had the importance and freshness of a new idea; New Englanders were self-conscious and delighted with it, possibly more eager to define it than love, and not insistent on distinguishing the two. [1] The cult of friendship was part of the romanticism of the times. When Fuller thanked Susan Prescott for giving her "the true life—the love of Trust and Honor," she was both anticipating the thanks dozens of friends would give her and naming the standard to which she would hold them and herself. Romanticism also fed the uninhibited sentimentality and passionate style of much discourse of the time, and the belief in irresistible, quasi-mystical "affinities" between persons. At the same time, in the 1830s and 1840s, friendship was becoming an intellectual phenomenon. Through their criticism of social institutions and materialism, intellectuals, especially the Transcendentalists, were beginning to think of themselves as a separate class, and this experience enhanced their need and appreciation of each other. The effort to nurture, analyze, and criticize intimacy, to share letters of friends, and to compare one friend with another, became habitual. Believing as they did in the richness of individuality and the infinite powers of consciousness, they found few occupations more valuable than sharing thought and feeling with a friend. Even Emerson, who found warmth toward people so difficult to sustain, believed friends "incomparably the richest informations of the power and order that lie at the heart of things." [2]

In the *Memoirs*, Fuller is treated most fully in her capacity as friend, with Channing quite simply regarding friendship as her vocation and Emerson calling her conversation the "most entertaining" in America. But these two men made no secret of the way they were initially repelled by her manner of dominating a group. Significantly, their antagonism found the same image, with Emerson saying "the men thought she carried too many guns" and Channing confessing that he avoided "one so armed from head to foot in saucy sprightliness." [3] For both, closer acquaintance with Fuller, particularly a tête-à-tête, broke down their resistance. Sarah Clarke attested to a similar double take in the process of becoming Fuller's friend, an experience of warfare that gave way to exhilarating peace—exhilarating because she found she was taken seriously as never before. Fuller had no tact. Wanting the substance of a person before her, she was too impatient for manners. But while Sarah Clarke felt Fuller's assault on her reserves and pretenses, the men were apparently wounded in their vanity and in their sense of what is proper to the gentler sex.

Once Fuller as warrior had broken through the shields of privacy or prejudice, she could lay down arms and disclose herself as the friend of striking talents. Certainly she was exacting and often difficult in this second phase, demanding friendship on her own terms. But her friendship was rare and original, for it drew on the provinces, as then understood, of both sexes. She was always active, searching, critical—the qualities she called "masculine"; but the "feminine" attributes—loyalty, nurture, tenderness, passion—were there too, now galvanized by the "masculine." With modern psychological insight, she understood that the secret, even shameful, aspects of the personality had to be exposed and understood for the integrated, or ideal, self to flourish. The intimate moral effect of her friendship is similar in all accounts and well summed up by James Clarke, who wrote her,

> What should I ever have been but for you? I am not much now, but what I am, I owe in a large degree to your influence. You roused my heart with high hopes, you raised my aims from paltry amusements to those which tasked the head and fed the soul. You inspired me with a great ambition to distinguish myself above my fellows, and made me see the worth and meaning of life. Whatever we owe to those who give us confidence in ourselves, who make us believe we *are* something distinct and can do something special, who arouse

our individual consciousness by an intelligent sympathy with
tendencies and feelings we ourselves only half understand—all
this I owe to you. You gave me to myself. [4]

And remarkably, once he came to know Fuller, Channing
translated his early fear of her emasculating power into a
source of virile strength: "The very thought of her aroused
manliness to emulate the vigorous freedom, with which one
was assured, that wherever placed she was that instant
acting." [5]

Not everyone seized the offer of such friendship. The
volatile young poet, Ellery Channing, refused the prospect of
having his ideal self always held before him, liking to "grow
backward" as much as forward. The pugnacious Unitarian
reformer, Theodore Parker, rejected the initial conditions of
her friendship. He and Fuller never became close, according
to Caroline Healey Dall, because both "required a sort of
personal submission before newcomers could be admitted to
a cordial understanding." A few young women felt "put on"
by Fuller and allowed "no chance"; one of them, "jealous of
another's influence," as Emerson put it privately, resisted
"with petulance." The women who welcomed her intimacy
probably did so with the quality of reasoned courage
disclosed by the odd locution of Sarah Shaw nearly four
decades after Fuller's death: "I feel proud that I had the
sense to love and venerate her as I did." [6] To be Fuller's
friend took a certain daring.

Though it fused her disparate energies, sharpened her
identity, served her differing needs as they emerged, and
brought something new to the culture of New England, the
art of friendship alone could not be her vocation. The sheer
exercise of her formidable personality could not long conceal
the absence of real function. Thus Fuller excited herself with
her own extemporaneous gifts but regretted that they did not
readily translate into writing and judged that her need of a
companion to "call out" her best "bespeaks a second-rate
mind." [7] And as we shall see, on the two occasions when she
tried to make relationships fill the need of a vocation, she did
the greatest injustice to herself and to reality. But all her

friendships worked eventually to move her toward her vocation: by exorcising some of her fantasies and exercising many of her anomalous drives, friendship helped to accustom Fuller to reality and society to Margaret Fuller.

Her earliest friendships were essentially rescues, usually conducted by older women, eager to engage the girl who was either isolating or aggressively alienating herself through self-pity, self-dramatization, and ignorance of all arts of friendship. Despite their differences, the coquettish British visitor Ellen Kilshaw, the earnest schoolmistress Susan Prescott, and the cosmopolitan author of a manual on etiquette Eliza Farrar all worked to domesticate the young Fuller, to make the ideal of womanhood, stretched just slightly, fit her better. Thus, after Fuller's ebullient and sharp-tongued behavior had put off a number of Cambridge matrons, Eliza Farrar, who admired her greatly, "undertook to mould her externally, to make her less abrupt, less self-asserting, more *comme il faut* in ideas, manners, and even costume." [8] Apparently, Fuller was grateful to this urbane and generous friend, who had time and skills her own mother lacked and could temporarily serve as role model.

Eliza Farrar introduced her to a number of women her age and younger who became devoted companions. Intense relationships with one or another young woman were a constant element in her life from her late teens to her early thirties when she left New England. There was Anna Barker, the talented Southern kinswoman of Farrar's, whose beauty moved Emerson to call her "that very human piece of divinity" [9] and Fuller to confide in her journal: "It is so true that a woman may be in love with a woman, and a man with a man" (II:16). Her relation with Anna reminded her of the love between brilliant de Staël and beautiful Récamier. Later, Fuller made a friend of a young student, the "gypsy-like," mischievous, and gifted Caroline Sturgis. Their early correspondence is marked by rhetoric of ecstasy, jealousy, withdrawal, and cautious return. The fervor and erotic overtones of these relationships beg for analysis.

It is possible that these women were more than half-consciously mimicking the intimacies of the romantic movement in Europe. Fuller had introduced to an enthralled circle of friends the fictionalized *Conversations with a Child*, supposedly a record of Goethe's friendship with Bettina Brentano, daughter of a wealthy merchant. But she had come to judge it somewhat distasteful, with its "air of an elderly guardian flirting cautiously with a giddy, inexperienced ward," or a "Father Confessor" using his office "to gratify his curiosity." More pleased by the relation between the spirited girl and Karoline von Günderode, eight years older, a canoness of a religious order, Fuller translated part of their correspondence. In this extravagant exhibit of romantic friendship, each mind was "at equal expense of keeping up its fires." Fiery indeed was the relation between the two women, particularly when Günderode fell victim to despair like "a chasm here in the breast" (Bettina: "can I not fill it? this chasm?" Günderode: "That also would pain me"). Or when Bettina writes: "Thou hast said that thy desire is to be free; but I do not desire to be free, but to take root in thee, a wood-rose refreshing itself in its own fragrance, it opens its bosom to the sun, but there if the earth crumbles away from its roots, all is over . . . when I think of the fiery radiance with which thou has so oft shone through my soul—abide with me yet." [10] Günderode's hot-and-cold magic, her brew of ideality and ardor, was not unlike that which Fuller served up to Barker and Sturgis.

But in America at this period, the language of Eros in female friendship was not unique to the talk and letters of Fuller's literary friends; it was a broader cultural phenomenon. A native explanation for it is connected to the cult of "true womanhood." Though initially backed by the need to make women satisfied and productive in the narrowed sphere of the home, the notion that women were essentially different from men began to produce unexpected and slightly subversive results. The myth that women alone possessed purity and spirituality undermined the case for heterosexuality and even for confinement to the nuclear family. For women could not expect to share these qualities with coarse, corrupted men and would need to look beyond the home for "kindred spirits." They would generate a "sisterhood of sensibility" in religious and reform organizations and especially in friendships. [11] One might further imagine that, since women brought up on this ideology were trained to believe that only men were burdened with sexual feeling, when such feeling arose in them they would not entirely recognize it for what it was. Rather, interpreting it as a potent effusion of the spirit, they would share this too with their dearest friends. Under the governing assumption that they shared purity, women could safely vent amorous feelings without needing to examine them. A side effect of the cult of true womanhood was thus an elaborate system of permitted passion. A thin line here separates healthy emotional freedom from damaging self-deception. Fuller probably recognized this both in her instinctive retreat from the emotional exhaustion of her meetings with Barker and in her mysterious remark that her connection with Sturgis had been "redeemed from the search after Eros" (II:18).

When the intensity diminished, quieter relations, like those Fuller sustained with other women, prevailed. Then the situations of her friends became opportunities to struggle with the problems of women: the unreflective reading habits of one, the need of another for more thoughtful companions, the stultifying marriage of a gifted poet, the paralyzing motherhood of a girl not yet developed. Such friendships could also become the theater for her self-expression of a laboratory in which she could test acceptance of her own anomalous yearnings.

Her friendships with men—though those with women were said to be six times more numerous—were equally important in keeping alive her hope for recognition and for the emergence somehow of a vocation. Harvard students, they were, for the most part, better equipped than the women to meet her on intellectual grounds and to sustain the energies charged by her father's pedagogy. She appears to have been content, in her Cambridge years, with the platonic nature of these relations. The single exception was her distant cousin George Davis. "His mirth," she wrote, "unsettled all things from their foundations"; [12] she might have hoped that his famous wit was token of a courageous inconoclasm. His failure to reciprocate her feelings hurt her briefly, but other stimulating companions, especially James Clarke, offered compensation.

When the pattern of her life was changed at twenty-three by the family's move to the farm at Groton, forty miles from Boston, correspondence with these friends assumed greater importance. Like the regular course of study she assigned herself in her spare time (German, French, and English Romanticism, European and American history, architecture, and astronomy), the correspondence in which she discussed her reading and thoughts was an antidote to the standard women's work she now did in keeping house, caring for the illnesses of her mother and grandmother, and sewing. ("Plain sewing is decidedly immoral," Fuller firmly opined. [13]) She also tutored the four youngest of her six siblings—Ellen, Arthur, Richard, and Lloyd—for five to eight hours a day. Though her father promised her a trip to Europe as a reward, and though he read American history with her, Fuller often felt frozen with resentment over the loss of the social and intellectual life of Cambridge. And, in an anecdote from September 1835, we get some measure of the stiffness he exhibited even when he meant to be tender. She had fallen into an illness—then called "brain fever" [14]—which it was feared she might not survive. "Habitually so sparing in tokens of affection," her father expressed his feelings for her more strongly than he had ever done: "My dear, I have been thinking of you in the night, and I cannot remember that you have any *faults*. You have defects, of course, as all mortals have, but I do not know that you have a single fault." [15] She had barely recovered her health when the long-planned course of her life was deflected by his sudden death from cholera on October 1.

Two new kinds of relationship were among the consequences of this shock to Fuller. In the first, she stepped into Timothy's shoes, acting as helpmeet to her mother and father to the children; in the second she remained in part the child in painful search for the father who had withheld himself up to the ultimate withdrawal. She took the first role when she called the younger children to her father's corpse and pledged on her knees that, "if she had ever been ungrateful or unfilial to her father, she would atone for it by fidelity to her brothers and sisters." [16] She kept her vow, first by fighting for her sister's right to education against her narrow-minded domineering Uncle Abraham, who took it upon himself to settle his brother's meager estate. She complained bitterly that she was deprived by gender of legal authority over the children. Then, with a devotion little recognized in the Fuller of the *Memoirs*, she set herself to learn how to handle the family business and financial matters, for which she felt she had little skill but her mother no capacity at all. Painfully she relinquished the long-cherished dream of going with the Farrars and an attractive new friend, Sam Ward, to Europe, where Harriet Martineau would have introduced her to the larger literary world for which she longed. For two years she taught school to help support the family—first in Bronson Alcott's controversial Temple School, then in Providence. In her frequent letters to all members of her family, she shepherded them individually and kept them in touch with each other. Thus she watched over the business careers of her brothers Eugene in New Orleans and William Henry in Cincinnati, and the uneasy marriage of Ellen to the quixotic poet Ellery Channing, helping them all plan where and how to live. In Arthur first, then Richard, she invested her own ambitions for a while, worked to finance their professional training, and advised them even about women. With poignant empathy, she arranged for education or treatment for the retarded brother, Lloyd. And her mother, no longer overshadowed by the domineering Timothy, became the object of unremitting affection; from near or far, Fuller devised comforts for her, or company and help with her garden. She scrutinized members of her family, like her friends, through the lens of their ideal development as she saw it, but she was generally hardheaded about their practical needs. She could be hurt by their failure to confide in her, but she learned to feel toward them a realistic acceptance that, as we shall see, anticipated her later friendships abroad.

The loss of her father, which forced her to become the head of the family, also left unresolved her need for simple affection; Timothy had always offered instead intellectual

rigor and pride in her. Thus, at thirty, she recalls in her
journal her childish desire for another relation with him:
"When I recollect how deep the anguish, how deeper still the
want with which I walked alone in hours of childish passion
and called for a father, after saying the word a hundred
times, till it was stifled by sobs, how great seems the duty
that name imposes." [17] The duty Timothy had shunned was
showing his daughter what to do with what he had made her:
how to unify the "masculine" and "feminine" poles in her
character. Instead, he had abandoned her to a society in
which she could only be useless and freakish.

Eventually, a feeling of respect and "relenting tenderness" [18] replaced the longing, resentment, and confusion she
felt in relation to her father. But first she would try to find
personal coherence and self-definition through two men.
Such projects are disastrous from their inception, burdening
relationships with a load they cannot bear. As if to lighten
the burden, Fuller tried to simplify her nature (and
necessarily distorted it), electing in the first case to deny her
sex and in the second to force herself into the role of
conventional woman. To make matters still worse, she fixed
on two men who were peculiarly ill-adapted for such
experiments.

Emerson was the first of these, and one of the most
important friends in her life. A man she had longed to meet
for years before she managed it, she continued to regard him
with love and reverence long after she discerned how little he
could directly help or understand her. Each became for the
other a touchstone for values attractively alien, and their
friendship did much to clarify for both the bounds their
temperaments set on them. Eight years older than Fuller,
Emerson must have first drawn her by his likeness to
Timothy in reserve and intellectual earnestness. More
important, he seemed to offer what Timothy could not, an
end to her anomalous social status—if not something to do, at
least a way to be. Calling his influence more "beneficial"
than that of "any American," Fuller wrote, "from him I first
learned what is meant by an inward life" (II:23). Early in
their friendship, he read aloud his "Nature," the conclusion

of which may have sounded to her like a solution. "Build therefore your own world," he had written. "As fast as you can conform your life to the pure idea in your mind, that will unfold its great proportions. . . . The advancing spirit . . . shall draw beautiful faces, warm hearts, wise discourse, and heroic acts, around its way, until evil is no more seen." In short, through his Transcendental faith he held out to her an alternative to the inhospitable social world, to American historical reality—a world fashioned after her individuality, not resistant to it.

In the beginning there was a pleasing reciprocity. When they met in 1836, Emerson, like Fuller, was grieving, and the loss of his brother Charles was such that the "very sober joy" in his second wife Lidian—one of the most frail, pious, and self-sacrificing of the Transcendentalists [19]—could not compensate for it. In exchange for the private world of consciousness, of introspective power and private harmony, Fuller tendered the best of real society, sharing her world of friendship. Sometimes Emerson was exuberantly grateful for the company of Fuller and the young friends—Caroline Sturgis, Anna Barker, Sam Ward—whom she freely shared with him: "your poor hermit . . . will come yet to know the world through your eyes." But just as Fuller eventually felt constrained by Emerson's ahistorical and solipsistic "inwardness," so did Emerson resist breaking out of his inveterate reserve. A tension developed as part of their friendship, for which both used the same striking word. Emerson's use of Montaigne's phrase, "Oh, *my friends*, there are no friends," was for Fuller "a paralyzing conviction," while Emerson confided in his journal after one of her visits, "Life too near paralyzes art." [20] What they had to offer one another was great, but given the ascetic basis of his craft and her need for vital relation, the threat of mutual paralysis was always near.

Other threats were more covert. One was emotional dishonesty bred of the cult of friendship and heightened by the mystique of Transcendentalism. This was expressed most simply by Fuller's and Emerson's complicity in refusing to recognize the effect of their intimacy on Lidian, who was also quite at a loss to express her discomfort. A more

complex (and potentially more destructive) evasion was
involved in the way in which, teaching self-reliance, Emerson
instilled expectations, even dependencies, for which he was
unable to take responsibility. One contradiction lay between
Emerson's belief that each person should follow his or her
own interior convictions and his wish that those convictions
should take on the coloration of Emerson's own. Another
contradiction was Fuller's: she could not separate her desire
to forge an independent and richly synthesized self from a
desire to have that self accepted, even sanctioned, by a
person of Emerson's stature. Early in 1840, when her
strenuous work on *The Dial* threw her into more regular and
tantalizing contact with him, she broached indirectly her
desire for such comprehensive acceptance. In a letter to her
dear Waldo, she constructed a parable about herself as a
"poor traveler of the desert" who toiled all day to reach a
distant palm: "But when he reached it, alas! it had grown too
high to shade the weary man at its foot." At the end she asks,
"Why do I write thus to one who must ever regard the
deepest tones of my nature as those of childish fancy or
worldly discontent."[21] Why, indeed, we might ask, if it were
not that Emerson, like the palm, was giving Fuller ambiguous
signals, alternately inviting her to approach with her vision
and her society and withdrawing from her intensity with
chill, lofty complacency?

As the year advanced, they both moved to deepen their
friendship, but from fatally diverse motivations. Emerson
contemplated writing an essay on friendship, though to
Fuller he confessed to being "perplexed lately with a droll
experience of limitation as if our faculties set a limit on our
affections."[22] In exploring the field with Fuller as guide, he
sought to identify his limits; by contrast, Fuller sought
through the connection with Emerson to arrive at her
greatest potential. (In such a contest, the conservative
objective prevails.) She resolved to make the palm stoop for
the weary traveler. Thus she wrote on an undated sheet of a
journal, surely from this period and about Emerson,

> I am bent on being his only friend myself. There is enough of
> me would I but reveal it. Enough of woman to sympathize

with all his feelings, enough of man to appreciate all thoughts[.] I could be a perfect friend and it would make me a nobler person. I would never indulge towards him that need of devotion which lies at the depth of my being. He measures too much, he is too reasonable. I could not be my truest childlike self. But I might be my truest manlike self. [23]

The passage is full of interesting contradictions. The sense that he draws on her "masculine" and "feminine" qualities counters her feeling that she cannot be "childlike" (by which she usually means playful, mystical, or fanciful) but only "manlike." And the effort to be noble, to refuse self-indulgence and spontaneity counters the bald possessiveness of the first sentence. We sense, under the confusion, the wish for wholeness and vocation narrowly construed as an exclusive mutual dependency.

The wish became explicit in the summer of 1840, a season of crisis for Fuller. Sam Ward and Anna Barker, each of whom had roused tumultuous feelings in her, were in the last stages of a problematic courtship, [24] and Fuller was probably struggling to feel a generous joy in their union. Then her arduous editorial work conflicted with a series of religious experiences that Emerson mistrusted as unhealthy and transitory. In August, exhausted and vulnerable, she turned to Emerson, challenging him to enlarge the grounds of their friendship, which she "stigmatized" as "commercial." He wrote to Sturgis that Fuller had "taxed me on both your parts with a certain inhospitality of soul," had accused him of remaining a critical stranger to women willing to be friends "in the full and sacred sense." He was disposed at first to meet the challenge ("If I count & weigh, I love also"), but he little knew how. [25]

Judging by his letters and the one of hers that survives from the ensuing debate, we can assume she was making a demand on Emerson as insupportable as it was inevitable. Having resolved as a child to be "bright and ugly," but discovering as she grew that her capacity for strong feeling and her "violent bodily" need for action only increased, she experimented with the idea of subsuming all these energies within a vital and generous intelligence. In effect, she wanted

to enlarge her "manlike" side until it included the rest of her.
Choosing for her partner in this enterprise of boundless
mutual exploration a man of exceptional and bold thought,
she hoped to bridge the sexual distinctions in herself, perhaps
to abolish them. Then her assumption that Emerson could
not respond sexually to her because he was married probably
worked only to intensify the paradoxically passionate way in
which she argued for a meeting of spirit. In pushing the lid
off friendship, she was concealing her motives twice over:
hiding her urge to dependence in heroics over free
development and forcing the straining and ecstasy of sex into
the locutions of the mind.

Fortunately for the future of her independence and
self-awareness, Emerson refused her experiment. In an entry
in his journal responding to one of her lost letters, he
upbraids her as he never could directly:

> You would have me love you. What shall I love? Your body?
> The supposition disgusts you. What you have thought and
> said? Well, whilst you were thinking and saying them, but not
> now. I see no possibility of loving anything but what now is,
> and is becoming; your courage, your enterprize, your budding
> affection, your opening thought, your prayer, I can love, but
> what else. [26]

In its own way, this is as revealing about Emerson as Fuller's
private thought on being "his only friend" is about her. As
she sought an exclusive, mutual, and total comprehension, he
wanted from her and others only what was potential,
suggestive, and fleeting—what, in short, could be absorbed in
his own system. The fixed past or hard edge, the time-bound
and circumstantial dimension, the persistent challenging
otherness of a friend called up no response in him.

Emerson's developed theory of friendship is consistent
with this bias. When Fuller, angered by his insistence that she
was alien to him, threw in his face virtual quotations from his
essay—writing, "But did you not ask for a foe in your friend?
Did you not ask for a 'large formidable nature?' "
(II:25)—she was seeing only part of that theory, for in that

same essay he rationalized his retreat. Although he does not analyze it thus, it seems that, precisely because his requirements for friendship are so total (it is essential that in dialogue "each stands for the whole world"), the ideal friendship is threatening: "Though I prize my friends, I cannot afford to talk with them and study their visions, lest I lose my own." The safe way is confessedly the exploitation of life for the soul's benefit: "The soul environs itself with friends that it may enter into a grander self-acquaintance or solitude." Thus, as he encouraged intense relations with Fuller to pursue his understanding of friendship, so, when the essay is done, did he follow his own analysis and withdraw. "I see very dimly in writing on this topic," he wrote her on October 24. "Do not expect it of me for a very long time."[27]

Fuller accepted his plea to return with good will to their old footing, and they remained friends all of her life. But beyond the emotional obfuscation, their crisis had exposed differences about the value of friendship which had intellectual and even ideological implications. Of course, Fuller too made use of friends, but generally her friends were not symbols. Their value lay in mutual support and she created with them a vital, congenial society; they and one's response to them were a road to the real world, not a replacement of it. Even in her incoherent desire to be Emerson's "only friend" she never intended to take more than she gave. Where Emerson's mode was evasion—"hovering like an eagle, skimming like a swallow . . . but never with me, nor in the depths"[28]—hers was commitment—"Why am I to love my friend the less for any obstruction in his life? Is not the very time for me to love most tenderly when I must see his life in despite of seeming?" (II:12). Fidelity, in fact, was a crucial test of one's capacity for reality: "To me it seems that the man or woman who can become indifferent to those they have loved, can hardly be depended on for reality in anything."[29] She connected her conviction to her gender, when she begged not to be exiled from the dark hour of her friend: "The manly mind might love best in the triumphant hour; but the woman could no more stay from the foot of

the cross than from the transfiguration" (II:12a). In her last
visit with the Emersons, in 1844, she teased him lightly about
how Concord lacked "the animating influence of Discord," [30] but she was making a related point. Where she
differed from Emerson was in seeking to know the whole
selves of friends, in wanting to share their pain, and in
believing in the creative good of contrast. As we shall see,
these attitudes were echoed in her response to Emersonian
Transcendentalism and in her move away from it.

Only one more time, so far as we know, did she feel and
yield to the lust of dependency. That was in 1845 when,
shortly after her arrival at the Greeleys' in New York, she
met and fell in love with the German-Jewish businessman
James Nathan, aged thirty-four like herself. We know little
about this gentle, blue-eyed man beyond the facts that he
was an amateur of the arts, played lieder on his guitar for
Fuller, and later aspired to publish travel pieces. When the
Greeleys apparently showed disapproval of him, they met
secretly and undertook a vigorous correspondence. Far from
denying her sex as with Emerson, Fuller now adopted the
stance of the stereotypical woman, passive and fixed on her
man. But less than in any of her relationships did this work
to draw together her various energies. It filled her alternately
with frustrated restlessness and regressive yearnings for rest.
The language of birds and blossoms crowded out all her
thought, and his attraction almost obliterated her respect for
self. ("I am with you as never with any other one, I like to be
quite still and have you the actor and the voice. You have life
enough for both; you will indulge me in this dear
repose." [31])

Fuller's letters that feverish spring show how near
repressed passion lay to repressed filial and maternal longings.
In a poem to Nathan, for instance, she calls herself "mother
of thy spirit life,/ And so in law thy wife," names him her
"sire," and identifies their "mutual birth" with spiritual
procreation. [32] What holds together the roles she assumes
here—mother, child, and lover—is the quality of willed
self-effacement, the apparent choice, for the first and last

time in her life, of the vicarious existence then believed
woman's natural end. It is tempting to imagine that Fuller
was conducting another experiment, for the willfully
"feminine" role was as artificial for her as the willfully
"masculine" had been. It seems more likely, however, that
her sexuality was more aroused than ever before and that for
the emergency the "feminine" idiom was the nearest to hand.

This is not to say that she could now lay claim to
self-knowledge. In her communications with Nathan, she was
still the daughter of the Puritans. We do not have Nathan's
letters, but we can deduce that, although he was the
countryman of Bettina, he lacked the benefit of indoctrina-
tion into New England's codified Platonism. Thus, when she
wrote, "Are you my guardian to domesticate me in the body,
and attach it more firmly to the earth?" he took it as a sexual
invitation. But when he made advances Fuller was shocked at
the revelation of his "lower nature" and required apologies.
A modern reader may sympathize with the foreigner to New
England's ways and find Nathan's misunderstanding entirely
comprehensible. A modern reader may even doubt that he
had entirely misunderstood Fuller's meaning. Nathan did
learn enough to be wary and eventually to retreat, in the late
spring, returning to Europe, ostensibly for business. The
promised reunion never took place. Plainly, he was no match
for her on any level. From Europe he wrote only to ask
favors and letters of reference; and his ultimate refusal,
however sugar-coated, to return her letters held the menace
that he might put them to some use. [33]

Despite the pain, as in the crisis with Emerson, Fuller
made progress with reality. She was losing her ability to
deceive herself about the content of feeling. Months after
Nathan's departure she could write, "I have felt . . . a desire
for you that amounted almost to anguish." [34] Perhaps she
was also beginning to understand that the complexity of her
character could be expressed in no single relationship and
that even love could not replace her need of the world. Only
in Paris would she meet a man who could articulate all these
needs. She met no American who could.

Notes

1. Thus Fuller wrote, "Love is no nobler than friendship, no more worthy of permanent life; but it searches deeper and drinks more life-blood" (BPL MS, no date).

2. *Memoirs*, I, 57; "Nature," *Complete Essays and Other Writings of Ralph Waldo Emerson*, ed. Brooks Atkinson (New York: Random House, 1950), p. 25.

3. *Memoirs*, I, 308, 202; II, 6.

4. March 1, 1838, *Letters of James Freeman Clarke*, ed. John Wesley Thomas (Hamburg, Germany: Cram, de Gruyter & Co., 1957), p. 129. Clarke added, concurring with Channing's judgment, "this great and benign influence" is "what God has given you to work."

5. *Memoirs*, II, 114.

6. Barbara Welter, "The Merchant's Daughter: A Tale for Life," *New England Quarterly*, 52 (1969), 10; Emerson, Notebook on MFO; May 20, 1884, to Thomas Wentworth Higginson, BPL MS.

7. *Memoirs*, I, 107.

8. Higginson, p. 36. Of old Nantucket whaling stock, Eliza Farrar (1791-1870), born at Dunkirk during the French Revolution, passed her childhood in England, where she knew eminent reformers and artists. She came to America in her twenties and at thirty-seven married a Harvard professor; in 1836, she published *The Young Lady's Friend*, a popular and practical manual which, while conservative in its stance toward women's sphere, urged women "to find pleasure in intellectual effort."

9. Rusk, *Letters*, II, 228.

10. "Bettina Brentano and Her Friend Günderode," *Dial*, II (1841), 316, 323, 329; "Preface," *Günderode* (Boston: Burnham, 1842), p. 2. The language and values of friendship in *Günderode* most directly influenced Fuller's reminiscences about Ellen Kilshaw in the autobiographical romance.

11. See William R. Taylor and Christopher Lasch, "Two Kindred Spirits: Sorority and Family in New England 1839-1846," *New England Quarterly*, 36 (1963), 23-41.

12. Joseph Jay Deiss, *The Roman Years of Margaret Fuller* (New York: T.Y. Crowell, 1969), p. 58. Clarke's letters suggest that Davis feared her influence and was unwilling to share his problems with her (*Letters of James Freeman Clarke*, pp. 56-57, 79).

13. *Reminiscences of Ednah Dow Cheney* (Boston: Lee & Shepard, 1902), p. 201. Reporting the remark, Cheney explained, "many women content themselves with the thought of industry when stitching wristbands . . . while mind and soul are empty and unemployed," adding "Margaret was no sentimentalist who valued self-sacrifice for its own sake" (p. 202).

14. This illness has prompted much speculation. Georgianna Bruce Kirby thought it was typhoid fever and that it caused Fuller's spinal curvature which was mysteriously cured by a magnetic healer a decade later (*Years of Experience* [New York: G. P. Putnam's Sons, 1887], p. 213). (Cheney, however, thought the curvature was caused by Fuller's tight-corseting in her teens.) On the other hand, Alexander E. Jones finds the illness psychosomatic; in "Margaret Fuller's Attempts to Write Fiction" (*Boston Public Library Quarterly*, VI [April 1954], 67-73), he argues that a story she wrote involving George Davis and his wife precipitated gossip and made Fuller ill with guilt.

15. *Memoirs*, I, 154.

16. Higginson, p. 54.

17. *Memoirs*, II, 52.

18. Higginson, p. 32.

19. Though Lidian on the verge of marriage seemed to Sarah Clarke almost equal to Emerson and perhaps as independent in her thinking as Margaret Fuller, in coming years Lidian had many reservations about her husband's iconoclastic views (Ralph L. Rusk, *The Life of Ralph Waldo Emerson* [New York: Charles Scribner's Sons, 1949], pp. 215, 226).

20. Rusk, *Letters*, II, 238; Harry R. Warfel, "Margaret Fuller and Ralph Waldo Emerson," *PMLA*, 50 (1935), 583-84, 586. For further analysis of this friendship, see also Carl F. Strauch, "Hatreds Swift Repulsions: Emerson, Margaret Fuller, and Others," *Studies in Romanticism*, 7 (1968), 65-103, and Bell Gale Chevigny, "Growing Out of New England: The Emergence of Margaret Fuller's Radicalism," *Women's Studies*, 4, No. 3 (1976).

21. *Memoirs*, I, 289-91.

22. Rusk, *Letters*, II, 248. Even when he engaged the task fully, he put it oddly—"I am determined by the help of heaven to suck this orange dry" (*Letters*, II, 332)—as if the task were finite and could try a man's patience.

23. Sheet enclosed in Emerson's Notebook on MFO. Until the argot of this circle is decoded, only intuition can help us measure the intensity of relationships. In reading letters or journal pieces as amorous in tone as this directed to "friend," "brother," or "sister," we suspect either that the tone is artificially warm or the appellation artificially cool. I choose the latter interpretation for Fuller's letter to Emerson in 1840.

24. Though Ward had hoped to live the life of an Emersonian scholar, he wrote later that his love for Anna, who was raised with the expectations of a society woman, made him desirous of satisfying "not only her feelings but her tastes by choosing the "lucrative profession" of business (David Baldwin, "Puritan Aristocrat in the Age of Emerson: A Study of Samuel Gray Ward," Dissertation, University of Pennsylvania, 1961, pp. 143-44). Apparently, Fuller took Ward's part and Emerson, infatuated by the confidences of the lovely Anna, took hers.

25. *Memoirs*, I, 288; Rusk, *Letters*, II, 325.

26. *The Journals and Miscellaneous Notebooks of Ralph Waldo Emerson*, eds. A. W. Plumstead and Harrison Hayford (Cambridge, Mass.: Harvard University Press, 1969), VII, 400.

27. "Friendship," *Complete Essays*, 235, 226; Rusk, *Letters*, II, 353.

28. July 12, 1840, to Caroline Sturgis, Tappan Papers, Houghton.

29. BPL MS, no date.

30. Higginson, p. 100.

31. *Love-Letters of Margaret Fuller, 1845-1846*, introduction by Julia Ward Howe (New York: D. Appleton, 1903), p. 41.

32. *Ibid.*, p. 90.

33. On November 27, 1846, he wrote enigmatically that her letters were "dear as ever to me and to a married man not quite unimportant," but that after the death of either they should be burned unread. His will, however, stipulated that they be published (Houghton MS).

34. *Love-Letters*, p. 180.

CONTEMPORARIES ON FULLER

1. Her vocation, William Henry Channing [1852]

In the *Memoirs*, Channing sought to resolve Fuller's dilemma with all the finality of an epitaph.

She was, indeed The Friend. This was her vocation. [*Memoirs*, II, 40]

2. Her influence on individuals, James Freeman Clarke [1852]

"There were many of my friends whom I understood more easily and sympathized with more readily than you," James Clark wrote Fuller on September 9, 1833, "yet we became connected (was it not so?) by the best, the most enduring part of our being" (*Letters of James Freeman Clarke*, p. 61). Their relationship remained warm and relatively uncomplicated. He shared both her passion for German literature, which they studied intensely together in Cambridge, and her adventurous interest in the Western frontier, where his Unitarian ministry took him in 1833. From there he confided in the "best friend of my mind" all the difficulties of his adjustment; feeling her superiority to other women put her beyond ordinary needs, he also freely confessed his love for other women. In the *Memoirs*, he described her theory and practice of friendship in the early 1830s. (The quoted phrase in the first sentence is Goethe's; Fuller inscribed it in the front of a journal she gave Clarke in 1832.)

a. ... One thing only she demanded of all her friends, – that they should have some "extraordinary generous seeking," that they should not be satisfied with the common routine of life, – that they should aspire to something higher, better, holier, than they had now attained. Where this element of aspiration existed, she demanded no originality of intellect, no greatness of soul. If these were found, well; but she could love, tenderly and truly, where they were not. But for a worldly

character, however gifted, she felt and expressed something very like contempt. At this period, she had no patience with self-satisfied mediocrity. She afterwards learned patience and unlearned contempt; but at the time of which I write, she seemed, and was to the multitude, a haughty and supercilious person, – while to those whom she loved, she was all the more gentle, tender and true.

Margaret possessed, in a greater degree than any person I ever knew, the power of so magnetizing others, when she wished, by the power of her mind, that they would lay open to her all the secrets of their nature. She had an infinite curiosity to know individuals, – not the vulgar curiosity which seeks to find out the circumstances of their outward lives, but that which longs to understand the inward springs of thought and action in their souls. This desire and power both rested on a profound conviction of her mind in the individuality of every human being. A human being, according to her faith, was not the result of the presence and stamp of outward circumstances, but an original *monad*, with a certain special faculty, capable of a certain fixed development, and having a profound personal unity, which the ages of eternity might develop, but could not exhaust. I know not if she would have stated her faith in these terms, but some such conviction appeared in her constant endeavor to see and understand the germinal principle, the special characteristic, of every person whom she deemed worthy of knowing at all. Therefore, while some persons study human nature in its universal laws, and become great philosophers, moralists and teachers of the race, – while others study mankind in action, and, seeing the motives and feelings by which masses are swayed, become eminent politicians, sagacious leaders, and eminent in all political affairs, – a few, like Margaret, study character, and acquire the power of exerting profoundest influence on individual souls.

b. I am disposed to think, much as she excelled in general conversation, that her greatest mental efforts were made in intercouse with individuals. All her friends will unite in the testimony, that whatever they may have known of wit and eloquence in others, they have never seen one who, like her, by the conversation of an hour or two, could not merely entertain and inform, but make an epoch in one's life. We all dated back to this or that conversation with Margaret, in which we took a complete survey of great subjects, came to some clear view of a difficult question, saw our way open before us to a higher plane of life, and were led to some definite resolution or purpose which has had a bearing on all our subsequent career. For Margaret's conversation turned, at such times, to life, – its destiny, its duty, its prospect. With comprehensive glance she would survey the past, and sum up, in a few brief words, its results; she would then turn to the future, and by a natural order, sweep through its chances and alternatives, – passing ever into a more earnest tone, into a more serious view, – and then bring all to bear on the present, till its duties grew plain, and its opportunities attractive. . . .

I recall many such conversations. I remember one summer's day, in which we rode together, on horseback, from Cambridge to Newton, – a day all of a piece, in which my eloquent companion helped me to understand my past life and her own, – a day which left me in that calm repose which comes to us, when we clearly apprehend what we ought to do, and are ready to attempt it. I recall other mornings when, not having seen her for a week or two, I would walk with her for hours, beneath the lindens or in the garden, while we related to each other what we had read in our German studies. And I always left her astonished at the progress of her mind, at the amount of new thoughts she had garnered, and filled with a new sense of the worth of knowledge, and the value of life.

There were other conversations, in which, impelled by the strong instinct of utterance, she would state, in words of tragical pathos, her own needs and longings, – her demands on life, – the struggles of mind, and of heart, – her conflicts with self, with nature, with the limitations of circumstances, with insoluble problems with an unattainable desire. She seemed to feel relief from the expression of these thoughts, though she gained no light from her companion. Many such conversations I remember, while she lived in Cambridge, and one such in Groton; but afterwards, when I met her, I found her mind risen above these struggles, and in a self-possessed state which needed no such outlet for its ferment. [*Memoirs*, *I*, *64-66*, *107-109*]

3. Her "truth-speaking power," Sarah Freeman Clarke, no date

James' older sister, Sarah Clarke (1808-1896), was one of the first women to take up art as a professional and one of the many intensely attached to Fuller. In 1843 she traveled in the West with her brother and Fuller and illustrated *Summer on the Lakes*. Well-connected in the Transcendentalist circle, she appears to have been somewhat diffident there. In a letter to Fuller, she contrasted her "genial presence" with the intimidating effect Sam Ward, William Channing, and Emerson had on her. After Fuller's death she wrote the following recollection.

In looking for the causes of the great influence possessed by Margaret Fuller over her pupils, companions, and friends, I find something in the fact of her unusual truth-speaking power. She not only did not speak lies after our foolish social customs, but she met you fairly. She broke her lance upon your shield. Encountering her glance, something like an electric shock was felt. Her eye pierced through your disguises. Your outworks fell before her first assault, and you were at her mercy. And then began the delight of true intercourse. Though she spoke rudely searching words, and told you startling truths, though she broke down your little shams and defenses, you felt exhilarated by the compliment of being found out, and even that she had cared to find you out. I think this was what attracted or bound us to her. We expected good from such a new condition of our relations, and good usually came of it.

No woman ever had more true lovers among those of her own sex, and as many men she also numbered among her friends. She had an immense appetite for social intercourse. When she met a new person she met him courageously, sincerely, and intimately. She did not study him to see beforehand how he might bear the shock of truth, but offered her best of direct speech at once. Some could not or would not hear it, and turned away; but often came back for more, and some of these became her fast friends.

Many of us recoiled from her at first; we feared her too powerful dominion over us, but as she was powerful, so she was tender; as she was exacting, she was generous. She demanded our best, and she gave us her best. To be with her was the most powerful stimulus, intellectual and moral. It was like the sun shining upon plants and causing buds to open into flowers. This was her gift, and she could no more help exercising it than the sun can help shining.... *[Higginson, pp. 117-18]*

4. Her conversion of skeptics,
William Henry Channing [1852]

In this account of Fuller at twenty, Channing compares Fuller, as so many others did, with de Staël's romantic heroine, Corinne.

About 1830, . . . we often met in the social circles of Cambridge, and I began to observe her more nearly. At first, her vivacity, decisive tone, downrightness, and contempt of conventional standards, continued to repel. She appeared too *intense* in expression, action, emphasis, to be pleasing, and wanting in that *retenue* which we associate with delicate dignity. Occasionally, also, words flashed from her of such scathing satire, that prudence counselled the keeping at safe distance from a body so surcharged with electricity. Then, again, there was an imperial — shall it be said imperious? — air, exacting deference to her judgments and loyalty to her behests, that prompted pride to retaliatory measures. She paid slight heed, moreover, to the trim palings of etiquette, but swept through the garden-beds and into the doorway of one's confidence so cavalierly, that a reserved person felt inclined to lock himself up in his sanctum. Finally, to the cooly-scanning eye, her friendships wore a look of such romantic exaggeration, that she seemed to walk enveloped in shining fog of sentimentalism. In brief, it must candidly be confessed, that I then suspected her of affecting the part of a Yankee Corinna.

But soon I was charmed, unaware, with the sagacity of her sallies, the profound thoughts carelessly dropped by her on transient topics, the breadth and richness of culture manifested in her allusions or quotations, her easy comprehension of new views, her just discrimination, and, above all, her *truthfulness.* "Truth at all cost," was plainly her ruling maxim. This it was that made her criticism so trenchant, her contempt of pretence so quick and stern, her speech so naked in frankness, her gaze so searching, her whole attitude so alert. Her estimates of men, books, manners, events, art, duty, destiny, were moulded after a grand ideal; and she was a severe judge from the very loftiness of her standard. Her stately deportment, border though it might on arrogance, but expressed high-heartedness. Her independence, even if haughty and rash, was the natural action of a self-centered will, that waited only fit occasion to prove itself heroic. Her earnestness to read the hidden

history of others was the gauge of her own emotion. The enthusiasm
that made her speech so affluent, when measured by the average scale,
was the unconscious overflow of a poetic temperament. And the ardor
of her friends' affection proved the faithfulness of her love. Thus gradually the mist melted away, till I caught a glimpse of her real self. We
were one evening talking of American literature, – she contrasting its
boyish crudity, half boastful, half timid, with the tempered, manly
equipoise of thorough-bred European writers, and I asserting that in its
mingled practicality and aspiration might be read bright auguries; when,
betrayed by sympathy, she laid bare her secret hope of what Woman
might be and do, as an author, in our Republic. The sketch was an
outline only, dashed off with a few swift strokes, but therein appeared
her own portrait, and we were strangers no more. [*Memoirs*, II, 6-8]

5. Her character, Elizabeth Hoar, April 3, 1839

A woman of considerable intellectual power who had been
the betrothed of Emerson's brother Charles, Elizabeth Hoar
remained a neighbor and close friend of the Emersons' after
Charles' early death in 1836. She was later a spirited and
devoted friend of Fuller's as well. She made a distinction
between Emerson and Fuller (similiar to one Fuller would
later draw [II:19]) when she wrote, "He is a ray of white
light, & she a prism—If not so pure & *calm*, yet she has all the
elements of the ray in her varied being" (Ralph L. Rusk, *Life
of Ralph Waldo Emerson*, p. 253). In a letter to Hannah L.
Chappell, Hoar offered an early impression of Fuller.

My dear Hannah,

Both your letters found me at Mr. Emerson's, but I waited until I came
home, to answer them. Miss Fuller has been there for a week past, and I
have not yet learned the art of self-regulation so far as to be able to do
anything when she is near. I see so few people who are anything but
pictures or furniture, to me, that the stimulus of such a person is great
and overpowering for the time. And indeed, if I saw all the people
whom I think of as desirable, and if I *could* help myself, I do not think
I should abate any of my interest in her. Her wit, her insight into

characters, – such that she seems to read them aloud to you as if they
were printed books, her wide range of thought and cultivation, – the
rapidity with which she appropriates all knowledge, joined with habits
of severe mental discipline (so rare in women, and in literary men not
technically "men of science"); her passionate love of all beauty, her
sympathy with all noble effort; then her energy of character and the
regal manner in which she takes possession of society wherever she is,
and creates her own circumstances; all these things keep me full of
admiration – not astonished, but pleased admiration – and, as "genius"
does always (*vide* R. W. E. on "Genius"), inspire me with new life, new
confidence in my own power, new desires to fulfill "the possible" in
myself. You would, perhaps, have an impression of levity, of want of
tenderness, from her *superficial* manner. The mean hindrances of life,
the mistakes, the tedium, which eat into your soul, and will take no
form to you but the tragic, she takes up with her defying wit and sets
them down in comic groups and they cease to be "respectabilities."
You feel at first as if this included ridicule or disregard of the sufferings
they bring to you; but not so. Her heart is helpfully sympathizing with
all striving souls. And she has overcome so much extreme physical and
mental pain, and such disappointments of external fortune, that she has
a right to play as she will with these arrows of fate. She is a high-
minded and generous servant of Duty, and a Christian (not a *traditional*
Christian, not made one by *authority*) in her idea of life. But this is all
catalogue; you cannot write down Genius, and I write it more because I
am thinking about her than from any hope of doing her justice. Only
her presence can give you the meaning of the name Margaret Fuller, and
this not once or twice, but as various occasions bring out the many
sides. And her power of bringing out Mr. Emerson has doubled my
enjoyment of that blessing to be in one house and room with him.
[Higginson, pp. 64-65]

6. Her effect on himself and others, .
Ralph Waldo Emerson [1852]

Almost as often as Emerson works in the *Memoirs* to quench
the prejudices surrounding Fuller's reputation, his own ambivalence rekindles them. Thus, in the same passage where he
calls her "the queen of some parliament of love," he also uses
language which invokes the hunter ("persons were her

game"), the soldier ("she disarmed the suspicions"), and the enforcer ("she extorted the secret of life"). And the arch mock-respect of his tone in discussing her passionate friendships with women in the last passage below reveals his discomfort with physical attraction and intensity.

a. ... I still remember the first half hour of Margaret's conversation. She was then twenty-six years old. She had a face and frame that would indicate fulness and tenacity of life. She was rather under the middle height; her complexion was fair, with strong fair hair. She was then, as always, carefully and becomingly dressed, and of ladylike self-possession. For the rest, her appearance had nothing prepossessing. Her extreme plainness, – a trick of incessantly opening and shutting her eyelids, – the nasal tone of her voice, – all repelled; and I said to myself, we shall never get far. It is to be said, that Margaret made a disagreeable first impression on most persons, including those who became afterwards her best friends, to such an extreme that they did not wish to be in the same room with her. This was partly the effect of her manners, which expressed an overweening sense of power, and slight esteem of others, and partly the prejudice of her fame. She had a dangerous reputation for satire, in addition to her great scholarship. The men thought she carried too many guns, and the women did not like one who despised them. I believe I fancied her too much interested in personal history; and her talk was a comedy in which dramatic justice was done to everybody's foibles. I remember that she made me laugh more than I liked; for I was, at that time, an eager scholar of ethics, and had tasted the sweets of solitude and stoicism, and I found something profane in the hours of amusing gossip into which she drew me, and, when I returned to my library, had much to think of the crackling of thorns under a pot. Margaret, who had stuffed me out as a philosopher, in her own fancy, was too intent on establishing a good footing between us, to omit any art of winning. She studied my tastes, piqued and amused me, challenged frankness by frankness, and did not conceal the good opinion of me she brought with her, nor her wish to please. She was curious to know my opinions and experiences. Of course, it was impossible long to hold out against such urgent assault. She had an incredible variety of anecdotes, and the readiest wit to give an absurd turn to whatever passed; and the eyes, which were so plain at first, soon swam with fun and drolleries, and the very tides of joy and superabundant life. . . .

b. She wore this circle of friends, when I first knew her, as a necklace of diamonds about her neck. They were so much to each other, that Margaret seemed to represent them all, and, to know her, was to acquire a place with them. The confidences given her were their best, and she held them to them. She was an active, inspiring companion and correspondent, and all the art, the thought, and the nobleness in New England, seemed, at that moment, related to her, and she to it. She was everywhere a welcome guest. The houses of her friends in town and country were open to her, and every hospitable attention eagerly offered. Her arrival was a holiday, and so was her abode. She stayed a few days, often a week, more seldom a month, and all tasks that could be suspended were put aside to catch the favorable hour, in walking, riding, or boating, to talk with this joyful guest, who brought wit, anecdotes, love-stories, tragedies, oracles with her, and, with her broad web of relations to so many fine friends, seemed like the queen of some parliament of love, who carried the key to all confidences, and to whom every question had been finally referred.

Persons were her game, specially, if marked by fortune, or character, or success; – to such was she sent. She addressed them with a hardihood, – almost a haughty assurance, – queen-like. Indeed, they fell in her way, where the access might have seemed difficult, by wonderful casualties; and the inveterate recluse, the coyest maid, the waywardest poet, made no resistance, but yielded at discretion, as if they had been waiting for her, all doors to this imperious dame. She disarmed the suspicion of recluse scholars by the absence of bookishness. The ease with which she entered into conversation made them forget all they had heard of her; and she was infinitely less interested in literature than in life. . . . Whatever romance, whatever virtue, whatever impressive experience, – this came to her; and she lived in a superior circle; for they suppressed all their commonplace in her presence.

c. It is certain that Margaret, though unattractive in person, and assuming in manners, so that the girls complained that "she put upon them," or, with her burly masculine existence, quite reduced them to satellites, yet inspired an enthusiastic attachment. I hear from one witness, as early as 1829, that "all the girls raved about Margaret Fuller," and the same powerful magnetism wrought as she went on, from year to year, on all ingenuous natures. The loveliest and the highest endowed women were eager to lay their beauty, their grace, the hospitalities of sumptuous homes, and their costly gifts, at her feet. When I expressed, one day, many years afterwards, to a lady who knew her well, some surprise at the homage paid her by men in Italy, – offers of marriage having there been made her by distinguished parties, – she replied: "There is nothing extraordinary in it. Had she been a man, any one of those fine girls of sixteen, who surrounded her here, would have married her: they were all in love with her, she understood them so well.". . .

I am to add, that she gave herself to her friendships with an entireness not possible to any but a woman, with a depth possible to few women. Her friendships, as a girl with girls, as a woman with women, were not unmingled with passion, and had passages of romantic sacrifice and of ecstatic fusion, which I have heard with the ear, but could not trust my profane pen to report. There were, also, the ebbs and recoils from the other party, – the mortal unequal to converse with an immortal, – ingratitude, which was more truly incapacity, the collapse of overstrained affections and powers. At all events, it is clear that Margaret, later, grew more strict, and values herself with her friends on having the tie now "redeemed from all search after Eros." So much, however, of intellectual aim and activity mixed with her alliances, as to breathe a certain dignity and myrrh through them all. She and her friends are fellow-students with noblest moral aims. She is there for help and for counsel. "Be to the best thou knowest ever 'true!' is her language to one." And that was the effect of her presence. Whoever conversed with her felt challenged by the strongest personal influence to a bold and generous life. . . . *[Memoirs, I, 202-203, 213-15, 280-82]*

FULLER'S WRITINGS

7. "Mariana," a story [1844]

Fuller published the story of Mariana in 1844 in *Summer on the Lakes* but had probably written it some years before. The second half of the story, omitted here, renders Mariana's marriage and death by the uncompromisingly partisan romantic formula favored by the young Fuller: women refuse to survive in a world of men unwilling to understand. The first half is generally taken to be a quasi-autobiographical account of Fuller's experience in the Prescotts' school. Certainly it is an attempt to reinterpret the isolating eccentricity of her teen-age years, when she sought to overwhelm or blackmail young girls into friendship. And the reality of the kindly "lady" of the story is strongly suggested by Fuller's letter of January 1830 to Susan Prescott: "your image shines as fair to my mind's eye as it did in 1825, when I left you with my heart overflowing with gratitude for your singular and judicious tenderness" (*Memoirs*, I, 57).

At first her school-mates were captivated with her ways; her love of wild dances and sudden song, her freaks of passion and of wit. She was always new, always surprising, and, for a time, charming.

But after a while, they tired of her. She could never be depended on to join in their plans, yet she expected them to follow out hers with their whole strength. She was very loving, even infatuated in her own affections, and exacted from those who had professed any love for her the devotion she was willing to bestow.

Yet there was a vein of haughty caprice in her character, and a love of solitude, which made her at times wish to retire apart, and at these times she would expect to be entirely understood, and let alone, yet to be welcomed back when she returned. She did not thwart others in their humors, but she never doubted of great indulgence from them.

Some singular habits she had, which, when new, charmed, but, after acquaintance, displeased her companions. She had by nature the same habit and power of excitement that is described in the spinning dervishes of the East. Like them she would spin until all around her were giddy, while her own brain, instead of being disturbed, was excited to great action. Pausing, she would declaim verses of others, or her own, or act many parts, with strange catchwords and burdens, that seemed to act with mystical power on her own fancy, sometimes stimulating her to convulse the hearers with laughter, sometimes to melt them to tears. When her power began to languish, she would spin again till fired to re-commence her singular drama, into which she wove figures from the scenes of her earlier childhood, her companions, and the dignitaries she sometimes saw, with fantasies unknown to life, unknown to heaven or earth.

This excitement, as may be supposed, was not good for her. It usually came on in the evening, and often spoiled her sleep. She would wake in the night, and cheat her restlessness by inventions that teased, while they sometimes diverted her companions.

She was also a sleep-walker; and this one trait of her case did somewhat alarm her guardians, who, otherwise, showed the profound ignorance as to this peculiar being, usual in the overseeing of the young. They consulted a physician, who said she would outgrow it, and prescribed a milk diet.

Meantime, the fever of this ardent and too early stimulated nature was constantly increased by the restraints and narrow routine of the boarding-school. She was always devising means to break in upon it. She had a taste – which would have seemed ludicrous to her mates, if they had not felt some awe of her, from the touch of genius and power that never left her – for costume and fancy dresses. There was always some sash twisted about her, some drapery, something odd in the arrangement of her hair and dress; so that the methodical preceptress dared not let her go out without a careful scrutiny and remodelling, whose soberizing effects generally disappeared the moment she was in the free air.

At last a vent was assured for her in private theatricals. Play followed play, and in these and the rehearsals, she found entertainment congenial with her. The principal parts, as a matter of course, fell to her lot; most of the good suggestions and arrangements came from her; and, for a time, she ruled mostly, and shone triumphant.

During these performances, the girls had heightened their bloom with artificial red; this was delightful to them, it was something so out of the way. But Mariana, after the plays were over, kept her carmine saucer on the dressing-table, and put on her blushes, regularly as the morning. When stared and jeered at, she at first said she did it because she thought it made her look pretty; but, after a while, she became petulant about it, – would make no reply to any joke, but merely kept up the habit.

This irritated the girls, as all eccentricity does the world in general, more than vice or malignity. They talked it over among themselves till they were wrought up to a desire of punishing, once for all, this sometimes amusing, but so often provoking non-conformist. And having obtained leave of the mistress, they laid, with great glee, a plan, one evening, which was to be carried into execution next day at dinner.

Among Mariana's irregularities was a great aversion to the meal-time ceremonial, – so long, so tiresome, she found it, to be seated at a certain moment, and to wait while each one was served, at so large a table, where there was scarcely any conversation; and from day to day it became more heavy to sit there, or go there at all; often as possible she excused herself on the ever-convenient plea of headache, and was hardly ever ready when the dinner-bell rang.

To-day the summons found her on the balcony, but gazing on the beautiful prospect. I have heard her say afterwards, that she had scarcely in her life been so happy, – and she was one with whom happiness was a still rapture. It was one of the most blessed summer days; the shadows of great white clouds empurpled the distant hills for a few moments, only to leave them more golden; the tall grass of the wide fields waved in the softest breeze. Pure blue were the heavens, and the same hue of pure contentment was in the heart of Mariana.

Suddenly on her bright mood jarred the dinner-bell. At first rose her usual thought, I will not, cannot go; and then the *must*, which daily life can always enforce, even upon the butterflies and birds, came, and she walked reluctantly to her room. She merely changed her dress, and never thought of adding the artificial rose to her cheek.

When she took her seat in the dining-hall, and was asked if she would be helped, raising her eyes, she saw the person who asked her was deeply rouged, with a bright glaring spot, perfectly round, on either cheek. She looked at the next, – same apparition! She then slowly passed her eyes down the whole line, and saw the same, with a suppressed smile distorting every countenance. Catching the design at once, she deliberately looked along her own side of the table, at every schoolmate in turn; every one had joined in the trick. The teachers strove to be grave, but she saw they enjoyed the joke. The servants could not suppress a titter.

When Warren Hastings stood at the bar of Westminster Hall, – when the Methodist preacher walked through a line of men, each of whom greeted him with a brickbat or rotten egg, – they had some preparation for the crisis, though it might be very difficult to meet it with an impassible brow. Our little girl was quite unprepared to find herself in the midst of a world which despised her, and triumphed in her disgrace.

She had ruled like a queen, in the midst of her companions; she had shed her animation through their lives, and loaded them with prodigal favors, nor once suspected that a popular favorite might not be loved. Now she felt that she had been but a dangerous plaything in the hands of those whose hearts she never had doubted.

Yet the occasion found her equal to it, for Mariana had the kind of spirit which, in a better cause, had made the Roman matron truly say of her death-wound, "It is not painful, Poetus." She did not blench, – she did not change countenance. She swallowed her dinner with apparent composure. She made remarks to those near her, as if she had no eyes.

The wrath of the foe, of course, rose higher, and the moment they were freed from the restraints of the dining room, they all ran off, gayly calling, and sarcastically laughing, with backward glances, at Mariana, left alone.

Alone she went to her room, locked the door, and threw herself on the floor in strong convulsions. These had sometimes threatened her life, in earlier childhood, but of later years she had outgrown them. Schoolhours came, and she was not there. A little girl, sent to her door, could get no answer. The teachers became alarmed, and broke it open. Bitter was their penitence, and that of her companions, at the state in which they found her. For some hours terrible anxiety was felt, but at last nature, exhausted, relieved herself by a deep slumber.

From this Mariana arose an altered being. She made no reply to the expressions of sorrow from her companions, none to the grave and kind, but undiscerning, comments of her teacher. She did not name the source of her anguish, and its poisoned dart sank deeply in. This was the thought which stung her so: – "What, not one, not a single one, in the hour of trial, to take my part? not one who refused to take part against me?" Past words of love, and caresses, little heeded at the time, rose to her memory, and gave fuel to her distempered heart. Beyond the sense of burning resentment at universal perfidy, she could not get. And Mariana, born for love, now hated all the world.

The change, however, which these feelings made in her conduct and appearance, bore no such construction to the careless observer. Her gay freaks were quite gone, her wildness, her invention. Her dress was uniform, her manner much subdued. Her chief interest seemed to be now in her studies, and in music. Her companions she never sought; but they, partly from uneasy, remorseful feelings, partly that they really liked her much better now that she did not puzzle and oppress them, sought her continually. And here the black shadow comes upon her life, the only stain upon the history of Mariana.

They talked to her, as girls having few topics naturally do, of one another. Then the demon rose within her, and spontaneously, without design, generally without words of positive falsehood, she became a genius of discord amongst them. She fanned those flames of envy and jealousy which a wise, true word from a third person will often quench forever; and by a glance, or seemingly light reply, she planted the seeds of dissension, till there was scarcely a peaceful affection, or sincere intimacy, in the circle where she lived, and could not but rule, for she was one whose nature was to that of the others as fire to clay.

It was at this time that I came to the school, and first saw Mariana. Me she charmed at once, for I was a sentimental child, who, in my early ill health, had been indulged in reading novels, till I had no eyes for the common. It was not, however, easy to approach her. Did I offer to run and fetch her handkerchief, she was obliged to go to her room, and would rather do it herself. She did not like to have people turn over for her the leaves of the music-book as she played. Did I approach my stool to her feet, she moved away as if to give me room. The bunch of wild flowers, which I timidly laid beside her plate, was left untouched. After some weeks, my desire to attract her notice really preyed upon me; and one day, meeting her alone in the entry., I fell upon my knees, and, kissing her hand, cried, "O, Mariana, do let me love you, and try to love me a little!" But my idol snatched away her hand, and laughing wildly, ran into her room. After that day, her manner to me was not only cold, but repulsive, and I felt myself scorned.

Perhaps four months had passed thus, when, one afternoon, it became obvious that something more than common was brewing.

Dismay and mystery were written in many faces of the older girls;
much whispering was going on in corners.

In the evening, after prayers, the principal bade us stay; and, in a
grave, sad voice, summoned forth Mariana to answer charges to be made
against her.

Mariana stood up and leaned against the chimneypiece. Then eight
of the older girls came forward, and preferred against her
charges, — alas! too well founded, of calumny and falsehood.

At first she defended herself with self-possession and eloquence.
But when she found she could no more resist the truth, she suddenly
threw herself down, dashing her head with all her force against the iron
hearth, on which a fire was burning, and was taken up senseless.

The affright of those present was great. Now that they had perhaps
killed her, they reflected it would have been as well if they had taken
warning from the former occasion, and approached very carefully a
nature so capable of any extreme. After a while she revived, with a faint
groan, amid the sobs of her companions. I was on my knees by the bed,
and held her cold hand. One of those most aggrieved took it from me,
to beg her pardon, and say, it was impossible not to love her. She made
no reply.

Neither that night, nor for several days, could a word be obtained
from her, nor would she touch food; but, when it was presented to her,
or any one drew near from any cause, she merely turned away her head,
and gave no sign. The teacher saw that some terrible nervous affection
had fallen upon her — that she grew more and more feverish. She knew
not what to do.

Meanwhile, a new revolution had taken place in the mind of the
passionate but nobly-tempered child. All these months nothing but the
sense of injury had rankled in her heart. She had gone on in one mood,
doing what the demon prompted, without scruple, and without fear.

But at the moment of detection, the tide ebbed, and the bottom of
her soul lay revealed to her eye. How black, how stained, and sad!
Strange, strange, that she had not seen before the baseness and cruelty
of falsehood, the loveliness of truth! Now, amid the wreck, uprose the
moral nature, which never before had attained the ascendant. "But,"
she thought, "too late sin is revealed to me in all its deformity, and
sin-defiled, I will not, cannot live. The main-spring of life is broken."

The lady who took charge of this sad child had never well
understood her before, but had always looked on her with great

tenderness. And now love seemed, – when all around were in the
greatest distress, fearing to call in medical aid, fearing to do without
it, – to teach her where the only balm was to be found that could heal
the wounded spirit.

One night she came in, bringing a calming draught. Mariana was
sitting as usual, her hair loose, her dress the same robe they had put on
her at first, her eyes fixed vacantly upon the whited wall. To the
proffers and entreaties of her nurse, she made no reply.

The lady burst into tears, but Mariana did not seem even to observe
it.

The lady then said, "O, my child, do not despair; do not think that
one great fault can mar a whole life! Let me trust you; let me tell you
the griefs of my sad life. I will tell you, Mariana, what I never expected
to impart to any one."

And so she told her tale. It was one of pain, of shame, borne not
for herself, but for one near and dear as herself. Mariana knew the
dignity and reserve of this lady's nature. She had often admired to see
how the cheek, lovely, but no longer young, mantled with the deepest
blush of youth, and the blue eyes were cast down at any little emotion.
She had understood the proud sensibility of her character. She fixed
her eyes on those now raised to hers, bright with fast-falling tears. She
heard the story to the end, and then, without saying a word, stretched
out her hand for the cup.

She returned to life, but it was as one who had passed through the
valley of death. The heart of stone was quite broken in her, – the fiery
will fallen from flame to coal. When her strength was a little restored,
she had all her companions summoned, and said to them, – "I deserved
to die, but a generous trust has called me back to life. I will be worthy
of it, nor ever betray the trust, or resent injury more. Can you forgive
the past?"

And they not only forgave, but, with love and earnest tears,
clasped in their arms the returning sister. They vied with one another in
offices of humble love to the humbled one; and let it be recorded, as an
instance of the pure honor of which young hearts are capable, that
these facts, known to some forty persons, never, so far as I know,
transpired beyond those walls.

It was not long after this that Mariana was summoned home. She
went thither a wonderfully instructed being, though in ways those who
had sent her forth to learn little dreamed of.

Never was forgotten the vow of the returning prodigal. Mariana could not *resent*, could not *play false*. The terrible crisis, which she so early passed through, probably prevented the world from hearing much of her. A wild fire was tamed in that hour of penitence at the boarding-school, such as has oftentimes wrapped court and camp in a destructive glow. *[Memoirs, I, 42-52]*

8. To Almira Barlow, November 19, 1830

In a very different style, parodying both herself and her detractors, Fuller wrote to an intimate of her twenties, Almira Barlow, wife of a clergyman and later resident at Brook Farm. (The friend of the second sentence was Elizabeth Randall, who long fascinated James Clarke.)

... Many things have happened since I echoed your farewell laugh. Elizabeth and I have been fully occupied. She has cried a great deal, fainted a good deal, and played the harp most of all. I have neither fertilized the earth with my tears, edified its inhabitants by my delicacy of constitution, nor wakened its echoes to my harmony, – yet some things have I achieved in my own soft feminine style. I hate glare, thou knowest, and have hitherto successfully screened my virtues therefrom. I have made several garments fitted for the wear of American youth; I have written six letters, and received a correspondent number; I have read one book, – a piece of poetry entitled, "Two Agonies," by M. A. Browne, (pretty caption, is it not?) – and J. J. Knapp's trial; I have given advice twenty times, – I have taken it once; I have gained two friends and recovered two; I have felt admiration four times, honor once, and disgust twice; I have been a journey, and showed my penetration in discovering the beauties of Nature through a thick and never-lifted shroud of rain; I have turned two new leaves in the book of human nature; I have got a new pink bag (beautiful!). I have imposed on the world, time and again, by describing your Lynn life as the perfection of human felicity, and adorning my visit there with all sorts of impossible adventures, – thus at once exhibiting my own rich invention and the credulous ignorance of my auditors (light and dark, you know, dear, give life to a picture); I have had tears for others' woes, and patience for my own, – in short, to climax this journal of many-colored deeds and chances, so well have I played my part, that in the self-same night I was styled by two several persons, "a sprightly young lady," and "a Syren!!" Oh rapturous sound! I have reached the goal of my ambition. Earth has nothing fairer or brighter to offer. *"Intelligency,"* was nothing to it. A "supercilious," "satirical," "affected," "pedantic," "Syren"!!!! Can the *olla-podrida* of human nature present a compound of more varied ingredients, or higher gusto?

Loveliest of created ministers wives! I have egotized as became a friend so interesting as myself, to one so sympathizing as thyself. For the present I pause, when, oh when shalt thou gather strength to come and hear the remainder? . . .

P.S. Write soon and let the letter be sentimental. Sentiment now bears unbounded sway in the palace of my heart. But write soon or the tide may ebb. *[Houghton MS copy]*

9. To James Freeman Clarke *[March-April 1830]*

From 1829 until the Fullers left Cambridge in 1833, James Clarke, a distant relation, was in almost daily contact with Fuller. Her early letters, signed "your cousin only thirty-seven degrees removed" were lighthearted. But when he pressed her on March 27, 1830, for more confidentiality, she replied with this letter. The disillusionment described here refers to her attraction to her witty cousin George Davis, whose indifference had made her ill the year before.

I thank you for your note. Ten minutes before I received it, I scarcely thought that anything again would make my stifled heart throb so warm a pulse of pleasure. Excuse my cold doubts, my selfish arrogance, — you will, when I tell you that this experiment has before had such uniform results; those who professed to seek my friendship, and whom, indeed, I have often truly loved, have always learned to content themselves with that inequality in the connection which I have never striven to veil. Indeed, I have thought myself more valued and better beloved, because the sympathy, the interest, were all on my side. True! such regard could never flatter my pride, nor gratify my affections, since it was paid not to myself, but to the need they had of me; still, it was dear and pleasing, as it has given me an opportunity of knowing and serving many lovely characters; and I cannot see that there is anything else for me to do on earth. And I should rejoice to cultivate generosity, since (see that *since*) affections gentler and more sympathetic are denied me.

I would have been a true friend to you: ever ready to solace your pains and partake your joy as far as possible. Yet I cannot but rejoice that I have met a person who could discriminate and reject a proffer of this sort. Two years ago I should have ventured to proffer you friendship, indeed, on seeing such an instance of pride in you; but I have gone through a sad process of feeling since, and those emotions, so necessarily repressed, have lost their simplicity, their ardent beauty. *Then*, there was nothing I might not have disclosed to a person capable of comprehending, had I ever seen such a one! Now there are many voices of the soul which I imperiously silence. This results not from any particular circumstance or event, but from a gradual ascertaining of realities.

I cannot promise you any limitless confidence, but I *can* promise that no timid caution, no haughty dread shall prevent my telling you the truth of my thoughts on any subject we may have in common. Will this satisfy you? Oh let it! suffer me to know you. *[Memoirs, I, 66-68]*

10. To James Freeman Clarke, July 6, 1832

While it is true, as Emerson says, that Fuller sometimes charged her friends with ingratitude, as often she apologized for such self-indulgence, as here.

I believe I behaved very badly the other evening. I did not think so yesterday. I had been too surprised and vexed to recover very easily, but to-day my sophistries have all taken wing, and I feel that nothing good could have made me act with such childish petulance and bluntness towards one who spoke from friendly emotions. Be at peace: I will astonish you by my repose, mildness, and self-possession. No, that is silly; but I believe it cannot be right to be on such terms with any one, that, on the least vexation, I indulge my feelings at his or her expense. We will talk less, but we shall be very good friends still, I hope. Shall not we? *[Memoirs, I, 79]*

11. To James Freeman Clarke, February 1, 1835

Typically mixing literary and personal analysis, Fuller here
writes from Groton to Clarke at Louisville, Kentucky; he had
recently written her about the new Polish immigrants. In
referring to Lane Seminary in Cincinnati, whose students
were agitating against slavery and working in the black
community until official censure resulted in their mass
resignation, she shows a plain preference for practical struggle
over oratory.

Dear James,

My mind has been so strongly turned towards you these several days
that though I owe you no letter I must write. Often in reading or
meditating, thoughts strike which I think I wish so much I could communicate to my friend James. If he could only come in this evening as
he used to at Cambridge I could pour forth such a flood. And he − he
would gravely listen and then − rise abruptly and go out as if he were
disgusted with all I had said but − a month or more after he would
come out with an answer which showed that he had thought about it
and if he did not agree at least had not been disgusted. Ah well a day
this delightful ⟨cousinwise⟩ contact of character is over for ever. The
thought makes me melancholy. . . .

So − where was I? Oh about Reinhard's memoirs − did you, dear
"Minister" ever read them for I am going to quote from them for some
time − So if you have not read them do so and partic^y Letter IX and
noting what is said therein of the method we should take in examining
revelation give me your opinion thereon. *Do it in form* − I want
it − Observe the valuable results of his six years patient industry, admire that truly German spirit which produces fruits of such perfect
ripeness, those habits of patient investigation, that freedom of spirit
joined with candour and humility − See how beautifully his life passed,
spirit constantly victorious over the rebellion of matter, every hour
employed in pursuits as useful as elegant, that genuine charity, that
consistent sweetness and humility − He gave away the fruits of his own
soul to the poor: How delightful his domestic life. Oh my friend how
lovely is the picture of a good man! I *hope* it is not flattered − Read it
and see if it does not affect you as it does me − I think you will find

passages which may be useful to [you] partic^y on the way in which he made general literature and great love of philosophy part of his religious character. Similar thoughts have occupied your own mind. He seems to have performed what you could conceive and wish therefore are capable of performing. You will not agree with his doctrine but that is nothing – And tell me how goes your Unitarianism – Before you went to the west I remember you were grafting sundry notions of your own on that most rational system. Have you decided yet how regeneration is to be accomplished. . . .

Now let me ask you some questions for I feel impertinent tonight – How many hours a day do you study and *what*: anything except sermon writing. Do you feel more or less alone than when with us. Is the promised freedom *joyous* or joyless? Which do you learn most from the book of Nature, Goethe or St Paul – and are you going to stay in the West always? – How are you friends the Poles? My desire to go to the West is revived by the doings at Lane Seminary – That sounds from afar so like the conflict of keen life. There is the greatest fuss about slavery in *this* little nook. An idle gentleman weary of his ease has taken to philanthropy as a profession and here are incessant lectures. I rarely go but I attended to hear the English emissary Thompson whom you must have read about in the papers. I wish you or any of my friends who need forming as speakers [remainder of letter is missing].
[Clarke Papers, Houghton]

12. To William Henry Channing,
July 1841, July 1842, and no date

Character analysis and interpretation of friendship was the indispensable core of her correspondence with W. H. Channing, who, despite his lavish praise in the *Memoirs*, appears often to have criticized Fuller's forthrightness and her insistent closeness. In the first of the three letters below, she distinguishes her ideal of friendship from his and Emerson's.

a. The more I think of it, the more deeply do I feel the imperfection of your view of friendship, which is the same Waldo E. takes in that letter on Charles' death. It is very noble, but not enough for our manifold nature. Our friends should be our incentive to Right, but not only our guiding but our prophetic stars. To love by right is much, to love by faith is more; both are the entire love without which heart, mind, and soul cannot be alike satisfied. We love and ought to love one another not merely for the absolute worth of each but on account of a mutual fitness of temporary character. We are not merely one another's priests or gods, but ministering angels, exercising in the part the same function as the Great Soul in the whole, of seeing the perfect through the imperfect, nay, making it come there. Why am I to love any friend the less for any obstruction in his life? is not the very time for me to love most tenderly when I must see his life in despite of seeming; when he *shows it* me I can only admire: I do not *give* myself. I am *taken captive.* . . .

Do not, I implore you, whether from pride or affection, wish to exile me from the dark hour. The manly mind might love best in the triumphant hour, but the woman could no more stay from the foot of the cross than from the transfiguration. And I am fit to be the friend of an immortal mortal because I know both these sympathies.   *[BPL MS]*

b. . . . I would have my friends tender of me, not because I am frail, but because I am capable of strength; – patient, because they see in me a principle that must, at last, harmonize all the exuberance of my character. I did not well understand what you felt, but I am willing to admit that what you said of my "over-great impetuosity" is just. You will, perhaps, feel it more and more. It may at times hide my better self. When it does, speak, I entreat, as harshly as you feel. Let me be always sure I know the worst. I believe you will be thus just, thus true, for we are both servants of Truth. *[Memoirs, II, 65-66]*

c. I like to hear you express your sense of my defects. The word "arrogance" does not, indeed, appear to me to be just; probably because I do not understand what you mean. But in due time I doubtless shall; for so repeatedly have you used it, that it must stand for something real in my large and rich, yet irregular and unclarified nature. But though I like to hear you, as I say, and think somehow your reproof does me good, by myself, I return to my native bias, and feel as if there was plenty of room in the universe for my faults, and as if I could not spend time in thinking of them, when so many things interest me more. I have no defiance or coldness, however, as to these spiritual facts which I do not know; but I must follow my own law, and bide my time, even if, like Oedipus, I should return a criminal, blind and outcast, to ask aid from the gods. Such possibilities, I confess, give me great awe; for I have more sense than most, of the tragic depths that may open suddenly in the life. Yet, believing in God, anguish cannot be despair, not guilt perdition. I feel sure that I have never willfully chosen, and that my life has been docile to such truth as was shown it. In an environment like mine, what may have seemed too lofty or ambitious in my character was absolutely needed to keep the heart from breaking and enthusiasm from extinction. *[Memoirs, II, 111-12]*

13. On talk with Ellery Channing, August 28, 1842

The poet, Ellery Channing (1818-1901), who had married Ellen Fuller in 1841, analyzed Margaret's character when they met in Concord the next year. Apparently, his cousin, W. H. Channing, had written critically in the same vein. Fuller's journal records her struggle with their strictures.

All these evenings it has rained and we could not go out. Ellery has come into my room, but it has not been pleasant. The indoor darkness seemed to cloud his mind: he was entirely different from what he is beneath the open sky. The first night he began by railing at me as artificial. "It dont strike me when you are alone with me, he says, but it does when others are present. You dont follow out the fancy of the moment, you converse, you have treasured thoughts to tell, you are disciplined, artificial." I pleaded guilty, and observed that I supposed it must be so, with one of my continuity of thought or earnestness of character. – As to that, says he, I shall not like you the better for your excellence. I dont know what is the matter, I feel strongly attracted towards you, but there is a drawback in my mind, I dont know exactly what. You will always be wanting to grow forward, now I like to grow backward too. You are too ideal. Ideal people anticipate their lives, and they make themselves and every body around them restless, by always being beforehand with themselves, & so on in the very tone of William's damning letter.

I listened attentively, for what he said was excellent, following up the humor of the moment he arrests admirable thoughts on the wing. But I cannot but see, that what they say of my or other obscure lives is true of every prophetic, of every tragic character, — And then I like to have them make me look [on] that side, and reverence the lovely forms of nature, & the shifting moods, and the clinging instincts. But I must not let them disturb me. There is one only guide, the voice in the heart that asks — Was thy wish sincere? If so thou canst not stray from nature, nor be so perverted but she will make thee true again. I must take my own path, and learn from them all, without being paralyzed for to day. We need great energy, and self-reliance to endure to day. My age may not be the best, my position may be bad, my character ill formed, but thou, Oh Spirit, hast no regard to aught but the seeking heart, and if I try to walk upright will guide me? What despair must he feel who after a whole life passed in trying to build up himself, resolves that it would have been far better, if he had kept still as the clod of the valley, or yielded easily as the leaf to every breeze. A path has been appointed me. I have walked in it as steadily as I could. "I am what I am." That which I am not, teach me in the others. I will bear the pain of imperfection, but not of doubt. Waldo must not shake me in my worldliness, nor William in the fine motion that that [sic] has given me what I have of life, nor this child of genius, make me lay aside the armour without which I had lain bleeding on the field long since, but if they can keep closer to Nature, and learn to interpret her as souls, also, — let me learn from them what I have not. [*"Margaret Fuller's 1842 Journal,"* ed. Joel Myerson, <u>Harvard Library Bulletin</u>, *21 (1973), 329]*

14. *To Samuel Gray Ward [September 1839]*

In the summer of 1835, Fuller escaped the family routine in Groton on a delightful tour of upstate New York with the Farrars and the engaging Sam Ward, who shared her enthusiasm for nature and art. After he returned from Italy laden with prints and engravings thrilling to Fuller, they fell into an exuberant intimacy; she dubbed him "Raffaello," and he, seven years younger, called her "Mother." On what appears to be a later copy by Fuller of this passionate accusation to Ward, she noted, "I believe in the first days of Sept[r] 1839."

To ———

You love me no more – How did you pray me to draw near to you! What words were spoken in impatience of separation! How did you promise to me, ay, and doubtless to yourself, too, of all we might be to one another, We are near and with Spring's fairest flowers I poured out my heart to you – At an earlier period I would fain have broke the tie that bound us, for I knew myself incapable of feeling or being content to inspire an ordinary attachment. As soon as I saw a flaw I would have broke the tie. You would not – you resented, yet with what pathetic grace, any distrust on my part. Forever, ever are words of which you have never been, are not now afraid.

You call me your best of friends, your dearest friend, you say that you always find yourself with me. I doubt not the depth of your attachment, doubt not that you feel my worth. But the confiding sweetness, the natural and prompt expression are gone – are they gone forever?

You do not wish to be with me; why try to hide it from me, from yourself? You are not interested in any of my interests, my friends, my pursuits are not yours. If you tell me of yours, it is like a matter of duty, not because you cannot help it, and must write or speak to relieve the full heart and mind.

The sympathizing contemplation of the beautiful in Nature, in Art is over for us. That for which I loved you first, and which made that love a shrine at which I could rest upon my wearing pilgrimage – Now – moons wax and wane, suns rise and set, the summer segment of the beautiful circle is filled, and since the first flush on the cheek of June we have not once seen, felt, admired together. You come here – to go away again, and make a call upon me in the parlor while you stay! You write to me – to say you would not write before and ask me why I do not write. You write me to go and see Michel's work by myself! You send me your books and pictures to ask me what I think of them! Thus far at least we have walked no step together and my heart deceives me widely if this be love, or if we live as friends should live!

Yet, spite of all this, sometimes I believe when I am with you, and come what may, I will be faithful myself, I will not again draw back, it shall be all your fault if we break off again. I will wait – I will not complain. I will exact nothing – I will make every allowance for the restlessness of a heart checked in its love, a mind dissatisfied with its pursuits. I will bear in mind that my presence is like to recall all you have need to forget and will try to believe that you would not be with me, that I "spoil you for your part on life's dull scene," or as you have said, "call up the woman in you."

You say you love me as ever, forever. I will, if I can, rely upon your word, believing you must deem me entitled to unshrinking frankness.

You have given me the sacred name of Mother, and I will be as indulgent, as tender, as delicate (if possible) in my vigilance, as if I had borne you beneath my heart instead of in it. But oh, it is waiting like the Mother beside the sepulchre for the resurrection, for all I loved in you is at present dead and buried, only a light from the tomb shines now and then in your eyes. . . . *[Houghton MS]*

15. To Samuel Gray Ward (?), no date

Some scholars have plausibly believed that this letter was addressed to Sam Ward and have therefore dated it in the year he married, 1840. Certainly the themes articulated here are characteristic of Fuller's critical thirtieth year: the agony over sexual definition, the isolation expressed in terms of the absence of familial ties, the proud sense of self-generation, the joyous release that accompanied pain.

I want words to express the singularity of all my past relations; yet let me try.

From a very early age I have felt that I was not born to the common womanly lot. I knew I should never find a being who could keep the key of my character: that there would be none on whom I could always lean, from whom I could always learn; that I should be a pilgrim and sojourner on earth, and that the birds and foxes would be surer of a place to lay the head than I. You understand me, of course; such beings can only find their homes in hearts. All material luxuries, all the arrangements of society, are mere conveniences to them.

This thought, all whose bearings I did not, indeed, understand, affected me sometimes with sadness, sometimes with pride. I mourned that I never should have a thorough experience of life, never know the full riches of my being; I was proud that I was to test myself in the sternest way, that I was always to return to myself, to be my own priest, pupil, parent, child, husband, and wife. All this I did not understand as I do now; but this destiny of the thinker, and (shall I dare to say it?) of the poetic priestess, sibylline, dwelling in the cave, or amid the Lybian sands, lay yet enfolded in my mind. Accordingly, I did not look on any of the persons, brought into relation with me, with common womanly eyes.

Yet, as my character is, after all, still more feminine than masculine, it would sometimes happen that I put more emotion into a state than I myself knew. I really was capable of attachment, though it never seemed so till the hour of separation. And if a connexion was torn up by the roots, the soil of my existence showed an unsightly wound, which long refused to clothe itself in verdure.

With regard to yourself, I was to you all that I wished to be. I knew that I reigned in your thoughts in my own way. And I also lived with you more truly and freely than with any other person. We were truly friends, but it was not friends as men are friends to one another, or as brother and sister. There was, also, that pleasure, which may, perhaps, be termed conjugal, of finding oneself in an alien nature. Is there any tinge of love in this? Possibly! At least, in comparing it with my relation to ———, I find *that* was strictly fraternal. I valued him for himself. I did not care for an influence over him, and was perfectly willing to have one or fifty rivals in his heart. * *

* * I think I may say, I never loved. I but see my possible life reflected on the clouds. As in a glass darkly, I have seen what I might feel as child, wife, mother, but I have never really approached the close relations of life. A sister I have truly been to many – a brother to more – a fostering nurse to, oh how many! The bridal hour of many a spirit, when first it was wed, I have shared, but said adieu before the wine was poured out at the banquet. And there is one I always love in my poetic hour, as the lily looks up to the star from amid the waters; and another whom I visit as the bee visits the flower, when I crave sympathy. Yet those who live would scarcely consider that I am among the living – and I am isolated, as you say.

My dear ———, all is well; all has helped me to decipher the great poem of the universe. I can hardly describe to you the happiness which floods my solitary hours. My actual life is yet much clogged and impeded, but I have at last got me an oratory where I can retire and pray. With your letter, vanished a last regret. You did not act or think unworthily. It is enough. As to the cessation of our confidential intercourse, circumstances must have accomplished that long ago; my only grief was that you should do it with your own free will, and for reasons that I thought unworthy. I long to honor you, to be honored by you. Now we will have free and noble thoughts of one another, and all that is best of our friendship shall remain. *[Memoirs, I, 98-101]*

16. On Anna Barker, no date

Anna Barker met Margaret Fuller when they were both under twenty. Anna's beauty seemed to the young Fuller a perfect counterpart to her own intelligence and had the effect of releasing repressed feeling. Fuller's language in this journal entry years later, especially the quotation from Goethe (which means "it is not a question of man or woman"), suggests that a strong impetus to this love was her desire to resolve her sexual identity by passionately transcending sex itself. As late as October 7, 1839, a visit from Anna still had power to overwhelm her, as she wrote to Caroline Sturgis: "The nights of talk and days of agitation, the tides of feeling which have been poured upon and from my soul have been too much for my strength of body or mind" (Tappan Papers, Houghton). In the next October, Anna married Sam Ward, and although friendly relations were maintained, Fuller's feeling for both diminished, perhaps in part because Anna required Ward to abandon the scholar's life and enter business. Frequently quoted, the journal entry below is usually bowdlerized so as to minimize the heat of Fuller's feeling and the coolness of her withdrawal.

. . . Many things interested me, but nothing so much as a large engraving of Madame Recamier in her boudoir. I have so often thought over the intimacy between her & Madame De Stael.

It is so true that a woman may be in love with a woman and a man with a man. I like to be sure of it because undoubtedly it is the same love we shall feel when we are angels, — when we ascend to the only fit place for the Mignons, where —

"Sie fragen nicht nach Mann und Weib."

It is regulated by the same law as that of love between persons of different sexes, only it is purely intellectual and spiritual, unprofaned by any mixture of lower instincts, undisturbed by any need of consulting temporal interests; its law is the desire of the spirit to realize a whole, which makes it seek in another being what it finds not in itself. Thus the beautiful seek the strong; the mute seeks the eloquent, the butterfly settles on the dark flower. Why did Socrates so love Alcibiades? Why did Korner love Schneider? How natural is the love of Wallenstein for Max; that of De Stael for De Recamier, mine for ———. I loved ——— for a time with as much passion as I was then strong enough to feel. Her face was always gleaming before me, her voice was always echoing in my ear, all poetic thoughts clustered round the dear image. This love was for me a key which unlocked many a treasure which I still possess; it was the carbuncle (emblematic gem!) which cast light into many of the darkest caverns of human nature. She loved me, too, though not so much, — because her nature was "less high, less grave, less large, less deep" — but she loved more tenderly, less passionately. She loved me, for I well remember her suffering when she first could feel my faults, & knew one part of the exquisite veil rent away, how she wished to stay apart, and weep the whole day. Then again that night when she leaned on me, & her eyes were such a deep violet blue like the night, as they never were before & we both felt such a strange mystic thrill, & knew what we had never known before. How well too, can I now account for that desire which I often had to get away from her & be alone with Nature, which displeased her so, for she wished to be with me all the time.

I do not love her now with passion, for I have exhausted her idea & she does not stimulate my fancy — she does not represent the beautiful to me now, — she is only one beautiful object. Then, she has never had a chance to get a hold on my heart by the thousand links of intimacy, — we have been so little together, all was from the elective affinities. But still I love her with a sort of pallid, tender romance, & feel towards her as I can to no other woman. I thought of all this as I looked at Madame Recamier. . . . [Houghton MS copy]

17. To Caroline Sturgis, January 10, 1839

In the mid-1830s, Fuller met Caroline Sturgis (1819-1888), a talented poet and painter and a vivacious, sometimes rebellious young woman. (Even in middle age, her manner of "delicate and casual irreverence" bemused young Henry James.) She became one of Fuller's closest friends: "With her," Fuller said, "I can talk of anything. She is like me. She is able to look facts in the face. We enjoy the clearest, widest, most direct communication" (*Memoirs*, I, 206). In the first years, Fuller directed her reading and urged her to seek elevating companionship: "To laugh a whole evening at vulgar nondescripts," she chided, is a pastime "much more excusable in a chameleon like me" (*Memoirs*, I, 203-204). Sturgis appears not to have found Fuller's tone in letters, like the one below from Groton, unduly overbearing. For example, she wrote in a letter to Fuller on August 28, 1841: "You have more to pardon than any other & you are the most generous of all. I hope I shall never again wrong you & myself as I have done" (Tappan Papers, Houghton).

My dear Cary,

The mountain and the valley express it exactly – We do not soar up direct like the lark! but our advance is always in the undulating line. You are *down* now but think how long you were *up* at Naushon. You must expect a season of dimness and grey discontent.

　　As to the premonitions of action and passion, I know the Titanic era must come ere long, but, oh Cary, do nothing to hasten it. Ward it off as long as possible by occupation. Give yourself time to ripen and strengthen for that tremendous strife. They never entered Olympus, those Titans, rather chained to earth, they vented their smouldering rage in volcanoes, "at which Jove laughs" – Do thou build high and strong the ladder before thou dost try to climb – The modelling seemed to me the very thing for you at this juncture. You can pursue that without hurting yourself, and it seems to suit the cant of your mind. Let books alone – you have other and better hieroglyphics before you.

Tell me all about the pictures you see, that bit of Poussin was admirable.

No doubt I was somewhat pained by your want of affection towards me while in Boston, but I did not dislike you, on the contrary I loved you as much as was consistent with the crowded, wearied state of my mind at that time. And not being upborne by excitement I had time to feel bodily pain and fatigue. But, I could not seriously think there was any danger of your ceasing to love me. There is so much in me which you do not yet know and have faculties to apprehend that you will not be able I believe, to get free of me for some years.

I send you many of Jas Clarke's letters. On reading them over they seemed to me among the most valuable I possessed. There are allusions to the 3 love affairs which formed him into manhood which I wish were not there. But all that is dead and gone, the pain and passion have passed with experience. I know he would entirely confide in my judgment as to the propriety of showing them. Perhaps some things may slightly disgust you in detail but I think when you have got through and look at it as whole you will think it a fine picture of an intellectual friendship, and an interesting history of the growth of a practical character. I think many critiques on books and pictures will interest you. And it will let you see how large a class of men feel towards women, more clearly than you could in books. . . . *[Tappan Papers, Houghton]*

18. To Caroline Sturgis [early 1840s]

The undated letter below was doubtless written in the early 1840s, when Fuller was editor of *The Dial*, which published some of Sturgis' work. The mysterious notion of redemption from the search after Eros may refer to Fuller's decision, late in 1839, not to press Sturgis for declarations of love. In another letter, Fuller explained, "I am of too ardent and sympathetic a nature not to feel these mental ruptures keenly at the time, but where I see good reason I can be patient, indulgent, attentive. . . ." (Tappan Papers, Houghton)

Monday eve^g

Dear Caroline,

I think what is poetical in your verses is of the purest tone. And even where most unmusical and unfinished they have the great beauty of being written to the dictation of Nature. The most irregular pulses beat with the mighty heart.

I hope you will be induced to perfect yourself in this mode of expression for the degree to which you have succeeded surprizes me. Your verse is almost as good as your best prose; with practice I think you would be most free in rhythm. Self-adopted chains well suit ambitious natures.

Some of these strains are to me of ineffable pathos. To live in your life is soothing and mystical to me even as the pine forest. Show me whenever you can what you write, what you do, I shall not often answer it directly, for such is not my way, but each drop will swell the wave of thought, of life, – till you hear the rebound.

One thing I admire at in you is your steadiness of nature. Now I am often and not least tonight tired to death of the earnestness of my life. I long to do something frivolous to go on a journey or plunge into externals somehow. I never can, my wheel whirls round again.

I build on our friendship now with trust, for I think it is redeemed from "the search after Eros." We may commune without exacting too much one from the other – Intercourse may be suspended at times, but not eventually broken off. Believe me worthy to know your nature as I believe you worthy to know mine. Believe as I do that our stars will culminate at the same point. . . . *[Tappan Papers, Houghton]*

19. To Harriet Martineau [late 1830s]

Fuller and Martineau sustained their friendship after the latter returned to Europe. After Fuller read Martineau's *Society in America*, published in 1837, she felt obliged to write her friend about how the book disappointed her. Although she later reprimanded her countrymen for their unreflective and testy response to the criticism of foreigners, she showed a patriotic reflex here. This is a copy of the letter Fuller made in her journal, published without date in the

Memoirs. Whether or not Martineau received the same version of this, she appears to have taken criticism from a younger woman badly and in turn criticized Fuller publicly in her *Autobiography* (IV:14).

On its first appearance, the book was greeted by a volley of coarse and outrageous abuse, and the nine days' wonder was followed by a nine days hue-and-cry. It was garbled, misrepresented, scandalously illtreated. This was all of no consequence. The opinion of the majority you will find expressed in a late number of the North American Review. I should think the article, though ungenerous, not more so than great part of the critiques upon your book.

The minority may be divided into two classes: The one, consisting of those who knew you but slightly, either personally, or in your writings. These have now read your book; and seeing in it your high ideal standard, genuine independence, noble tone of sentiment, vigor of mind and powers of picturesque description, they value your book very much, and rate you higher for it.

The other comprises those who were previously aware of these high qualities, and who, seeing in a book to which they had looked for a lasting monument to your fame, a degree of presumptuousness, irreverence, inaccuracy, hasty generalization, and ultraism on many points, which they did not expect, lament the haste in which you have written, and the injustice which you have consequently done to so important a task, and to your own powers of being and doing. To this class I belong.

I got the book as soon as it came out, – long before I received the copy endeared by your handwriting, – and devoted myself to reading it. I gave myself up to my natural impressions, without seeking to ascertain those of others. Frequently I felt pleasure and admiration, but more frequently disappointment, sometimes positive distaste.

There are many topics treated of in this book of which I am not a judge; but I do pretend, even where I cannot criticize in detail, to have an opinion as to the general tone of thought. When Herschel writes his Introduction to Natural Philosophy, I cannot test all he says, but I cannot err about his fairness, his manliness, and wide range of knowledge. When Jouffroy writes his lectures, I am not conversant with all his topics of thought, but I can appreciate his lucid style and admirable method. When Webster speaks on the currency, I do not understand the subject, but I do understand his mode of treating it, and can see what a blaze of light streams from his torch. When Harriet Martineau writes about America, I often cannot test that rashness and inaccuracy of which I hear so much, but I can feel that they exist. A want of soundness, of habits of patient investigation, of completeness, of arrangement, are felt throughout the book: and, for all its fine descriptions of scenery, breadth of reasoning, and generous daring, I cannot be happy in it, because it is not worthy of my friend, and I think a few months given to ripen it, to balance, compare, and mellow, would have made it so. * *

Certainly you show no spirit of harshness towards this country in general. I think your tone most kindly. But many passages are deformed by intemperance of epithet.** Would your heart, could you but investigate the matter, approve such overstatement, such a crude, intemperate tirade as you have been guilty of about Mr. Alcott, – a true and noble man, a philanthropist, whom a true and noble woman, also a philanthropist, should have delighted to honor; whose disinterested and resolute efforts, for the redemption of poor humanity, all independent and faithful minds should sustain, since the "broadcloth" vulgar will be sure to assail them; a philosopher, worthy of the palmy times of ancient Greece; a man whom Carlyle and Berkely, whom you so uphold, would delight to honor; a man whom the worldlings of Boston hold in as much horror as the worldlings of ancient Athens did Socrates. They smile to hear their verdict confirmed from the other side of the Atlantic, by their censor, Harriet Martineau.

I do not like that your book should be an abolition book. You might have borne your testimony as decidedly as you pleased; but why leaven the whole book with it? The subject haunts us on almost every page. It *is* a great subject, but your book had other purposes to fulfil.

I have thought it right to say all this to you, since I felt it. I have shrunk from the effort, for I fear that I must lose you. Not that I think all authors are like Gil Blas' archbishop. No: if your heart turns from me, I shall still love you, still think you noble. I know it must be so trying to fail of sympathy, at such a time, where we expect it. And, besides, I felt from the book that the sympathy between us is less general than I had supposed, it was so strong on several points. It is strong enough for me to love you ever, and I could no more have been happy in your friendship, if I had not spoken out now. *[Memoirs, I, 192-94]*

20. To her mother, September 5, 1837

The voluminous correspondence with members of her family mostly treats pressing practical questions: money, health, education, employment. A very few letters to her only sister, Ellen, about ten years younger, survive. On August 25, 1836, she urged the pretty teen-aged orphan, "Do not be concerned about your faded frocks; if you are neat and lady-like in your manners they will not injure you with any person whose good opinion is worth having," and instructs her to pray for strength "to rise above the opinion of this world as far as vanity is concerned" (Houghton MS). There is no evidence that Ellen was intellectual, but when her right to education was threatened by her domineering uncle, Abraham, Fuller, now teaching in Providence, rose fiercely to the occasion and wrote her mother from Concord.

My very dear Mother,

Do not suffer the remarks of that sordid man to give you any uneasiness — Proceed to act as we agreed when I was with you. It is perfectly clear to my mind that the arrangements we then made are the right ones, and I do not fear to hold myself responsible for the consequences.

If Abraham Fuller continues to annoy you in this manner I am decidedly of opinion that the management of our affairs had better be transferred to someother lawyer. . . . We pay Abraham and we could as well pay another man who would confine himself to his proper part of managing the money. You must, my dear Mother, steadily consider yourself as the guardian of the children. You must not let his vulgar insults make you waver as to giving the children advantages to which they would be well entitled if the property were only a third of what it now is. I cannot like you think that feelings of kindness, however narrow the mind of the writer, could induce him to taunt you or Eugene or say things which he knows to be false. Do not suffer yourself to be puzzled or scared by such stuff. . . .

Fit out the children for school, and let not Lloyd be forgotten. You incur an awful responsibility by letting him go so neglected any longer. I shall get Ellen a place at Mrs. Urquhart's if possible; if not, I may take her to Providence, for I hear of no better place. She shall not be treated in this shameful way, bereft of proper advantages and plagued and cramped in the May of life. If I stay at Providence and Abraham manages to trouble you about money before we can get other arrangements made I will pay her bills, if I do not stay there, I will put the affair into the hands of a lawyer: we will see if she is not to have a year's schooling from twelve to eighteen. I am not angry but I am determined. I am sure that my Father, if he could see me, would approve the view I take. . . . If I do not stay I will let her have my portion of our income with her own. . . . *[Houghton MS]*

21. To Arthur Fuller, December 31, 1837

While she was in Providence, struggling with uncongenial work to send her siblings through school, she made clear to Arthur, then fifteen, how important his achievement was.

. . . You express gratitude for what I have taught you. It is in your power to repay me a hundred fold by making every exertion now to improve. I did not teach you as I would, yet I think the confinement and care I took of you children, at a time when my mind was so excited by many painful feelings, have had a very bad effect upon my health. I do not say this to pain you, or to make you more grateful to me, (for, probably, if I had been aware at the time what I was doing, I might not have sacrificed myself so,) but I say it that you may feel it your duty to fill my place and do what I may never be permitted to do. Three precious years at the best period of life I gave all my best hours to you children – let me not see you idle away time which I have always valued so, let me not find you unworthy of the love I felt for you. Those three years would have enabled me to make great attainments which now I never may. Do you make them in my stead, that I may not remember that time with sadness. *[Houghton MS]*

22. To Richard Fuller, May 25, 1841

More letters to Richard, fourteen years younger, survive than to her other brothers or Ellen. Richard's distaste for business, his love of study and life simple and close to nature, his uncertainty about a career, his vulnerability with women–all evoked in her letters a high degree of imaginative involvement and solicitude. When this was written from Concord, their troubling youngest brother, Lloyd, had been sent to the school at Brook Farm.

My dear Richard,

... I am living here the quiet country life you would enjoy. Here are hens, cows, pigs! and what I like better wildflowers and a nest of singing birds. By the way, I don't think you could gratify Mrs. Ward more than on the Sunday you go to Jamaica to get her a bouquet of wild flowers. Borrow a tin pail or box and wet them when you put them in; they may thus be brought to town perfectly fresh. Mr. Emerson works five or six hours a day in his garden and his health which was in a very low state this spring improves day by day. He has a friend with him of the name of Henry Thoreau who has come to live with him and be his working man this year. H.T. is three and twenty, has been through college and kept a school, is very fond of classic studies, and an earnest thinker yet intends being a farmer. He has a great deal of practical sense, and as he has bodily strength to boot, he may look to be a successful and happy man. He has a boat which he made himself, and rows me out on the pond. Last night I went out quite late and staid til the moon was almost gone, heard the whip-poor-will for the first time this year. There was a sweet breeze full of apple-blossom fragrance which made the pond swell almost into waves. I had great pleasure. I think of you in these scenes, because I know you love them too. By and by when the duties are done, we may expect to pass summer days together.

I have had a letter from Lloyd, stating that "he did not like the community as he expected, for he has to work when he does not wish to"!!

> very affectionately
> your sister M. *[Houghton MS]*

23. On Emerson's influence, no date

These lines to James Clarke about Emerson's importance for her indicate how his influence led her away from external place and action and even hint at a healthy fear of becoming dependent on him.

You question me as to the nature of the benefits conferred upon me by Mr. E.'s preaching. I answer, that his influence has been more beneficial to me than that of any American, and that from him I first learned what is meant by an inward life. Many other springs have since fed the stream of living waters, but he first opened the fountain. That the "mind is its own place," was a dead phrase to me, till he cast light upon my mind. Several of his sermons stand apart in memory, like landmarks of my spiritual history. It would take a volume to tell what this one influence did for me. But perhaps I shall some time see that it was best for me to be forced to help myself. *[Memoirs, I, 194-95]*

24. To Ralph Waldo Emerson, January 7, 1839

This is Emerson's transcript of a Groton letter from Fuller. Her teasing tone is a mark of the free equality they had achieved. On April 24, 1840, she wrote in a similar vein, "When I am a Queen, if so unfortunate as to come to the throne in a northern climate, I will have greenhouses innumerable. . . . I shall only give you sweet pea or lavendar because you are merely a philosopher and a farmer, not a hero, nor a sentimentalist" (Rusk, *Letters*, II, 291).

How could you omit your Lecture? I stayed in town only to hear it, & shall have no chance at another this winter. Could you not have taken some other time for your "slight indisposition." I fancied L. was worse, & had passed from diet on ricewater to nothing at all. I sent a maiden to inquire at Mrs. A.'s & she returned all smiles to tell me that Mrs E was quite well, that Mr E. had lost a night's rest!! but had since rode to Waltham, walked five miles, sawed wood, & by use of these mild remedies was now perfectly restored Imagine my indignation: Lose a night's rest! as if an intellectual person ever had a night's rest; one too of that sect who are supposed to be always

> "Lying broad awake, & yet
> Remaining from the body, & apart
> In intellect, & power, & will, to hear
> Time flowing in the middle of the night,
> And all things creeping to the day of doom"

– that such an one should adjourn a lecture on Genius because he has lost a nights sleep.

I would tell you of my visit in town, but that I have uttered the record in so circulating a medium, that I cannot but fancy it may have vibrated as far as Concord. Lest it should not, I will say, that three things were specially noteworthy. First, a talk with Mr. Alcott, in which he appeared to me so great, that I am inclined to think he deserves your praise, and that he deceived neither you nor himself in saying that I had not yet seen him. Beside his usual attitude and closeness to the ideal, he showed range, grasp, power of illustration, and precision of statement such as I never saw in him before. I will begin him again and read by faith awhile.

There was a book of studies from Salvator Rosa, from the Brimmer donation, at the Athenaeum, which I looked over with great delight and got many thoughts for my journal. There was at last an interview with Mr. Allston. He is as beautiful as the town-criers have said, and deserves to be Mr. Dana's Olympus, Lares, and Penates, as he is. He got engaged upon his Art, and flamed up into a galaxy of Platonism. Yet what he said was not as beautiful as his smile of genius in saying it. Unfortunately, I was so fascinated, that I forgot to make myself interesting, and shall not dare to go and see him. *[Rusk, Letters, II, 178n. and Higginson, p. 95]*

25. To Ralph Waldo Emerson, September 29, 1840

The emotionally charged debate on friendship raged through two months of 1840, until, on October 22, Emerson called it off, apologizing for his coldness and urging Fuller, as a "woman of sense and sentiment," to return to their old footing of exchanging "reasonable words" (Rusk, *Letters*, II, 352-53). The letter below is the only one of Fuller's letters from the period that survives, copied in Emerson's hand. It is in response to his of September 25, in which he said: "Now in your last letter, you . . . do say . . . that I am yours and yours shall be, let me dally how long soever in this or that temporary relation. I on the contrary do constantly aver that you and I are not inhabitants of one thought of the Divine Mind, but of two thoughts, that we meet and treat like foreign states, one maritime, one inland, whose trade and laws are essentially unlike. . . . Our friend is part of our fate; those who dwell in the same truth are friends; those who are exercised on different thoughts are not, and must puzzle each other for the time" (Rusk, *Letters*, II, 336-37). Here she upbraids him for retreating from some of the bolder assertions in his essay while revealing between the lines that her need for support on the eve of the Ward-Barker wedding has reduced her to passionate dependency. She confronts his charge, spoken or implicit, that she sought power. She also defends a complex of responses and drives in herself which are not susceptible to rational analysis but are essential to her still unfocused vitality. When the air cleared, these differences would become the ground of her sharpened independence. (The ellipsis after the second paragraph is Rusk's.)

I have felt the impossibility of meeting far more than you; so much, that if you ever know me well, you will feel that the fact of my abiding by you thus far, affords a strong proof that we are to be much to one another. How often have I left you despairing & forlorn. How often have I said, This light will never understand my fire; this clear eye will never discern the law by which I am filling my circle; this simple force will never interpret my need of manifold being.

Dear friend on one point misunderstand me less. I do not love power other than every vigorous nature delights to feel itself living. To violate the sanctity of relations – I am as far from it as you can be. I make no claim. I have no wish which is not dictated by a feeling of truth. Could I lead the highest angel captive by a look, that look I would not give, unless prompted by true love: I am no usurper. I ask only mine own inheritance. If it be found that I have mistaken its boundaries, I will give up the choicest vineyard, the fairest flowergarden, to its lawful owner. . . .

In me I did not think you saw the purity, the singleness, into which, I have faith that all this darting motion, & restless flame shall yet be attempered & subdued. I felt that you did not for me the highest office of friendship, by offering me the clue of the labyrinth of my own being. Yet I thought you appreciated the fearlessness which shrinks from no truth in myself & others, & trusted me, believing that I knew the path for myself. O it must be that you have felt the worth of that truth which has never hesitated to infringe our relation, or aught else, rather than not vindicate itself. If you have not seen this stair on which God has been so untiringly leading me to himself, you have indeed been wholly ignorant of me. Then indeed, when my soul, in its childish agony of prayer, stretched out its arms to you as a father, – did you not see what was meant by this crying for the moon; this sullen rejection of playthings which had become unmeaning? Did you then say, "I know not what this means; perhaps this will trouble me; the time will come when I shall hide my eyes from this mood"; – then you are not the friend I seek.

But did not you ask for a "foe" in your friend? Did not you ask for a "large formidable nature"? But a beautiful foe, I am not yet, to you. Shall I ever be? I know not. My life is now prayer. Through me sweetest harmonies are momently breathing. Shall they not make me beautiful, – Nay, beauty? Shall not all vehemence, all eccentricity, be purged by these streams of divine light? I have, in these hours, but one pain; The sense of the infinite exhausts & exalts: it cannot therefore possess me wholly; else, were I also one wave of gentlest force. Again I shall cease to melt & flow; again I shall seek & pierce & rend asunder.

But oh, I am now full of such sweet certainty. never never more can it be utterly shaken. All things have I given up to the Central Power, myself, you also; yet, I cannot forbear adding, dear friend. I am now so at home, I know not how again to wander & grope, seeking my place in another soul. I need to be recognized. After this, I shall be claimed, rather than claim, yet if I speak of facts, it must be as I see them.

To L. my love. In her, I have always recognized the saintly element. *That*, better than a bible in my hand, shows that it cannot be to me wholly alien. Yet am I no saint, no anything, but a great soul born to know all, before it can return to the creative fount. *[Rusk, Letters, II, 340-41n.]*

26. To Ralph Waldo Emerson, October 1841

After autumn 1840, both Emerson and Fuller worked to salvage their friendship. When she withdrew he begged her to return, but jocularly: "Hast thou no bowels of compassion

for this Stylite solitude?" (Rusk, *Letters*, II, 380). Almost
jocularly, he apologized for disappointing Caroline, Sam,
Anna, and her: "They say in heaven I am a very awkward
lover of my friends . . . but a sincere one. My love reacts on
me like the recoiling gun: it is pain" (Rusk, *Letters*, II, 438).
During her annual visit to Concord the next year, they
resumed what he termed "these strange, cold-warm,
attractive-repelling conversations with Margaret" on friendship, but now, on her side, the demands gave way to
appreciative analysis of their differences. This letter,
postdated October 1841 and marked "letter written at
Concord from room to room," was apparently delivered by
his child, also called Waldo, with some of Emerson's writing,
on which she comments in the first lines.

How true and majestical it reads: Surely you must have said it this time.
The page flows too, and we have no remembrance of "mosaic or
medal."

Dear Waldo, I know you do not regard our foolish critiques, except in
the true way to see whether you have yet got the best *form* of
expression. What do we know of when you should stop writing or how
you should live? In these pages I seem to hear the music rising I so long
have wished to hear, and am made sensible to the truth of the passage
in one of your letters "Life, like the nimble Tartar &c
     I like to be in your library when you are out of it. It seems a sacred
place. I came here to find a book, that I might feel more life and be
worthy to sleep, but there is so much soul here I do not need a book.
When I come to yourself, I cannot receive you, and you cannot give
yourself; it does not profit. But when I cannot find you the beauty and
permanence of your life come to me.
     "She (Poesie) has ascended from the depths of a nature, and only
by a similar depth, shall she be apprehended!" – I want to say while I
am feeling it, what I have often (not always) great pleasure in
feeling – how long it must be, before I am able to meet you, – I see
you – and fancied it nearer than it was, you were right in knowing the
contrary.
     How much, much more I would fain say and cannot. I am too
powerfully drawn while with you, and cannot advance a step, but when

away I have learned something. Not yet to be patient and faithful and holy however, but only have taken off the shoes, to tread the holy ground. I shall often depart through the ranges of manifold being, but as often return to where I am tonight. *[Rusk, Letters, II, 455n.]*

27. On Lidian Emerson, September 2, 1842

From the journal Fuller kept during her 1842 stay in Concord we get a glimpse of what her friendship with Emerson cost his wife, Lidian. Fuller's simultaneously searching and evasive response to the situation is characteristic for her during this period; she also assumed a radical distinction between herself and other women. (Waldo, Emerson's first-born, had died at five years of age in January, and "Mamma," Emerson's mother, was living at his house.)

[September] 2^d It is a most brilliant day, & I stole the morning from my writing to take Lidian and then Mamma to ride. L. has had a slow fever which has confined her to her chamber almost ever since I came, & I have not been attentive to her as I should have been, if I had thought she cared about it. I did not go into her room at all for a day or two, simply because I was engaged all the time and kept expecting to see her down stairs. When I *did* go in, she burst into tears, at sight of me, but laid the blame on her nerves, having taken opium &c. I felt embarrassed, & did not know whether I ought to stay or go. Presently she said something which made me suppose she thought W. passed the evenings in talking with me, & a painful feeling flashed across me, such as I have not had, all has seemed so perfectly understood between us. I said that I was with Ellery or H[enry] T[horeau] both of the eve gs & that W. was writing in the study.

I thought it all over a little, whether I was considerate enough. As to W. I never keep him from any such duties, any more than a book would. – He lives in his own way, & he dont soothe the illness, or morbid feelings of a friend, because he would not wish any one to do it *for him*. It is useless to expect it; what does it signify whether he is with me or at his writing. L. knows perfectly well, that he has no regard for me or any one that would make him wish to be with me, a minute longer than I could fill up the time with thoughts.

As to my being more his companion that cannot be helped, his life is in the intellect not the affections. He has affection for me, but it is because I quicken his intellect. – I dismissed it all, as a mere sick moment of L's.

Yesterday she said to me, at dinner, I have not yet been out, will you be my guide for a little walk this afternoon. I said I am engaged to walk with Mr E. but – (I was going to say, I will walk with you first,) when L. burst into tears. The family were all present, they looked at their plates. Waldo looked on the ground, but soft & serene as ever. I said "My dear Lidian, certainly I will go with you." "No! she said I do not want you to make any sacrifice, but I do feel perfectly desolate, and forlorn, and I thought if I once got out, the fresh air would do me good, and that with you, I should have courage, but go with Mr E. I will not go"

I hardly knew what to say, but I insisted on going with her, & then she insisted on going so that I might return in time for my other walk. Waldo said not a word: he retained his sweetness of look, but never offered to do the least thing. I can never admire him enough at such times; he is so true to himself. In our walk and during our ride this morn g L. talked so fully that I felt reassured except that I think she will always have these pains, because she has always a lurking hope that Waldo's character will alter, and that he will be capable of an intimate union; now I feel convinced that it will never be more perfect between them two. I do not believe it will be less: for he is sorely troubled by imperfections in the tie, because he dont believe in any thing better. – And where he loved her first, he loves her always. Then the influence of any one with him would be just in proportion to independence of him, combined with pure love of him for his own sake. Yet in reply to all L. said, I would not but own that though I thought it was the only way, to take him for what he is, as he wishes to be taken, and though my experience of him has been, for that very reason, so precious to me, I dont know that I could have fortitude for it in a more intimate relation. Yet nothing could be nobler, nor more consoling than to be his wife, if one's mind were only thoroughly made up to the truth. – As for myself, if I have not done as much as I ought for L. it is that her magnanimity has led her to deceive me. I have really thought that she was happy to have me in the house solely for Waldo's sake, and my own, and she is, I know, in the long account, but there are pains of every day which I am apt to neglect for others as for myself. – But

Truth, spotless Truth, and Prayer and Love shall yield a talisman to teach me how to steer.

I suppose the whole amount of the feeling is that women cant bear to be left out of the question. And they dont see the whole truth about one like me, if they did they would understand why the brow of Muse or Priestess must wear a shade of sadness. On my side I dont remember them enough. They have so much that I have not, I cant conceive of their wishing for what I have. (*enjoying* is not the word: these I know are too generous for that) But when Waldo's wife, & the mother of that child that is gone thinks me the most privileged of women, & that E[lizabeth] H[oar] was happy because her love was snatched away for a life long separation, & thus she can know none but ideal love: it does seem a little too insulting at first blush. — And yet they are not altogether wrong. [*"Margaret Fuller's 1842 Journal," ed. Joel Myerson, Harvard Library Bulletin, 21 (1973), 331-32]*

28. On marriages, September 4, 1842

In contrast to her lack of sympathy for Lidian's feelings, Fuller's journal two days later reveals considerable anxiety for the marital happiness of her sister, Ellen. Ellery Channing, Ellen's husband since the previous September, had preceded her to Concord to find them winter lodgings. On September 2, he showed Fuller a letter from Caroline Sturgis urging him to visit her at Naushon (on the way to Martha's Vineyard and Nantucket). Explaining his confidence that "when I am once united to E[llen] again, I shall never be separated from her," he told her of his desire to pay a last visit to Caroline, with whom he had a romantic friendship. Though Fuller had been "entirely in favor of his going," she was in vicarious agony when her sister arrived before his return. The passage has special interest also because of its cryptic allusions to the difference between Fuller's and Emerson's feelings about marriage, a topic they discussed much that summer.

Aft[ernoon]. Waldo came into my room to read me what he has written in his journal about marriage, & we had a long talk. He listens with a soft wistful look to what I say, but is nowise convinced. It was late in a dark afternoon, the fine light in that red room always so rich, cast a beautiful light upon him, as he read and talked. *Since* I have found in his journal two sentences that represent the two sides of his thought.

In time

"Marriage should be a covenant to secure to either party the sweetness and the handsomeness of being a calm continuing inevitable benefactor to the other."

In eternity

"Is it not enough that souls shoul meet in a law, in a thought, obey the same love, demonstrate the same idea. These alone are the nuptials of minds. I marry you for better, not for worse, I marry impersonally."

I shall write to him about it.

At night Mamma & Lidian came down too & sat in my room. I was no longer engrossed in writing & talking, & my anxiety increased as the hour for the stage was approaching lest Ellen should arrive unaccompanied by Ellery. W. declared it was impossible to happen, but I saw well enough he was as anxious as I. At last the stage stopped in a violent rain. W. went to the door & sure enough it was my poor little prodigal. "Is Mr Channing here" "No, but Margaret is" & in he brought her

I thought I should faint, but recovered myself directly. I did not wish to frighten her & I did not let her know where Ellery was gone. She behaved sweetly, though so disappointed at not finding him. I saw at once that she was less selfish than formerly.

Waldo was now distressed *for me*: he called me out, & offered to go down to Boston this very evening, & bring me back news if I would. But I would not let him & then he said he should go in the morning early. I shall never forget the tender sympathy he showed me at this time. We talked sometime & when I came back I found I had left Ellen too long alone. She felt as if E. must be ill, & she had better go to him in B[oston] next morning "He may not be there" said I. "Why, he must," says she "where else could he be?" I made no reply – how people can ever bear the task of dissembling or concealing I cant think, one minute of it is so painful.

I passed a wretched night, yet was much entertained, for she talked all through the night & I wanted to hear about what she had to say. In

the middle of the night she got up unpacked her trunk to get it & set
E's picture (an ugly thing that I should not think she would value) on
the mantelpiece that she might see it. Then an hour or two after she
said "M. are you asleep," "No" – "I hope you will like Ellery so that
he may enjoy being with you: he needs the stimulus of such minds. He
values Cary's very much: he reads her letters a great deal: Do you know
whether he has seen her?" – I believe, he has, said I, & I *thought* "poor
deluded innocent" – Then I thought over all these relations once more,
but I still came to the same result that I always do. If I were Waldo's
wife, or Ellery's wife, I should acquiesce in all these relations, since
they needed them. I should expect the same feeling from my husband,
& I should think it little in him not to have it. I felt I should never
repent of advising Ellery to go whatever happened. Well, he came back
next day, and All's Well that Ends Well. It was I that suppose always
thought that he & others will surely do as they intend, & that's a great
mistake.

Mamma & Lidian sympathized with me almost with tears, Waldo
looked radiant, & H[enry] T[horeau] as if his tribe had won a victory.
Well it was a pretty play, since it turned out no tragedy at last. Ellery
told Ellen at once how it was, and she took it just as she ought.
[*"Margaret Fuller's 1842 Journal,"* ed. Joel Myerson, Harvard Library
Bulletin, 21 (1973), 335-36]

29. On changing assessment of Emerson, August 25, 1842

During the same visit, Fuller noted in her journal that she and
Waldo "no longer act powerfully on one another" and wrote
in a letter probably to W. H. Channing, a penetrating
summary of their relations. We note at the end her sharp
awareness that in her connection with him she turned away
from history, society, and action.

... After the first excitement of intimacy with him, – when I was
made so happy by his high tendency, absolute purity, the freedom and
infinite graces of an intellect cultivated much beyond any I had
known, – came with me the questioning season. I was greatly
disappointed in my relation to him. I was, indeed, always called on to
be worthy, – this benefit was sure in our friendship. But I found no

intelligence of my best self; far less was it revealed to me in new modes; for not only did he seem to want the living faith which enables one to discharge this holiest office of a friend, but he absolutely distrusted me in every region of my life with which he was unacquainted. The same trait I detected in his relations with others. He had faith in the Universal, but not in the Individual Man; he met men, not as a brother, but as a critic. Philosophy appeared to chill instead of exalting the poet.

But now I am better acquainted with him. His "accept" is true; the "I shall learn," with which he answers every accusation, is no less true. No one can feel his limitations, in fact, more than he, though he always speaks confidently from his present knowledge as all he has yet, and never qualifies or explains. He feels himself "shut up in a crystal cell," from which only "a great love or a great task could release me," and hardly expects either from what remains in this life. But I already see so well how these limitations have fitted him for his peculiar work, that I can no longer quarrel with them; while from his eyes looks out the angel that must sooner or later break every chain. Leave him in his cell affirming absolute truth; protesting against humanity, if so he appears to do; the calm observer of the courses of things. Surely, "he keeps true to his thought, which is the great matter." He has already paid his debt to his time; how much more he will give we cannot know; but already I feel how invaluable is a cool mind, like his, amid the warring elements around us. As I look at him more by his own law, I understand him better; and as I understand him better, differences melt away. My inmost heart blesses the fate that gave me birth in the same clime and time, and that has drawn me into such a close bond with him as, it is my hopeful faith, will never be broken but from sphere to sphere even more hallowed. * * *

What did you mean by saying I had imbibed much of his way of thought? I do indeed feel his life stealing gradually into mine; and I sometimes think that my work would have been more simple, and my unfolding to a temporal activity more rapid and easy, if we had never met. But when I look forward to eternal growth, I am always aware that I am far larger and deeper for him. His influence has been to me that of lofty assurance and sweet serenity. He says, I come to him as the European to the Hindoo, or the gay Trouvére to the Puritan in his steeple hat. Of course this implies that our meeting is partial. I present to him the many forms of nature and solicit with music; he melts them all into spirit and reproves performance with prayer. When I am with God alone, I adore in silence. With nature I am filled and grow only. With most men I bring words of now past life, and do actions suggested by the wants of their natures rather than my own. But he stops me from doing anything, and makes me think. [*Memoirs*, II, 67-69]

30. To Elizabeth Peabody, December 26, 1844

Also in the journal of her 1842 visit to Concord, Fuller recorded a pleasant visit with the newlywed Nathaniel Hawthorne and his wife Sophia Peabody at the Old Manse. Youngest of the three remarkable Peabody sisters, Sophia wrote a rapturous sonnet to Fuller in appreciation of the Conversations, called "To a Priestess of the Temple Not Made with Hands." If his wife's adoration of Fuller troubled Hawthorne, he overcame it and other antisocial feelings at the time. Fuller wrote, "He walked home with me; we stopped some time to look at the moon she was struggling with clouds. H. said he should be much more willing to die than two months ago, for he had had some real possession in life, but still he never wished to leave this earth; it was beautiful enough. He expressed, as he always does, many fine perceptions. I like to hear the lightest thing he says" ("Margaret Fuller's 1842 Journal," ed. Joel Myerson, p. 325). Yet with the eldest Peabody, Elizabeth (1804-1894), Fuller was never close; Elizabeth wrote after Fuller's death that she did not count herself among Fuller's intimate friends "as she decidedly wished I should not." This is intriguing, as the two women had so much in common: both were charter members of the Transcendental Club, both teachers at Alcott's school; Elizabeth hosted and recorded Fuller's Conversations and participated in work of *The Dial*. (In this last capacity, she often got things confused, according to Fuller.) Although a competitive feeling may explain Fuller's coolness, Elizabeth Peabody's own account of their meeting in 1827 or 1828 suggests other possibilities: "Margaret said almost nothing, but I think she was laughing at me, for which there seemed good

cause. I was impressed strongly with her perfect good nature. . . . She had no malice in her heart" (Emerson, Notebook on MFO, Houghton). Such monumental modesty or
self-effacement of character might well have dismayed or
threatened Fuller. In her only surviving letter to Peabody,
written from New York, Fuller implies as much and, probably drawing on her own experience, warns the older woman on
the mental confusion and self-destructiveness of dependency.

. . . Let me answer, in brief, to the most interesting part of your letter.
Probably, I have, as you say, a large share of prudence by nature. It has
not, however, been large enough to save me from being much
disappointed, in various relations, by a want of delicacy and tenderness
from those who had seemed capable of it. But, perceiving similar faults
in me, and yet knowing my heart capable of pure and intelligent love, I
believe them so, too, and that we shall be better and do better as we
grow.

The tone of your letter was so mild, and its spirit so
comprehensive, that I felt as if you *must* be nearer peace than I had
ever expected to find you in this world. Yet your tendency to
extremes, as to personal attachments, is so strong, I am afraid you will
not wholly rise above it.

The persons whom you have idolized can never, in the end, be
ungrateful, and, probably, at the time of retreat they still do justice to
your heart. But, so long as you must draw persons too near you, a
temporary recoil is sure to follow. It is the character striving to defend
itself from a heating and suffocating action upon it.—

A little, only a little less of this in you would give your powers the
degree of fresh air they need. Could you be as generous and
sympathetic, yet never infatuated; then the blur, the haste, the tangle
would disappear, and neither I nor any one could refuse to understand
you.

I admit that I have never done you justice. There is so much in you
that is hostile to my wishes, as to character, and especially as to the
character of woman; how could I be quite candid! Yet when I have
looked at you, truly, I have also looked steadily, and always feel myself
in your debt that you cordially pardon all that must be to you
repressing and unpleasant in me.

To the care of the fair spirit that sometimes looks out so full through your features and your conduct I commend you. It must finally give you back all your friends.... *[Houghton MS copy]*

31. To Richard Fuller, March 2, 1845

While Fuller was living in New York, she looked to her brother Richard to take on the family responsibility. She explained to him the radical difference that the move meant for her.

... You say you feel worthy and able to be my friend. That I believe this, I did not think any further proof was needed on my side than the great confidence I placed in you during the latter part of our sojourn in Cambridge. On yours I am inclined to ask of you to take as far as possible my place in the family. To show refined consideration for Mother, take judicious care of Lloyd. You have felt as if my honor and the development of my powers, was really precious to you. I have now a position where I can devote myself entirely to use its accessions, a noble career is before me yet. I want to be unimpeded by cares which I cannot, at this distance, attend to properly. I want that my friends should *wish* me now to act in my public career rather than towards them personally. I have given almost all my young energies to personal relations. I no longer feel inclined to this and wish to share and impel the general stream of thought.... *[Houghton MS]*

32. To James Nathan, [spring 1845]

Thanks to the vigorous efforts of Fuller's family, no one knew of her strange intimacy with James Nathan until her correspondence emerged before an astonished New England in 1903. Spring had come early in New York in 1845, and Fuller wrote nearly daily to her "Liebster." The rebirth of life in the woods around the Greeleys' Manhattan home on Turtle Bay reflected all too irresistibly the sprouting of passion for Nathan. The conclusion of this letter inspired the offensive advances of Nathan, who failed to understand that for New Englanders license was the province of poetry alone. Apparently his peace offering, a puppy named Josey, was made and received without irony.

Sunday afternoon

The true lovely time is come at last. The leaves and grasses are out, so that the wind can make soft music, as it sweeps along, instead of the rattling and sobbing of winter. A dear little shower is refreshing the trees and they grow greener and fairer every moment in gratitude. (I write so badly, because the wind shakes my paper too as well as the other leaves, but I can't bear to shut the window.)

You must use your moderation about our interviews, and as you know best. I like best to rely entirely upon you, yet keep time as much as possible with the enchanting calls of outward nature. It is nothing to be together in the parlour, or in the street, and we are not enough so among the green things. To-day the lilacs are all in blossom, and the air is full of a perfume which causes ecstasy.

I hear you with awe assert power over me and feel it to be true. It causes awe, but not dread, such as I felt sometime since at the approach of this mysterious power, for I feel deep confidence in my friend and know that he will lead me on in a spirit of holy love and that all I may learn of nature and the soul will be legitimate. The destiny of each human being is no doubt great and peculiar, however obscure its rudiments to our present sight, but there are also in every age a few in whose lot the meaning of that age is concentrated. I feel that I am one of those persons in my age and sex. I feel chosen among women. I have deep mystic feelings in myself and intimations from elsewhere. I could not, if I would, put into words these spirit facts, indeed they are but swelling germs as yet, and all I do for them is to try to do nothing that might blight them. Yet as you say you need forget your call, so have I need of escaping from this overpowering sense. But when forced back upon myself, as now, though the first turnings of the key were painful, yet the inner door makes rapturous music too upon its golden hinge. What it hides, you perhaps know, as you read me so deeply; indeed, some things you say seem as if you did. Yet do not, unless you must. You look at things so without their veils, yet that seems noble and antique to me. I do it when you hold me by the hand, yet, when I feel how you are thinking, I sometimes only say: Psyche was but a mortal woman, yet as the bride of Love, she became a daughter of the gods too. But had she learned in any other way this secret of herself, all had been lost, the plant and flower and fruit.

But it is impossible to say these things, at least for me. They are myself, but not clearly defined to myself. With you, all seems to assume such palpable reality, though you do not forget its inner sense either. I love to hear you read off the secret, and yet you sometimes make me tremble too. I confide in you, as this bird, now warbling without, confides in me. You will understand my song, but you will not translate it into language too human. I wish, I long to be human, but divinely human. Let the soul invest every act of its abode with somewhat of its own lightness and subtlety. Are you my guardian to domesticate me in the body, and attach it more firmly to the earth? Long it seemed, that it was only my destiny, to say a few words to my youth's companions and then depart. I hung lightly as an air-plant. Am I to be rooted on earth, ah! choose for me a good soil and a sunny place, that I may be a green shelter to the weary and bear fruit enough to pay for staying.

Au revoir! Adieu! [*Love-Letters of Margaret Fuller, 1845-1846* (New York: D. Appleton, 1903), pp. 18-21]

33. To James Nathan, May 9, 1845

It would be difficult to say which of the effects Nathan had on Fuller was stronger: the awakening of her sensuality or the putting to sleep of her mind. They combine to give her letters a powerfully narcotic tone. Two impulses made for her self-effacement. One was the desire to have a child. (A month after Nathan's flight, she wrote Sturgis: "It seems as if I was learning everything, that every element of beauty and power was being reproduced in my frame, but only in my son shall they appear, not in me, his unknown but happy mother" [Tappan Papers, Houghton].) The other—expressed here for the last time in her life—was the desire to be a child.

Friday evening

Dearest,

I must begin by "babbling of green fields." Though it be true, as you say that this region of beautiful symbols is not the highest, I do find such relief in the soft trance, the still rapture they can give. I live in their life and am nourished by it, as the infant from the mother's breast. Do you not cease to love this region too. You shall upbear me to the stars, when your energies overflow, and I feel sure that you will not find me incompetent to be received in the region of ideas. But let me sometimes hold you by the hand to linger with me here and listen while the grass grows; it does me so much good, the soft warm life close to the earth. Perhaps it is, that I was not enough a child at the right time, and now am too childish; but will you not have patience with that?

The tulips are out now and the crimson ones seem to me like you. They fill gloriously with the sunlight, and the petals glow like gems, while the black stamens in the cup of the flower look so rich and mystical. I have gathered two and put them in my vase, but the perfume is almost overpowering; there are also two golden ones, that have rooted themselves on the edge of a grassy bank. I do not know how they could get there; it was a strange elopement from the regular flower-bed, but the effect is beautiful of flowers so *vornehm* willing to be wild.

I have been sitting in the twilight in the spot where we have been several times. Always something unpleasant occurred when we were there, but it has all endeared us to one another and ennobled the relation. And now a shrub has starred itself all over with white flowers and bends over the place. The young moon bent her pure crescent above the rocks, my parapet behind; the waves stole in, vibrating through the silence with insidious murmur. *Spülen!* – how expressive is the German word; we have none like it. In this enchanting solitude, I thought of thee, of thy great thoughts. I have well understood all that has been told me. Do not hesitate to unfold the whole, only, indeed, in the musical order. I feel sure of being equal to it. Indeed, it seems as if there had been a gradual and steady preparation in me to hear it all. It will not be in vain that we have met. Whatever be your destiny, whether you be born to give form to these ideas, or are only the harbinger, the father of him who is to come, – that they have been uttered on earth and found their due vibration, predicts that their fulfilment is near. Man shall stand upon the earth as Man, and no more content himself with specific titles and partial claims.

My dearest, I feel a deep desire to utter myself, to answer the inspirations of your life from my inmost soul, but I cannot. The easy powers, the superficial eloquence all fail me here. The little wings on my feet upbear me in the world, but they are not strong enough here. You would have to take me to heart and read my silence, but I believe you will.

Since I began to write, I grow more powerless, whether that you are thinking of me now, or from the sense of your thoughts that have been poured upon me, I do not know this time. But often I feel, that you are thinking of me and it takes away all power of thought or motion. You say it will not always be so, that by-and-bye it will stimulate me to be more myself. This may be. There is at present so much for me to assimilate and absorb. Could I indeed but let it rest in me till I grow to the stature of what I feel. You know how it will be, since you have the secret of this vital energy. You must know how it works in all forms of life, especially in mine, with which you are now in conjunction. I feel the most tender reliance, and also faith, that I shall never be a trouble to you. I observe, that it is with you, as it has been with me in many cases. You attract beings so much, that after a while it is too much for their good or your pleasure. Then comes the painful retrograde motion. But I feel confident that my angel will not let it be so with me. I have never been able to go a step, where you did not take me. Now, when I want you most, I feel that I cannot seek you, unless you do me. So not even by a thought shall I be permitted to follow you, where I cannot accompany.

Now there is more and far better to be said, but again I cannot. Yet it is delightful to know that you will read all that is left unsaid. Now why say anything? – but it is sweet to express all one can. *[Love-Letters of Margaret Fuller, 1845-1846, (New York: D. Appleton, 1903) pp. 76-79]*

PART

III

The
Transcendentalist

Teacher, Editor, Literary Critic

In many ways, the Transcendentalist movement, which preoccupied Margaret Fuller during her last eight years in New England, seemed richly designed to meet her needs. As a new cultural presence, as a spiritual revolt, and, in its ambivalent way, as a social force, the movement did much to mitigate her isolation, to strengthen her self-esteem, and, as she came to identify her differences from its members, chiefly Emerson, to sharpen her sense of direction. As we shall see, the direction she ultimately took presents symbolically a powerful critique of the movement.

Her cultural appetites made Margaret Fuller a freak in her own land. "Fitted by genius and culture to mingle as an equal in the most refined circles of Europe," according to Channing, she was stuck with "the very decent, yet drudging, descendants of the prim Puritans." [1] Through Transcendentalism, some aspects of the Europe she could not visit—the Europe of literary romanticism and German philosophical idealism—and even the exotic India of Hindu thought approached Massachusetts. For a loose enclave of high-minded readers, like an educated elite in an underdeveloped country, passed around their copies of Carlyle and Coleridge, de Staël and Goethe, Kant, Schelling, Fichte, and the *Bhagavadgita*, and, half digesting them, half recreated them in their own image. Fuller's participation in this exchange should not be confused with assimilation; when she left America, Emerson characterized her still as "an exotic in New England, a foreigner from some more sultry and expansive climate" (V:4). But for a long while, the group was stimulating and intellectually gratifying to her.

As a spiritual revolt, the Transcendentalist movement served a more profound need. Transcendentalism was the culmination of a long process in which the divine authority of New England's original Calvinism was internalized. The liberal Unitarian Dr. William Ellery Channing had hastened the process by replacing Calvinist determinism with individual responsibility, and by replacing the subjection of man to a wrathful God with the intuitive discovery of a benevolent God in the human soul. But by the 1830s Dr. Channing was still an exception. More than internalizing divinity, Unitarianism had secularized it, more than encouraging the intuitive authority of the private individual, it had sanctioned the "rational" authority of public institutions and the marketplace. It had become, as Emerson stigmatized it, "the corpse-cold Unitarianism of Harvard College and Brattle Street." While Dr. Channing thought Christianity, generously interpreted, could house the most rebellious spirit, Emerson felt cramped by all molds, religious and secular. In quitting the ministry in 1832, Emerson was repudiating external authority; and in retiring to Concord, he dramatized his belief that authority could lie only in intuition and feeling, in a self that was not merely godlike but was god itself. Abandoning his reliance on historical Christianity and, as nearly as possible, on the history of his time as well, he sought through creative perception to realize moments of divine harmony between the self and the universe; then he published this enlarged selfhood to the world. It is small wonder that fires of outrage reanimated the Unitarian corpse and that gentle Dr. Channing feared Emerson's followers would "fall into a kind of 'ego-theism.' " Dr. Channing's nephew, William Henry Channing, and many of his generation would not be deterred by doctrinal fears. They heard in Transcendentalism the simple and irresistible call: "Trust, dare and be; infinite good is ready for your asking; seek and find. All that your fellows can claim or need is that you should become, in fact, your highest self; fulfill, then, your ideal." [2]

Margaret Fuller, chilled by the family Unitarianism and yearning since childhood for release of an emotional nature repressed by intellectuality, must have felt that the logic of personal and of universal history met in the Transcendental faith. The transformation of "self-consciousness" from a painful social experience into an exalted and creative condition must have had overwhelming appeal. Within such a movement a young woman who could only cut an outlandish figure in conventional New England might escape into a free realm where her extravagant ambition to grow and feel was sanctioned philosophically and seemed to be genuinely welcomed. The limits of this welcome emerge after her death in the ambivalence of some of the Transcendentalists' accounts of her unorthodox manner in New England and in their censorship of her unorthodox behavior in Italy. But, for the most part, Fuller saw simply that the Transcendentalists embraced more of her than others did and was for the time grateful.

As a social force, Transcendentalism was divided and ambiguous, and I can only point to some of the problems here. The movement's origins were in a class which until the Jacksonian era had so often combined broad culture with political and social power that intellectuality itself had come to be unconsciously identified with that class. Thus, as Frederickson notes, "In driving class privilege from the seat of authority, the Jacksonians seemed to have driven out intellect as well." But beginning with his address, "The American Scholar," Emerson seemed to construe his very detachment from traditions of the past and institutions of the present as a source of new power and meaning for American society. [3] Though Emerson offered no program for social change, he offered an alternative set of values which some readers (notably Theodore Parker, W. H. Channing, and George Ripley) translated into such a program; seizing "the Newness" in this spirit, they joined the growing ranks of active reformers in the 1840s. But Emerson did not, and while he was feared in some quarters as a radical critic of the established order, he was at that time also an advocate of caution with men and organizations seeking to change that order.

Until the 1850s, Emerson was critical of the established social order only secondarily or implicitly. As with church authority, so with political or social authority: Emerson sought to strip it of historic specificity and to internalize it. "His method of self-renewal," writes Sacvan Bercovitch, "consisted in arrogating the meaning of America to himself"—America, that is, as an *idea* which springs from no political or social institution, but from "the purest minds" only. To put it simply, he was more concerned to "represent" a mythic and potential America than to confront the actual one. Consequently, his ideology was hostile to both elements of social reform—organization and action. His refusal of political and social sectarianism was consistent with his rejection of sectarianism in religion. The truth in behavior could be measured only by its radical social isolation: "It is only as a man puts off all foreign support and stands alone that I see him to be strong and to prevail. He is weaker by every recruit to his banner." Then to adopt a cause was to take the part for the whole; this was the same as the refusal of true spiritual consciousness and hence tainted with the material: "Each 'cause' as it is called—say Abolition, Temperance, say Calvinism, or Unitarianism—becomes speedily a little shop, where the article, let it have been at first never so subtle and ethereal, is now made up into portable and convenient cakes, and retailed in small quantities to suit purchasers." Only in detachment from society and its causes, he argued, can the self achieve harmonious unity with the higher Reality in which all contradictions are dissolved. Eventually and mysteriously, by scrupulously shunning "manipular attempts to realize the world of thought," the "transformation of genius into practical power" will be effected. [4]

Fuller's needs for self-development made her more receptive to Emerson's deliberate distancing of social pressures, his action by spiritual example, than to those Transcendentalists who chose direct and sometimes organized action. His perspective on Transcendentalism seemed to offer her a broader synthesis of energies than friendship alone did. But when Emerson's synthesis was most complete—that is to say, most independent of and detached from material and historical reality—it was actually most alien to her. Emerson's perspective was in fact nearly as debilitating to her real strength as the dream of all-sufficing friendship had been; it tempted her to absolutize the inner self and to live as if she could elude entirely the limits of time and place and sex. Fuller never succumbed fully to the lure of such privatization, despite its glorious claims, partly because the roles the movement gave her—teacher, editor, and literary critic—required rigorous and semipublic work. More fundamentally, as we shall now see, her nurture, her nature, and her sex itself worked to keep her from as fully transcending material reality and reducing the complexity of experience as Emerson, especially in these early years of his career, strove to do.

Fuller's self-nurture led her to Transcendentalism by a route which was primarily neither religious nor philosophical but literary. Though a youthful mystical experience drew her to a liberal Christianity, her faith was tentative and eclectic to the verge, for her time, of heresy. (Honesty obligated even her devoted Clarke to call her life goals only "almost Christian.") Merely one of her resources, her faith was not her chief source of energy. And with philosophy she often had to struggle, confessing to failure to understand Fichte and Jacobi, and complaining that even a "feasting" with Plato was not new nourishment. ("Plato's thoughts have, indeed, so passed into our intellectual life that I feel as if only returning to my native mountain air while with these philosophers and cannot be quite enough a disciple.") She read Locke, de Staël on Locke, Kant and the post-Kantians largely as a means of better understanding romantic literature, especially from Germany. She wrote that, at twenty-one, oppressed by emotional disappointments, family cares, and social obligations, "I took up the study of German, and my progress was like the rebound of a string pressed almost to bursting." [5] In German she read Lessing, Novalis, Tieck, Schiller, Körner, Richter, and, above all, Goethe.

Goethe expressed her desire for knowledge gained through passionate, broad, and subtle experience; and the wisdom and high influence of his female characters sustained and inspired her. At the age of twenty-two, she felt that Goethe perfectly comprehended every feeling she had ever had. By a reflex equally self-centered and generous, then, she began dreaming of writing a life of Goethe. Ironically, she thought she would have to go to Europe to learn the details of the private life of the writer who had so liberated her spirit, for no American scholar would share them with a lady. Most enlightened men she knew refused even to read Goethe on grounds of moral reprobation. Although she never transformed her voluminous notes into a biography, she was in her essays and letters for a great part of the next decade an avid publicist of the literature of Goethe and other Germans, and published her translation of *Eckermann's Conversations with Goethe*. She also offered classes in the language, read and discussed the literature for months with Dr. Channing, and forced Emerson to examine and largely overcome his prejudices against Goethe. Her commitment to Goethe was the basis for her largest single contribution to Transcendental intellectual life and gave her a staunch support for her resistance to Emersonian detachment.

In addition to her learning, her volatile nature played its role in this resistance. Her appetite for the clash and color of participation made her confess to Emerson on reading "Nature" again that she delighted "more in thought-living than in living thought." [6] And her sex was a third factor, though she was included in the Transcendentalist circle more in spite than because of it. Her sex gave her a primary and inescapable sense of otherness; the ensuing habit of perceiving duality would work against a desire or capacity for absorption into mystic unity. These influences would finally move her to a position and way of life not only dramatically different from Emerson's but implicitly critical of his. Even during her years of closest involvement with the Transcendentalists, differences from them emerged.

What was perhaps most alien and striking even to these lovers of art was the "passionate love for the beautiful" that Hedge remarked in Fuller, the sensual vitality which in New England earned her the labels "pagan," "exotic," and "Bacchante." The training of her father, despite his own austerity, had its influence here. Having drunk in the classics first, she found the Christian teachings made her cry out "for her dear old Greek gods"; by contrast, Christian "spirituality seemed nakedness." [7] (Indeed, her matured spiritual longing was for a life "more complete and various" than Christ's; in 1842 she imagined a second Messiah with "the calm beauty and physical fulness of a Greek God, with the deep consciousness of a Moses, with the holy love and purity of Jesus." [8]) We understand better what Fuller found so reinforcing in Goethe when we learn that Emerson early complained that the German poet's work failed to "transport" him out of the "dominion of the senses." Objecting to "the velvet life he led," and finding in his writing "luxuriously" a "new and worse offence," Emerson leveled his verdict: "the Puritan in me accepts no apology for bad morals in such as he." A further mark of the kinship between Fuller and Goethe is that both, chilled in northern Protestant cultures, were to be warmed by the same Rome and to feel reborn there—and both divined it in advance. Fuller wrote in the winter of 1841, "Once I was almost all intellect; now I am almost all feeling. Nature vindicates her rights, and I feel all Italy glowing beneath the Saxon crust." This penchant for physical happiness informed even her criticism. Although she never, in New England, praised sensuality as such, although she ranked the "priestly vocation" in art second to none, she was too alive to beauty to let these standards interfere with aesthetic pleasure. And she missed this sensual vitality when it was absent in others. Thus, in her otherwise adulatory review of Emerson's second volume of essays, she voices this mild criticism of him, who worked so deliberately against the flat horizontal of his world: "We doubt this friend raised himself too early to the perpendicular and did not lie along the ground long enough to hear the secret whispers of our parent life. We could wish he might be thrown by conflicts on the lap of mother earth, to see if he would not rise again with added powers." [9]

Apparently opposing this sensuousness is her Puritan impulse to unblinkingly acknowledge pain, limitation, and even evil. (Actually both qualities are rooted in the same refusal to turn from material reality, a refusal which often set her at odds with friends seeking precisely to transcend it.) Sometimes this impulse took the form of hardheaded practicality, born of the limits imposed on her as a woman, especially after she began to struggle to help support her family. Even earlier, when James Clarke professed the Transcendentalist faith in the power of human will which Emerson shared, Fuller maintained passionately that circumstances had incalculable power over character. Elsewhere she wrote that she wanted "to know and feel my pain, to investigate its nature and its source" (III:5). Fuller forces us to re-examine the classic assumption that women's appreciation of pain is masochistic. She shows that it can also spring from realism, a desire to know life as fiercely as one can, and, when its breadth is denied, to make the most of its depth and height.

Her more philosophical acceptance of evil as "a growth of nature, and one condition of the development of good" (V:8) is related to this tendency. Her definition of evil as an obstruction which forces us to creative accomplishment owes much to her intimate bodily experience, to her physical frailty, her chronic bouts of migraine, and her brushes with death. "Our Father, let not the heaviest shower be spared," she prayed, "let not the gardener forbear his knife till the fair hopeful tree of existence be brought to its fullest blossom and fruit!"[10] But since Emerson, in his theory of compensation, also saw the uses for growth of limitation and loss, it is important to note the subtle difference in emphasis. While Emerson stresses the precious instant of mystic unity when man "parts with his individuality, leaves all thought of private stake, personal feeling, and in compensation . . . has in some sort the strength of the whole," Fuller's attention was rather to the cause and the effect on the self of religious crisis; "I have lived to know that the secret of all things is pain, and that nature travaileth most painfully with her noblest product."[11] Here we have a second distinction. For Emerson, mystic harmony was the end; his mode was timeless and relatively static. For Fuller, religious crisis and vision was part of a process involving pain and change; her mode was relatively dynamic.

This difference influences a third, which concerns the response to risk, challenge, and conflict. In *Summer on the Lakes*, Fuller constructed a dialogue in which Emerson, thinly disguised as "Self-Poise" argues, "No leaps, no starts will avail us, by patient crystallization alone the equal temper of wisdom is attainable. . . . The better part of wisdom is a sublime prudence, a pure and patient truth that will receive nothing it is not sure it can permanently lay to heart. Of our study there should be in proportion two-thirds of rejection to one of acceptance." To this Fuller's persona, "Free Hope," retorts, "To me it seems that it is madder never to abandon oneself, than often to be infatuated; better to be wounded, a captive, and a slave, than always to walk in armor." Her conviction, as un-Emersonian as it was unladylike, that conflict and confrontation are more productive of truth than serenity, figured in a letter to Clarke written before she was twenty. Here she sketched a man of genius (a typical incognito) who, adoring "the bright phantoms of his mind's creation," grew to intellectual manhood. Then "I wished this being might be launched into the world of realities, his heart glowing with the ardor of an immortal toward perfection, his eyes searching everywhere to behold it; I wished he might collect into one burning point those withering, palsying convictions, which, in the ordinary routine of things so gradually pervade the soul; that he might suffer, in brief space, agonies of disappointment commensurate with his unpreparedness and confidence." Out of this accelerated and dialectical clash of idealism and reality, she felt sure, "such a man would suddenly dilate in a form of Pride, Power, and Glory—a centre round which asking, aimless hearts might rally." [1] [2]

All these forces in Fuller—her fidelity to material actuality (whether in the form of sensual beauty or of pain and limitation), her preference for dynamic process, and her attraction to conflict and confrontation—worked to lead her away from the lure inherent in Emersonian Transcendentalism of pure transparent unity with the eternal. This is not to say that she ever wholly abandoned the love of spirit that drew her to Transcendentalism. Rather, especially after she left New England, she was increasingly stimulated by the need to imbed her values in material and social reality—and the more intransigent the reality, the better.

Teaching, the first vocation the Transcendentalist movement provided for Fuller, was a traditional one for women. But Fuller characteristically stretched traditional roles, and her first position was in a school soon to be dogged by scandal. This was Bronson Alcott's Temple School, where the Transcendentalist activist Elizabeth Peabody was also teaching. All of Alcott's convictions now look innocent enough. Believing with Wordsworth that children were nearer than adults to their celestial origins, he thought that education should be directed toward their knowledge of their inner natures. His chief method toward this end was Socratic conversation, in which he pursued the children's understanding of themselves and of the Gospels. Basing his pedagogy on friendship, not authority, and valuing more than most Transcendentalists the individual's relation to the group, Alcott submitted all questions of discipline to the assembled children. Punishment was customarily the brief exclusion of the child from the conversations, though once Alcott required a recreant child to strike him. But when the two volumes of his *Conversations with Children on the Gospels* were published in late 1836 and early 1837, tempers grew so hot in Boston that a mob threatened to attack Alcott's Friday meeting of Sunday-school teachers. He was charged with heresy for treating the children as spiritual authorities, blasphemy for stripping Jesus of any special divinity, and obscenity for discussing, however indirectly, the physical aspects of birth. Coupled with the financial panic of 1837, this public hysteria resulted in the loss of many pupils and eventually the closing of the school. [13]

Fuller, however, was pleased by the contrast between Alcott's pedagogy and her father's, especially Alcott's preference for the development of character, confidence, and self-understanding over the mastery of mechanical details and for free-ranging thought over discipline. She defended him against all detractors. But privately she noted that Alcott's spirituality lacked robust vitality and excluded the material and the complex.

Given Alcott's dwindling resources, and the meagerness of supplements earned by her teaching German, French, and Italian to women, Fuller accepted the handsome offer of one thousand dollars a year to teach for the man Alcott considered—hastily, it emerged—his chief disciple, Hiram Fuller. (No relation to Margaret Fuller, he was a disciple of Alcott's only insofar as he could make that lucrative.) There, at the Greene Street School in Providence, the boys were said to be overawed by Fuller or undone by her sarcasm, but her success was great with the girls in their late teens, many of whom left the school when she did. Adapting Alcott's goals, her main object in teaching moral philosophy was to upset their received notions and stimulate fresh thought. As Anna Gale noted in her journal on January 5, 1838, "Miss Fuller said that Dr. Wayland's thoughts would lay upon our minds, like dry husk, unless they take root sufficiently deep to produce one little thought of our own." [14] Introducing controversial subjects, such as evil, reincarnation, militant reform, and the millenium, Fuller shared her own uncertainties as well as her convictions while carefully "calling out" her pupils' independent views.

Despite the gratifications of her teaching years, Fuller continually regretted the loss of concentrated leisure for thought and the necessary abandonment of her Goethe biography. From Boston, in 1837, she wrote Hedge with fretful wit, "I faint with desire to think and surely shall, the first opportunity, but some outward requisition is ever knocking at the door of my mind and I am as ill placed as regards a chance to think as a haberdasher's prentice or the President of Harvard University." In Providence the next year, the "suppression and accommodation" required of her made it worse. Emerson's attempts to pacify her made her burst out, "I hate everything that is reasonable just now, 'wise limitations' and all. I have behaved much too well for some time past; it has spoiled my peace. . . . Isolation is necessary to me, as to others. Yet I keep on 'fulfilling all my duties,' as the technical phrase is, except to myself." [15]

Exhausted and frustrated, she resigned her post in December 1838, writing Channing, "I do not wish to teach again at all." In the same letter she added, "But I foresee circumstances that may make it wrong for me to obey my wishes," and asked Channing, then in Cincinnati—"an excellent starting point for my brothers," she thought—to "investigate the possibility of setting up school for sixty girls." [16] Although she later found a location in Illinois where her brother Arthur established a school, she never taught again in a formal institution.

But her feeling for education as a process of opening the self to meaningful life remained with her, evolving as her sense of meaningful life changed. In Boston education would next mean helping women of her own class to find new resources and self-respect, in New York providing tools of survival to the poor and orphaned and a new start to prisoners and prostitutes, and in France and England uniting workers as a class. Finally, in Italy education meant nothing less than a people preparing itself for unremitting struggle. But all this lay ahead; first she had to learn better what she meant by fulfilling her duty to herself.

On the list of enlightened acts toward women in the nineteenth century, the Transcendentalists' making a woman the editor of their literary organ ranks low. Long before they were meeting regularly in 1837 as the "Symposium Club" according to Alcott, "Hedge's Club" according to the rest of them, or the "Transcendental Club" according to the world, Frederic Hedge had proposed that his friends create a literary periodical. Late in 1839, the Club agreed on the need for a journal to compete with the conservative or theological or stridently partisan ones in New England which failed either to publish or to appeal to them. Theodore Parker proposed that Emerson be editor, with Fuller and Hedge as assistants. Because this duty conflicted with his freedom, Emerson transferred it to Fuller, and Ripley agreed to handle the business end. As Fuller's enthusiasm for the literature of Europe had sharpened her interest in the evolution of an authentic American literature, she consented. No sooner was the journal a reality than Hedge retreated, confessing candidly his fear that public identification with Transcendentalism would open him to charges of atheism. "I believe we all feel much alike in regard to this Journal," Emerson wrote Fuller; "we all wish it to be but do not wish to be in any way personally responsible for it." [17]

Nevertheless, Emerson helped—largely redrafting, for example, her introductory address to the first issue of *The Dial* in July 1840. The "conductors of this work," he said, joined with those in New England who determine to "make new demands on literature, and to reprobate that rigor of our conventions of religion and education which is turning us to stone, which renounces hope, which looks only backward, which asks only such a future as the past, which suspects improvement, and holds nothing so much in horror as new views and the dreams of youth." Proposing "not to multiply books, but to report life," they would draw less on professional writers than on "the discourse of the living, and the portfolios which friendship has opened to us." [18]

Thus put to the test, friendship was often found wanting. Since contributors were unpaid, Fuller was obliged to use all her arts of stimulation and entreaty to get them, and for 136 pages of one issue had hastily to provide 85 pages from her own notebooks. Then, when she was able to secure such spontaneous and heartfelt work as Emerson had solicited, it often fell short of her critical standards. Unwilling to accept writing she judged slipshod, she tried to summon the tact to reject some pieces by young Thoreau—too contrived, in her estimation—without discouraging him. And she risked what she called "impertinence" by criticizing a passage of Emerson's she felt had "rather *l'air bourgeois*"; "I think when you look again you will think you have not said what you meant to say." Under Fuller, *The Dial* published more quasi-mystical fiction, criticism of the arts, and discussion of German romanticism than it did subsequently. But she tried to be impartial, and later defended her practice of publishing representative pieces even when she did not like them against Emerson's preference for satisfying his own taste: "I wish my tastes and sympathies still more expansive than they are, instead of more severe. Here we differ." [19]

Apparently, her tolerance was nowhere shared, and the extreme divergences between members of the circle gaped even wider in print. Despite Fuller's hope of conducting *The Dial* in "a spirit neither of dogmatism nor of compromise," outside critics often found the first and contributors complained of the second. After the first issue, Emerson wrote, "I hope our Dial will get to be a little *bad*." [20] Alcott judged the journal timid and conventional for not publishing in every issue his widely satirized "Orphic Sayings," while feisty Parker was not abashed to say *The Dial* needed a beard. These rivaling calls for virile boldness seemed to drive Fuller into an uncharacteristically "feminine" neutrality and made the *Dial* she produced less challenging than any of her later work. Though Higginson wrote in 1884 that the cumulative effect of the journal on his generation was liberating, the magazine was too eclectic to galvanize a community, let alone to win a circulation over three hundred.

For Fuller, the recalcitrance of writers, the steady overwork, and the controversial response were exhausting. As a last indignity, the journal's financial instability resulted in her earning two free copies of each issue but never the promised annual salary of two hundred dollars. Although *The Dial* kept Margaret Fuller busy, it was not the action she craved. In spring 1842, she resigned. Partly out of respect for the sacrifice she had made, Emerson wrote that there should be "rotation in martyrdom" and took over the chief editing task. [21]

Fuller's poems, stories, and art and music criticism are too subjective or diffuse to provide much interest now. But her essays—literary, feminist, and political—though lacking in the structural firmness that might have come with a regular education, are historically important and well worth our attention. Her literary criticism both for *The Dial* and later for the *New York Tribune* is widely regarded as the best—with the possible exception of Poe's—produced in this country before 1850. Thus it is disturbing that, in the *Memoirs*, Clarke, Emerson, and Channing all but ignore her work for *The Dial* and give hardly more attention to her critical writing than to the opinion of friends who found it inferior to her conversation. Moreover, even Channing, the one of the three who seems to have struggled hardest against his sexual prejudices, attributes her literary powers to her lack of womanly fulfillment. ("The very glow of her poetic enthusiasm was but an outflush of trustful affection; the very restlessness of her intellect was the confession that her heart had found no home. . . . her absorption in study [was] the natural vent of emotions, which had met no object worthy of life-long attachment.") One can hardly disprove such contentions, but the argument from sex could as well run that in literary study and writing, the limitations of woman's status are apparently baffled and eluded, for thought transcends gender. That Fuller saw literary endeavor as a way of escaping female shackles is borne out in her "Short Essay on Critics," in which she names the candor she wants "manliness"—by which she meant forthright humanness—and calls the habit of respect speaking "man to man." [22]

Moreover, she found in the romantic school of criticism which she absorbed through Goethe and Carlyle a natural arena for the blend of abilities she regarded as "masculine" and "feminine." In her "Short Essay on Critics," she distinguished between the "subjective class" of critics, whose impressionistic pieces, eschewing reflection and analysis, only "characterize the critic," and the "apprehensive class who can go out of themselves and enter fully into a foreign existence." As a third and superior class, the "comprehensive" critics, like the apprehensive, judge a work "by its own law" but also by a broader law (which she never defines explicitly) because they perceive "the analogies of the universe, and how they are regulated by an absolute, invariable principle. . . ." This ideal critic, then, is "not merely a poet, not merely a philosopher, not merely an observer, but tempered of all three." [23] Paralleling her pattern for friendships, such criticism coupled the capacities for warm empathy and for coolheaded, informed evaluation. And, as with friendship, the literature she studied enlarged her experience. Hence she was as widely curious in her critical role as she was eclectic in her editorial role. Distinguishing between literature for the ages, which she compared critically with the best in its field, and literature for the day, which she chose usually simply to describe, she welcomed both.

The values she brought to criticism were romantic and Transcendentalist. Most conspicuous are her requirement—which Longfellow failed to meet—that imagination, a gift of nature, be spontaneous, not contrived or derivative, and her preference for authors who exhibit "resolute will" or "earnestness of soul" or penetrating vision—what Matthew Arnold would call "high seriousness." Though spiritual and moral, these biases were not moralistic; and indeed she deplored the public need for "a moral" and for the depiction of conventional mores in literary productions.

Her enduring love for complex reality, coupled with her high moral idealism, made her an incomparable mediator between timid Americans and the variously threatening Goethe, Byron, and Sand. She saw that Goethe's worldliness, his daring (especially in *Elective Affinities*, which centers on marital infidelity), Byron's morbidity, and Sand's free passion, if scrutinized in the context of their age and their options, could enlighten and liberate the understanding. Her concern for the development of an inherently American literature, expressing the peculiar genius of American life, was equally great, and related. Richly acquainted through books with continental culture and afflicted neither with the Anglophilism nor continental xenophobia of many New Englanders, Fuller expected immigrants to enhance, not detract from, this country's cultural life. From the eventual fusion of the races she expected a unique culture, free from the prejudices that fettered European culture.

Finally, this critic sought personal synthesis by turning her "manly" attention to female characters, women writers, and that rare male novelist of feminist persuasion, Charles Brockden Brown. Significantly, she wrote more such pieces for the *New York Tribune* than for New England's *Dial*. The explanation for these pieces requires a section of its own (IV). For the editor who began her career by apologizing for being a woman could never have written them had she been confined to the experiences described in this part. While Transcendentalism was adventurous enough to make room for her talent, it was not itself capable of increasing her esteem and understanding of her sex. What she needed, as we shall see, was to generate experiments of her own in talking and working with women.

Notes

1. *Memoirs*, II, 36.
2. David P. Edgell, *William Ellery Channing: An Intellectual Portrait* (Boston: Beacon Press, 1955), p. 122; *Memoirs*, II, 13.
3. George M. Frederickson, *The Inner Civil War: Northern Intellectuals and the Crisis of the Union* (New York: Harper & Row, 1965), pp. 9-10.
4. Bercovitch, *The Puritan Origins of the American Self* (New Haven: Yale University Press, 1975), p. 173; *Complete Essays and Other Writings of Ralph Waldo Emerson*, ed. Brooks Atkinson (New York: Random House, 1950), pp. 169 ("Self-Reliance"), 98 ("The Transcendentalist"), 364 ("Experience"). I am indebted to Myra Jehlen for calling to my attention some of these aspects of Emerson.
5. *Memoirs*, I, 133; January 27, 1839, to Caroline Sturgis, Tappan Papers, Houghton; *Kindred Papers*, p. 359.
6. April 12, 1849, Higginson, p. 310.

7. *Memoirs*, I, 93; Barbara M. Cross, *The Educated Woman in America: Selected Writings of Catharine Beecher, Margaret Fuller, and M. Carey Thomas* (New York: Teachers College Press, 1965), p. 122.

8. Frederick Augustus Braun, *Margaret Fuller and Goethe* (New York: Henry Holt, 1910), p. 255. The version in *Memoirs* (II, 92) tellingly omits the phrase "physical fulness."

9. Braun, p. 151; *Correspondence of Thomas Carlyle and Ralph Waldo Emerson* (Boston: James R. Osgood, 1883), I, 30-31; *Memoirs*, II, 58; *The Writings of Margaret Fuller*, ed. Mason Wade (New York: The Viking Press, 1941), p. 393. Fuller's Concord journal of 1842 provides a striking example of her difference from Emerson on the sufficiency of physical beauty. Noting that Emerson's response to a moonlit night was to remark that "each twinkling light breaking there summons to demand the whole secret," Fuller disagreed: "the beauty does not stimulate me to ask *why*?, and press to the centre, I was satisfied for the moment, full as if my existence were filled out, for nature had said the very word that was lying in my heart" ("Margaret Fuller's 1842 journal," ed. Joel Myerson, *Harvard Library Bulletin*, 21 [1973], 324).

10. *Kindred Papers*, p. 360.

11. "The Genuine Man," *Young Emerson Speaks: Unpublished Discourses on Many Subjects*, ed. Arthur C. McGiffert, Jr. (Boston: Houghton Mifflin Co., 1938), p. 186; *Kindred Papers*, p. 359.

12. *Summer on the Lakes in 1843* (1844); rpt. Nieuwkoop: B. De Graaf, 1972), 130-31; *Memoirs*, I, 69-70.

13. Dorothy McCuskey, *Bronson Alcott, Teacher* (New York: Macmillan, 1940), pp. 82-113.

14. E. A. Hoyt and L. S. Brigham, "Glimpses of Margaret Fuller: The Greene Street School and Florence," *New England Quarterly*, 29 (1956), 88.

15. *Writings*, ed. Wade, p. 548; Providence, March 1, 1838, Higginson, p. 90.

16. Providence, December 9, 1838, BPL MS.

17. Ralph L. Rusk, *The Life of Ralph Waldo Emerson* (New York: Charles Scribner's Sons, 1949), pp. 275-76.

18. *The Dial*, I (July 1840), 1-4.

19. Higginson, pp. 157, 167; see Bernard Rosenthal, "*The Dial*, Transcendentalism, and Margaret Fuller," *English Language Notes*, 8 (September 1970), 28-36.

20. *Memoirs*, II, 25; Rusk, *Letters*, II, 316.

21. Arthur Brown, *Margaret Fuller* (New York: Twayne, 1964), p. 62.

22. *Memoirs*, II, 37; *Writings*, ed. Wade, p. 228.

23. "A Short Essay on Critics," *Writings*, ed. Wade, pp. 223-29.

CONTEMPORARIES ON FULLER

1. Her teaching in Providence, Anna Gale, 1838

These entries in Anna Gale's journal at the Greene Street School offer portraits of Miss Fuller serious and Miss Fuller jolly, in both cases helping the girls to discard the feelings convention imposed on them and to find their own.

a. . . . We were led to speak of the various idols which people have, such as Money, Fame and Power. Beauty was mentioned, but Miss Fuller thought we could not love Beauty too well if we looked up through Nature to Nature's God. The possession of it could not injure us, if we were contented with simply being beautiful. Speaking of gratitude to God Miss F. asked us if we thought it was a natural impulse of our nature. If she had asked me in particular I should unhesitatingly have answered that it was. She then asked us if we could think of any particular instance in our lives – if ever anything had occurred so particularly agreeable and pleasant that our first thought was to fall upon our knees and thank God; or whether we should do thus only because we have been taught to do so. She then referred us to little children. If you give them anything new they do not stop and thank you, but you must tell them to do it over and over again. This I have seen done too often to doubt its truth, and I concluded that my opinion was going to be proved entirely wrong, though for once I did not like to give it up. But Miss Fuller said that she had never been taught to feel this gratitude, and there had been instances in her life when she thought this feeling sprung up spontaneously. She thought we naturally possessed such a feeling, but it was destroyed by being drilled into us when children. Children think they are born to be happy, – that everybody is to contribute to their happiness – and it is hard for them to think it otherwise; but it is a lesson that they learn the first time they are shut up in a closet. Miss Fuller said that we are apt to make a wrong estimate of happiness. We see those who are young, rich and beautiful, and we think they must be the happiest; but it is not so. The balance of happiness is more equal than we imagine. We cannot judge of the happiness of others.

b. . . . Miss Landon was a poetess who caused us some amusement. Her poetry is not very valuable. It is very sentimental, being mostly about broken hearts, forlorn lovers, and those who have been disappointed in their love. One of the young ladies asked if Miss Landon's heart had been broken. Miss F. said she did not know; that if it had it was probably mended. Some broken hearts get mended again, fastened together by putty or something, whilst others always remain broken. Miss F. said if we read her poetry we must sigh over it, or we should be much behindhand; for many ladies read it, and wept over it. It would introduce us to many ladies with swanlike necks; more ladies with swanlike necks than were in this school. Miss Landon is now about twenty-eight. *[E. A. Hoyt and L. S. Brigham, "Glimpses of Margaret Fuller: The Greene Street School and Florence," New England Quarterly, 29 (1956) 93-94]*

2. An afternoon with Fuller,
Nathaniel Hawthorne, August 22, 1842

During her Concord visits, Fuller became friendly enough with Hawthorne to write in 1844 that she felt "more like a sister to H., or rather more that he might be a brother to me, than ever with any man before" (Mason Wade, *Margaret Fuller: Whetstone of Genius*, p. 113). Hawthorne, who remained on the critical fringe of Transcendentalism and was much later one of Fuller's most famous and vehement detractors, (VI:7) left a record in his notebooks of a typically spontaneous Transcendental afternoon with her. (He and Sophia Peabody had been married only a month earlier.)

. . . After leaving the book at Mr. Emerson's, I returned through the woods, and entering Sleepy Hollow, I perceived a lady reclining near the path which bends along its verge. It was Margaret herself. She had been there the whole afternoon, meditating or reading; for she had a book in her hand, with some strange title, which I did not understand, and have forgotten. She said that nobody had broken her solitude, and was just giving utterance to a theory that no inhabitant of Concord ever visited Sleepy Hollow, when we saw a whole group of people entering the sacred precincts. Most of them followed a path that led them remote from us; but an old man passed near us, and smiled to see Margaret lying on the ground, and me sitting by her side. He made some remark about the beauty of the afternoon, and withdrew himself into the shadow of the wood. Then we talked about Autumn — and about the pleasures of getting lost in the woods — and about the crows, whose voices Margaret had heard — and about the experiences of early childhood, whose influence remains upon the character after the collection of them has passed away — and about the sight of mountains from a distance, and the view from their summits — and about other matters of high and low philosophy. In the midst of our talk we heard footsteps above us, on the high bank; and while the intruder was still hidden among the trees, he called to Margaret, of whom he had gotten a glimpse. Then he emerged from the green shade; and, behold, it was Mr. Emerson, who, in spite of his clerical consecration, had found no better way of spending the Sabbath than to ramble among the woods. He appeared to have had a pleasant time; for he said that there were Muses in the woods to-day, and whispers to be heard in the breezes. It being now nearly six o'clock, we separated, Mr. Emerson and Margaret towards his house, and I towards mine, where my little wife was very busy getting tea. . . . *[Hawthorne, American Notebooks, ed. Claude M. Simpson (Columbus: Ohio State University Press, 1972), pp. 342-43]*

3. Her writing and talk, Edgar Allan Poe, August 1846

For the *Broadway Journal*, Poe wrote an essay essentially in praise of Fuller's writing. Meeting her in literary circles in New York, he seems to have been agreeably impressed, as witness his description of her reading here, and only later became antagonistic (III: 13). The first passage below follows a criticism of her diction for "vulgarity" and "barbarism."

a . . . In spite of these things, however, and of her frequent unjustifiable Carlyleisms (such as that of writing sentences which are no sentences, since, to be parsed, reference must be had to sentences preceding), the style of Miss Fuller is one of the very best with which I am acquainted. In general effect, I know no style which surpasses it. It is singularly piquant, vivid, terse, bold, luminous; leaving details out of sight, it is everything that a style need be. . . .

b. . . . What poet, in especial, but must feel at least the better portion of himself more fairly represented in even his commonest sonnet (earnestly written) than in his most elaborate or most intimate personalities?

I put all this as a general proposition, to which Miss Fuller affords a marked exception – to this extent, that her personal character and her printed book are merely one and the same thing. We get access to her soul *as* directly from the one as from the other – no *more* readily from this than from that – easily from either. Her acts are bookish, and her books are less thoughts than acts. Her literary and her conversational manner are identical. Here is a passage from her *Summer on the Lakes*:

The rapids enchanted me far beyond what I expected; they are so swift that these cease to *seem* so – you can think only of their *beauty*. The fountain beyond the Moss islands I discovered for myself, and thought it for some time an *accidental* beauty which it would not do to *leave*, lest I might never see it again. After I found it *permanent*, I returned many times to watch the play of its crest. In the little waterfall beyond, Nature seems, as she often does, to have made a *study* for some larger design. She delights in this – a sketch within a sketch – a dream within *a dream*. Wherever we see it, the lines of the great buttress in the fragment of stone, the hues of the waterfall, copied in the flowers that *star* its bordering mosses, we are *delighted*; for all the lineaments become *fluent*, and we mold the scene in congenial thought with its *genius*.

Now all this is precisely as Miss Fuller would speak it. She is perpetually saying just such things in just such words. To get the conversational woman in the mind's eye, all that is needed is to imagine her reciting the paragraph just quoted; but first let us have the personal woman. She is of the medium height; nothing remarkable about the figure; a profusion of lustrous light hair; eyes a bluish gray, full of fire; capacious forehead; the mouth when in repose indicates profound sensibility, capacity for affection, for love – when moved by a slight smile, it becomes even beautiful in the intensity of this expression; but the upper lip, as if impelled by the action of involuntary muscles, habitually uplifts itself, conveying the impression of a sneer. Imagine, now, a person of this description looking you at one moment earnestly

in the face, at the next seeming to look only within her own spirit or at
the wall; moving nervously every now and then in her chair; speaking in
a high key, but musically, deliberately (not hurriedly or loudly), with a
delicious distinctness of enunciation – speaking, I say, the paragraph in
question, and emphasizing the words which I have italicized, not by
impulsion of the breath (as is usual) but by drawing them out as long as
possible, nearly closing her eyes the while – imagine all this, and we
have both the woman and the authoress before us. *[Complete Works of
Edgar Allan Poe (New York: G. P. Putnam's Sons, 1902), IX, 13-14,
17-19]*

4. A satirical portrait, James Russell Lowell, 1848

In "A Fable for Critics," James Russell Lowell snipes at a
number of American authors, including himself, and more
than once at Fuller, who disparaged his verse in her essay on
American literature. "Let murderers be shut, to grow wiser
and cooler,/ At hard labor for life on the works of Miss
–––," he urges; later he alludes to her as the "Pythoness."
But his fullest attack, in which she bears the name of an
autobiographical character in her *Woman in the Nineteenth
Century*, exhibits well what Higginson (p. 216) called the
"tomahawk theory" of criticism: "men revenged literary
slights by personal abuse."

> "... But there comes Miranda, Zeus! where shall I flee to?
> She has such a penchant for bothering me too!
> She always keeps asking if I don't observe a
> Particular likeness 'twixt her and Minerva;
> She tells me my efforts in verse are quite clever; –
> She's been travelling now, and will be worse than ever;
> One would think, though, a sharp-sighted noter she'd be
> Of all that's worth mentioning over the sea,
> For a woman must surely see well, if she try,
> The whole of whose being's a capital I:
> She will take an old notion, and make it her own,
> By saying it o'er in her Sibylline tone,

Or persuade you 'tis something tremendously deep,
By repeating it so as to put you to sleep;
And she well may defy any mortal to see through it,
When once she has mixed up her infinite *me* through it,
There is one thing she owns in her own single right,
It is native and genuine — namely, her spite;
Though, when acting as censor, she privately blows
A censer of vanity 'neath her own nose."
Here Miranda came up, and said, " Phoebus! you know
That the Infinite Soul has its infinite woe,
As I ought to know, having lived cheek-by-jowl,
Since the day I was born, with the Infinite Soul;
I myself introduced, I myself, I alone,
To my Land's better life authors solely my own,
Who the sad heart of earth on their shoulders have taken,
Whose works sound a depth by Life's quiet unshaken,
Such as Shakespeare, for instance, the Bible, and Bacon,
Not to mention my own works; Time's nadir is fleet,
And, as for myself, I'm quite out of conceit —"

"Quite out of conceit! I'm enchanted to hear it,"
Cried Apollo aside. " Who'd have thought she was near it?
To be sure, one is apt to exhaust those commodities
One uses too fast, yet in this case as odd it is
As if Neptune should say to his turbots and whitings,
' I'm as much out of salt as Miranda's own writings '
(Which, as she in her own happy manner has said,
Sound a depth, for 'tis one of the functions of lead).
She often has asked me if I could not find
A place somewhere near me that suited her mind;
I know but a single one vacant, which she,
With her rare talent that way, would fit to a T.
And it would not imply any pause or cessation
In the work she esteems her peculiar vocation, —
She may enter on duty today, if she chooses,
And remain Tiring-woman for life to the Muses."

Miranda meanwhile has succeeded in driving
Up into a corner, in spite of their striving,

A small flock of terrified victims, and there,
With an I-turn-the-crank-of-the-Universe air
And a tone which, at least to *my* fancy, appears
Not so much to be entering as boxing your ears,
Is unfolding a tale (of herself, I surmise,
For 'tis dotted as thick as a peacock's with I's). . . .
[Poetical works of James Russell Lowell
(Boston: Houghton Mifflin, 1904), IV, 62-64]

FULLER'S WRITINGS

5. On suspension of belief [1829-30]

Fuller's young friends described her in her Cambridge years as "a wonder of intellect, who had yet no religion" (*Memoirs*, I, 205). At nineteen, she wrote to one of them about religious belief, revealing a pattern of complex aspiration that would remain with her—the desire for absolute truth balanced by hunger for various experience, a belief in final resolution coupled with a need for reality even if it should prove painful, and a commitment to growth and change.

I have hesitated much whether to tell you what you ask about my religion. You are mistaken! I have not formed an opinion. I have determined not to form settled opinions at present. Loving or feeble natures need a positive religion, a visible refuge, a protection, as much in the passionate season of youth as in those stages nearer to the grave. But mine is not such. My pride is superior to any feelings I have yet experienced: my affection is strong admiration, not the necessity of giving or receiving assistance or sympathy. When disappointed, I do not ask or wish consolation, – I wish to know and feel my pain, to investigate its nature and its source; I will not have my thoughts diverted or my feelings soothed; 'tis therefore that my young life is so singularly barren of illusions. I know, I feel the time must come when this proud and impatient heart shall be stilled, and turn from the ardors of Search and Action, to lean on something above. But – shall I say it? – the thought of that calmer era is to me a thought of deepest sadness; so remote from my present being is that future existence, which still the mind may conceive. I believe in Eternal Progression. I believe in a God, a Beauty and Perfection to which I am to strive all my life for assimilation. From these two articles of belief, I draw the rules by which I strive to regulate my life. But though I reverence all religions as necessary to the happiness of man, I am yet ignorant of the religion of Revelation. Tangible promises! well defined hopes! are things of which I do not *now* feel the need. At present, my soul is intent on this

life, and I think of religion as its rule; and, in my opinion, this is the
natural and proper course from youth to age. . . . [_Memoirs_, I, 135-36]

6. On mystical experience at twenty-one [1840]

From Rome, Fuller wrote Emerson that she had come to
mistrust the mystical experiences of her New England years.
We do not know how she felt finally about an early
experience whose impact led her to write nine years
afterward, "Since that day I have never more been
completely engaged in self." From our perspective, this
journal recollection demonstrates how the frustration of her
position and the discipline of repressed desire and ambition
could explode in a vision of the self subsumed in the "All."

It was Thanksgiving day, (Nov., 1831,) and I was obliged to go to
church, or exceedingly displease my father. I almost always suffered
much in church from a feeling of disunion with the hearers and dissent
from the preacher; but to-day, more than ever before, the services
jarred upon me from their grateful and joyful tone. I was wearied out
with mental conflicts, and in a mood of most childish, child-like
sadness. I felt within myself great power, and generosity, and
tenderness; but it seemed to me as if they were all unrecognized, and as
if it was impossible that they should be used in life. I was only
one-and-twenty; the past was worthless, the future hopeless; yet I could
not remember ever voluntarily to have done a wrong thing, and my
aspiration seemed very high. I looked round the church, and envied all
the little children; for I supposed they had parents who protected them,
so that they could never know this strange anguish, this dread
uncertainty. I knew not, then, that none could have any father but
God. I knew not, that I was not the only lonely one, that I was not the
selected Oedipus, the special victim of an iron law. I was in haste for all
to be over, that I might get into the free air.* *
    I walked away over the fields as fast as I could walk. This was my
custom at that time, when I could no longer bear the weight of my
feelings, and fix my attention on any pursuit; for I do believe I never
voluntarily gave way to these thoughts one moment. The force I
exerted I think, even now, greater than I ever knew in any other

character. But when I could bear myself no longer, I walked many hours, till the anguish was wearied out, and I returned in a state of prayer. Today all seemed to have reached its height. It seemed as if I could never return to a world in which I had no place, – to the mockery of humanities. I could not act a part, nor seem to live any longer. It was a sad and sallow day of the late autumn. Slow processions of sad clouds were passing over a cold blue sky; the hues of earth were dull, and gray, and brown, with sickly struggles of late green here and there; sometimes a moaning gust of wind drove late, reluctant leaves across the path; – there was no life else. In the sweetness of my present peace, such days seem to me made to tell man the worst of his lot; but still that November wind can bring a chill of memory.

I paused beside a little stream, which I had envied in the merry fulness of its spring life. It was shrunken, voiceless, choked with withered leaves. I marvelled that it did not quite lose itself in the earth. There was no stay for me, and I went on and on, till I came to where the trees were thick about a little pool, dark and silent. I sat down there. I did not think; all was dark, and cold, and still. Suddenly the sun shone out with that transparent sweetness, like the last smile of a dying lover, which it will use when it has been unkind all a cold autumn day. And, even then, passed into my thought a beam from its true sun, from its native sphere, which has never since departed from me. I remembered how, a little child, I had stopped myself one day on the stairs, and asked, how came I here? How is it that I seem to be this Margaret Fuller? What does it mean? What shall I do about it? I remembered all the times and ways in which the same thought had returned. I saw how long it must be before the soul can learn to act under these limitations of time and space, and human nature; but I saw, also, that it *must* do it, – that it must make all this false true, – and sow new and immortal plants in the garden of God, before it could return again. I saw there was no self; that selfishness was all folly, and the result of circumstance; that it was only because I thought self real that I suffered; that I had only to live in the idea of the *all*, and all was mine. This truth came to me, and I received it unhesitatingly; so that I was for that hour taken up into God. In that true ray most of the relations of earth seemed mere films, phenomena. * *

My earthly pain at not being recognized never went deep after this hour. I had passed the extreme of passionate sorrow; and all check, all failure, all ignorance, have seemed temporary ever since. When I consider that this will be nine years ago next November, I am astonished that I have not gone on faster since; that I am not yet sufficiently purified to be taken back to God. Still, I did but touch then on the only haven of Insight. . . . *[Memoirs, I, 139-41]*

7. Credo, 1842

By November 16, 1837, the Transcendentalists had stirred up such outrage and ridicule that Fuller snapped in a letter to Sturgis that she didn't know what people meant by the "nonsense" they circulated about the group. She granted that her "active mind" was "busy with large topics" and that she numbered Emerson, George Ripley, and Alcott among her friends. "*But* if it is meant that I cherish any opinions which interfere with domestic duties, cheerful courage and judgment in the practical affairs of life, I challenge any or all in the little world which knows me to prove such deficiency from any acts of mine since I came to woman's estate" (Tappan Papers, Houghton). Inevitably, however, she caught the contagion of philosophy. She tried to "shun a premature narrowness," to follow "the path of progress, not of renunciation" trod by her "priests" of "Pagan greatness" (*Memoirs*, II, 86). But pantheism and repudiation of dogma had two adverse effects: it made some of her writing diffuse to the point of unintelligibility and some spiritually unacceptable to her editors. From a credo written one night in 1842, I have extracted only her theory of good and evil and the reservations about Jesus censored in Channing's presentation of it in the *Memoirs* (II, 88-92).

There is a spirit uncontainable and uncontained, – Within it all manifestation is contained, whether of good (accomplishment) or evil (obstruction). To itself its depths are unknown. By living it seeks to know itself, thus evolving plants, animals, men, suns, stars, angels, and, it is to be presumed an infinity of forms not yet visible in the horizon of this being who now writes.

Its modes of operation are twofold. First, as genius inspires genius, love love, angel-mother brings forth angel-child. This is the uninterrupted generation, or publication of spirit taking upon itself *congenial forms*. Second, conquering *obstruction*, finding the like in the unlike. This is a secondary generation, a new dynasty, as virtue for simplicity, faith for oneness, charity for pure love. . . .

God, we say, is Love. If we believe this we must trust Him. Whatever has been permitted by the law of being must be *for* good, and only *in time not good*. We do trust Him and are led forward by experience. Sight gives experience of outward life, faith of inward. We then discern, however faintly, the necessary harmony of the two lives. The moment we have broken through an obstruction, not accidentally, but by the aid of faith, we begin to realize why any was permitted. We begin to interpret the universe and deeper depths are opened with each soul that is convinced. For it would seem that the Divine expressed His meaning to Himself more distinctly in man than in the other forms of our sphere, and through him uttered distinctly the Hallelujah which the other forms of nature only intimate.

Wherever man remains imbedded in nature, whether from sensuality or because he is not yet awakened to consciousness, the purpose of the whole remains unfulfilled, hence our displeasure when man is not in a sense *above* nature. Yet when he is not bound so closely with all other manifestations, as duly to express their spirit, we are also displeased. He must be at once the highest form of nature and conscious of the meaning she has been striving successively to unfold through those below him. . . .

But when I say to you, also, that though I think [the events of the Old and the New Testaments] really happened, it is of no consequence to me whether it did or not, that the ideal truth such illustrations present to me, is enough, and that if the mind of St. John, for instance, had conceived the whole and offered it to us as a poem, to me, as far as I know, it would be just as real. You see how wide the gulf that separates me from the Christian Church. . . . Do you not place Christ then in a higher place than Socrates, for instance, or Michael Angelo? Yes! Because if his life was not truer, it was deeper, and he is a representative of the ages. But then I consider the Greek Apollo as one also!

. . . For myself, I believe in Christ because I can do without him; because the truth he announces I see elsewhere intimated; because it is foreshadowed in the very nature of my own being. But I do not wish to do without him. He is constantly aiding and answering me. Only I will not lay any undue and exclusive emphasis on him. When he comes to me I will receive him; when I feel inclined to go by myself, I will. I do not reject the church either. Let men who can with sincerity live in it. I would not — for I believe far more widely than any body of men I know. And as nowhere I worship less than in the places set apart for that purpose, I will not seem to do so. The blue sky seen above the opposite roof preaches better than any brother, because, at present, a freer, simpler medium of religion. When great souls arise again that dare to be entirely free, yet are humble, gentle, and patient, I will listen, if they wish to speak.

. . . I am grateful here, as everywhere, where spirit bears fruit in fulness. It attests the justice of my desires; it kindles my faith; it rebukes my sloth; it enlightens my resolve. But so does the Apollo, and the beautiful infant, and the summer's earliest rose. It is only one modification of the same harmony. Jesus breaks through the soil of the world's life, like some great river through the else inaccessible plains and valleys. I bless its course. I follow it. But it is a part of the All. There is nothing peculiar about it, but its form. . . .

All future manifestations will come, like this, — not to destroy the law and the prophets but to fulfill. But as an Abraham called for a Moses, a Moses for a David, so does Christ for another ideal. . . .

We want a life more complete and various than that of Christ. We have had the Messiah to reconcile and teach, let us have another to live out all the symbolical forms of human life with the calm beauty and physical fulness of a Greek god, with the deep consciousness of a Moses, with the holy love and purity of Jesus. Amen! . . . [Frederick Braun, Margaret Fuller and Goethe (New York: Henry Holt, 1910), pp. 250-57]

8. To Richard Fuller, August 11, 1842

On October 25, 1841, Fuller had written her brother Richard, "There are few characters so vigorous and of such sustained self-impulse that they do not need frequent unexpected difficulties to awaken and keep in exercise their powers." Writing from Cambridge the next year, she offered him an intimate illustration of this conviction that good grows out of painful experience in recalling her bitter associations with the Groton farm where she had suffered grave illness and her father had died.

. . . You were too young to feel how trying are the disorders of a house which has lost its head, the miserable perplexities which arose in our affairs, the wounds your mother underwent in that time of deep dejection from the unfeeling and insolent conduct of many who had been kept in check by respect for your father, her loneliness and sense of unfitness for the new and heavy burden of care. It will be many years yet, before you can appreciate the conflicts of my mind, as I doubted whether to give up all which my heart desired for a path for which I had no skill, and no call, except that *some one* must tread it, none else was ready. The Peterborough hills and the Waschusetts are associated in my mind with many hours of anguish, as great I think as I am capable of feeling. I used to look at them, towering to the sky, and feel that I, too, from my birth had longed to rise, but I felt crushed to earth, yet again a nobler spirit said *that* could never be. The good knight may come forth scarred and maimed from the unequal contest, shorn of his strength and unsightly to the careless eye, but the same fire burns within and deeper than ever, and he may be conquered but *never subdued*.

But if these beautiful hills, and wide, rich fields saw this sad lore well learned they also saw some precious lessons given too, of faith, of fortitude, of self-command, and a less selfish love. There too in solitude the mind acquired more power of concentration and discerned the beauty of a stricter method. There the heart was awakened to sympathize with the ignorant, to pity the vulgar, and hope for the seemingly worthless, for a need was felt of realizing the only reality, the divine soul of this visible creation, which cannot err and will not sleep, which cannot permit evil to be permanent or its aim of beauty to be eventually frustrated in the smallest particular. *[Houghton MS]*

9. On conversation with Alcott [circa 1837]

When the Temple School aroused Boston's wrath in the spring of 1837, Fuller heard that Hedge was planning to "cut up Alcott." She wrote begging him not to lend the patronage of his wit "to the ugly blinking owls, who are now hooting from their snug tenements, overgrown rather with nettles than with ivy, at his star of purest ray serene." Instead, she thought, he should write "a long beautiful, wise-like article, showing the elevated air, and at the same time the practical defects of his system" (Higginson, p. 78). After a long talk with Alcott, she recorded in her journal her objections to Transcendental mysticism.

Mr. A. "O for the safe and natural way of Intuition! I cannot grope like a mole in the gloomy passages of experience. To the attentive spirit, the revelation contained in books is only so far valuable as it comments upon, and corresponds with, the universal revelation. Yet to me, a being social and sympathetic by natural impulse, though recluse and contemplative by training and philosophy, the character and life of Jesus have spoken more forcibly than any fact recorded in human history. This story of incarnate Love has given me the key to all mysteries, and showed me what path should be taken in returning to the Fountain of Spirit. Seeing that other redeemers have imperfectly fulfilled their tasks, I have sought a new way. They all, it seemed to me, had tried to influence the human being at too late a day, and had laid their plans too wide. They began with men; I will begin with babes. They began with the world; I will begin with the family. So I preach the Gospel of the Nineteenth Century."

M. "But, preacher, you make *three* mistakes.

You do not understand the nature of Genius or creative power.

You do not understand the reäction of matter on spirit.

You are too impatient of the complex; and, not enjoying variety in unity, you become lost in abstractions, and cannot illustrate your principles." *[Memoirs, I, 171-72]*

10. On last day at Greene Street School [December 1838]

When Fuller resigned from the Greene Street School she wrote bitterly, "I have here been always in a false position and my energies been consequently much repressed," and "I am wearied out and I have gabbled and simpered and given my mind to the public view these two years back, till there seems to be no good left in me" (Higginson, pp. 91-92, 94). Her record of her last day, while in a wholly different temper, gives some notion of why teaching was so draining for her.

... Then [I summoned] the older girls who have been most under my care. There were about forty present.

I began by telling them that I thought them now sufficiently instructed to appreciate, in some degree, the difficulties by which I had been oppressed while teaching them. I gave an account of the false impressions which were given me of the position I should there occupy. I gave some idea of the barbarous ignorance in which I found them, appealed to their remembrance and told some facts in confirmation of these extraordinary statements. I showed them how all my efforts had, necessarily, been directed to stimulate their minds, and prepare them for discipline, and how I had been obliged to leave undone much that I should, under other circumstances have deemed indispensable. I told them I was sensible that my successor finding so much still to do would think I had done nothing, and that I left the charge of defending my character with them. I thanked them for the favorable opinion of my government they had so generously expressed. But though they could none of them remember instances in which I had been unjust, I remembered three, and specified the persons (all of whom were present, sobbing as if their hearts would break).

I thanked them for the moral beauty of their conduct towards me, said that an appeal to conscience had never failed to be answered, and that I had the happiness of being confirmed in the belief that young persons, generally, would be governed by appeals to their higher nature.

I spoke with a clear conscience of the care which I had taken to avoid interfering with the opinions or prejudices of their parents, however opposed to my own. I had always spoken of truth I offered as *my* view of truth and felt that I had not only in words but in heart combined tolerance and delicacy with perfect frankness. . . . *[BPL MS]*

11. Preface to *Eckermann's Conversations with Goethe, 1839*

After resigning from teaching, Fuller completed her translation of *Eckermann's Conversations with Goethe*, which George Ripley, the versatile founder of Brook Farm, published in 1839 as part of a series of books in translation. (The venture was no more profitable than *The Dial*, and Fuller received nothing.) The warmth of her support of Goethe in her introduction to this volume, at a time when he was under regular and vehement attack from the conservative *North American Review*, took nerve and independence. In *The Dial* of July 1841, she published a longer essay on Goethe (here omitted for reasons of space), in which she demonstrated with groundbreaking insight how his works expressed Goethe's spiritual development. In it she occasionally mocks the moralism of her readers, as when she wrote of the storm of indignation that greeted *Elective Affinities*: "The reason probably is the subject, any discussion of the validity of the marriage vow making society tremble to its foundation; and secondly the cold manner in which it is done. All that is in the book would be bearable to most minds if the writer had had less the air of a spectator, and had larded his work here and there with ejaculations of horror and surprise" (*The Writings of Margaret Fuller*, ed. Mason Wade, p. 262). But in general the essay is more diffuse and deferential to her readers' sensibilities than in the Translator's Preface excerpted here.

. . . And here it may not be amiss to give some intimation (more my present limits do not permit) of the grounds on which Goethe is to myself an object of peculiar interest and constant study.

I hear him much assailed by those among us who know him, some few in his own language but most from translations of *Wilhelm Meister* and *Faust*. These, his two great works in which he proposed to himself the enigma of life and solved it after his own fashion, were naturally enough selected in preference to others for translating. This was for all but the translators unfortunate, because these two, above all others, require a knowledge of the circumstances and character from which they rose, to ascertain their scope and tendency.

It is sneeringly said, "Those persons who are so fanatical for German literature always say, if you object to any of their idols, that you are not capable of appreciating them." And it is truly though oftentimes too impatiently said. The great movement in German literature is too recent to be duly estimated even by those most interested to examine it. The waves have scarcely yet ebbed from this new continent, and those who are visiting its shores see so much that is new and beautiful that of their many obligations to the phenomenon the chief is as yet that of the feeling of fresh creative life at work there.

No wonder that they feel vexed at those who declare from an occasional peep through a spyglass that they see no new wonders for geology; that they can botanize all the flowers, and find nothing worthy of fresh attempts at classification; and that there are no birds except a few sea-gulls. Would these hasty critics but recollect how long it was before similar movements in Italy, Spain, France, and England found their proper place in the thoughts of other nations, they would not think fifty years' investigation too much for fifty years' growth, and would no longer provoke the ire of those who are lighting their tapers at the German torch. Meanwhile it is silly to be in a pet always; and disdainful answers have been recognized as useless since Solomon's time or earlier. What could have been the reason they were not set aside while that wise prince lived, once for all?

The objections usually made, though not without a foundation in truth, are such as would answer themselves on a more thorough acquaintance with the subject. In France and England there has seemed an approximation of late to juster views. Yet in a recent number of *Blackwood's Magazine* has appeared an article as ignorant (and that is a strong word) as anything that has ever been written about Goethe.

The objections, so far as I know them, may be resolved into these classes —

He is not a Christian;

He is not an idealist;

He is not a democrat;

He is not Schiller.

If by Christian be meant the subordination of the intellectual to the spiritual, I shall not deny that with Goethe the reverse was the case. He sought always for unity; but the want with him was chiefly one of the intellect. A creative activity was his law. He was far from insensible to spiritual beauty in the human character. He has embodied it in its finest forms; but he merely put it in what seemed to him its place as the keystone of the social arch, and paints neither that nor any other state with partiality. Such was his creed as a writer. "I paint," he seems to say, "what I have seen; choose from it or take it all, as you will or can." In his love of form Goethe was a Greek; constitutionally and by the habit of his life averse to the worship of sorrow. His God was rather the creative and uplifting than the paternal spirit; his religion, that all his powers must be unfolded; his faith, "that nature could not dispense with immortality." In the most trying occasions of his life he referred

to "the great idea of duty which alone can hold us upright."
Renunciation, the power of sacrificing the temporary for the
permanent, is a leading idea in one of his great works, *Wilhelm Meister*.
The thought of the Catholic Dante is repeated in his other great work,
Faust, where Margaret by her innocence of heart and the resolute
aversion to the powers of darkness which her mind in its most shattered
state does not forget, redeems not only her own soul, but that of her
erring lover. The virgin Ottilia, who immolates herself to avoid the
possibility of spotting her thoughts with passion, gives to that much
abused book *Die Wahlverwandtschaften* the pathetic moral of the
pictures of the Magdalen. His two highest characters, Natalia and
Macaria, are representations of beneficence and heavenly wisdom.
Iphigenia by her steadfast truth hallows all about her and disarms the
powers of hell. Such traits as these may be accumulated; yet it remains
not the less true that Goethe was not what is called a spiritual writer.
Those who cannot draw the moral for themselves had best leave his
books alone; they require the power as life does. This advantage only
does he give or intend to give you, of looking at life brought into a
compass convenient to your eye by a great observer and artist, and at
times when you can look uninterrupted by action, undisturbed by
passion.

He was not an idealist; that is to say, he thought not so much of
what might be as what is. He did not seek to alter or exalt Nature, but
merely to select from her rich stores. Here indeed, even as an artist, he
would always have stopped short of the highest excellence if he had not
at times been inspired beyond his knowledge and his will. Had his views
been different, his peculiar powers of minute, searching, and extended
observation would have been much injured; as instead of looking at
objects with the single aim of ascertaining their properties, he would
have examined them only to gain from them what most favored his
plans. I am well satisfied that "he went the way that God and Nature
called him."

He was an aristocrat. And in the present day hostility arises
instinctively against one who does not believe in the people and whose
tastes are in favor of a fixed external gradation. My sympathies are with
the great onward movement now obvious throughout the civilized
world; my hope is that we may make a fair experiment whether men
can be educated to rule themselves and communities be trusted to
choose their own rulers. This is, it seems, the present tendency of the

ages; and had I influence, I would not put a straw in the way. Yet a minority is needed to keep these liberals in check and make them pause upon their measures long enough to know what they are doing; for as yet the caldron of liberty has shown a constant disposition to overboil. The artist and literary man is naturally thrown into this body by his need of repose and a firm ground to work in his proper way. Certainly Goethe by nature belonged on that side; and no one who can understand the structure of his mind, instead of judging him by his outward relations, will impute to him unworthy motives or think he could, being what he was, hold other opinions. And is not this all which is important? The gates that keep out the water while the ship is building have their place also, as well as the ship itself or the wind which fills the sails. To be sincere, consistent, and intelligent in what one believes is what is important; a higher power takes care of the rest.

In reply to those who object to him that he is not Schiller, it may be remarked that Shakespeare was not Milton, nor Ariosto Tasso. It was indeed unnecessary that there should be two Schillers, one being sufficient to represent a certain class of thoughts and opinions. It would be well if the admirers of Schiller would learn from him to admire and profit by his friend and coadjutor, as he himself did.

Schiller was wise enough to judge each nature by its own law, great enough to understand greatness of an order different from his own. He was too well aware of the value of the more beautiful existences to quarrel with the rose for not being a lily, the eagle for not being a swan.

I am not fanatical as to the benefits to be derived from the study of German literature. I suppose indeed that there lie the life and learning of the century, and that he who does not go to those sources can have no just notion of the workings of the spirit in the European world these last fifty years or more; but my tastes are often displeased by German writers, even by Goethe — of German writers the most English and Greek. To cultivate the tastes we must go to another school; but I wish that we could learn from the Germans habits of more liberal criticism, and leave this way of judging from comparison or personal predilections. If we must draw parallels, we ought to be sure that we are capable of a love for all greatness as fervent as that of Plutarch's time. Perhaps it may be answered that the comparison between Goethe and Schiller began in Germany; it did so, but arose there from circumstances with which we have nothing to do. Generally the wise German criticizes with the positive degree and is well aware of the danger in using the comparative.

For the rest no one who has a higher aim in reading German books than mere amusement; no one who knows what it is to become acquainted with a literature as literature, in its history of mutual influences, diverse yet harmonious tendencies, can leave aside either Schiller or Goethe; but far, far least the latter. It would be leaving Augustus Ceasar out of the history of Rome because he was not Brutus.

Having now confessed to what Goethe is not, I would indicate as briefly as possible what to me he is.

Most valuable as a means of balancing the judgment and suggesting thought from his antagonism to the spirit of the age. He prefers the perfecting of the few to the slight improvement of the many. He believes more in man than men, effort than success, thought than action, nature than providence. He does not insist on my believing with him. I would go up often into this fortress, and look from its battlements to see how goes the fight below. I need not fear to be detained. He knows himself too well to ask anything of another except to know him.

As one of the finest lyric poets of modern times. Bards are also prophets; and woe be to those who refuse to hear the singer, to tender him the golden cup of homage. Their punishment is in their fault.

As the best writer of the German language, who has availed himself of all its advantages of richness and flexibility and added to them a degree of lightness, grace, clearness, and precision beyond any other writer of his time; who has more than any other tended to correct the fantastic, cumbrous, centipede style indigenous to Germany.

As a critic on art and literature, not to be surpassed in independence, fairness, powers of sympathy, and largeness of view.

As almost the finest observer of his time of human nature, and almost as much so of external nature. He has great delicacy of penetration, and a better tact at selecting objects than almost any who has looked at the time of which I am a child. Could I omit to study this eighty years' journal of my parent's life, traced from so commanding a position by so sure a hand, and one informed by so keen and cultivated an eye? Where else shall we find so large a mirror or one with so finely decorated a frame?

As a mind which has known how to reconcile individuality of character with universality of thought; a mind which, whatever be its faults, ruled and relied on itself alone; a nature which knew its law and revolved on its proper axis, unrepenting, never bustling, always active, never stagnant, always calm.

A distinguished critic speaks of Goethe as the conqueror of his century. I believe I do not take so admiring a view of the character of Goethe as this, his only competent English critic. I refer to Mr. Carlyle. But so far as attaining the object he himself proposed, a choice of aim, a "wise limitation," and unwearied constancy in the use of means; so far as leaving behind the limbo of self-questioning uncertainty in which most who would fain think as well as act are wading, and bringing his life into an uninterrupted harmony with his thought, he did indeed conquer. He knew both what he sought and how to seek it — a great matter!

I am not a blind admirer of Goethe. I have felt what others feel, and seen what others see. I too have been disturbed by his aversion to pain and isolation of the heart. I also have looked in vain for the holy and heroic elements. Nor do I believe that any degree of objectivity is inconsistent with a partiality for what is noblest in individual characters. Shakespeare is a proof to the contrary. As a critic he does not treat subjects masterfully. He does not give you at once a central point, and make you feel the root of the matter; but you must read his essays as aggregates of thoughts, rather clustering round than unfolding the subject. In his later years he lost his architectural vigor; and his works are built up like the piles in Piranesi's *Visions* of galleries and balconies connected only by cobweb ladders. Many of his works I feel to be fragmentary and inadequate. I am even disposed to deny him the honors most generally awarded him — those of the artist. I think he had the artist's eye and the artist's hand, but not the artist's love of structure.

But I will stop here, and wait until the time when I shall have room to substantiate my charges. I flatter myself I have now found fault enough to prove me a worthy critic after the usual fashion. Mostly I prefer leveling upward, in the way recommended by Goethe in speaking of the merchants he met while traveling.

While it is so undesirable that any man should receive what he has not examined, a far more frequent danger is that of flippant irreverence. Not all that the heavens contain is obvious to the unassisted eye of the careless spectator. Few men are great; almost as few able to appreciate greatness. The critics have written little upon the *Iliad* in all these ages which Alexander would have thought worth keeping with it in his golden box. Nor Shakespeare nor Dante nor Calderon has as yet found a sufficient critic, though Coleridge and the Schlegels have lived since they did. The greatness of Goethe his nation has felt for more than half a century; the world is beginning to feel it, but time may not yet have ripened his critic; especially as the grand historical standpoint is the only one from which a comprehensive view could be taken of him.

Meanwhile it is safer to take off the hat and shout *Vivat!* to the conqueror who may become a permanent sovereign than to throw stones and mud from the gutter. The star shines, and that it is with no borrowed light his foes are his voucher. And every planet is a portent to the world; but whether for good or ill, only he can know who has science for many calculations. Not he who runs can read these books, or any books of any worth. I am content to describe him in the terms Hamlet thought sufficiently honorable to him he honored most:

> He was a man, *take him for all in all*,
> We shall not look upon his like again.

As such worth our study – and more to us than elder great men, because of our own day and busied most with those questions which lie nearest us. . . . *[The Writings of Margaret Fuller, ed. Mason Wade, (New York: The Viking Press, 1941), pp. 233-40]*

12. On hopes for The Dial, 1840

When she committed herself to working strenuously for Transcendentalism by editing *The Dial*, Fuller was probably more deeply committed to the work of spiritual regeneration in America—and opposed to materialism, social institutions, even social reforms and action—than at any other time. Reflecting all this, the following letter, to an unknown correspondent, also reveals quiescence unwonted in Fuller and her belief that the position of women limited her capacity to participate in the movement.

Since the Revolution, there has been little, in the circumstances of this country, to call out the higher sentiments. The effect of continued prosperity is the same on nations as on individuals, – it leaves the nobler faculties undeveloped. The need of bringing out the physical resources of a vast extent of country the commercial and political fever incident to our institutions, tend to fix the eyes of men on what is local and temporary, on the external advantages of their condition. The superficial diffusion of knowledge, unless attended by a correspondent deepening of its sources, is likely to vulgarize rather than to raise the thought of a nation, depriving them of another sort of education through sentiments of reverence, and leading the multitude to believe themselves capable of judging what they but dimly discern. They see a wide surface, and forget the difference between seeing and knowing. In this hasty way of thinking and living they traverse so much ground that they forget that not the sleeping railroad passenger, but the botanist, the geologist, the poet, really see the country, and that, to the former, "a miss is as good as a mile." In a word, the tendency of circumstances has been to make our people superficial, irreverent, and more anxious to get a living than to live mentally and morally. This tendency is no way balanced by the slight literary culture common here, which is mostly English, and consists in a careless reading of publications of the day, having the same utilitarian tendency with our own proceedings. The infrequency of acquaintance with any of the great fathers of English lore marks this state of things.

New England is now old enough, — some there have leisure enough, — to look at all this; and the consequence is a violent reäction, in a small minority, against a mode of culture that rears such fruits. They see that political freedom does not necessarily produce liberality of mind, nor freedom in church institutions — vital religion; and, seeing that these changes cannot be wrought from without inwards, they are trying to quicken the soul, that they may work from within outwards. Disgusted with the vulgarity of a commercial aristocracy, they become radicals; disgusted with the materialistic working of "rational" religion, they become mystics. They quarrel with all that is, because it is not spiritual enough. They would, perhaps, be patient if they thought this the mere sensuality of childhood in our nation, which it might outgrow; but they think that they see the evil widening, deepening, — not only debasing the life, but corrupting the thought of our people, and they feel that if they know not well what should be done, yet that the duty of every good man is to utter a protest against what is done amiss.

Is this protest undiscriminating? are these opinions crude? do these proceedings threaten to sap the bulwarks on which men at present depend? I confess it all, yet I see in these men promise of a better wisdom than in their opponents. Their hope for man is grounded on his destiny as an immortal soul, and not as a mere comfort-loving inhabitant of earth, or as a subscriber to the social contract. It was not meant that the soul should cultivate the earth, but that the earth should educate and maintain the soul. Man is not made for society, but society is made for man. No institution can be good which does not tend to improve the individual. In these principles I have confidence so profound, that I am not afraid to trust those who hold them, despite their partial views, imperfectly developed characters, and frequent want of practical sagacity. I believe, if they have opportunity to state and discuss their opinions, they will gradually sift them, ascertain their grounds and aims with clearness, and do the work this country needs. I hope for them as for "the leaven that is hidden in the bushel of meal, till all be leavened." The leaven is not good by itself, neither is the meal; let them combine, and we shall yet have bread.

Utopia it is impossible to build up. At least, my hopes for our race on this one planet are more limited than those of most of my friends. I accept the limitations of human nature, and believe a wise acknowledgment of them one of the best conditions of progress. Yet every noble scheme, every poetic manifestation, prophesies to man his eventual destiny. And were not man ever more sanguine than facts at the moment justify, he would remain torpid, or be sunk in sensuality. It is on this ground that I sympathize with what is called the "Transcendental party," and that I feel their aim to be the true one. They acknowledge in the nature of man an arbiter for his deeds, – a standard transcending sense and time, – and are, in my view, the true utilitarians. They are but at the beginning of their course, and will, I hope, learn how to make use of the past, as well as to aspire for the future, and to be true in the present moment.

My position as a woman, and the many private duties which have filled my life, have prevented my thinking deeply on several of the great subjects which these friends have at heart. I suppose, if ever I become capable of judging, I shall differ from most of them on important points. But I am not afraid to trust any who are true, and in intent noble, with their own course not to aid in enabling them to express their thoughts whether I coincide with them or not.

On the subject of Christianity, my mind is clear. If Divine, it will stand the test of any comparison. I believe the reason it has so imperfectly answered to the aspirations of its Founder is, that men have received it on external grounds. I believe that a religion, thus received, may give the life an external decorum, but will never open the fountains of holiness in the soul.

One often thinks of Hamlet as the true representative of idealism in its excess. Yet if, in his short life, man be liable to some excess, should we not rather prefer to have the will palsied like Hamlet, by a deep-searching tendency and desire for poetic perfection, than to have it enlightened by worldly sagacity, as in the case of Julius Caesar, or made intense by pride alone, as in that of Coriolanus?

After all, I believe it is absurd to attempt to speak on these subjects within the limits of a letter. I will try to say what I mean in print some day. Yet one word as to "the material," in man. Is it not the object of all philosophy, as well as of religion and poetry, to prevent its prevalence? Must not those who see most truly be ever making statements of the truth to combat this sluggishness, or worldliness? What else are sages, poets, preachers, born to do? Men go an undulating course, — sometimes on the hill, sometimes in the valley. But he only is in the right who in the valley forgets not the hill-prospect, and knows in darkness that the sun will rise again. That is the real life which is subordinated to, not merged in, the ideal; he is only wise who can bring the lowest act of his life into sympathy with its highest thought. And this I take to be the one only aim of our pilgrimage here. I agree with those who think that no true philosophy will try to ignore or annihilate the material part of man, but will rather seek to put it in its place, as servant and minister to the soul. *[Memoirs, II, 26-31]*

13. *"American Literature," 1846*

In her *Papers on Literature and Art* (1846), Fuller published a comprehensive essay on the state of American literature. Subtitled "Its position in the present time, and prospects for the future," it surveyed the scene from classical genre to new reportage. To fill out the picture she appended to the essay her *Tribune* reviews of Hawthorne (the most promising American fiction writer, in her estimation), the neglected Gothic novelist Charles Brockden Brown, and the highly esteemed Longfellow (whose poetry she had reviewed only at Greeley's insistence, as she felt no rapport with it).

The essay won the antagonism of Poe and Lowell, and her criticism of Longfellow offended many readers. But Poe faulted her for praising friends like Ellery Channing and acquaintances like Cornelius Mathews, for slighting Lowell and omitting himself: "She is grossly dishonest," he wrote a friend. "She abuses Lowell, for example, (the best of our poets, perhaps) on account of a personal quarrel with him. She has omitted all mention of me for the same reason—although, a short time before the issue of her book, she praised me highly in the Tribune.... She praised 'Witchcraft' because Mathews (who toadies her) wrote it. In a word, she is an ill-tempered and very inconsistent old maid—avoid her." Poe's own inconsistency is revealed a year later in a letter disparaging Lowell's "Fable for Critics" which concludes, "Lowell is a ranting abolitionist and *deserves* a good using up" (*The Letters of Edgar Allan Poe*, ed. John Ward Ostrom, II, 355, 427).

Omitted from Fuller's essay here is her description of two little-known works, Mathews' *Witchcraft* and Sylvester Judd's, *Margaret, or the Real and Ideal*; extracts from the Hawthorne and Brown reviews follow.

Some thinkers may object to this essay, that we are about to write of that which has, as yet, no existence.

For it does not follow because many books are written by persons born in America that there exists an American literature. Books which imitate or represent the thoughts and life of Europe do not constitute an American literature. Before such can exist, an original idea must animate this nation and fresh currents of life must call into life fresh thoughts along its shores.

We have no sympathy with national vanity. We are not anxious to prove that there is as yet much American literature. Of those who think and write among us in the methods and of the thoughts of Europe, we are not impatient; if their minds are still best adapted to such food and such action. If their books express life of mind and character in graceful forms, they are good and we like them. We consider them as colonists and useful schoolmasters to our people in a transition state; which lasts rather longer than is occupied in passing, bodily, the ocean which separates the new from the old world.

We have been accused of an undue attachment to foreign continental literature, and, it is true, that in childhood, we had well nigh "forgotten our English," while constantly reading in other languages. Still, what we loved in the literature of continental Europe was the range and force of ideal manifestation in forms of national and individual greatness. A model was before us in the great Latins of simple masculine minds seizing upon life with unbroken power. The stamp both of nationality and individuality was very strong upon them; their lives and thoughts stood out in clear and bold relief. The English character has the iron force of the Latins, but not the frankness and expansion. Like their fruits, they need a summer sky to give them more sweetness and a richer flavour. This does not apply to Shakespeare, who has all the fine side of English genius, with the rich colouring, and more fluent life, of the Catholic countries. Other poets, of England also, are expansive more or less, and soar freely to seek the blue sky, but take it as a whole, there is in English literature, as in English character, a reminiscence of walls and ceilings, a tendency to the arbitrary and conventional that repels a mind trained in admiration of the antique spirit. It is only in later days that we are learning to prize the peculiar greatness which a thousand times outweighs this fault, and which has enabled English genius to go forth from its insular position and conquer such vast dominion in the realms both of matter and of mind.

Yet there is, often, between child and parent, a reaction from excessive influence having been exerted, and such an one we have experienced, in behalf of our country, against England. We use her language, and receive, in torrents, the influence of her thought, yet it is, in many respects, uncongenial and injurious to our constitution. What suits Great Britain, with her insular position and consequent need to concentrate and intensify her life, her limited monarchy, and spirit of trade, does not suit a mixed race, continually enriched with new blood from other stocks the most unlike that of our first descent, with ample field and verge enough to range in and leave every impulse free, and abundant opportunity to develope a genius, wide and full as our rivers, flowery, luxuriant and impassioned as our vast prairies, rooted in strength as the rocks on which the Puritan fathers landed.

That such a genius is to rise and work in this hemisphere we are confident; equally so that scarce the first faint streaks of that day's dawn are yet visible. It is sad for those that foresee, to know that they may not live to share its glories, yet it is sweet, too, to know that every act and word, uttered in the light of that foresight, may tend to hasten or ennoble its fulfilment.

That day will not rise till the fusion of races among us is more complete. It will not rise till this nation shall attain sufficient moral and intellectual dignity to prize moral and intellectual, no less highly than political, freedom, not till, the physical resources of the country being explored, all its regions studded with towns, broken by the plow, netted together by railways and telegraph lines, talent shall be left at leisure to turn its energies upon the higher department of man's existence. Nor then shall it be seen till from the leisurely and yearning soul of that riper time national ideas shall take birth, ideas craving to be clothed in a thousand fresh and original forms.

Without such ideas all attempts to construct a national literature must end in abortions like the monster of Frankenstein, things with forms, and the instincts of forms, but soulless, and therefore revolting. We cannot have expression till there is something to be expressed.

The symptoms of such a birth may be seen in a longing felt here and there for the sustenance of such ideas. At present, it shows itself, where felt, in sympathy with the prevalent tone of society, by attempts at external action, such as are classed under the head of social reform. But it needs to go deeper, before we can have poets, needs to penetrate beneath the springs of action, to stir and remake the soil as by the action of fire.

Another symptom is the need felt by individuals of being even sternly sincere. This is the one great means by which alone progress can be essentially furthered. Truth is the nursing mother of genius. No man can be absolutely true to himself, eschewing cant, compromise, servile imitation, and complaisance, without becoming original, for there is in every creature a fountain of life which, if not choked back by stones and other dead rubbish, will create a fresh atmosphere, and bring to life fresh beauty. And it is the same with the nation as with the individual man.

The best work we do for the future is by such truth. By use of that, in whatever way, we harrow the soil and lay it open to the sun and air. The winds from all quarters of the globe bring seed enough, and there is nothing wanting but preparation of the soil, and freedom in the atmosphere, for ripening of a new and golden harvest.

We are sad that we cannot be present at the gathering in of this harvest. And yet we are joyous, too, when we think that though our name may not be writ on the pillar of our country's fame, we can really do far more towards rearing it, than those who come at a later period and to a seemingly fairer task. *Now*, the humblest effort, made in a noble spirit, and with religious hope, cannot fail to be even infinitely useful. Whether we introduce some noble model from another time and clime, to encourage aspiration in our own, or cheer into blossom the simplest wood-flower that ever rose from the earth, moved by the genuine impulse to grow, independent of the lures of money or celebrity; whether we speak boldly when fear or doubt keep others silent, or refuse to swell the popular cry upon an unworthy occasion, the spirit of truth, purely worshipped, shall turn our acts and forbearances alike to profit, informing them with oracles which the latest time shall bless.

Under present circumstances the amount of talent and labour given to writing ought to surprise us. Literature is in this dim and struggling state, and its pecuniary results exceedingly pitiful. From many well known causes it is impossible for ninety-nine out of the hundred, who wish to use the pen, to ransom, by its use, the time they need. This state of things will have to be changed in some way. No man of genius writes for money; but it is essential to the free use of his powers, that he should be able to disembarrass his life from care and perplexity. This is very difficult here; and the state of things gets worse and worse, as less and less is offered in pecuniary meed for works demanding great devotion of time and labour (to say nothing of the ether engaged) and the publisher, obliged to regard the transaction as a matter of business, demands of the author to give him only what will find an immediate market, for he cannot afford to take any thing else. This will not do! When an immortal poet was secure only of a few copyists to circulate his works, there were princes and nobles to patronize literature and the arts. Here is only the public, and the public must learn how to cherish the nobler and rarer plants, and to plant the aloe, able to wait a hundred years for its bloom, or its garden will contain, presently, nothing but potatoes and pot-herbs. We shall have, in the course of the next two or three years, a convention of authors to inquire into the causes of this state of things and propose measures for its remedy. Some have already been thought of that look promising, but we shall not announce them till the time be ripe; that date is not distant, for the difficulties increase from day to day, in consequence of the system of cheap publication, on a great scale.

The ranks that led the way in the first half century of this republic were far better situated than we, in this respect. The country was not so deluged with the dingy page, reprinted from Europe, and patriotic vanity was on the alert to answer the question, "Who reads an American book?" And many were the books written, worthy to be read, as any out of the first class in England. They were, most of them, except in their subject matter, English books.

The list is large, and, in making some cursory comments, we do not wish to be understood as designating *all* who are worthy of notice, but only those who present themselves to our minds with some special claims. In history there has been nothing done to which the world at large has not been eager to award the full meed of its deserts. Mr. Prescott, for instance, has been greeted with as much warmth abroad as here. We are not disposed to undervalue his industry and power of clear and elegant arrangement. The richness and freshness of his materials is such that a sense of enchantment must be felt in their contemplation. We must regret, however, that they should have been first presented to the public by one who possesses nothing of the higher powers of the historian, great leading views, or discernment as to the motives of action and the spirit of an era. Considering the splendor of the materials the books are wonderfully tame, and every one must feel that having once passed through them and got the sketch in the mind, there is nothing else to which it will recur. The absence of thought, as to that great picture of Mexican life, with its heroisms, its terrible but deeply significant superstitions, its admirable civic refinement, seems to be quite unbroken.

Mr. Bancroft is a far more vivid writer; he has great resources and great command of them, and leading thoughts by whose aid he groups his facts. But we cannot speak fully of his historical works, which we have only read and referred to here and there.

In the department of ethics and philosophy, we may inscribe two names as likely to live and be blessed and honoured in the later time. These are the names of Channing and of Emerson.

Dr. Channing had several leading thoughts which corresponded with the wants of his time, and have made him in it a father of thought. His leading idea of "the dignity of human nature" is one of vast results, and the peculiar form in which he advocated it had a great work to do in this new world. The spiritual beauty of his writings is very great; they are all distinguished for sweetness, elevation, candour, and a severe devotion to truth. On great questions, he took middle ground, and sought a panoramic view; he wished also to stand high, yet never forgot what was above more than what was around and beneath him. He was not well acquainted with man on the impulsive and passionate side of his nature, so that his view of character was sometimes narrow, but it was always noble. He exercised an expansive and purifying power on the atmosphere, and stands a godfather at the baptism of this country.

The Sage of Concord has a very different mind, in every thing except that he has the same disinterestedness and dignity of purpose, the same purity of spirit. He is a profound thinker. He is a man of ideas, and deals with causes rather than effects. His ideas are illustrated from a wide range of literary culture and refined observation, and embodied in a style whose melody and subtle fragrance enchant those who stand stupified before the thoughts themselves, because their utmost depths do not enable them to sound his shallows. His influence does not yet extend over a wide space; he is too far beyond his place and his time, to be felt at once or in full, but it searches deep, and yearly widens its circles. He is a harbinger of the better day. His beautiful elocution has been a great aid to him in opening the way for the reception of his written word.

In that large department of literature which includes descriptive sketches, whether of character or scenery, we are already rich. Irving, a genial and fair nature, just what he ought to be, and would have been, at any time of the world, has drawn the scenes amid which his youth was spent in their primitive lineaments, with all the charms of his graceful jocund humor. He has his niche and need never be deposed; it is not one that another could occupy.

The first enthusiasm about Cooper having subsided, we remember more his faults than his merits. His ready resentment and way of showing it in cases which it is the wont of gentlemen to pass by in silence, or meet with a good humored smile, have caused unpleasant associations with his name, and his fellow citizens, in danger of being tormented by suits for libel, if they spoke freely of him, have ceased to speak of him at all. But neither these causes, nor the baldness of his plots, shallowness of thought, and poverty in the presentation of character, should make us forget the grandeur and originality of his sea-sketches, nor the redemption from oblivion of our forest-scenery, and the noble romance of the hunter-pioneer's life. Already, but for him, this fine page of life's romance would be almost forgotten. He has done much to redeem these irrevocable beauties from the corrosive acid of a semi-civilized invasion.

Miss Sedgwick and others have portrayed, with skill and feeling, scenes and personages from the revolutionary time. Such have a permanent value in proportion as their subject is fleeting. The same charm attends the spirited delineations of Mrs. Kirkland, and that amusing book, "A New Purchase." The features of Hoosier, Sucker, and Wolverine life are worth fixing; they are peculiar to the soil, and indicate its hidden treasures; they have, also, that charm which simple life, lived for its own sake, always has, even in rude and all but brutal forms.

What shall we say of the poets? The list is scanty; amazingly so, for there is nothing in the causes that paralyze other kinds of literature that could affect lyrical and narrative poetry. Men's hearts beat, hope, and suffer always, and they must crave such means to vent them; yet of the myriad leaves garnished with smooth stereotyped rhymes that issue yearly from our press, you will not find, one time in a million, a little piece written from any such impulse, or with the least sincerity or sweetness of tone. They are written for the press, in the spirit of imitation or vanity, the paltriest offspring of the human brain, for the heart disclaims, as the ear is shut against them. This is the kind of verse which is cherished by the magazines as a correspondent to the tawdry pictures of smiling milliners' dolls in the frontispiece. Like these they are only a fashion, a fashion based on no reality of love or beauty. The inducement to write them consists in a little money, or more frequently the charm of seeing an anonymous name printed at the top in capitals.

We must here, in passing, advert also to the style of story current in the magazines, flimsy beyond any texture that was ever spun or even dreamed of by the mind of man, in any other age and country. They are said to be "written for the seamstresses," but we believe that every way injured class could relish and digest better fare even at the end of long days of exhausting labour. There are exceptions to this censure; stories by Mrs. Child have been published in the magazines, and now and then good ones by Mrs. Stephens and others; but, take them generally, they are calculated to do a positive injury to the public mind, acting as an opiate, and of an adulterated kind, too.

But to return to the poets. At their head, Mr. Bryant stands alone. His range is not great, nor his genius fertile. But his poetry is purely the language of his inmost nature, and the simple lovely garb in which his thoughts are arranged, a direct gift from the Muse. He has written nothing that is not excellent, and the atmosphere of his verse refreshes and composes the mind, like leaving the highway to enter some green, lovely, fragrant wood.

Halleck and Willis are poets of society. Though the former has written so little, yet that little is full of fire, — elegant, witty, delicate in sentiment. It is an honour to the country that these occasional sparks, struck off from the flint of commercial life, should have kindled so much flame as they have. It is always a consolation to see one of them sparkle amid the rubbish of daily life. One of his poems has been published within the last year, written, in fact, long ago, but new to most of us, and it enlivened the literary thoroughfare, as a green wreath might some dusty, musty hall of legislation.

Willis has not the same terseness or condensed electricity. But he has grace, spirit, at times a winning pensiveness, and a lively, though almost wholly sensuous, delight in the beautiful.

Dana has written so little that he would hardly be seen in a more thickly garnished galaxy. But the masculine strength of feeling, the solemn tenderness and refined thought displayed in such pieces as the "Dying Raven," and the "Husband and Wife's Grave," have left a deep impression on the popular mind.

Longfellow is artificial and imitative. He borrows incessantly, and mixes what he borrows, so that it does not appear to the best advantage. He is very faulty in using broken or mixed metaphors. The ethical part of his writing has a hollow, secondhand sound. He has, however, elegance, a love of the beautiful, and a fancy for what is large and manly, if not a full sympathy with it. His verse breathes at times much sweetness; and, if not allowed to supersede what is better may promote a taste for good poetry. Though imitative, he is not mechanical.

We cannot say as much for Lowell, who, we must declare it, though to the grief of some friends, and the disgust of more, is absolutely wanting in the true spirit and tone of poesy. His interest in the moral questions of the day has supplied the want of vitality in himself; his great facility at versification has enabled him to fill the ear with a copious stream of pleasant sound. But his verse is stereotyped; his thought sounds no depth, and posterity will not remember him.

R. W. Emerson, in melody, in subtle beauty of thought and expression, takes the highest rank upon this list. But his poems are mostly philosophical, which is not the truest kind of poetry. They want the simple force of nature and passion, and, while they charm the ear and interest the mind, fail to wake far-off echoes in the heart. The imagery wears a symbolical air, and serves rather as illustration, than to delight us by fresh and glowing forms of life.

We must here mention one whom the country has not yet learned to honour, perhaps never may, for he wants artistic skill to give complete form to his inspiration. This is William Ellery Channing, nephew and namesake of Dr. C., a volume of whose poems, published three or four years ago in Boston, remains unknown, except to a few friends, nor, if known, would they probably, excite sympathy, as those which have been published in the periodicals have failed to do so. Yet some of the purest tones of the lyre are his, the finest inspirations as to the feelings and passions of men, deep spiritual insight, and an entire originality in the use of his means. The frequently unfinished and obscure state of his poems, a passion for forcing words out of their usual meaning into one which they may appropriately bear, but which comes upon the reader with an unpleasing and puzzling surprise, may repel, at first glance, from many of these poems, but do not mar the following sublime description of the beings we want, to rule, to redeem, to re-create this nation, and under whose reign alone can there be an American literature, for then only could we have life worth recording. . . .

A series of poems, called "Man in the Republic," by Cornelius Mathews, deserves a higher meed of sympathy than it has received. The thoughts and views are strong and noble, the exhibition of them imposing. In plastic power this writer is deficient. His prose works sin in exuberance, and need consolidating and chastening. We find fine things, but not so arranged as to be seen in the right places and by the best light. In his poems Mr. Mathews is unpardonably rough and rugged; the poetic substance finds no musical medium in which to flow. Yet there *is* poetic substance which makes full chords, if not a harmony. . . .

Meanwhile, the most important part of our literature, while the work of diffusion is still going on, lies in the journals, which monthly, weekly, daily, send their messages to every corner of this great land, and form, at present, the only efficient instrument for the general education of the people.

Among these, the Magazines take the lowest rank. Their object is principally to cater for the amusement of vacant hours, and, as there is not a great deal of wit and light talent in this country, they do not even this to much advantage. More wit, grace, and elegant trifling, embellish the annals of literature in one day of France than in a year of America.

The Reviews are more able. If they cannot compare, on equal terms, with those of France, England, and Germany, where, if genius be rare, at least a vast amount of talent and culture are brought to bear upon all the departments of knowledge, they are yet very creditable to a new country, where so large a portion of manly ability must be bent on making laws, making speeches, making rail-roads and canals. They are, however, much injured by a partisan spirit, and the fear of censure from their own public. This last is always slow death to a journal; its natural and only safe position is to *lead*; if, instead, it bows to the will of the multitude, it will find the ostracism of democracy far more dangerous than the worst censure of a tyranny could be. It is not half so dangerous to a man to be immured in a dungeon alone with God and his own clear conscience, as to walk the streets fearing the scrutiny of a thousand eyes, ready to veil, with anxious care, whatever may not suit the many-headed monster in its momentary mood. Gentleness is dignified, but caution is debasing; only a noble fearlessness can give wings to the mind, with which to soar beyond the common ken, and learn what may be of use to the crowd below. Writers have nothing to do but to love truth fervently, seek justice according to their ability, and then express what is in the mind; they have nothing to do with consequences, God will take care of those. The want of such noble courage, such faith in the power of truth and good desire, paralyze mind greatly in this country. Publishers are afraid; authors are afraid; and if a worthy resistance is not made by religious souls, there is danger that all the light will soon be put under bushels, lest some wind should waft from it a spark that may kindle dangerous fire. . . .

The life of intellect is becoming more and more determined to the weekly and daily papers, whose light leaves fly so rapidly and profusely over the land. Speculations are afloat, as to the influence of the electric telegraph upon their destiny, and it seems obvious that it should raise their character by taking from them in some measure, the office of gathering and dispersing the news, and requiring of them rather to arrange and interpret it.

This mode of communication is susceptible of great excellence in the way of condensed essay, narrative, criticism, and is the natural receptacle for the lyrics of the day. That so few good ones deck the poet's corner, is because the indifference or unfitness of editors, as to choosing and refusing, makes this place, at present, undesirable to the poet. It might be otherwise.

The means which this organ affords of diffusing knowledge and sowing the seeds of thought where they may hardly fail of an infinite harvest, cannot be too highly prized by the discerning and benevolent. Minds of the first class are generally indisposed to this kind of writing;

what must be done on the spur of the occasion and cast into the world so incomplete, as the hurried offspring of a day or hour's labour must generally be, cannot satisfy their judgment, or do justice to their powers. But he who looks to the benefit of others, and sees with what rapidity and ease instruction and thought are assimilated by men, when they come thus, as it were, on the wings of the wind, may be content, as an unhonoured servant to the grand purposes of Destiny, to work in such a way at the Pantheon which the Ages shall complete, on which his name may not be inscribed, but which will breathe the life of his soul.

The confidence in uprightness of intent, and the safety of truth, is still more needed here than in the more elaborate kinds of writing, as meanings cannot be fully explained nor expressions revised. Newspaper writing is next door to conversation, and should be conducted on the same principles. It has this advantage: we address, not our neighbour, who forces us to remember his limitations and prejudices, but the ideal presence of human nature as we feel it ought to be and trust it will be. We address America rather than Americans. . . .

. . . But we have omitted many things in this slight sketch, for the subject, even in this stage, lies as a volume in our mind, and cannot be unrolled in completeness unless time and space were more abundant. Our object was to show that although by a thousand signs, the existence is foreshown of those forces which are to animate an American literature, that faith, those hopes are not yet alive which shall usher it into a homogeneous or fully organized state of being. The future is glorious with certainties for those who do their duty in the present, and, lark-like, seeking the sun, challenge its eagles to an earthward flight, where their nests may be built in our mountains, and their young raise their cry of triumph, unchecked by dullness in the echoes. . . .

Hawthorne (Mosses from an Old Manse) . . . The volume before us shares the charms of Hawthorne's earlier tales; the only difference being that his range of subjects is a little wider. There is the same gentle and sincere companionship with Nature, the same delicate but fearless scrutiny of the secrets of the heart, the same serene independence of petty and artificial restrictions, whether on opinions or conduct, the same familiar, yet pensive sense of the spiritual or demoniacal influences that haunt the palpable life and common walks of men, not

by many apprehended except in results. We have here to regret that
Hawthorne, at this stage of his mind's life, lays no more decisive hand
upon the apparition – brings it no nearer than in former days. We had
hoped that we should see, no more as in a glass darkly, but face to face.
Still, still brood over his page the genius of revery and the nonchalance
of Nature, rather than the ardent earnestness of the human soul which
feels itself born not only to see and disclose, but to understand and
interpret such things. Hawthorne intimates and suggests, but he does
not lay bare the mysteries of our being.

The introduction to the "Mosses," in which the old manse, its
inhabitants and visitants are portrayed, is written with even more than
his usual charm of placid grace and many strokes of his admirable good
sense. Those who are not, like ourselves, familiar with the scenes and its
denizens, will still perceive how true that picture must be; those of us
who are thus familiar will best know how to prize the record of objects
and influences unique in our country and time.

"The Birth Mark" and "Rapaccini's Daughter," embody truths of
profound importance in shapes of aerial elegance. In these, as here and
there in all these pieces, shines the loveliest ideal of love, and the
beauty of feminine purity (by which we mean no mere acts or
abstinences, but perfect single truth felt and done in gentleness) which
is its root.

"The Celestial Railroad," for its wit, wisdom, and the graceful
adroitness with which the natural and material objects are interwoven
with the allegories, has already won its meed of admiration.
"Fire-worship" is a most charming essay for its domestic sweetness and
thoughtful life. "Goodman Brown" is one of those disclosures we have
spoken of, of the secrets of the breast. Who has not known such a trial
that is capable indeed of sincere aspiration toward that only good, that
infinite essence, which men call God. Who has not known the hour
when even that best beloved image cherished as the one precious
symbol left, in the range of human nature, believed to be still pure gold
when all the rest have turned to clay, shows, in severe ordeal, the
symptoms of alloy. Oh, hour of anguish, when the old familiar faces
grow dark and dim in the lurid light – when the gods of the hearth,
honoured in childhood, adored in youth, crumble, and nothing, nothing is
left which the daily earthly feelings can embrace – can cherish with unbroken faith! Yet some survive that trial more happily than young Goodman Brown. They are those who have not sought it – have never of

their own accord walked forth with the Tempter into the dim shades of Doubt. Mrs. Bull-Frog is an excellent humourous picture of what is called to be "content at last with substantial realities!!" The "Artist of the Beautiful" presents in a form that is, indeed, beautiful, the opposite view as to what *are* the substantial realities of life. Let each man choose between them according to his kind. Had Hawthorne written "Roger Malvin's Burial" alone, we should be pervaded with the sense of the poetry and religion of his soul. . . .

Charles Brockden Brown (Ormond; or The Secret Witness and Wieland or the Transformation) . . . Brown is great as ever human writer was in showing the self-sustaining force of which a lonely mind is capable. He takes one person, makes him brood like the bee, and extract from the common life before him all its sweetness, its bitterness, and its nourishment.

We say makes *him*, but it increases our own interest in Brown that, a prophet in this respect of a better era, he has usually placed this thinking royal mind in the body of a woman. This personage too is always feminine, both in her character and circumstances, but a conclusive proof that the term *feminine* is not a synonym for *weak*. Constantia, Clara Wieland, have loving hearts, graceful and plastic natures, but they have also noble thinking minds, full of resource, constancy, courage. The Marguerite of Godwin, no less, is all refinement, and the purest tenderness, but she is also the soul of honour, capable of deep discernment and of acting in conformity with the inferences she draws. The man of Brown and Godwin has not eaten of the fruit of the tree of knowledge and been driven to sustain himself by sweat of his brow for nothing, but has learned the structure and laws of things, and become a being, rational, benignant, various, and desirous of supplying the loss of innocence by the attainment of virtue. So his woman need not be quite so weak as Eve, the slave of feeling or of flattery: she also has learned to guide her helm amid the storm across the troubled waters.

The horrors which mysteriously beset these persons, and against which, so far as outward facts go, they often strive in vain, are but a representation of those powers permitted to work in the same way throughout the affairs of this world. Their demoniacal attributes only represent a morbid state of the intellect, gone to excess from want of balance with the other powers. There is an intellectual as well as a

physical drunkenness, and which no less impels to crime. Carwin, urged
on to use his ventriloquism, till the presence of such a strange agent
wakened the seeds of fanaticism in the breast of Wieland, is in a state
no more foreign to nature than that of the wretch executed last week,
who felt himself drawn as by a spell to murder his victim because he
had thought of her money and the pleasures it might bring him, till the
feeling possessed his brain that hurls the gamester to ruin. The victims
of such agency are like the soldier of the Rio Grande, who, both legs
shot off and his life-blood rushing out with every pulse, replied serenely
to his pitying comrades that "he had now that for which the soldier
enlisted." The end of the drama is not in this world, and the fiction
which rounds off the whole to harmony and felicity before the curtain
falls, sins against truth, and deludes the reader. The Nelsons of the
human race are all the more exposed to the assaults of fate that they
are decorated with the badges of well-earned glory. Who, but feels as
they fall in death, or rise again to a mutilated existence, that the end is
not yet? Who, that thinks, but must feel that the recompense is, where
Brown places it, in the accumulation of mental treasure, in the severe
assay by fire that leaves the gold pure to be used sometime—somewhere.

Brown, man of the brooding eye, the teeming brain, the deep and
fervent heart; if thy country prize thee not and has almost lost thee out
of sight, it is that her heart is made shallow and cold, her eye dim, by
the pomp of circumstance, the love of gross outward gain. She cannot
long continue thus, for it takes a great deal of soul to keep a huge body
from disease and dissolution. As there is more soul thou wilt be more
sought, and many will yet sit down with thy Constantia to the meal and
water on which she sustained her full and thoughtful existence, who
could not endure the ennui of aldermanic dinners, or find any relish in
the imitation of French cookery. To-day many will read the words, and
some have a cup large enough to receive the spirit, before it is lost in
the sand on which their feet are planted.

Brown's high standard of the delights of intellectual communion
and of friendship correspond with the fondest hopes of early days. But
in the relations of real life, at present, there is rarely more than one of
the parties ready for such intercourse as he describes. On the one side
there will be dryness, want of perception or variety, a stupidity unable
to appreciate life's richest boon when offered to its grasp, and the finer
nature is doomed to retrace its steps, unhappy as those who having

force to raise a spirit cannot retain or make it substantial, and stretch out their arms only to bring them back empty to the breast. *[Papers on Literature, II, 122-34, 137-40, 142, 144-46, 148-50]*

14. "Modern British Poets," 1846

In this essay, Fuller discussed the nine poets who made the English romantic movement (excluding Keats, still little known in America, whom she appears not to have read): the "singers," Campbell, Moore, and Scott; the realist Crabbe; the ill-fated Shelley and Byron, "mournful in their beauty"; and the poet-philosophers, Coleridge and Wordsworth (her favorites), and Southey. In her treatment of Byron, we see a fair sample of her critical range, her sympathetic interpretation of him, and her need to measure him by his superiors. (Professor Teufelsdröckh is the protagonist of Carlyle's *Sartor Resartus* who resolved to turn his back on the romantic excess symbolized for him by Goethe.)

. . . The unfortunate Byron (*unfortunate* I call him because "mind and destiny are but two names for one idea,") has long been at rest; the adoration and the hatred of which he was the object are both dying out. His poems have done their work; a strong personal interest no longer gives them a factitious charm, and they are beginning to find their proper level. Their value is twofold – immortal and eternal, as records of thoughts and feelings which must be immortally and eternally interesting to the mind of individual man; historical, because they are the most complete chronicle of a particular set of impulses in the public mind.

How much of the first sort of value the poems of Byron possess, posterity must decide, and the verdict can only be ascertained by degrees; I for one should say not much. There are many beautiful pictures; infinite wit, but too local and temporary in its range to be greatly prized beyond his own time; little originality; but much vigor, both of thought and expression; with a deep, even a passionate love of the beautiful and grand. . . .

It is worthy of remark that Byron's moral perversion never paralyzed or obscured his intellectual powers, though it might have lowered their aims. With regard to the plan and style of his works, he showed strong good sense and clear judgment. The man who indulged such narrowing egotism, such irrational scorn, would prune and polish without mercy the stanzas in which he uttered them; and this bewildered Idealist was a very bigot in behoof of the commonsensical satirist, the almost peevish Realist — Pope.

Historically these poems are valuable as records of that strange malady, that sickness of the soul, which has, in our day, cankered so visibly the rose of youth. It is common to speak of the Byronic mood as morbid, false, and foolish; it is the two former, and, if it could be avoided, would most assuredly be the latter also. But how can it always be avoided? Like as a fever rages in the blood before we are aware, even so creeps upon the soul this disease, offspring of a moral malaria, an influence impalpable till we feel its results within ourselves. Since skilful physicians are not always at hand, would it not be better to purify the atmosphere than to rail at the patient? Those who have passed through this process seem to have wondrous little pity for those who are still struggling with its horrors, and very little care to aid them. Yet if it be disease, does it not claim pity, and would it not be well to try some other remedy than hard knocks for its cure? What though these sick youths do mourn and lament somewhat wearisomely, and we feel vexed, on bright May mornings, to have them try to persuade us that this beautiful green earth, with all its flowers and bird-notes, is no better than a vast hospital? Consider, it is a relief to the delirious to rave audibly, and few, like Professor Teufelsdrock, have strength to keep a whole Satanic school in the soul from sprouting aloud. . . . There is no getting rid of the epidemic of the season, however annoying and useless it may seem. You cannot cough down an influenza; it will cough you down.

Why young people will just now profess themselves so very miserable, for no better reason than that assigned by the poet to some "inquiring friends,"

> "Nought do I mourn I e'er possessed,
> I grieve that I cannot be blessed;"

I have here no room to explain. Enough that there has for some time prevailed a sickliness of feeling, whose highest water-mark may be found in the writings of Byron. He is the "power man" (as the Germans call him, meaning perhaps the *power-loom*!) who has woven into one

tissue all those myriad threads, tear-stained and dull-gray, with which
the malignant spiders of speculation had filled the machine shop of
society, and by so doing has, though I admit, unintentionally, conferred
benefits upon us incalculable for a long time to come. He has lived
through this experience for us, and shown us that the natural fruits of
indulgence in such a temper are dissonance, cynicism, irritability, and
all uncharitableness. Accordingly, since his time the evil has lessened.
With this warning before them, let the young examine that world,
which seems at times so deformed by evils and endless contradictions,

> "Control them and subdue, transmute, bereave
>   Of their bad influence, and the good receive."

Grief loses half its charm when we find that others have endured the
same to a higher degree, and lived through it. Nor do I believe that the
misanthropy of Byron ever made a single misanthrope; that his
scepticism, so uneasy and sorrowful beneath its thin mask of levity,
ever made a single sceptic. I know those whom it has cured of their yet
half-developed errors. I believed it has cured thousands.

As supplying materials for the history of opinion, then, Byron's
poems will be valuable. And as a poet, I believe posterity will assign him
no obscure place, though he will probably be classed far beneath some
who have exercised a less obvious or immediate influence on their own
times; beneath the noble Three of whom I am yet to speak, whose
merits are immortal, because their tendencies are towards immortality,
and all whose influence must be a growing influence; beneath Southey,
Coleridge, and Wordsworth. . . .

In earlier days the greatest poets addressed themselves more to the
passions or heart-emotions of their fellow-men than to their thoughts or
mind-emotions. The passions were then in their natural state, and held
their natural places in the character. They were not made sickly by a
false refinement, or stimulated to a diseased and incessantly craving
state. Men loved and hated to excess, perhaps; but there was nothing
factitious in their love or hatred. The tone of poetry, even when
employed on the most tragic subjects, might waken in the hearer's heart
a chord of joy; for in such natural sorrow there was a healthful life, an
energy which told of healing yet to come and the endless riches of love
and hope.

How different is its tone in Faust and Manfred; how false to simple
nature, yet how true to the time! As the mechanism of society has

become more complex, and must be regulated more by combined efforts, desire after individuality brings him who manifests it into a state of conflict with society. This is felt from a passion, whether it be love or ambition, which seeks to make its own world independent of trivial daily circumstances, and struggles long against the lessons of experience, which tell it that such singleness of effort and of possession cannot be, consistently with that grand maxim of the day, *the greatest happiness of the greatest number*. Not until equally enlightened and humble, can the human being learn that individuality of character is not necessarily combined with individuality of possession, but depends alone on the zealous observance of truth. Few can be wise enough to realize with Schiller, that "to be truly immortal one must live in the whole." The mind struggles long, before it can resolve on sacrificing any thing of its impulsive nature to the requisitions of the time. And while it struggles it mourns, and these lamentations compose the popular poetry. Men do not now look in poetry for a serene world, amid whose vocal groves and green meads they may refresh themselves after the heat of action, and in paradisaical quiet listen to the tales of other days. No! dissatisfied and represt, they want to be made to weep, because, in so doing, they feel themselves in some sense free.

All this conflict and apparently bootless fretting and wailing mark a transition-state — a state of gradual revolution, in which men try all things, seeking what they hold fast, and feel that it is good. But there are some, the pilot-minds of the age, who cannot submit to pass all their lives in experimentalizing. They cannot consent to drift across the waves in the hope of finding *somewhere* a haven and a home; but, seeing the blue sky over them, and believing that God's love is every where, try to make the best of that spot on which they have been placed, and, not unfrequently, by the aid of spiritual assistance, more benign than that of Faust's Lemures, win from the raging billows large territories, whose sands they can convert into Eden bowers, tenanted by lovely and majestic shapes. . . . [*Papers on Literature, I, 74-78, 80-81*]

15. "Miss Barrett's Poems," January 4, 1845

In her review of *A Drama of Exile: And Other Poems*, written a month after she began work for the *Tribune*, we feel

Fuller's identification with Elizabeth Barrett's free spirit, frail health, and erudition (even the overuse of it, which Fuller criticizes here, as her own friends did a few months later with regard to her own *Woman in the Nineteenth Century* [IV:8]).

What happiness for the critic when, as in the present instance, his task is, mainly, how to express a cordial admiration; to indicate an intelligence of beauties, rather than regret for defects!

We have read these volumes with feelings of delight far warmer than the writer, in her sincerely modest preface, would seem to expect from any reader, and cannot hesitate to rank her, in vigour and nobleness of conception, depth of spiritual experience, and command of classic allusion, above any female writer the world has yet known.

In the first quality, especially, most female writers are deficient. They do not grasp a subject with simple energy, nor treat it with decision of touch. They are, in general, most remarkable for delicacy of feeling, and brilliancy or grace in manner.

In delicacy of perception, Miss Barrett may vie with any of her sex. She has what is called a true woman's heart, although we must believe that men of a fine conscience and good organization will have such a heart no less. Signal instances occur to us in the cases of Spenser, Wordsworth and Tennyson. The woman who reads them will not find hardness or blindness as to the subtler workings of thoughts and affections.

If men are often deficient on this score; women, on the other hand, are apt to pay excessive attention to the slight tokens, the little things of life. Thus, in conduct or writing, they tend to weary us by a morbid sentimentalism. From this fault Miss Barrett is wholly free. Personal feeling is in its place; enlightened by Reason, ennobled by Imagination. The earth is no despised resting place for the feet, the heaven bends wide above, rich in starry hopes, and the air flows around exhilarating and free. . . .

In the "Drama of Exile" and the "Vision of Poets," where she aims at a Miltonic flight or Dantesque grasp — not in any spirit of rivalry or imitation, but because she is really possessed of a similar mental scope — her success is far below what we find in the poems of feeling and experience; for she has the vision of a great poet, but little in proportion of his plastic power. She is at home in the Universe; she sees its laws; she sympathises with its motions. She has the imagination all compact – the healthy archetypal plant from which all forms may be divined, and, so far as now existent, understood. Like Milton, she sees the angelic hosts in real presence; like Dante, she hears the spheral concords and shares the planetary motions. But she cannot, like Milton, marshal the angels so near the earth as to impart the presence other than by sympathy. He who is near her level of mind may, through the magnetic sympathy, see the angels with her. Others will feel only the grandeur and sweetness she expresses in these forms. Still less can she, like Dante, give, by a touch, the key which enables ourselves to play on the same instrument. She is singularly deficient in the power of compression. There are always far more words and verses than are needed to convey the meaning, and it is a great proof of her strength, that the thought still seems strong, when arrayed in a form so Briarean clumsy and many-handed.

We compare her with those great poets, though we have read her preface and see how sincerely she deprecates any such comparison, not merely because her theme is the same as theirs, but because, as we must again repeat, her field of vision and nobleness of conception are such, that we cannot forbear trying her by the same high standard to see what she lacks. . . .

We have already said, that, as a poet, Miss Barrett is deficient in plastic energy, and that she is diffuse. We must add many blemishes of overstrained and constrained thought and expression. The ways in which words are coined or forced from their habitual meanings does not carry its excuse with it. We find no gain that compensates the loss of elegance and simplicity. One practice which has already had its censors of using the adjective for the noun, as in the cases of "The cry of the Human," "Leaning from the Golden," we, also, find offensive, not only to the habitual tastes, but to the sympathies of the very mood awakened by the writer.

We hear that she has long been an invalid, and, while the knowledge of this increases admiration for her achievements and delight at the extent of the influence – so much light flowing from the darkness of the sick room, – we seem to trace injurious results, too. There is often a want of pliant and glowing life. The sun does not always warm the marble. We have spoken of the great book culture of this mind. We must now say that this culture is too great in proportion to that it has received from actual life. The lore is not always assimilated to the new form; the illustrations sometimes impede the attention rather than help its course; and we are too much and too often reminded of other minds and other lives.

Great variety of metres are used, and with force and facility. But they have not that deep music which belongs to metres which are the native growth of the poet's mind. In that case, others may have used them, but we feel that, if they had not, he must have invented them; that they are original with him. Miss Barrett is more favoured by the grand and thoughtful, than by the lyric muse.

We have thus pointed out all the faults we could find in Miss Barrett, feeling that her strength and nobleness deserves this act of high respect. She has no need of leniency, or caution.... [*Papers on Literature*, II, 22-25, 28-29]

16. "French Novelists of the Day," February 1, 1845

In this essay for the *Tribune*, Fuller discussed Balzac, the "modern Mephistopheles, 'the spirit that denieth' "; Eugène Sue, the Socialist crusader for whom Timothy Fuller named his first son; and her favorite, George Sand. In her discussion of Sand—which her brother Arthur eliminated from the essay in the posthumous *Life Without and Life Within*—we see passionate sympathy in conflict with morality that laments, as Hawthorne did later with Hester Prynne, Sand's lack of "quite clean hands."

George Sand we esteem to be a person of strong passions, but of original nobleness and a love of right sufficient to guide them all to the service of worthy aims. But she fell upon evil times. She was given in marriage according to the fashion of the old regime; she was taken from a convent where she had heard a great deal about the law of God and the example of Jesus, into a society where no vice was proscribed if it would wear the cloak of hypocrisy. She found herself impatient of deception and loudly called by passion: she yielded; but she could not do so as others did, sinning against what she owned to be the rule of right and the will of Heaven. She protested; she examined; she assailed. She "hacked into the roots of things," and the bold sound of her ax called around her every foe that finds a home amid the growth of civilization. Still she persisted. "If it be real," thought she, "it cannot be destroyed; as to what is false, the sooner it goes the better; and I for one had rather perish beneath its fall than wither in its shade."

Schiller puts into the mouth of Mary Stuart these words as her only plea: "The world knows the worst of me; and I may boast that though I have erred, I am better than my reputation." Sand may say the same. All is open, noble; the free descriptions, the sophistry of passion are at least redeemed by a desire for truth as strong as ever beat in any heart. To the weak or unthinking the reading of such books may not be desirable, for only those who take exercise as men can digest strong meat. But to anyone able to understand the position and circumstances, we believe this reading cannot fail of bringing good impulses, valuable suggestions, and it is quite free from that subtle miasma which taints so large a portion of French literature, not less since the Revolution than before. This we say to the foreign reader. To her own country Sand is a boon precious and prized both as a warning and a leader, for which none there can be ungrateful. She has dared to probe its festering wounds, and if they be not past all surgery, she is one who, most of any, helps toward a cure.

Would indeed the surgeon had come with quite clean hands! A woman of Sand's genius, as free, as bold, and pure from even the suspicion of error, might have filled an apostolic station among her people. Then with what force had come her cry, "If it be false, give it up; but if it be true, keep to it − one or the other!" . . .

For some years Sand has quitted her post of assailant. She has seen that it is better to seek some form of life worthy to supersede the old than rudely to destroy it, heedless of the future. Her fire is bending towards philanthropic measures. She does appear to possess much of the constructive faculty, and though her writings command a great pecuniary compensation and have a wide sway, it is rather for their tendency than for their thought. She has reached no commanding point of view from which she may give orders to the advanced corps. She is still at work with others in the trench, though she works with more force than almost any.

In power indeed Sand bears the palm above any of the novelists. She is vigorous in conception, often great in the apprehension and the contrast of characters. She knows passion, as has been well hinted, at a white heat, when all the lower particles are remolded by its power. Her descriptive talent is very great, and her poetic feeling exquisite. She wants but little of being a poet, but that little is indispensable. Yet she keeps us always hovering on the borders of the enchanted fields. She has to a signal degree that power of exact transcript from her own mind of which almost all writers fail. There is no veil, no half-plastic integument between us and the thought. We vibrate perfectly with it.

This is her chief charm, and next to it is one in which we know no French writer that resembles her except Rousseau, though he indeed is vastly her superior in it. This is, of concentrated glow. Her nature glows beneath the words, like fire beneath the ashes, deep — deep!

Her best works are unequal; in many parts written hastily or carelessly or with flagging spirits. They all promise far more than they perform; the work is not done masterly; she has not reached that point where a writer sits at the helm of his own genius. Sometimes she plies the oar; sometimes she drifts. But what greatness she has is genuine; there is no tinsel of any kind, no drapery carefully adjusted or chosen gesture about her. May Heaven lead her at last to the full possession of her best self, in harmony with the higher laws of life! . . . [The Writings of Margaret Fuller, ed. Mason Wade, (New York: The Viking Press, 1941) pp. 305-308]

PART

IV

The Feminist

> You will be surprised when you hear me say that the history
> of the Transcendental movement stretched along two hundred
> years, beginning with a woman's life and work in 1637, and
> ending with a woman's work and death in 1850. The arc,
> which we call transcendental, was subtended by a chord, held
> at first by Anne Hutchinson, and lost in the Atlantic waves
> with Margaret Fuller. [1]

So lectured Caroline Healey Dall, a veteran feminist, at the
end of the century; in her youth, she had been Fuller's
disciple. But though Fuller's life and work had made possible
such a feminist interpretation of Transcendentalism, for
herself feminism emerged slowly and initially as a part of her
engagement with Transcendentalism.

In a sense, it is remarkable that Fuller became a feminist
at all. Certainly identification with other women did not
come easily to her. In the absence of a movement, criticism
of other women was the natural recourse of a woman seeking
to break out of the limited world her sisters seemed to
accept, and this was accentuated in Fuller's case by her goals
of unlimited self-development. To defend herself from
discouragement, Fuller cultivated in private her sense of
exceptionality and presented herself publicly as a woman of
singular destiny. Her feminism never eradicated these habits.
On the other hand, beginning in girlhood, her interest in
herself had made her genuinely curious about other women
and intensely attracted to some of them. Gradually, a sense
of women as a group and a desire to work for them emerged.
The first expression of her concern was an enterprise
motivated partly by financial need: the offering of a series of
"Conversations" for women, beginning in November 1839, a
few months before she began to work on *The Dial*. Very
likely inspired by heady sessions with the Transcendentalist
Club, the Conversations nourished a sense of herself and of
possible vocations which eventually· led her far beyond the
Concord circle and its aims.

In a letter to Sophia Ripley, Fuller proposed to assemble
a circle of "well-educated and thinking women"; her object

was to help them "systematize thought and give a precision and clearness in which our sex are so deficient, chiefly, I think, because they have so few inducements." Thus employing Timothy Fuller's standards, she aimed to answer the questions he could not. The women were to ask, "What were we born to do: and how shall we do it?" and, more specifically, to ascertain "how we may make best use of our means of building up the life of thought upon the life of action." She felt confident of success if the women would participate, would abjure "coterie criticism" and "that sort of vanity in them which wears the garb of modesty." At the first meeting she explained further that the extensive but superficial education currently granted women of her class deprived them of the abilities and the "mother wisdom and wit" their less schooled but more genuinely productive grandmothers had; and unlike men, who "reproduce all that they learn" in college and worldly careers, "women learn without any attempt to reproduce." Her choice of the word "reproduce" for the intellectual achievement she sought was not casual. She had thought long and painfully before preferring the quick "children of the muse" to the "lovely children of a human birth," who brought to their mothers "slow and neutralizing cares." [2]

Paying a small fee, about twenty-five women—eventually more than forty would appear—gathered at noon once a week for two hours in the shabby parlor of Elizabeth Peabody. (After leaving Alcott's school, that tireless handmaiden of the movement had set up a Transcendentalist townhouse, a cultural oasis on West Street in Boston, from which she sold or loaned foreign literature and published native works on a small scale.) These participants were almost all from eminent families or were accomplished in their own right or prominent then or later in the abolitionist and feminist struggles: women like Elizabeth Bliss Bancroft, Eliza Farrar, Lydia Cabot Parker, Lidian Emerson, Mary, Sophia, and Elizabeth Peabody, Lydia Maria Child, and Maria White. In the first series, Fuller chose Greek mythology to discuss, seeing it as "playful as well as deep," although even here some "Christian ladies," unhappy that "heathen Greeks should be envied," had to be persuaded that the Greeks had achieved a more mature civilization than the Christians. [3] The Conversations continued for five winters and also treated fine arts, ethics, education, and women, especially their influence on family, school, church, society, and literature.

Her method in the Conversations, adapted from her teaching experiments, was first to offer a short introduction to the subject, suggesting ideas they might pursue, then to invite responses, definitions, criticisms. There were no reading assignments, no regular written ones. Some issues intriguing to us now are blurred in the records women kept of these conversations, where the actual exchanges are rendered telegraphically or smothered in enthusiastic generality. If one account suggests it was an open exchange of ideas, teaching intellectual self-reliance, another hints that it was Fuller's dazzling solo, inspiring a trancelike worship. It seems likely that both interpretations were valid at one time or another in the course of five winters and that they were not felt to be contradictory. In a gathering of this sort (with virtually no precedent save Ann Hutchinson's much bolder group) led by such an unusually well-educated and articulate woman, the question of equality between her and the other women was not as pressing as it would become later. No Transcendentalist brooded over this sort of dilemma. And Fuller was offering the women liberation as she had come to know it—the Transcendentalist brew of enthusiasm for self and others and ideas. Thus, in all likelihood, neither Fuller nor her students would see irony in her way of describing their harmonious communication: "Our relation is now perfectly true, and I do not think they will ever interrupt me" (IV:11).

For the women the experience was plainly instructive as well as exhilarating. Whether in the final analysis it worked to liberate them or subtly to gild their cages depends on our perspective. From a short-range feminist point of view or a radical political one, we might agree with Harriet Martineau's strictures (IV:4) and find that this Yankee version of the salon both overindulged the women and mystified the real issues of their lives. If any records of her later Conversation series—especially those on women and education—had survived, we might gain an altogether different impression. But the existing records suggest that nothing Fuller said directly perjured True Womanhood; on the contrary, she clearly endorsed women's "special" capacity for love and morality. In her treatment of the fine arts, she also affirmed women's sense of duty, though, of course, in her own idiom. Describing self-knowledge, "the path of the true soul," as "enacted poesy," she pointed out that "the disturbing influence of other wills," which had "as much right to their own action as we to ours," prevented its complete attainment. As in her friendships, she urged living in terms of the ideal, but, if the record is faithful, she was more conservative about the possibility; the fine arts—"one compensation for the necessary prose of life"—should console women for life's limitations. Not only did Fuller soft-pedal open emancipation, but she preferred—at least at first—to discuss topics "quite separated from all exciting local subjects." [4] She consciously avoided controversial social questions and refused outright to discuss abolition (IV:12). Contrasted with Angelina Grimké's speaking tour, which culminated in 1838 with an antislavery appeal before the Massachusetts State Legislature, Fuller's "parlatorio," as Emerson styled it, was mild amusement indeed.

But if we take a liberal or a long-range feminist view, Martineau's criticism seems to miss the point. Fuller's very premise that women should nurture their serious responses to each other as well as their obligations to family and society was trail-blazing. The "vindication of woman's right to think" which Elizabeth Cady Stanton later found in the Conversations, [5] was subtly subversive; for thinking women the precincts of love stretched beyond the hearth and morality was reinformed with free choice and personal responsibility. Even in her treatment of Greek mythology, Fuller taught by analogy the importance of free will, the enlightened mind, and moral awakening. [6]

In Fuller's own development the Conversations played a similarly ambiguous role. While their content delayed her acquisition of sophisticated political attitudes and understanding, their form initiated a break from the Transcenden-

talists. For the form of the Conversations was her own invention, it satisfied some of her special needs, and it gave her
clearer authority than her previous activities had done and a
foretaste of social involvement. At first, Fuller expected little
for herself from the experience. After the first weeks, she
reported that, while she was relieved not to have had the
feeling she dreaded "of display, of a paid Corinne," she was
"never driven home for ammunition, never put to any expense, never truly called out." As the women in the group
could not challenge her intellectually, the relation between
them and Fuller must have been marked more by gratitude
and generosity than by mutuality or solidarity. After her last
Conversation, Fuller virtually confessed to her diary that
such altruism—however flattering its reception—could not satisfy her: "It was the last time, and they were pleasant. They
love me and fancy I am good and wise. Oh that it gave me
more pleasure to do *a little* good, and give *a little* happiness.
But there is no modesty or moderation in me." [7]

The letter she wrote to Elizabeth Hoar after the same
meeting was much more positive, however: "How noble has
been my experience of such relations now for six years, and
with so many and so various minds! Life is worth living, is it
not?" And there are indications that Fuller began to draw on
more of her resources for this group than elsewhere. For
Elizabeth Peabody, who had seen Fuller perform also at the
Transcendental Club, wrote, in refutation of the general
axiom that men best draw out women, "Certain it is that
Margaret never appears, when I see her, either so brilliant and
deep in thought, or so desirous to please, or so
heart-touching, as in this very party." [8]

Peabody's observation was made after the first
Conversation in the second winter, which took place
November 5, 1840, less than two weeks after Emerson
begged off from their tormented debate on friendship. The
juxtaposition of Fuller's failure with Emerson and her success
with the women is dramatically revealing. The point is not
that Emerson was cold and the women warm, though this is
true. The point is rather that what she had asked of Emerson,
comprehension and acceptance of all her faculties, was
inappropriate and necessarily obscure; driving her demand

were the masked urges to power and submission. With the women she was simply making use of her diverse energies—intellectual and erotic, poetic and moral. She was engaged in an activity in which her enthusiastic emotionality was fused with disciplined thought. Triggered as it was by her intimate experience of unused and directionless energy, her sympathetic work with the women began to show her the way to wholeness, the free exercise of her power. She would become whole and power would become real in her intelligent and committed action for those who lacked it.

At the same time, her experience in the Conversations led her to esteem women more. In February 1841, she dashed off an angry note to Channing in which pride in her sex was still outweighed by resentment of man's power. "I wish I were a man, and then there would be *one*," she flashed. "There are women much less unworthy to live than you, Men; the best are so unripe, the wisest so ignoble, the truest so cold!" [9]

By 1843, however, in a long essay for the July issue of *The Dial*, her ideas had ripened to the point where she could argue that to restrain women's self-development was to inhibit that of the whole human race. This essay, "The Great Lawsuit: Man versus Men: Woman versus Women," was her most Transcendentalist work, applying that system to herself and her sex, and it was also a summary of the views she held in New England on self and society. A year later she expanded the essay into the book *Woman in the Nineteenth Century*, which represented two sorts of advances in her development: a quickened sense of independence and of psychological integrity and a new attention to the claims of society and politics. Her experiences between the writing of essay and book greatly influenced these changes. At the time the essay was published, she was traveling in the Great Lakes region, a venture which did much to wean her from dependence on the thought of New England. The trip also had the long-overdue effect of moving Margaret Fuller permanently into the larger world, as her book *Summer on the Lakes in 1843* prompted Horace Greeley to offer her a job with the *New York Tribune*. In autumn 1844, before undertaking her new job, she gave herself a holiday with

Caroline Sturgis, her favorite companion for New England fortnights, in handsome Fishkill, on the Hudson not far from New York. There she expanded the *Dial* essay, which Greeley had agreed to publish as a book.

Although her old enemies, loneliness and migraine, the "great vulture" with "iron talons," tormented her as she wrote, she saw them clearly now as the price paid for independence as a woman and for the fusion of qualities she was effecting at last. "I think the black jailer laughs now, hoping that while I want to show that Woman can have the free, full action of intellect, he will prove in my own self that she has not physical force to bear it," she wrote in her journal. Autonomy becomes the weapon by which she might prevail.

> I have no fetters, and when one perceives how others are bound in false relations, this surely should be regarded as a privilege. And so varied have been my sympathies, that this isolation will not, I trust, make me cold, ignorant, nor partial. My history presents much superficial, temporary tragedy. The Woman in me kneels and weeps in tender rapture; the Man in me rushes forth, but only to be baffled. Yet the time will come, when, from the union of this tragic king and queen, shall be born a radiant sovereign self.

Action from feeling should heal the breach and prevent tears or bafflement. [10]

The experience of revising *Woman in the Nineteenth Century* approximated such ideal action. Fuller knew well that with this work she was repudiating an earlier otherworldly and ultra "feminine" dream of action and choosing one bound up with mundane circumstance, a relatively "virile" form, perhaps, except that she embraced it as a woman and on woman's behalf. "Formerly," she wrote at this time, "the pen did not seem to me an instrument capable of expressing the spirit of a life like mine." The alternatives she had sought belong to the myth of Fuller as sibyl or Corinne, of Fuller at her most breathless in the Conversations:

An enchanter's mirror, on which, with a word, could be made to rise all apparitions of the universe, grouped in new relations; a magic ring, that could transport the wearer, himself invisible, into each region of grandeur or beauty; a divining-rod, to tell where lie the secret fountains of refreshment; a wand, to invoke elemental spirits—only such as these seemed fit to embody one's thoughts with sufficient swiftness and force. In earlier years I aspired to wield the sceptre or the lyre; for I loved with wise design and irresistible command to mould many to one purpose, and it seemed all that man could desire to breathe in music and speak in words, the harmonies of the universe.

Resolutely and without regret, she breaks the spell: "But the golden lyre was not given to my hand. . . . Let me use, then, the slow pen." The tone, even the rhythm, of her intentions changes dramatically. "I will make no formal vow to the long-scorned Muse. . . . but I will court excellence, so far as an humble heart and open eye can merit it, and, if I may gradually grow to some degree of worthiness in this mode of expression, I shall be grateful." Though the humility may have been in some measure a pose too, the commitment to a new métier was not, and Fuller kept this vow to herself the rest of her life. Her pen, of course, was never slow, and she wrote to Channing in mid-November, "I have finished the pamphlet, though the last day it kept spinning out beneath my hand. . . . I felt a delightful glow, as if I had put a good deal of my true life in it, and as if, should I go away now, the measure of my foot-print would be left on the earth." [11]
Fuller's feeling of psychic wholeness is reflected in her treatment in this book of the vexed question whether female nature is distinct from male. As always, she left it open, but now from intuitive fidelity to freedom and an unwillingness to be restrictive, not from tormented indecision. [12] On the one hand, she concurs with the cultural conviction that woman's nature was distinct—or, in her own idiom, "electrical in movement, intuitive in function, spiritual in tendency"—that it is "more native to inspire and receive the poem, than it is to create it." But she insists, on

the other hand, that this female essence never appears unmixed: "two sides of the great radical dualism," male and female, "are perpetually passing into one another," and "there is no wholly masculine man, no purely feminine woman." Moreover, distinguishing "Muse," the woman in whom the "feminine" qualities preponderate, from "Minerva," in whom the "masculine" prevails, Fuller argues that in the present state of society, Minerva should be encouraged more than Muse (IV:13).

The eloquent portrait of Fuller's "friend" Miranda in this work triumphantly mirrors Fuller's Minerva. This is also an idealized self-portrait which contrasts sharply with that in the 1840 autobiographical fragment (I:5). Timothy's training, earlier characterized as his "one great mistake," is now seen as stemming not from a "sentimental reverence for Woman but a firm belief in the equality of the sexes." Where previously she argued that he trained her as a boy at the expense of her girlhood, now she sees that he addressed her "as a living mind," not a plaything. Where the effect earlier was a life "devoured in the bud," now it is ability to take "her place easily, not only in the world of organized being, but in the world of mind. A dignified sense of self-dependence was given as all her portion, and she found it a sure anchor." No doubt both the ease and unity of youth projected in this version and the difficulty and division in the 1840 account are polemical strategies dictated by perceptions available to her at different times. But why, after three years, do pride and courage supplant despair in her memory of her extraordinary youth? Surely the intervening experience of wholeness in conducting the Conversations goes far to explain the change. And again the act of engaging all her thought and feeling in writing the book represented a healing of the breach.

The structure of the Conversations—women seeking by themselves to find and develop their own powers—also informs the fervent and reiterated theme of independence in the book. By "independence" she means a combination of the Transcendentalist virtue of self-reliance and the activist one of "self-impulse." She means that, believing woman made for man, man disqualifies himself from representing woman, and that, until she represents herself, woman is "only an overgrown child." She means that celibacy and solidarity among women are honorable and essential.

In its attitudes toward society—the effects society has on women, the role women should take in society—the argument of *Woman in the Nineteenth Century* is a curiously hybrid affair. Here, calls for various social reforms and even for militant action sound through the old music of pure Transcendentalist asocial individualism. This dissonance comes partly from Fuller's perennial uneasiness with pure Transcendentalism and partly from the growing social concern which was drawing her to New York. Thus she begins by applying to women the Transcendentalist tenet that "the highest ideal Man can form of his own powers is that which he is destined to attain." In this phase of her thought, "What Woman needs is not as a woman to act or rule, but as a nature to grow, as an intellect to discern, as a soul to live freely and unimpeded, to unfold such powers as were given her when we left our common home." But grafted onto this lofty philosophizing is the homely democratic faith of the Declaration of Independence: "All men are born free and equal." The latter notion leads her to praise the abolitionist movement she had chosen to ignore in her Conversations and to admire its activists, Angelina Grimké and Abby Kelley. In her revision she also calls upon women to respond en masse to the threatened annexation of Texas; and she heralds public speaking and petition carrying by women, widely censored as immodest and offensive, as the exercise of "moral power" men have abjured. Fuller allows that she adopts contradictory systems of analysis of the cause and cure of human ill, veering from the internal and individual to the social and institutional and back. But she believes at this stage that neither system alone is adequate; we should blend the wisdom of Fourier, the critic of society, with that of Goethe, the critic of the soul.

Such eclecticism frees her to write with flexibility and with a candor remarkable for the time on marriage and, in the revision, on sexuality and prostitution. Marriage, in her view, is honorable in linking individuals who cherish mutual freedom, but is debased by possessiveness and the motive of security. It becomes odious when used as a standard by which to cast out the brilliant George Sand or Mary Wollstonecraft, whose very gifts may make conventional liaisons unacceptable. She does not openly argue for women's sexual needs, but the claim for equality in passion begins to emerge from her high-minded appeal for equality in purity, purity that is a proud choice, not a matter of restraint or ignorance. On the forbidden topic of prostitution, she urges her middle-class readers to think about how their own idleness and vain love of display pressure poor women into desperate competition.

In the context of feminist thought, *Woman* presented a broader but much less single-minded attack on the question of woman than its chief predecessors had done. Mary Wollstonecraft, for example, steeped in the republican and rationalist thought of the Enlightenment and fired by the revolutionary atmosphere of fifty years earlier, had called for full equality in a consistent, rationalist fashion. Fuller's comparatively romantic and unsystematic treatment represented an advance past Wollstonecraft's *Vindication of the Rights of Woman* chiefly in its insistence that woman must take responsibility for her own liberation.

In America, Catharine Beecher and the Grimké sisters, like Wollstonecraft, had very recently written out of a political urgency which Fuller was only beginning to feel. But the political difference between the Grimkés and Beecher was polar. Stirred by an abhorrence of slavery and a partial identification with the slaves, the Grimké sisters freed and fulfilled themselves by moving from their slaveholding family, through a strong religious commitment, to the abolitionist movement. The censure of these women for speaking in the 1830s provided a major impetus to the women's-rights movement, and the sisters dedicated their lives to fighting the double oppression. Enemies of the clergy and the vested interests of the nation, the Grimkés argued for absolute equality and were the first so clearly to give the lie to Tocqueville's fancy of the woman whose mature freedom lies in self-repression.

By contrast, Catharine Beecher explicitly endorsed and even extended Tocqueville's reasoning. For her the emergency was the nation's imminent dissolution—the consequence of expansion, heightening competition, and growing sectional conflict—witnessed daily in the microcosm of the family. Only hierarchy, a firmly differentiated character in women, and the discipline of deference, could save the day; for such willed submission was the mark of superior moral sensibility whose influence, if genuinely and uniformly based in the home, would, according to Beecher, spread irresistibly beyond it to the nation at large. (Fuller's drives toward power and dependency in her relation to Emerson would, in Beecher's terms, be sanctioned by marriage and made grandiose by patriotism.) The nature of a woman who saved America was radically different from the nature of one who liberated herself and slaves. As conservatism bound Beecher to sexual stereotypes, political radicalism freed the Grimkés from them. Thus while Sarah Grimké argued in *Letters on the Equality of the Sexes* that only "the forgetfulness of sex" will enable us to fulfill the Creator's design, Catharine Beecher insisted that only women's cultivation of a character "refined in intellect . . . benevolent in feeling . . . unassuming and unambitious, 'gentle and easy to be entreated' " would work to influence men, and through them, the nation. [13]

While I can find no concrete evidence that Fuller had yet read the work of either the Grimkés or Beecher, [14] she echoes at moments the thought of both. Beneath her glamorous veil, Muse is simply the wife in Catharine Beecher's vision, and insofar as Fuller assumes sexual difference and awards superiority to women, she is bound to that conservative tradition. But Minerva and the Miranda portrait are granted greater vividness than Muse. And Fuller has acid scorn for those who feel woman must be sheltered in the inner circle: "Those who think the physical circumstances of Woman would make a part in the affairs of national government unsuitable, are by no means those who think it impossible for negresses to endure field-work, even during pregnancy, or for sempstresses to go through their killing labors." At such moments, and with the calls to action, Fuller moves for the first time toward the Grimkés' radicalism, though she appears not yet aware of its cost.

Transcendentalist idealism separates her from both traditions, and is at once radical in its independence and heroic iconoclasm and conservative in its obliviousness to social conditions.

Fuller's combination of commitment to women and lack of systematic analysis made her book widely influential at the same time that it failed to contribute markedly to any school of thought. Men friendly to Fuller, especially Theodore Parker, W. H. Channing, and James Clarke, and students of the Conversations, especially Caroline Healey Dall, Elizabeth Peabody, and Ednah Dow Cheney, all gave the feminist movement active support; Cheney noted that after her death women's clubs named for Fuller sprang up all over the West. In 1848, the drafters of the Seneca Falls Declaration of Sentiments may have taken their cue from Fuller's use of the Declaration of Independence; certainly they systematically bodied forth most of Fuller's points. In 1852, Sarah Grimké urged the first Women's Rights Convention in Pennsylvania to adopt as their watchword Fuller's prayer, "Give me truth; cheat me by no illusion." And Paulina Wright Davis, at the Worcester Convention in 1850, lamented her death at the moment when so many were hoping this "leader of thought" would come home to lead the movement. [15]

It is unlikely that Fuller would have taken such a public role. Active feminism had worked to clarify for her the ways in which pure Transcendentalism was inadequate for her; it showed her that there were vocations which drew on all her qualities and initiated her career of activist journalism; it was leading her into fuller engagements with the world. She never lost her feminist perspective, but it triggered a process of political analysis and action which carried her beyond struggle for women alone. She never ceased caring for women, but the distancing, altruistic mode disappeared. At the same time, in her own life she at last recognized and claimed the freedom she needed for herself. In a sense, only by ceasing to be a leader of women could Margaret Fuller become—for those women who could *see* the meaning of her life in its last years—a model.

Notes

1. "Transcendentalism in New England, A Lecture delivered before the Society for Philosophical Enquiry" (Boston: Roberts Bros., 1897) p. 6. Ednah Dow Cheney had made a very similar point in a lecture on Fuller given at the Congress of American Advancement of Women in New Orleans, in November 1895.

2. *Memoirs*, II, 324-29; Mason Wade, *Margaret Fuller: Whetstone of Genius* (New York: The Viking Press, 1940), p. 81; Although Oberlin had begun in 1833 to offer women a college education and Mount Holyoke opened in 1837, very few women and apparently none in Fuller's acquaintance availed themselves of these controversial opportunities. And Elizabeth Peabody's "Historical School" for women seemed to have lacked Fuller's inspiring emphasis on self-development.

3. *Memoirs*, I, 329-30.

4. *Memoirs*, I, 341, 329.

5. *History of Woman Suffrage*, eds. Elizabeth Cady Stanton, Susan B. Anthony, and Matilda Joslyn Gage, (1881; rpt. New York: Arno and *The New York Times*, I, 1969), 801.

6. I am indebted to Barbara Welter for this last observation.

7. *Memoirs*, I, 332; Higginson, p. 303. A curious fact, which may support my notion of the group's incomplete solidarity, is that both women who kept the most extensive records known of the Conversations—Elizabeth Peabody and Caroline Healey Dall—believed that Fuller did not like them (see II:30 and Houghton MS).

8. *Memoirs*, I, 351, 340.

9. Higginson, p. 112.

10. *Memoirs*, II, 135, 136.

11. *Memoirs*, II, 138; Higginson, p. 201.

12. For many readers, including George Eliot, this was wisdom: "Some of the best things she says are on the folly of absolute definitions of woman's nature and absolute demarcations of woman's mission" ("Margaret Fuller and Mary Wollstonecraft," *Leader*, VI (1855), 988-89; rpt. in *Essays of George Eliot*, ed. Thomas Pinney [New York: Columbia University Press, 1963], p. 203).

13. *Letters on the Equality of the Sexes, and the Condition of Woman*, quoted in *The Roots of American Feminist Thought*, eds. James L. and Sheila M. Cooper (Boston: Allyn and Bacon, 1973), p. 71 *Essay on Slavery and Abolitionism with Reference to the Duty of American Females* (1843), quoted by Kathryn Kish Sklar, *Catharine Beecher: A Study in American Domesticity* (new Haven: Yale University Press, 1973), p. 136.

14. For the *Tribune* of October 30, 1845, Fuller reviewed Catharine Beecher's *Duty of American Women to Their Country*; she was interested particularly in Beecher's projected training of teachers.

15. *Reminiscences of Ednah Dow Cheney* (Boston: Lee & Shepard, 1902,) p. 193; *History of Woman Suffrage*, I, 355, 217.

CONTEMPORARIES ON FULLER

1. Her eighth Conversation
[December 1839]

This letter from an unidentified woman who visited Fuller's eighth Conversation in December 1839 conveys the atmosphere of festivity and solemnity, seriousness and childlike spontaneity that emerges from many accounts. Whether Fuller actually dressed elegantly for the Conversations, as this writer suggests, or whether this was "simply an effect of a general impression of magnificence made by her genius," as Emerson insisted, has been much debated. Here Fuller's appearance is taken as part of the general celebration and mutual desire to give pleasure.

Christmas made a holiday for Miss Fuller's class, but it met on Saturday, at noon. As I sat there, my heart overflowed with joy at the sight of the bright circle, and I longed to have you by my side, for I know not where to look for so much character, culture, and so much love of truth and beauty, in any other circle of women and girls. The names and faces would not mean so much to you as to me, who have seen more of the lives, of which they are the sign. Margaret, beautifully dressed, (don't despise that, for it made a fine picture,) presided with more dignity and grace than I had thought possible. The subject was Beauty. Each had written her definition, and Margaret began with reading her own. This called forth questions, comments, and illustrations, on all sides. The style and manner, of course, in this age, are different, but the question, the high point from which it was considered, and the earnestness and simplicity of the discussion, as well as the gifts and graces of the speakers, gave it the charm of a Platonic dialogue. There was no pretension or pedantry in a word that was said. The tone of remark and question was simple as that of children in a school class; and, I believe, every one was gratified. *[Memoirs, I, 332-33]*

2. Record of Conversation on March 22, 1841, Elizabeth Peabody

Elizabeth Peabody's notes on the Conversations from the second winter preserve something of the tone and method of these gatherings and show the depth of Fuller's immersion at this time in Transcendentalist philosophy. The participants at the March 22 meeting were probably Anna Shaw, Caroline Sturgis, Elizabeth Peabody, Lidian Emerson, Almira Barlow, and Ellen Hooper.

The question of the day was, What is life?

Let us define, each in turn, our idea of living. Margaret did not believe we had, any of us, a distinct idea of life.

A. S. thought so great a question ought to be given for a written definition. "No," said Margaret, "that is of no use. When we go away to think of anything, we never do think. We all talk of life. We all have some thought now. Let us tell it. C———, what is life?"

C——— replied, – "It is to laugh, or cry, according to our organization."

"Good," said Margaret, "but not grave enough. Come, what is life? I know what I think; I want you to find out what you think."

Miss P. replied, – "Life is division from one's principle of life in order to a conscious reorganization. We are cut up by time and circumstance, in order to feel our reproduction of the eternal law."

Mrs. E., – "We live by the will of God, and the object of life is to submit," and went on into Calvinism.

Then came up all the antagonisms of Fate and Freedom.

Mrs. H. said, – "God created us in order to have a perfect sympathy from us as free beings."

Mrs. A. B. said she thought the object of life was to attain absolute freedom. At this Margaret immediately and visibly kindled.

C. S. said, – "God creates from the fulness of life, and cannot but create; he created us to overflow, without being exhausted, because what he created, necessitated new creation. It is not to make us happy, but creation is his happiness and ours."

Margaret was then pressed to say what she considered life to be.

Her answer was so full, clear, and concise, at once, that it cannot but be marred by being drawn through the scattering medium of my memory. But here are some fragments of her satisfying statement.

She began with God as Spirit, Life, so full as to create and love eternally, yet capable of pause. Love and creativeness are dynamic forces, out of which we, individually, as creatures, go forth bearing his image, that is, having within our being the same dynamic forces, by which we also add constantly to the total sum of existence, and shaking off ignorance, and its effects, and by becoming more ourselves, *i e.*, more divine; — destroying sin in its principle, we attain to absolute freedom, we return to God, conscious like himself, and, as his friends, giving, as well as receiving, felicity forevermore. In short, we become gods, and able to give the life which we now feel ourselves able to receive.

On Saturday morning, Mrs. L. E. and Mrs. E. H. were present, and begged Margaret to repeat the statement concerning life, with which she closed the last conversation. Margaret said she had forgotten every word she said. She must have been inspired by a good genius, to have so satisfied everybody, — but the good genius had left her. She would try, however, to say what she thought, and trusted it would resemble what she had said already. She then went into the matter, and, true enough, she did not use a single word she used before. *[Memoirs, I, 345-47]*

3. Conversations for men and women,
Elizabeth Peabody [April 1841]

The women attending the Conversations prevailed upon Fuller to invite men to an additional series of Conversations on Greek mythology in March and April 1841. Though she hoped their superior education would enrich the discussion and "prevent the wandering and keep us from prejudice," it seems to have been the least successful of her series. In the stark record she kept at nineteen, Caroline Healey described a quarrel about the necessity of sin for the salvation of human beings. Emerson argued that man should never recognize evil and that "Good was always present to the soul;—and was all the true soul took note of. It was a duty not to look!" According to Healey, Fuller countered that "she believed evil to be a good in the grand scheme of things. . . . In one word, she would not accept the world—for she felt within herself the power to reject it—did she not believe evil working in it for good! Man had gained more than he lost by his fall." Emerson's stiff last word in this account was "that to imagine it possible to fall was to *begin* to fall" (Healey, *Margaret and Her Friends*, pp. 113-18). In her summary of the series and of that debate, Elizabeth Peabody discerns some of the basic differences which led Fuller from Emersonian thought to a more active and political viewpoint.

Margaret's plan, in these conversations, was a very noble one, and, had it been seconded, as she expected, they would have been splendid. She thought, that, by admitting gentlemen, who had access, by their classical education, to the whole historical part of the mythology, her own comparative deficiency, as she felt it, in this part of learning, would be made up; and that taking her stand on the works of art, which were the final development in Greece of these multifarious fables, the whole subject might be swept from zenith to nadir. But all that depended on others entirely failed. Mr. W. contributed some isolated facts, — told the etymology of names, and cited a few fables not so commonly known as most; but, even in the point of erudition, which Margaret did not profess, on the subject, she proved the best informed of the party, while no one brought an idea, except herself.

Her general idea was, that, upon the Earth-worship and Sabaeanism of earlier ages, the Grecian genius acted to humanize and idealize, but, still, with some regard to the original principle. What was a seed, or a root, merely, in the Egyptian mind, became a flower in Greece, — Isis, and Osiris, for instance, are reproduced in Ceres and Proserpine, with some loss of generality, but with great gain of beauty; Hermes, in Mercury, with only more grace of form, though with great loss of grandeur; but the loss of grandeur was also an advance in philosophy, in this instance, the brain in the hand being the natural consequence of the application of Idea to practice, — the Hermes of the Egyptians.

I do not feel that the class, by their apprehension of Margaret, do any justice to the scope and depth of her views. They come, — myself among the number, — I confess, — to be entertained; but she has a higher purpose. She, amid all her infirmities, studies and thinks with the seriousness of one upon oath, and there has not been a single conversation this winter, in either class, that had not in it the spirit which giveth life. Just in proportion to the importance of the subject, does she tax her mind, and say what is most important; while, of necessity, nothing is reported from the conversations but her brilliant sallies, her occasional paradoxes of form, and, sometimes, her impatient reacting upon dulness and frivolity. In particular points, I know, some excel her; in particular departments I sympathize more with some other persons; but, take her as a whole, she has the most to bestow on others by conversation of any person I have ever known. I cannot conceive of any species of vanity living in her presence. She distances all who talk with her.

Mr. E. only served to display her powers. With his sturdy reiteration of his uncompromising idealism, his absolute denial of the fact of human nature, he gave her opportunity and excitement to unfold and illustrate her realism and acceptance of conditions. What is so noble is, that her realism is transparent with idea. – her human nature is the germ of a divine life. She proceeds in her search after the unity of things, the divine harmony, not by exclusion, as Mr. E. does, but by comprehension, –,and so, no poorest, saddest spirit, but she will lead to hope and faith. *[Memoirs, I, 348-50]*

4. *"Gorgeous Pedants," Harriet Martineau [1877]*

Though Martineau never attended Fuller's Conversations, she probably influenced the way they are remembered more than anyone who did. The vehemence of this criticism, from *Harriet Martineau's Autobiography*, of Fuller's life during the period of the Conversations was doubtless prompted by Fuller's devasting remarks on *Society in America*, which had been published in the *Memoirs* (II: 19). (Martineau wrote in her diary in November 1839, "I suffered a great deal from her letter," though she also found its spirit "very noble" [*Harriet Martineau's Autobiography*, ed. Maria Weston Chapman, II, 319].) Preoccupied with Fuller's esoteric themes and her reputedly opulent dress, Martineau found no social purpose served by the Conversations. The two groups of "elect"–abolitionists and Conversationalists–actually had largely overlapping membership, but Martineau's charge that Fuller willfully neglected abolition is certainly justified.

. . . The difference between us was that while she was living and moving in an ideal world, talking in private and discoursing in public about the most fanciful and shallow conceits which the transcendentalists of Boston took for philosophy, she looked down upon persons who acted instead of talking finely, and devoted their fortunes, their peace, their repose, and their very lives to the preservation of the principles of the republic. While Margaret Fuller and her adult pupils sat "gorgeously dressed," talking about Mars and Venus, Plato and Göthe, and fancying themselves the elect of the earth in intellect and refinement, the liberties of the republic were running out as fast as they could go, at a breach which another sort of elect persons were devoting themselves to repair: and my complaint against the "gorgeous" pedants was that they regarded their preservers as hewers of wood and drawers of water, and their work as a less vital one than the pedantic orations which were spoiling a set of well-meaning women in a pitiable way. All that is settled now. It was over years before Margaret died. I mention it now to show, by an example already made public by Margaret herself, what the difference was between me and her, and those who followed her lead. This difference grew up mainly after my return from America. We were there intimate friends; and I am disposed to consider that period the best of her life, except the short one which intervened between her finding her real self and her death. She told me what danger she had been in from the training her father had given her, and the encouragement to pedantry and rudeness which she derived from the circumstances of her youth. She told me that she was at nineteen the most intolerable girl that ever took a seat in a drawing-room. Her admirable candour, the philosophical way in which she took herself in hand, her genuine heart, her practical insight, and, no doubt, the natural influence of her attachment to myself, endeared her to me, while her powers, and her confidence in the use of them, led me to expect great things from her. . . .

How it might have been with her if she had come to Europe in 1836, I have often speculated. As it was, her life in Boston was little short of destructive. I need but refer to the memoir of her. In the most pedantic age of society in her own country, and in its most pedantic city, she who was just beginning to rise out of pedantic habits of thought and speech relapsed most grievously. She was not only completely spoiled in conversation and manners: she made false estimates of the objects and interests of human life. She was not content with pursuing, and inducing others to pursue, a metaphysical idealism destructive of all genuine feeling and sound activity: she mocked at objects and efforts of a higher order than her own, and despised those

who, like myself, could not adopt her scale of valuation. All this might
have been spared, a world of mischief saved, and a world of good
effected, if she had found her heart a dozen years sooner, and in America instead of Italy. It is the most grievous loss I have almost ever
known in private history – the deferring of Margaret Fuller's married
life so long. [*Harriet Martineau's Autobiography*, ed. *Maria Weston
Chapman (Boston: James R. Osgood & Co., 1877), II, 381-83*]

5. Her influence on young women,
Ednah Dow Cheney [1902]

The career of Ednah Cheney (1824-1904) represents a partial
rebuttal of Martineau. She went on from the Conversations
to become involved in reforms ranging from "free religion"
to Freedman's Aid. After the Civil War her optimism and
idealism centered on women's rights; she played an active,
though moderate, role in the struggles for suffrage and education. In 1902, she wrote of Fuller: "To this day, I am astonished to find how large a part of 'what I am when I am most
myself' I have derived from her" (*Reminiscences*, p. 101).

I was eager enough for any intellectual advantage, but I had imbibed
with the unthinking eagerness of a schoolgirl the common prejudices
against Miss Fuller, and although I believed that I should
learn from her, I had no idea that I should esteem, and, much more,
love her. I found myself in a new world of thought; a flood of light
irradiated all that I had seen in nature, observed in life, or read in
books. Whatever she spoke of revealed a hidden meaning, and everything seemed to be put into true relation. Perhaps I could best express
it by saying that I was no longer the limitation of myself, but I felt that
whole wealth of the universe was open to me. It was this consciousness
of the illimitable ego, the divinity in the soul, which was so real to
Margaret herself, and what she meant in her great saying "I accept the
universe," which gave her that air of regal superiority which was mis-
interpreted as conceit.

Perhaps I can best give you an idea of what she was to me by an
answer which I made to her. One day when she was alone with me, and
I feel as if I could now feel her touch and hear her voice, she said, "Is
life rich to you?" and I replied, "It is since I have known you." Such

was the response of many a youthful heart to her, and herein was her wonderful influence. She did not make us her disciples, her blind followers. She opened the book of life to us and helped us to read it for ourselves. . . .

. . . The first mistake that the world has made in its effort to comprehend this large nature is in considering her, not as a typical woman, but as an exceptional one, whose powers were masculine, and who wielded some magic sword which she alone had strength to grasp. . . . With all the force of her intellect, all the strength of her will, all her self-denial and power of thought, she was essentially and thoroughly a woman, and she won her victories not by borrowing the peculiar weapons of man, but by using her own with courage and skill. [*Reminiscences of Ednah Dow Cheney* (Boston: Lee & Shepard, 1902), pp. 205, 193-94)]

6. "The Great Lawsuit," Sophia Peabody Hawthorne [July 1843]

The difference between the awe Sophia Hawthorne felt for Fuller's Conversations and the distaste she evinces below for Fuller's *Dial* essay, "The Great Lawsuit: Man versus Men; Woman versus Women," suggests that marriage had softened Sophia as feminism sharpened Fuller. The letter below was to Sophia's mother, whose earlier independence as a schoolmistress in Salem did not prevent her from finding Fuller's language in *Woman* "offensive to delicacy" (Julian Hawthorne, *Nathaniel Hawthorne and His Wife*, I, 258).

. . . What do you think of the speech which Queen Margaret Fuller has made from the throne? It seems to me that if she were married truly, she would no longer be puzzled about the rights of woman. This is the revelation of woman's true destiny and place, which never can be *imagined* by those who do not experience the relation. In perfect, high union there is no question of supremacy. Souls are equal in love and intelligent communion, and all things take their proper places as inevitably as the stars their orbits. Had there never been false and profane marriages, there would not only be no commotion about woman's rights, but it would be Heaven here at once. Even before I was married, however, I could never feel the slightest interest in this movement. It

then seemed to me that each woman could make her own sphere
quietly, and also it was always a shock to me to have women mount the
rostrum. Home, I think, is the great arena for women, and there, I am
sure, she can wield a power which no king or conqueror can cope with.
I do not believe any man who ever knew one noble woman would ever
speak as if she were an inferior in any sense: it is the fault of ignoble
women that there is any such opinion in the world. *[Julian Hawthorne,
Nathaniel Hawthorne and his Wife (Boston: James R. Osgood & Co.
1855), I, 257]*

7. Woman in the Nineteenth Century,
Edgar Allan Poe, August 1846

A reviewer of *Woman in the Nineteenth Century* protested in
the *Broadway Journal*: "Her most direct writing is on a
subject no virtuous woman can treat justly. No woman is a
true woman who is not wife and mother." Poe, later writing
an essay on Fuller for the same journal, disavowed his
colleague's remarks. In the passage below, Poe differs from
Cheney's later view (IV: 5) that Fuller was a representative
woman.

Woman in the Nineteenth Century is a book which few women in the
country could have written, and no woman in the country would have
published, with the exception of Miss Fuller. In the way of independence, of unmitigated radicalism, it is one of the "Curiosities of
American Literature," and Doctor Griswold should include it in his
book. I need scarcely say that the essay is nervous, forcible, thoughtful,
suggestive, brilliant, and to a certain extent scholarlike – for all that
Miss Fuller produces is entitled to these epithets – but I must say that
the conclusions reached are only in part my own. Not that they are too
bold, by any means – too novel, too startling, or too dangerous in their
consequences, but that in their attainment too many premises have
been distorted, and too many analogical inferences left altogether out
of sight. I mean to say that the intention of the Deity as regards sexual
differences – an intention which can be distinctly comprehended only
by throwing the exterior (more sensitive) portions of the mental retina
casually over the wide field of universal analogy – I mean to say that
this intention has not been sufficiently considered. Miss Fuller has

erred, too, through her own excessive subjectiveness. She judges woman by the heart and intellect of Miss Fuller, but there are not more than one or two dozen Miss Fullers on the whole face of the earth. *[Complete Works of Edgar Allan Poe (New York: G. P. Putnam's Sons, 1902), IX, 7-8]*

8. Woman in the Nineteenth Century, Caroline Sturgis, March 4, 1845

One indication of the degree of mutual respect between Fuller and her friends is the freedom with which some of them criticized her writing. Thus Lydia Maria Child wrote her on August 23, 1844, thanking her for *Summer in the Lakes*; "Shall I tell you what always, more or less, mars my pleasure? . . . The stream is abundant and beautiful; but it always seems to be *pumped*, rather than to *flow*. . . . your house is too full; there is too much furniture for your rooms. This is the result of a higher education than popular writers usually have; but it stands much in the way of extensive popularity (Houghton MS). And Caroline Sturgis criticized *Woman in the Nineteenth Century* in the letter below. Fuller responded on March 13, 1845, that she found her remarks "very true"; but she added that the need for the book was proved "by the ardent interest it excites in those who have never known me. Those, you know, are the persons to whom it is addressed, and they do feel their wounds probed, and healing promised by it. The opposition and the sympathy it excites are both great, and you will laugh to hear that it is placarded here as 'Great Book of the Age' " (Tappan Papers, Houghton).

Thank you for the pamphlet, dear Margaret. I have read it through but the style troubles me very much. I cannot free myself from a feeling of great consciousness in all you write. There is a recurrence of comparisons, illustrations, & words, which is not pleasing. There seems to be a want of vital powers as if you had gathered flowers and planted them in a garden but had left the roots in their own soil. It is full of suggestions like everything else in this age, but one living child is worth a whole series of tableaux. It is not a book to take to heart and that is what a book upon woman should be. It makes me sad that it is necessary such an one should be written but since it is so it cannot but do

good to lift the veil as you have done — how hard a thing to do! The
book is good for me in giving me a glimpse of many things, and I am
like a child peeping into a confectioner's store & wishing to go & taste
all the sugar swans and frosted cakes. . . . *[Houghton MS]*

9. *Woman in the Nineteenth Century.* John Neal, March 4, 1845

When Fuller invited John Neal (1793-1876) to address her
students in Providence on the destiny and vocation of
women, her feminist thought was greatly stimulated. A flamboyant intellectual from Maine, Neal was a teacher of drawing and fencing, an editor, a lawyer, a poet and historical
romancer famous for composition at breakneck speed, and an
ardent Benthamite polemicist. "I knew none who was so
truly a man," Fuller wrote; but he also made her uneasy: "I
should not like to have my motives scrutinized as he should
scrutinize them" (BPL MS). Though he wrote her from Port-
land that a quick skimming assured him that *Woman* was "a
most desirable companion for life," his utilitarian approach
made him essentially impatient with it.

My dear Miss Fuller

You go for thought — I for action. You find action in your path at
every step Instead of making faces at him and bullying him off the
field, you sit down by the wayside and begin magnetizing him. Now I
dont believe in anything upon earth of a tranquilizing nature, where
men and women are at stake — I go for the whip and spur — the lash of
the cartman's whip and bark of the sheperds [sic] dog: in other words I
go for making people get up and *take care of themselves.* Women are
fools — beyond all question. But who made them so? Their fathers-
husbands-brothers — and all the lawgivers and mighty of earth — per-
suading them to believe, the simpletons, while they are held in the most
degrading thraldom, as mere instruments of pleasure and show, that
they are *not* slaves in the worst sense of the term, & calling upon them
to teach what they have never been allowed to learn (politics and law
and history for example — or the definition of liberty, secondly the
Constitution of the U.S.) and to be satisfied with unqualified, hopeless

and perpetual dependence upon Man – ⟨encouraged⟩ to prattle about an identity of interests, which identity consists in mans *making* the law, *interpreting* the law, and *carrying* the law into ⟨execution⟩, without being questioned or impeded for one single moment by the efforts of *woman*. But enough – I tell you that there is no hope for woman, till she has a hand in making the law – no chance for her till her *vote* is worth as much as a mans vote. When it is – woman will not be fobbed off with sixpence a day for the very work a man would get a dollar for – making a shift to live, God knows how, to say nothing of shirts. But enough – we must have a talk together, if I am ever to persuade you into a right view of the subject. All you and others are doing to elevate woman, is only fitted to make her feel more sensibly the long abuse of her understanding, when she comes to her senses. You might as well educate slaves – and still keep them in bondage.*[Houghton MS]*

10. Her feminism, Horace Greeley [1852]

"Margaret's book is going to *sell*," exulted Horace Greeley (1811-1872) to a friend, "I tell you it has the real stuff in it" (Arthur W. Brown, *Margaret Fuller*, pp. 76-77). The sale in one week of a first edition of one thousand copies proved him right.

Mary Cheney Greeley, greatly impressed by Fuller during visits to Boston, had urged her husband to offer Fuller a job on the *New York Daily Tribune* and a room in their ramshackle mansion on the East River. He was at first a maladroit host. He scolded her for her addiction to strong tea and resolved to "escape the fascination which she seemed to exert over the eminent and cultivated persons, mainly women, who came to our out-of-the-way dwelling to visit her, and who seemed generally to regard her with a strangely Oriental adoration" (*Memoirs*, II, 156). His private view of the women's-rights struggle shows in the classic judgment he makes in *Recollections of a Busy Life* (p. 178): "Noble and great as she was, a good husband and two or three bouncing babies would have emancipated her from a good deal of cant and nonsense." Though they later became warm friends, in the early phase he noted with satisfaction the inconsistency in her feminism.

... One other point of tacit antagonism between us may as well be noted. Margaret was always a most earnest, devoted champion on the Emancipation of Women, from their past and present condition of inferiority, to an independence on Men. She demanded for them the fullest recognition of Social and Political Equality with the rougher sex; the freest access to all stations, professions, employments, which are open to any. To this demand I heartily acceded. It seemed to me, however, that her clear perceptions of abstract right were often overborne, in practice, by the influence of education and habit; that while she demanded absolute equality for Woman, she exacted a deference and courtesy from men to women, *as* women, which was entirely inconsistent with that requirement. In my view, the equalizing theory can be enforced only by ignoring the habitual discrimination of men and women, as forming separate *classes*, and regarding all alike as simply *persons*, – as human beings. So long as a lady shall deem herself in need of some gentleman's arm to conduct her properly out of a dining or ball-room, – so long as she shall consider it dangerous or unbecoming to walk half a mile alone by night, – I cannot see how the "Woman's Rights" theory is ever to be anything more than a logically defensible abstraction. In this view Margaret did not at all concur, and the diversity was the incitement to much perfectly good-natured, but nevertheless sharpish sparring between us. Whenever she said or did anything implying the usual demand of Woman on the courtesy and protection of Manhood, I was apt, before complying, to look her in the face and exclaim with marked emphasis, – quoting from her "Woman in the Nineteenth Century," – *"Let them be sea-captains if they will!"* Of course, this was given and received as raillery, but it did not tend to ripen our intimacy or quicken my esteem into admiration. ...
[*Memoirs*, II, 155-56]

FULLER'S WRITINGS

11. On first Conversation, second winter, November 8, 1840

Fuller wrote the letter below to W. H. Channing after the second winter of Conversations had just begun. The first meeting took place at the beginning of November 1840, just after Emerson had finally repelled her demand for anomalous friendship. In the *Memoirs*, Emerson blandly reports, "By all accounts it was the best of all her days"; characteristically, it was followed by great physical discomfort. (The initiais supplied below are taken from the copy Emerson made of the letter in his notebook.)

Sunday

On Wednesday I opened with my class. It was a noble meeting. I told them the great changes in my mind, and that I could not be sure they would be satisfied with me now, as they were when I was in deliberate possession of myself. I tried to convey the truth, and though I did not arrive at any full expression of it, they all, with glistening eyes, seemed melted into one love. Our relation is now perfectly true, and I do not think they will ever interrupt me. [A] sat beside me, all glowing; and the moment I had finished, she began to speak. She told me afterwards, she was all kindled, and none there could be strangers to her more. I was really delighted by the enthusiasm of Mrs. [F.] I did not expect it. All her best self seemed called up, and she feels that these meetings will be her highest pleasure. [E.H.] too, was most beautiful. I went home with Mrs. F., and had a long attack of nervous headache. She attended anxiously on me, and asked if it would be so all winter. I said, if it were I did not care; and truly I feel just now such a separation from pain and illness, — such a consciousness of true life, while suffering most, — that pain has no effect but to steal some of my time. *[Memoirs, I, 339-40]*

12. On abolition, to Maria Weston Chapman, December 26, 1840

In the 1830s, Maria Chapman (1806-1885), a talented and courageous woman, faced angry mobs as an abolitionist, edited Garrison's *Liberator*, satirized the clergy when they attacked the Grimké sisters, and became a close friend to Harriet Martineau, whose biography she later wrote. In December 1840, she wrote Fuller asking her to support the annual Anti-Slavery Fair and to devote a Conversation to abolition. During that year the woman question had twice been raised in the abolition movement. At its annual convention in May, the American Anti-Slavery Society had split over Garrison's persistent support of women's speaking in public and holding office in the Society. Then the refusal to seat women at the World's Convention of the anti-slavery forces in London aroused active indignation. Apparently, these events stirred Fuller's hopes that the causes of slave and of woman would be seriously joined. But, disappointed in a convention she attended—or using disappointment as an excuse—she retreated again from this still alien atmosphere, and wrote from Jamaica refusing Chapman.

My dear Mrs. Chapman,

I received your note but a short time before I went to the conversation party. There was no time for me to think what I should do or even ascertain the objects of the Fair. Had I known them I could not by any slight suggestion have conveyed my views of such movements. And a conversation on the subject would interrupt the course adopted by my class. I therefore merely requested Miss Peabody to show the papers and your note to me before I began on the subject before us.

The Abolition course commands my respect, as do all efforts to relieve and raise suffering human nature. The faults of the party are such that it seems to me must always be incident to the partizan spirit. All that was noble and pure in their zeal has helped us all. For disinterestedness and constancy of many individuals among you I have a high respect. Yet my own path leads a different course and often leaves me quite ignorant what you are doing as in the present instance of your Fair.

Very probably to one whose heart is so engaged as yours in particular measures this indifference will seem incredible or even culpable. But if indifferent I have not been intolerant: I have wronged none of you by a hasty judgement or careless words, and, when I have not investigated a case so as to be sure of my own opinion, have, at least, never chimed in with the popular hue and cry. I have always wished that efforts originating in a grievous sympathy, or a sense of right should have fair play; have had firm faith that they must, in some way, produce eventual good.

The late movements in your party have interested me more than those which had for their object the enfranchisement of the African only. Yet I presume I should still feel sympathy with your aims only not with your measures. Yet I should like to be more fully acquainted with both. The late convention I attended hoping to hear some clear account of your wishes as to religious institutions and the social position of woman. But not only I heard nothing that pleased me, but no clear statement from any one. Have you in print what you consider an able exposition of the views of yourself and friends? – Or if not, should you like yourself to give me an account of how these subjects stand in your mind? As far as I know you seem to me quite wrong as to what is to be done for woman! She needs new helps I think, but not such as you propose. But I should like to know your view and your grounds more clearly than I do.

> With respect
> S. M. Fuller *[BPL MS]*

13. *Woman in the Nineteenth Century [1845]*

When Fuller was writing her essay on women, she talked to Emerson, who noted in his journal: "The conversation turned upon the state & duties of Woman. As always, it was historically considered, & had a certain falseness so. For me, today, Woman is not a degraded person with duties forgotten, but a docile daughter of God with her face heavenward endeavoring to hear the divine word & to convey it to me" (*Journals and Miscellaneous Notebooks of Ralph Waldo Emerson*, eds. W. H. Gilman and J. E. Parsons, VII, 372). Notwithstanding the staggering failure of irony in the last phrase, the passage suggests how this work was a turning point for Fuller. She was rejecting a view that made women timeless and affirming the historical perspective Emerson found false. Especially in revising the essay, she helped women see themselves as defined by generations of tradition and present circumstances. She offered them a past against which to shape their future and achieve some measure of selfhood and power in the present.

In organization, *Woman in the Nineteenth Century* is rather loose and digressive, but the outline Fuller provides in the final several pages is a useful guide to her main argument. While trying to preserve the style, I have cut some of the more lengthy illustrations of her chief ideas.

Preface. The following essay is a reproduction, modified and expanded, of an article published in "The Dial, Boston, July, 1843," under the title of "The Great Lawsuit. – Man *versus* Men; Woman *versus* Women."

This article excited a good deal of sympathy, and still more interest. It is in compliance with wishes expressed from many quarters that it is prepared for publication in its present form.

Objections having been made to the former title, as not sufficiently easy to be understood, the present has been substituted as expressive of the main purpose of the essay; though, by myself, the other is preferred, partly for the reason others do not like it, – that is, that it requires some thought to see what it means, and might thus prepare the reader to meet me on my own ground. Besides, it offers a larger scope, and is, in that way, more just to my desire. I meant by that title to intimate the fact that, while it is the destiny of Man, in the course of the ages, to ascertain and fulfil the law of his being, so that his life shall be seen, as a whole, to be that of an angel or messenger, the action of prejudices and passions which attend, in the day, the growth of the individual, is continually obstructing the holy work that is to make the earth a part of heaven. By Man I mean both man and woman; these are the two halves of one thought. I lay no especial stress on the welfare of either. I believe that the development of the one cannot be effected without that of the other. My highest wish is that this truth should be distinctly and rationally apprehended, and the conditions of life and freedom recognized as the same for the daughters and the sons of time; twin exponents of a divine thought.

I solicit a sincere and patient attention from those who open the following pages at all. I solicit of women that they will lay it to heart to ascertain what is for them the liberty of law. It is for this, and not for any, the largest, extension of partial privileges that I seek. I ask them if interested by these suggestions, to search their own experience and intuitions for better, and fill up with fit materials the trenches that hedge them in. From men I ask a noble and earnest attention to anything that can be offered on this great and still obscure subject, such as I have met from many with whom I stand in private relations.

And may truth, unpolluted by prejudice, vanity or selfishness, be granted daily more and more as the due of inheritance, and only valuable conquest for us all!   *November, 1844.*

Woman in the Nineteenth Century.

> "Frailty, thy name is *Woman*."
> "The Earth waits for her Queen."

The connection between these quotations may not be obvious, but it is strict. Yet would any contradict us, if we made them applicable to the other side, and began also,

> "Frailty, thy name is *Man*."
> "The Earth waits for its King?"

Yet Man, if not yet fully installed in his powers, has given much earnest of his claims. Frail he is indeed, – how frail! how impure! Yet often has the vein of gold displayed itself amid the baser ores, and Man has appeared before us in princely promise worthy of his future.

If, oftentimes, we see the prodigal son feeding on the husks in the fair field no more his own, anon we raise the eyelids, heavy from bitter tears, to behold in him the radiant apparition of genius and love, demanding not less than the all of goodness, power and beauty. We see that in him the largest claim finds a due foundation. That claim is for no partial sway, no exclusive possession. He cannot be satisfied with any one gift of life, any one department of knowledge or telescopic peep at the heavens. He feels himself called to understand and aid Nature, that she may, through his intelligence, be raised and interpreted; to be a student of, and servant to, the universe-spirit; and king of his planet, that, as an angelic minister, he may bring it into conscious harmony with the law of that spirit.

In clear, triumphant moments, many times, has rung through the spheres the prophecy of his jubilee; and those moments, though past in time, have been translated into eternity by thought; the bright signs they left hang in the heavens, as single stars or constellations, and, already, a thickly sown radiance consoles the wanderer in the darkest night. . . .

Such marks have been made by the footsteps of *man* (still, alas! to be spoken of as the *ideal* man), wherever he has passed through the wilderness of *men*, and whenever the pigmies stepped in one of those, they felt dilate within the breast somewhat that promised nobler stature and purer blood. They were impelled to forsake their evil ways of decrepit scepticism and covetousness of corruptible possessions. Convictions flowed in upon them. They, too, raised the cry: God is living, now, to-day; and all beings are brothers, for they are his children. Simple words enough, yet which only angelic natures can use or hear in their full, free sense.

These were the triumphant moments; but soon the lower nature took its turn, and the era of a truly human life was postponed.

Thus is man still a stranger to his inheritance, still a pleader, still a pilgrim. Yet his happiness is secure in the end. And now, no more a glimmering consciousness, but assurance begins to be felt and spoken, that the highest ideal Man can form of his own powers is that which he is destined to attain. Whatever the soul knows how to seek, it cannot fail to obtain. This is the Law and the Prophets. Knock and it shall be opened; seek and ye shall find. It is demonstrated; it is a maxim. Man no longer paints his proper nature in some form, and says, "Prometheus had it; it is God-like;" but "Man must have it; it is human." However disputed by many, however ignorantly used, or falsified by those who do receive it, the fact of an universal, unceasing revelation has been too clearly stated in words to be lost sight of in thought; and sermons preached from the text, "Be ye perfect," are the only sermons of a pervasive and deep-searching influence. . . .

Yet, no doubt, a new manifestation is at hand, a new hour in the day of Man. We cannot expect to see any one sample of completed being, when the mass of men still lie engaged in the sod, or use the freedom of their limbs only with wolfish energy. The tree cannot come to flower till its root be free from the cankering worm, and its whole growth open to air and light. While any one is base, none can be entirely free and noble. Yet something new shall presently be shown of the life of man, for hearts crave, if minds do not know how to ask it. . . .

Meanwhile, not a few believe . . . that the idea of Man, however imperfectly brought out, has been far more so than that of Woman . . . that she, the other half of the same thought, the other chamber of the heart of life, needs now take her turn in the full pulsation, and that improvement in the daughters will best aid in the reformation of the sons of this age.

It should be remarked that, as the principle of liberty is better understood, and more nobly interpreted, a broader protest is made in behalf of Woman. As men become aware that few men have had a fair chance, they are inclined to say that no women have had a fair chance. The French Revolution, that strangely disguised angel, bore witness in favor of Woman, but interpreted her claims no less ignorantly than those of Man. Its idea of happiness did not rise beyond outward enjoyment, unobstructed by the tyranny of others. The title it gave was "citoyen," "citoyenne;" and it is not unimportant to Woman that even this species of equality was awarded her. Before, she could be condemned to perish on the scaffold for treason, not as a citizen, but as a subject. The right with which this title then invested a human being was that of bloodshed and license. The Goddess of Liberty was impure. As we read the poem addressed to her, not long since, by Beranger, we can scarcely refrain from tears as painful as the tears of blood that flowed when "such crimes were committed in her name." Yes! Man, born to purify and animate the unintelligent and the cold, can, in his madness, degrade and pollute no less the fair and the chaste. Yet truth was prophesied in the ravings of that hideous fever, caused by long ignorance and abuse. Europe is conning a valued lesson from the blood-stained page. The same tendencies, further unfolded, will bear good fruit in this country. . . . This country is as surely destined to elucidate a great moral law, as Europe was to promote the mental culture of Man.

Though the national independence be blurred by the servility of individuals; though freedom and equality have been proclaimed only to leave room for a monstrous display of slave-dealing and slave-keeping; though the free American so often feels himself free, like the Roman, only to pamper his appetites and his indolence through the misery of his fellow-beings; still it is not in vain that the verbal statement has been made, "All men are born free and equal." There it stands a golden certainty wherewith to encourage the good, to shame the bad. The New World may be called clearly to perceive that it incurs the utmost penalty if it reject or oppress the sorrowful brother. And, if men are deaf, the angels hear. But men cannot be deaf. It is inevitable that an external freedom, an independence of the encroachments of other men, such as has been achieved for the nation, should be so also for every member of it. That which has once been clearly conceived in the intelligence cannot fail, sooner or later, to be acted out. . . .

. . . We have waited here long in the dust; we are tired and hungry; but the triumphal procession must appear at last.

Of all its banners, none has been more steadily upheld, and under none have more valor and willingness for real sacrifices been shown, than that of the champions of the enslaved African. And this band it is, which, partly from a natural following out of principles, partly because many women have been prominent in that cause, makes, just now, the warmest appeal in behalf of Woman.

Though there has been a growing liberality on this subject, yet society at large is not so prepared for the demands of this party, but that its members are, and will be for some time, coldly regarded as the Jacobins of their day.

"Is it not enough," cries the irritated trader, "that you have done all you could to break up the national union, and thus destroy the prosperity of our country, but now you must be trying to break up family union, to take my wife away from the cradle and the kitchen-hearth to vote at polls, and preach from a pulpit? Of course, if she does such things, she cannot attend to those of her own sphere. She is happy enough as she is. She has more leisure than I have, – every means of improvement, every indulgence."

"Have you asked her whether she was satisfied with these *indulgences*?"

"No, but I know she is. She is too amiable to desire what would make me unhappy, and too judicious to wish to step beyond the sphere of her sex. I will never consent to have our peace disturbed by any such discussions."

" 'Consent – you?' it is not consent from you that is in question – it is assent from your wife."

"Am not I the head of my house?"

"You are not the head of your wife. God has given her a mind of her own."

"I am the head, and she the heart."

"God grant you play true to one another, then! I suppose I am to be grateful that you did not say she was only the hand. If the head represses no natural pulse of the heart, there can be no question as to your giving your consent. Both will be of one accord, and there needs but to present any question to get a full and true answer. There is no need of precaution, of indulgence, nor consent. But our doubt is whether the heart *does* consent with the head, or only obeys its decrees with a passiveness that precludes the exercise of its natural powers or a repugnance that turns sweet qualities to bitter, or a doubt that lays waste the fair occasions of life. It is to ascertain the truth that we propose some liberating measures." . . .

It may well be an Anti-Slavery party that pleads for Woman, if we consider merely that she does not hold property on equal terms with men; so that, if a husband dies without making a will, the wife, instead of taking at once his place as head of the family, inherits only a part of his fortune, often brought him by herself, as if she were a child, or ward only, not an equal partner.

We will not speak of the innumerable instances in which profligate and idle men live upon the earnings of industrious wives; or if the wives leave them, and take with them the children, to perform the double duty of mother and father, follow from place to place, and threaten to rob them of the children, if deprived of the rights of a husband, as they call them, planting themselves in their poor lodgings, frightening them into paying tribute by taking from them the children, running into debt at the expense of these otherwise so overtasked helots. . . . But I would not deal with "atrocious instances," except in the way of illustration, neither demand from men a partial redress in some one matter, but go to the root of the whole. If principles could be established, particulars would adjust themselves aright. Ascertain the true destiny of Woman; give her legitimate hopes, and a standard within herself; marriage and all other relations would by degrees be harmonized with these.

But to return to the historical progress of this matter. Knowing that there exists in the minds of men a tone of feeling toward women as toward slaves, such as is expressed in the common phrase, "Tell that to women and children;" that the infinite soul can only work through them in already ascertained limits; that the gift of reason, Man's highest prerogative, is allotted to them in much lower degree; that they must be kept from mischief and melancholy by being constantly engaged in active labor, which is to be furnished and directed by those better able to think, &c., &c., – we need not multiply instances, for who can review the experience of last week without recalling words which imply, whether in jest or earnest, these views, or views like these, – knowing this, can we wonder that many reformers think that measures are not likely to be taken in behalf of women, unless their wishes could be publicly represented by women?

"That can never be necessary," cry the other side. "All men are privately influenced by women; each has his wife, sister, or female friends, and is too much biased by these relations to fail of representing their interests; and, if this is not enough, let them propose and enforce their wishes with the pen. The beauty of home would be destroyed, the delicacy of the sex be violated, the dignity of halls of legislation degraded, by an attempt to introduce them there. Such duties are inconsistent with those of a mother;" and then we have ludicrous pictures of ladies in hysterics at the polls, and senate-chambers filled with cradles.

But if, in reply, we admit as truth that Woman seems destined by nature rather for the inner circle, we must add that the arrangements of civilized life have not been, as yet, such as to secure it to her. Her circle, if the duller, is not the quieter. If kept from "excitement," she is not from drudgery. Not only the Indian squaw carries the burdens of the camp, but the favorites of Louis XIV accompany him in his journeys, and the washerwoman stands at her tub, and carries home her work at all seasons, and in all states of health. Those who think the physical circumstances of Woman would make a part in the affairs of national government unsuitable, are by no means those who think it impossible for negresses to endure field-work, even during pregnancy, or for sempstresses to go through their killing labors.

As to the use of the pen, there was quite as much opposition to Woman's possessing herself of that help to free agency as there is now to her seizing on the rostrum or the desk; and she is likely to draw, from a permission to plead her cause that way, opposite inferences to what might be wished by those who now grant it.

As to the possibility of her filling with grace and dignity any such position, we should think those who had seen the great actresses, and heard the Quaker preachers of modern times, would not doubt that Woman can express publicly the fulness of thought and creation, without losing any of the peculiar beauty of her sex. What can pollute and tarnish is to act thus from any motive except that something needs to be said or done. Woman could take part in the processions, the songs, the dances of old religion; no one fancied her delicacy was impaired by appearing in public for such a cause.

As to her home, she is not likely to leave it more than she now does for balls, theatres, meetings for promoting missions, revival meetings, and others to which she flies, in hope of an animation for her existence commensurate with what she sees enjoyed by men. Governors of ladies'-fairs are no less engrossed by such a charge, than the governor of a state by his; presidents of Washingtonian societies no less away from home than presidents of conventions. If men look straitly to it, they will find that, unless their lives are domestic, those of the women will not be. A house is no home unless it contain food and fire for the mind as well as for the body. The female Greek, of our day, is as much in the street as the male to cry, "What news?" We doubt not it was the same in Athens of old. The women, shut out from the market-place, made up for it at the religious festivals. For human beings are not so constituted that they can live without expansion. If they do not get it in one way, they must in another, or perish.

As to men's representing women fairly at present, while we hear from men who owe to their wives not only all that is comfortable or graceful, but all that is wise, in the arrangement of their lives, the frequent remark, "You cannot reason with a woman," — when from those of delicacy, nobleness, and poetic culture, falls the contemptuous phrase "women and children," and that in no light sally of the hour, but in works intended to give a permanent statement of the best experiences, — when not one man, in the million, shall I say? no, not in the hundred million, can rise above the belief that Woman was made *for Man*, — when such traits as these are daily forced upon the attention, can we feel that Man will always do justice to the interests of Woman? Can we think that he takes a sufficiently discerning and religious view of her office and destiny *ever* to do her justice, except when prompted by sentiment, — accidentally or transiently, that is, for the sentiment will vary according to the relations in which he is placed? The lover, the poet, the artist, are likely to view her nobly. The father and the philosopher have some chance of liberality; the man of the world, the legislator for expediency, none.

Under these circumstances, without attaching importance, in themselves, to the changes demanded by the champions of Woman, we hail them as signs of the times. We would have every arbitrary barrier thrown down. We would have every path laid open to Woman as freely as to Man. Were this done, and a slight temporary fermentation allowed to subside, we should see crystallizations more pure and of more various beauty. We believe the divine energy would pervade nature to a degree unknown in the history of former ages, and that no discordant collision, but a ravishing harmony of the spheres, would ensue.

Yet, then and only then will mankind be ripe for this, when inward and outward freedom for Woman as much as for Man shall be acknowledged as a *right*, not yielded as a concession. As the friend of the negro assumes that one man cannot by right hold another in bondage, so should the friend of Woman assume that Man cannot by right lay even well-meant restrictions on Woman. If the negro be a soul, if the woman be a soul, apparelled in flesh, to one Master only are they accountable. There is but one law for souls, and, if there is to be an interpreter of it, he must come not as man, or son of man, but as son of God.

Were thought and feeling once so far elevated that Man should esteem himself the brother and friend, but nowise the lord and tutor, of Woman, — were he really bound with her in equal worship, — arrangements as to function and employment would be of no consequence. What Woman needs is not as a woman to act or rule, but as a nature to grow, as an intellect to discern, as a soul to live freely and unimpeded, to unfold such powers as were given her when we left our common home. If fewer talents were given her, yet if allowed the free and full employment of these, so that she may render back to the giver his own with usury, she will not complain; nay, I dare to say she will bless and rejoice in her earthly birth-place, her earthly lot. Let us consider what obstructions impede this good era, and what signs give reason to hope that it draws near.

I was talking on this subject with Miranda, a woman, who, if any in the world could, might speak without heat and bitterness of the position of her sex. Her father was a man who cherished no sentimental

reverence for Woman, but a firm belief in the equality of the sexes. She
was his eldest child, and came to him at an age when he needed a
companion. From the time she could speak and go alone, he addressed
her not as a plaything, but as a living mind. Among the few verses he
ever wrote was a copy addressed to this child, when the first locks were
cut from her head; and the reverence expressed on this occasion for
that cherished head, he never belied. It was for him the temple of
immortal intellect. He respected his child, however, too much to be an
indulgent parent. He called on her for clear judgment, for courage, for
honor and fidelity; in short, for such virtues as he knew. In so far as he
possessed the keys to the wonders of this universe, he allowed free use
of them to her, and, by the incentive of a high expectation, he forbade,
so far as possible, that she should let the privilege lie idle.

Thus this child was early led to feel herself a child of the spirit. She
took her place easily, not only in the world of organized being, but in
the world of mind. A dignified sense of self-dependence was given as all
her portion, and she found it a sure anchor. Herself securely anchored,
her relations with others were established with equal security. She was
fortunate in a total absence of those charms which might have drawn to
her bewildering flatteries, and in a strong electric nature, which repelled
those who did not belong to her, and attracted those who did. With
men and women her relations were noble – affectionate without
passion, intellectual without coldness. The world was free to her, and
she lived freely in it. Outward adversity came, and inward conflict; but
that faith and self-respect had early been awakened which must always
lead, at last, to an outward serenity and an inward peace.

Of Miranda I had always thought as an example, that the restraints
upon the sex were insuperable only to those who think them so, or who
noisily strive to break them. She had taken a course of her own, and no
man stood in her way. Many of her acts had been unusual, but excited
no uproar. Few helped, but none checked her; and the many men who
knew her mind and her life, showed to her confidence as to a brother,
gentleness as to a sister. And not only refined, but very coarse men
approved and aided one in whom they saw resolution and clearness of
design. Her mind was often the leading one, always effective.

When I talked with her upon these matters, and had said very much
what I have written, she smilingly replied: "And yet we must admit
that I have been fortunate, and this should not be. My good father's

early trust gave the first bias, and the rest followed, of course. It is true that I have had less outward aid, in after years, than most women; but that is of little consequence. Religion was early awakened in my soul, — a sense that what the soul is capable to ask it must attain, and that, though I might be aided and instructed by others, I must depend on myself as the only constant friend. This self-dependence, which was honored in me, is deprecated as a fault in most women. They are taught to learn their rule from without, not to unfold it from within.

"This is the fault of Man, who is still vain, and wishes to be more important to Woman than, by right, he should be."

"Men have not shown this disposition toward you," I said.

"No; because the position I early was enabled to take was one of self-reliance. And were all women as sure of their wants as I was, the result would be the same. But they are so overloaded with precepts by guardians, who think that nothing is so much to be dreaded for a woman as originality of thought or character, that their minds are impeded by doubts till they lose their chance of fair, free proportions. The difficulty is to get them to the point from which they shall naturally develop self-respect, and learn self-help.

"Once I thought that men would help to forward this state of things more than I do now. I saw so many of them wretched in the connections they had formed in weakness and vanity. They seemed so glad to esteem women whenever they could.

" 'The soft arms of affection,' said one of the most discerning spirits, 'will not suffice for me, unless on them I see the steel bracelets of strength.'

"But early I perceived that men never, in any extreme of despair, wished to be women. On the contrary, they were ever ready to taunt one another, at any sign of weakness, with,

> 'Art thou not like the women, who, —

The passage ends various ways, according to the occasion and rhetoric of the speaker. When they admired any woman, they were inclined to speak of her as 'above her sex.' Silently I observed this, and feared it argued a rooted scepticism, which for ages had been fastening on the heart, and which only an age of miracles could eradicate. Ever I have been treated with great sincerity; and I look upon it as a signal instance of this, that an intimate friend of the other sex said, in a fervent moment, that I 'deserved in some star to be a man.' He was much surprised when I disclosed my view of my position and hopes, when I declared my faith that the feminine side, the side of love, of beauty, of holiness, was now to have its full chance, and that, if either were better, it was better now to be a woman; for even the slightest achievement of good was furthering an especial work of our time. He smiled incredulously. 'She makes the best she can of it,' thought he. 'Let Jews believe the pride of Jewry, but I am of the better sort, and know better.'

"Another used as highest praise, in speaking of a character in literature, the words 'a manly woman.'

"So in the noble passage of Ben Jonson:

> 'I meant the day-star should not brighter ride,
>   Nor shed like influence from its lucent sea;
> I meant she should be courteous, facile, sweet,
>   Free from that solemn vice of greatness, pride;
> I meant each softest virtue there should meet,
>   Fit in that softer bosom to abide,
> Only a learned and a *manly* soul
>   I purposed her, that should with even powers
> The rock, the spindle, and the shears control
>   Of destiny, and spin her own free hours.' "

"Methinks," said I, "you are too fastidious in objecting to this. Jonson, in using the word 'manly,' only meant to heighten the picture of this, the true, the intelligent fate, with one of the deeper colors."

"And yet," said she, "so invariable is the use of this word where a heroic quality is to be described, and I feel so sure that persistence and courage are the most womanly no less than the most manly qualities, that I would exchange these words for others of a larger sense, at the risk of marring the fine tissue of the verse. Read, 'A heavenward and instructed soul,' and I should be satisfied. Let it not be said, wherever there is energy or creative genius, 'She has a masculine mind.' "

This by no means argues a willing want of generosity toward Woman. Man is as generous towards her as he knows how to be.

Wherever she has herself arisen in national or private history, and nobly shone forth in any form of excellence, men have received her, not only willingly, but with triumph. Their encomiums, indeed, are always, in some sense, mortifying; they show too much surprise. "Can this be you?" he cries to the transfigured Cinderella; "well, I should never have thought it, but I am very glad. We will tell every one that you have '*surpassed your sex.*' "

In every-day life, the feelings of the many are stained with vanity. Each wishes to be lord in a little world, to be superior at least over one; and he does not feel strong enough to retain a life-long ascendency over a strong nature. . . .

But not only is Man vain and fond of power, but the same want of development, which thus affects him morally, prevents his intellectually discerning the destiny of Woman. The boy wants no woman, but only a girl to play ball with him, and mark his pocket handkerchief. . . .

It is not the transient breath of poetic incense that women want; each can receive that from a lover. It is not life-long sway; it needs but to become a coquette, a shrew, or a good cook, to be sure of that. It is not money, nor notoriety, nor the badges of authority which men have appropriated to themselves. If demands, made in their behalf, lay stress on any of these particulars, those who make them have not searched deeply into the need. The want is for that which at once includes these and precludes them; which would not be forbidden power, lest there be temptation to steal and misuse it; which would not have the mind perverted by flattery from a worthiness of esteem: it is for that which is the birthright of every being capable of receiving it, – the freedom, the religious, the intelligent freedom of the universe to use its means, to learn its secret, as far as Nature has enabled them, with God alone for their guide and their judge.

Ye cannot believe it, men; but the only reason why women ever assume what is more appropriate to you, is because you prevent them from finding out what is fit for themselves. Were they free, were they wise fully to develop the strength and beauty of Woman; they would never wish to be men, or man-like. The well-instructed moon flies not from her orbit to seize on the glories of her partner. No; for she knows that one law rules, one heaven contains, one universe replies to them alike. It is with women as with the slave:

> "Vor dem Sklaven, wenn er die Kette bricht,
> Vor dem freien Menschen erzittert nicht."

Tremble not before the free man, but before the slave who has chains to break.

In slavery, acknowledged slavery, women are on a par with men. Each is a work-tool, an article of property, no more! In perfect freedom, such as is painted in Olympus, in Swedenborg's angelic state, in the heaven where there is no marrying nor giving in marriage, each is a purified intelligence, an enfranchised soul, – no less.

> "Jene himmlische Gestalten
> Sie fragen nicht nach Mann und Weib,
> Und keine kleider, keine Falten
> Umgeben den verklarten Leib.". . .

. . . Civilized Europe is still in a transition state about marriage; not only in practice but in thought. It is idle to speak with contempt of the nations where polygamy is an institution or seraglios a custom, while practices far more debasing haunt, well-nigh fill, every city and every town, and so far as union of one with one is believed to be the only pure form of marriage, a great majority of societies and individuals are still doubtful whether the earthly bond must be a meeting of souls, or only supposes a contract of convenience and utility. Were Woman established in the rights of an immortal being, this could not be. She would not, in some countries, be given away by her father with scarcely more respect for her feelings than is shown by the Indian chief who sells his daughter for a horse, and beats her if she runs away from her new home. Nor, in societies where her choice is left free, would she be perverted, by the current of opinion that seizes her, into the belief that she must marry, if it be only to find a protector, and a home of her own. Neither would Man, if he thought the connection of permanent importance, form it so lightly. He would not deem it a trifle, that he was to enter into the closest relations with another soul, which, if not eternal in themselves, must eternally affect his growth. Neither, did he believe Woman capable of friendship, would he, by rash haste, lose the chance of finding a friend in the person who might, probably, live half a century by his side. Did love, to his mind, stretch forth into infinity, he would not miss his chance of its revelations, that he might the sooner rest from his weariness by a bright fireside, and secure a sweet and graceful attendant "devoted to him alone." Were he a step higher, he would not carelessly enter into a relation where he might not be able to do the duty of a friend, as well as a protector from external ill, to the other party, and have a being in his power pining for sympathy, intelligence and aid, that he could not give.

What deep communion, what real intercourse is implied in sharing the joys and cares of parentage, when any degree of equality is admitted between the parties! It is true that, in a majority of instances, the man looks upon his wife as an adopted child, and places her to the other children in the relation of nurse or governess, rather than that of parent. Her influence with them is sure; but she misses the education which should enlighten that influence, by being thus treated. It is the order of nature that children should complete the education, moral and mental, of parents, by making them think what is needed for the best culture of human beings, and conquer all faults and impulses that interfere with their giving this to these dear objects, who represent the world to them. Father and mother should assist one another to learn what is required for this sublime priesthood of Nature. But, for this, a religious recognition of equality is required.

Where this thought of equality begins to diffuse itself, it is shown in four ways.

First; – The household partnership. In our country, the woman looks for a "smart but kind" husband; the man for a "capable, sweet-tempered" wife. The man furnishes the house; the woman regulates it. Their relation is one of mutual esteem, mutual dependence. Their talk is of business; their affection shows itself by practical kindness. They know that life goes more smoothly and cheerfully to each for the other's aid; they are grateful and content. The wife praises her husband as a "good provider;" the husband, in return, compliments her as a "capital housekeeper." This relation is good as far as it goes.

Next comes a closer tie, which takes the form either of mutual idolatry or of intellectual companionship. The first, we suppose, is to no one a pleasing subject of contemplation. The parties weaken and narrow one another; they lock the gate against all the glories of the universe, that they may live in a cell together. To themselves they seem the only wise; to all others, steeped in infatuation; the gods smile as they look forward to the crisis of cure; to men, the woman seems an unlovely syren; to women, the man an effeminate boy.

The other form, of intellectual companionship, has become more and more frequent. Men engaged in public life, literary men, and artists, have often found in their wives companions and confidants in thought no less than in feeling. And, as the intellectual development of Woman has spread wider and risen higher, they have, not unfrequently, shared the same employment; as in the case of Roland and his wife, who were friends in the household and in the nation's councils, read, regulated home affairs, or prepared public documents together, indifferently. It is very pleasant, in letters begun by Roland and finished by his wife, to see the harmony of mind, and the difference of nature; one thought, but various ways of treating it. . . . The page of [Madame Roland's] life is one of unsullied dignity. Her appeal to posterity is one against the injustice of those who committed such crimes in the name of Liberty. She makes it in behalf of herself and her husband. I would put beside it, on the shelf, a little volume, containing a similar appeal from the verdict of contemporaries to that of mankind, made by Godwin in behalf of his wife, the celebrated, the by most men detested, Mary Wolstonecraft. In his view, it was an appeal from the injustice of those who did such wrong in the name of virtue. Were this little book interesting for no other cause, it would be so for the generous affection evinced under the peculiar circumstances. This man had courage to love and honor this woman in the face of the world's sentence, and of all that was repulsive in her own past history. He believed he saw of what soul she was, and that the impulses she had struggled to act out were noble, though the opinions to which they had led might not be thoroughly weighed. He loved her, and he defended her for the meaning and tendency of her inner life. It was a good fact.

Mary Wolstonecraft, like Madame Dudevant (commonly known as George Sand) in our day, was a woman whose existence better proved the need of some new interpretation of Woman's Rights than anything she wrote. Such beings as these, rich in genius, of most tender sympathies, capable of high virtue and a chastened harmony, ought not to find themselves, by birth, in a place so narrow, that, in breaking bonds, they become outlaws. Were there as much room in the world for such, as in Spenser's poem for Britomart, they would not run their heads so wildly against the walls, but prize their shelter rather. They find their way, at last, to light and air, but the world will not take off the brand it has set upon them. The champion of the Rights of Woman found, in Godwin, one who would plead that cause like a brother. He who delineated with such purity of traits the form of Woman in the Marguerite, of whom the weak St. Leon could never learn to be worthy, – a pearl indeed whose price was above rubies, – was not false in life to the faith by which he had hallowed his romance. He acted, as he wrote, like a brother. This form of appeal rarely fails to touch the basest man: – "Are you acting toward other women in the way you would have men act towards your sister?" George Sand smokes, wears male attire, wishes to be addressed as "Mon frère;" – perhaps, if she found those who were as brothers indeed, she would not care whether she were brother or sister. We rejoice to see that she, who expresses such a painful contempt for men in most of her works, as shows she must have known great wrong from them, depicts, in "La Roche Mauprat," a man raised by the workings of love from the depths of savage sensualism to a moral and intellectual life. It was love for a pure object, for a steadfast woman, one of those who, the Italian said, could make the "stair to heaven."

This author, beginning like the many in assault upon bad institutions, and external ills, yet deepening the experience through comparative freedom, sees at last that the only efficient remedy must come from individual character. These bad institutions, indeed, it may always be replied, prevent individuals from forming good character, therefore we must remove them. Agreed; yet keep steadily the higher aim in view. Could you clear away all the bad forms of society, it is vain, unless the individual begin to be ready for better. There must be a parallel movement in these two branches of life. And all the rules left by Moses availed less to further the best life than the living example of one Messiah.

Still the mind of the age struggles confusedly with these problems, better discerning as yet the ill it can no longer bear, than the good by which it may supersede it. But women like Sand will speak now and cannot be silenced; their characters and their eloquence alike foretell an era when such as they shall easier learn to lead true lives. But though such forebode, not such shall be parents of it. Those who would reform the world must show that they do not speak in the heat of wild impulse; their lives must be unstained by passionate error; they must be severe lawgivers to themselves. They must be religious students of the divine purposes with regard to man, if they would not confound the fancies of a day with the requisitions of eternal good. Their liberty must be the liberty of law and knowledge. But as to the transgressions against custom which have caused such outcry against those of noble intention, it may be observed that the resolve of Eloisa to be only the mistress of Abelard, was that of one who saw in practice around her the contract of marriage made the seal of degradation. Shelley feared not to be fettered, unless so to be was to be false. Wherever abuses are seen, the timid will suffer; the bold will protest. But society has a right to outlaw them till she has revised her law; and this she must be taught to do, by one who speaks with authority, not in anger or haste. . . .

We might mention instances, nearer home, of minds, partners in work and in life, sharing together, on equal terms, public and private interests, and which wear not, on any side, the aspect of offence shown by those last-named: persons who steer straight onward, yet, in our comparatively free life, have not been obliged to run their heads against any wall. But the principles which guide them might, under petrified and oppressive institutions, have made them warlike, paradoxical, and, in some sense, Pariahs. The phenomena are different, the law is the same, in all these cases. Men and women have been obliged to build up their house anew from the very foundation. If they found stone ready in the quarry, they took it peaceably; otherwise they alarmed the country by pulling down old towers to get materials. . . .

The fourth and highest grade of marriage union is the religious, which may be expressed as pilgrimage toward a common shrine. This includes the others: home sympathies and household wisdom, for these pilgrims must know how to assist each other along the dusty way; intellectual communion, for how sad it would be on such a journey to have a companion to whom you could not communicate your thoughts and aspirations as they sprang to life; who would have no feeling for the prospects that open, more and more glorious as we advance; who would never see the flowers that may be gathered by the most industrious traveller! It must include all these. . . .

Another sign of the times is furnished by the triumphs of Female Authorship. These have been great, and are constantly increasing. Women have taken possession of so many provinces for which men had pronounced them unfit, that, though these still declare there are some inaccessible to them, it is difficult to say just *where* they must stop.

The shining names of famous women have cast light upon the path of the sex, and many obstructions have been removed. When a Montague could learn better than her brother, and use her lore afterwards to such purpose as an observer, it seemed amiss to hinder women from preparing themselves to see, or from seeing all they could, when prepared. Since Somerville has achieved so much, will any young girl be prevented from seeking a knowledge of the physical sciences, if she wishes it? De Stael's name was not so clear of offence; she could not forget the Woman in the thought; while she was instructing you as a mind, she wished to be admired as a Woman; sentimental tears often dimmed the eagle glance. Her intellect, too, with all its splendor, trained in a drawing-room, fed on flattery, was tainted and flawed; yet its beams make the obscurest school-house in New England warmer and lighter to the little rugged girls who are gathered together on its wooden bench. She may never through life hear her name, but she is not the less their benefactress.

The influence has been such, that the aim certainly is, now, in arranging school instruction for girls, to give them as fair a field as boys. As yet, indeed, these arrangements are made with little judgment or reflection; just as the tutors of Lady Jane Grey, and other distinguished women of her time, taught them Latin and Greek, because they knew nothing else themselves, so now the improvement in the education of girls is to be made by giving them young men as teachers, who only teach what has been taught themselves at college, while methods and topics need revision for these new subjects, which could better be made by those who had experienced the same wants. Women are, often, at the head of these institutions; but they have, as yet, seldom been thinking women, capable of organizing a new whole for the wants of the time, and choosing persons to officiate in the departments. And when some portion of instruction of a good sort is got from the school, the far greater proportion which is infused from the general atmosphere of society contradicts its purport. Yet books and a little elementary instruction are not furnished in vain. Women are better aware how great and rich the universe is, not so easily blinded by narrowness or partial views of a home circle. "Her mother did so before her" is no longer a sufficient excuse. Indeed, it was never received as an excuse to mitigate the severity of censure, but was adduced as a reason, rather, why there should be no effort made for reformation.

Whether much or little has been done, or will be done, – whether women will add to the talent of narration the power of systematizing, – whether they will carve marble, as well as draw and paint, – is not important. But that it should be acknowledged that they have intellect which needs developing – that they should not be considered complete, if beings of affection and habit alone – is important.

Yet even this acknowledgment, rather conquered by Woman than proferred by Man, has been sullied by the usual selfishness. Too much is

said of women being better educated, that they may become better
companions and mothers *for men*. They should be fit for such
companionship, and we have mentioned, with satisfaction, instances
where it has been established. Earth knows no fairer, holier relation
than that of a mother. It is one which, rightly understood, must both
promote and require the highest attainments. But a being of infinite
scope must not be treated with an exclusive view to any one relation.
Give the soul free course, let the organization, both of body and mind,
be freely developed, and the being will be fit for any and every relation
to which it may be called. The intellect, no more than the sense of
hearing, is to be cultivated merely that Woman may be a more valuable
companion to Man, but because the Power who gave a power, by its
mere existence signifies that it must be brought out toward perfection.

In this regard of self-dependence, and a greater simplicity and fulness of being, we must hail as a preliminary the increase of the class
contemptuously designated as "old maids."

We cannot wonder at the aversion with which old bachelors and
old maids have been regarded. Marriage is the natural means of forming
a sphere, of taking root in the earth; it requires more strength to do this
without such an opening; very many have failed, and their
imperfections have been in every one's way. They have been more
partial, more harsh, more officious and impertinent, than those
compelled by severer friction to render themselves endurable. Those
who have a more full experience of the instincts have a distrust as to
whether the unmarried can be thoroughly human and humane, such as
is hinted in the saying, "Old maids' and bachelors' children are well
cared for," which derides at once their ignorance and their
presumption.

Yet the business of society has become so complex, that it could
now scarcely be carried on without the presence of these despised
auxiliaries; and detachments from the army of aunts and uncles are
wanted to stop gaps in every hedge. They rove about, mental and moral
Ishmaelites, pitching their tents amid the fixed and ornamented homes
of men.

In a striking variety of forms, genius of late, both at home and
abroad, has paid its tribute to the character of the Aunt and the Uncle,
recognizing in these personages the spiritual parents, who have supplied
defects in the treatment of the busy or careless actual parents.

They also gain a wider, if not so deep experience. Those who are not intimately and permanently linked with others, are thrown upon themselves; and, if they do not there find peace and incessant life, there is none to flatter them that they are not very poor, and very mean. . . . Not "needing to care that she may please a husband," a frail and limited being, [the spinster's] thoughts may turn to the centre, and she may, by steadfast contemplation entering into the secret of truth and love, use it for the good of all men, instead of a chosen few, and interpret through it all the forms of life. It is possible, perhaps, to be at once a priestly servant and a loving muse. . . .

Even among the North American Indians, a race of men as completely engaged in mere instinctive life as almost any in the world, and where each chief, keeping many wives as useful servants, of course looks with no kind eye on celibacy in Woman, it was excused in the following instance mentioned by Mrs. Jameson. A woman dreamt in youth that she was betrothed to the Sun. She built her a wigwam apart, filled it with emblems of her alliance, and means of an independent life. There she passed her days, sustained by her own exertions, and true to her supposed engagement.

In any tribe, we believe, a woman, who lived as if she was betrothed to the Sun, would be tolerated, and the rays which made her youth blossom sweetly, would crown her with a halo in age. . . .

The electrical, the magnetic element in Woman has not been fairly brought out at any period. Everything might be expected from it; she has far more of it than Man. This is commonly expressed by saying that her intuitions are more rapid and more correct. . . .

Women who combine this organization with creative genius are very commonly unhappy at present. They see too much to act in conformity with those around them, and their quick impulses seem folly to those who do not discern the motives. This is an usual effect of the apparition of genius, whether in Man or Woman, but is more frequent with regard to the latter, because a harmony, an obvious order and self-restraining decorum, is most expected from her. . . .

Sickness is the frequent result of this overcharged existence. To this region, however misunderstood, or interpreted with presumptuous carelessness, belong the phenomena of magnetism, or mesmerism, as it is now often called, where the trance of the Ecstatica purports to be produced by the agency of one human being on another, instead of, as in her case, direct from the spirit.

The worlding has his sneer at this as at the services of religion. "The churches can always be filled with women"—"Show me a man in one of your magnetic states, and I will believe."

Women are, indeed, the easy victims both of priestcraft and self-delusion; but this would not be, if the intellect was developed in proportion to the other powers. They would then have a regulator, and be more in equipoise, yet must retain the same nervous susceptibility while their physical structure is such as it is.

It is with just that hope that we welcome everything that tends to strengthen the fibre and develop the nature on more sides. When the intellect and affections are in harmony; when intellectual consciousness is calm and deep; inspiration will not be confounded with fancy.

> Then, "she who advances
> With rapturous, lyrical glances,
> Singing the song of the earth, singing
> Its hymn to the Gods,"

will not be pitied as a mad-woman, nor shrunk from as unnatural. . . .

In our own country, women are, in many respects, better situated than men. Good books are allowed, with more time to read them. They are not so early forced into the bustle of life, nor so weighed down by demands for outward success. The perpetual changes, incident to our society, make the blood circulate freely through the body politic, and, if not favorable at present to the grace and bloom of life, they are so to activity, resource, and would be to reflection, but for a low materialist tendency, from which the women are generally exempt in themselves, though its existence, among the men, has a tendency to repress their impulses and make them doubt their instincts, thus often paralyzing their action during the best years.

But they have time to think, and no traditions chain them, and few conventionalities, compared with what must be met in other nations. There is no reason why they should not discover that the secrets of nature are open, the revelations of the spirit waiting, for whoever will seek them. When the mind is once awakened to this consciousness, it will not be restrained by the habits of the past, but fly to seek the seeds of a heavenly future. . . .

Women who speak in public, if they have a moral power, such as has been felt from Angelina Grimke and Abby Kelly, — that is, if they speak for conscience' sake, to serve a cause which they hold sacred, — invariably subdue the prejudices of their hearers, and excite an interest proportionate to the aversion with which it had been the purpose to regard them.

A passage in a private letter so happily illustrates this, that it must be inserted here.

Abby Kelly in the Town-House of ———.

"The scene was not unheroic — to see that woman, true to humanity and her own nature, a centre of rude eyes and tongues, even gentlemen feeling licensed to make part of a species of mob around a female out of her sphere. As she took her seat in the desk amid the great noise, and in the throng, full, like a wave, of something to ensue, I saw her humanity in a gentleness and unpretension, tenderly open to the sphere around her, and, had she not been supported by the power of the will of genuineness and principle, she would have failed. It led her to prayer, which, in Woman especially, is childlike; sensibility and will going to the side of God and looking up to him; and humanity was poured out in aspiration.

"She acted like a gentle hero, with her mild decision and womanly calmness. All heroism is mild, and quiet, and gentle, for it is life and possession; and combativeness and firmness show a want of actualness. She is as earnest, fresh and simple, as when she first entered the crusade. I think she did much good, more than the men in her place could do, for Woman feels more as being and reproducing — this brings the subject more into home relations. Men speak through, and mostly from intellect, and this addresses itself to that in others which is combative."

For Woman, if, by a sympathy as to outward condition, she is led to aid the enfranchisement of the slave, must be no less so, by inward tendency, to favor measures which promise to bring the world more thoroughly and deeply into harmony with her nature. When the lamb takes place of the lion as the emblem of nations, both women and men will be as children of one spirit, perpetual learners of the word and doers thereof, not hearers only.

A writer in the New York Pathfinder, in two articles headed "Femality," has uttered a still more pregnant word than any we have named. He views Woman truly from the soul, and not from society, and the depth and leading of his thoughts are proportionably remarkable. He views the feminine nature as a harmonizer of the vehement elements, and this has often been hinted elsewhere; but what he expresses most forcibly is the lyrical, the inspiring and inspired apprehensiveness of her being. . . .

There are two aspects of Woman's nature, represented by the ancients as Muse and Minerva. It is the former to which the writer in the Pathfinder looks. It is the latter which Wordsworth has in mind, when he says,

> "With a placid brow,
> Which woman ne'er should forfeit, keep thy vow."

The especial genius of Woman I believe to be electrical in movement, intuitive in function, spiritual in tendency. She excels not so easily in classification, or recreation, as in an instinctive seizure of causes, and a simple breathing out of what she receives, that has the singleness of life, rather than the selecting and energizing of art.

More native is it to her to be the living model of the artist than to set apart from herself any one form in objective reality; more native to inspire and receive the poem, than to create it. In so far as soul is in her completely developed, all soul is the same; but in so far as it is modified in her as Woman, it flows, it breathes, it sings, rather than deposits soil, or finishes work; and that which is especially feminine flushes, in blossom, the face of earth, and pervades, like air and water, all this seeming solid globe, daily renewing and purifying its life. Such may be the especially feminine element spoken of as Femality. But it is no more the order of nature that it should be incarnated pure in any form, than that the masculine energy should exist unmingled with it in any form.

Male and female represent the two sides of the great radical dualism. But, in fact, they are perpetually passing into one another. Fluid hardens to solid, solid rushes to fluid. There is no wholly masculine man, no purely feminine woman.

History jeers at the attempts of physiologists to bind great original laws by the forms which flow from them. They make a rule; they say from observation what can and cannot be. In vain! Nature provides exceptions to every rule. She sends women to battle, and sets Hercules spinning; she enables women to bear immense burdens, cold, and frost; she enables the man, who feels maternal love, to nourish his infant like a mother. . . . Presently she will make a female Newton, and a male Syren.

Man partakes of the feminine in the Apollo, Woman of the masculine as Minerva.

What I mean by the Muse is that unimpeded clearness of the intuitive powers, which a perfectly truthful adherence to every admonition of the higher instincts would bring to a finely organized human being. It may appear as prophecy or as poesy. It enabled Cassandra to foresee the results of actions passing round her; the Seeress to behold the true character of the person through the mask of his customary life. (Sometimes she saw a feminine form behind the man, sometimes the reverse.) It enabled the daughter of Linnaeus to see the soul of the flower exhaling from the flower. . . . Of this sight of the world of causes, this approximation to the region of primitive motions, women I hold to be especially capable. Even without equal freedom with the other sex, they have already shown themselves so; and should these faculties have free play, I believe they will open new, deeper and purer sources of joyous inspiration than have as yet refreshed the earth.

Let us be wise, and not impede the soul. Let her work as she will. Let us have one creative energy, one incessant revelation. Let it take what form it will, and let us not bind it by the past to man or woman, black or white. Jove sprang from Rhea, Pallas from Jove. So let it be.

If it has been the tendency of these remarks to call Woman rather to the Minerva side, – if I, unlike the more generous writer, have spoken from society no less than the soul, – let it be pardoned! It is love that has caused this, – love for many incarcerated souls, that might be freed, could the idea of religious self-dependence be established in them, could the weakening habit of dependence on others be broken up. . . .

It is, therefore, only in the present crisis that the preference is given to Minerva. The power of continence must establish the legitimacy of freedom, the power of self-poise the perfection of motion.

Every relation, every gradation of nature is incalculably precious, but only to the soul which is poised upon itself, and to whom no loss, no change, can bring dull discord, for it is in harmony with the central soul.

If any individual live too much in relations, so that he becomes a stranger to the resources of his own nature, he falls, after a while, into a distraction, or imbecility, from which he can only be cured by a time of isolation, which gives the renovating fountains time to rise up. With a society it is the same. Many minds, deprived of the traditionary or instinctive means of passing a cheerful existence, must find help in self-impulse or perish. It is therefore that, while any elevation, in the view of union, is to be hailed with joy, we shall not decline celibacy as the great fact of the time. It is one from which no vow, no arrangement, can at present save a thinking mind. For now the rowers are pausing on their oars; they wait a change before they can pull together. All tends to illustrate the thought of a wise contemporary. Union is only possible to those who are units. To be fit for relations in time, souls, whether of Man or Woman, must be able to do without them in the spirit.

It is therefore that I would have Woman lay aside all thought, such as she habitually cherishes, of being taught and led by men. I would have her, like the Indian girl, dedicate herself to the Sun, the Sun of Truth, and go nowhere if his beams did not make clear the path. I would have her free from compromise, from complaisance, from helplessness, because I would have her good enough and strong enough to love one and all beings, from the fulness, not the poverty of being. . . .

Once, two fine figures stood before me, thus. The father of very intellectual aspect, his falcon eye softened by affection as he looked down on his fair child; she the image of himself, only more graceful and brilliant in expression. I was reminded of Southey's Kehama; when, lo, the dream was rudely broken! They were talking of education, and he said,

"I shall not have Maria brought too forward. If she knows too much, she will never find a husband; superior women hardly ever can."

"Surely," said his wife, with a blush, "you wish Maria to be as good and wise as she can, whether it will help her to marriage or not."

"No," he persisted, "I want her to have a sphere and a home, and some one to protect her when I am gone." . . .

But men do *not* look at both sides, and women must leave off asking them and being influenced by them, but retire within themselves, and explore the ground-work of life till they find their peculiar secret. Then, when they come forth again, renovated and baptized, they will know how to turn all dross to gold, and will be rich and free though they live in a hut, tranquil if in a crowd. Then their sweet singing shall not be from passionate impulse, but the lyrical overflow of a divine rapture, and a new music shall be evolved from this many-chorded world.

Grant her, then, for a while, the armor and the javelin. Let her put from her the press of other minds, and meditate in virgin loneliness. The same idea shall reappear in due time as Muse, or Ceres, the all-kindly, patient Earth-Spirit.

Among the throng of symptoms which denote the present tendency to a crisis in the life of Woman, . . . I have attempted to select a few.

One of prominent interest is the unison upon the subject of three male minds, which, for width of culture, power of self-concentration and dignity of aim, take rank as the prophets of the coming age, while their histories and labors are rooted in the past. . . .

Swedenborg approximated to that harmony between the scientific and poetic lives of mind, which we hope from the perfected man. The links that bind together the realms of nature, the mysteries that accompany her births and growths, were unusually plain to him. He seems a man to whom insight was given at a period when the mental frame was sufficiently matured to retain and express its gifts. . . . His idea of Woman is sufficiently large and noble to interpose no obstacle to her progress. His idea of marriage is consequently sufficient. Man and Woman share an angelic ministry; the union is of one with one, permanent and pure. . . .

As apostle of the new order, of the social fabric that is to rise from love, and supersede the old that was based on strife, Charles Fourier comes next, expressing, in an outward order, many facts of which Swedenborg saw the secret springs. The mind of Fourier, though grand and clear, was, in some respects, superficial. He was a stranger to the highest experiences. His eye was fixed on the outward more than the inward needs of Man. Yet he, too, was a seer of the divine order, in its musical expression, if not in its poetic soul. He has filled one department of instruction for the new era, and the harmony in action, and freedom for individual growth, he hopes, shall exist. . . .

He, too, places Woman on an entire equality with Man, and wishes to give to one as to the other that independence which must result from intellectual and practical development.

Those who will consult him for no other reason, might do so to see how the energies of Woman may be made available in the pecuniary way. The object of Fourier was to give her the needed means of self-help, that she might dignify and unfold her life for her own happiness, and that of society. The many, now, who see their daughters liable to destitution, or vice to escape from it, may be interested to examine the means, if they have not yet soul enough to appreciate the ends he proposes.

On the opposite side of the advancing army leads the great apostle of individual culture, Goethe. Swedenborg makes organization and union the necessary results of solitary thought. Fourier, whose nature was, above all, constructive, looked to them too exclusively. Better institutions, he thought, will make better men. Goethe expressed, in every way, the other side. If one man could present better forms, the rest could not use them till ripe for them.

Fourier says, As the institutions, so the men! All follies are excusable and natural under bad institutions.

Goethe thinks, As the man, so the institutions! There is no excuse for ignorance and folly. A man can grow in any place, if he will.

Ay! but, Goethe, bad institutions are prison-walls and impure air, that make him stupid, so that he does not will.

And thou, Fourier, do not expect to change mankind at once, or even "in three generations," by arrangement of groups and series, or flourish of trumpets for attractive industry. If these attempts are made by unready men, they will fail.

Yet we prize the theory of Fourier no less than the profound suggestion of Goethe. Both are educating the age to a clearer consciousness of what Man needs, what Man can be; and better life must ensue. . . .

. . . That for which I most respect [Mrs. Jameson] is the decision with which she speaks on a subject which refined women are usually afraid to approach, for fear of the insult and scurrile jest they may encounter; but on which she neither can nor will restrain the indignation of a full heart. I refer to the degradation of a large portion of women into the sold and polluted slaves of men, and the daring with which the legislator and man of the world lifts his head beneath the heavens, and says, "This must be; it cannot be helped; it is a necessary accompaniment of *civilization*."

So speaks the *citizen*. Man born of Woman, the father of daughters, declares that he will and must buy the comforts and commercial advantages of his London, Vienna, Paris, New York, by conniving at the moral death, the damnation, so far as the action of society can insure it, of thousands of women for each splendid metropolis.

O men! I speak not to you. It is true that your wickedness . . . is its own punishment. Your forms degraded and your eyes clouded by secret sin; natural harmony broken and fineness of perception destroyed in your mental and bodily organization; God and love shut out from your hearts by the foul visitants you have permitted there: incapable of pure marriage; incapable of pure parentage; incapable of worship; O wretched men, your sin is its own punishment! You have lost the world in losing yourselves. Who ruins another has admitted the worm to the root of his own tree, and the fuller ye fill the cup of evil, the deeper must be your own bitter draught. But I speak not to you — you need to teach and warn one another. And more than one voice rises in earnestness. And all that *women* say to the heart that has once chosen the evil path is considered prudery, or ignorance, or perhaps a feebleness of nature which exempts from similar temptations.

But to you, women, American women, a few words may not be addressed in vain. . . . To you . . . it is more especially my business to address myself on this subject, and my advice may be classed under three heads:

Clear your souls from the taint of vanity.

Do not rejoice in conquests, either that your power to allure may be seen by other women, or for the pleasure of rousing passionate feelings that gratify your love of excitement.

It must happen, no doubt, that frank and generous women will excite love they do not reciprocate, but, in nine cases out of ten, the woman has, half consciously, done much to excite. In this case, she shall not be held guiltless, either as to the unhappiness or injury of the lover. Pure love, inspired by a worthy object, must ennoble and bless, whether mutual or not; but that which is excited by coquettish attraction of any grade of refinement, must cause bitterness and doubt, as to the reality of human goodness, so soon as the flush of passion is over. And, that you may avoid all taste for these false pleasures,

> "Steep the soul
> In one pure love, and it will last thee long." . . .

A little while since I was at one of the most fashionable places of public resort. I saw there many women, dressed without regard to the season or the demands of the place, in apery, or, as it looked, in mockery, of European fashions. I saw their eyes restlessly courting attention. I saw the way in which it was paid; the style of devotion, almost an open sneer, which it pleased those ladies to receive from men whose expression marked their own low position in the moral and intellectual world. Those women went to their pillows with their heads full of folly, their hearts of jealousy, or gratified vanity; those men, with the low opinion they already entertained of Woman confirmed. These were American *ladies*; that is, they were of that class who have wealth and leisure to make full use of the day, and confer benefits on others. They were of that class whom the possession of external advantages makes of pernicious example to many if these advantages be misused.

Soon after, I met a circle of women, stamped by society as among the most degraded of their sex. "How," it was asked of them, "did you come here?" for by the society that I saw in the former place they were shut up in a prison. The causes were not difficult to trace: love of dress, love of flattery, love of excitement. They had not dresses like the other ladies, so they stole them; they could not pay for flattery by distinctions, and the dower of a worldly marriage, so they paid by the profanation of their persons. In excitement, more and more madly sought from day to day, they drowned the voice of conscience.

Now I ask you, my sisters, if the women at the fashionable house be not answerable for those women being in the prison?

As to position in the world of souls, we may suppose the women of the prison stood fairest, both because they had misused less light, and because loneliness and sorrow had brought some of them to feel the need of better life, nearer truth and good. This was no merit in them, being an effect of circumstance, but it was hopeful. But you, my friends (and some of you I have already met), consecrate yourselves without waiting for reproof, in free love and unbroken energy, to win and to diffuse a better life. Offer beauty, talents, riches, on the altar; thus shall ye keep spotless your own hearts, and be visibly or invisibly the angels to others.

I would urge upon those women who have not yet considered this subject, to do so. Do not forget the unfortunates who dare not cross your guarded way. If it do not suit you to act with those who have organized measures of reform, then hold not yourself excused from acting in private. Seek out these degraded women, give them tender sympathy, counsel, employment. Take the place of mothers, such as might have saved them originally. . . .

Women are accustomed to be told by men that the reform is to come *from them*. "You," say the men, "must frown upon vice; you must decline the attentions of the corrupt; you must not submit to the will of your husband when it seems to you unworthy, but give the laws in marriage, and redeem it from its present sensual and mental pollutions."

This seems to us hard. Men have, indeed, been, for more than a hundred years, rating women for countenancing vice. But, at the same time, they have carefully hid from them its nature, so that the preference often shown by women for bad men arises rather from a confused idea that they are bold and adventurous, acquainted with regions which women are forbidden to explore, and the curiosity that ensues, than a corrupt heart in the woman. As to marriage, it has been inculcated on women, for centuries, that men have not only stronger passions than they, but of a sort that it would be shameful for them to share or even understand; that, therefore, they must "confide in their husbands," that is, submit implicitly to their will; that the least appearance of coldness or withdrawal, from whatever cause, in the wife is wicked, because liable to turn her husband's thoughts to illicit indulgence; for a man is so constituted that he must indulge his passions or die!

Accordingly, a great part of women look upon men as a kind of wild beasts, but "suppose they are all alike;" the unmarried are assured by the married that, "if they knew men as they do," that is, by being married to them, "they would not expect continence or self-government from them." . . .

"In the heart of every young woman," says [a] female writer . . . addressing herself to the husband, "depend upon it, there is a fund of exalted ideas; she conceals, represses, without succeeding in smothering them. *So long as these ideas in your wife are directed to* you, *they are, no doubt, innocent*, but take care that they be not accompanied with *too much* pain. In other respects, also, spare her delicacy. Let all the antecedent parts of your life, if there are such, which would give her pain, be concealed from her; *her happiness and her respect for you would suffer from this misplaced confidence.* Allow her to retain that flower of purity, *which should distinguish her, in your eyes, from every other woman.*" We should think so truly, under this canon. Such a man must esteem purity an exotic that could only be preserved by the greatest care. Of the degree of mental intimacy possible, in such a marriage, let every one judge for himself!

On this subject, let every woman, who has once begun to think, examine herself; see whether she does not suppose virtue possible and necessary to Man, and whether she would not desire for her son a virtue which aimed at a fitness for a divine life, and involved, if not asceticism, that degree of power over the lower self, which shall "not exterminate the passions, but keep them chained at the feet of reason." The passions, like fire, are a bad master; but confine them to the hearth and the altar, and they give life to the social economy, and make each sacrifice meet for heaven. . . .

If women are to be bond-maids, let it be to men superior to women in fortitude, in aspiration, in moral power, in refined sense of beauty! You who give yourselves "to be supported," or because "one must love something," are they who make the lot of the sex such that mothers are sad when daughters are born.

It marks the state of feeling on this subject that it was mentioned, as a bitter censure on a woman who had influence over those younger than herself, – "She makes those girls want to see heroes?"

"And will that hurt them?"

"Certainly; how *can* you ask? They will find none, and so they will never be married."

"*Get* married" is the usual phrase, and the one that correctly indicates the thought; but the speakers, on this occasion, were persons too outwardly refined to use it. They were ashamed of the word, but not of the thing. . . .

I now touch on my own place and day, and, as I write, events are occurring that threaten the fair fabric approached by so long an avenue. . . . Last week brought news which threatens that a cause . . . of Americans in general . . . is in danger, for the choice of the people threatens to rivet the chains of slavery and the leprosy of sin permanently on this nation, through the Annexation of Texas!

Ah! if this should take place, who will dare again to feel the throb of heavenly hope, as to the destiny of this country? The noble thought that gave unity to all our knowledge, harmony to all our designs, – the thought that the progress of history had brought on the era, the tissue of prophecies pointed out the spot, where humanity was, at last, to have a fair chance to know itself, and all men be born free and equal for the eagle's flight, – flutters as if about to leave the breast, which, deprived of it, will have no more a nation, no more a home on earth.

Women of my country! – Exaltadas! if such there be, – women of English, old English nobleness, who understand the courage of Boadicea, the sacrifice of Godiva, the power of Queen Emma to tread the red-hot iron unharmed, – women who share the nature of Mrs. Hutchinson, Lady Russell, and the mothers of our own revolution, – have you nothing to do with this? You see the men, how they are willing to sell shamelessly the happiness of countless generations of fellow-creatures, the honor of their country, and their immortal souls, for a money market and political power. Do you not feel within you that which can reprove them, which can check, which can convince them? You would not speak in vain; whether each in her own home, or banded in unison.

Tell these men that you will not accept the glittering baubles, spacious dwellings, and plentiful service, they mean to offer you through these means. Tell them that the heart of Woman demands nobleness and honor in Man, and that, if they have not purity, have not mercy, they are no longer fathers, lovers, husbands, sons of yours.

This cause is your own, for, as I have before said, there is a reason why the foes of African Slavery seek more freedom for women; but put it not upon that ground, but on the ground of right.

If you have a power, it is a moral power. The films of interest are not so close around you as around the men. If you will but think, you cannot fail to wish to save the country from this disgrace. Let not slip the occasion, but do something to lift off the curse incurred by Eve.

You have heard the women engaged in the Abolition movement accused of boldness, because they lifted the voice in public, and lifted the latch of the stranger. But were these acts, whether performed judiciously or no, *so* bold as to dare before God and Man to partake the fruits of such offence as this?

You hear much of the modesty of your sex. Preserve it by filling the mind with noble desires that shall ward off the corruptions of vanity and idleness. A profligate woman, who left her accustomed haunts and took service in a New York boarding-house, said "she had never heard talk so vile at the Five Points, as from the ladies at the boarding-house." And why? Because they were idle; because, having nothing worthy to engage them, they dwelt, with unnatural curiosity, on the ill they dared not go to see.

It will not so much injure your modesty to have your name, by the unthinking, coupled with idle blame, as to have upon your soul the weight of not trying to save a whole race of women from the scorn that is put upon *their* modesty.

Think of this well! I entreat, I conjure you, before it is too late. It is my belief that something effectual might be done by women, if they would only consider the subject, and enter upon it in the true spirit, – a spirit gentle, but firm, and which feared the offence of none, save One who is of purer eyes than to behold iniquity.

And now I have designated in outline, if not in fulness, the stream which is ever flowing from the heights of my thought.

In the earlier tract I was told I did not make my meaning sufficiently clear. In this I have consequently tried to illustrate it in various ways, and may have been guilty of much repetition. Yet, as I am anxious to leave no room for doubt, I shall venture to retrace, once more, the scope of my design in points, as was done in old-fashioned sermons.

Man is a being of two-fold relations, to nature beneath, and intelligences above him. The earth is his school, if not his birth-place; God his object; life and thought his means of interpreting nature, and aspiring to God.

Only a fraction of this purpose is accomplished in the life of any one man. Its entire accomplishment is to be hoped only from the sum of the lives of men, or Man considered as a whole.

As this whole has one soul and one body, any injury or obstruction to a part, or to the meanest member, affects the whole. Man can never be perfectly happy or virtuous, till all men are so.

To address Man wisely, you must not forget that his life is partly animal, subject to the same laws with Nature.

But you cannot address him wisely unless you consider him still more as soul, and appreciate the conditions and destiny of soul.

The growth of Man is two-fold, masculine and feminine.

So far as these two methods can be distinguished, they are so as

Energy and Harmony;

Power and Beauty;

Intellect and Love;
or by some such rude classification; for we have not language primitive
and pure enough to express such ideas with precision.

These two sides are supposed to be expressed in Man and Woman,
that is, as the more and the less, for the faculties have not been given
pure to either, but only in preponderance. There are also exceptions in
great number, such as men of far more beauty than power, and the
reverse. But, as a general rule, it seems to have been the intention to
give a preponderance on the one side, that is called masculine, and on
the other, one that is called feminine.

There cannot be a doubt that, if these two developments were in
perfect harmony, they would correspond to and fulfil one another, like
hemispheres, or the tenor and bass in music.

But there is no perfect harmony in human nature; and the two
parts answer one another only now and then; or, if there be a persistent
consonance, it can only be traced at long intervals, instead of
discoursing an obvious melody.

What is the cause of this?

Man, in the order of time, was developed first; as energy comes
before harmony; power before beauty.

Woman was therefore under his care as an elder. He might have
been her guardian and teacher.

But, as human nature goes not straight forward, but by excessive
action and then reaction in an undulated course, he misunderstood and
abused his advantages, and became her temporal master instead of her
spiritual sire.

On himself came the punishment. He educated Woman more as a
servant than a daughter, and found himself a king without a queen.

The children of this unequal union showed unequal natures, and,
more and more, men seemed sons of the handmaid, rather than
princess.

At last, there were so many Ishmaelites that the rest grew
frightened and indignant. They laid the blame on Hagar, and drove her
forth into the wilderness.

But there were none the fewer Ishmaelites for that.

At last men became a little wiser, and saw that the infant Moses
was, in every case, saved by the pure instincts of Woman's breast. For,
as too much adversity is better for the moral nature than too much
prosperity, Woman, in this respect, dwindled less than Man, though in
other respects still a child in leading-strings.

So Man did her more and more justice, and grew more and more kind.

But yet — his habits and his will corrupted by the past — he did not clearly see that Woman was half himself; that her interests were identical with his; and that, by the law of their common being, he could never reach his true proportions while she remained in any wise shorn of hers.

And so it has gone on to our day; both ideas developing, but more slowly than they would under a clearer recognition of truth and justice, which would have permitted the sexes their due influence on one another, and mutual improvement from more dignified relations.

Wherever there was pure love, the natural influences were, for the time, restored.

Wherever the poet or artist gave free course to his genius, he saw the truth, and expressed it in worthy forms, for these men especially share and need the feminine principle. The divine birds need to be brooded into life and song by mothers.

Wherever religion (I mean the thirst for truth and good, not the love of sect and dogma) had its course, the original design was apprehended in its simplicity, and the dove presaged sweetly from Dodona's oak.

I have aimed to show that no age was left entirely without a witness of the equality of the sexes in function, duty and hope.

Also that, when there was unwillingness or ignorance, which prevented this being acted upon, women had not the less power for their want of light and noble freedom. But it was power which hurt alike them and those against whom they made use of the arms of the servile, — cunning, blandishment, and unreasonable emotion.

That now the time has come when a clearer vision and better action are possible — when Man and Woman may regard one another as brother and sister, the pillars of one porch, the priests of one worship.

I have believed and intimated that this hope would receive an ampler fruition, than ever before, in our own land.

And it will do so if this land carry out the principles from which sprang our national life.

I believe that, at present, women are the best helpers of one another.

Let them think; let them act; till they know what they need.

We only ask of men to remove arbitrary barriers. Some would like to do more. But I believe it needs that Woman show herself in her native dignity, to teach them how to aid her; their minds are so encumbered by tradition. . . .

You ask, what use will she make of liberty, when she has so long been sustained and restrained?

I answer; in the first place, this will not be suddenly given. I read yesterday a debate of this year on the subject of enlarging women's rights over property. It was a leaf from the class-book that is preparing for the needed instruction. The men learned visibly as they spoke. The champions of Woman saw the fallacy of arguments on the opposite side, and were startled by their own convictions. With their wives at home, and the readers of the paper, it was the same. And so the stream flows on; thought urging action, and action leading to the evolution of still better thought.

But were this freedom to come suddenly, I have no fear of the consequences. Individuals might commit excesses, but there is not only in the sex a reverence for decorums and limits inherited and enhanced from generation to generation, which many years of other life could not efface, but a native love, in Woman as Woman, of proportion, of "the simple art of not too much," – a Greek moderation, which would create immediately a restraining party, the natural legislators and instructors of the rest, and would gradually establish such rules as are needed to guard, without impeding, life. . . .

But if you ask me what offices they may fill, I reply – any. I do not care what case you put; let them be sea-captains, if you will. I do not doubt there are women well fitted for such an office. . . .

I think women need, especially at this juncture, a much greater range of occupation than they have, to rouse their latent powers. A party of travellers lately visited a lonely hut on a mountain. There they found an old woman, who told them she and her husband had lived there forty years. "Why," they said, "did you choose so barren a spot?" She "did not know; *it was the man's notion.*"

And, during forty years, she had been content to act, without knowing why, upon "the man's notion." I would not have it so.

In families that I know, some little girls like to saw wood, others to use carpenters' tools. Where these tastes are indulged, cheerfulness and good-humour are promoted. Where they are forbidden, because "such things are not proper for girls," they grow sullen and mischievous.

Fourier had observed these wants of women, as no one can fail to do who watches the desires of little girls, or knows the ennui that haunts grown women, except where they make to themselves a serene little world by art of some kind. He, therefore, in proposing a great variety of employments, in manufactures or the care of plants and animals, allows for one third of women as likely to have a taste for masculine pursuits, one third of men for feminine.

Who does not observe the immediate glow and serenity that is diffused over the life of women, before restless or fretful, by engaging in gardening, building, or the lowest department of art? Here is something that is not routine, something that draws forth life towards the infinite.

I have no doubt, however, that a large proportion of women would give themselves to the same employments as now, because there are circumstances that must lead them. Mothers will delight to make the nest soft and warm. Nature would take care of that; no need to clip the wings of any bird that wants to soar and sing, or finds in itself the strength of pinion for a migratory flight unusual to its kind. The difference would be that *all* need not be constrained to employments for which *some* are unfit.

I have urged upon the sex self-subsistence in its two forms of self-reliance and self-impulse, because I believe them to be the needed means of the present juncture.

I have urged on Woman independence of Man, not that I do not think the sexes mutually needed by one another, but because in Woman this fact has led to an excessive devotion, which has cooled love, degraded marriage, and prevented either sex from being what it should be to itself or the other.

I wish Woman to live, *first* for God's sake. Then she will not make an imperfect man her god, and thus sink to idolatry. Then she will not take what is not fit for her from a sense of weakness and poverty. Then, if she finds what she needs in Man embodied, she will know how to love, and be worthy of being loved.

By being more a soul, she will not be less Woman, for nature is perfected through spirit.

Now there is no woman, only an overgrown child.

That her hand may be given with dignity, she must be able to stand alone. I wish to see men and women capable of such relations as are depicted by Landor in his Pericles and Aspasia, where grace is the natural garb of strength, and the affections are calm, because deep. The softness is that of a firm tissue, as when

"The gods approve
The depth, but not the tumult of the soul,
A fervent, not ungovernable love."

A profound thinker has said, "No married woman can represent the female world, for she belongs to her husband. The idea of Woman must be represented by a virgin."

But that is the very fault of marriage, and of the present relation between the sexes, that the woman *does* belong to the man, instead of forming a whole with him. Were it otherwise, there would be no such limitation to the thought.

Woman, self-centred, would never be absorbed by any relation; it would be only an experience to her as to man. It is a vulgar error that love, *a* love, to Woman is her whole existence; she also is born for Truth and Love in their universal energy. Would she but assume her inheritance, Mary would not be the only virgin mother. Not Manzoni alone would celebrate in his wife the virgin mind with the maternal wisdom and conjugal affections. The soul is ever young, ever virgin.

And will not she soon appear? —the woman who shall vindicate their birthright for all women; who shall teach them what to claim, and how to use what they obtain? Shall not her name be for her era Victoria, for her country and life Virginia? Yet predictions are rash; she herself must teach us to give her the fitting name.

An idea not unknown to ancient times has of late been revived, that, in the metamorphoses of life, the soul assumes the form, first of Man, then of Woman, and takes the chances, and reaps the benefits of either lot. Why then, say some, lay such emphasis on the rights or needs of Woman? What she wins not as Woman will come to her as Man.

That makes no difference. It is not Woman, but the law of right, the law of growth, that speaks in us, and demands the perfection of each being in its kind – apple as apple, Woman as Woman. Without adopting your theory, I know that I, a daughter, live through the life of Man; but what concerns me now is, that my life be a beautiful, powerful, in a word, a complete life in its kind. Had I but one more moment to live I must wish the same. Suppose, at the end of your cycle, your great world-year, all will be completed, whether I exert myself or not (and the supposition is *false*, – but suppose it true), am I to be indifferent about it? Not so! I must beat my own pulse true in the heart of the world; for *that* is virtue, excellence, health. . . . *[Woman in the Nineteenth Century and Kindred Papers (1874; rpt. New York: Greenwood Press, 1968)]*

14. On man and woman, no date

In one of her journals, Fuller allows herself more whimsy and bitterness over the relation between the sexes than she did in *Woman in the Nineteenth Century*.

Woman–Man.—Woman is the flower, man the bee. She sighs out melodious fragrance, and invites the winged laborer. He drains her cup, and carries off the honey. She dies on the stalk; he returns to the hive, well fed, and praised as an active member of the community. *[Life Without and Life Within, p. 349]*

PART

V

The Social Critic
and Journalist

The long detour of Margaret Fuller's career before the period of social and political activity raises questions about the influence of her father's public life. The numerous letters she wrote her father during his terms in the House of Representatives (1817-25) are too self-conscious to yield more than the most tentative clues. By turns gossipy, erudite, and sentimental, they refer seldom to public life, and her request that he send newspapers to her at Miss Prescott's school comes as a surprise. More characteristically, her references to his work suggest a precocious amusement and detachment. When only ten, she asked him to send her the speeches of Mr. Randolph (probably John Randolph of Roanoke), which she judged "Keen, witty (though satirical), and eloquent," adding, "I never troubled my head much about any of the speeches except yours unless to laugh at the endless repetition observable in some." Again, in 1825, she teased him about asserting so positively in one season that Adams will prevail and wavering in the next. [1]

It was not until the mid-1830s that Fuller developed a solid respect for political activity. At that time, Timothy Fuller, preparing a history of his country and perhaps seeking to renew on a healthier footing his old closeness to his daughter, drew her into the study of American history and Jefferson's letters. "A *genuine man*," as she saw him, Jefferson persuaded her that a citizen "need not stoop to be a demagogue, he need not swagger his Demosthenian thunders on every petty local question, he need not despise, nay he ought not to disregard general literature, nor elegant pursuits." [2] Jefferson led her thus to distinguish a political activity which is consistent with culture and dignity from "the paltry game of local politics" which she had always despised and continued to scorn the rest of her life. Jefferson also voiced the belief in America's special democratic destiny that later informed Fuller's *Woman in the Nineteenth Century* and her *Tribune* writing. Most important, this study gave her the exciting sensation, perhaps for the first time, of usefully belonging to her "time and place" (V:5). But the promise hinted here of a social and political vocation was so effectively canceled after her father's death in 1835 that in

July 1842 she responded to the Dorr rebellion in the streets of Providence more like a Federalist than a daughter of a "Jacobin." Unequivocally rejecting her time and place, she wrote that she never felt a greater "aversion to my environment," and prayed to the "Eternal" for a heart purged from "this hot haste about ephemeral trifles" (V:6).

As we shall see, this prim repudiation of contemporary political action in 1842 began as early as the next year to give way; by gradual stages, corresponding to her various removes from New England—to the West, to New York, and to Europe—it was transformed into interest, then enthusiasm, and finally active engagement. Fuller's conservative period coincides with the high tide of her friendship with Emerson, with the years in which she found his anti-historical bias most attractive. Conservatism for both was a matter of taste, a function of skeptical temperament. But their shared skepticism about the systems of other men drove them in different directions. Emerson's skepticism threw him back, especially in his public persona, on the unbroken unity between the self-reliant self and the perfected *ideas* of America, while Fuller's made her doubt systems even of her own making and finally forced her outward to observe with sharpening curiosity the actual conditions of Americans and to collect what nuggets of meaning she could derive from them. But this evolution was slow and nowhere in sight when, in the last months of 1840, she refused to join in George Ripley's communal society and even to discuss abolition in her Conversations. Since she later became a warm advocate of Utopian socialism and abolition this early resistance bears examination.

Different as Brook Farm was from Emerson's "crystal cell," it too began with a door slammed on the church. Convinced that the Christian life could not flourish under existing social conditions, George Ripley resigned his ministry in the effort to create an exemplary society in small. More dedicated than worldly-wise, he chose as the site of the Brook Farm Institute of Agriculture and Education 170 acres in West Roxbury, most of them gravel. Established as a joint-stock company, it was designed "to combine the thinker and the worker, as far as possible, in the same individual" and to gather people together as equals who would run, according to their several tastes and talents, a farm and school freed of "the pressure of our competitive institutions." Implicitly, it was expected to disclose a new social order. Experimental Utopias, though mostly conceived in Europe, were spawned furiously in America, the land that James Madison told Harriet Martineau was "useful in proving things before held impossible." By benefiting and uniting people of all classes, the communitarian socialism of Robert Owen or Charles Fourier was deliberately shaped to minimize class struggle and to preclude revolution. Although George and Sophia Ripley had read Fourier and, as we shall see, in 1844 converted Brook Farm into a Fourierist "phalanx," they began in 1840 with native Transcendental spontaneity. [3]

Nevertheless the Ripleys early efforts to enlist Alcott, Emerson, and Fuller all failed. Alcott was shaping his own utopia, and Emerson declined to move from his "present prison to a prison a little larger." Fuller's refusal was more complex. Her resentful years in Groton had robbed farm life of glamour, and her bitter memory of her father's strict regimen made her resist forced social planning. Emerson's influence too speaks in her caveat "We are not ripe to reconstruct society yet," and in the unconscious vanity of her assertion that she is "so unrelated" to society that the corruption of her times has left no mark on her. Craving an association based on "destinies," not "efforts," she noted in her journal that she belonged "to a constellation, not a phalanx," and judged far nobler the "man entirely unpledged, unbound" than one committed to any doctrine. [4] All this was bravado, not boldness. Nevertheless, Fuller enjoyed the ferment Brook Farm produced and frequently visited there, offering Conversations and listening to confidences, and walking in the pinewoods. As she came to know the place, she tentatively endorsed the communal principle while sustaining her objection to the haste and blind optimism of its execution.

In 1844, the Ripleys, influenced by Albert Brisbane, the chief American disciple of Fourier, remodeled the Farm as closely as they could after Fourier's phalanx. Fourier was the first writer of the period to base a critique of bourgeois society squarely on a materialist reading of human nature. Civilization, he argued, had failed because it had suppressed passions inseparable from the human condition. He proposed, by accepting and utilizing the passions, to create small exemplary communities, or phalanxes, in which labor would be freed from coercion, and sexuality no longer repressed. Funded by private capital, the phalanx would share profits according to a reshuffled hierarchy of labor, capital, and talent. What was penetrating and advanced in Fourier's thought was offset by wild prophetic fantasies and an obsession with mathematics which led him to insist on precise proportions for the buildings in the community. Brisbane was a reformer enamoured of technology, a man in whom mathematics and compassion seemed to nourish each other, yet for his American readers he was shrewd enough to edit out the master's madness and his modern sexual thought. Omitting Fourier's millenial seas of lemonade and playing down the radical-feminist and free-love implications of his sanction of "passional attraction," Brisbane stressed the validity of "attractive industry"—the pursuit of a variety of preferences in labor—and of divided wealth. Notwithstanding these sober adjustments, many in the Transcendental community fell away in horror from the mechanical organization of labor by "Groups and Series." Fuller continued to visit, doubtful but curious, missing "leisure and liberality" but finding, despite "a good deal of sound to the machinery," that "the wheels seemed to turn easily." [5] After she left Massachusetts, as we shall see, the seriousness of Fourier's grasp of social oppression held increasing interest for her.

In a similar way, her early response to the abolitionists was marked by a defensive individualism. Nowhere did the Transcendentalists of Emerson's persuasion so clearly subscribe to a class consciousness—even while denying they

were a class—as in their response in the 1830s and 1840s to
the abolitionists. For the fiercest and most organized
opposition to the abolitionists came from "gentlemen of
property and standing." Pressure groups, which included
what they called "despicable outcasts," threatened the
authority of local elites, and the abolitionists' direct appeal
to women and children was seen as an incursion on
patriarchal authority. [6] Although the Transcendentalists did
not share these fears and opposed slavery in principle, they
felt the abolitionists' concerns were necessarily external and
vulgarly sectarian: their audience was the faceless crowd and
their language had to be shrill enough to be heard. The style
of the abolitionists, their heat and vehemence, combined
with their threat to individualism, nearly distracted Fuller for
years from the content of their exhortations. In this period,
she praised the elder Channing for "standing apart from the
conflicts of the herd" in his book *Slavery* (1836): "So
refreshing its calm, benign atmosphere, after the pestilence-
bringing gales of the day." Invective and strained rhetoric
immediately deafened her, and she criticized the polemical
tone of Theodore Parker and her friend W. H. Channing:
"Truth needs no such weapons." [7] But her neglect of
abolition in the Boston Conversations contrasts with her
awakened interest in *Woman in the Nineteenth Century* and
her *New York Tribune* contributions. Going west with Sarah
and James Clarke in the summer of 1843 helped to change
her attitudes.

Of course, Fuller did not see slaves on that trip but rather
the new settlers and the Indian tribes those settlers were
driving out. In the narrative made from her journals, *Summer
on the Lakes*, her steadily growing appreciation for both
groups began to break the spell of New England elitism. In
her writing about the Indians, it is often hard to separate the
fresh insight from the platitude, her self-examination from
her complacency. As the book opens, the "quiet satisfaction"
she felt at seeing that Niagara matched its description gave
way, when she let her own response emerge, to an
"undefined dread" and the irrepressible fantasy of an Indian
ambush (V:10). Her candor here about her conditioned fear

may have helped her later, when she encountered actual Indians, to write about them with vividness and sensitivity. She perpetually identifies them with the gorgeous and immense landscape of the West. Indians and land become, as they would for Thoreau, measures for the white man, for his use of the earth and its creatures, for his honesty, magnaminity, and reverence. [8] But romanticizing the Indian past was hardly novel; it linked her to the Whig critics of Jackson's ruthless Indian policy. Then too, her preoccupation with the degradation of the contemporary Indian may have sprung either from a kindred sense of oppression or from its opposite, an inability to break through their discomforting otherness. Whatever its source, her shame and indignation at the crimes of her own race were genuine and made her keen to find in books on Indians and in the whites she met the psychohistory of racism, the inevitable "aversion of the injurer for him he has degraded." We may be amused by her presumption in writing, after staying alone several days near the Indian encampment of Mackinaw Island, "I feel acquainted with the soul of this race," but her sympathetic exposure to the Indians may have fed her later interest in blacks.

As the frontier exposed the democratic experiment at its baldest extreme, Fuller looked to the white settlements for a "new order." She saw the relative disconnectedness of the white settler from the wilderness first in his complacent instinct to spit into Niagara Falls and ludicrously to offer himself there as a guide. (This Fuller compared to asking for an usher to point out the moon.) In Chicago she saw only negatives: "I like not the petty intellectualities, cant, and bloodless theory there at home, but this merely instinctive existence, to those who live it so 'first rate,' 'off hand' and 'go ahead,' pleases me no better." The dreary alternative appeared to be importation of Yankee narrowness and calculation in the men or of European standards of culture in the unhappy women, who usually had been dragged unwillingly and unprepared into the West. But people like William Clarke, James' brother, who took her on a wagon tour of northern Illinois, began to feed her hope for a new culture; she was enchanted by William's tales and "unstudied lore, the unwritten poetry which common life presents to a strong and gentle mind. It was a great contrast to the subtleties of analysis, the philosophical strainings of which I had seen so much." By the end of this voyage in which she had made her bed on a bar-room floor and shot the rapids with aplomb in an Indian canoe, she called it "pleasant" to hear "rough men tell pieces out of their own common lives, in place of the frippery talk of some fine circle with its conventional sentiment, and timid, second-hand criticism" (Writing later on travel books by women, she noted that journeying stretched the authors' minds.) [9] Such experiences educated her tastes and perceptions and, perhaps, prepared her for the diversity of New York.

The challenge of adapting to the frontier coupled with the difficulty of talking her way into the exclusively male preserves of the Harvard Library to complete research for her book must have eased her transition to demotic New York as the first female member of the working press. In 1844, Harlem was farmland and Central Park pasture for goats and turf for squatters, but to the south, muddy and reeking streets notwithstanding, the city seethed with life and Greeley's *New York Tribune* on Nassau Street missed little of it. The *Tribune* began publication in 1841 as a paper dedicated first to the elevation of the masses—the reading public generated by the new penny papers—and second to the success of the liberal Whigs. Greeley hoped to crowd out the sensational rival penny papers by his commitment to morality, social progress, and the arts.

The *Tribune* reflected what mattered to Greeley, the pride and excitement in the city that had dazzled the farm boy and the indignation over social injustice that staggered him when he saw the victims of the panic of 1837 and that made him for a while an ardent Fourierist. Greeley was no radical: he sympathized with woman's claim for justice but rejected divorce reform and suffrage; he opposed through legal forms the extension of slaveholding territory but attacked abolitionists for divisiveness; and he was appalled by working conditions but fought labor unionism and strikes. Yet he was compassionate and open-minded and, as an editor, progressive or outspoken enough to be often embattled in his attacks on the Mexican War or nativism and his support of the Irish or Fourier. An associate recalled that Greeley was never so happy as when at bay, and he was never more attacked and warlike than in the nearly two years when Fuller worked with him. [10] This was the man and the journal that could help her pick up the thread dropped ten years before, root her again in her time and place, and set her in action.

"Mr. Greeley I like, nay more, love. He is, in his habits, a—plebian; in his heart, a noble man. His abilities, in his own way, are great. He believes in mine to a surprising extent. We are true friends," she wrote to her brother Eugene. Glossing over the bumpy beginning of their relationship, this description was accurate. They were both perhaps more useful friends to each other than to Mary Greeley, who paid back Horace for his single-minded attention to his paper with her whimsically tyrannical mothering of their son "Pickie," whom all three adored. Until she moved into town, Fuller made their home less the "Castle Doleful" Greeley later called it, drawing callers for Mary and becoming deeply attached to Pickie. Horace, whom she found as "disinterestedly generous" as her mother, was the first in a long while who could "teach" her many things. [11]

"I like living here," she wrote Sarah Shaw, "All flows freely and I find I don't dislike wickedness and wretchedness more than pettiness and coldness. My own individual life is easy to lead." It was not her uncomplicated love for Horace Greeley that made possible these remarkable claims, and certainly not her contorted and wasted passion for the deft social climber James Nathan. More than the various stimulation they provided, it was the city, the bracing concreteness of its problems, her own growing mastery and complete freedom of action, her vast audience and their responsiveness, that gave her that exhilarating sense of mobility and engagement. All this made her relish "this great field which opens before me," and exult that she had "never been so well situated." [12]

Margaret Fuller's New York was literary soirees or meetings with old Isaac Hopper, the intrepid Underground Railroad engineer and last Quaker in knee breeches, who was now planning the first halfway house for female convicts. (Hopper Home still functions on the Lower East Side, not far from its original site on Twelfth Street.) It was trysts with Nathan at Lydia Maria Child's house or at the office of Dr. Leger, the magnetic healer who reportedly cured her spinal curvature. [13] It was tours of galleries and studios, or (with W. H. Channing, then a city missionary) of schools, hospitals, asylums, prisons, or that sink of poverty and crime, the Five Points area. It was concerts, or the Tabernacle lecture of Cassius M. Clay, the charismatic antislavery publisher whose press had been destroyed in Kentucky. New York was the refuge of Danish adventurer, Harro Harring, who brought news of Mazzini, Garibaldi, and revolution in Europe, whose novel Fuller impetuously helped finance from her slender reserves. It was also the refuge of thousands of Irish whose mass flight from the potato famine made them a social problem in their new home, and it was the great harbor embraced by the "wood of masts" that she found better than any poem. Standing in the city, Fuller felt "the life blood rushing from an entire continent to swell her heart." [14]

Fuller's life was integral to her work, and most of it went into her writing. Greeley had hired her to fill the spot vacated by Albert Brisbane (later filled by George Ripley) and he expected her to report on social conditions as well as lend literary prestige to the paper. Book reviews often became occasions for her social commentary, and in the nearly two hundred articles she wrote in New York, she supported all his major causes as well as generating some of her own. The ignorance and deviousness attributed to the Irish she analyzed as "the faults of an oppressed race" (V:16), and she welcomed the persecuted Jews and Germans. She inveighed against the war in Mexico, Southern slavery, and Northern prejudice, and she defended even the rhetoric of Cassius Clay, called fanatical by his enemies. She mocked the cowardice of publishers, when one house broke a contract with Harring because his book was "not duly orthodox." [15] She demanded more enlightened education and broader employment for the poor and for women. She played on the guilt of the rich to win support for charitable institutions, and she urged them to supply both companionship and furniture for Hopper Home.

No longer preoccupied with ideal friendship or restricted to acquaintance in her class, Fuller's concern for women in trouble could flourish, and her feminism grew with her social awareness. According to Dall, Nathan had heard of her interest in "abandoned women" and first approached her for advice about a young woman he had seduced in Germany who had followed him to America. Fuller not only talked with the woman and "saved her from further profanation," but provided "safety and a home" to others in similar difficulties. [16] Though Fuller's advocacy in her articles about women prisoners has more than a touch of *noblesse oblige*, in the context of prevailing convictions, her approach was advanced. Penologists then held that "if a girl had natural warmth and passion, even a single sexual experience made her capable of any crime." And Tocqueville, visiting prisons in America, was told by a corrections officer that "the reformation of girls, who have contracted bad morals, is a chimera which it is hopeless to pursue." [17] In this atmosphere, Fuller's support of Eliza Farnham's controversial rehabilitation program at Sing Sing was imaginative and bold. Her energetic commitment to these women was simply the practical application of her theory of evil reasserted in her attack in the *Tribune*, March 4, 1846, on capital punishment; she argued that the Creative spirit "has permitted the temporary existence of evil as a condition necessary to bring out [in persons] free agency and individuality of character." Moreover, her involvement was backed by respect. As she wrote to Nathan, after visiting the women at Hopper Home, "I like them better than most women I meet, because, if any good is left, it is so genuine, and they make no false pretensions nor cling to shadows." [18]

As her job as a reporter gave her access to worlds hitherto closed to a woman of her class, a deepening concern for other oppressed groups—immigrants, blacks, the poor, the blind, the insane—followed. The modern reader may feel in this concern the same ambivalence as in her attitude to the Indians. Liberal as her reportage was for the time, it was still eminently genteel muckraking: the Jew is subjected to age-old stereotyping, the poor to kindly pity. Her inexperience with social issues coupled with that unquestioned confidence in the authority of her own feelings made her naive or condescending in these pieces as often she was moving and advanced. They should be read as apprentice exercises through which she groped her way toward her more informed, critical, and independent role of foreign correspondent.

The failure of many of her old friends to approve her new career forced her to understand how she had changed. "They think I ought to produce something excellent, while I am satisfied to aid in the great work of popular education," she confided to a friend. "I never regarded literature merely as a collection of exquisite products, but rather as a means of mutual interpretation. Feeling that many are reached and in some degree helped, the thoughts of every day seem worth noting, though in a form that does not inspire me." She no longer needed that old intoxication, much of it self-induced, of reaching for a unique, unprecedented form of expression. The pursuit of writing as "mutual interpretation," as a process in which the writer, impatient with static products, joins with forces for social change, was demanding enough. While with *The Dial* she aimed not "at leading public opinion, but at stimulating each man to think for himself," [19] the stimulus of a mass audience and her goal of popular education began to reverse these objectives. Then the urgency of social issues all around her and the discipline of Greeley's deadlines effectively destroyed her desire with the Dial to have "the will palsied like Hamlet by a deep-searching tendency."

But when it came to solutions for social ills, Fuller had difficulty in taking a new direction. For specific institutions she could outline pragmatic reforms, but deep-seated social problems aroused only lofty hopes for a wise national policy. Though in her editorial pieces she liked to conjure up the image of purifying fire, it remained spiritual metaphor as long as she was in America. Though she claimed, on January 17, 1846, that "we ourselves belong to the 'extreme left' of the Army of Progress," she declined to act in a "spirit of defiance and haste." Instead, she depended on the twin bastions which were her Jeffersonian and Transcendentalist heritage: her confidence in the high moral destiny of America and her faith in the self-determining powers of the individual. In *Woman* she had written, "This country is as surely destined to elucidate a great moral law, as Europe was to promote the mental culture of Man," (IV:13), and at the beginning of her *Tribune* career, she was sanguine about America fulfilling Heaven's "great promise." But a year later, after the annexation of Texas and on the eve of war with Mexico, the promise had become ambiguous: the national eagle still "will lead the van" in the coming time "but whether to soar upward to the sun or to stoop for helpless prey, who now dares promise?" After the first victory of the war, she wrote contemptuously, "our stars have lighted us only to the ancient heathen—the vulgar path of national aggrandizement." And in her last month in New York, "Our hopes as to National honor and goodness are almost wearied out, and we feel obliged to turn to the Individual and to the Future for consolation." [20]

This second recourse—her faith in the potency of the individual leader, in the leaven that would lift up the masses, as she liked to put it—seemed at first more sound. "If nations go astray, the narrow path may always be found and followed by the individual man," she wrote on July 4, 1845, adding further, "Let men feel that in private lives, more than in public measures, must the salvation of the country lie." [21] But for the January 1, 1846, *Tribune*, she gloomily remarked that there was "no great genius at this day living," and her national commentary remained dispirited from then until she left the country.

Not only had the great leaders dropped from view, but the doctrine of self-determination also seemed increasingly irrelevant, as she fixed her attention on those who through poverty, degradation, or ignorance were denied the wherewithal of self-determination. As with her response to the prisoners, education and moral enlightenment came first to the mind of this woman who owed so much to self-culture, but in New York the proportions of the task seemed massive. She never offered a threat to established power, but at moments she began to glimpse that other institutions had to be transformed before the oppressed could really learn, and that the privileged, for all their education, were necessarily oppressors. Confident only that the solutions could not emerge from any political party, she glanced, rather fleetingly to be sure, at the creation of new institutions, the promise of leadership from the people, and the dream of a classless society. [22]

In this connection, one of the most tantalizing suggestions in the *Tribune* archives is Fuller's translation, published August 5, 1845, of a letter from the Paris correspondent of the *Deutsche Schnellpost*, a German-immigrants' newspaper. Among her regular contributions to the *Tribune* were reviews of European journals and a survey of news from abroad, often light or bizarre. But this article, occupying half of the *Tribune*'s front page, drew on the rich recent political experience of Europe and argued, as Fuller had done and would continue to do, that political progress does not necessarily bring social progress in its wake. According to this analyst, probably Heinrich Börnstein, the requisite "wider principles" would be found neither in abstract humanism nor "too sensual" communism, but in the socialism where both converged. Moreover, this socialist school was no party but a loosely associated group of laborers and hounded philosophers like Marx or Ruge. The author then deplores Marx's criticism of Bauer in the *Holy Family* (just published that year) and Ruge's of Marx, though he is confident too that truth arises from such contacts, and he closes with a long quotation from Engels' *Condition of the working Class in England*. This is surely among the very earliest notices of Marx and Engels in America. More remarkable is the closeness between Fuller's ideas at this point and Börnstein's. It is interesting to speculate about what might have happened had communication opened between the two journalists, and had Fuller followed the thought of Marx and Engels in the next three years. In the *Communist Manifesto* she might have approached answers to questions that were to become increasingly pressing for her when, in Europe, no patriotic idealism veiled reality, and she confronted class division in all its nakedness.

In August 1846, she sailed for England as one of the first American correspondents of either sex and as companion to the philanthropic Marcus Spring, his wife, Rebecca, and

young son, Eddie. In asking Sam Ward for a loan of five
hundred dollars, she regretted briefly that she had not seen
Europe with him ten years before: "It would have given my
genius wings" and compensated for "my painful youth." But
disappointment had brought her into "liberal communion
with the woful [sic] struggling crowd of fellowmen." In a
rare lapse of prophetic powers, she wrote that now her mind
and character were "too much formed" to be much changed
by Europe; instead it would offer her a "new field of
observation" for her career as journalist. [2 4]

In Great Britain, exploration of social conditions and new
tendencies crowded out most of the time she would earlier
have spent with culture and "genius." Thus she had only one
day for the British Museum and omitted visiting most of the
private galleries. The memory of Burns' rebuke to the
aristocracy earns more space in her writing than her visit to
once-cherished Wordsworth. She regretted that Wordsworth's
"habits of seclusion" deafened him "to the voice which cries
loudly from other parts of England, and will not be stilled by
sweet poetic suasion or philosophy, for it is the cry of men in
the jaws of destruction." (These words contrast sharply with
her earlier praise for the sweet detachment of Channing's
anti-slavery book.) She listened with interest to British
reformers, though she did not fail to reproach them for their
wars with China and Ireland. Style was still a consideration
with her, and George Dawson, James Martineau, and
W. J. Fox could not match Channing's eloquence or Parker's
"sustained flow," but she cared more now about the
"homely adaptation of their thought to common wants." She
wrote enthusiastically about improvement of tenements, the
public baths of Edinburgh and public laundries of London,
and the Mechanics Institute of Liverpool whose director
quoted *The Dial* in urging self-reliance on his students.
Everywhere she noted the energetic versatility of British
women: working in publishing and art, stocking the
provincial museums, and creating new educational institutions for working people. [2 5]

Galvanizing her intensified attention to reform was the
vivid and omnipresent shock of poverty in England. Dogging
her progress through all the celebrated cities was the

unforgettable sight of the industrial slums, especially their worn female victims "too dull to carouse" and their children fed on opium. "Poverty in England has terrors of which I never dreamed at home," she wrote; yet we know she had toured the slums of Five Points with Channing. What her unconscious adherence to the democratic rhetoric of America made her miss at home the European tradition of critical political rhetoric laid bare in England.

While England made her urge intelligent men of means to take steps before it was too late, the more volatile and precarious state of affairs in France pointed to more drastic and wholesale change. In 1847, the rapid growth of two different tendencies was preparing the explosion that in the next year would blast Louis Philippe off the throne. The bourgeois liberals and educated industrial workers, who wanted the political freedoms won in the French Revolution complemented socially by the means to exercise and enjoy it, represented one tendency. The theoreticians who analyzed the ills of capitalism and built alternative socialist Utopias—the Saint-Simonians and the Fourieriests—led the other. [27] Fuller met Victor-Prosper Considérant, Fourier's chief disciple, [28] and very likely met Pierre Leroux, who had broken from Saint-Simon to build a system of his own; both men were active in the revolutionary government the next year. (Leroux had founded *La Revue Indépendente*, the journal which published a translation of Fuller's essay on American literature and invited her to write more pieces.) Everywhere she saw signs of frustration and ferment: Paris workers attending night school, and Lyons weavers too oppressed to do so. She met Pierre-Jean de Béranger, jailed for satirical songs which kept alive the spirit of the Revolution, and she read incendiary leaflets in the street. As in England, her dispatches gave more space to social concerns—prostitution, a school for the mentally retarded, the new crèches (or day-care centers)—than to cultural ones. She made time, however, to pay homage to the manuscripts of Rousseau, "the precursor of all we most prize," whose "spirit was intimate with the fundamental truths of human nature and fraught with prophecy. [29]

Fuller's swift public tour was paralleled by a rushing private voyage. As Europe heated up for revolution, Fuller's experiences and encounters were preparing her for fundamental and irrevocable change in her personal life. If she had come to Europe still hoping to join the expedient Nathan, that hope was effectively killed when she received a letter in Edinburgh announcing his engagement to a German woman. Shortly afterward, descending Ben Lomond after a four-mile climb, she was separated from Marcus Spring, failed to find the path, and was forced to spend a dangerous night alone on a narrow ledge, keeping in constant motion to survive the cold mist that mounted in visionary shapes. She resisted the lures of fatal passivity and was found in the morning by a rescue party of shepherds. Her "mental experience," she wrote in her dispatch, was "most precious and profound," a "presentation of stern, serene realities," and apparently it was also cathartic. [30] She not only relinquished pursuit of Nathan, but also effectively quit all longing for misty embraces, whether of man or idea.

At the same time, Europeans who had admired her *Woman* and her newly issued *Papers on Literature and Art* were giving her a handsome reception, and made her feel life rich with tangible possibilities. "As soon as I reached England," she confided to Caroline Sturgis, "I found how right we were in supposing there was elsewhere a greater range of interesting character among the men, than with us." To Richard she amplified, "from their habits of conversation so superior to those of Americans, I am able to come out a great deal more than I can at home, and they seem proportionately interested." But her pleasure sprang less from the men than from herself. "I find myself in my element in European society," she wrote Emerson. "It does not, indeed, come up to my ideal, but so many of the encumbrances are cleared away that used to weary me in America, that I can enjoy a freer play of faculty and feel, if not like a bird in the air, at least as easy as a fish in water." [31] It did not come up to her ideal, but made her freer: she all but confesses that idealism confined her. Even before she reached Italy, which would move her from active

liberalism to radicalism, Europe was offering her two crucial
sensations America never did: the shock of class consciousness and the warm bath of personal (and implicitly physical)
self-acceptance. Tocqueville's knot was coming undone. She
was more than ready for the liberating influence of Mazzini
in London and of Mickiewicz and Sand in Paris, who would
help her discover how to move against the two pressures,
social and religious, that bound American women in place.

   She met Giuseppe Mazzini in her last month in England.
Driven by political urgency nearly twenty years earlier to
abandon his literary aspirations, Mazzini was well suited to
help her channel the powerful indignation the tour of Great
Britain had stirred. (Mazzini's premise that you cannot
transform the inward man if he works fourteen hours a
day [32] now made more sense than Emerson's doctrine of
"the infinitude of the private man.") Barred from Italy
fifteen years before, Mazzini had tirelessly pursued his vision
of a united and Republican Europe to be initiated by a
Republican Italy centered in Rome, to be informed by a new
religious synthesis, "the religion of Humanity," and to move
toward the eventual fusion of all classes into one. After the
failure of uprisings in northern Italy, he had been working
quietly in London raising money to revive his "Young Italy"
abroad. Appealing to the sentimental pity of the British
upper classes for Italian children exploited as organ-grinders
and vendors of white mice, he had opened a free school for
Italian workmen where he added a fourth R to the traditional
three: revolution—thinly guised as history and geography.
Harro Harring introduced Fuller to Mazzini, who knew her
work through the Carlyles and invited her to speak at his
school's anniversary celebration. Despite the reservations
about Christianity she and Mazzini shared, for the *Tribune*
she compared the students to the disciples of Judaea and
predicted that these poor Italian boys could be in these times
more effective than an Orphic poet with their people. Her
language is symptomatic of the effect this ascetic and
charismatic figure—dressed perpetually in velvet mourning for
Italy—had, especially on women with whom he felt a special
affinity.

Mazzini's real importance for Fuller lay in his incorporating many of the values she still cherished while helping her to abandon those beginning to fail her and endorse new ones she needed. He shared her conviction that self-education was our first duty, but he generalized it until it held the secret of immortality: "Humanity is like a man who lives indefinitely and is always learning," he wrote. Like her, he located the destructive force in materialism, but he coupled it with the individualism Fuller had, until recently, cherished uncritically; thus he attacked America as "the negative, individualistic, materialistic school." He pitted against such individualism the "collective thought," the determination learned from the Saint-Simonians to subordinate the parts of society to the whole. Thus he brought a new selflessness to nationalism, which was for him the prelude to the "association" of all humanity. What put teeth in this roseate vision was his conviction that *war*, undertaken by the subject people without the intervention of foreign governments, was the sole recourse for Italy. While Fuller's ideas remained more secular and less hopeful than Mazzini's, the unshakable collectivity of his vision helped her to move intellectually past her floundering dependence on heroes and men of good will, and his calm acceptance of the need for armed struggle undermined her fading faith in reform; both developments were preconditions for her own radicalism. Recognizing Fuller's value, Mazzini sent off letters of introduction to his mother and many allies on the continent, and Fuller felt committed enough to his plan to smuggle him disguised in her party into Italy. But she did not give herself over to hero worship. Even in her first account, while she called him "the most beauteous person I have seen," she added subtly, "He is one in whom holiness has purified, but somewhat dwarfed the man." [33]

By contrast, Adam Mickiewicz, the great Polish poet, whom she met shortly before leaving Paris, was one in whom holiness must have seemed only to amplify the man. Mickiewicz shared with Mazzini a love of literature and the will to put it aside to struggle for freedom, a devotion to the land of his birth, a commitment to fight for its nationhood and republicanism throughout Europe. Their political differences lay primarily in Mickiewicz's mystical authoritarianism—his subscription to Catholicism and his deference to the Pope and the Bonapartes. Of crucial importance to Fuller was the stress he laid on women's rights. By way of introduction, she sent him a volume of the poems of Emerson, whom Mickiewicz much admired. It is worth note that the Emerson he had quoted frequently in support of his own inflammatory lectures at the Collège de France was sometimes distorted in the process. Though he cited Emerson on intuition, self-reliance, and organic connectedness, he went far beyond his source when he tied these values to a heroic agrarian folk that would redeem the world. And for all his apocalypticism, Mickiewicz needed time and space more than Emerson, who, he declared, "isolates us too much, not taking into account epoch, nation or earth. Emerson's man dangles one knows not where." [34]

Meeting Fuller was, for Mickiewicz, one of those experiences which "consoles and fortifies." He found her a "*true* person," the only "woman to whom it has been given to touch what is decisive in the present world and to have a presentiment of the world of the future." But his first letter to her suggests he believed she needed still more rooting in the physical present: "For you the first step of your deliverance . . . is to know whether you are to be permitted to remain a virgin." So ripe was Fuller for sexual "deliverance" that she apparently took no offense at his presumption. Moreover, she saw in Mickiewicz the longed-for synthesis: "I found in him the man I had long wished to see, with the intellect and passions in due proportion for a full and healthy human being, with a soul constantly inspiring," she wrote Emerson. [35]

To Emerson's neighbor, Elizabeth Hoar, Fuller described her equally powerful encounter with George Sand. In Sand, Fuller recognized her own androgynous ideal, the forehead and eyes "beautiful," the lower part of the face "strong and masculine," these elements fused by "the expression of *goodness*, wholeness, and power, that pervaded the whole,—the truly human heart and nature that shone in the eyes." Enjoying the sense of so rich, so prolific, so ardent a genius," she adds, "I liked the woman in her, too, very much; I never liked a woman better." Most striking is the change in Fuller's response to Sand's sexual habits. Though her boldness in defending Sand in her writing for America had shocked her readers, it was always qualified. "Those who would reform the world must show that they do not speak in the heat of wild impulse," she had cautioned in *Woman* (IV:23), and in her *Tribune* review she cried, "Would indeed the surgeon had come with quite clean hands!"(III:16). Now, in the freer atmosphere of France, she writes without apology that Sand's "range" was too great for any one man permanently to "interest and command her," and sums up: "She needs no defence, but only to be understood, for she has bravely acted out her nature, and always with good intentions" (V:13). Nearly three years later, Fuller was to write of her own passion, "for bad or for good, I acted out my character" (VI:48); the echo is strong proof of the sanction Sand's extraordinary influence provided for the younger woman.

How often Fuller saw Sand we do not know, but she regretted she had not more time to give to "this real and important relation" with Mickiewicz. But the Springs' itinerary was for Italy, and Fuller left Paris with mixed feelings. "It pains me to come away, having touched only the glass over the picture," she wrote. But on the other hand, she had never been entirely comfortable with the "slippery" French: "My French teacher says, I speak and act like an Italian, and I hope, in Italy I shall find myself more at home." [36]

Reluctant as she was to leave these extraordinary influences, Sand's freedom and wholeness, Mickiewicz' exhortations to free herself sexually, and Mazzini's inspiration to devote herself actively combined to propel her toward the land and the city her earliest study had taught her to love. Rome would prove more a home than any she had known. Here historical events would combine with Fuller's

unleashed capacity for growth and change to offer her her
most comprehensive definition of self, her most satisfying
and radical work.

Notes

1. December 20, 1824; November 22, 1820; January 31, 1825, Houghton Ms.

2. Houghton MS.

3. Arthur Eugene Bestor, Jr., *Backwoods Utopias: The Sectarian and Owenite
Phases of Communitarian Socialism in America, 1663-1827* (Philadelphia: University of Pennsylvania Press, 1950), pp. 1-10.

4. *Journals of Ralph Waldo Emerson*, eds. E. W. Emerson and W. E. Forbes
(Boston: Houghton Mifflin Co., 1910), V, 473: *Memoirs*, II, 57, 58-59, 73.

5. Georgianna Bruce Kirby, *Years of Experience* (New York: G. P. Putnam's
Sons, 1887), p. 186.

6. Leonard L. Richards, *Gentlemen of Property and Standing: Anti-Abolition-
ist Mobs in Jacksonian America* (New York: Oxford University Press, 1970), pp.
58-62.

7. *Memoirs*, I, 129-30; letter to Mary Rotch and Miss Gifford, February 5,
1843, Houghton MS. An earlier letter to James Clarke (II:11) hinted, however,
that should action replace theory she would be ready for it.

8. Thoreau first urged her to make a book of her notes, and the digressive and
subjective narrative structure very likely influenced his *A Week on the Concord
and Merrimack Rivers*; the use of the Indian as a measure appears, of course, in
Walden.

9. Rusk, *Letters*, III, 200-201n.; *Summer on the Lakes in 1843* (1844; rpt.
Nieuwkoop: B. De Graaf, 1972), pp. 67, 249; *Kindred Papers*, p. 287.

10. James Parton, *Life of Horace Greeley* (New York: Mason Bros., 1855),
pp. 263-65. See also Glyndon G. Van Deusen, *Horace Greeley: Nineteenth-
Century Crusader* (Philadelphia: University of Pennsylvania Press, 1953).

11. Higginson, 209; *Memoirs*, II, 51.

12. February 25, 1845, Jay Papers, Houghton; Higginson, p. 208.

13. Kirby, p. 213.

14. *Tribune*, September 8, 1845.

15. *Tribune*, September 8, 1845.

16. Copy of May 29, 1908, letter to Higginson, Houghton MS.

17. W. David Lewis, "The Female Criminal and the Prisons of New York,
1825-45," *New York History*, 42 (1961), 217.

18. *Love-Letters of Margaret Fuller, 1845-1846* (New York: D. Appleton,
1903), p. 114.

19. *Memoirs*, II, 164, BPL MS.

20. *Tribune*, January 1, 1845; January 1, 1846; May 21, 1846; July 8, 1846.
See also Francis E. Kearns, "Margaret Fuller's Social Criticism," Dissertation,
University of North Carolina, 1960, Ch. IV.

21. See also January 1, 1845, where she asserts that "ten just men" can save
the nation.

22. See especially "Prince's Poems (August 13, 1845), "Thom's Poems" (August 22, 1845), and "Mrs. Norton's Child of the Islands" (July 26, 1845), reprinted together as "Poets of the People," *Papers on Literature*, II, 1-21.

23. Heinrich Börnstein often wrote dispatches for the *Schellpost* and was at that time proprietor, in Paris, of *Vorwärts*, a radical paper that published people named in the article—Weitling, Ruge, and Marx—and later started a paper in St. Louis with Bernays, also named here.

24. March 3, 1845, Samuel Gray Ward Papers, Houghton.

25. *At Home and Abroad*, pp. 132-133, 168, 174, 162, 127.

26. *At Home and Abroad*, p. 171.

27. Georges Duveau, *1848: The Making of a Revolution*, trans. Anne Carter (New York: Random House, 1967), pp. 209-212.

28. She wrote Channing that Considérant and his associates were "full of hope and their Propaganda has a real and increasing influence as is proved by the taunts which every other party has in store. . . ." BPL MS.

29. *At Home and Abroad*, p. 207.

30. *At Home and Abroad*, p. 155.

31. *Memoirs*, II, 172; September 27, 1846, Houghton MS; *Memoirs*, II, 184.

32. Gwilym O. Griffith, *Mazzini: Prophet of Modern Europe* (New York: Harcourt Brace, 1932), p. 177.

33. Gaetano Savemini, *Mazzini*, trans. I.M. Rawson (New York: Crowell-Collier, 1962), p. 57 Denis Mack Smith, *Italy: A Modern History* (Ann Arbor: University of Michigan Press, 1969), p. 13; *Memoirs*, II, 173.

34. Edmund Ordon, "Mickiewicz and Emerson," *University of Buffalo Studies* No. 1 (July 1956), p. 43.

35. Leopold Wellisz, *The Friendship of Margaret Fuller d'Ossoli and Adam Mickiewicz* (New York: Polish Book Importing Co., 1947), pp. 18, 13; *Memoirs*, II, 207.

36. *Memoirs*, II, 201-202.

CONTEMPORARIES ON FULLER

1. At Brook Farm, Georgianna Bruce Kirby [1887]

Whether Hawthorne modeled Zenobia of *The Blithedale Romance* (his Brook Farm novel of 1852) on Margaret Fuller and, if so, whether in malice or admiration, has been hotly contested for over a hundred years. And the record of Fuller at Brook Farm is also controversial. One of the residents, Amelia Russell, recalled, "When listening to her wonderful conversations, which by the way, were limited to one person—herself—and straining my mind to comprehend her meaning, I must own I have sometimes wished her English was rather plainer" (Lindsay Swift, *Brook Farm*, p. 212). But Georgianna Bruce, who deferentially burned pastilles to purify Fuller's room and brought her coffee in their only china, recalled in her memoir below that she found in Fuller a candid—and possibly earthy—realism.

... There was no *mother* at the community of sufficiently large intellect, experience and courage to advise and sustain vigorous, natural young men and maidens in any important emergency. Had Mrs. Sophia Ripley been a mother, possessing the prescience and tact begotten of maternal love, it would have been better for all of us. Unfortunately, she was a sisterly rather than a wifely woman. She was gentle, refined, well informed, but narrow and, compared with the others, artificial. While you were in her mood or state of mind, she accepted you with all amiability; when you were groping in the dark, or tempest-tossed, she helplessly abandoned you to your fate, perhaps condemned you, as those always condemn who are incapable of understanding others.

Many of us did her great injustice by demanding of her that with which nature had not endowed her, viz., broad and deep human sympathy. We felt ourselves at times sadly in need of a wise, motherly friend, and because Sophia was the wife of the president, and especially because she was over forty, we insisted that years should give the required experience and looked to her for the help we could not expect from one another. But she was not equal to the position. Indeed I knew of no one but Margaret Fuller who would have been. How all-sufficient we should have found *her* wonderfully comprehensive judgment and tenderness. But how often should we have encountered a Margaret Fuller outside in the world when we needed her? [*Years of Experience (New York: G. P. Putnam's Sons, 1887), pp. 172-73]*

2. Her *Tribune* writing and concern for prostitutes, Horace Greeley [1852]

Although Greeley complained that Fuller wrote slowly, she did meet her obligation of writing three pieces—two literary and one on a social theme—per week, and he usually gave them the lead position on page one. What apparently warmed Greeley most toward her was her honesty, her personal generosity, and her ready sympathy for social "inferiors," whether servants or "ruined" women.

Her earlier contributions to the Tribune were not her best, and I did not at first prize her aid so highly as I afterwards learned to do. She wrote always freshly, vigorously, but not always clearly; for her full and intimate acquaintance with continental literature, especially German, seemed to have marred her felicity and readiness of expression in her mother tongue. While I never met another woman who conversed more freely or lucidly, the attempt to commit her thoughts to paper seemed to induce a singular embarrassment and hesitation: She could write only when in the vein; and this needed often to be waited for through several days, while the occasion sometimes required an immediate utterance. The new book must be reviewed before other journals had thoroughly dissected and discussed it else the ablest critique would command no general attention, and perhaps be, by the greater number, unread. That the writer should wait the flow of inspiration, or at least the recurrence of elasticity of spirits and relative health of body, will not seem unreasonable to the general reader; but to the inveterate hack-horse of the daily press, accustomed to write at any time, on any subject, and with a rapidity limited only by the physical ability to form the requisite pen-strokes, the notion of waiting for a brighter day, or a happier frame of mind, appears fantastic and absurd. He would as soon think of waiting for a change in the moon. Hence, while I realized that her contributions evinced rare intellectual wealth and force, I did not value them as I should have done had they been written more fluently and promptly. They often seemed to make their appearance "a day after the fair." . . .

Of her writings I do not purpose to speak critically. I think most of her contributions to the Tribune, while she remained with us, were characterized by a directness, terseness, and practicality, which are wanting in some of her earlier productions. Good judges have confirmed my own opinion, that, while her essays in the Dial are more elaborate and ambitious, her reviews in the Tribune are far better adapted to win the favor and sway the judgment of the great majority of readers. But, one characteristic of her writings I feel bound to commend, – their absolute truthfulness. She never asked how this would sound, nor whether that would do, nor what would be the effect of saying anything; but simply, "Is it the truth? Is it such as the public should know?" And if her judgment answered, "Yes," she uttered it; no matter what turmoil it might excite, nor what odium it might draw down on her own head. . . .

I have known few women, and scarcely another maiden, who had the heart and the courage to speak with such frank compassion, in mixed circles, of the most degraded and outcast portion of the sex. The contemplation of their treatment, especially by the guilty authors of their ruin, moved her to a calm and mournful indignation, which she did not attempt to suppress nor control. Others were willing to pity and deplore; Margaret was more inclined to vindicate and to redeem. She did not hesitate to avow that on meeting some of these abused, unhappy sisters, she had been surprised to find them scarcely fallen morally below the ordinary standard of Womanhood, – realizing and loathing their debasement; anxious to escape it; and only repelled by the sad consciousness that for them sympathy and society remained only so long as they should persist in the ways of pollution. Those who have read her "Woman," may remember some daring comparisons therein suggested between these Pariahs of society and large classes of their respectable sisters; and that was no fitful expression, – no sudden outbreak, – but impelled by her most deliberate convictions. I think, if she had been born to large fortune, a house of refuge for all female outcasts desiring to return to the ways of Virtue, would have been one of her most cherished and first realized conceptions. [*Memoirs*, II, 154-55, 157-60]

3. As a female journalist, "T. L.," March 7, 1846

A response in a rival newspaper to one of Fuller's reviews for the *Tribune* shows how naïve was her hope that critics might speak together "as man to man." On March 4, 1846, Fuller had reviewed *A Defence of Capital Punishment* by George B. Cheever, attacking both the author's position and his rigid presentation. Though writing that she had "neither skill nor patience" to unravel Cheever's "sophistical reasoning," she went on to outline its chief flaws and called for a "noble and strong opponent, putting forth all his power for conscience's sake." Fuller's antagonist, "T. L." began his assault, excerpted below, by ignoring her: "It was probably from the pen of [the *Tribune*'s] fair correspondent, but we shall regard it as the Editor's own work." Fuller replied with spirit in the March 10 *Tribune*: "We were not aware that the Bible, or the welfare of human beings were subjects improper for the consideration of 'females' whether 'fair' or otherwise. We had always supposed that, in the field of literature, the meeting was not between man and woman, but between mind and mind." (Ole Bull [1810-1880] was a Norwegian violinist and composer about whom Fuller wrote three pieces during his American tour; the *Harbinger*, edited by George Ripley from 1845 to 1849, was a Fourierist journal which aimed to treat "the great questions in social science, politics, literature, and the arts.")

... We cannot ... help remarking, by the way, on the very chivalrous course pursued by these heroic philanthropists [of the *Tribune* school]. Having abandoned that field in which alone it is possible to have a satisfactory discussion of this subject, and that, too, after repeated challenges of their own which had been most promptly met, these most valiant men have the meanness and cowardice to skulk behind a female, who, however personal and abusive she might be, could not, especially on such questions as these, be treated as a proper and legitimate adversary. Of course no reply will be made to that very modest lady who has so foolishly, and with so much vanity, suffered herself to be thrust forward in an argument for which she herself admits, "she has neither skill nor patience." Indeed, although this most admirable representative of the school of "love and philanthropy" and of the "spiritual insight" seems quite at home in such very common language as "monstrous," "detestable," "horrible," "demoniac," "diabolical," &c, yet she should know that the proper discussion of the question so rashly ventured upon requires more than this; and that it is indeed quite a different matter from doing up the slop literature of the *Tribune*, or writing unmeaning rhapsodies on the unutterable ideas of Ole Bull, or repeating the cant and drivel of the Harbinger about Dante and Beethoven, or praising the chaste "creations" of that most chaste and "spiritual" creature, George Sand. . . . *[Morning Courier and New-York Enquirer, March 7, 1846]*

4. Letter of introduction, Ralph Waldo Emerson, July 31, 1846

It is significant that so few of Fuller's friends commented on her journalism. But James Clarke, a regular reader of the *Tribune*, wrote her about her articles: "They seem to me to be better written than any thing of yours I have read. There is more ease, grace, freedom & point to them. The thoughts and sentiments are such as must do good, & I am extremely glad that you have such an excellent organ through which to speak to the public" (July 26, 1845, Houghton MS). In contrast, Emerson remarked wryly, "The muses have feet, to be sure, but it is an odd arrangement that selects them for the treadmill" (Rusk, *Letters*, III, 268). When she was leaving New York, he visited her to give her the following introduction to his combative friend of many years, Thomas Carlyle. Carlyle's own responses to Margaret Fuller were summed up after her death: "Such a predetermination to *eat* this big Universe as her oyster or her egg, and to be absolute empress of all height and glory in it that her heart could conceive, I have not before seen in any human soul" (*Correspondence of Thomas Carlyle and Ralph Waldo Emerson*, II, 212).

I send this letter by Margaret Fuller, of whose approach I believe I wrote you some word. There is no foretelling how you visited and crowded English will like our few educated men or women, and in your learned populace my luminaries may easily be overlooked. But of all the travellers whom you have so kindly received from me, I think of none, since Alcott went to England, whom I so much desired that you should see and like, as this dear old friend of mine. For two years now I have scarcely seen her, as she has been at New York, engaged by Horace Greeley as a literary editor of his *Tribune* newspaper. This employment was made acceptable to her by good pay, great local and personal conveniences of all kinds, and unbounded confidence and respect from Greeley himself, and all other parties connected with this influential journal (of 30,000 subscribers, I believe). And Margaret Fuller's work as critic of all new books, critic of the drama, of music, and good arts in New York, has been honorable to her. Still this employment is not satisfactory to me. She is full of all nobleness, and with the generosity native to her mind and character appears to me an exotic in New England, a foreigner from some more sultry and expansive climate. She is, I suppose, the earliest reader and lover of Goethe in this Country, and nobody here knows him so well. Her love too of whatever is good in French, and specially in Italian genius, give her the best title to travel. In short, she is our citizen of the world by quite special diploma. And I am heartily glad that she has an opportunity of going abroad that pleases her. . . . [*Correspondence of Thomas Carlyle and Ralph Waldo Emerson (Boston: James R. Osgood & Co., 1883) II, 115-16]*

FULLER'S WRITINGS

5. On American history [1833-34]

One of her few pleasures during the Groton farm years was the renewal of study—now on a more equal footing—with her father. The attitudes she developed then toward American history helped make possible her later role with the *Tribune*. We note that she needed heroes to mediate between her emotional requirements and her new interest in society.

American History! Seriously, my mind is regenerating as to my country, for I am beginning to appreciate the United States and its great men. The violent antipathies, – the result of an exaggerated love for, shall I call it by so big a name as the "poetry of being?" – and the natural distrust arising from being forced to hear the conversation of half-bred men, all whose petty feelings were roused to awkward life by the paltry game of local politics, – are yielding to reason and calmer knowledge. Had I but been educated in the knowledge of such men as Jefferson, Franklin, Rush! I have learned how to know them partially. And I rejoice, if only because my father and I can have so much in common on this topic. All my other pursuits have led me away from him; here he has much information and ripe judgment. But, better still, I hope to feel no more that sometimes despairing, sometimes insolently contemptuous, feeling of incongeniality with my time and place. Who knows but some proper and attainable object of pursuit may present itself to the cleared eye? At any rate, wisdom is good, if it brings neither bliss nor glory. [*Memoirs*, I, 149]

6. On the Dorr rebellion, July 1842

Fuller's chief contact with American popular history in the making occurred when she visited. in Providence during a mass protest led by Thomas Wilson Dorr. The archaic constitution of Rhode Island severely limited male suffrage and made for obsolete apportionment of members to the state legislature. A redrafted instrument did not satisfy Dorr, who tried to seize the Providence arsenal; his failures led to his flight and the mass imprisonment of his supporters. In the following account, Fuller is more struck by the social distortions the struggle caused than the issues it addressed. It is interesting that she connects "vestal" purity (of her Quaker friend Mary Rotch of New Bedford) with abhorrence of political struggle; only five years later in Italy, she effectively linked sexual fulfillment with political enthusiasm.

A letter at Providence would have been like manna in the wilderness. I came into the very midst of the fuss, and, tedious as it was at the time, I am glad to have seen it. I shall in future be able to believe real, what I have read with a dim disbelief of such times and tendencies. There is, indeed, little good, little cheer, in what I have seen: a city full of grown-up people as wild, as mischief-seeking, as full of prejudice, careless slander, and exaggeration, as a herd of boys in the play-ground of the worst boarding-school. Women whom I have seen, as the domestic cat, gentle, graceful, cajoling, suddenly showing the disposition, if not the force, of the tigress. I thought I appreciated the monstrous growths of rumor before, but I never did. The Latin poet, though used to a court, has faintly described what I saw and heard often, in going the length of a street. It is astonishing what force, purity and wisdom it requires for a human being to keep clear of falsehoods. These absurdities, of course, are linked with good qualities, with energy of feeling, and with a love of morality, though narrowed and vulgarized by the absence of the intelligence which should enlighten. I had the good discipline of trying to make allowance for those making none, to be charitable to their want of charity, and cool without being cold. But I don't know when I have felt such an aversion to my environment, and prayed so earnestly day by day, – "O, Eternal, purge from my inmost heart this hot haste about ephemeral trifles," and "keep back thy servant from presumptuous sins; let them not have dominion over me."

What a change from the almost vestal quiet of "Aunt Mary's" life, to all this open-windowed, open-eyed screaming of "poltroon," "nefarious plan," "entire depravity," &c. &c.. [Memoirs, II, 64-65]

7. On communal experiments, October 18, 1840

When George Ripley first broached his plan for Brook Farm to Fuller, she had just been spending idyllic days boating at Newbury with Caroline Sturgis. Her first response, in her journal, is indulgently playful: she offers a far more anarchic and romantic alternative.

... As we glided along the river, I could frame my community far more naturally and rationally than [Ripley]. A few friends should settle upon the banks of a stream like this, planting their homesteads. Some should be farmers, some woodmen, others bakers, millers, &c. By land, they should carry to one another the commodities; on the river they should meet for society. At sunset many, of course, would be out in their boats, but they would love the hour too much ever to disturb one another. I saw the spot where we should discuss the high mysteries that Milton speaks of. Also, I saw the spot where I would invite select friends to live through the noon of night, in silent communion. When we wished to have merely playful chat, or talk on politics or social reform, we would gather in the mill, and arrange those affairs while grinding the corn. What a happy place for children to grow up in! Would it not suit little ––– to go to school to the cardinal flowers in her boat, beneath the great oak-tree? I think she would learn more than in a phalanx of juvenile florists. But, truly, why has such a thing never been? One of these valleys so immediately suggests an image of the fair company that might fill it, and live so easily, so naturally, so wisely. Can we not people the banks of some such affectionate little stream? I distrust ambitious plans, such as Phalansterian organizations!

[Ripley] is quite bent on trying his experiment. I hope he may succeed; but as they were talking the other evening, I thought of the river, and all the pretty symbols the tide-mill presents, and felt if I could at all adjust the economics to the more simple procedure, I would far rather be the miller, hoping to attract by natural affinity some congenial baker, "und so weiter." However, one thing seems sure, that many persons will soon, somehow, somewhere, throw off a part, at least, of these terrible weights of the social contract, and see if they cannot lie more at ease in the lap of Nature. I do not feel the same interest in these plans, as if I had a firmer hold on life, but I listen with much pleasure to the good suggestions. [*Memoirs, II, 45-47*]

8. On an early stay at Brook Farm [1841]

The following record, probably of her first visit to Brook
Farm, which opened in April 1841, provides a good sample
of her theoretical and temperamental objections to the
Ripleys' community.

On Friday I came to Brook Farm. The first day or two here is desolate.
You seem to belong to nobody, – to have a right to speak to nobody;
but very soon you learn to take care of yourself, and then the freedom
of the place is delightful.

It is fine to see how thoroughly Mr. and Mrs. R. act out, in their
own persons, what they intend.

All Saturday I was off in the woods. In the evening we had a
general conversation, opened by me, upon Education, in its largest
sense, and on what we can do for ourselves and others. I took my usual
ground: The aim is perfection; patience the road. The present object is
to give ourselves and others a tolerable chance. Let us not be too
ambitious in our hopes as to immediate results. Our lives should be
considered as a tendency, an approximation only. Parents and teachers
expect to do too much. They are not legislators, but only interpeters to
the next generation. Soon, very soon, does the parent become merely
the elder brother of his child; – a little wiser, it is to be hoped. ———
differed from me as to some things I said about the gradations of
experience, – that "to be brought prematurely near perfect beings
would chill and discourage." He thought it would cheer and console. He
spoke well, – with a youthful nobleness. _____ said "that the most
perfect person would be the most impersonal" – philosophical bull
that, I trow – "and, consequently, would impede us least from God."
Mr. R. spoke admirably on the nature of loyalty. The people showed a
good deal of the *sans-culotte* tendency in their manners, – throwing
themselves on the floor, yawning, and going out when they had heard
enough. Yet, as the majority differ from me, to begin with, – that
being the reason this subject was chosen, – they showed, on the whole,
more respect and interest than I had expected. As I am accustomed to
deference, however, and need it for the boldness and animation which
my part requires, I did not speak with as much force as usual. Still, I
should like to have to face all this; it would have the same good effects
that the Athenian assemblies had on the minds obliged to encounter
them.

Sunday. A glorious day: — the woods full of perfume. I was out all the morning. In the afternoon, Mrs. R. and I had a talk. I said my position would be too uncertain here, as I could not work. ——— said: —"They would all like to work for a person of genius. They would not like to have this service claimed from them, but would like to render it of their own accord." "Yes," I told her; "but where would be my repose, when they were always to be judging whether I was worth it or not. It would be the same position the clergyman is in, or the wandering beggar with his harp. Each day you must prove yourself anew. You are not in immediate relations with material things."

We talked of the principles of the community. I said I had not a right to come, because all the confidence in it I had was as an *experiment* worth trying, and that it was a part of the great wave of inspired thought. ——— declared they none of them had confidence beyond this; but they seem to me to have. Then I said, "that though I entirely agreed about the dignity of labor, and had always wished for the present change, yet I did not agree with the principle of paying for services by time, neither did I believe in the hope of excluding evil, for that was a growth of nature, and one condition of the development of good." We had valuable discussion on these points.

All Monday morning in the woods again. Afternoon, out with the drawing party; I felt the evils of want of conventional refinement, in the impudence with which one of the girls treated me. She has since thought of it with regret, I notice; and, by every day's observation of me, will see that she ought not to have done it.

In the evening, a husking in the barn. Men, women, and children, all engaged. It was a most picturesque scene, only not quite light enough to bring it out fully. I staid and helped about half an hour, then took a long walk beneath the stars.

Wednesday. I have been too much absorbed to-day by others, and it has made me almost sick. Mrs. ——— came to see me, and we had an excellent talk, which occupied nearly all the morning. Then Mrs. ——— wanted to see me, but after a few minutes I found I could not bear it, and lay down to rest. Then ——— came. Poor man; — his feelings and work are wearing on him. He looks really ill now. Then ——— and I went to walk in the woods. I was deeply interested in all she told me. If I were to write down all she and four other married women have confided to me, these three days past, it would make a cento, on one subject, in five parts. Certainly there should be some great design in my life; its attractions are so invariable.

In the evening, a conversation on Impulse. The reason for choosing this subject is the great tendency here to advocate spontaneousness, at the expense of reflection. It was a much better conversation than the one before. None yawned, for none came, this time, from mere curiosity. There were about thirty-five present, which is a large enough circle. Many engaged in the talk. I defended nature, as I always do; – the spirit ascending through, not superseding, nature. But in the scale of Sense, Intellect, Spirit, I advocated tonight the claims of Intellect, because those present were rather disposed to postpone them. On the nature of Beauty we had good talk. ––– spoke well. She seemed in a much more reverent humor than the other night, and enjoyed the large plans of the universe which were unrolled. –––, seated on the floor, with the light falling from behind on his long gold locks, made, with sweet, serene aspect, and composed tones, a good exposé of his way of viewing things.

Saturday. Well, good-by, Brook Farm. I know more about this place than I did when I came; but the only way to be qualified for a judge of such an experiment would be to become an active, though unimpassioned, associate in trying it. Some good things are proven, and as for individuals, they are gainers. Has not ––– vied, in her deeds of love, with "my Cid," and the holy Ottilia? That girl who was so rude to me stood waiting, with a timid air, to bid me good-by. Truly, the soft answer turneth away wrath.

I have found myself here in the amusing position of a conservative. Even so is it with Mr. R. There are too many young people in proportion to the others. I heard myself saying, with a grave air, "Play out the play, gentles." Thus, from generation to generation, rises and falls the wave. [_Memoirs, II, 73-78_]

9. On return to Brook Farm [1842]

In a journal or letter, Fuller summarized another visit. Her phrase, "liberty of law," which she uses here and in _Woman in the Nineteenth Century_, is an allusion to the Fourierist conviction that universal law will be expressed in the absolute liberty of the individual.

Here I have passed a very pleasant week. The tone of the society is much sweeter than when I was here a year ago. There is a pervading spirit of mutual tolerance and gentleness, with great sincerity. There is no longer a passion for grotesque freaks of liberty, but a disposition, rather, to study and enjoy the liberty of law. The great development of mind and character observable in several instances, persuades me that this state of things affords a fine studio for the soul-sculptor. To a casual observer it may seem as if there was not enough of character here to interest, because there are no figures sufficiently distinguished to be worth painting for the crowd; but there is enough of individuality in free play to yield instruction; and one might have, from a few months' residence here, enough of the human drama to feed thought for a long time. *[Memoirs, II, 78]*

10. *Summer on the Lakes in 1843 [1844]*

Published by Charles C. Little and James Brown of Boston, *Summer on the Lakes* may have been intended as a corrective to Dickens' *American Notes*, an infamous caricature of western manners in 1842, but it has its own bite. For Greeley, it was "one of the clearest and most graphic delineations, ever given, of the Great Lakes, of the Prairies, and of the receding barbarism, and the rapidly advancing, but rude, repulsive semi-civilization, which were contending with most unequal forces for the possession of those rich lands. I still consider 'Summer on the Lakes' unequalled, especially in its pictures of the Prairies and of the sunnier aspects of Pioneer life" (*Memoirs*, II, 152-53). Fuller initiated here a style of seeing and writing which would become more lean and pointed in the coming years. To concentrate on her social thought, I have here omitted her flamboyant digressions (one forty pages long on a German seeress), her survey of literature on the Indian, and many passages of physical description.

Niagara. . . . When I first came, I felt nothing but a quiet satisfaction. I found that drawings, the panorama, &c. had given me a clear notion of the position and proportions of all objects here; I knew where to look for everything, and everything looked as I thought it would. . . .

But all great expression, which, on a superficial survey, seems so easy as well as so simple, furnishes, after a while, to the faithful observer, its own standard by which to appreciate it. Daily these proportions widened and towered more and more upon my sight, and I got, at last, a proper foreground for these sublime distances. Before coming away, I think I really saw the full wonder of the scene. After a while it so drew me into itself as to inspire an undefined dread, such as I never knew before, such as may be felt when death is about to usher us into a new existence. The perpetual trampling of the waters seized my senses. I felt that no other sound, however near, could be heard, and would start and look behind me for a foe. I realized the identity of that mood of nature in which these waters were poured down with such absorbing force, with that in which the Indian was shaped on the same soil. For continually upon my mind came, unsought and unwelcome, images, such as never haunted it before, of naked savages stealing behind me with uplifted tomahawks; again and again this illusion recurred, and even after I had thought it over, and tried to shake it off, I could not help starting and looking behind me.

As picture, the falls can only be seen from the British side. There they are seen in their veils, and at sufficient distance to appreciate the magical effects of these, and the light and shade. From the boat, as you cross, the effects and contrasts are more melodramatic. On the road back from the whirlpool, we saw them as a reduced picture with delight. But what I liked best was to sit on Table Rock, close to the great fall. There all power of observing details, all separate consciousness, was quite lost.

Once, just as I had seated myself there, a man came to take his first look. He walked close up to the fall, and, after looking at it a moment, with an air as if thinking how he could best appropriate it to his own use, he spat into it.

This trait seemed wholly worthy of an age whose love of *utility* is such that the Prince Puckler Muskau suggests the probability of men coming to put the bodies of their dead parents in the fields to fertilize them, and of a country such as Dickens has described; but these will not, I hope, be seen on the historic page to be truly the age or truly the America. A little leaven is leavening the whole mass for other bread. . . .

The Great Lakes. Coming up the river St. Clair, we saw Indians for the first time. They were camped out on the bank. It was twilight, and their blanketed forms, in listless groups or stealing along the bank, with a lounge and a stride so different in its wildness from the rudeness of the white settler, gave me the first feeling that I really approached the West.

The people on the boat were almost all New-Englanders, seeking their fortunes. They had brought with them their habits of calculation, their cautious manners, their love of polemics. It grieved me to hear these immigrants, who were to be the fathers of a new race, all, from the old man down to the little girl, talking, not of what they should do, but of what they should get in the new scene. It was to them a prospect, not of the unfolding nobler energies, but of more ease and larger accumulation. It wearied me, too, to hear Trinity and Unity discussed in the poor, narrow, doctrinal way on these free waters; but that will soon cease; there is not time for this clash of opinions in the West, where the clash of material interests is so noisy. They will need the spirit of religion more than ever to guide them, but will find less time than before for its doctrine. This change was to me, who am tired of the war of words on these subjects, and believe it only sows the wind to reap the whirlwind, refreshing, but I argue nothing from it; there is nothing real in the freedom of thought at the West, — it is from the position of men's lives, not the state of their minds. So soon as they have time, unless they grow better meanwhile, they will cavil and criticise, and judge other men by their own standard, and outrage the law of love every way, just as they do with us. . . .

I come to the West prepared for the distaste I must experience at its mushroom growth. I know that, where "go ahead" is the only motto, the village cannot grow into the gentle proportions that successive lives and the gradations of experience involuntarily give. In older countries the house of the son grew from that of the father, as naturally as new joints on a bough, and the cathedral crowned the whole as naturally as the leafy summit the tree. This cannot be here. The march of peaceful is scarce less wanton than that of warlike invasion. The old landmarks are broken down, and the land, for a season, bears none, except of the rudeness of conquest and the needs of the day, whose bivouac-fires blacken the sweetest forest glades. I have come prepared to see all this, to dislike it, but not with stupid narrowness to distrust or defame. On the contrary, while I will not be so obliging as to confound ugliness with beauty, discord with harmony, and laud and be contented with all I meet, when it conflicts with my best desires and tastes, I trust by reverent faith to woo the mighty meaning of the scene, perhaps to foresee the law by which a new order, a new poetry, is to be evoked from this chaos, and with a curiosity as ardent, but not so selfish, as that of Macbeth, to call up the apparitions of future kings from the strange ingredients of the witch's caldron. Thus I will not grieve that all the noble trees are gone already from this island to feed this caldron, but believe it will have Medea's virtue, and reproduce them in the form of new intellectual growths, since centuries cannot again adorn the land with such as have been removed. . . .

Chicago. There can be no two places in the world more completely thoroughfares than this place and Buffalo. They are the two correspondent valves that open and shut all the time, as the life-blood rushes from east to west, and back again from west to east.

Since it is their office thus to be the doors, and let in and out, it would be unfair to expect from them much character of their own. To make the best provisions for the transmission of produce is their office, and the people who live there are such as are suited for this, — active, complaisant, inventive, business people. There are no provisions for the student or idler; to know what the place can give, you should be at work with the rest; the mere traveller will not find it profitable to loiter there as I did. . . .

The only thing I liked at first to do was to trace with slow and unexpecting step the narrow margin of the lake. Sometimes a heavy swell gave it expression; at others, only its varied coloring, which I found more admirable every day, and which gave it an air of mirage instead of the vastness of ocean. Then there was a grandeur in the feeling that I might continue that walk, if I had any seven-leagued mode of conveyance to save fatigue, for hundreds of miles without an obstacle and without a change.

But after I had ridden out, and seen the flowers, and observed the sun set with that calmness seen only in the prairies, and the cattle winding slowly to their homes in the "island groves," — most peaceful of sights, — I began to love, because I began to know the scene, and shrank no longer from "the encircling vastness."

It is always thus with the new form of life; we must learn to look at it by its own standard. At first, no doubt, my accustomed eye kept saying, if the mind did not, What! no distant mountains? What! no valleys? But after a while I would ascend the roof of the house where we lived, and pass many hours, needing no sight but the moon reigning in the heavens, or starlight falling upon the lake, till all the lights were out in the island grove of men beneath my feet, and felt nearer heaven that there was nothing but this lovely, still reception on the earth; no towering mountains, no deep tree-shadows, nothing but plain earth and water bathed in light. . . .

Notwithstanding all the attractions I thus found out by degrees on the flat shores of the lake, I was delighted when I found myself really on my way into the country for an excursion of two or three weeks. We set forth in a strong wagon, almost as large, and with the look of those used elsewhere for transporting caravans of wild beasts, loaded with everything we might want, in case nobody would give it to us, — for buying and selling were no longer to be counted on, — with a pair of strong horses, able and willing to force their way through mud-holes and amid stumps, and a guide, equally admirable as marshal and companion, who knew by heart the country and its history, both natural and artificial, and whose clear hunter's eye needed neither road nor goal to guide it to all the spots where beauty best loves to dwell. . . .

Papaw Grove, Illinois. Next day we crossed the river. We ladies crossed on a little foot-bridge, from which we could look down the stream, and see the wagon pass over at the ford. A black thunder-cloud was coming up; the sky and waters heavy with expectation. The motion of the wagon, with its white cover, and the laboring horses, gave just the due interest to the picture, because it seemed as if they would not have time to cross before the storm came on. However, they did get across, and we were a mile or two on our way before the violent shower obliged us to take refuge in a solitary house upon the prairie. In this country it is as pleasant to stop as to go on, to lose your way as to find it, for the variety in the population gives you a chance for fresh entertainment in every hut, and the luxuriant beauty makes every path attractive. In this house we found a family "quite above the common," but, I grieve to say, not above false pride, for the father, ashamed of being caught barefoot, told us a story of a man, one of the richest men, he said, in one of the Eastern cities, who went barefoot, from choice and taste. . . .

That night we rested, or rather tarried, at a grove some miles beyond, and there partook of the miseries, so often jocosely portrayed, of bedchambers for twelve, a milk dish for universal handbasin, and expectations that you would use and lend your "hankercher" for a towel. But this was the only night, thanks to the hospitality of private families, that we passed thus; amd it was well that we had this bit of experience, else might we have pronounced all Trollopian records of the kind to be inventions of pure malice.

With us was a young lady who showed herself to have been bathed in the Britannic fluid, wittily described by a late French writer, by the impossibility she experienced of accomodating herself to the indecorums of the scene. We ladies were to sleep in the bar-room, from which its drinking visitors could be ejected only at a late hour. The outer door had no fastening to prevent their return. However, our host kindly requested we would call him, if they did, as he had "conquered them for us," and would do so again. We had also rather hard couches (mine was the supper-table); but we Yankees, born to rove, were altogether too much fatigued to stand upon trifles, and slept as sweetly as we would in the "bigly bower" of any baroness. But I think England sat up all night, wrapped in her blanket-shawl, and with a neat lace cap upon her head, – so that she would have looked perfectly the lady, if any one had come in, – shuddering and listening. I know that she was very ill next day, in requital. She watched, as her parent country watches the seas, that nobody may do wrong in any case, and deserved to have met some interruption, she was so well prepared. However, there was none, other than from the nearness of some twenty sets of powerful lungs, which would not leave the night to a deathly stillness. In this house we had, if not good beds, yet good tea, good bread, and wild strawberries, and were entertained with most free communications of opinion and history from our hosts. Neither shall any of us have a right to say again that we cannot find any who may be willing to hear all we may have to say. "A's fish that comes to the net," should be painted on the sign at Papaw Grove. . . .

Rock River, Illinois. There was a peculiar charm in coming here, where the choice of location, and the unobtrusive good taste of all the arrangements, showed such intelligent appreciation of the spirit of the scene, after seeing so many dwellings of the new settlers, which showed plainly that they had no thought beyond satisfying the grossest material wants. Sometimes they looked attractive, these little brown houses, the natural architecture of the country, in the edge of the timber. But almost always, when you came near the slovenliness of the dwelling, and the rude way in which objects around it were treated, when so little care would have presented a charming whole, were very repulsive.

Seeing the traces of the Indians, who chose the most beautiful sites for their dwellings, and whose habits do not break in on that aspect of Nature under which they were born, we feel as if they were the rightful lords of a beauty they forbore to deform. But most of these settlers do not see it at all; it breathes, it speaks in vain to those who are rushing into its sphere. Their progress is Gothic, not Roman, and their mode of cultivation will, in the course of twenty, perhaps ten years, obliterate the natural expression of the country.

This is inevitable, fatal; we must not complain, but look forward to a good result. Still, in travelling through this country, I could not but be struck with the force of a symbol. Wherever the hog comes, the rattlesnake disappears; the omnivorous traveller, safe in its stupidity, willingly and easily makes a meal of the most dangerous of reptiles, and one which the Indian looks on with a mystic awe. Even so the white settler pursues the Indian, and is victor in the chase. . . .

Oregon, Illinois. The great drawback upon the lives of these settlers, at present, is the unfitness of the women for their new lot. It has generally been the choice of the men, and the women follow, as women will, doing their best for affection's sake, but too often in heartsickness and weariness. Beside, it frequently not being a choice or conviction of their own minds that it is best to be here, their part is the hardest, and they are least fitted for it. The men can find assistance in field labor, and recreation with the gun and fishing-rod. Their bodily strength is greater, and enables them to bear and enjoy both these forms of life.

The women can rarely find any aid in domestic labor. All its various and careful tasks must often be performed, sick, or well, by the mother and daughters, to whom a city education has imparted neither the strength nor skill now demanded.

The wives of the poorer settlers, having more hard work to do than before, very frequently become slatterns; but the ladies, accustomed to a refined neatness, feel that they cannot degrade themselves by its absence, and struggle under every disadvantage to keep up the necessary routine of small arrangements.

With all these disadvantages for work, their resources for pleasure are fewer. When they can leave the housework, they have not learnt to ride, to drive, to row, alone. Their culture has too generally been that given to women to make them "the ornaments of society." They can dance, but not draw; talk French, but know nothing of the language of flowers; neither in childhood were allowed to cultivate them, lest they should tan their complexions. Accustomed to the pavement of Broadway, they dare not tread the wild-wood paths for fear of rattlesnakes!

Seeing much of this joylessness, and inaptitude, both of body and mind, for a lot which would be full of blessings for those prepared for it, we could not but look with deep interest on the little girls, and hope they would grow up with the strength of body, dexterity, simple tastes, and resources that would fit them to enjoy and refine the Western farmer's life.

But they have a great deal to war with in the habits of thought acquired by their mothers from their own early life. Everywhere the fatal spirit of imitation, of reference to European standards, penetrates, and threatens to blight whatever of original growth might adorn the soil.

If the little girls grow up strong, resolute, able to exert their faculties, their mothers mourn over their want of fashionable delicacy. Are they gay, enterprising, ready to fly about in the various ways that teach them so much, these ladies lament that "they cannot go to school, where they might learn to be quiet." They lament the want of "education" for their daughters, as if the thousand needs which call out their young energies, and the language of nature around, yielded no education.

Their grand ambition for their children is to send them to school in some Eastern city, the measure most likely to make them useless and unhappy at home. I earnestly hope that, erelong, the existence of good schools near themselves, planned by persons of sufficient thought to meet the wants of the place and time, instead of copying New York or Boston, will correct this mania. Instruction the children want to enable them to profit by the great natural advantages of their position; but methods copied from the education of some English Lady Augusta are as ill suited to the daughter of an Illinois farmer, as satin shoes to climb the Indian mounds. An elegance she would diffuse around her, if her mind were opened to appreciate elegance; it might be of a kind new, original, enchanting, as different from that of the city belle as that of the prairie torch-flower from the shop-worn article that touches the cheek of that lady within her bonnet.

To a girl really skilled to make home beautiful and comfortable, with bodily strength to enjoy plenty of exercise, the woods, the streams, a few studies, music, and the sincere and familiar intercourse, far more easily to be met with here than elsewhere, would afford happiness enough. Her eyes would not grow dim, nor her cheeks sunken, in the absence of parties, morning visits, and milliners' shops.

As to music, I wish I could see in such places the guitar rather than the piano, and good vocal more than instrumental music.

The piano many carry with them, because it is the fashionable instrument in the Eastern cities. Even there, it is so merely from the habit of imitating Europe, for not one in a thousand is willing to give the labor requisite to insure any valuable use of the instrument.

But out here, where the ladies have so much less leisure, it is still less desirable. Add to this, they never know how to tune their own instruments, and as persons seldom visit them who can do so, these pianos are constantly out of tune, and would spoil the ear of one who began by having any.

The guitar, or some portable instrument which requires less practice, and could be kept in tune by themselves, would be far more desirable for most of these ladies. It would give all they want as a household companion to fill up the gaps of life with a pleasant stimulus or solace, and be sufficient accompaniment to the voice in social meetings.

Singing in parts is the most delightful family amusement, and those who are constantly together can learn to sing in perfect accord. All the practice it needs, after some good elementary instruction, is such as meetings by summer twilight and evening firelight naturally suggest. . . .

Chicago again and nearby lakes. At Chicago I read again Philip Van Artevelde, and certain passages in it will always be in my mind associated with the deep sound of the lake, as heard in the night. I used to read a short time at night, and then open the blind to look out. The moon would be full upon the lake, and the calm breath, pure light, and the deep voice harmonized well with the thought of the Flemish hero. When will this country have such a man? It is what she needs; no thin Idealist, no coarse Realist, but a man whose eye reads the heavens, while his feet step firmly on the ground, and his hands are strong and dexterous for the use of human implements. A man religious, virtuous, and — sagacious; a man of universal sympathies, but self-possessed; a man who knows the region of emotion, though he is not its slave; a man to whom this world is no mere spectacle, or fleeting shadow, but a

great, solemn game, to be played with good heed, for its stakes are of
eternal value, yet who, if his own play be true, heeds not what he loses
by the falsehood of others; — a man who hives from the past, yet
knows that its honey can but moderately avail him; whose
comprehensive eye scans the present, neither infatuated by its golden
lures, nor chilled by its many ventures; who possesses prescience, as the
wise man must, but not so far as to be driven mad to-day by the gift
which discerns to-morrow; — when there is such a man for America, the
thought which urges her on will be expressed. . . .

One day we ladies gave, under the guidance of our host, to visiting
all the beauties of the adjacent lakes, — Nomabbin, Silver, and Pine
Lakes. On the shore of Nomabbin had formerly been one of the finest
Indian villages. Our host said, that once, as he was lying there beneath
the bank, he saw a tall Indian standing at gaze on the knoll. He lay a
long time, curious to see how long the figure would maintain its
statue-like absorption. But at last his patience yielded, and, in moving,
he made a slight noise. The Indian saw him, gave a wild, snorting sound
of indignation and pain, and strode away.

What feelings must consume their hearts at such moments! I
scarcely see how they can forbear to shoot the white man where he
stands.

But the power of fate is with the white man, and the Indian feels
it. This same gentleman told of his travelling through the wilderness
with an Indian guide. He had with him a bottle of spirit which he meant
to give him in small quantities, but the Indian, once excited, wanted the
whole at once. "I would not," said Mr. ———, "give it him, for I
thought, if he got really drunk, there was an end to his services as a
guide. But he persisted, and at last tried to take it from me. I was not
armed; he was, and twice as strong as I. But I knew an Indian could not
resist the look of a white man, and I fixed my eye steadily on his. He
bore it for a moment, then his eye fell; he let go the bottle. I took his
gun and threw it to a distance. After a few moments' pause, I told him
to go and fetch it, and left it in his hands. From that moment he was
quite obedient, even servile, all the rest of the way."

This gentleman, though in other respects of most kindly and liberal
heart, showed the aversion that the white man soon learns to feel for
the Indian on whom he encroaches, — the aversion of the injurer for
him he has degraded. After telling the anecdote of his seeing the Indian
gazing at the seat of his former home,

"A thing for human feelings the most trying,"

and which, one would think, would have awakened soft compassion — almost remorse — in the present owner of that fair hill, which contained for the exile the bones of his dead, the ashes of his hopes, he observed: "They cannot be prevented from straggling back here to their old haunts. I wish they could. They ought not be permitted to drive away *our* game." *Our* game, — just heavens! . . .

On the bank of Silver Lake we saw an Indian encampment. A shower threatened us, but we resolved to try if we could not visit it before it came on. We crossed a wide field on foot, and found the Indians amid the trees on a shelving bank; just as we reached them, the rain began to fall in torrents, with frequent thunderclaps, and we had to take refuge in their lodges. These were very small, being for temporary use, and we crowded the occupants much, among whom were several sick, on the damp ground, or with only a ragged mat between them and it. But they showed all the gentle courtesy which marks their demeanor towards the stranger, who stands in any need; though it was obvious that the visit, which inconvenienced them, could only have been caused by the most impertinent curiosity, they made us as comfortable as their extreme poverty permitted. They seemed to think we would not like to touch them; a sick girl in the lodge where I was, persisted in moving so as to give me the dry place; a woman, with the sweet melancholy eye of the race, kept off the children and wet dogs from even the hem of my garment.

Without, their fires smouldered, and black kettles, hung over them on sticks, smoked and seethed in the rain. An old, theatrical-looking Indian stood with arms folded, looking up to the heavens, from which the rain dashed and the thunder reverberated; his air was French-Roman; that is, more Romanesque than Roman. The Indian ponies, much excited, kept careering through the wood, around the encampment, and now and then, halting suddenly, would thrust in their intelligent, though amazed faces, as if to ask their masters when this awful pother would cease, and then, after a moment, rush and trample off again.

At last we got away, well wetted, but with a picturesque scene for memory. At a house where we stopped to get dry, they told us that this wandering band (of Pottawattamies), who had returned on a visit, either from homesickness, or need of relief, were extremely destitute.

The women had been there to see if they could barter for food their head-bands, with which they club their hair behind into a form not unlike a Grecian knot. They seemed, indeed, to have neither food, utensils, clothes, nor bedding; nothing but the ground, the sky, and their own strength. Little wonder if they drove off the game!

Part of the same band I had seen in Milwaukie, on a begging dance. The effect of this was wild and grotesque. They wore much paint and feather head-dresses. "Indians without paint are poor coots," said a gentleman who had been a great deal with, and really liked, them; and I like the effect of the paint on them; it reminds of the gay fantasies of nature. With them in Milwaukie was a chief, the finest Indian figure I saw, more than six feet in height, erect, and of a sullen, but grand gait and gesture. He wore a deep-red blanket, which fell in large folds from his shoulders to his feet, did not join in the dance, but slowly strode about through the streets, a fine sight, not a French-Roman, but a real Roman. He looked unhappy, but listlessly unhappy, as if he felt it was of no use to strive or resist. . . .

Returning to the boarding-house, which was also a boarding-school, we were sure to be greeted by gay laughter.

This school was conducted by two girls of nineteen and seventeen years; their pupils were nearly as old as themselves. The relation seemed very pleasant between them; the only superiority – that of superior knowledge – was sufficient to maintain authority, – all the authority that was needed to keep daily life in good order.

In the West, people are not respected merely because they are old in years; people there have not time to keep up appearances in that way; when persons cease to have a real advantage in wisdom, knowledge, or enterprise, they must stand back, and let those who are oldest in character "go ahead," however few years they may count. There are no banks of established respectability in which to bury the talent there; no napkin of precedent in which to wrap it. What cannot be made to pass current, is not esteemed coin of the realm. . . .

Mackinaw. Late at night we reached this island of Mackinaw, so famous for its beauty, and to which I proposed a visit of some length. It was the last week in August, at which time a large representation from the Chippewa and Ottawa tribes are here to receive their annual payments from the American government. As their habits make travelling easy and inexpensive to them, neither being obliged to wait for steamboats, or write to see whether hotels are full, they come hither by thousands, and those thousands in families, secure of accomodation on the beach, and food from the lake, to make a long holiday out of the occasion. There were near two thousand encamped on the island already, and more arriving every day.

As our boat came in, the captain had some rockets let off. This greatly excited the Indians, and their yells and wild cries resounded along the shore. Except for the momentary flash of the rockets, it was perfectly dark, and my sensations as I walked with a stranger to a strange hotel, through the midst of these shrieking savages, and heard the pants and snorts of the departing steamer, which carried away all my companions, were somewhat of the dismal sort; though it was pleasant, too, in the way that everything strange is; everything that breaks in upon the routine that so easily incrusts us.

I had reason to expect a room to myself at the hotel, but found none, and was obliged to take up my rest in the common parlor and eating-room, a circumstance which insured my being an early riser.

With the first rosy streak, I was out among my Indian neighbors, whose lodges honeycombed the beautiful beach, that curved away in long, fair outline on either side the house. They were already on the alert, the children creeping out from beneath the blanket door of the lodge, the women pounding corn in their rude mortars, the young men playing on their pipes. . . .

. . . The first afternoon I was there, looking down from a near height, I felt that I never wished to see a more fascinating picture. It was an hour of the deepest serenity; bright blue and gold, with rich shadows. Every moment the sunlight fell more mellow. The Indians were grouped and scattered among the lodges; the women preparing food, in the kettle or frying-pan, over the many small fires; the children, half naked, wild as little goblins, were playing both in and out of the water. Here and there lounged a young girl, with a baby at her back, whose bright eyes glanced, as if born into a world of courage and of joy, instead of ignominious servitude and slow decay. Some girls were cutting wood, a little way from me, talking and laughing, in the low musical tone, so charming in the Indian women. Many bark canoes were upturned upon the beach, and, by that light, of almost the same amber as the lodges; others coming in, their square sails set, and with almost arrowy speed, though heavily laden with dusky forms, and all the apparatus of their household. Here and there a sail-boat glided by, with a different but scarce less pleasing motion.

It was a scene of ideal loveliness, and these wild forms adorned it, as looking so at home in it. All seemed happy, and they were happy that day, for they had no fire-water to madden them, as it was Sunday, and the shops were shut. . . .

They talked a great deal, and with much variety of gesture, so that I often had a good guess at the meaning of their discourse. I saw that, whatever the Indian may be among the whites, he is anything but taciturn with his own people; and he often would declaim, or narrate at length. Indeed, it is obvious, if only from the fables taken from their stores by Mr. Schoolcraft, that these tribes possess great power that way.

I liked very much to walk or sit among them. With the women I held much communication by signs. They are almost invariably coarse and ugly, with the exception of their eyes, with a peculiarly awkward gait, and forms bent by burdens. This gait, so different from the steady and noble step of the men, marks the inferior position they occupy. I had heard much eloquent contradiction of this. . . .

Notwithstanding the homage paid to women, and the consequence allowed them in some cases, it is impossible to look upon the Indian women without feeling that they *do* occupy a lower place than women among the nations of European civilization. The habits of drudgery expressed in their form and gesture, the soft and wild but melancholy expression of their eye, reminded me of the tribe mentioned by Mackenzie, where the women destroy their female children, whenever they have a good opportunity; and of the eloquent reproaches addressed by the Paraguay woman to her mother, that she had not, in the same way, saved her from the anguish and weariness of her lot.

More weariness than anguish, no doubt, falls to the lot of most of these women. They inherit submission, and the minds of the generality accomodate themselves more or less to any posture. Perhaps they suffer less than their white sisters, who have more aspiration and refinement, with little power of self-sustenance. But their place is certainly lower, and their share of the human inheritance less.

Their decorum and delicacy are striking, and show that, when these are native to the mind, no habits of life make any difference. Their whole gesture is timid, yet self-possessed. They used to crowd round me, to inspect little things I had to show them, but never press near; on the contrary, would reprove and keep off the children. Anything they took from my hand was held with care, then shut or folded, and returned with an air of lady-like precision. They would not stare, however curious they might be, but cast sidelong glances. . . .

I have spoken of the hatred felt by the white man for the Indian: with white women it seems to amount to disgust, to loathing. How I could endure the dirt, the peculiar smell, of the Indians, and their dwellings, was a great marvel in the eyes of my lady acquaintance; indeed, I wonder why they did not quite give me up, as they certainly looked on me with great distaste for it. "Get you gone, you Indian dog," was the felt, if not the breathed, expression towards the hapless owners of the soil; — all their claims, all their sorrows quite forgot, in abhorrence of their dirt, their tawny skins, and the vices the whites have taught them.

A person who had seen them during great part of a life expressed his prejudices to me with such violence, that I was no longer surprised that the Indian children threw sticks at him, as he passed. A lady said: "Do what you will for them, they will be ungrateful. The savage cannot be washed out of them. Bring up an Indian child, and see if you can attach it to you." The next moment, she expressed, in the presence of one of those children whom she was bringing up, loathing at the odor left by one of her people, and one of the most respected, as he passed through the room. When the child is grown, she will be considered basely ungrateful not to love the lady, as she certainly will not; and this will be cited as an instance of the impossibility of attaching the Indian.

Whether the Indian could, by any efforts of love and intelligence from the white man, have been civilized and made a valuable ingredient in the new state, I will not say; but this we are sure of, — the French Catholics, at least, did not harm them, nor disturb their minds merely to corrupt them. The French they loved. But the stern Presbyterian, with his dogmas and his task-work, the city circle and the college, with their niggard concessions and unfeeling stare, have never tried the experiment. It has not been tried. Our people and our government have sinned alike against the first-born of the soil, and if they are the fated agents of a new era, they have done nothing, — have invoked no god to keep them sinless while they do the hest of fate.

Worst of all is it, when they invoke the holy power only to mask their iniquity; when the felon trader, who, all the week, has been besotting and degrading the Indian with rum mixed with red pepper, and damaged tobacco, kneels with him on Sunday before a common altar, to tell the rosary which recalls the thought of Him crucified for love of suffering men, and to listen to sermons in praise of "purity"!!

"My savage friends," cries the old, fat priest, "you must, above all things, aim at *purity*."

Oh! my heart swelled when I saw them in a Christian church. Better their own dog-feasts and bloody rites than such mockery of that other faith.

"The dog," said an Indian, "was once a spirit; he has fallen for his sin and was given by the Great Spirit, in this shape, to man, as his most intelligent companion. Therefore we sacrifice it in highest honor to our friends in this world, — to our protecting geniuses in another."

There was religion in that thought. The white man sacrifices his own brother, and to Mammon, yet he turns in loathing from the dog-feast. . . .

Amalgamation would afford the only true and profound means of civilization. But nature seems, like all else, to declare that this race is fated to perish. Those of mixed blood fade early, and are not generally a fine race. They lose what is best in either type, rather than enhance the value of each, by mingling. There are exceptions, — one or two such I know of, — but this, it is said, is the general rule. . . .

The Chippewas have lately petitioned the State of Michigan, that they may be admitted as citizens; but this would be vain, unless they could be admitted, as brothers, to the heart of the white man. And while the latter feels that conviction of superiority which enabled our Wisconsin friend to throw away the gun, and send the Indian to fetch it, he needs to be very good, and very wise, not to abuse his position. But the white man, as yet, is a half-tamed pirate, and avails himself as much as ever of the maxim, "Might makes right." All that civilization does for the generality is to cover up this with a veil of subtle evasions and chicane, and here and there to rouse the individual mind to appeal to Heaven against it.

I have no hope of liberalizing the missionary, of humanizing the sharks of trade, of infusing the conscientious drop into the flinty bosom of policy, of saving the Indian from immediate degradation and speedy death. The whole sermon may be preached from the text, "Needs be that offences must come, yet woe unto them by whom they come." Yet, ere they depart, I wish there might be some masterly attempt to reproduce, in art or literature, what is proper to them, — a kind of beauty and grandeur which few of the every-day crowd have hearts to feel, yet which ought to leave in the world its monuments, to inspire the thought of genius through all ages. . . .

By the premature death of Mrs. Schoolcraft was lost a mine of poesy, to which few had access, and from which Mrs. Jameson would have known how to coin a series of medals for the history of this ancient people. We might have known in clear outline, as now we shall not, the growths of religion and philosophy, under the influences of this climate and scenery, from such suggestions as nature and the teachings of the inward mind presented.

Now we can only gather that they had their own theory of the history of this globe; had perceived a gap in its genesis, and tried to fill it up by the intervention of some secondary power, with moral sympathies. They have observed the action of fire and water upon this earth; also that the dynasty of animals has yielded to that of man. With these animals they have profound sympathy, and are always trying to restore to them their lost honors. On the rattlesnake, the beaver, and the bear, they seem to look with a mixture of sympathy and veneration, as on their fellow settlers in these realms. There is something that appeals powerfully to the imagination in the ceremonies they observe, even in case of destroying one of these animals. . . .

The Indian is steady to that simple creed which forms the basis of all his mythology; that there is a God and a life beyond this; a right and wrong which each man can see, betwixt which each man should choose; that good brings with it its reward, and vice its punishment. His moral code, if not as refined as that of civilized nations, is clear and noble in the stress laid upon truth and fidelity. And all unprejudiced observers bear testimony, that the Indians, until broken from their old anchorage by intercourse with the whites, — who offer them, instead, a religion of which they furnish neither interpretation nor example, — were singularly virtuous, if virtue be allowed to consist in a man's acting up to his own ideas of right. . . .

I have not wished to write sentimentally about the Indians, however moved by the thought of their wrongs and speedy extinction. I know that the Europeans who took possession of this country felt themselves justified by their superior civilization and religious ideas. Had they been truly civilized or Christianized, the conflicts which sprang from the collision of the two races might have been avoided; but this cannot be expected in movements made by masses of men. The mass has never yet been humanized, though the age may develop a human thought. Since those conflicts and differences did arise, the hatred which sprang from terror and suffering, on the European side, has naturally warped the whites still further from justice.

The Indian, brandishing the scalps of his wife and friends, drinking their blood, and eating their hearts, is by him viewed as a fiend, though, at a distant day, he will no doubt be considered as having acted the Roman or Carthaginian part of heroic and patriotic self-defence, according to the standard of right and motives prescribed by his religious faith and education. Looked at by his own standard, he is virtuous when he most injures his enemy, and the white, if he be really the superior in enlargement of thought, ought to cast aside his inherited prejudices enough to see this, to look on him in pity and brotherly goodwill, and do all he can to mitigate the doom of those who survive his past injuries.

In McKenney's book is proposed a project for organizing the Indians under a patriarchal government; but it does not look feasible, even on paper. Could their own intelligent men be left to act unimpeded in their behalf, they would do far better for them than the white thinker, with all his general knowledge. But we dare not hope the designs of such will not always be frustrated by barbarous selfishness, as they were in Georgia. *There* was a chance of seeing what might have been done, now lost for ever.

Yet let every man look to himself how far this blood shall be required at his hands. Let the missionary, instead of preaching to the Indian, preach to the trader who ruins him, of the dreadful account which will be demanded of the followers of Cain, in a sphere where the accents of purity and love come on the ear more decisively than in ours. Let every legislator take the subject to heart, and, if he cannot undo the effects of past sin, try for that clear view and right sense that may save us from sinning still more deeply. And let every man and every woman, in their private dealings with the subjugated race, avoid all share in embittering, by insult or unfeeling prejudice, the captivity of Israel. . . .

Homeward bound. In the boat many signs admonished that we were floating eastward. A shabbily-dressed phrenologist laid his hand on every head which would bend, with half-conceited, half-sheepish expression, to the trial of his skill. Knots of people gathered here and there to discuss points of theology. A bereaved lover was seeking religious consolation in – Butler's Analogy, which he had purchased for that purpose. However, he did not turn over many pages before his attention was drawn aside by the gay glances of certain damsels that came on board at Detroit, and, though Butler might afterwards be seen sticking from his pocket, it had not weight to impede him from many a feat of lightness and liveliness. I doubt if it went with him from the boat. Some there were, even, discussing the doctrines of Fourier. It seemed pity they were not going to, rather than from, the rich and free country where it would be so much easier than with us to try the great experiment of voluntary association, and show beyond a doubt that "an ounce of prevention is worth a pound of cure," a maxim of the "wisdom of nations" which has proved of little practical efficacy as yet. . . . *[Summer on the Lakes in 1843* (1844; rpt. Nieuwkoop: B. De Graaf, 1972)]

11. On visit to Sing Sing, October 20, 1844

The sources of reform in the 1840s were often garish, but rarely more so than in the case of Eliza Farnham. Her beliefs in phrenology and in a female superiority so great as to obviate the need for rights somehow fused to make her a pioneer in rehabilitation for women prisoners. Appointed matron of the women's prison of Sing Sing in 1844 after a rebellion there, she suspended the rule of silence, rewarded the well-behaved with bouquets of flowers, started a library, and taught writing and handicrafts. At Fuller's suggestion, Georgianna Bruce left Brook Farm to work (despite protests of her fellow-utopians) as Farnham's assistant. Ultimately, the anger of the prison chaplain over Farnham's reading *Oliver Twist* aloud to the inmates on Sunday "to awaken good resolutions" led to Farnham's forced resignation in 1848 and the setback for nearly forty years of women's prison reform. (Nothing daunted, the next year Farnham took off for California with a group of unmarried women to foster decorum amid the chaos of the Gold Rush.) Here is Fuller's account in a letter to Elizabeth Hoar of her first visit to Sing Sing with Caroline Sturgis and William Channing.

(For a fair sample of Channing's pious effulgence, compare
his redaction of the following in the *Memoirs* [II, 144-45].)

... We have just been passing Sunday at Sing Sing. We went with
William Channing: he staid at the chaplain's, we at the prison. It was a
noble occasion for his eloquence, and I never felt more content than
when at the words "Men and brethren" all those faces were upturned
like a sea swayed by a single wind, and the shell of brutality burst apart
at the touch of love divinely human. He visited several of them in their
cells and the incidents that came were moving.

On Sunday they all are confined in their cells after twelve at noon
that the keepers may have rest from their weekly fatigues, but I was
allowed to have some of the women out to talk with, and the interview
was very pleasant. These women were among the so-called worst but
nothing could be more decorous than their conduct, and frank too. All
passed much as in one of my Boston classes. I told them I was writing
about Woman; and, as my path had been a favoured one, I wanted to
gain information of those who had been tempted to pollution and
sorrow. They seemed to reply in the same spirit in which I asked.
Several, however, expressed a wish to see me alone, as they could then
say *all*, which they could not bear to before one another: and I intend
to go there again, and take time for this. It is very gratifying to see the
influence these few months of gentle and intelligent treatment have had
upon these women; indeed it is wonderful, and even should the state
change its policy affords the needed text for treatment of the subject.
[Emerson Notebook on MFO]

12. On talk to prisoners, December 25, 1844

Among Fuller's papers at the Houghton Library is an undated
fragment of remarks she made on a political prisoner,
probably in an address to the Sing Sing inmates: "He felt, as I
believe many of you do, though with less reason, that those
who put him there had no right to do it. He felt, with as
much truth, that many without the prison walls were far
worse than those within. But when once there, did he waste
his time in useless repinings or anger that could only poison
his own heart—Not so!" She went on to describe how the

prisoner studied to improve himself. There is no original of Fuller's talk to the women at Sing Sing on Christmas Day 1844, and Channing's version, below, is doubtless distended to some degree by his own pomposity.

I have passed other Christmas days happily, but never felt as now, how fitting it is that this festival should come among the snows and chills of winter: for, to many of you, I trust, it is the birth-day of a higher life, when the sun of good-will is beginning to return, and the evergreen of hope gives promise of the eternal year. * * *

Some months ago, we were told of the riot, the license, and defying spirit which made this place so wretched, and the conduct of some now here was such that the world said: — "Women once lost are far worse than abandoned men, and cannot be restored." But, no! It is not so! I know my sex better. It is because women have so much feeling, and such a rooted respect for purity, that they seem so shameless and insolent, when they feel that they have erred and that others think ill of them. They know that even the worst of men would like to see women pure as angels, and when they meet man's look of scorn, the desperate passion that rises is a perverted pride, which might have been their guardian angel. Might have been! Rather let me say, which may be; for the great improvement so rapidly wrought here gives us all warm hopes. * * *

Be not in haste to leave these walls. Yesterday, one of you, who was praised, replied, that "if she did well she hoped that efforts would be made to have her pardoned." I can feel the monotony and dreariness of your confinement, but I entreat you to believe that for many of you it would be the greatest misfortune to be taken from here too soon. You know, better than I can, the temptations that await you in the world; and you must now perceive how dark is the gulf of sin and sorrow, towards which they would hurry you. Here, you have friends indeed; friends to your better selves; able and ready to help you. Born of unfortunate marriages, inheriting dangerous inclinations, neglected in childhood, with bad habits and bad associates, as certainly must be the case with some of you, how terrible will be the struggle when you leave this shelter! O, be sure that you are fitted to triumph over evil, before you again expose yourselves to it! And, instead of wasting your time and strength in vain wishes, use this opportunity to prepare yourselves for a better course of life, when you are set free. . . .

And never be discouraged; never despond; never say, "It is too late." Fear not, even if you relapse again and again. Many of you have much to contend with. Some may be so faulty, by temperament or habit, that they can never on this earth lead a wholly fair and harmonious life, however much they strive. Yet do what you can. If in one act, – for one day, – you can do right, let that live like a point of light in your memory; for if you have done well once you can again. If you fall, do not lie grovelling; but rise upon your feet once more, and struggle bravely on. And if aroused conscience makes you suffer keenly, have patience to bear it. God will not let you suffer more than you need to fit you for his grace. At the very moment of your utmost pain, persist to seek his aid, and it will be given abundantly. *[Memoirs, II, 146-48]*

13. *"Our City Charities," March 19, 1845*

"The pauper establishments that belong to a great city take the place of the skeleton at the banquets of old. They admonish us of stern realities. . . ." Thus in the *Tribune*, Fuller opened her survey of "our city charities"—the Bellevue Alms House, the Farm School, the Asylum for the Insane, and the Penitentiary of Blackwell's Island. Now she was in a position to hold up for emulation the enlightened policies of Farnham at Sing Sing and the pleasant and humane atmosphere of the Bloomingdale Asylum for the Insane—an institution in the Harlem heights which she had visited to report on a Valentine's Day dance. Her persuasive strategies—picturesque portraiture and appeals to the self-interest of potential benefactors—were, according to Greeley, remarkably effective with the rich.

. . . At the Alms House there is every appearance of kindness in the guardians of the poor, and there was a greater degree of cleanliness and comfort than we had expected. But the want of suitable and sufficient employment is a great evil. The persons who find here either a permanent or temporary refuge have scarcely any occupation provided except to raise vegetables for the establishment, and prepare clothing for themselves. The men especially have the most vagrant, degraded air, and so much indolence must tend to confirm them in every bad habit. We were told that, as they are under no strict discipline, their labor at the various trades could not be made profitable; yet surely the means of such should be provided, even at some expense. Employments of various kinds must be absolutely needed, if only to counteract the bad effects of such a position. Every establishment in aid of the poor should be planned with a view to their education. There should be instruction, both practical and in the use of books, openings to a better intercourse than they can obtain from their miserable homes, correct notions as to cleanliness, diet, and fresh air. A great deal of pain would be lost in their case, as with all other arrangements for the good of the many, but here and there the seed would fall into the right places, and some members of the downtrodden million, rising a little from the mud, would raise the whole body with them. . . .

From the Alms house we passed in an open boat to the Farm School. We were unprepared to find this, as we did, only a school upon a small farm, instead of one in which study is associated with labor. The children are simply taken care of and taught the common English branches till they are twelve years old, when they are bound out to various kinds of work. We think this plan very injudicious. It is bad enough for the children of rich parents, not likely in after life to bear a hard burden, and who are, at any rate, supplied with those various excitements required to develope the character in the earliest years; it is bad enough, we say, for these to have no kind of useful labor mingled with their plays and studies. Even these children would expand more, and be more variously called forth, and better prepared for common life, if another course were pursued. But in schools like this at the farm, where the children, on leaving it, will be at once called on for adroitness and readiness of mind and body, and where the absence of natural ties and the various excitements that rise from them inevitably give to life a mechanical routine calculated to cramp and chill the character, it would be peculiarly desirable to provide various occupations, and such as are calculated to prepare for common life. As to economy of time, there is never time lost, by mingling other pursuits with the studies of children; they have vital energy enough for many things at once, and learn more from books when their attention is quickened by other kinds of culture. . . .

Hence we passed to the Asylum for the Insane. Only a part of this building is completed and it is well known that the space is insufficient. Twice as many are inmates here as can be properly accomodated. A tolerable degree, however, of order and cleanliness is preserved. We could not but observe the vast difference between the appearance of the insane here and at Bloomingdale, or other institutions where the number of attendants and nature of the arrangements permit them to be the object of individual treatment; that is, where the wants and difficulties of each patient can be distinctly and carefully attended to. At Bloomingdale, the shades of character and feeling were nicely kept up, decorum of manners preserved, and the insane showed in every way that they felt no violent separation betwixt them and the rest of the world, and might easily return to it. The eye, though bewildered seemed lively, and the tongue prompt. But *here*, insanity appeared in its more stupid, wild, or despairing forms. They crouched in corners; they had no eye for the stranger, no heart for hope, no habitual expectation of light. Just as at the Farm School, where the children show by their unformed features and mechanical movements that they are treated by wholesale, so do these poor sufferers. It is an evil incident to public establishments, and which only a more intelligent public attention can obviate. . . .

Passing to the Penitentiary, we entered on one of the gloomiest scenes that deforms the great metropolis. Here are the twelve hundred, who receive the punishment due to the vices of so large a portion of the rest. And under what circumstances! Never was punishment treated more simply as a social convenience, without regard to pure right, or a hope of reformation. . . .

The want of proper matrons, or any matrons, to take the care so necessary for the bodily or mental improvement or even decent condition of the seven hundred women assembled here, is an offence that cries aloud. It is impossible to take the most cursory survey of this assembly of women; especially it is impossible to see them in the Hospital, where the circumstances are a little more favorable, without seeing how many there are in whom the feelings of innocent childhood are not dead, who need only good influences and steady aid to raise them from the pit of infamy and woe into which they have fallen. And, if there was not one that could be helped, at least Society owes them the insurance of a decent condition while here. We trust that interest on the subject will not slumber.

The recognized principles of all such institutions which have any higher object than the punishment of fault, (and we believe few among us are so ignorant as to avow that as the only object, though they may, from want of thought, act as if it were,) are — Classification as the first step, that the bad may not impede those who wish to do well; 2d. Instruction, practical, oral, and by furnishing books which may open entirely new hopes and thoughts to minds oftener darkened than corrupted; 3d. A good Sanitary system, which promotes self-respect, and through health and purity of body, the same in mind. . . .

We hope to see the two thousand poor people, and the poor children, better situated in their new abode, when we visit them again. The Insane Asylum will gain at once by enlargement of accomodations; but more attendance is also necessary, and, for that purpose, the best persons should be selected. We saw, with pleasure, tame pigeons walking about among the most violent of the insane, but we also saw two attendants with faces brutal and stolid. Such a charge is too delicate to be intrusted to any but excellent persons. . . . There is no reason why New York should not become a model for other States in these things. There is wealth enough, intelligence, and good desire enough, and surely, need enough. If she be not the best cared for city in the world, she threatens to surpass in corruption London and Paris. Such bane as is constantly poured into her veins demands powerful antidotes. *[New York Tribune, March 19, 1845, p. 1]*

14. On *The Narrative of Frederick Douglass*, June 10, 1845

In 1845, the *Tribune* published at least seven pieces by Fuller against slavery. Perhaps making amends to Maria Weston Chapman for her earlier indifference (IV:12), Fuller twice reviewed her annual abolition anthology. Frederick Douglass' *Narrative* was among the most powerful of the many slave narratives published in the 1830s and 1840s. In praising it, Fuller, like Harriet Beecher Stowe, subscribed to what George Frederickson has called "romantic racialism"—a benign attitude toward racial "peculiarities." This *Tribune* review concluded with a long quotation (omitted here) in which Douglass demolished the notion that the slave's songs prove his contentment.

Frederick Douglass has been for some time a prominent member of the abolition party. He is said to be an excellent speaker – can speak from a thorough personal experience – and has upon the audience, besides, the influence of a strong character and uncommon talents. In the book before us he has put into the story of his life the thoughts, the feelings, and the adventures that have been so affecting through the living voice; nor are they less so from the printed page. He has had the courage to name persons, times, and places, thus exposing himself to obvious danger, and setting the seal on his deep convictions as to the religious need of speaking the whole truth. Considered merely as a narrative, we have never read one more simple, true, coherent, and warm with genuine feeling. It is an excellent piece of writing, and on that score to be prized as a specimen of the powers of the black race, which prejudice persists in disputing. We prize highly all evidence of this kind, and it is becoming more abundant. The cross of the Legion of Honor has just been conferred in France on Dumas and Souliè, both celebrated in the paths of light literature. Dumas, whose father was a general in the French army, is a mulatto; Souliè, a quadroon. He went from New Orleans, where, though to the eye a white man, yet, as known to have African blood in his veins, he could never have enjoyed the privileges due to a human being. Leaving the land of freedom, he found himself free to develop the powers that God had given.

Two wise and candid thinkers – the Scotchman Kinmont, prematurely lost to this country, of which he was so faithful and generous a student, and the late Dr. Channing, – both thought that the African race had in them a peculiar element, which, if it could be assimilated with those imported among us from Europe, would give to genius a development, and to the energies of character a balance and harmony, beyond what has been seen heretofore in the history of the world. Such an element is indicated in their lowest estate by a talent for melody, a ready skill at imitation and adaptation, an almost indestructible elasticity of nature. It is to be remarked in the writings both of Souliè and Dumas, full of faults, but glowing with plastic life and fertile in invention. The same torrid energy and saccharine fulness may be felt in the writings of this Douglass, though his life, being one of action or resistance, has been less favorable to *such* powers than one of a more joyous flow might have been.

The book is prefaced by two communications – one from Garrison, and one from Wendell Phillips. That from the former is in his usual over-emphatic style. His motives and his course have been noble and generous; we look upon him with high respect; but he has indulged in violent invective and denunciation till he has spoiled the temper of his mind. Like a man who has been in the habit of screaming himself hoarse to make the deaf hear, he can no longer pitch his voice on a key agreeable to common ears. Mr. Phillips's remarks are equally decided, without this exaggeration in the tone. Douglass himself seems very just and temperate. We feel that his view, even of those who have injured him most, may be relied upon. He knows how to allow for motives and influences. Upon the subject of religion, he speaks with great force, and not more than our own sympathies can respond to. The inconsistencies of slaveholding professors of religion cry to Heaven. We are not disposed to detest, or refuse communion with them. Their blindness is but one form of that prevalent fallacy which substitutes a creed for a faith, a ritual for a life. We have seen too much of this system of atonement not to know that those who adopt it often began with good intentions, and are, at any rate, in their mistakes worthy of the deepest pity. But that is no reason why the truth should not be uttered, trumpet-tongued, about the thing. "Bring no more vain oblations;" sermons must daily be preached anew on that text. Kings, five hundred years ago, built churches with the spoils of war; clergymen to-day command slaves to obey a gospel which they will not allow them to read, and call themselves Christians amid the curses of their fellow-men. The world ought to get on a little faster than this, if there be really any principle of improvement in it. The kingdom of heaven may not at the beginning have dropped seed larger than a mustard-seed, but even from that we had a right to expect a fuller growth than we can believe to exist, when we read such a book as this of Douglass. Unspeakably affecting is the fact that he never saw his mother at all by daylight.

"I do not recollect of ever seeing my mother by the light of day. She was with me in the night. She would lie down with me, and get me to sleep, but long before I waked she was gone."

The following extract presents a suitable answer to the hackneyed argument drawn by the defender of slavery from the songs of the slave, and is also a good specimen of the powers of observation and manly heart of the writer. We wish that every one may read his book, and see what a mind might have been stifled in bondage — what a man may be subjected to the insults of spendthrift dandies, or the blows of mercenary brutes, in whom there is no whiteness except of the skin, no humanity except in the outward form, and of whom the Avenger will not fail yet to demand, "Where is thy brother?" . . . [*Life Without and Life Within*, pp. 121-23]

15. On the United States Exploring
Expedition, June 28, 1845

Although Fuller had been disappointed in the *Narrative of the United States Exploring Expedition* (1844) by Commander Charles Wilkes, she was interested in the problems his findings raised. In the *Tribune*, she linked her appeal for objective scientific study with her anthropological curiosity and her growing hatred for cultural imperialism.

Slight as the intercourse held by the Voyager with the South Sea Islands is, his narrative is always more prized by us than those of the missionary and traders, who, though they have better opportunity for full and candid observation, rarely use it so well, because their minds are biased towards their special objects. It is deeply interesting to us to know how much and how little God has accomplished for the various nations of the larger portion of the earth, before they are brought into contact with the civilization of Europe and the Christian religion. To suppose it so little as most people do, is to impugn the justice of Providence. We see not how any one can contentedly think that such vast multitudes of living souls have been left for thousands of years without manifold and great means of instruction and happiness. To appreciate justly how much these have availed them, to know how far they are competent to receive new benefits, is essential to the philanthropist as a means of aiding them, no less than it is important to the philosopher who wishes to see the universe as God made it, not as some men think he *ought to* have made it.

The want of correct knowledge, and a fair appreciation of the uncultivated man as he stands, is a cause why even the good and generous fail to aid him, and contact with Europe has proved so generally more of a curse than a blessing. It is easy enough to see why our red man, to whom the white extends the Bible or crucifix with one hand, and the rum-bottle with the other, should look upon Jesus as only one more Manitou, and learn nothing from his precepts or the civilization connected with them. The Hindoo, the South American Indian, who knew their teachers first as powerful robbers, and found themselves called upon to yield to violence not only their property, personal freedom, and peace, but also the convictions and ideas that had been rooted and growing in their race for ages, could not be

otherwise than degraded and stupefied by a change effected through
such violence and convulsion. But not only those who came with fire
and sword, crying, "Believe or die;" "Understand or we will scourge
you;" "Understand *and* we will only plunder and tyrannize over
you," – not only these ignorant despots, self-deceiving robbers, have
failed to benefit the people they dared esteem more savage than
themselves, but the worthy and generous have failed from want of
patience and an expanded intelligence. Would you speak to a man? first
learn his language. Would you have the tree grow? learn the nature of
the soil and climate in which you plant it. Better days are coming, we
do hope, as to these matters – days in which the new shall be
harmonized with the old, rather than violently rent asunder from it;
when progress shall be accomplished by gentle evolution, as the stem of
the plant grows up, rather than by the blasting of rocks, and blindness
or death of the miners. . . . *[Life Without and Life Within, pp. 141-42]*

16. "The Irish Character,"
June 28, 1845

In the 1840s, the tides of immigration swollen by the potato
famine led to the development of reactionary anti-Irish and
anti-Catholic nativism and the secret societies that in the
1850s became the Know-Nothing party. Already there had
been anti-Irish riots, and employment notices bore the
formula "No Irish need apply." Fuller's warm defense of the
Irish sprang from the habitual interest she took in servants
wherever she visited and her support of an independent Irish
republic. (In this cause, Robert Emmet, Lord Edward
Fitzgerald, John Philpot Curran, and Daniel O'Connell were
leading agitators.) When the following article elicited angry
objections, she wrote another, calling American desire for
gratitude feudalistic and urging on her readers the "great
patriotic work . . . of mutual education." In Europe her
commitment to American hospitality to refugees would only
grow.

In one of the eloquent passages quoted in the *"Tribune"* of Wednesday,
under the head, "Spirit of the Irish Press," we find these words:
    "Domestic love, almost morbid from external suffering, prevents

him (the Irishman) from becoming a fanatic and a misanthrope, and reconciles him to life."

This recalled to our mind the many touching instances known to us of such traits among the Irish we have seen here. We have known instances of morbidness like this. A girl sent "home," after she was well established herself, for a young brother, of whom she was particularly fond. He came, and shortly after died. She was so overcome by his loss that she took poison. The great poet of serious England says, and we believe it to be his serious thought though laughingly said, "Men have died, and worms have eaten them, but not for love." Whether or not death may follow from the loss of a lover or child, we believe that among no people but the Irish would it be upon the loss of a young brother. . . .

They are able, however, to make the sacrifice of even these intense family affections in a worthy cause. We knew a woman who postponed sending for her only child, whom she had left in Ireland, for years, while she maintained a sick friend who had no one else to help her.

The poetry of which I have spoken shows itself even here, where they are separated from old romantic associations, and begin the new life in the New World by doing all its drudgery. We know flights of poetry repeated to us by those present at their wakes, — passages of natural eloquence, from the lamentations for the dead, more beautiful than those recorded in the annals of Brittany or Roumelia. . . .

It is the genius which will enable Emmet's appeal to draw tears from the remotest generations, however much they may be strangers to the circumstances which called it forth. It is the genius which beamed in chivalrous loveliness through each act of Lord Edward Fitzgerald, – the genius which, ripened by English culture, favored by suitable occasions, has shed such glory on the land which has done all it could to quench it on the parent hearth.

When we consider all the fire which glows so untamably in Irish veins, the character of her people, considering the circumstances, almost miraculous in its goodness, we cannot forbear, notwithstanding all the temporary ills they aid in here, to give them a welcome to our shores. Those ills we need not enumerate; they are known to all, and we rank among them, what others would not, that by their ready service to do all the hard work, they make it easier for the rest of the population to grow effeminate, and help the country to grow too fast. But that is her destiny, to grow too fast: there is no use talking against it. Their extreme ignorance, their blind devotion to their priesthood, their pliancy in the hands of demagogues, threaten continuance of these ills, yet, on the other hand, we must regard them as most valuable elements in the new race. They are looked upon with contempt for their want of aptitude in learning new things; their ready and ingenious lying; their eye-service. These are the faults of an oppressed race, which must require the aid of better circumstances through two or three generations to eradicate. Their virtues are their own; they are many, genuine, and deeply-rooted. Can an impartial observer fail to admire their truth to domestic ties, their power of generous bounty, and more generous gratitude, their indefatigable good-humor (for ages of wrong which have driven them to so many acts of desperation, could never sour their blood at its source), their ready wit, their elasticity of nature? They are fundamentally one of the best nations of the world. Would they were welcomed here, not to work merely, but to intelligent sympathy, and efforts, both patient and ardent, for the education of their children! No sympathy could be better deserved, no efforts wiselier timed. Future Burkes and Currans would know how to give thanks for them, and Fitzgeralds rise upon the soil — which boasts the magnolia with its kingly stature and majestical white blossoms, — to the same lofty and pure beauty. Will you not believe it, merely because that bog-bred youth you placed in the mud-hole tells you lies, and drinks to cheer himself in those endless diggings? You are short-sighted, my friend; you do not look to the future; you will not turn your head to see what may have been the influences of the past. You have not examined your own breast to see whether the monitor there has not commanded you to do your part to counteract these influences; and yet the Irishman appeals to you, eye to eye. He is very personal himself, — he expects a personal interest from you. Nothing has been able to destroy this hope, which was the fruit of his nature. We were much touched by O'Connell's direct appeal to the queen, as "Lady!" But she did not listen, — and we fear few ladies and gentlemen will till the progress of Destiny compels them. *[Kindred Papers, pp. 321-25]*

17. "Children's Books," February 5, 1845

After Fuller's death, Greeley reminisced at length about her love of children. She was an enthralling narrator, mimic, and playmate, he recalled, "never lofty, nor reserved, nor mystical" (*Memoirs*, II, 160). In growing appreciation of her father's educational method, she urged *Tribune* readers who were mature enough to "revive with force and beauty the thoughts and scenes of childhood" to turn their talents to writing children's books.

There is too much amongst us of the French way of palming off false accounts of things on children, "to do them good," and showing nature to them in a magic lantern "purified for the use of childhood," and telling stories of sweet little girls and brave little boys, — O, all so good, or so bad! and above all, so *little*, and everything about them so little! Children accustomed to move in full-sized apartments, and converse with full-grown men and women, do not need so much of this baby-house style in their literature. They like, or would like if they could get them, better things much more. They like the *Arabian Nights*, and *Pilgrim's Progress*, and *Bunyan's Emblems*, and *Shakspeare*, and the *Iliad* and *Odyssey* — at least, they used to like them: and if they do not now, it is because their taste has been injured by so many sugar-plums. The books that were written in the childhood of nations suit an uncorrupted childhood now. They are simple, picturesque, robust. Their moral is not forced, nor is the truth veiled with a well-meant but sure-to-fail hypocrisy. Sometimes they are not moral at all, — only free plays of the fancy and intellect. These, also, the child needs, just as the infant needs to stretch its limbs, and grasp at objects it cannot hold. We have become so fond of the moral, that we forget the nature in which it must find its root; so fond of instruction, that we forget development.

Where ballads, legends, fairy-tales, *are* moral, the morality is heart-felt: if instructive, it is from the healthy common sense of mankind, and not for the convenience of nursery rule, nor the "peace of schools and families." . . .

Children need some childish talk, some childish play, some childish books. But they also need, and need more, difficulties to overcome, and a sense of the vast mysteries which the progress of their intelligence shall aid them to unravel. This sense is naturally their delight, as it is their religion, and it must not be dulled by premature explanations or subterfuges of any kind. . . . [*Kindred Papers*, pp. 311-13]

18. On travel in England and Scotland,
August 1846 [to January 1847]

On August 1, 1846, while Fuller set sail with the Springs on the steamer *Cambria*, she took leave of her great newspaper audience, in whom she boasted she had found "nothing petty or provincial": "Farewell to New York city, where twenty months have presented me with a richer and more varied exercise for thought and life, than twenty years could in any other part of these United States." She had come to feel confidence in this "great city struggling up through the love of money" (*Tribune*, Jan. 14, 1846). In Europe, however, she saw and felt social and economic inequities more keenly than at home and sought out remedies and reformers. The following selections are from the first ten of her thirty-three dispatches to the *Tribune*.

The day after our arrival we went to Manchester. There we went over the magnificent warehouse of ——— Phillips, in itself a Bazaar ample to furnish provision for all the wants and fancies of thousands. In the evening we went to the Mechanics' Institute, and saw the boys and young men in their classes. I have since visited the Mechanics' Institute at Liverpool, where more than seventeen hundred pupils are received, and with more thorough educational arrangements; but the excellent spirit, the desire for growth in wisdom and enlightened benevolence, is the same in both. For a very small fee, the mechanic, clerk, or apprentice, and the women of their families, can receive various good and well-arranged instruction, not only in common branches of an English education, but in mathematics, composition, the French and German languages, the practice and theory of the Fine Arts, and they are ardent in availing themselves of instruction in the higher branches. I found large classes, not only in architectural drawing, which may be supposed to be followed with a view to professional objects, but landscape also, and as large in German as in French. They can attend many good lectures and concerts without additonal charge, for a due place is here assigned to music as to its influence on the whole mind. The large and well furnished libraries are in constant requisition, and the books in most constant demand are not those of amusement, but of a solid and permanent interest and value. Only for the last year in

Manchester, and for two in Liverpool, have these advantages been extended to girls; but now that part of the subject is looked upon as it ought to be, and begins to be treated more and more as it must and will be wherever true civilization is making its way. One of the handsomest houses in Liverpool has been purchased for the girls' school, and room and good arrangement been afforded for their work and their play. Among other things they are taught, as they ought to be in all American schools, to cut out and make dresses. . . .

I heard a most interesting letter read from a tradesman in one of the country towns, whose daughters are self-elected instructors of the people in the way of cutting out from books and pamphlets fragments on the great subjects of the day, which they send about in packages, or paste on walls and doors. He said that one such passage, pasted on a door, he had seen read with eager interest by hundreds to whom such thoughts were, probably, quite new, and with some of whom it could scarcely fail to be as a little seed of a large harvest. Another good omen I found in written tracts by Joseph Barker, a working-man of the town of Wortley, published through his own printing-press.

How great, how imperious the need of such men, of such deeds, we felt more than ever, while compelled to turn a deaf ear to the squalid and shameless beggars of Liverpool, or talking by night in the streets of Manchester to the girls from the Mills, who were strolling bareheaded, with coarse, rude, and reckless air, through the streets, or seeing through the windows of the gin-palaces the women seated drinking, too dull to carouse. The homes of England! their sweetness is melting into fable; only the new Spirit in its holiest power can restore to those homes their boasted security of "each man's castle," for Woman, the warder, is driven into the street, and has let fall the keys in her sad plight. . . .

I understand there is an intellectual society of high merit in Glasgow, but we were there only a few hours, and did not see any one. Certainly the place, as it may be judged of merely from the general aspect of the population and such objects as may be seen in the streets, more resembles an *Inferno* than any other we have yet visited. The people are more crowded together, and the stamp of squalid, stolid misery and degradation more obvious and appalling. The English and Scotch do not take kindly to poverty, like those of sunnier climes; it makes them fierce or stupid, and, life presenting no other cheap pleasure, they take refuge in drinking. . . .

But from all these sorrowful tokens I by no means inferred the falsehood of the information, that here was to be found a circle rich in intellect and in aspiration. The manufacturing and commercial towns, burning focuses of grief and vice, are also the centres of intellectual life, as in forcing-beds the rarest flowers and fruits are developed by use of impure and repulsive materials. Where evil comes to an extreme, Heaven seems busy in providing means for the remedy. Glaring throughout Scotland and England is the necessity for the devoutest application of intellect and love to the cure of ills that cry aloud, and, without such application, erelong help *must* be sought by other means than words. Yet there is every reason to hope that those who ought to help are seriously, though slowly, becoming alive to the imperative nature of this duty; so we must not cease to hope, even in the streets of Glasgow, and the gin-palaces of Manchester, and the dreariest recesses of London. . . .

The castle of Stirling is as rich as any place in romantic associations. We were shown its dungeons and its Court of Lions, where, says tradition, wild animals, kept in the grated cells adjacent, were brought out on festival occasions to furnish entertainment for the court. So, while lords and ladies gay danced and sang above, prisoners pined and wild beasts starved below. This, at first blush, looks like a very barbarous state of things, but, on reflection, one does not find that we have outgrown it in our present so-called state of refined civilization, only the present way of expressing the same facts is a little different. Still lords and ladies dance and sing, unknowing or uncaring that the laborers who minister to their luxuries starve or are turned into wild beasts. Man need not boast his condition, methinks, till he can weave his costly tapestry without the side that is kept under looking thus sadly. . . .

We crossed the moorland in a heavy rain, and reached Newcastle late at night. Next day we descended into a coal-mine; it was quite an odd sensation to be taken off one's feet and dropped down into darkness by the bucket. The stables under ground had a pleasant Gil-Blas air, though the poor horses cannot like it much; generally they see the light of day no more after they have once been let down into these gloomy recesses, but pass their days in dragging cars along the rails of the narrow passages, and their nights in eating hay and dreaming of grass!! When we went down, we meant to go along the gallery to the place where the miners were then at work, but found this was a walk of a mile and a half, and, beside the weariness of picking one's steps slowly along by the light of a tallow candle, too wet and dirty an enterprise to be undertaken by way of amusement; so, after proceeding half a mile or so, we begged to be restored to our accustomed level, and reached it with minds slightly edified and face and hands much blackened. . . .

In Sheffield I saw the sooty servitors tending their furnaces. I saw them also on Saturday night, after their work was done, going to receive its poor wages, looking pallid and dull, as if they had spent on tempering the steel that vital force that should have tempered themselves to manhood. . . .

I visited the model prison at Pentonville; but though in some respects an improvement upon others I have seen, – though there was the appearance of great neatness and order in the arrangements of life, kindness and good judgment in the discipline of the prisoners, – yet there was also an air of bleak forlornness about the place, and it fell far short of what my mind demands of such abodes considered as redemption schools. But as the subject of prisons is now engaging the attention of many of the wisest and best, and the tendency is in what seems to me the true direction, I need not trouble myself to make crude and hasty suggestions; it is a subject to which persons who would be of use should give the earnest devotion of calm and leisurely thought.

The same day I went to see an establishment which gave me unmixed pleasure; it is a bathing establishment put at a very low rate to enable the poor to avoid one of the worst miseries of their lot, and which yet promises *to pay*. Joined with this is an establishment for washing clothes, where the poor can go and hire, for almost nothing, good tubs, water ready heated, the use of an apparatus for rinsing, drying, and ironing, all so admirably arranged that a poor woman can in three hours get through an amount of washing and ironing that would, under ordinary circumstances, occupy three or four days. Especially the drying closets I contemplated with great satisfaction, and hope to see in our own country the same arrangements throughout the cities, and even in the towns and villages. Hanging out the clothes is a great exposure for women, even when they have a good place for it; but when, as is so common in cities, they must dry them in the house, how much they suffer! . . . As long as we are so miserable as to have any very poor people in this world, *they* cannot put out their washing, because they cannot earn enough money to pay for it, and, preliminary to something better, washing establishments like this of London are desirable. . . .

And though I wish to return to London "in the season" when that city is an adequate representative of the state of things in England, I am glad I did not at first see all that pomp and parade of wealth and luxury in contrast with the misery, squalid, agonizing, ruffianly, which stares one in the face in every street of London, and hoots at the gates of her palaces more ominous a note than ever was that of owl or raven in the portentous times when empires and races have crumbled and fallen from inward decay.

It is impossible, however, to take a near view of the treasures created by English genius, accumulated by English industry, without a prayer, daily more fervent, that the needful changes in the condition of this people may be effected by peaceful revolution, which shall destroy nothing except the shocking inhumanity of exclusiveness, which now prevents their being used for the benefit of all. May their present possessors look to it in time! *[At Home and Abroad, pp. 121-22, 124, 159-61, 164-65, 186-87, 170-71]*

19. On meeting Carlyle [December 1846]

It was the "wild bugle call" of Carlyle writing on German authors which had first attracted James Clarke and Fuller to their German studies. But years later, in a *Tribune* review, she was caustic about Carlyle's bullying, insulting way with the reader in his *Letters and Speeches of Oliver Cromwell*. When she met him in London, she enjoyed his wit and laughter and chided Emerson, "Carlyle is worth a thousand of you for that;–he is not ashamed to laugh, when he is amused, but goes on in a cordial human fashion" (*Memoirs*, I, 185). For his part, Carlyle found her "a strange, lilting, lean old maid, not nearly such a bore as I expected" (Mason Wade, *Margaret Fuller: Whetstone of Genius*, p. 186). From their meetings comes the most famous of Fuller anecdotes, in which Carlyle responded to Fuller's "I accept the universe," with the devastating mutter, "By Gad, she'd better!"

I have not yet spoken of one of *our* benefactors, Mr. Carlyle, whom I saw several times. I approached him with more reverence after a little experience of England and Scotland had taught me to appreciate the strength and height of that wall of shams and conventions which he more than any man, or thousand men, — indeed, he almost alone, — has begun to throw down. Wherever there was fresh thought, generous hope, the thought of Carlyle has begun the work. He has torn off the veils from hideous facts; he has burnt away foolish illusions; he has awakened thousands to know what it is to be a man, — that we must live, and not merely pretend to others that we live. He has touched the rocks and they have given forth musical answer; little more was wanting to begin to construct the city.

But that little was wanting, and the work of construction is left to those that come after him: nay, all attempts of the kind he is the readiest to deride, fearing new shams worse than the old, unable to trust the general action of a thought, and finding no heroic man, no natural king, to represent it and challenge his confidence.

Accustomed to the infinite wit and exuberant richness of his writings, his talk is still an amazement and a splendor scarcely to be faced with steady eyes. He does not converse, — only harangues. It is the usual misfortune of such marked men (happily not one invariable or inevitable) that they cannot allow other minds room to breathe and show themselves in their atmosphere, and thus miss the refreshment and instruction which the greatest never cease to need from the experience of the humblest. Carlyle allows no one a chance, but bears down all opposition, not only by his wit and onset of words, resistless in their sharpness as so many bayonets, but by actual physical superiority, raising his voice and rushing on his opponent with a torrent of sound. This is not the least from unwillingness to allow freedom to others; on the contrary, no man would more enjoy a manly resistance to his thought; but it is the impulse of a mind accustomed to follow out its own impulse as the hawk its prey, and which knows not how to stop in the chase. Carlyle, indeed, is arrogant and overbearing, but in his arrogance there is no littleness or self-love: it is the heroic arrogance of some old Scandinavian conqueror, — it is his nature and the untamable impulse that has given him power to crush the dragons. You do not love him, perhaps, nor revere, and perhaps, also, he would only laugh at you if you did; but you like him heartily, and like to see him the powerful smith, the Siegfried, melting all the old iron in his furnace till it glows to a sunset red, and burns you if you senselessly go too near. He seemed to me quite isolated, lonely as the desert; yet never was man more fitted to prize a man, could he find one to match his mood. He finds such, but only in the past. He sings rather than talks. He pours upon you a kind of satirical, heroical, critical poem, with regular cadences, and generally catching up near the beginning some singular epithet, which serves as a *refrain* when his song is full, or with which as with a knitting-needle he catches up the stitches if he has chanced now and then to let fall a row. For the higher kinds of poetry he has no sense, and his talk on that subject is delightfully and gorgeously absurd; he sometimes stops a minute to laugh at it himself, then begins anew with fresh vigor; for all the spirits he is driving before him seem to him as Fata Morganas, ugly masks, in fact, if he can but make them turn about, but he laughs that they seem to others such dainty Ariels. He puts out his chin sometimes till it looks like the beak of a bird, and his eyes flash bright instinctive meanings like Jove's bird; yet he is not calm and grand enough for the eagle: he is more like the falcon, and yet not of gentle blood enough for that either. He is not exactly like anything but himself, and therefore you cannot see him without the most hearty refreshment and good-will, for he is original, rich, and strong enough to afford a thousand faults; one expects some wild land in a rich kingdom. His talk, like his books, is full of pictures, his critical strokes masterly; allow for his point of view, and his survey is admirable. He is a large subject; I cannot speak more or wiselier of him now, nor needs it; his works are true, to blame and praise him, the Siegfried of England, great and powerful, if not quite invulnerable, and of a might rather to destroy evil than legislate for good. At all events, he seems to be what Destiny intended, and represents fully a certain side; so we make no remonstrance as to his being and proceeding for himself, though we sometimes must for us.... *[At Home and Abroad, pp. 183-85]*

20. On the Carlyles and Mazzini, November 16, 1846

Fuller was slower to get to know Jane Carlyle, of the "sad and charming" eyes, "for who can speak while her husband is there?" But later she found her "full of grace, sweetness, and talent." One of Mrs. Carlyle's closest friends was the exiled Mazzini. Fuller's early descriptions of him for the *Tribune* are steeped in generalized idealism: "The name of Joseph Mazzini is well known to those among us who take an interest in the cause of human freedom, who, not content

with the peace and ease bought for themselves by the
devotion and sacrifices of their fathers, look with anxious
interest on the suffering nations who are preparing for a
similar struggle" (*At Home and Abroad*, p. 181). More
revealing is the letter she wrote in Paris to Emerson recalling
an evening with Mazzini and the Carlyles. It sharpened her
sense of Carlyle's disturbing affinity with sheer might and her
own growing social commitment.

... I only saw them once more, when they came to pass an evening
with us. Unluckily, Mazzini was with us, whose society, when he was
there alone, I enjoyed more than any. He is a beauteous and pure
music; also, he is a dear friend of Mrs. C.; but his being there gave the
conversation a turn to "progress" and ideal subjects, and C. was fluent
in invectives on all our "rose-water imbecilities." We all felt distant
from him, and Mazzini, after some vain efforts to remonstrate, became
very sad. Mrs. C. said to me, "These are but opinions to Carlyle; but to
Mazzini, who has given his all, and helped bring his friends to the
scaffold, in pursuit of such subjects, it is a matter of life and death."

All Carlyle's talk, that evening, was a defence of mere
force, — success the test of right; — if people would not behave well,
put collars round their necks; — find a hero, and let them be his slaves,
&c. It was very Titanic, and anti-celestial. I wish the last evening had
been more melodious. However, I bid Carlyle farewell with feelings of
the warmest friendship and admiration. We cannot feel otherwise to a
great and noble nature, whether it harmonize with our own or not. I
never appreciated the work he has done for his age till I saw England. I
could not. You must stand in the shadow of that mountain of shams, to
know how hard it is to cast light across it.

Honor to Carlyle! *Hoch!* Although in the wine with which we
drink this health, I, for one, must mingle the despised "rose-water." ...
[*Memoirs*, II, 187-88]

21. *On English and French character and the*
Chamber of Deputies, December 1846 [and March 1847]

In Paris, Fuller indulged in reflections on national
characteristics, a favorite pastime. When she was still in New

York, she had remarked that "the French are the only nation
that will dance on the brink of the gulf down which we
plunge into the infinite unknown," and had wished her
"nervous driving nation" might learn to emulate their grace,
consciousness, and nimble wit (*Tribune*, July 9, 1845; June
7, 1845).

a. I sit down here in Paris to narrate some recollections of London. The
distance in space and time is not great, yet I seem in wholly a different
world. Here in the region of wax-lights, mirrors, bright wood fires,
shrugs, vivacious ejaculations, wreathed smiles, and adroit courtesies, it
is hard to remember John Bull, with his coal-smoke, hands in pockets,
except when extended for ungracious demand of the perpetual
half-crown, or to pay for the all but perpetual mug of beer. John, seen
on that side, is certainly the most churlish of clowns, and the most
clownish of churls. But then there are so many other sides! When a
gentleman, he is so truly the gentleman, when a man, so truly the man
of honor! His graces, when he has any, grow up from his inmost heart.
    Not that he is free from humbug; on the contrary, he is prone to
the most solemn humbug, generally of the philanthropic or otherwise
moral kind. But he is always awkward beneath the mask, and can never
impose upon anybody – but himself. Nature meant him to be noble,
generous, sincere, and has furnished him with no faculties to make
himself agreeable in any other way or mode of being. 'Tis not so with
your Frenchman, who can cheat you pleasantly, and move with grace in
the devious and slippery path. You would be almost sorry to see him
quite disinterested and straightforward, so much of agreeable talent and
naughty wit would thus lie hid for want of use. But John, O John, we
must admire, esteem, or be disgusted with thee. [*At Home and Abroad*,
pp. *169-70*]

b. It is very amusing to be in the Chamber of Deputies when some dull
person is speaking. The French have a truly Greek vivacity; they cannot
endure to be bored. Though their conduct is not very dignified, I
should like a corps of the same kind of sharp-shooters in our legislative
assemblies when honorable gentlemen are addressing their constituents
and not the assembly, repeating in lengthy, windy, clumsy paragraphs
what has been the truism of the newspaper press for months previous,
wickedly wasting the time that was given us to learn something for

ourselves, and help our fellow-creatures. In the French Chamber, if a man who has nothing to say ascends the tribune, the audience-room is filled with the noise as of myriad beehives; the President rises on his feet, and passes the whole time of the speech in taking the most violent exercise, stretching himself to look imposing, ringing his bell every two minutes, shouting to the representatives of the nation to be decorous and attentive. In vain: the more he rings, the more they won't be still. I saw an orator in this situation, fighting against the desires of the audience, as only a Frenchman could, — certainly a man of any other nation would have died of embarrassment rather, — screaming out his sentences, stretching out both arms with an air of injured dignity, panting, growing red in the face; but the hubbub of voices never stopped an instant. At last he pretended to be exhausted, stopped, and took out his snuff-box. Instantly there was a calm. He seized the occasion, and shouted out a sentence; but it was the only one he was able to make heard. They were not to be trapped so a second time. When any one is speaking that commands interest, as Berryer did, the effect of this vivacity is very pleasing, the murmur of feeling that rushes over the assembly is so quick and electric, — light, too, as the ripple on the lake. I heard Guizot speak one day for a short time. His manner is very deficient in dignity, — has not even the dignity of station; you see the man of cultivated intellect, but without inward strength; nor is even his panoply of proof. [*At Home and Abroad, pp. 208-09]*

*22. On famine, Fourier, and
the Lyons weavers [March and April 1847]*

Before leaving New York, Fuller had perceived that France was peculiarly bewitched. She wrote in the January 1, 1846, *Tribune*: "France is in an uneasy dream—she knows she has been very sick, has had terrible remedies administered, and ought to be getting thoroughly well, which she is not. Louis Philippe watches by her pillow, doses and bleeds her, so that she cannot fairly try her strength, and find whether something or other has been done. But Louis Philippe and Metternich must soon, in the course of nature, leave this scene; and then there will be none to keep out air and light from the chamber, and the patients will be roused and

ascertain their true condition." Among the signs of life she
noted in France were a refuge for female ex-prisoners
(though she judged it "too formal" and ignorant of "human
nature") and an evening school for workers which she
proposed to emulate at home, "should I ever return." In her
dispatches of March and April 1847, she voiced new
appreciation of Fourier. The second passage is from her
account of the young mother who introduced Fuller to the
cramped garrets of the weavers of Lyons.

a. . . . The poorer classes have suffered from hunger this winter. All
signs of this are kept out of sight in Paris. A pamphlet, called "The
Voice of Famine," stating facts, though in the tone of vulgar and
exaggerated declamation, unhappily common to productions on the
radical side, was suppressed almost as soon as published; but the fact
cannot be suppressed, that the people in the provinces have suffered
most terribly amid the vaunted prosperity of France.

While Louis Philippe lives, the gases, compressed by his strong
grasp, may not burst up to light; but the need of some radical measures
of reform is not less strongly felt in France than elsewhere, and the
time will come before long when such will be imperatively demanded.
The doctrines of Fourier are making considerable progress, and
wherever they spread, the necessity of some practical application of the
precepts of Christ, in lieu of the mummeries of a worn-out ritual,
cannot fail to be felt. The more I see of the terrible ills which infest the
body politic of Europe, the more indignation I feel at the selfishness or
stupidity of those in my own country who oppose an examination of
these subjects, – such as is animated by the hope of prevention. The
mind of Fourier was, in many respects, uncongenial to mine. Educated
in an age of gross materialism, he was tainted by its faults. In attempts
to reorganize society, he commits the error of making soul the result of
health of body, instead of body the clothing of soul; but his heart was
that of a genuine lover of his kind, of a philanthropist in the sense of
Jesus, – his views were large and noble. His life was one of devout
study on these subjects, and I should pity the person who, after the
briefest sojourn in Manchester and Lyons, – the most superficial
acquaintance with the population of London and Paris, – could seek to
hinder a study of his thoughts, or be wanting in reverence for his
purposes. But always, always, the unthinking mob has found stones on

the highway to throw at the prophets. *[At Home and Abroad, pp. 205–206]*

b. . . . I admired her graceful manner of introducing us into those dark little rooms, and she was affectionately received by all her acquaintance. But alas! that voice, by nature of such bird-like vivacity, repeated again and again, "Ah! we are all very unhappy now." "Do you sing together, or go to evening schools?" "We have not the heart. When we have a piece of work, we do not stir till it is finished, and then we run to try and get another; but often we have to wait idle for weeks. It grows worse and worse, and they say it is not likely to be any better. We can think of nothing, but whether we shall be able to pay our rent. Ah! the work-people are very unhappy now." This poor, lovely little girl, at an age when the merchant's daughters of Boston and New York are just gaining their first experiences of "society," knew to a farthing the price of every article of food and clothing that is wanted by such a household. Her thought by day and her dream by night was, whether she should long be able to procure a scanty supply of these, and Nature had gifted her with precisely those qualities, which, unembarrassed by care, would have made her and all she loved really happy; and she was fortunate now, compared with many of her sex in Lyons, – of whom a gentleman who knows the class well said: "When their work fails, they have no resource except in the sale of their persons. There are but these two ways open to them, weaving or prostitution, to gain their bread." And there are those who dare to say that such a state of things is *well enough*, and what Providence intended for man, – who call those who have hearts to suffer at the sight, energy and zeal to seek its remedy, visionaries and fanatics! To themselves be woe, who have eyes and see not, ears and hear not, the convulsions and sobs of injured Humanity!

My little friend told me she had nursed both her children, – though almost all of her class are obliged to put their children out to nurse; "but," said she, "they are brought back so little, so miserable, that I resolved, if possible, to keep mine with me." Next day in the steamboat I read a pamphlet by a physician of Lyons in which he recommends the establishment of *Crèches*, not merely like those of Paris, to keep the children by day, but to provide wet-nurses for them. Thus, by the infants receiving nourishment from more healthy persons, and who under the supervision of directors would treat them well, he hopes to counteract the tendency to degenerate in this race of sedentary workers, and to save the mothers from too heavy a burden of care and labor, without breaking the bond between them and their children, whom, under such circumstances, they could visit often, and see them taken care of as they, brought up to know nothing except how to weave, cannot take care of them. Here, again, how is one reminded of Fourier's observations and plans, still more enforced by the recent developments at Manchester as to the habit of feeding children on opium, which has grown out of the position of things there. *[At Home and Abroad, pp. 215-16]*

23. On meeting George Sand, January 18 and March 17, 1847

The life and work of George Sand offered one version of the public and private radicalism toward which Fuller was moving. Waiting in Paris for Sand to return from her provincial chateau, Fuller heard that rumors about her were not exaggerated. She delighted in Sand's living with Chopin "on the footing of combined means, independent friendship!" Assured that Sand "takes rank in society like a man, for the weight of her thoughts," Fuller noted that she was paid less for them than Balzac, Dumas, or Sue. Finally Sand returned. In New York, Fuller had published her support of Sand in the *Tribune*; but this account of their meeting and of her deeper acceptance of the woman, sent to Elizabeth Hoar, was for friends' eyes only.

At last, however, she came; I went to see her at her house, Place d'Orleans. I found it a handsome modern residence. She had not answered my letter, written about a week before, and I felt a little anxious lest she should not receive me; for she is too much the mark of impertinent curiosity, as well as too busy, to be easily accessible to strangers. I am by no means timid, but I have suffered, for the first time in France, some of the torments of *mauvaise honte*, enough to see what they must be to many.

It is the custom to go and call on those to whom you bring letters, and push yourself upon their notice; thus you must go quite ignorant whether they are disposed to be cordial. My name is always murdered by the foreign servants who announce me. I speak very bad French; only lately have I had sufficient command of it to infuse some of my natural spirit in my discourse. This has been a great trial to me, who am eloquent and free in my own tongue, to be forced to feel my thoughts struggling in vain for utterance.

The servant who admitted me was in the picturesque costume of a peasant, and, as Madame Sand afterward told me, her god-daughter, whom she had brought from her province. She announced me as "*Madame Salere*," and returned into the ante-room to tell me, "*Madame says she does not know you.*" I began to think I was doomed to a rebuff, among the crowd who deserve it. However, to make assurance sure, I said, "Ask if she has not received a letter from me." As I spoke, Madame S. opened the door, and stood looking at me an instant. Our eyes met. I never shall forget her look at that moment. The doorway made a frame for her figure; she is large, but well-formed. She was dressed in a robe of dark violet silk, with a black mantle on her shoulders, her beautiful hair dressed with the greatest taste, her whole appearance and attitude, in its simple and lady-like dignity, presenting an almost ludicrous contrast to the vulgar caricature idea of George Sand. Her face is a very little like the portraits, but much finer; the upper part of the forehead and eyes are beautiful, the lower, strong and masculine, expressive of a hardy temperament and strong passions, but not in the least coarse; the complexion olive, and the air of the whole head Spanish, (as, indeed, she was born at Madrid, and is only on one side of French blood.) All these details I saw at a glance; but what fixed my attention was the expression of *goodness*, nobleness, and power, that pervaded the whole, – the truly human heart and nature that shone in the eyes. As our eyes met, she said, "*C'est vous*," and held out her hand. I took it, and went into her little study; we sat down a moment, then I said, "*Il me fait de bien de vous voir*," and I am sure I said it with my whole heart, for it made me very happy to see such a woman, so large and so developed a character, and everything that *is* good in it so *really* good. I loved, shall always love her.

She looked away, and said, "*Ah! vous m'avez écrit une lettre charmante*." This was all the preliminary of our talk, which then went on as if we had always known one another. She told me, before I went away, that she was going that very day to write to me; that when the servant announced me she did not recognize the name, but after a minute it struck her that it might be *La dame Americaine*, as the foreigners very commonly call me, for they find my name hard to remember. She was very much pressed for time, as she was then preparing copy for the printer, and, having just returned, there were many applications to see her, but she wanted me to stay then, saying, "It is better to throw things aside, and seize the present moment." I staid a good part of the day, and was very glad afterwards, for I did not see her again uninterrupted. Another day I was there, and saw her in her circle. Her daughter and another lady were present, and a number of gentlemen. Her position there was of an intellectual woman and good friend, – the same as my own in the circle of my acquaintance as distinguished from my intimates. Her daughter is just about to be married. It is said, there is no congeniality between her and her mother; but for her son she seems to have much love, and he loves and admires her extremely. I understand he has a good and free character, without conspicuous talent.

Her way of talking is just like her writing, – lively, picturesque, with an undertone of deep feeling, and the same skill in striking the nail on the head every now and then with a blow.

We did not talk at all of personal or private matters. I saw, as one sees in her writings, the want of an independent, interior life, but I did not feel it as a fault, there is so much in her of her kind. I heartily enjoyed the sense of so rich, so prolific, so ardent a genius. I liked the woman in her, too, very much; I never liked a woman better.

For the rest I do not care to write about it much, for I cannot, in the room and time I have to spend, express my thoughts as I would; but as near as I can express the sum total, it is this. S—— and others who admire her, are anxious to make a fancy picture of her, and represent her as a Helena (in the Seven Chords of the Lyre); all whose mistakes are the fault of the present state of society. But to me the truth seems to be this. She has that purity in her soul, for she knows well how to love and prize its beauty; but she herself is quite another sort of person. She needs no defence, but only to be understood, for she has bravely acted out her nature, and always with good intentions. She might have loved one man permanently, if she could have found one contemporary with her who could interest and command her throughout her range; but there was hardly a possibility of that, for such a person. Thus she has naturally changed the objects of her affection, and several times. Also, there may have been something of the Bacchante in her life, and of the love of night and storm, and the free raptures amid which roamed on the mountain-tops the followers of Cybele, the great goddess, the great mother. But she was never coarse, never gross, and I am sure her generous heart has not failed to draw some rich drops from every kind of wine-press. When she has done with an intimacy, she likes to break it off suddenly, and this has happened often, both with men and women. Many calumnies upon her are traceable to this cause.

I forgot to mention, that, while talking, she *does* smoke all the time her little cigarette. This is now a common practice among ladies abroad, but I believe originated with her.

For the rest, she holds her place in the literary and social world of France like a man, and seems full of energy and courage in it. I suppose she has suffered much, but she has also enjoyed and done much, and her expression is one of calmness and happiness. I was sorry to see her *exploitant* her talent so carelessly. She does too much, and this cannot last forever; but "Teverino" and the "Mare au Diable," which she has lately published, are as original, as masterly in truth, and as free in invention, as anything she has done.

Afterwards I saw Chopin, not with her, although he lives with her, and has for the last twelve years. I went to see him in his room with one of his friends. He is always ill, and as frail as a snow-drop, but an exquisite genius. He played to me, and I liked his talking scarcely less. Madame S. loved Liszt before him; she has thus been intimate with the two opposite sides of the musical world. Mickiewicz says, "Chopin talks with spirit, and gives us the Ariel view of the universe. Liszt is the eloquent *tribune* to the world of men, a little vulgar and showy certainly, but I like the tribune best." It is said here, that Madame S. has long had only a friendship for Chopin, who, perhaps, on his side prefers to be a lover, and a jealous lover; but she does not leave him, because he needs her care so much, when sick and suffering. About all this, I do not know; you cannot know much about anything in France, except what you see with your two eyes. Lying is ingrained in "*la grande nation*," as they so plainly show no less in literature than life. [*Memoirs*, I, 194-99]

PART

VI

The Radical
in Italy

Looking back from her new Roman vantage point in May 1847, Fuller wrote, "Paris is the very focus of the intellectual activity in Europe. There I found every topic intensified, clarified, reduced to portable dimensions; there is the cream of all the milk, but I am not strong enough to live on cream, at present." She thought half-apologetically of her "trance of repose" in Italy among "people so indolently joyous" [1] as a respite, an indulgence of weary body and hungry senses; she always intended to return to Paris, in her mind the school for the most advanced social thought. She may have heard there of Louis Blanc, who had carried socialism about as far as it could go while still abjuring class struggle. His popular pamphlet proposed "social workshops" to be financed by the state, controlled by the workers, and open to all seeking employment. In another year such schemes and social reality itself were "intensified" and "clarified" to a degree neither Fuller nor Blanc could have anticipated. For in February 1848, the working class joined with the middle class in overthrowing the bourgeois monarchy of Louis Philippe and made Louis Blanc the member for the extreme left of the Provisional Government. But his promised "right to work" and his workshops were sabotaged and travestied as the actual irreconcilability of the needs of the two classes emerged, and four months later the bourgeois republicans crushed the workers in pitched battle. These events gave birth to modern political consciousness, serving, as Marx saw it, to reveal that "bourgeois republic signifies the unlimited despotism of one class over other classes" and to redefine revolution from then on as class struggle. [2]

Fuller never returned to Paris, and she would not have expressed the meaning of 1848 as Marx did. But she watched events in Paris with excitement and a precocious awareness that they were effecting irreversible change in political consciousness. Hindsight tempts us to believe Italy held her by teaching her more fundamental lessons than she would learn in the school of Paris. She learned that the needs of her body could not be met by a mere vacation in Italy to be followed by renewed intellectual vigor and continued physical deprivation. In Italy she took a lover and bore a child, acts of self-discovery and release which, as we shall see, tended more to complement than to conflict with her political development. Then, Fuller's political education up to 1847 prepared her to understand the evolving situation in Italy better than that of Paris. In effect, she had to experience the national struggles of Italy, which partly echoed America's past, before she could appreciate, even intellectually, the social challenges and class struggles of Paris, which prefigured the political future of the world.

Since the political experiences of Italy and of Fuller are so interconnected in what follows, it may be helpful at the outset to outline and distinguish them. In Italy—with the partial exception of Milan—there were none of those conditions which bred social ferment in Paris: the living memory of the balked French Revolution, the stimulating and abundant activity of social theorists, the tradition of student insurgency, and the rise of an industrial proletariat and consequently of class consciousness. Even nationalist ideas were virtually nonexistent in Italy until the French Revolution and Napoleon's notion of Italy had suggested them. And with the Congress of Vienna of 1814, Italy was again subjected to reactionary and foreign domination. Metternich's remark that Italy was only a "geographical expression" was borne out not only by the division of Italy into eight separate states but also by its almost total control by Austria. In the north, rich Lombardy and Venetia were part of the Austrian Empire, and Hapsburgs sat on the throne of Tuscany, Parma, and Modena; in the south the Kingdom of Naples, or the Two Sicilies, ruled by a Spanish Bourbon, was virtually an Austrian protectorate; and the Papal States, which belted Italy across the middle, deferred to Vienna. Only in the northwest, in the Kingdom of Piedmont (also called Sardinia) was there a relatively independent and native Italian dynasty, the House of Savoy, represented since 1831 by the intermittently liberal Charles Albert. Although the unsuccessful risings of the Carbonari and Mazzini's Giovine Italia gave sporadic life to the notion of an independent, constitutional, and unified Italy, there was no real change until the election in 1846 of the liberal Pope Pius IX. Proclaiming universal amnesty for political prisoners, the Pope later included laymen in a council of state and authorized a civic guard, a symbol of order to conservatives, independence to liberals, and revolutionary readiness to radicals. By these measures Pius IX simultaneously undermined his temporal power and excited Italians in other states to press for reforms.

From 1847, when Fuller arrived in Italy, to the middle of 1849, the Risorgimento, or national revival, accelerated rapidly. In 1847, a spirit of moderate liberalism, dictated chiefly by the work of the exiled priest Vicenzo Gioberti, prevailed. Depicting an idealized and reformed Papacy presiding over a loose federation of Italian kingdoms and duchies protected by the armed force of Charles Albert, Gioberti made Mazzini's scheme of republican union seem romantic madness. But in 1848, reforms, uprisings, and revolutions in Italy and the rest of Europe began to generate popular demands for more radical change and to expose the inability of the moderates, the Pope, and Charles Albert to accomplish it. Pressures for the formation of a unified Republic led to the Pope's flight from Rome and the return of Mazzini. In 1849, Charles Albert abdicated after military defeat, but the creation of a democratic Roman Republic fired the zeal of young men all over Italy. They flocked to Rome's defense when the new French president, Louis Napoleon, sent his army to destroy the Republic and restore the Pope. With the French victory, the Pope initiated a fierce reaction and Austria regained her hegemony over Italy. (It was not until a decade after the fall of Rome and Fuller's death that two men, both by then enemies of Mazzini—Garibaldi with his military triumphs and Cavour with his Machiavellian diplomatic gifts—achieved Mazzini's goal of unifying Italy.)

To the Italian experience Fuller brought a political awareness which had grown swiftly after she abandoned New England and the apolitical posture she had cultivated there. What she learned in New York of social inequity and unprincipled and aggressive foreign policy began to undermine her faith in the saving power of leaders or the reliability of "divine destiny," though no new systemic criticism and no fundamental solution replaced it. Her travel in England and France sharpened her sense of social crisis.

What she had perceived as inequity in America now began to look like hopeless class division, but, like most of her contemporaries and virtually all of her class, Fuller could barely frame the problem in these terms. The inspiration of Mazzini and the experience of revolution in a country industrially and politically less mature than England and France provided a necessary transition to the modern radical analysis toward which she was moving when her life ended.

In replacing the spiritual literary exemplar with the practice of direct, exemplary action, Mazzini satisfied Fuller's earliest bias, learned from the Romans and long suspended in her contact with the Transcendentalists. His doctrine that war was the inevitable instrument of nationalism fell in with her temperamental penchant for conflict and her growing impatience with reform. While he strengthened her radical bent in these ways, the political implications of his romantic collective vision were more ambiguous, and the impact on Fuller was complex. As a repudiation of individualism, his habit of considering people in the mass was progressive; as a bulwark against class analysis, it was reactionary. Mazzini was not unaware of class; in 1844, he distinguished the class owning land, credit, and capital from that dispossessed of all but their hands, and he wrote that political revolution alone was inadequate to the needs of the latter. But he argued that the political revolution necessarily came prior to the social one. Moreover, he did not conceive of social revolution dialectically; rather it was a process of absorption and dissolution whereby each new era moves toward a more perfect equilibrium adding social elements to the preceding era. The form of social change he favored, for his time, was the voluntary association of workers into ever-larger units. Class warfare he considered antipathetic to the collective principle, immoral, and unjust. In short, his republican and nationalist priorities fed his desire to minimize the differences between classes and kept his perspective essentially bourgeois. Consequently, he rarely used the word "proletariat," preferring the more comprehensive and evocative "people." And although he used "people" variously to designate all classes in a nation, or the population neither aristocratic nor clerical, or the class subject to the bourgeoisie, it is significant that he usually meant "the middle and lower middle classes and the tradespeople," excluding the laboring classes beneath them. [3]

While Fuller's friends and acquaintances were generally drawn from the upper-class intelligentsia, the effect of Mazzini's collective approach was to direct her attention as never before to the "people" of Rome, especially to the middle and lower-middle classes which preoccupied him. (Indeed, she often remarked on the absence, even fear, of political consciousness in the lower classes, especially among peasants.) But her attention carried her beyond her mentor in some respects. For while both Mazzini's long exile and political priorities led him to minimize gradations and conflicts of social need in his countrymen, Fuller's lifelong interest in the education and fulfillment of individuals made her curious about just such questions when she turned to the group. Greeting the rapid development of the Roman crowds with great excitement, she was also a sharp observer of their relationship to political events and of the growth of their autonomy. Finally, as we shall see, this attention led her to make some class distinctions which in turn made her want a more thoroughgoing social revolution than Mazzini did.

Fuller's ceaseless scrutiny of the state of consciousness in the people and in herself gave most of her twenty-one dispatches from Italy more concentrated force and shapeliness than anything else she wrote. The effect she achieves in the dispatches as a whole is panoramic: it involves quick sketching of conditions in Germany, Austria, and France, with shrewd predictions of the political and social evolution to be expected in those countries, denser drawing of the mounting struggles throughout Italy with their interlocking dynamics, and a close, slowly evolving portrait of the Pope and the people of Rome. She is especially absorbed by the Pope's gradual decline in leadership and the people's steady rise in self-determination. Sometimes these dispatches show the marks of haste, for the imminent departure of a steamer often kept Fuller from even reading them over. Sometimes they are crabbed or obscure when her involvement was too intense to permit leisurely exposition, but the old self-indulgent attitudinizing is absent. More partisan than anything she did before, her writing in this last period is more intimately a part of her action and her feeling, in no way an expression of a choice in which something else is sacrificed. In these dispatches, all her values are intact and so focused and actualized that they make her accounts of hopefulness, restlessness, political suspense, and battle, riveting even now. Caught up in Mazzini's vision and the dazzling excitement of events, she tends to overestimate the Italians' power and the likelihood of victory and to underestimate the real limitations on Charles Albert's options and, for a while, the value of Garibaldi. But she is otherwise perspicacious. Urgency drives the old wishfulness out of her social analysis. And in her assessments of the motives of rulers and priests, she draws on a fund of skeptical insight wholly new in her writing. Something of the bite and flash said to characterize her conversation at last dominates her work.

Fuller arrived in Italy when enthusiasm for Gioberti and "Gioberti's Pope," Pius IX, prevailed in the progressive middle class, which judged Mazzini's goal of fusion premature, his measures desperate and doomed. While Fuller's preference for Mazzini's vision held firm, in the open and optimistic political atmosphere of 1847 she met people entertaining a variety of views. Her friendship with the remarkable Marchesa Costanza Arconati Visconti, formed soon after her arrival in Rome, paved the way for these connections. Nine years older than Fuller, this gracious woman, with "a mind strong, clear, precise and cultivated," had just returned from twenty-six years of political exile with her husband, during which time their salon had been a center of liberalism, both literary and political. Now settled in Florence, they collaborated actively with other Catholic federalists, finding Gioberti, as she told Fuller, the "pole-star for us who are not republicans." [4] Arconati was in a position to introduce Fuller to political activists, leading writers, and intelligent women, and she showered her with books, journals, and occasional gifts of money. She readily became the woman closest to Fuller in Europe. Their correspondence is remarkable both for simple affection and candid exchange of political information and opinion, sometimes sharply divergent.

An altogether different friendship was formed in those stimulating spring days [5] when, wandering in St. Peter's after vespers one day, Fuller was separated from the Springs, and a young man, handsome though somewhat melancholy in expression, offered to assist her in finding them. Giovanni Angelo Ossoli was like Costanza Arconati only in noble birth. His father and one of his brothers were high-ranking papal functionaries and the other two brothers were colonels in the Pope's Guardia Nobile. From the priests he had received only the minimal education requisite to follow their lead. But, though a good Catholic, Ossoli did not believe the Pope should hold temporal power and was interested in a unified and republican Italy. After he escorted her home, Fuller wrote of the encounter to her friend Mickiewicz, who had followed up his original challenge to her virginity by exhorting her to "breathe life through your pores," to saturate herself with Italian life, and in admiring Italian women to remember that she too was beautiful. Now more vigorously he urged her to prolong her good moments, not to leave lightly those drawn to her like "the little Italian" she met in the church. Much later, Fuller wrote her sister that Ossoli had proposed marriage shortly after their meeting, "but the connection seemed so every way unfit, I did not hesitate a moment" (VI:48). Unfit, she must have felt, because he was ten years younger and had none of her intellectual accomplishments or curiosity. On the other hand, their very differences satisfied old and interlocking needs of both. Ossoli, the youngest of six children, close only to his two sisters, and still grieving for the mother who died when he was six, needed a confident, even authoritative, woman. And in responding to his beauty, gentleness, and capacity for devotion, Fuller was cherishing the "feminine" in him, as she had valued in Ward, Nathan, her brother Richard, and others, the way they eluded "masculine" stereotyping. She said later he was most like her brother Eugene, of whom she had written in a journal three years earlier, "How all but infinite the mystery by which sex is stamped on the germ! . . . Impossible to trace. Here am I the child of masculine energy and Eugene of feminine loveliness." [6] In moving toward Ossoli she would be confirming her ideal of androgyny and of a union where character flourishes free of expectations fixed by sex.

But first she evaded him and even, by a curious recoil, pursued an American painter, Thomas Hicks, virtually demanding his intimacy and succeeding in arousing that mixture of devotion and panic she had elicited in other men. We have no letters between them except their first, but they seem to have settled into an enduring friendship. When she confessed to *Tribune* readers that she could not describe Italy without long residence in districts untouched by foreigners and "without an intimacy of feeling, an abandonment to the spirit of the place impossible to most Americans," [7] she may have been referring to Hicks' inhibitions as well as her own.

So strong was the diffuse attraction of Rome that it was painful to her to resume the tour with the Springs in June. But the gifted acquaintances of Costanza Arconati in Florence, Milan, and Bellagio did much to compensate. Despite a political stalemate in Florence, she saw that "within, Tuscany burns" and was thrilled by the "rush of thought to the new vent" of the freed press. In Milan, she met some of the young radicals who would form a provisional government in the uprising next year; she admired them more than the great writer, Manzoni, feeling Italy needed "a more active faith" than his doctrine of "pray and wait." [8] By the end of the summer, Fuller had covered more ground in Italy than Mazzini, who before his exile knew only Genoa and Tuscany, and she was getting in position to make judgments and commitments of her own.

In Venice, she declined to travel further with the Springs, even though they were going on to Germany, for, as Goethe himself had done, she was dreaming of Rome. As she wrote to Richard Fuller, "I should always suffer the pain of Tantalus thinking of Rome, if I could not see it more thoroughly . . . for it was all *outside* the two months . . . I had only just begun to live with their life." [9] To others she wrote of a change in her feelings, of a desire to move "inward." In this new context, the indispensable word of the Transcendentalists meant a complex of things wholly changed:

a desire to be done with sight-seeing, to ignore art, to concentrate on the fundamentals—living economically, speaking the language of the "common people," mastering the "great future" of Italy. As moving "inward" earlier signified to Fuller the self's desire for transcendence, now it reflected the self's desire for immanence, for rooting itself in the material and the actual.

An "inward" life may also have meant a life responsive at last to the stirrings of desire, sharpened perhaps by regret over her restraint with Nathan, by her flight from Ossoli, and now by more uncanny sympathetic insinuations from Mickiewicz. She must not limit her life to books and dreams, he wrote during the summer: "You have pleaded the freedom of women in a masculine and frank style. Live and act as you write. . . . I have seen you, with all your knowledge, and all your imagination, and all your literary reputation, living in a bondage harder than that of a servant. . . . The relations that are right for you are those which develop and free your spirit while answering the legitimate needs of your body. You are the only judge of those needs." If she was to be a woman of the new epoch, he argued, she must part from her traveling companions and seek freedom. [10] Whatever its source, it was a "strong impulse" that led her back to Ossoli in October 1847, very soon to become his lover.

Later, in stoic accents dictated by hard times, she wrote her sister, "I neither rejoice or grieve—for bad or for good I acted out my character" (VI:48). At the time, it was the act of loving Ossoli—and all that stood for—that made her character clearer, more cohesive, than it had been. How Fuller changed by loving Ossoli has been much misunderstood. Most biographers of her century suggested that the pose of the arrogant eccentric was simply cast aside, revealing the Victorian "true woman." [11] Some in our century see the modern, sexually balanced woman burning at last through Puritan repression. But there never was much "true womanhood" about Fuller's feelings. It is entirely possible that she never married; she lived apart from Ossoli until their last year, as much from choice as from the need of secrecy; and, though she grew markedly tender, the deference was all on his side. And sexual fulfillment was immensely important, but it was so because her love for Ossoli was bound up with a series of new convictions shaping Fuller's character.

"The Italians sympathize with my character and understand my organization as no other people ever did," she wrote her mother at this time. "They admire the ready eloquence of my nature, and highly prize my intelligent sympathy (such as they do not often find in foreigners) with their sufferings in the past and their hopes for the future." [12] Plainly, the relation between Fuller and Ossoli was part of this broader dynamic of understanding and sympathy, which was a matter not simply of mutually delighted temperaments but of idealistic and revolutionary recognition. Evidence that their love grew in this spirit is Ossoli's daring the wrath of his family by enlisting in the largely nationalist Civic Guard on November 15. At the same time, Fuller sought a "divorce" from the English and American circle. Much later, W. H. Hurlbut, an American acquaintance who found Ossoli an "underdeveloped and uninteresting Italian," speculated, "she probably married him as a representative of an imagined possibility in the Italian character which I have not yet been able to believe in." [13] This surmise is sound; all her life Fuller had committed herself to "imagined possibilities"—in herself, her friends, the Indians, her students, the ladies of Boston, and the prostitutes of New York—but in Italy for the first time Fuller's commitment to possibility was total.

The experience of Italy then satisfied and fused the disparate longings of a lifetime; emotional fullness and heroic action at last came together. Moreover, it clarified for her the source of her frustrations with America in her time. She felt the impulse and meaning of the American Revolution alive in Italy as they were not at home except in the abolitionist cause, which she now learned to honor. And she worked to revitalize that spirit in her homeland by exhibiting for Americans its rebirth in Italy. Hence we have the curious picture of Fuller late in 1847 suffering from all that is "peculiarly American and English," wishing she could shut out the sound of the language, while pouring it out to exhort her countrymen. Or we see her refusing until 1850 the entreaties of Emerson and her family to repatriate because she had most to say to America from Italy. This refusal richly symbolizes the ways in which she repudiated Emerson's perspective. At stake was more than the rejection of the life of the mind for the life of action. Fuller and Emerson differed over nothing less than the relation of the individual to American destiny, the autonomy of that destiny, and their understanding of national growth. Emerson's identification of the individual's "latent conviction" with the "universal sense" of Americans, his "conflation of the private with the national dream," made ordinary action beside the point and, despite all the excitement it generated, posed no critical cutting edge to established society. Fuller's response to Italy ("Italy receives me as a long-lost child, and I feel myself at home here") meant the fundamental abandonment of her attempt to be a "representative" American in Emerson's sense, the acceptance of her otherness, and her wish to use that very otherness to cut through to an American essence that was betraying itself with accelerating speed. For Emerson, a great American destiny would unfold with a speed directly related to America's autonomy, to her success in extracting "this tape-worm of Europe from the brain of our countrymen"; he offered his representative self as a guide to fulfilling that destiny. Fuller denied the specialness and autonomy of American destiny; she offered the actual struggle of a foreign people as a guide to completing the American Revolution, and entering a brotherhood of nations. Emerson's model of national growth was singular and organic; the nation and the reliant self unfold together in the unique context of a beneficent American nature. Fuller's model was multiple and morally dialectic; nations change under the pressure of challenges posed them by other societies. [14]

So Fuller remained in Italy, understanding that only in this way could she hope to prize her nationality, only by invoking Rome's imminent future could she serve America's present. In this posture she differed not only with Emerson at home but with the other Americans who came as "passionate pilgrims" to Europe. Quite precisely she inverted Cooper's formulation of 1838: "The Roman glorifies himself in what his ancestors have been, the Americans in what his posterity *will* be." Her evolving bias led her beyond those who sought in Europe, especially in "eternal Rome," unchanging values to use in distinguishing and consciously shaping values suited to their still formless and mutable home. When this ideal and static Europe conjured out of American need exploded in reolution, especially when Rome erupted in sudden turmoil, the pilgrims were devastated, and their reflexes were conservative. [15] With regard to the Italians, it had long been the habit of these devotees to distinguish between Rome as a temple of art and her apparently unrelated and unworthy race of custodians and tenants, famous only for theft, beggary, and voluble lying. Americans could not abruptly regard this same people as the stuff of heroic struggle, and the assessment of Fuller's skeptical acquaintance— "impulsive and ill-disciplined children of passion"—ranked with the kinder judgments. Fuller observed succinctly that "there is an antagonism of race." [16]

Unlike the other pilgrims, Fuller was prepared even before she saw Rome to welcome rapid social progress, for her father had taught her to value chiefly the secular democratic virtues and military pride of ancient Rome, and Mazzini had led her to believe these would swiftly be recovered. Moreover, she gradually threw off most traces of her culture's prejudices against Italians. Indeed, her developing attitude toward them is the core of the drama in her dispatches, although at first the character of Pius IX engaged her interest more than the people did. Pius IX was a man of incompatible impulses. On the one hand liberal enough to see the need for reform and Italian enough to resent the interference of the Austrians, he was on the other hand thoroughly devoted to the interests of the church. While his reforms and nationalist sympathies built popular support for the Papacy, they had the effect of limiting his temporal power. (Much later, when he had tasted the bitter fruits of his liberal nationalism, the Catholic in him recovered with reactionary virulence, eventually issuing the Syllabus of Errors, defining the doctrine of papal infallibility, and rejecting the modern world wholesale.) While Fuller never failed to note that his position was inherently contradictory, she was moved by his "goodness" and his apparently sincere spiritual depth. (The reasons appear partly autobiographical, especially when she laid a tender stress on the sight of him "absorbed in his devotions," or wrote, "It makes me very happy to be for once in a place ruled by a father's love." It is as if she spent on the Pope for the last time her orphaned feelings of dependency and the fervent spirituality of her adolescence, before exorcising them forever.) but at the same time, her growing knowledge of the people was leading her to praise them, though sometimes at first as children who were maturing, cultivating such skills as "prudence," "wise docility," and "singular discretion." [17] By December she was regretting that the Pope was still fearful of his people—that he had, for instance, barred the display of other states' flags at the inauguration of the new Council. That a group of American expatriates had, like Betsy Ross, sewn a flag for the occasion, gaily inquiring of newcomers about the current number of states at home, only made Fuller feel worse about this prohibition.

In the last months of 1847, the growing demand for liberty in the political sphere was strangely matched in Fuller's private life by a feeling of widened freedom combined with deepened engagement. The shock of happiness made her impatient with her fate, with not having had money to come to Italy long ago, and "find those that belong to me, or at least try my experiments; then my health would never have sunk, nor the best years of my life been wasted in useless friction." *Useless friction?* Only something on the order of a revelation could have evoked this laconic dismissal of those years of searching, of rapture and agony. We have to read the letters of this period as a sort of code in which she protects the conspiracies sometimes of Mazzini's friends, sometimes of her heart. Her letters to friends written in New England seven to ten years earlier were also in code, but that was the sign of self-mystification and repression, this of purpose and release hidden only from outsiders. "I have not been so well since I was a child," she wrote her mother, "nor so happy ever, as during the last six weeks." [18]

It was the old story: this clear and simple joy was betrayed by biology, and early in the new year she discovered she was pregnant. One desolate cry to Caroline Sturgis is all that survives of her feelings. The desolation of a woman in the nineteenth century, of chronic poor health, finding herself pregnant at thirty-seven, hardly needs explanation. But in Fuller's case there were factors that made it harder to bear: the loss of freedom of action just as she had begun to taste it, the bitter awareness that the social and economic questions she would now be addressing were all too domestic, her recent discovery that Uncle Abraham had remained angry at his impertinent niece, leaving her no legacy, [19] and her by then philosophical opposition to all but perfect marriages. Even the weather conspired against her; it was an unceasingly foul winter in Rome, raining steadily the first three months of her pregnancy. In January 1849, her *Tribune* letters took a virulently anti-Catholic turn, attacking the superstition, the antipathy to reform, and the repression of women imbedded in the faith. She deplored the Pope's fear of being called a Protestant Pope and, with a true Yankee reflex, found disgustingly abject the sight of the new municipal officers kissing his foot. Some of her animus may have sprung from her resentment over an aspect of her dilemma—the impossibility, for a Protestant, of getting a papal dispensation to marry Ossoli, should she have wanted to do so, without the knowledge and probably the consent of his father. The old Marchese would have been appalled by her age, her lack of wealth and status, and especially her republicanism, and would have disowned Ossoli. With his father's death in February, Ossoli's position worsened; his eldest brother, Giusseppe, forced him to move from his father's rooms to his sister's and would have welcomed the opportunity provided by such an inappropriate marriage to disinherit him. Ossoli stood by Fuller, but she found thin comfort in a love made of "all fondness, but no help" (VI:22).

Fuller seems to have turned with relief from the impasse of the private struggle to the exhilaration of the public one. In the first months of 1848, uprisings flared like a string of firecrackers lacing Europe. Italy took the initiative, as Mazzini had prophesied. First Sicily, teased beyond endurance by the false promises of Ferdinand II, rose, and Naples, following, forced from the king a popular constitution. His example led Charles Albert of Piedmont and the Grand Duke of Tuscany to grant constitutions, and they in turn obliged the Pope to follow suit. Meanwhile, the Milanese, in imitation of the Boston Tea Party, boycotted the tobacco and lotteries heavily taxed by the Austrians; the result was fierce repression. The February revolution in Paris inspired the uprising in Vienna and the consequent flight of Metternich in early March; this last stroke triggered the "Five Glorious Days" of street-fighting in Milan, which issued in the expulsion of the Austrian garrison. At the same time, Venice proclaimed itself an independent republic. Seeing an opportunity to rule a unified northern Italy, Charles Albert declared war on Austria and invaded Lombardy. Italian troops swarmed up from Tuscany, Naples, and even the Papal States to help rout the Austrians from Lombardy, then from Venetia.

In the middle of these events, Mickiewicz, the man Fuller most wished to see again, if she returned to France, came to Rome to recruit a legion from the Poles in exile there. She probably confided in him, for after he left with his legion for Florence, he wrote urging her to shake off melancholy dreams and scolding her for her terror over "very natural, very common suffering."[20] By March and April, she had recovered her joy, now in a fiercer strain. She exulted in the fall of Louis Philippe and the revolutionary courage of the troops marshaled in Rome. "It is a time such as I always dreamed of; and that fire burns in the hearts of men around me which can keep me warm," she wrote. "Have I something to do here? or am I only to cheer on the warriors, and after write the history of their deeds? The first is all I have done yet, but many have blessed me for my sympathy, and blest me by the action it impelled."[21]

For all her force of sympathy, her political acumen grew more rapidly. She began to develop a perspective that gave her a remarkable measure of independence from the three leading nationalist tendencies. She had from the outset considered the goal of the Giobertists, a federation of Italian states under Pius IX, too modest. And they were finally discredited at the end of April by the Pope's Allocution disclaiming responsibility for the very war he had implicitly blessed and by his recall of his forces. As for the supporters of Charles Albert, she was no more deceived by the

republicans who thought they could use him than by
Giobertists who called him "Sword of Pius IX"; behind the
mask of the crusader she early discerned the opportunistic
empire builder. Charles Albert, however, was himself
deceived. Trying by vague gestures to appease and
appropriate all factions, his vacillation (which earned him the
name *Re Tentenna*, or King Wobble) became habitual and he
ended by neutralizing himself. Moving with such unstable
allies against the overwhelming might of the Austrians was
bad enough. But the inexperience of the Italian military,
their foolish scorn for gaudy Garibaldi and his guerrilla
legion, freshly arrived from Uruguay, and the noncooperation
and sabotage of the Lombardy peasants, worn out from
Napoleonic incursions, also told against him. Then he lost the
troops of Rome, and the King of Naples called home his
army to help bombard insurgents in his own cities (for which
he was nicknamed King Bomba). Finally, the general triumph
of counterrevolution in Paris and Prague killed the hope for
French military support and guaranteed the return in force of
Austria. In July 1848, driven back from Venetia, back from
Lombardy, Charles Albert signed an armistice.

Fuller's allegiance to Mazzini and the republicans remained strong, but she showed, especially in the spring of
1848, a disposition to be critical of him. An early indication,
which does not mention Mazzini, was her strident celebration
in the *Tribune* of the "nobility" of the "laboring classes" in
the February revolution in Paris and of the merging there of
social and political revolution. In affirming class struggle in
Paris, Fuller was boldly taking the step explicitly refused by
both the Utopian socialists and Mazzini. She was also moving
beyond her exhortations to Americans to regenerate their
revolution by emulating the spirit of the Italian republicans;
the Paris revolution, an internal struggle of classes, was for
Americans a more ominous model, calling not for
regeneration but for drastic change. She urged her
countrymen to "learn in time for a preventive wisdom" how
to forge a "true democracy" (VI:25).

In her next dispatch, she criticized Mazzini directly,
writing that, even with his great dream of "political
emancipation, Mazzini saw "not all," that he ignored or

denied "that of which the cry of Communism, the systems of
Fourier, etc. are but the forerunners." She declined to
elaborate "in the small print of the *Tribune*" (VI:27), and we
are left to wonder about several things. It is extremely
unlikely that she had read or heard of the *Communist
Manifesto*, printed two months earlier in London. [22] But she
might have been reacting against fresh news from Milan,
where Mazzini had recently arrived. When a delegation of
tailors approached him demanding better working conditions,
Mazzini insisted on their subordinating even those just needs
to the great struggle for Italy. It is possible that her position,
initially more conservative than Mazzini's, had become more
radical, as she had familiarized herself with the people he still
preferred to consider abstractly and had seen how the process
of revolution had schooled and tempered them. But it is also
possible that she was thinking along different lines, not of a
class struggle but of restructuring the family. It is probable
that she was contemplating both kinds of social revolution at
once; however far apart they later became, they lay then, in
the cradle, side by side.

Support for this last interpretation comes from a letter
written on May 29 to her friend Mary Rotch, just before
Fuller left Rome to hide her swelling belly in the country.
"You must always love me *whatever* I do," she begins, with
the anomaly and danger of her condition on her mind. "I
depend on that. And this thought puts me in mind to ask
whether you are not aware that I am as great an associationist
as W. Channing, himself, that is to say as firm a believer that
the next form society will take in remedy of the dreadful ills
that now consume it will be voluntary association in small
communities. The present forms are become unwieldy." If
she slips into social thought to keep from confessing private
fact here, it would not be the first time. But they may have
been connected: if she was not married, saw no clear way to
becoming married, and was not enthusiastic about the
institution of marriage, it is likely she was contemplating
social arrangements that would tolerate, even endorse, such
irregular arrangements and help support her child. (We note
that for the first time she does not take exception to
Fourier's materialism on behalf of the spirit; in fact, this

dimension of her rhetoric is almost completely eliminated after Fuller was touched by the material facts of politics and pregnancy.) When she goes on to say, "But what I think on this subject I hope to have force and time to explain in print. Not in the Tribune," [23] the echo of this unexplained reserve about the *Tribune* rings like a prohibition. The explanation may lie in the outcome of the debate on Fourierism, in the columns of their newspapers, between Henry J. Raymond of the *Courier and Enquirer* and Greeley, in the winter of 1846-47. Unable to rattle Greeley in his defense of Fourier's economic thought, Raymond had finally assailed Fourier for asserting that passions were intrinsically good and restraint evil. Though Greeley vigorously denied that socialism as Americans understood it provided for any such criminal license, the debate soon and abruptly ended. [24] That Raymond was right about Fourier Fuller would not have known from Albert Brisbane's sanitized presentation of Fourier for Americans but may well have learned about after arriving in Europe. In fact, Fourier was a pioneering radical feminist, not only advocating sexual equality but also criticizing in detail the institutions of marriage and the family. Fuller's reiterated mention of his name in public and private writing suggests he was in possession of a scheme of values she wanted and increasingly needed to accept.

To Mary Rotch she confided that she hoped "in the silence and retirement of the country" to write more about this and other subjects. She sent to Hicks (now embroiled in the Paris revolution and soon to shelter two fugitive insurgents there) her personal papers, a cache of newspaper clippings, and a forlorn note, mentioning neither marriage nor pregnancy, to be opened in the event of her death. Then she packed up her collection of newspapers, books, tracts, pamphlets, and government documents, along with her daguerrotype of Ossoli, and set out for Aquila in the Abruzzi mountains. Letting her friends imagine she was in another town, she relied on Ossoli to forward her letters, bank drafts, and newspapers.

At first, she settled happily in this town encircled by snow-covered mountains. Daily she walked or rode a donkey by "grain fields enamelled with the brilliant blue corn-flower and red poppy . . . like nothing in America." She rejoiced that the peasants were "remote from the corruptions of foreign travel"; they in turn called her "simpatica" and blessed her as she passed. "They are people whom I could love and live with. Bread and grapes among them would suffice me," she wrote Emerson. She told Arconati that she tried to catch up with her hundred correspondents, but devoted the "great part of the day" to a history of the Italian struggle, which she predicted would take three months: "It grows upon me." [25] By that time *double-entendre* was second nature and the alibi of a writing retreat so convenient for her confinement that we cannot be sure of the reality of her stated intentions at this time. But loneliness and fear of the future soon began to assail her. Refusing Richard's entreaties to return home, she begged him to sell the last of her property, as Greeley's last remittance had been lost. After two months, to be close enough for Ossoli, who was now working for his uncle, to visit her Sundays, she moved to rooms by the river in the ancient town of Rieti.

This was the moment, however, that Charles Albert was driven back by the Austrians to Milan and then to his own domain. Provocatively, the Austrians moved within the Papal States to attack Bologna, and the Civic Guard, including Ossoli, was kept in suspense awaiting the Pope's response. Ossoli was suddenly confronted by the dilemma of neoclassical tragedy, but the love and honor he had to choose between wore modern dress: his love was a militant begging for news of her revolutionary friends in Milan and honor was the equivocating Pope. So torn was Fuller that she began one letter to Ossoli raging at Pius IX ("Oh! how unworthy the Pope is! He seems now a man without a heart! And this traitor of a Carlo Alberto! they'll be damned for all the centuries to come.') and ended it with an unusual effusion of tenderness ("I love you in these important days better than ever. The moon has been so beautiful these last nights, it has pained me not to have your company"). Three days later, fear for her life made her reflect bitterly, "Not often does destiny demand a greater price for some happy moments," but she added quickly, "Never do I repent of our affection." [26] For once her self-interest and the Pope's cold caution coincided. The Pope declined to send the guard to assist the Bolognese, who drove back the Austrians without it. Ossoli was thus free to come at the end of August to Rieti and remained until September 5, when their son, Angelo Eugenio Filippo Ossoli, was born.

Though she had written in her journal years before of her maternal longing ("I have no child of my own, and the woman in me so craves this experience it seems the want of it must paralyze me") and had intensely loved a few children, Fuller was unprepared for the actual shock of motherly feeling: "I know nothing about it." She marveled over the baby's "really delicate ways, like a dancer," and the people in the house called him "*Angiolino*, because he is so lovely." [27] (She and Ossoli took their cue and called the baby Angelino.) The loss of her milk, the avaricious schemes of the women in the house, the landlord's efforts to seduce the nurse—nothing could destroy this new rapture. She urged Ossoli to devise a way to bring the child to Rome, but he felt it imprudent. In their letters the next month they came near assuming conventional sex roles. His anxiety was the Pope's appointment of an unpopular minister, hers the job of finding a wet nurse. Then he had to find a legal way of baptizing the baby, and she a means of protecting the baby from a smallpox epidemic when there was no vaccine in Rieti. Finally Ossoli found vaccine and sent it from Rome. He also secured a devious form whereby he could pose as proxy for the absent parents at the child's baptism and omit the names of the parents; this subterfuge would hardly have been necessary had they been married. Unfortunately, Ossoli's nephew who had helped with this scheme became godfather, instead of Mickiewicz, who was their first and richly appropriate choice.

Needing both to secure the ten dollars Greeley paid for each dispatch and to be near the struggle, Fuller returned to Rome, the mere sight of which moved her more than ever before. She was just in time for the crisis, made inevitable by six months of tension between the Pope and his advisers on the one hand and the Civic Guard and the volatile democratic clubs, or *circoli*, on the other. The Pope's appointment as minister of Pellegrino Rossi was an open affront to the *circoli*; Rossi had in exile become Louis Philippe's ambassador and friend of the conservative bourgeois Guizot. Inspired by Venice's resistance and the growth of democracy in Tuscany, the *circoli* called for war with Austria and a new constitution, both opposed by Rossi. Working alone, contemptuous of the people, Rossi sought to preserve the temporal power of the Pope from the forces both of reaction and revolution; he assumed nearly dictatorial power and called on the papal troops to back it. These same troops made no move when Rossi was murdered before their eyes on November 15. Nine days later, disguised as a plain monk, the Pope fled to the shelter of the King of Naples.

Fuller's maternal tenderness worked in no way to blunt the fierce satisfaction she took in the end of Rossi or her bitter grief over the weakness of the Pope. In the context of this treachery, Mazzini seemed to stand alone "on a sunny height" and she never again qualified her praise. She resumed writing for the *Tribune* and urged that America send a sensitive and forceful ambassador, remarking that were it "another century" she might ask for the position herself. At this point, Fuller's selfhood seemed only fortified, not domesticated, by motherhood. Though she rushed to spend a week with the baby at Christmas, she needed equally to be in Rome to witness its triumphs. She was present for the opening of the Constituent Assembly (the first ever elected in Italy by universal manhood suffrage), when Garibaldi marched with the other deputies, for the proclamation of the Republic, and for the arrival of Mazzini in the great "Third Rome" of his vision. Unfortunately, we do not know what she made of the social measures of the republicans—the abolition of flour taxes, the provision of work to the unemployed artists and tailors, the confiscation and redistribution of Church landholdings, the conversion of the office of the Holy Inquisition into apartments for the poor of Trastevere—which wrought a social revolution second only to that in Paris the year before. [28]

In March 1849, as the dying embers of revolution flared

briefly again all over Europe, Charles Albert, whose defeat the year before had given Italy over to the republicans, broke his armistice with Austria. His defeat at Custoza within his own kingdom eleven days later had the effect of winning the country back for the moderates. [29] Meanwhile, the Pope had been preparing for reaction, secretly applying for the intervention of his four nearest neighbors. By April, armies of Naples and Austria were moving toward Rome from the south and the north by land, and Spanish ships were steaming from the west. As for the French, Fuller had speculated even in January on the likelihood of French intervention, but others, including Mazzini, gave the new president, Louis Napoleon, the benefit of the doubt, recalling his youthful involvement with the Carbonari. Her instincts here were more sound, for with the swing to the right of the French Republic, the president judged that a swift victory at Rome was a solid means of securing Catholic support. Hence he offered an expeditionary force ostensibly as a stabilizing agent.

"I have never yet felt afraid when really in the presence of danger, though sometimes in its apprehension," [30] Fuller once wrote. The formula helps us to understand the disparity between her acceptance of the exaggerated fears in Rieti of Garibaldi (VI:40), a man she was unusually slow to understand, and her composure when she actually met his legion (VI:2d), or between the recurrent morbid predictions that burden her letters at this time and her refusal to leave Rome in its greatest emergency. For after three weeks with her child in the spring of 1849, she returned to Rome, which soon she could not leave again.

Within days after her return the French landed and were marching toward Rome, ignoring the high-sounding phrases from their own constitution painted on the walls by the road. Both the Romans, who thought the French would not attack a republic, and the French, confident that Italians never fight, were mistaken. On April 30, the French attacked Rome and were driven back by the forces of Garibaldi, who was restrained by a fatally optimistic Mazzini from driving them into the sea. On this day, Fuller received a note from the

Princess Cristina Trivulzio Belgioioso (whom Mazzini had put
in charge of the hospitals) asking her to direct the Hospital of
Fate Bene Fratelli on the small island in the Tiber.

Belgioioso was a remarkable woman who, for youthful
anti-Austrian activity, had spent many years in exile
presiding, like Arconati, over a brilliant salon. Unlike
Arconati, however, she was ardent, flamboyantly beautiful,
and emancipated. She had had several lovers; she had
conducted Fourier-like experiments on her estates, providing
communal quarters, schools, and a factory for impoverished
peasants; and when she heard in Naples of the "Five Glorious
Days" at Milan, she chartered a steamship to carry volunteers
there. She even offered to create and lead a truly popular
political party for Charles Albert. With some moral
hesitation, Arconati herself had introduced Fuller to
Belgioioso more than a year before. Eventually Arconati
turned on the princess, finding scandalous her appearances at
political clubs and cafés and her demagogic marches with
tricolor banners on the streets. How close Belgioioso and
Fuller became and how much her freedom may have inspired
Fuller's we do not know. But Fuller honored her in print for
her intrepid dedication and for eluding the political
narrowness of the Italian nobility.

After the French were driven back to their camp, there
was a month of suspense. While Garibaldi's guerrillas were
harassing King Bomba's troops back to Naples, Mazzini was
tricked into negotiations by which the French bought time to
gain reinforcements. Scenting a rat, Fuller dubbed the May
negotiations the "Second Act of the French farce." The
diaries of Emelyn and William Story, her nearest friends at
that time, make rather an operetta of the siege. They describe
drifting from a rally to the theater, putting in time hearing
"some very bad music" or running charitable errands, like
taking money to the hospital for the princess, who had been
three days without sleep. "Then we went to Spillman's to get
her an ice-cream to cool her parched throat, and while we
were there came screaming and hooting a crowd which
dragged along two cardinals' carriages magnificently painted
and gilt. These with pickaxes and clubs they broke entirely to
pieces and set fire to, crying out, "this is the blood of the

poor!—'E il sangue dei poveri!' " Then back to princess, the ice miraculously intact. [3][1]

Very different was the drama of Fuller in those days, rarely glimpsing Ossoli with his troops in the Vatican gardens, and getting notes from the nurse in Rieti threatening to abandon the child if money wasn't sent, and working long hours at the hospital. In this capacity she subverted the official detachment of America and acted as ambassador for the other America she was urging into life in her dispatches. Being locked in Rome to tend wounded heroes while her own child lay possibly neglected in the unreachable hills must have wrought displacements in her feelings. Finally it worked to break down the ferocity of her partisan zeal and her enthusiasm for martyrdom. She was especially broken after June 3, when the French, strengthened by seasoned troops from the Algerian wars, launched a surprise attack. Then followed a month of battle, and the hospitals began to fill. "You say, you are glad I have had this great opportunity for carrying out my principles," she wrote in anguish to the stiffly righteous Channing; she confessed her courage failed her at last. Lamenting over "the beautiful young men, mown down in their stately prime," she burst out, "I forget the great ideas, to sympathize with the poor mothers, who had nursed their precious forms, only to see them all lopped and gashed" (VI:45). Yet what made the image of "these noble, bleeding martyrs, my brothers" so potent for Fuller was precisely their "great ideas." And so she wrote wearily, yawing back and forth between the irreconcilable poles of her feeling, "After the attempt at revolution in France failed, could I have influenced Mazzini, I should have prayed him to capitulate, and yet I feel that no honorable terms can be made with such a foe, and that the only way is *never* to yield; but the sound of musketry, the sense that men were perishing in a hopeless contest, had become too terrible for my nerves." And she described a last meeting with Mazzini after the French entered Rome on July 4, in a way that accented her limitations:

> Mazzini had suffered millions more than I could; he had borne his fearful responsibility; he had let his dearest friends perish;

he had passed all these nights without sleep; in two short months, he had grown old; all the vital juices seemed exhausted; his eyes were all blood-shot; his skin orange; flesh he had none; his hair was mixed with white; his hand was painful to the touch; but he had never flinched, never quailed; had protested in the last hour against surrender; sweet and calm, but full of a more fiery purpose than ever; in him I revered the hero, and owned myself not of that mould. [32]

All that made for her joy when the revolution was rising—the fusion of lover and partisan—worked to redouble her anguish when it came crashing down.

For one more moment she felt the synthesis, but it was the wholeness not of joy but of desperate courage. That was on June 30, after a night of unusually heavy bombardment from the French camp. She called Lewis Cass, Jr., the United States chargé d'affaires, to her rooms to give him papers for her family in the event of her death. She explained that she planned to spend the night with her husband, who commanded a battery on the Pincian hill. Cass wrote later: "That being the highest and most exposed position in Rome, and directly in the line of the bombs from the French camp, it was not to be expected, she said, that he could escape the dangers of another night such as the last, and that therefore it was her intention to remain with him and share his fate." [33] They survived, but the Roman Republic did not, and rarely after that did she experience the strength that comes from the integrity of self.

"Private hopes of mine are fallen with the hopes of Italy. I have played for a new stake and lost it," she wrote to Richard. Had the Republic triumphed, Fuller might have witnessed the culmination of the stunning development of the people and the evolution of new institutions. She might have raised her son in that salutary atmosphere. For her and for Ossoli—whose bravery and authority during the siege had won him a promotion—work for the Republic would have emerged and commitment continued to give their lives form. The proud inhospitality of most Romans to the entering French troops fired Fuller's hope for "perpetual resistance"; but she also noted that beggars began again to "swarm" as soon as the "black ravens" of the Church came out of hiding. [34] The last work she did for the Republic was to secure passports and American protection for some of the republican leaders—beyond this nothing, not even writing, as she was no longer able to face pain "without the power to aid." As for Ossoli, reared for a life he had repudiated, the life he was making for himself now lay in ruins, and he was bitterly depressed.

All that was left them was the life of their son—and that barely, as they found him starving in Rieti. Living together at last and caring for the sick child in Rieti and then in Florence provided a private happiness that Fuller and probably Ossoli had not known since childhood. Partly because the future had just been emptied of all promise, and partly because nothing drew her away from the baby's growth and the "power and sweetness" of Ossoli's presence, Fuller lived for the first time wholly in the present. Of the child's response to her, she wrote a friend, "So sweet this unimpassioned love; it knows not dark reactions, it does not idealize, and cannot be daunted by the faults of its object. . . . I wish you had a child. Nothing else can take the worst bitterness out of life." [35]

Ossoli's love for her was apparently of a piece with the child's feeling, adding essentially devotion and responsibility. It had no element of romantic challenge and freed her for self-acceptance, from the curse of forever "anticipating" her life. When she told Arconati he had "little of what is called intellectual development" but that having seen "the great faults in characters of enthusiasm and genius," his unspoiled instincts, quiet sense of duty, and constant affection held "the highest value" for her, [36] she was not simply apologizing or bravely accepting him *faute de mieux*. She was recognizing the crucial distinction between others, who "loved me with a mixture of fancy and enthusiasm, excited by my talent at embellishing life," and Ossoli, who "loves me from simple affinity" (VI:51). Nowhere is more light shed on her relations with Ossoli, or with her mother, than when she compares the tenderness of their love for her and expresses confidence that they, in particular, will love each other when they meet.

This is not to say that her liaison with Ossoli fed only the pathological hungers of her childhood, though it did that. ("Since my father's death," she wrote Ward, "I have never been so well as at present." [37]) Saying "In him I found a home, and one that interferes with no tie" (VI:46a), suggests that this relationship combined her childish and orthodox needs with her mature and independent ones. For now that she knew genuine love, she also knew, accepted, and conceivably welcomed its limits. It had taken her almost all of her life to grasp the two lucid conditions of the love she needed: that it could only be simple, and that it could not be all-consuming. She found her tie to Ossoli barred her from very little, and she even thought about how to guarantee the same freedom for him.

But Fuller had learned nothing in her progress out of New England if not that private happiness is a delusion when cut off from work in the world with others. Though in Florence she cultivated, with man and child, a circle of generous friends and a round of simple pleasures, she had no access to the work she required. The precious synthesis came to her only in contorted glimpses, as when, sitting with her child in the elegant parks of a Florence again under despotic rule, she watched the human panorama, lovely children, little dogs, "M. de Coaveilles who helped betray Rome and the elegant Austrian officers who will be driven out of Italy when Angelino is a man" (VI:50). In this dream of revolution she was no participant.

Then it became clear that even private happiness was as chancy as public struggle. Police surveillance and the fear of spies dogged the couple on one side, the need of money on the other. Friends and family had helped sustain them through loans and presents, but now the child was better, and they had to find some livelihood. [38] Fuller resumed work on her history of Italy. Surviving accounts of this book are inconsistent. Though it might have been only a pretext for her isolation in Rieti, she plainly had saved a vast assortment of materials for four years. Though at one point in the last year she disparaged what she had accomplished, more often she spoke of it as the most important thing she had done. Except for her long researches on Goethe's life, it was the only work she did not toss off. Emelyn Story told friends she had held the manuscript in her hands, but Elizabeth Barrett Browning said that on the eve of her departure for America Fuller spoke as if it were far from finished. Apparently, she sent a description or a part of it to publishers in England, who rejected it because they had either too little or—for the conservative British audience—too much to go on. In any case, she had played out her hand: time and resources were gone. She was convinced there was nowhere to turn but to America.

Homesick and pregnant in Aquila, Fuller had daydreamed of a single day's return home, but even in fantasy feared rejection there. A year later, a dream of visiting Anna Ward in her Lenox home was more explicit:

> The place seemed quite beautiful to me and I saw the mountains from the window. While I was looking, you & Sam came in with a number of persons I did not know. You all talked of things about which I knew nothing and nobody spoke to me or drew me from my window. At last I suggested that I had been gone a long time and you replied carelessly, "O yes, I think I have not seen you since Wednesday." You must not be so indifferent when I *do* come.

The fear expressed here of alienation, the inaccessibility of beauty, and the hostility of society was apt enough, but indifference was the wrong word for the American response. When the story of Ossoli and their child unleashed what she termed "the social inquisition of the United States," she might have been grateful for a little indifference.[39]

Early in 1850, Frederika Bremer, a Swedish visitor to America wrote that rumors of "a Fourierest or Socialist marriage, without the external ceremony" provoked sudden attacks and eloquent defenses in Fuller's circle. It is provocative that no originals survive of letters in which she broke the news at home, and that there are no records of a wedding date. It is likely she offered no details about her marriage and gave only general reasons for delaying the announcement. In a letter to Fuller, Sarah Clarke complained frankly that she found herself "in a most unpleasant position" because she had no hard facts and "the world said injurious things of you which we were not authorized to deny"; she concluded, with penetration, "to me it seemed that you were more afraid of being thought to have submitted to the ceremony of marriage than to have omitted it." Fuller's terse and proud stance indeed suggests this possibility: that by revealing little of her marriage she signaled the unorthodox way in which she viewed it and fended off the embrace of society, the belated initiation into the stifling rites of "true womanhood." Knowing the grim futility of having her marriage understood by her own criteria, she thus refused to be understood by those of society. The simpler explanation is, of course, that she was lying, that she had never been married, or was married well after she had conceived or given birth. Respectability helped to prevent most of her biographers from choosing this last interpretation of her sparing and cryptic explanations. There is also the potent identification of Margaret Fuller with truthfulness. Yet she was no stranger to partisan exaggeration and had used subterfuge for Ossoli and the child. That Ossoli, too, wrote his sisters of his marriage only from Florence adds to the mystery, which with present information remains unresolvable. [40]

Whether or not Fuller was taking home a finished book and a legitimate marriage may never be ascertained, but the ideas for her book and the nature of her relationship with Ossoli virtually guaranteed a cool welcome. When Elizabeth Barrett Browning said Fuller would be thrown to the wolves in America for her "socialistic" opinions, she was surely not referring to her support of Italian republicanism, which had broad liberal approval in America and which the Brownings themselves, though more mildly, shared. We do not know why Mrs. Browning judged her "one of the out and out *Reds*," but it is possible that Fuller talked with her about both aspects of socialism: organizing the workers and reorganizing the family. In her last month in Florence she was returning mentally to Paris, studying what had happened in 1848 in its more critical revolution. She was examining both its liberal sources in Lamartine's massive *Histoire des Girondins*, which in 1847 had reawakened enthusiasm for the moderate goals of the French Revolution, and its socialist roots in Louis Blanc's *L'Histoire des Dix Ans, 1830-40*, a five-volume attack on the reign of the bourgeoisie. This rich study suggests she was preparing to write something more broadly historical and possibly theoretical than her impressions of the Italian struggle. If so, and if she had lived to sort out her judgments of Mazzini and to have analyzed the difference between nationalist and social revolution, the loss of this book is incalculably greater than is generally imagined. In addition to studying European events, she was writing to the Springs inquiring eagerly about their impressions of the North American Phalanx in Red Bank, New Jersey. In the rhetoric of this Fourierist colony, no sexual distinction affected work responsibility and rights, and the "relationship of the sexes" was a question freely to be settled "by woman herself." [41] If her book developed these two socialist strands and the connection between them, it might have had some difficulty finding a publisher or an audience in America. (A letter from Sarah Clarke put it mildly that a personal account of her experiences would probably prove more lucrative than what she was writing. [42]) And even if the book never saw the light, Fuller's notions of sexual relationships and roles were probably too advanced for the North American Phalanx, and the French socialist notions too extreme for even Greeley to entertain. Among the letters she carried on board the merchantman "Elizabeth" on May 17, 1850, was one freshly received from Marcus and Rebecca Spring, the most forward-looking of her friends, who, having taken counsel with Emerson and Channing, urged her to remain abroad. [43]

She was returning to those she loved and who loved her, but her way of loving now was somewhat alien to her old friends; it was bound up with a knowledge of self and society they did not share and were no more likely to grasp under conditions of life in America than she had done. The love of her friends is perhaps best revealed by the letters of her brother and W. H. Channing after her death. In order to copy extracts of her papers for publication, Richard wrote to his sister, Ellen, that he had employed a copyist who promised discretion. He himself would copy from those "objectionable to be shown to him," but if she found papers which he himself should not see, Ellen or their mother should copy the extracts themselves. Channing's aggressiveness thirty years later is simply the other side of the coin from Richard's shrinking from knowing all about his "beautiful and dear sister." Having heard that Higginson was writing a new biography, he wrote a redundant and ranting letter, insisting that Higginson stress her perfection, the spiritual, ideal, and moral character of her genius, her practical wisdom, and her "all-pervading, all-refining religiousness." Then he added, in confidence, his assurance that "my estimate of this noble person was juster, deeper, purer, truer, loftier than has ever been given elsewhere.[44] (Channing was, ironically, one to whom Fuller wrote with unusual candor about the limitations of her marriage.) Apparently, the American myth of the ideal woman required the refusal of knowledge of her even after death.

Fuller's fear of the sea voyage—her superstitious dread for herself and Angelino, her recollection that a fortuneteller warned Ossoli against it—was the outward sign of her intimate understanding that the person she had become could never go home to America. The long trajectory of her short life was not circular. To respect herself and her insistent energy she had first to use what was at hand in America, to go the route of idealism, transcendence of the material aspects of her condition. When this had made her strong enough, she left New England and began in New York to apply her energy more directly to the material reality of her self and her world; but her mystified sexuality and her dependence on notions of divinely ordained national destiny show that she was still subject to American limitations of mind. Only in Italy did she come to understand the meaning of her most intimate prayer, "Give me truth; cheat me by no illusion." She learned that reality was what she had meant, though her culture had taught her to call it truth. She learned that love, made of generous commitment to the autonomy of both persons, was only obscured by her obsession with ideal passion, and that the need to recast relations between sexes and between classes was only obscured by her country's idealistic pride.

Fuller faced death all the way home. First the captain of the "Elizabeth" died of smallpox, then Angelino, infected, struggled nine days for his life. Late on July 18, 1850, the mate told them they would dock the next day and everyone packed. But near four in the morning a storm drove them into the sands of Fire Island, the cargo of Carrara marble broke through the hold, and the ship stuck fast, canted sideways. There followed twelve hours of shipwreck. As the cabin gave way, the passengers scrambled across the ravaged deck to the relative safety of the forecastle; Fuller thus abandoned her manuscript and materials. [45] As the light came up, they could make out the shore, fifty yards away, and eventually people appeared, but these were salvage pirates not rescuers. (Later, to his horror, Channing learned that some of those on shore would have attempted rescue had they known anyone "important" was on board.) For some time, they watched each other over the roiling waves, then, the captain's widow, clinging to a plank, as the ship's boats had been lost, made it to shore with a sailor. Fuller would not follow, refusing to be separated from Ossoli and the child. The mate and all but four seamen then abandoned them. At last, the steward seized the child and leaped into the sea, but both drowned before reaching shore. Shortly afterward, Ossoli was washed away, apparently without Fuller, in her distraught condition, grasping the fact. [46] As she sat at the foremast, her hair loose over her white nightdress, facing America, the cook heard her say, "I see nothing but death before me." [47] It was an extreme image of her condition. So she stayed, until the wave broke that tore her away, poised, arrested, frozen in her final hesitation, staring at the unresponsive land.

Notes

1. Letter to Mary Rotch, Eliza Farrar's Quaker aunt, Houghton MS.

2. Karl Marx, *The Eighteenth Brumaire of Louis Bonaparte* (New York: International Publishers, 1963), p. 24.

3. Gaetano Salvemini, *Mazzini*, trans. I. M. Rawson (New York: Crowell-Collier, 1962), p. 146.

4. *Memoirs*, II, 220; Emma Detti, *Margaret Fuller Ossoli e i suoi corrispond-enti* (Florence, Italy: Le Monnier, 1942), p. 229.

5. Emelyn Story, the source of the anecdote, did not specify the date, and we do not know why W. H. Channing penned "Holy Thursday" into her account for publication in the *Memoirs*. Holy Thursday fell on April 1 in 1847.

6. Detti, pp. 312-13, 309; Emerson, Notebook on MFO, p. 270.

7. *At Home and Abroad*, p. 220.

8. *Ibid*., p. 231, 237.

9. May 29, 1848, Houghton MS.

10. Detti, p. 312.

11. Thus Sarah Josepha Hale, in *Woman's Record* (New York: Harper & Bros., 1853), suggested that Fuller's loss of her taste for German literature before her death might be a sign of redemption. And a British reviewer of the *Memoirs* wrote that "from the time she became a mother till the final tragedy, . . . she was an altered woman and evinced a greatness of soul and heroism of character so grand that we feel disposed to extend to her whole career the admiration and sympathy inspired by the closing scenes" (*Westminster Review*, LXVII [April 1852]). In *Portraits of American Women* (Boston: Houghton Mifflin Co., 1919), Gamaliel Bradford offers the most concise version of this school: he says she learned in Italy that "the height of self-culture is to forget culture and to forget self" (p. 162).

12. Joseph Jay Deiss, *The Roman Years of Margaret Fuller* (New York: T. Y. Crowell, 1969), p. 86.

13. *Letters and Journals of Thomas Wentworth Higginson 1846-1906*, ed. Mary Higginson (New York: Negro Universities Press, 1969), pp. 29-30.

14. "Self-Reliance," *Complete Essays and Other Writings of Ralph Waldo Emerson*, ed. Brooks Atkinson (New York: Random House, 1950), p. 145; Sacvan Bercovitch, *The Puritan Origins of the American Self* (New Haven: Yale University Press, 1975), p. 173; letter to Elizabeth Hoar, September 1847, Memoirs, II, 220; "Culture," *Complete Essays*, p. 725. My discussion of Emerson here, as elsewhere, centers on the years of Fuller's life. After her death, his notions of action, the state, and the individual, underwent a series of changes. First, in the fifties, he joined in the widespread opposition in the North to the Fugitive Slave Law and endorsed collective disobedience to the state and heroic action like John Brown's. Second, he so fiercely supported the North's prosecution of the Civil War that he argued that government should have "in any crisis of the state, the absolute powers of a dictator," and found the Lincoln of the Emancipation Proclamation as triumphantly "representative" as he had Brown. Third, joining a number of citizens' organizations, he proposed one more conservative than them all, a National Academy of Literature and Art, which would compose "a jury to sit upon abnormal anomalous pretensions to genius, such as puzzle the public mind now and then." (See George M. Frederickson, *The Inner Civil War* (New York: Harper & Row, 1965), pp. 177-79.) I am less concerned here with his change—with how the pressures of history, of age, of prestige, made him desert his early radical individualism—than with his constancy. Whether contemporary issues engaged him or not, he always identified himself with American destiny so snugly that he could offer neither himself nor his thought as a cutting edge to that destiny. Thus, even after her death, he could neither have understood nor shared Fuller's enthusiasm for alternative, non-American, heroism nor her interest in radical reorganization of class and family structure.

15. See William Salomone, "The Nineteenth Century Discovery of Italy An Essay in American Cultural History," *American Historical Review*, LXXIII (June 1968), pp. 1359-91.

16. *Memoirs*, II, 324; letter to Richard Fuller, February 23, 1849, Houghton MS. In the latter she deprecates Americans' mistrust of the "too demonstrative, too fiery, too impressionable" Hungarians, Poles, and Italians and scorns their preference for "the loyal, slow moving Germans" and the Russians' "gentlemanly servility."

17. *At Home and Abroad*, pp. 263, 260, 244, 247, 280.

18. *Memoirs*, II, p. 223. In April 1848, she alluded to this new habit of half-revelation in a letter to a friend: "I love Rome more every hour, but I do not like to write details, or really to let anyone know anything about it. I pretend to, perhaps, but in reality I do not betray the secrets of my love." (BPL MS).

19. When all the bequests were paid, her share of the estate came to less than a thousand dollars.

20. Detti, p. 315.

21. *Memoirs*, II, 236-37.

22. It is interesting that Fuller's assessments of events in Italy and of the failings of Charles Albert were usually consistent with those that Marx and Engels were publishing at the same time in the *Neue Rheinische Zeitung*. (Marx and Engels began in 1851 sending dispatches of their own to the *New York Tribune*; their first series was on the German revolution and counterrevolution.)

23. May 29, 1848, Houghton MS.

24. In his *Life of Horace Greeley* (New York: Mason Bros., 1855), James Parton offers an extensive summary of the debate.

25. *Memoirs*, II, 244, 242-43.

26. August 15 and 18, 1848, Houghton MS.

27. Faith Chipperfield, *In Quest of Love* (New York: Coward-McCann, 1957), p. 266. *Memoirs*, II, 298.

28. Priscilla Robertson, *Revolutions of 1848: A Social History* (Princeton: Princeton University Press, 1967), p. 365. Mazzini felt these measures implied no socialism, as he told Clough (*The Poems and Prose Remains of Arthur Hugh Clough*, [London: Macmillan, 1869] I, 143). Fuller's enthusiasm for similar reforms in Paris, described in her 1849 diary, suggests she warmly welcomed them in Rome (Leona Rostenberg, "Margaret Fuller's Roman Diary," *Journal of Modern History*, 12 [1940], 218).

29. Robertson, p. 360.

30. *Memoirs*, II, 250.

31. Henry James, *William Wetmore Story and His Friends* (Boston: Houghton Mifflin Co., 1903), I, 155.

32. *Memoirs*, II, 267-68. Mazzini's extraordinary concern for individuals, even at the height of the siege, is nowhere more plain than in his letter of June 9, 1849, to Fuller begging her to "be *woman* and forgive" his not writing, explaining that every minute problem of the war "comes down to me," and exclaiming in final proof, "I scarcely even write a few words to my mother" (Deiss, p. 259).

33. Detti, pp. 343-44.

34. Deiss, p. 276; *At Home and Abroad*, p. 418.

35. BPL MS copy, no date.

36. *Memoirs*, II, 316-17.

37. February 24, 1850, Samuel Gray Ward Papers, Houghton.

38. Why Fuller did not resume writing for the *Tribune* is unclear; Deiss (p.302-303) speculates that it was because rumors of her "free love" liaison were afloat in New York.

39. March 18, 1849, Samuel Gray Ward Papers, Houghton; letter to Emelyn Story, November 30, 1849, Houghton MS copy.

40. Bremer, *The Homes of the New World* (1853; rpt. New York: Negro Universities Press, 1968) I, 710; Houghton MS. In her *Life of Margaret Fuller* (New York: E. P. Dutton, 1942), Madeleine Stern offers the most persuasive argument that Fuller and Ossoli were married. Because there are no records of a marriage in Rome (in the Vatican Library, the Protestant Archives, or the Vicariate of Rome), because they were often in spring 1848 on day trips outside Rome, and because in April 1849 each writes the other lamenting that they cannot be together on April 4, suggesting it is an important anniversary (VI:40) Stern believes they were married on April 4, 1848, in a town outside Rome. She does not address the problems they would have had in paying to keep quiet such a sensational union taking place anywhere in the Papal States. If they were married in remote Rieti, the records were destroyed in an American air raid in 1943.

Detti and Deiss are both more influenced by a letter Ossoli's sister Angela wrote Ellen Channing on March 9, 1851, saying that her brother had written from Florence that he and Fuller were married there after baptizing their son in Rieti (Houghton MS). But while Detti hypothesizes the marriage took place in an unrecorded visit to Florence immediately after Angelo's baptism in 1848, Deiss assumes that it took place after they moved to Florence in fall 1849. The chapel Deiss alludes to as a possible scene of the marriage (p. 292) matches the description by Fuller's friend Hurlbut (*Memoirs*, II, 321-22) of a convent church, San Salvatore al Monte, near San Miniato; at that time, according to Enzo Settesoldi of the Opera del Duomo Archives in Florence, no marriage could be performed there.

The marriage question remains wide open. Although for their marriage to be legal and their child legitimate in Italy, they would have had to be married according to canonical law and the Council of Trent, it is possible that they were married by an American official or a Protestant minister. The fact that Ossoli drew up a document making Angelo his heir and entitling him to all rights and privileges of the Ossoli name may be interpreted variously: 1) they were not married when Angelo was born; 2) Ossoli was compensating for having married outside the church; 3) a Catholic marriage had to be kept secret.

41. *Letters of Elizabeth Barrett Browning*, ed. F. G. Kenyon (New York: Macmillan, 1898), I. 428; John Humphrey Noyes, *History of American Socialisms* (1870; rpt. New York: Hillary House, 1961), p. 460.

42. March 5, 1850, Houghton MS.

43. Although both the Springs insisted their advice was based on the greater advantage she would have in publishing her book from Italy than at home, it is not difficult to read between the lines their incapacity to face the shock of her union with Ossoli. Thus Rebecca adds, "if you return you will lose the power to write as well for you would not be so happy and your friend [though canceled by a later pen, this indiscreet last word is still legibile] (whom with much pleasure we now learn from Hicks is your old friend Giovanni) would not and could not be so happy here as in his own beautiful Italy—what could repay him, and what could with you take the place of such [illegible] as the Brownings and others you mention? ... It is because we love you we say 'stay!'" (April 14, 1850, Houghton MS).

44. August 22, 1853, Houghton MS; April, 1883, BPL MS.

45. There is some debate about when the ship sank, the captain's widow indicating it was five hours earlier (*At Home and Abroad*, p. 45). Upon hearing news of the wreck, Emerson immediately dispatched Thoreau to the site of the wreck to obtain all the details he could and to retrieve the manuscript, if possible. He failed to find it, but among the Fuller Papers at Harvard is a document ignored by all her biographers which maintains that the bodies of Fuller and Ossoli were washed up on shore some days later. Writing on June 29, 1901, to Mrs. Anna Parker Pruyn, Arthur Dominy maintains that his father, Felix, agent of Underwriters of New York City and correspondent for the *New York Tribune*, said that the bodies, matching the descriptions of Ossoli and Fuller (all the other women's bodies had been accounted for), were boxed and sent by a vessel commanded by Captain James Wick to Greeley, who "refused to have anything to do with them." Fearful he was breaking the law by having the bodies on board, the captain and another man buried them in the dead of night on Coney Island. Later he said he was sure he could not again find the spot, as the night was so dark and his terror so great.

46. Although according to the *Memoirs* Fuller and Ossoli were torn off the deck at the same instant, two accounts writtten at the time of the wreck say Ossoli went first (*At Home and Abroad*, pp. 446, 451). In one of these Fuller refused to try to save herself; in the other the seamen "had just persuaded her to trust herself to a plank, in the belief that Ossoli and their child had already started for the shore, when just as she was stepping down, a great wave broke over the vessel and swept her into the boiling deep." (pp. 450-51). So many people had the impression that Fuller wished to die that when Higginson was writing his biography of Fuller a number of her friends pressed him to strive to eradicate it. It is impossible to know whether or not at the end she chose to die, but if she made that choice under such circumstances, it need not be taken to reflect back on her recent life. More interesting and subtler is the question of whether or not she had already given up, as Margaret Allen argues in "The Political and Social Criticism of Margaret Fuller," *South Atlantic Quarterly*, 72 [Autumn 1973] 560-73). Allen believes that "the triumph of reaction, tyranny, and naked force," crushed Fuller's spirit, for she hears in Fuller's "political reactions during the later years of her life. . . . a prominent note of perfectionist absolutism that yearns for complete solutions and scorns the half measures of politicians. It seems a quintessentially American trait." Hence, according to Allen, Fuller could take refuge neither in cynicism nor the tragic sense. Putting aside the question how either tragic vision or cynicism might have helped her radical activism survive, the charge of perfectionist absolutism is one Fuller's late writing sometimes bears out. It is my view, however, that her openness and sensitivity to the actual complexity of experience was never so great as in the last year of her life. After the fall of Rome, the most devastating of her losses, she was indeed emotionally exhausted and longed for a quiet life and occasionally for death. But then her celebration of the Italians' resistance to the French, her desire to visit and analyze their fortifications, her intensive study of the revolutionary wave, and her continued curiosity about new social experiments are all incompatible with the sort of mental surrender Allen alludes to. What might have produced a fatal despair off the coast of Fire Island was the prospect of trying to hoard and use this slender store of hard-sought resiliency in a country so marked by "perfectionist absolutism."

47. *At Home and Abroad*, p. 446.

CONTEMPORARIES ON FULLER

1. Defense of her political work,
James Russell Lowell, July 12, 1849

In March 1849 a copy of Lowell's satirical *Fable for Critics* (III:7) reached Rome, embittering Fuller ("I shall never again be perfectly, religiously generous . . . I am worse than I was" [Houghton MS]). Lowell's friend William Story rebuked him: "The joke of 'Tiring-woman to the Muses' is too happy; but because fate has really been unkind to her, and because she depends on her pen for her bread-and-water (and that is nearly all she has to eat), and because she is her own worst enemy, and because through her disappointment and disease, which (things) embitter every one, she has struggled most stoutly and manfully, I could have wished you had let her pass scot-free" (Henry James, *William Wetmore Story and his Friends*, I, 171). Previously unaware that she was poor, Lowell regretted his attack, and later his wife and former patron of Fuller's Conversations, Maria White, worked to quell malicious rumors about Fuller's marriage. On June 27, 1849, Bishop John Hughes of New York City called for a collection "for the relief and support of the Pope" and, labeling the Roman Republic a reign of terror, noted that no foreign ambassador recognized it—excepting of course "the female plenipotentiary" of the *Tribune*. This blast gave Lowell his opportunity.

. . . The Roman revolutionists have been denounced as bloodthirsty rabble who coerced the orderly citizens by terror. This would be a priori an absurdity, even had it not appeared that no city could be so vigorously and successfully defended except by a unanimous people. It is a disgrace to America that she is not represented at Rome by a man with brain enough and heart enough to sympathize with the struggle of a race in whom fifteen centuries of bad government have not extinguished the memory of a glorious past. Bishop Hughes says sneeringly that the Roman Republic has been recognized only by the "female plenipotentiary of the Tribune." It is a pity that America could not be always as adequately represented. But Miss Fuller has not merely contented herself with the comparatively cheap sympathy of words, though even brave words are much if spoken at the right time. We learn from private letters that, the last American left in Rome, she was doing her duty in the hospitals as a nurse for the wounded, thus performing also her mission as woman. Women have been sainted at Rome for less, and the Bishop is welcome to his sneer.

We cannot too often repeat that it is Slavery which has benumbed the heart of the American people. It is one chain which binds down the oppressed of whatever race or complexion all over the world. As long as we have our own private sham to maintain, we are co-partners with all other speculators in sham, wherever they may be. . . . [*National Anti-Slavery Standard*, July 12, 1849, p. 26]

2. In Rome with Ossoli, Emelyn Story [1852]

After Fuller's death, Emelyn Story prepared a little manuscript book of recollections. All but the third, seventh, and eighth passages below are reprinted in the *Memoirs*, but there great liberties are taken with style and occasionally with tone and content. Thus although Channing omitted the third passage below, writing on the manuscript itself that he doubted its accuracy, in the fifth passage, he penned into Fuller's bedside confession her concern for her "husband," a word striking for its absence from all of Fuller's accounts of Ossoli.

a. As soon as she heard of our arrival [in Rome, November 1847] she stretched forth a friendly, cordial hand, and greeted us most warmly. She gave us great assistance in our search for convenient lodgings, and we were soon happily established near her. Our intercourse was henceforth most frequent and intimate and knew no cloud nor coldness. Daily we were much together, and daily felt more sensible of the worth and value of our friend. To me she seemed so unlike what I had known her in America, that I continually said to her "how have I misjudged you – you are not [at] all such a person as I took you to be in America." To this she replied, "I am not the same person, I am in many respects another, my life has new channels now and how thankful I am that I have been able to come out into larger interests – but partly, you did not know me at home in the true light." I did not know her much personally, when in Boston; but through her friends, who were mine also, I learned to think of her as a person on intellectual stilts, with a large share of arrogance and little sweetness of temper. How unlike to this was she now – so delicate so simple confiding and affectionate with a true womanly heart and soul sensitive and generous, and, what was to me a still greater surprise, possessed with broad charity, that she could cover with its mantle the faults and defects of those about her.

We soon became acquainted with the young Marquis Ossoli, and met him frequently at Margaret's rooms. He appeared to be of a reserved and gentle nature, with quiet, gentleman-like manners, and there was something melancholy in the expression of his face, which make one desire to know more of him. In figure, he was tall and of slender frame, dark eyes and hair and we judged that he was about thirty years of age, possibly younger.

b. [In that fall of 1847, Ossoli] became her constant visitor and as in those days Margaret watched with zeal and intense interest the tide of political events, his mind was also turned in the direction of Liberty and better government. Whether or not Ossoli unassisted would have been able to emancipate himself from the influence of his family and early education, both eminently conservative and narrow, may be a question but that he did throw off the shackles is true and that he gave the cause of Roman liberty his warm espousal is most certain – Margaret had known Mazzini in London, and partaken of his schemes for the future of his country and was watching with great interest the current events, as well as taking pains to inform herself in regard to action of all parties with a view to write a history of the Period. Ossoli brought her every intelligence that might be of interest to her and busied himself in learning the views of both parties that she might be able to view the matter impartially.

Here I may say, that in the estimation of most those who were in Italy at this time the loss of Margaret's history and notes is a great and irreparable one. No one could have possessed so many avenues of direct information from both sides – While she was the friend and correspondent of Mazzini and knew the springs of action of his party – through her husband's family and connections, she knew the other view. So that whatever might be the value of her deductions, her facts could not have been other than of highest value in this age of incorrect report and perverted statement. Together, Margaret and Ossoli went to the meetings of either side – and to her he carried all the flying reports of the day, such as he had heard in the café, or through his friends.

c. Not long after our coming to Rome, the old Marquis Ossoli died and as Angelo was his youngest ⟨son⟩ and only unmarried ⟨one⟩, the care of his father during his last illness fell upon him. A few hasty moments of these days of anxiety he went to pass with Margaret, who tried to console him in his deep affliction. When at length his Father died, he told Margaret that he ⟨loved her and⟩ must marry her or be miserable. She still refused to look upon him as a lover and insisted that it was not fitting, that it was best he should marry a younger woman – that she would be his friend but not his wife. In this way it rested for some time during which we saw Ossoli pale, dejected and unhappy. He was always with her but in a sort of hopeless, desperate manner attending her, until at length he convinced her of this love and she married him.

d. [In the spring of 1849] when it was certain that the French had landed forces at Civita Vecchia and would attack Rome, Ossoli took station with his men on the walls of the Vatican gardens, where he remained faithfully to the end of the attack. Margaret had, at the same time, the entire charge of one of the hospitals (the name of which I have forgotten), and was the assistant of the Princess Belgiojoso, in charge of "*dei Pellegrini*," where, during the first day they received seventy wounded men, French and Romans.

Night and day Margaret was occupied and with the princess so ordered and disposed the hospitals that their conduct was truly admirable. All the work was skilfully divided, so that there was no confusion or hurry, and from the chaotic condition in which these places had been left by the priests, who previously had charge of them, they brought perfect regularity and discipline. Of money they had very little and they were obliged to give their own time and thoughts in its place. From the Americans in Rome, they raised a subscription for the aid of the wounded of either party, but besides this, they had scarcely any money to use. I have been through the wards with Margaret, and seen how comforting was her presence to the poor suffering men. "How long will the Signora stay?" "When will the Signora come again?" they eagerly asked. For each one's peculiar tastes she had a care: to one she carried books; to another she told the news of the day; and listened to another's oft-repeated tale of wrongs, as the best sympathy she could give. They raised themselves up on their elbows, to get the last glimpse of her as she was going away. There were some of the poor sturdy fellows of Garibaldi's Legion there, and to them she listened, as with delight they spoke of their chief, of his courage and skill; for he seemed to have won the hearts of his men in a remarkable manner.

One thing I may as well say in this connection. It happened, that some time before the coming of the French, while Margaret was travelling in the country quite by herself, as she perhaps was returning from a visit to her child, who was out at nurse in the country, that she rested for an hour or two at a little wayside *osteria*. While there, she was startled by the *padrone*, who, with great alarm, rushed into the room, and said, "We are quite lost! here is the Legion Garibaldi! and these men always pillage and if we do not give all up to them without pay they will kill us." Margaret looked out upon the road and saw that it was quite true that the legion was coming thither with all speed for a moment she said that she felt uncomfortably such was the exaggerated account of the conduct of the men that she thought it quite possible that they would take her horses and so leave her without the means of proceeding upon her journey. They came and she had determined to offer them a lunch at her own expense, having faith that gentleness and courtesy was the best protection from injury. Accordingly, as soon as they arrived, and came boisterously into the *osteria*, she rose, and said to the *Padrone*, "Give these good men wine and bread on my account for after their ride they must need refreshment." Immediately the noise and confusion subsided with respectful bows to her they seated themselves and partook of the lunch giving her an account of their journey. When she was ready to go and her *vettura* was at the door, they waited upon her, took down the steps, and assisted her in with much gentleness and respectfulness of manner, and she drove off, wondering how men with such natures could have the reputation they had. And so far as we could gather except in this instance, their conduct was of a most disorderly kind.

e. [After an exhausting day at the hospital,] she called me to her bedside and said that I must consent for her sake to keep the secret she was about to confide— Then she told me where her child was, and when it was born and gave me certain papers and parchment documents which I was to keep, and, in the event of her death I was to take the boy to her mother in America and confide him to her care and that of her friend Caroline Tappan.

The papers thus given me I had perfect liberty to read but after she had told me her story I desired no confirmation of this fact, beyond what her words had given me. One or two of the papers she opened, and we together read them One was written on parchment in Latin, and was a certificate, given by the priest who married them, saying that Angelo Eugene Ossoli was the legal [words illegible] heir of whatever title and fortune should come to his father. To this was affixed his seal with those of the other witnesses, and the Ossoli crest was drawn in full upon the paper. There was also a book, in which Margaret had written the history of her acquaintance and marriage with Ossoli, and of the birth of her child. In giving that to me, she said "If I do not survive to tell this myself to my family, this book will be to them invaluable therefore keep it for them, if I live, it will be of no use for my word will be all that they will ask." I took the papers and locked them up, never feeling any desire to look into them, as I never did, and as she gave them to me, I returned them to her, when I left Rome for Switzerland.

After this, she often spoke to me of the necessity there had been and still existed for her keeping her marriage a secret. At the time, I argued in favor of her making it public but subsequent events have shown me the wisdom of her decision— The explanation she gave me of the secret marriage was this: They were married soon after (I think, but am not positive) the death of the old Marquis Ossoli. The estate he had left was undivided and the two brothers, attached to the Papal household, were to be the executors. This property was not large, but when fairly divided would bring to each a little property, an income sufficient, with Roman economy for life in Rome. Every one knows, that law is subject to ecclesiastical influence in Rome, and that marriage with a Protestant would be destructive to all prospects of favorable administration. Beside being of another Religious Faith, there was in this case the additional crime of having married a Liberal, – one who had publicly interested herself in favor of radical views – Taking the two together, there was good reason to suppose, that, if it were known, Ossoli must be a beggar, and a banished man, under the existing government But waiting a little while there was a chance (a fair one too), of an honorable post under the new form of government which everybody anticipated. Leaving Rome, too, at that time, was leaving the field wherein they might hope to work much good, and where they felt that they were needed. Ossoli's brothers had long before begun to look jealously upon him. Knowing his acquaintance with Margaret, they feared the influence she might exert over his mind in favor of Liberal sentiments and had not hesitated to threaten the Papal displeasure — Ossoli's education had been such, that it certainly argues an uncommon degree of character that he was so firm and single in his political views, and was indifferent to the pecuniary advantages which his former position offered.

For many years, the Ossoli family had been high in favor and in office in Rome and he had the same vista for his own future had he chosen to follow their lead. The Pope left for Mòle di Gaeta and then came a suspension of all Legal procedure — so that the estate was never divided before we left Italy and I do not know that it has ever been.

f. [During the siege of Rome] Ossoli's post was one of considerable danger he being in one of the most exposed places, and as Margaret saw his wounded and dying comrades, she felt that another shot might take him from her, or bring him to her care in the hospital — Eagerly she watched as the carts came up with their suffering loads, knowing that her worst fears might be confirmed. No argument of ours could persuade Ossoli to leave his post to take food or rest, Sometimes we went to him, and carried a concealed basket of provisions, but he shared it with so many of his fellows, that his own portion must have been almost nothing. Haggard, worn, and pale, he walked over the Vatican grounds with us, pointing out, now here, now there, where some poor fellow's blood sprinkled the wall. Margaret was with us, and for a few moments they could have an anxious talk about their child. . . .

To get to the child or to send to him was quite impossible and for days they were in complete ignorance about him. After waiting upon the Post Office with the anxiety that a Mother only can know at length a letter came but it only relieved her from her present anxiety with regard to the boy's health to give her another cause of uneasiness — the nurse declared that unless means were immediately found for sending her, in advance payment, a certain sum of money, she would altogether abandon the child. It seemed at first impossible to send money, the road was so insecure, the bearer of any parcel was likely to be seized by one party or the other and treated as a spy. But happily after much consideration, the sum was sent to the address of a physician who had charge to look after the child and I think it did reach its destination, and for a while answered the purpose of keeping the wretched nurse faithful to her charge.

g. Many of our countrymen who saw [Ossoli] could discover little in him but that was rather because he was not quickly interested in others, than that he lacked interesting points. He was always reserved, and when with Margaret preferred always to hear her talk even when she spoke a language he did not know than to talk himself or hear any one else.

His manner toward Margaret was devoted and lover-like to a striking degree — He cared not how trivial was the service if he might perform it for her — I remember to have seen him one morning after they had been married nearly two years, set off on an errand to get the handle of her parasol mended with as much genuine knightly zeal as if the charge had been a much weightier one. As he took it [he] said "How sweet it is to do little things for you never attend to such yourself always leave them to me for my pleasure." When she was ill he nursed and watched over her with the tenderness of woman. When she said to him, "How have you learned to be so good a nurse," he said, "My Father was ill, and I tended upon him." No service was too trivial, no sacrifice too great for him. He never wished her to give up any pleasure because he could not share it, but if she were interested, he would go with her to any house, leave her and call again to take her home. Such tender, unselfish love I have rarely before seen it made green her days, and gave her an expression of peace and serenity which before was a stranger to her face. "No companion in nature was ever so much to me as is Ossoli," does not this show that his soul was deep and full of emotion, for who that knew Margaret would believe that any other companion would have been agreeable to her in her communion with nature. What a beautiful picture is that of their return to Rome after a day spent on the Campagna!

h. A [word illegible] friend one who ⟨knew⟩ Margaret often during the last winter in Florence tells me that the child was not of a healthy [word illegible], that a physician who has passed much time in study of diseases of the Brain has said he would never have lived to be a man. *[BPL MS]*

*3. Evenings in Florence, Frederick Gale,
December 15 and 29, 1849*

On December 11, 1849, Frederick Gale wrote Anna, his sister and one of Fuller's former Greene Street students, that he had just met "the quondam Margaret Fuller—now transformed, by marriage, into no less a personage than the Marchioness of Ossoli," with husband and child both "depending upon her pen for a subsistence." Never one of Fuller's admirers, he concluded jubilantly, "Now that the scornful, manhating Margaret of 40 has got a husband, really no old maid need despair, while there is life in her body!" In his journal he offered two contradictory impressions of Fuller in exile from Rome.

a. In the eve to Mozier's house, where I met a large company — mostly artists — among them *Geo. P. Marsh* (was not introduced) and *Madame Ossioli* [*sic*] & the young *Marquis d'Ossioli*, her spouse. I found her much older & uglier than I had anticipated. There are wrinkles & lines in her face, old enough for 60! Her husband is handsome & hardly looks 30. She appeared sad & depressed to me — bent in body & in fact an old woman before her time. The political events in Italy in which she had embarked, as it were, by her marriage with the Marquis — a rebel against the Pope & Officer in the service of the Republicans, have probably contributed to this result. But I heard nothing like that tone of scorn & contempt which I expected in her conversation. I talked a good deal with her, & chiefly about the sad manner in which the progressive movements of the recent struggles have been managed.

b. In eve to Mozier's — met a large party of Americans — had a fine supper in which cold turkey, duck, maryonaise [*sic*], champagne & whisky punch played a prominent part — and the transcendental ex-editress of the Dial devoted herself with unmistakeable ardor to them all not even declining that vulgar, but comforting beverage – so un-fashionable for Boston blues, *the whisky punch*. I danced two cotillions with her & found her none the worse for the liquor – but merry & agreeable. Her spouse says nothing. The ladies left before 2, but a party of gentlemen told stories & renewed the potations somewhat later. *[E. A. Hoyt and L. S. Brigham, "Glimpses of Margaret Fuller: The Greene Street School and Florence,"* New England Quarterly, *29 (1956), 98]*

4. In Florence with Ossoli,
William Henry Hurlbut *[1852]*

Fresh from Harvard Divinity School, the South Carolinian W. H. Hurlbut (1827-1895) visited Florence for six weeks in March and April 1850. Later (spelling his name Hurlbert), he became an influential journalist, but his reminiscence of Fuller's and Ossoli's life in the Piazza Santa Maria Novella is unctuous with deference. Among his tales of Fuller's skill and bravery in resolving quarrels, her mornings of writing, evenings with friends, and occasional excursions to the hills with Ossoli, he offers valuable data on Ossoli and on Fuller's response to Florence in defeat.

... I cannot remember ever to have found Madame Ossoli alone, on those evenings when she remained at home. Her husband was always with her. The picture of their room rises clearly on my memory. A small square room, sparingly, yet sufficiently furnished, with polished floor and frescoed ceiling, – and, drawn up closely before the cheerful fire, an oval table, on which stood a monkish lamp of brass, with depending chains that support quaint classic cups for the olive oil. There, seated beside his wife, I was sure to find the Marchese, reading from some patriotic book, and dressed in the dark brown, red-corded coat of the Guardia Civica, which it was his melancholy pleasure to wear at home. So long as the conversation could be carried on in Italian, he used to remain, though he rarely joined in it to any considerable degree; but if a number of English and American visitors came in, he used to take his leave and go to the Café d'Italia, being very unwilling, as Madame Ossoli told me, to impose any seeming restraint, by his presence, upon her friends, with whom he was unable to converse. For the same reason, he rarely remained with her at the houses of her English or American friends, though he always accompanied her thither, and returned to escort her home.

I conversed with him so little that I can hardly venture to make any remarks on the impression which I received from his conversation, with regard to the character of his mind. Notwithstanding his general reserve and curtness of speech, on two or three occasions he showed himself to possess quite a quick and vivid fancy, and even a certain share of humor. I have heard him tell stories remarkably well. One tale, especially, which related to a dream he had in early life, about a treasure concealed in his father's house, which was thrice repeated, and made so strong an impression on his mind as to induce him to batter a certain panel in the library almost to pieces, in vain, but which received something like a confirmation from the fact, that a Roman attorney, who rented that and other rooms from the family, after his father's death, grew suddenly and unaccountably rich, — I remember as being told with great felicity and vivacity of expression. . . .

Though condemned by her somewhat uncertain position at Florence, as well as by the state of things in Tuscany at that time, to a comparative inaction, Madame Ossoli never seemed to lose in the least the warmth of her interest in the affairs of Italy, nor did she bate one jot of heart or hope for the future of that country. She was much depressed, however, I think, by the apparent apathy and prostration of the Liberals in Tuscany; and the presence of the Austrian troops in Florence was as painful and annoying to her, as it could have been to any Florentine patriot. When it was understood that Prince Lichtenstein had requested the Grand Duke to order a general illumination in honor of the anniversary of the battle of Novara, Madame Ossoli, I recollect, was more moved than I remember on any other occasion to have seen her. And she used to speak very regretfully of the change which had come over the spirit of Florence, since her former residence there. Then all was gayety and hope. Bodies of artisans, gathering recruits as they passed along, used to form themselves into choral bands, as they returned from their work at the close of the day, and filled the air with the chants of liberty. Now, all was a sombre and desolate silence. [*Memoirs, II, 326-29*]

5. Her last year, Elizabeth Barrett Browning [1852]

The elopement and move to Italy of Elizabeth Barrett (1806-1861) and Robert Browning (1812-1889) prevented Fuller's meeting them until autumn 1849. Despite her own spectacular middle-age romance Elizabeth reported she was taken "by surprise" when Fuller came to Florence "with a husband and child above a year old. Nobody had even suspected a word of this underplot, and her American friends stood in mute astonishment before this apparition of them here" (Henry James, *William Wetmore Story*, I, 130). But, Robert wrote, they conceived a "quick love and respect for her" and saw her several times, Ossoli less frequently (*Letters of Robert Browning*, collected by Thomas J. Wise, p. 33). Though Elizabeth's own republican ardor would grow in the coming decade, in 1850 she found Fuller's opinions wild and pictured an embattled woman: "Her face & soul were full of furrows, through continual wrestling with the world" (*Letters to Mrs. David Ogilvy*, eds., P.N. Heydon and P. Kelley, p. 31). And even in grief over her friend's death, she insisted Fuller's writings failed to do her justice ("Her written works are just naught. . . . Never read what she has written" [*Letters of Elizabeth Barrett Browning*, ed. F.G. Kenyon, II, 59]), always excepting the promised manuscript on Italy. The following letter was written to Mary Russell Mitford.

What still further depressed me during our latter days at Florence was the dreadful event in America – the loss of our poor friend Madame Ossoli, affecting in itself, and also through association with that past, when the arrowhead of anguish was broken too deeply into my life ever to be quite drawn out. Robert wanted to keep the news from me till I was stronger, but we live too *close* for him to keep anything from me, and then I should have known it from the first letter or visitor, so there was no use trying. The poor Ossolis spent part of their last evening in Italy with us, he and she and their child, and we had a note from her off Gibraltar, speaking of the captain's death from smallpox. Afterwards it appears that her child caught the disease and lay for days between life and death; *recovered*, and then came the final agony.

'Deep called unto deep,' indeed. Now she is where there is no more grief and 'no more sea;' and none of the restless in this world, none of the shipwrecked in heart ever seemed to me to want peace more than she did. We saw much of her last winter; and over a great gulf of differing opinion we both felt drawn strongly to her. High and pure aspiration she had – yes, and a tender woman's heart – and we honoured the truth and courage in her, rare in woman or man. The work she was preparing upon Italy would probably have been more equal to her faculty than anything previously produced by her pen (her other writings being curiously inferior to the impressions her conversation gave you); indeed, she told me it was the only production to which she had given time and labour. But, if rescued, the manuscript would be nothing but the raw material. I believe nothing was finished; nor, if finished, could the work have been otherwise than deeply coloured by those blood colours of Socialistic views, which would have drawn the wolves on her, with a still more howling enmity, both in England and America. Therefore it was better for her to go. Only God and a few friends can be expected to distinguish between the pure personality of a woman and her professed opinions. She was chiefly known in America, I believe, by oral lectures and a connection with the newspaper press, neither of them happy means of publicity. Was she happy in anything, I wonder? She told me that she never was. May God have made her happy in her death.

Such gloom she had in leaving Italy! So full she was of sad presentiment! Do you know she gave a *Bible* as a parting gift from her child to ours, writing in it "*In memory of* Angelo Eugene Ossoli" – a strange, prophetical expression? That last evening a prophecy was talked of jestingly – an old prophecy made to poor Marquis Ossoli, "that he should shun the sea, for that it would be fatal to him." I remember how she turned to me smiling and said, "Our ship is called the 'Elizabeth,' and I accept the omen." *[Letters of Elizabeth Barrett Browning, ed. F. G. Kenyon (New York: Macmillan, 1898), I, 459-60]*

6. The question of her marriage,
Ralph Waldo Emerson [1850-51]

"I have lost in her my audience"–with this scrawl in his journal, upon learning of Fuller's death, Emerson mourned an image of her that had actually faded years before. In writing Carlyle two weeks later, he looked almost coldly at what Fuller had become: "I doubt you never saw in her what was inestimable here. But she died in happy hour for herself. Her health was much exhausted. Her marriage would have taken her away from us all, & there was a subsistence yet to be secured, & diminished powers, & old age" (Rusk, *Letters*, IV, 224). Already he had talked with Channing about writing a life of Fuller, though, as he confessed to Ward, it would take considerable nerve: "I think it could really be done, if one would heroically devote himself, and a most vivacious book written, but it must be done *tête exaltée*, & in the tone of Spiridion, or even of Bettine, with the coolest ignoring of Mr Willis Mr Carlyle and Boston & London. . . . Nay, if for the glory & honour of Margaret such a hecatomb were prepared, and all scruples magnificently renounced, I think, when the first experiments came to be made, it might turn out to be a work above our courage" (*Letters*, IV, 222). There were difficulties obtaining materials and permission, and dilemmas of tact, but the problem of courage was the great one, and in a notebook Emerson kept for thinking through his memoir of Fuller, he confronted it head on in considering her marriage. The page of this notebook has been cut out after the mention of "Aglauron and Laurie," Fuller's work most critical of marriage. Very likely Emerson cited the passage in which a character speaks of the "sanctity" of marriage and praises it as "a means of bringing home to the mind the great idea of Duty."

Marriage W.H.C. fancied that M. had not married: that a legal tie was contrary to her view of a noble life. I, on the contrary, believed that she would speculate on this subject as all reformers do; but when it came to be a practical question to herself, she would feel that this was a tie which ought to have every solemnest sanction; that against the theorist was a vast public opinion, too vast to brave; an opinion of all nations & of all ages. See what she says in *Aglauron & Laurie*; which is as follows. [Page cut.] *[Emerson, Notebook on MFO]*

7. Chronology of her movements,
Ralph Waldo Emerson [1850-51]

At the end of his notebook, Emerson uses Fuller's letters to trace her activities. Rarely can we find such neat cancellation—here by the stroke of a pen through the word "perhaps"—of disturbing ambiguity.

. . . 1847 Jan 31 Paris
April 15 Rome May 7
1 July Florence
10 July Venice
Aug 9 Milan
26 Bellaggio Lake of Como
Sept 15 Florence at the Moziers
Oct 28 Rome 29 Oct *happy, alone,* & *free*
Nov 2 Rome
Rome of Dec 47 has spent sweetly 2 of the 6 mos she feels in Rome
House expenses $50 per month
16 Dec Rome
married ~~perhaps~~ in Oct. Nov. or Dec
1848 Jan 11 Rome
Rome, 25 Feb. 1848
17 March Rains & headach from 16 Dec
20 May 21 May goes to Rieti
July 3 Rieti
Rieti Sept 5 Angelo Eugene Ossoli was born . . .
[Emerson, Notebook on MFO]

8. Florentine gossip, Nathaniel Hawthorne, April 3, 1858

Hawthorne's reversal of feeling about Margaret Fuller was the opposite of Lowell's. From the affection of his record of their friendship in Concord in 1842 (III:2), Hawthorne moved to the malignant virtuosity of this passage written in a journal in Rome eight years after her death. It was suppressed by Sophia in her 1871 selection from Hawthorne's French and Italian notebooks, then published in 1884 by Julian, their son, in a new selection. Richard Fuller's son, Frederick, published a defense of his aunt, demonstrating that Hawthorne's informant, Mozier, was no intimate of Fuller's and contrasting the picture of Fuller and Ossoli drawn by those who were. Mozier's remarks about Ossoli's family and Fuller's literary development were simply wrong, and Mrs. Story's testimony about the Italian manuscript contradicts Mozier's. Sarah Clarke wrote that Mozier, a retired merchant turned sculptor, was an unscrupulous gossip driven by a desire to ingratiate himself with distinguished people (BPL MS). And Moncure Conway, who investigated in Rome the story of Ossoli's abysmal sculpture, found it to belong rather to "the career of one Germano, a poor and dishonest Italian whom Margaret had befriended until he was proved an imposter." (Mozier took Germano into his studio, possibly at her request, until it was learned that he had bought cheaply the work he was selling as his own and at extravagant prices.) Conway speculated that Mozier mentioned Germano to Hawthorne as an instance of Fuller's poor judgment, and that Julian had both incorrectly deciphered his father's notes and omitted an account of Mozier's attack on Fuller's moral character which alone could account for his father's vehemence (Transcript of Conway's letter from Rome, February 12, 1890, in hand of Arthur Fuller's daughter Edith, Houghton MS). Surely Fuller's frank response to sexual need lies at the heart of this assault. It is likely too that her combining sexual honesty with intellectual activity and political commitment in Rome was even more threatening to Hawthorne and that the ambivalence of his treatment of Zenobia in *The Blithedale Romance* (1852) reflects his response to what Fuller had become.

Despite the indignation of Fuller's friends, Julian offered no apology for exhuming this passage. In the *Boston Evening Transcript* of December 31, 1884, he boasted, "The majority of readers will, I think, not be inconsolable that poor Margaret Fuller has at last taken her place with the numberless other dismal frauds who fill the limbo of human pretension and failure." He was right about the majority, and the image Hawthorne sketched here has endured and

spawned scores of apocryphal tales as no image of Fuller's
defenders has done.

... [Mr. Mozier] called to see us last night, and talked for about two
hours in a very amusing and interesting style; his topics being taken
from his own personal experience, and shrewdly treated. He spoke
much of Greenough, whom he described as an excellent critic of art,
but possessed of not the slightest inventive genius. His statue of
Washington at the Capitol, is taken precisely from the Phidian Jupiter;
his Chanting Cherubs are copied in marble from two figures in a picture
by Raphael. He did nothing that was original with himself. From
Greenough, Mr. Mozier passed to Margaret Fuller, whom he knew well,
she having been an intimate of his during a part of her residence in
Italy. His developments about poor Margaret were very curious. He says
that Ossoli's family, though technically noble, is really of no rank
whatever; the elder brother, with the title of marquis, being at this very
time a working bricklayer, and the sisters walking the streets without
bonnets — that is, being in the station of peasant girls, in the female
populace of Rome. Ossoli himself, to the best of his belief, was
Margaret's servant, or had something to do with the care of her
apartments. He was the handsomest man whom Mr. Mozier ever saw,
but entirely ignorant even of his own language, scarcely able to read at
all, destitute of manners; in short, half an idiot, and without any
pretensions to be a gentleman. At Margaret's request, Mr. Mozier had
taken him into his studio, with a view to ascertain whether he was
capable of instruction in sculpture; but after four months' labor, Ossoli
produced a thing intended to be a copy of a human foot; but the "big
toe" was on the wrong side. He could not possibly have had the least
appreciation of Margaret, and the wonder is, what attraction she found
in this boor, this man without the intellectual spark — she that had
always shown such a cruel and bitter scorn of intellectual delinquency.
As from her towards him, I do not understand what feeling there could
have been, except it were purely sensual; as from him towards her,
there could hardly have been even this, for she had not the charm of
womanhood. But she was a woman anxious to try all things, and fill up
her experience in all directions; she had a strong and coarse nature, too,
which she had done her utmost to refine, with infinite pains, but which
of course could only be superficially changed. The solution of the
riddle lies in this direction; nor does one's conscience revolt at the idea

of thus solving it; for – at least, this is my own experience – Margaret has not left, in the heart and minds of those who knew her, any deep witness of her integrity and purity. She was a great humbug; of course with much talent, and much moral reality, or else she could not have been so great a humbug. But she had stuck herself full of borrowed qualities, which she chose to provide herself with, but which had no root in her.

Mr. Mozier added, that Margaret had quite lost all power of literary production, before she left Rome, though occasionally the charm and power of her conversation would reappear. To his certain knowledge, she had no important manuscripts with her when she sailed (she having shown him all she had, with a view to his securing their publication in America;) and the History of the Roman Revolution, about which there was so much lamentation, in the belief that it had been lost with her, never had existence. Thus there appears to have been a total collapse in poor Margaret, morally and intellectually; and tragic as her catastrophe was, Providence was, after all, kind in putting her, and her clownish husband, and their child, on board that fated ship. There never was such a tragedy as her whole story; the sadder and sterner, because so much of the ridiculous was mixed up with it, and because she could bear anything better than to be ridiculous. It was such an awful joke, that she should have resolved – in all sincerity, no doubt – to make herself the greatest, wisest, best woman of the age; and, to that end, she set to work on her strange, heavy, unpliable, and, in many respects, defective and evil nature, and adorned it with a mosaic of admirable qualities, such as she chose to possess; putting in here a splendid talent, and there a moral excellence, and polishing each separate piece, and the whole together, till it seemed to shine afar and dazzle all who saw it. She took credit to herself for having been her own Redeemer, if not her own Creator; and, indeed, she was far more a work of art than any of Mr. Mozier's statues. But she was not working on an inanimate substance, like marble or clay; there was something within her that she could not possibly come at, to re-create and refine it; and, by and by, this rude old potency bestirred itself, and undid all her labor in the twinkling of an eye. On the whole, I do not know but I like her the better for it, – the better, because she proved herself a very woman, after all, and fell as the weakest of her sisters might. *[The Portable Hawthorne, ed. Malcolm Cowley (New York: The Viking Press, 1948), pp. 594-97]*

9. *Meditation on her meaning, Henry James [1903]*

It is tempting to see Margaret Fuller lightly veiled in any
number of Henry James' characters—the mesmerizing or
predatory feminist, the expatriate lady with a dim,
scandalous past, the bold foreign correspondent, the young
American heroine seeking a richer freedom in Europe. James
was only seven when Fuller died, but his curiosity about his
predecessors, the pioneer Americans deliberately exiled in
Europe, was always vivid. It led him to write the life of
William Wetmore Story and his friends. "Among the ghosts
... of the little related, vanished world," none but Margaret
Fuller "looks out at me more directly and wistfully." It is
clearly as a ghost, to whet his imagination, that Fuller most
interested James, for he appeared ignorant of her republican
sympathies and repeated Elizabeth Browning's dismissal of
Fuller's writing. (Mrs. Browning's sense that Fuller's marriage
was an "underplot" also gives him his cue below.) We also
feel in this passage that even the few facts about Fuller he
knew were indigestible to his imagination and thus haunted
it.

... On March 24th, our kindly diarist [Emelyn Story] "went home
with Margaret and sat with her in her quiet little upper chamber all the
evening. W. came for me, and we stayed until a late hour of the night."
The unquestionably haunting Margaret-ghost, looking out from her
quiet little upper chamber at her lamentable doom, would perhaps be
never so much to be caught by us as on some such occasion as this.
What comes up is the wonderment of *why* she may, to any such degree,
be felt as haunting; together with other wonderments that brush us
unless we give them the go-by. It is not for this latter end that we are
thus engaged at all; so that, making the most of it, we ask ourselves
how, possibly, in our own luminous age, she would have affected us on
the stage of the "world," or as a candidate, if so we may put it, for the
cosmopolite crown. It matters only for the amusement of
evocation – since she left nothing behind her, her written utterance
being naught; but to what would she have corresponded, have
"rhymed," under categories actually known to us? Would she, in other
words, with her appetite for ideas and her genius for conversation, have

struck us but as a somewhat formidable bore, one of the worst kind, a culture-seeker without a sense of proportion, or, on the contrary, have affected us as a really attaching, a possibly picturesque New England Corinne?

Such speculations are, however, perhaps too idle; the *facts* of the appearance of this singular woman, who would, though conceit was imputed to her, doubtless have been surprised to know that talk may be still, after more than half a century, made about her — the facts have in themselves quite sufficient colour, and the fact in particular of her having achieved, so unaided and so ungraced, a sharp identity. This identity was that of the talker, the moral *improvisatrice*, or at least had been in her Boston days, when, young herself, she had been as a sparkling fountain to other thirsty young. In the Rome of many waters there were doubtless fountains that quenched, collectively, any individual gush; so that it would have been, naturally, for her plentiful life, her active courage and company, that the little set of friends with whom we are concerned valued her. She had bitten deeply into Rome, or, rather, *been*, like so many others, by the wolf of the Capitol, incurably bitten; she met the whole case with New England arts that show even yet, at our distance, as honest and touching; there might be ways for her of being vivid that were not as the ways of Boston. . . .

. . . The "underplot" was precisely another of the personal facts by which the lady could interest — the fact, that is, that her marriage should *be* an underplot, and that her husband, much *decaduto*, should make explanation difficult. These things, let alone the final catastrophe, in short, were not talk, but life, and life dealing with the somewhat angular Boston sibyl on its own free lines. All of which, the free lines overscoring the unlikely material, is doubtless partly why the Margaret-ghost, as I have ventured to call it, still unmistakably walks the old passages. . . . *[William Wetmore Story and his Friends, (Boston: Houghton, Mifflin & Co., 1903), I, 127-31]*

FULLER'S WRITINGS

10. On Genoa and Naples [April 1847]

Writing her first impressions of Naples for the *Tribune*, Fuller subscribed to the then typical tourist's distinction between eternal Italy and the degraded contemporary Italian. In the north, bad weather and Mazzini's contacts combined to reverse the judgment. (One of the passionate Genoese faces here praised belonged to Mazzini's mother, Maria. Fiercely devoted to her son, she was so taken by Fuller that she hinted to Mazzini that they should marry, forcing him to remind her of his vow of celibacy.)

The excessive beauty of Genoa is well known, and the impression upon the eye alone was correspondent with what I expected; but alas! the weather was still so cold I could not realize that I had actually touched those shores to which I had looked forward all my life, where it seemed that the heart would expand, and the whole nature be turned to delight. Seen by a cutting wind, the marble palaces, the gardens, the magnificent water-view of Genoa, failed to charm, – "I *saw, not felt*, how beautiful they were." Only at Naples have I found *my* Italy, and here not till after a week's waiting, – not till I began to believe that all I had heard in praise of the climate of Italy was fable, and that there is really no spring anywhere except in the imagination of poets. For the first week was an exact copy of the miseries of a New England spring; a bright sun came for an hour or two in the morning, just to coax you forth without your cloak, and then came up a villainous, horrible wind, exactly like the worst east wind of Boston, breaking the heart, racking the brain, and turning hope and fancy to an irrevocable green and yellow hue, in lieu of their native rose.

However, here at Naples I *have* at last found *my* Italy; I have passed through the Grotto of Pausilippo, visited Cuma, Baiae, and Capri, ascended Vesuvius, and found all familiar, except the sense of enchantment, of sweet exhilaration, this scene conveys.

"Behold how brightly breaks the morning!"

and yet all new, as if never yet described, for Nature here, most prolific and exuberant in her gifts, has touched them all with a charm unhackneyed, unhackneyable, which the boots of English dandies cannot trample out, nor the raptures of sentimental tourists daub or fade. Baiae had still a hid divinity for me, Vesuvius a fresh baptism of fire, and Sorrento — O Sorrento was beyond picture, beyond poesy, for the greatest Artist had been at work there in a temper beyond the reach of human art. . . .

At Genoa and Leghorn, I saw for the first time Italians in their homes. Very attractive I found them, charming women, refined men, eloquent and courteous. If the cold wind hid Italy, it could not the Italians. A little group of faces, each so full of character, dignity, and, what is so rare in an American face, the capacity for pure, exalting passion, will live ever in my memory, — the fulfilment of a hope! . . .

At Leghorn we changed the boat, and, retracing our steps, came now at last to Naples, — to this priest-ridden, misgoverned, full of dirty, degraded men and women, yet still most lovely Naples, — of which the most I can say is that the divine aspect of nature *can* make you forget the situation of man in this region, which was surely intended for him as a princely child, angelic in virtue, genius, and beauty, and not as a begging, vermin-haunted, image-kissing Lazzarone. [*At Home and Abroad*, pp. 217-19]

11. To Thomas Hicks, April 23, 1847

Soon after arriving in Rome, Fuller wrote this letter, which has never before been published, and whose immodesty and insistence has apparently embarrassed her biographers. Wanting to believe she was gentled by Italy, most of them have ignored the letter; the few who cite it omit or soften the more aggressive phrases and pass it off as a letter to Ossoli, glossing over the fact that he could not read English. Moreover, the existence in the Houghton Library of an unsigned letter which is clearly a reply to Fuller's letter has gone unremarked. The fact that Fuller wrote such an ardent letter to another man *after* meeting Ossoli (if indeed she met him during Easter week at the beginning of April as is generally believed) explodes the reassuring myth that her feeling for him was immediate and complete. With the utmost cordiality and regret, Fuller's correspondent replied on May 4:

> I would like to tell you all about myself, you would then see that there is but little fire in the hut and that could you enter you would find but a few embers on the hearth of a lonely ambitious man—one whose life has been as solitary as it is unknown—but at present I can tell you nothing. That great thoughts and the hope to do good deeds engross me, you have partly guessed, but my fate is as hidden from me as the lost names of the houses of Balbec.
>
> It was melancholy to read your thought that we shall know each other but a short time. But if we are kindred as you say, and our horoscope in some respects the same, now that we have met, can we ever be separated? You speak of my youth; is it by years then that *Life* is measured? Do you not perceive that my heart has grown gray? that the passion which sometimes lights my dull eye is like the smile found upon the lips of dead children? It is you who are young for every pulse of your being is full and warm with Love. Why would you be endeared to me? I am the child of autumn. . . . Do you not see that I cannot make you happy? May I hope not to offend you in writing so? *[Houghton MS]*

A postscript—"Kind enough to tell Eddy that I shall not be in the Studio today"—provided the clue which led me to other letters by Thomas Hicks, an American painter, and I found that the writing was by the same hand. Fuller met Hicks, who was, ironically, only twenty-three years old, when she first came to Rome; later she praised his work and his zeal for social reform in letters to an influential friend and to the *Tribune*. When she went to Rieti to have her baby, she sent her papers to Hicks for safekeeping. During the siege of Rome, he painted her portrait; after her death, he refused to part with it or her letters, which he told Ellen Channing were "sacredly confidential." In later years, Hicks became a prosperous portraitist, painting many famous people, including Lincoln and Harriet Beecher Stowe.

Dear Youth

You do not come to see me, so I can think of no way but this which is so awkward to pay the little debt of the other day. I do not know what you paid, if more than this money, you must tell me.

I do not understand why you do not seek me more, you said you were too hard at work and had not time. I tried to believe you, because you seem to me like one who always wishes to speak the truth exactly, but I could not. I can always find time to see any one I wish to; it seems to me it is the same with every one.

You are the only one whom I have seen here in whose eye I recognized one of my own kindred. I want to know and to love you and to have you love me: you said you have no friendliness of nature but that is not true; you are precisely one to need the music, the recognition of kindred minds. How can you let me pass you by, without full and free communication. I do not understand it, unless you are occupied by some other strong feeling. Very soon I must go from here, do not let me go without giving me some of your life. I wish this for both our sakes, for mine, because I have so lately been severed from congenial companionship, that I am suffering for want of it, for yours because I feel as if I had something precious to leave in your charge.

When we are together it does not seem to me, as if you were insensible to all this? Am I mistaken. Yet, after I had been with you, I could not meet you the next day as I wanted to, at the Palazzo Borghese I mean. I wanted to speak to you with frank affection, and I could not. Something prevents what is it? answer. [Houghton MS]

12. On the high tide of the Pope's popularity, May 1847

Hicks' rejection of Fuller was apparently eclipsed by her excitement over life in Rome. In her early enthusiasm for the rapport between the new Pope and the people, we note that her identification is with the Pope rather than the people. This passage is from a *Tribune* dispatch.

I have heard owls hoot in the Colosseum by moonlight, and they spoke more to the purpose than I ever heard any other voice upon that subject. I have seen all the pomps and shows of Holy Week in the church of St. Peter, and found them less imposing than an habitual acquaintance with the place, with processions of monks and nuns stealing in now and then, or the swell of vespers from some side chapel. I have ascended the dome, and seen thence Rome and its Campagna, its villas with their cypresses and pines serenely sad as nothing else in the world, and the fountains of the Vatican garden gushing hard by. I have been in the Subterranean to see a poor little boy introduced, much to his surprise, to the bosom of the Church; and then I have seen by torch-light the stone popes where they lie on their tombs, and the old mosaics, and virgins with gilt caps. It is all rich, and full, — very impressive in its way. St. Peter's must be to each one a separate poem.

The ceremonies of the Church have been numerous and splendid during our stay here; and they borrow unusual interest from the love and expectation inspired by the present Pontiff. He is a man of noble and good aspect, who, it is easy to see, has set his heart upon doing something solid for the benefit of man. But pensively, too, must one feel how hampered and inadequate are the means at his command to accomplish these ends. The Italians do not feel it, but deliver themselves, with all the vivacity of their temperament, to perpetual hurras, vivas, rockets, and torchlight processions. I often think how grave and sad must the Pope feel, as he sits alone and hears all this noise of expectation.

A week or two ago the Cardinal Secretary published a circular inviting the departments to measures which would give the people a sort of representative council. Nothing could seem more limited than this improvement, but it was a great measure for Rome. At night the Corso in which we live was illuminated, and many thousands passed through it in a torch-bearing procession. I saw them first assembled in the Piazza del Popolo, forming around its fountain a great circle of fire. Then, as a river of fire, they streamed slowly through the Corso, on their way to the Quirinal to thank the Pope, upbearing a banner on which the edict was printed. The stream of fire advanced slowly, with a perpetual surge-like sound of voices; the torches flashed on the animated Italian faces. I have never seen anything finer. Ascending the Quirinal they made it a mount of light. Bengal fires were thrown up, which cast their red and white light on the noble Greek figures of men and horses that reign over it. The Pope appeared on his balcony; the crowd shouted three vivas; he extended his arms; the crowd fell on their knees and received his benediction; he retired, and the torches were extinguished, and the multitude dispersed in an instant. *[At Home and Abroad, pp. 224-25]*

13. To William Henry Channing, May 7, 1847

This letter is among several written at the time which disclose a dramatic and conscious reworking of values, made necessary by Fuller's determination "to know the common people and to feel truly in Italy" and to better know herself.

I write not to you about these countries, of the famous people I see, of magnificent shows and places. All these things are only to me an illuminated margin on the text of my inward life. Earlier, they would have been more. Art is not important to me now. I like only what little I find that is transcendantly good, and even with that feel very familiar and calm. I take interest in the state of the people, their manners, the state of the race in them. I see the future dawning; it is in important aspects Fourier's future. But I like no Fourierites; they are terribly wearisome here in Europe; the tide of things does not wash through them as violently as with us, and they have time to run in the tread-mill of system. Still, they serve this great future which I shall not live to see. I must be born again. *[Memoirs, II, 209]*

14. On tributes to women in Italy, August 9, 1847

Although Fuller later expressed disappointment in most Italian women, whenever she found them in positions of strength or spotted any promise of it, as during her summer tour in 1847, she made enthusiastic notes; these items were in a *Tribune* dispatch.

Before reaching Perugia, I visited an Etrurian tomb, which is a little way off the road; it is said to be one of the finest in Etruria. The hill-side is full of them, but excavations are expensive, and not frequent. The effect of this one was beyond my expectations; in it were several female figures, very dignified and calm, as the dim lamp-light fell on them by

turns. The expression of these figures shows that the position of woman
in these states was noble. Their eagles' nests cherished well the female
eagle who kept watch in the eyrie. . . .

Passing from Florence, I came to Bologna, – learned Bologna;
indeed an Italian city, full of expression, of physiognomy, so to speak.
A woman should love Bologna, for there has the spark of intellect in
woman been cherished with reverent care. Not in former ages only, but
in this, Bologna raised a woman who was worthy to the dignities of its
University, and in their Certosa they proudly show the monument to
Matilda Tambroni, late Greek Professor there. Her letters, preserved by
her friends, are said to form a very valuable collection. In their
anatomical hall is the bust of a woman, Professor of Anatomy. In Art
they have had Properzia di Rossi, Elizabetta Sirani, Lavinia Fontana,
and delight to give their works a conspicuous place.

In other cities the men alone have their *Casino dei Nobili*, where
they give balls, *conversazioni*, and similar entertainments. Here women
have one, and are the soul of society.

In Milan, also, I see in the Ambrosian Library the bust of a female
mathematician. These things make me feel that, if the state of woman
in Italy is so depressed, yet a good-will toward a better is not wholly
wanting. Still more significant is the reverence to the Madonna and
innumerable female saints, who, if, like St. Teresa, they had intellect as
well as piety, became counsellors no less than comforters to the spirit
of men. *[At Home and Abroad, pp. 230, 232]*

15. *To Caroline Sturgis, August 22, 1847*

In this letter from Bellagio on Lake Como, Fuller's notions of
being "out of" the body and of a body transcendent may
puzzle the modern reader; her repudiation of pain and of
busy intellectuals will not. Revised and with mention of Mrs.
Greeley and the Springs omitted, this letter is in the *Memoirs*
(II, 216-17).

Dearest Carrie,

. . . I remember I wrote to you from Rome in the first weeks when I
was suffering terrible regrets and could not yet find myself at home in

Italy. I do not know whether you ever received that letter, but if not, I would not go back upon those things.

Rome was much poisoned for me so, but after a time, its genius triumphed and I became absorbed in its peculiar life. Again I suffered from parting, and have since resolved to return, and pass at least a part of the winter.

People may write and prate as they please about Rome, they cannot convey thus a portion of its spirit. It must be inhaled wholly, with the yielding of the whole heart. It is really something ⟨transcendental⟩ both spirit and body.

Those last glorious nights, in which I wandered about amid the old walls and columns, or sat by the fountains in the Piazza del Popolo, or by the river, were worth an age of pain both after and before only one hates pain in Italy.

Tuscany I did not like so well. It is a great place to study thoughts; the history of character and art. Indeed there I did really begin to study, as well as gaze and feel. But I did not like it. Florence is more in its spirit like Boston than like an Italian city. I knew a good many Italians, but they were busy and intellectual, not like those I had known before. But Florence is full of really good, really great pictures. There first I saw some of the great masters, Andrea del Sarto, in particular, one sees only there, and he is worth much. His wife, whom he always paints and for whom he was so infatuated reminds me of Mrs. Greely [sic]. She has just the same bad qualities, and in what is good the same wild nature, or the same of what is called deviltry. . . .

At Venice, the Springs left me, and it was high time, for I had become quite insupportable. I was always out of the body, and they, good friends, were *in.* I felt at times a wicked irritation against them for being the persons who took me away from France, which was no fault of theirs. Since I have been alone I have grown reasonable again, indeed in the first week floating about in [a] gondola, I seemed to find myself again. . . .

In Milan I stayed awhile and knew some radicals, young, and interested in ideas. Here, on the lake, I have fallen into contact with some of the high society, – duchesses, marquises, and the like. My friend here is a Marchioness who bears the name of *Visconti*; by my side I have formed connection with a fair and brilliant Polish lady, born Princess *Radzivill*. It is rather pleasant to come a little on the traces of

these famous histories; also, both these ladies take pleasure in telling me
of spheres so unlike mine, and do it well. . . . *[Houghton MS]*

16. On Austrian rule and need for revolution, October 1847

Returning from the lakes to Milan, Fuller found the city
elated by the arrival of a new pro-Italian archbishop and
outraged at the marching, on a flimsy pretext, of Austrian
troops across the border of Lombardy into the Papal States.
For the first time, in a dispatch to the *Tribune*, she spoke of
the inevitability of revolution.

The Austrian rule is always equally hated, and time, instead of melting
away differences, only makes them more glaring. The Austrian race
have no faculties that can ever enable them to understand the Italian
character; their policy, so well contrived to palsy and repress for a time,
cannot kill, and there is always a force at work underneath which shall
yet, and I think now before long, shake off the incubus. The Italian
nobility have always kept the invader at a distance; they have not been
at all seduced or corrupted by the lures of pleasure or power, but have
shown a passive patriotism highly honorable to them. In the middle
class ferments much thought, and there is a capacity for effort; in the
present system it cannot show itself, but it is there; thought ferments,
and will yet produce a wine that shall set the Lombard veins on fire
when the time for action shall arrive. The lower classes of the
population are in a dull state indeed. The censorship of the press
prevents all easy, natural ways of instructing them; there are no public
meetings, no free access to them by more instructed and aspiring minds.
The Austrian policy is to allow them a degree of material well-being,
and though so much wealth is drained from the country for the service
of the foreigners, yet enough must remain on these rich plains
comfortably to feed and clothe the inhabitants. Yet the great moral
influence of the Pope's action, though obstructed in their case, does
reach and rouse them, and they, too, felt the thrill of indignation at the
occupation of Ferrara. The base conduct of the police toward the
people, when, at Milan, some youths were resolute to sing the hymn in
honor of Pius IX., when the feasts for the Archbishop afforded so

legitimate an occasion, roused all the people to unwonted feeling. The nobles protested, and Austria had not courage to persist as usual. She could not sustain her police, who rushed upon a defenceless crowd, that had no share in what excited their displeasure, except by sympathy, and, driving them like sheep, wounded them *in the backs*. Austria feels that there is now no sympathy for her in these matters; that it is not the interest of the world to sustain her. Her policy is, indeed, too thoroughly organized to change except by revolution; its scope is to serve, first, a reigning family instead of the people; second, with the people to seek a physical in preference to an intellectual good; and, third, to prefer a seeming outward peace to an inward life. This policy may change its opposition from the tyrannical to the insidious; it can know no other change. Yet do I meet persons who call themselves Americans, – miserable, thoughtless Esaus, unworthy their high birthright, – who think that a mess of pottage can satisfy the wants of man, and that the Viennese listening to Strauss's waltzes, the Lombard peasant supping full of his polenta, is *happy enough*. Alas! I have the more reason to be ashamed of my countrymen that it is not among the poor, who have so much toil that there is little time to think, but those who are rich, who travel, – in body that is, they do not travel in mind. Absorbed at home by the lust of gain, the love of show, abroad they see only the equipages, the fine clothes, the food, – they have no heart for the idea, for the destiny of our own great nation: how can they feel the spirit that is struggling now in this and others of Europe? [*At Home and Abroad, pp. 239-40*]

17. On Rome and a National Guard for Florence, October 18, 1847

The Italians' response to the creation of a National Guard in Florence prompted Fuller's first comparison with the early days of the American Republic. She closed this letter by urging her fellow countrymen to offer some token of sympathy, suggesting, for instance, a cannon to be called the *Amerigo* or *Columbo* and "to be used by the Guard for salutes on festive occasions, if they should be so happy as to have no more serious need." (Such exhortations helped spur

the first mass meeting in America in support of Italian unity.
It took place on November 29 at the Broadway Tabernacle,
and Greeley was one of the sponsors.)

In the spring, when I came to Rome, the people were in the
intoxication of joy at the first serious measures of reform taken by the
Pope. I saw with pleasure their childlike joy and trust. With equal
pleasure I saw the Pope, who has not in his expression the signs of
intellectual greatness so much as of nobleness and tenderness of heart,
of large and liberal sympathies. Heart had spoken to heart between the
prince and the people; it was beautiful to see the immediate good
influence exerted by human feeling and generous designs, on the part of
a ruler. He had wished to be a father, and the Italians with that
readiness of genius that characterizes them, entered at once into the
relation; they, the Roman people, stigmatized by prejudice as so crafty
and ferocious, showed themselves children, eager to learn, quick to
obey, happy to confide.

Still doubts were always present whether all this joy was not
premature. The task undertaken by the Pope seemed to present
insuperable difficulties. It is never easy to put new wine into old
bottles, and our age is one where all things tend to a great crisis; not
merely to revolution, but to radical reform. From the people
themselves the help must come, and not from princes; in the new state
of things, there will be none but natural princes, great men. From the
aspirations of the general heart, from the teachings of conscience in
individuals, and not from an old ivy-covered church long since
undermined, corroded by time and gnawed by vermin, the help must
come. Rome, to resume her glory, must cease to be an ecclesiastical
capital; must renounce all this gorgeous mummery, whose poetry,
whose picture, charms no one more than myself, but whose meaning is
all of the past, and finds no echo in the future. Although I sympathized
warmly with the warm love of the people, the adulation of leading
writers, who were so willing to take all from the hand of the prince, of
the Church, as a gift and a bounty, instead of implying steadily that it
was the right of the people, was very repulsive to me. The moderate
party, like all who, in a transition state, manage affairs with a constant
eye to prudence, lacks dignity always in its expositions; it is
disagreeable and depressing to read them. . . .

I arrived in Florence, unhappily, too late for the great fête of the

12th of September, in honor of the grant of a National Guard. But I wept at the mere recital of the events of that day, which, if it should lead to no important results, must still be hallowed for ever in the memory of Italy, for the great and beautiful emotions that flooded the hearts of her children. The National Guard is hailed with no undue joy by Italians, as the earnest of progress, the first step toward truly national institutions and a representation of the people. Gratitude has done its natural work in their hearts; it has made them better. Some days before the fête were passed in reconciling all strifes, composing all differences between cities, districts, and individuals. They wished to drop all petty, all local differences, to wash away all stains, to bathe and prepare for a new great covenant of brotherly love, where each should act for the good of all. On that day they all embraced in sign of this, — strangers, foes, all exchanged the kiss of faith and love; they exchanged banners, as a token that they would fight for, would animate, one another. All was done in that beautiful poetic manner peculiar to this artist people; but it was the spirit, so great and tender, that melts my heart to think of. It was the spirit of true religion, — such, my Country! as, welling freshly from some great hearts in thy early hours, won for thee all of value that thou canst call thy own, whose groundwork is the assertion, still sublime though thou hast not been true to it, that all men have equal rights, and that these are *birth*-rights, derived from God alone.

I rejoice to say that the Americans took their share on this occasion, and that Greenough — one of the few Americans who, living in Italy, takes the pain to know whether it is alive or dead, who penetrates beyond the cheats of tradesmen and the cunning of a mob corrupted by centuries of slavery, to know the real mind, the vital blood, of Italy — took a leading part. I am sorry to say that a large portion of my countrymen here take the same slothful and prejudiced view as the English, and, after many years' sojourn, betray entire ignorance of Italian literature and Italian life, beyond what is attainable in a month's passage through the thoroughfares. . . . In reference to what I have said of many Americans in Italy, I will only add, that they talk about the corrupt and degenerate state of Italy as they do about that of our slaves at home. They come ready trained to that mode of reasoning which affirms that, because men are degraded by bad institutions, they are not fit for better. [*At Home and Abroad, pp. 242-43, 245-47*]

18. To Richard Fuller, October 29, 1847

Settled in cheap lodgings on Via del Corso and learning
Roman economies from Ossoli, Fuller reported to her
brother Richard, always her mainstay for financial help in
Europe. For the *Memoirs* (II, 221), the editors saw fit to
substitute for her unseemly and thrice reiterated happiness "I
. . . am contented" and to excise her pert reference to their
own class as "the mob." (Fuller's frequent reference to the
pleasure of being jostled by the "vivacious" and "good-
humored" Roman crowd must have been equally mysti-
fying.) Her last sentence was intended to comfort Richard,
who was breaking an engagement; and these were the words
that Emerson found so haunting and baffling to his wish to
see an honest woman in his dear friend (VI:7).

. . . I am trying all I can to economize in these little things, anxious to
keep the Roman expenses for six months within the limits of four
hundred dollars. Rome is not as cheap a place as Florence, but then I
would not give a pin to live in Florence. We have just had glorious times
with the October feasts, when all the Roman people were out. I am
now truly happy here really *in* Rome, so quiet and familiar; no longer,
like the mob, a staring, sight-seeing stranger, riding about finely dressed
in a coach to see the Muses and the Sibyls. I see these things now in the
natural manner, and am happy, yes I *am* happy here.

Goodbye, dear Richard, heaven bless you and show you how to
act. Keep free of false ties they are the curse of life, I find myself so
happy here, alone and free. *[Houghton MS]*

19. To Ralph Waldo Emerson, December 20, 1847

The struggle for subsistence combined with the drowsiness of
the first month of pregnancy (probably still unrecognized)
gave this letter its initially depressed tone. Fuller's
resentment of the need to exert herself and her curiously
prophetic image lend credence to the notion that she
submitted to drowning two and a half years later. Quarreling
with this interpretation is the resolute good sense of the
ending.

Nothing less than two or three years, free from care and forced labor, would heal all my hurts, and renew my life-blood at its source. Since Destiny will not grant me that, I hope she will not leave me long in the world, for I am tired of keeping myself up in the water without corks, and without strength to swim. I should like to go to sleep, and be born again into a state where my young life should not be prematurely taxed.

Italy has been glorious to me, and there have been hours in which I received the full benefit of the vision. In Rome, I have known some blessed, quiet days, when I could yield myself to be soothed and instructed by the great thoughts and memories of the place. But those days are swiftly passing. Soon I must begin to exert myself, for there is this incubus of the future, and none to help me, if I am not prudent to face it. So ridiculous, too, this mortal coil, – such small things!

I find how true was the lure that always drew me towards Europe. It was no false instinct that said I might here find an atmosphere to develop me in ways I need. Had I only come ten years earlier! Now my life must be a failure, so much strength has been wasted on abstractions, which only came because I grew not in the right soil. However, it is a less failure than with most others, and not worth thinking twice about. Heaven has room enough, and good chances in store, and I can live a great deal in the years that remain. *[Memoirs, II, 224-25]*

20. On Americans in Europe, abolitionists at home *[November 1847]*

In her New Year's letter for the *Tribune*, written in mid-November, Fuller caricatured the ignorance of most American tourists. (A fragment in the *Memoirs* [II, 222], surely her covering letter to Greeley for this dispatch, explained, "Since I have experienced the different atmosphere of the European mind, and been allied with it, nay, mingled in the bonds of love, I suffer more than ever from that which is peculiarly American or English.") But she found far warmer praise than before for the abolitionists and—perhaps with Mazzini's reinforcement—for dedicated youth.

The American in Europe, if a thinking mind, can only become more American. In some respects it is a great pleasure to be here. Although we have an independent political existence, our position toward Europe, as to literature and the arts, is still that of a colony, and one feels the same joy here that is experienced by the colonist in returning to the parent home. What was but picture to us becomes reality; remote allusions and derivations trouble no more: we see the pattern of the stuff, and understand the whole tapestry. There is a gradual clearing up on many points, and many baseless notions and crude fancies are dropped. Even the post-haste passage of the business American through the great cities, escorted by cheating couriers and ignorant *valets de place*, unable to hold intercourse with the natives of the country, and passing all his leisure hours with his countrymen, who know no more than himself, clears his mind of some mistakes, – lifts some mists from his horizon.

There are three species. First, the servile American, – a being utterly shallow, thoughtless, worthless. He comes abroad to spend his money and indulge his tastes. His object in Europe is to have fashionable clothes, good foreign cookery, to know some titled persons, and furnish himself with coffee-house gossip, by retailing which among those less travelled and as uninformed as himself he can win importance at home. I look with unspeakable contempt on this class, – a class which has all the thoughtlessness and partiality of the exclusive classes in Europe, without any of their refinement, or the chivalric feeling which still sparkles among them here and there. However, though these willing serfs in a free age do some little hurt, and cause some annoyance at present, they cannot continue long; our country is fated to a grand, independent existence, and, as its laws develop, these parasites of a bygone period must wither and drop away.

Then there is the conceited American, instinctively bristling and proud of – he knows not what. He does not see, not he, that the history of Humanity for many centuries is likely to have produced results it requires some training, some devotion, to appreciate and profit by. With his great clumsy hands, only fitted to work on a steam-engine, he seizes the old Cremona violin, makes it shriek with anguish in his grasp, and then declares he thought it was all humbug before he came, and now he knows it; that there is not really any music in these old things; that the frogs in one of our swamps make much finer, for they are young and alive. To him the etiquettes of courts and camps, the ritual of the Church, seem simply silly, — and no wonder, profoundly ignorant as he is of their origin and meaning. Just so the legends which are the subjects of pictures, the profound myths which are represented in the antique marbles, amaze and revolt him; as, indeed, such things need to be judged of by another standard than that of the Connecticut Blue-Laws. He criticises severely pictures, feeling quite sure that his natural senses are better means of judgment than the rules of connoisseurs, — not feeling that, to see such objects, mental vision as well as fleshly eyes are needed, and that something is aimed at in Art beyond the imitation of the commonest forms of Nature. This is Jonathan in the sprawling state, the booby truant, not yet aspiring enough to be a good schoolboy. Yet in his folly there is meaning; add thought and culture to his independence, and he will be a man of might: he is not a creature without hope, like the thick-skinned dandy of the class first specified.

The artistes form a class by themselves. Yet among them, though seeking special aims by special means, may also be found the lineaments of these two classes, as well as of the third, of which I am now to speak.

This is that of the thinking American, — a man who, recognizing the immense advantage of being born to a new world and on a virgin soil, yet does not wish one seed from the past to be lost. He is anxious to gather and carry back with him every plant that will bear a new climate and new culture. Some will dwindle; others will attain a bloom and stature unknown before. He wishes to gather them clean, free from noxious insects, and to give them a fair trial in his new world. And that he may know the conditions under which he may best place them in that new world, he does not neglect to study their history in this. . . .

. . . But we must stammer and blush when we speak of many things. I take pride here, that I can really say the liberty of the press works well, and that checks and balances are found naturally which suffice to its government. I can say that the minds of our people are alert, and that talent has a free chance to rise. This is much. But dare I further say that political ambition is not as darkly sullied as in other countries? Dare I say that men of most influence in political life are those who represent most virtue, or even intellectual power? Is it easy to find names in that career of which I can speak with enthusiasm? Must I not confess to a boundless lust of gain in my country? Must I not concede the weakest vanity, which bristles and blusters at each foolish taunt of the foreign press, and admit that the men who make these undignified rejoinders seek and find popularity so? Can I help admitting that there is as yet no antidote cordially adopted, which will defend even that great, rich country against the evils that have grown out of the commercial system in the Old World? Can I say our social laws are generally better, or show a nobler insight into the wants of man and woman? I do, indeed, say what I believe, that voluntary association for improvement in these particulars will be the grand means for my nation to grow, and give a nobler harmony to the coming age. But it is only of a small minority that I can say they as yet seriously take to heart these things; that they earnestly meditate on what is wanted for their country, for mankind, – for our cause is indeed the cause of all mankind at present. Could we succeed, really succeed, combine a deep religious love with practical development, the achievements of genius with the happiness of the multitude, we might believe man had now reached a commanding point in his ascent, and would stumble and faint no more. Then there is this horrible cancer of slavery, and the wicked war that has grown out of it. How dare I speak of these things here? I listen to the same arguments against the emancipation of Italy, that are used against the emancipation of our blacks; the same arguments in favor of the spoliation of Poland, as for the conquest of Mexico. I find the cause of tyranny and wrong everywhere the same, – and lo! my country! the darkest offender, because with the least excuse; forsworn to the high calling with which she was called; no champion of the rights of men, but a robber and a jailer; the scourge hid behind her banner; her eyes fixed, not on the stars, but on the possessions of other men.

How it pleases me here to think of the Abolitionists! I could never endure to be with them at home, they were so tedious, often so narrow, always so rabid and exaggerated in their tone. But, after all, they had a high motive, something eternal in their desire and life; and if it was not the only thing worth thinking of, it was really something worth living and dying for, to free a great nation from such a terrible blot, such a threatening plague. God strengthen them, and make them wise to achieve their purpose!

I please myself, too, with remembering some ardent souls among the American youth, who I trust will yet expand, and help to give soul to the huge, over-fed, too hastily grown-up body. May they be constant! "Were man but constant, he were perfect," it has been said; and it is true that he who could be constant to those moments in which he has been truly human, not brutal, not mechanical, is on the sure path to his perfection, and to effectual service of the universe.

It is to the youth that hope addresses itself; to those who yet burn with aspiration, who are not hardened in their sins. But I dare not expect too much of them. I am not very old; yet of those who, in life's morning, I saw touched by the light of a high hope, many have seceded. Some have become voluptuaries; some, mere family men, who think it quite life enough to win bread for half a dozen people, and treat them decently; others are lost through indolence and vacillation. Yet some remain constant;

> "I have witnessed many a shipwreck,
> Yet still beat noble hearts."

I have found many among the youth of England, of France, of Italy, also, full of high desire; but will they have courage and purity to fight the battle through in the sacred, the immortal band? Of some of them I believe it, and await the proof. If a few succeed amid the trial, we have not lived and loved in vain. [*At Home and Abroad, pp. 250-52, 254-56*]

21. On a nun taking the veil, December 30, 1847

In 1847, the Roman Christmas season blended the traditional religious ceremonies with political oratory and revolutionary enthusiasm over Verdi's inflammatory operas. Fuller's *Tribune* account of December 30 was cheerful except for her description of a novice taking the veil. No doubt her delight in Ossoli's intimacy informed her rage at this irreversible captivity.

On Sunday, I went to see a nun take the veil. She was a person of high family; a princess gave her away, and the Cardinal Ferreti, Secretary of State, officiated. It was a much less effective ceremony than I expected from the descriptions of travelers and romance-writers. There was no moment of throwing on the black veil; no peal of music; no salute of cannon. The nun, an elegantly dressed woman of five or six and twenty, − pretty enough, but whose quite worldly air gave the idea that it was one of those arrangements made because no suitable establishment could otherwise be given her, — came forward, knelt, and prayed; her confessor, in that strained, unnatural whine too common among preachers of all churches and all countries, praised himself for having induced her to enter on a path which would lead her fettered steps "from palm to palm, from triumph to triumph." Poor thing! she looked as if the domestic olives and poppies were all she wanted; and lacking these, tares and wormwood must be her portion. She was then taken behind a grating, her hair cut, and her clothes exchanged for the nun's vestments; the black-robed sisters who worked upon her looking like crows or ravens at their ominous feasts. All the while, the music played, first sweet and thoughtful, then triumphant strains. The effect on my mind was revolting and painful to the last degree. Were monastic seclusion always voluntary, and could it be ended whenever the mind required a change back from seclusion to common life, I should have nothing to say against it; there are positions of the mind which it suits exactly, and even characters that might choose it all through life; certainly, to the broken-hearted it presents a shelter that Protestant communities do not provide. But where it is enforced or repented of, no hell could be worse; nor can a more terrible responsibility be incurred than by him who has persuaded a novice that the snares of the world are less dangerous than the demons of solitude. [*At Home and Abroad*, pp. 271-72]

22. *To Caroline Sturgis Tappan, January 12, 1848*

A single record survives of Fuller's feelings upon discovering she was pregnant. Her confession is obscured by being imbedded in travelogue and by its melodramatic opacity of diction. The complaints were apparently so familiar that they did not awaken the suspicion of Caroline Sturgis, who was also distracted by her marriage one month before to William Tappan; Fuller did not explain herself to her confidante for another year.

My time in Lombardy and Switzerland was a series of beautiful pictures, dramatic episodes, not without some original life in myself. When I wrote to you from Como, I had a peaceful season. I floated on the lake with my graceful Polish countess, hearing her stories of heroic sorrow; or I walked in the delicious gardens of the villas, with many another summer friend. Red banners floated, children sang and shouted, the lakes of Venus and Diana glittered in the sun. The pretty girls of Bellaggio, with their coral necklaces, brought flowers to the "American countess," and "hoped she would be as happy as she deserved." Whether this cautious wish is fulfilled, I know not, but certainly I left all the glitter of life behind at Como.

My days at Milan were not unmarked. I have known some happy hours, but they all lead to sorrow; and not only the cups of wine, but of milk, seem drugged with poison for me. It does not *seem* to be my fault, this Destiny; I do not court these things, – they come. I am a poor magnet, with power to be wounded by the bodies I attract.

Leaving Milan, I had a brilliant day in Parma. I had not known Correggio before; he deserves all his fame. I stood in the parlor of the Abbess, the person for whom all was done, and Paradise seemed opened by the nymph, upon her car of light, and the divine children peeping through the vines. Sweet soul of love! I should weary of you, too; but it was glorious that day.

I had another good day, too, crossing the Apennines. The young crescent moon rose in orange twilight, just as I reached the highest peak. I was alone on foot; I heard no sound; I prayed.

At Florence, I was very ill. For three weeks, my life hung upon a thread. The effect of the Italian climate on my health is not favorable. I feel as if I had received a great injury. I am tired and woe-worn; often, in the bed, I wish I could weep my life away. However, they brought me gruel, I took it, and after a while rose up again. In the time of the vintage, I went alone to Sienna. This is a real untouched Italian place. This excursion, and the grapes, restored me at that time.

When I arrived in Rome, I was at first intoxicated to be here. The weather was beautiful, and many circumstances combined to place me in a kind of passive, childlike well-being. That is all over now, and, with this year, I enter upon a sphere of my destiny so difficult, that I, at present, see no way out, except through the gate of death. It is useless to write of it; you are at a distance and cannot help me; – whether accident or angel will, I have no intimation. I have no reason to hope I shall not reap what I have sown, and do not. Yet how I shall endure it I cannot guess; it is all a dark, sad enigma. The beautiful forms of art charm no more, and a love, in which there is all fondness, but no help, flatters in vain. I am all alone; nobody around me sees any of this. My

numerous friendly acquaintances are troubled if they see me ill, and
who so affectionate and kind as Mr. and Mrs. S[tory]? [*Memoirs, II,
231-33*]

23. To Costanza Arconati Visconti, January 14, 1848

Sharply contrasting with the morbid anxiety in her letter to
her best friend at home is the angry vivacity of this one to
her best friend abroad only two days later. Mazzini had
written and Fuller translated a widely circulated letter to Pius
IX urging him to lead a new Europe. "Do not contaminate
yourself with diplomacy, make no compact with fear, with
expediency, with the false doctrines of a *legality*, which is
merely a falsehood invented when faith failed," Mazzini
urged. "Do not fear excesses from the people once entered
upon this way; the people only commit excesses when left to
their own impulses without any guide whom they respect. Do
not pause before the idea of becoming a cause of war. . . .
The unity of Italy is a work of God. . . . It will be fulfilled,
with you or without you." (In private, the Pope is said to
have complained, "They want me to be a Napoleon, and I am
only a poor country parson" [G. O. Griffith, *Mazzini:
Prophet of Modern Europe*, p. 175].) It is hardly surprising
that the Countess Arconati wrote Fuller that she had found
Mazzini's letter "presumptuous," but she took no offense at
Fuller's reply below, and said only that she would try to love
Mazzini for her sake.

What black and foolish calumnies are these on Mazzini! It is as much
for his interest as his honor to let things take their course, at present.
To expect anything else, is to suppose him base. And on what act of his
life dares any one found such an insinuation? I do not wonder that you
were annoyed at his manner of addressing the Pope; but to me it seems
that he speaks as he should, — near God and beyond the tomb; not
from power to power, but from soul to soul, without regard to
temporal dignities. It must be admitted that the etiquette, Most Holy
Father, &c., jars with this. [*Memoirs, II, 233*]

24. On Sicilian insurrection and Roman weather, January 1848

The tension inherent in the political situation and in Fuller's personal life crackled in the frenetic and witty asperity of her second dispatch in January. (The orphan by her side in the church of Ara Coeli was Ossoli.)

Sicily is in full insurrection; and it is reported Naples, but this is not sure. There was a report, day before yesterday, that the poor, stupid king was already here, and had taken cheap chambers at the Hotel d'Allemagne, as, indeed, it is said he has always a turn for economy, when he cannot live at the expense of his suffering people. Day before yesterday, every carriage that the people saw with a stupid-looking man in it they did not know, they looked to see if it was not the royal runaway. But it was their wish was father to that thought, and it has not as yet taken body as fact. In like manner they report this week the death of Prince Metternich; but I believe it is not sure he is dead yet, only dying. With him passes one great embodiment of ill to Europe. As for Louis Philippe, he seems reserved to give the world daily more signal proofs of his base apostasy to the cause that placed him on the throne, and that heartless selfishness, of which his face alone bears witness to any one that has a mind to read it. . . .

To return to Rome: what a Rome! the fortieth day of rain, and damp, and abominable reeking odors, such as blessed cities swept by the sea-breeze — bitter sometimes, yet indeed a friend — never know. It has been dark all day, though the lamp has only been lit half an hour. The music of the day has been, first the atrocious *arias*, which last in the Corso till near noon, though certainly less in virulence on rainy days. Then came the wicked organ-grinder, who, apart from the horror of the noise, grinds exactly the same obsolete abominations as at home or in England, — the Copenhagen Waltz, "Home, sweet home," and all that! The cruel chance that both an English my-lady and a Councillor from one of the provinces live opposite, keeps him constantly before my window, hoping baiocchi. Within, the three pet dogs of my landlady, bereft of their walk, unable to employ their miserable legs and eyes, exercise themselves by a continual barking, which is answered by all the dogs in the neighborhood. An urchin returning from the laundress, delighted with the symphony, lays down his white bundle in the gutter, seats himself on the curb-stone, and attempts an imitation of the music of cats as a tribute to the concert. The door-bell rings. *Chi è?* "Who is it?" cries the handmaid, with unweariable senselessness, as if any one would answer, *Rogue*, or *Enemy*, instead of the traditionary *Amico, Friend*. Can it be, perchance, a letter, news of home, or some of the many friends who have neglected so long to write, or some ray of hope to break the clouds of the difficult Future? Far from it. Enter a man poisoning me at once with the smell of the worst possible cigars, not to be driven out, insisting I shall look upon frightful, ill-cut cameos, and worse-designed mosaics, made by some friend of his, who works in a chamber and will sell *so* cheap. Man of ill-odors and meanest smile! I am no Countess to be fooled by you. For dogs they were not even — dog-cheap.

A faint and misty gleam of sun greeted the day on which there was the feast to the Bambino, the most venerated doll of Rome. This is the famous image of the infant Jesus, reputed to be made of wood from a tree of Palestine, and which, being taken away from its present abode, — the church of Ara Coeli, — returned by itself, making the bells ring as it sought admittance at the door. It is this which is carried in extreme cases to the bedside of the sick. It has received more splendid gifts than any other idol. An orphan by my side, now struggling with difficulties, showed me on its breast a splendid jewel, which a doting grandmother thought more likely to benefit her soul if given to the Bambino, than if turned into money to give her grandchildren education and prospects in life. The same old lady left her vineyard, not to these children, but to her confessor, a well-endowed Monsignor, who occasionally asks this youth, his godson, to dinner! Children so placed are not quite such devotees to Catholicism as the new proselytes of America; — they are not so much patted on the head, and things do not show to them under quite the same silver veil. . . .

January 22, 2 o'clock, P.M.
Pour, pour, pour again, dark as night, — many people coming in to see me because they don't know what to do with themselves. I am very glad to see them for the same reason; this atmosphere is so heavy, I seem to carry the weight of the world on my head and feel unfitted for every exertion. As to eating, that is a bygone thing; wine, coffee, meat, I have resigned; vegetables are few and hard to have, except horrible

cabbage, in which the Romans delight. A little rice still remains, which I take with pleasure, remembering it growing in the rich fields of Lombardy, so green and full of glorious light. That light fell still more beautiful on the tall plantations of hemp, but it is dangerous just at present to think of what is made from hemp. . . .

This morning authentic news is received from Naples. The king, when assured by his own brother that Sicily was in a state of irresistible revolt, and that even the women quelled the troops, – showering on them stones, furniture, boiling oil, such means of warfare as the household may easily furnish to a thoughtful matron, – had, first, a stroke of apoplexy, from which the loss of a good deal of bad blood relieved him. His mind apparently having become clearer thereby, he has offered his subjects an amnesty and terms of reform, which, it is hoped, will arrive before his troops have begun to bombard the cities in obedience to earlier orders. [*At Home and Abroad*, pp. 296-301]

25. On revolution in Paris and Milan, March 29 and April 1, 1848

The February revolution in Paris inspired in Fuller her fiercest praise for class struggle and her first suggestion that her country had more to learn from it than from the American revolutionary past. The March rising in Milan exposed the insupportably divided loyalties of Pius IX; no sooner had the Italian in him rapturously blessed the troops marching against the Austrians in Milan than the Pope in him realized with anguish that he was warring against fellow Catholics.

This happened last week. The news of the dethronement of Louis Philippe reached us just after the close of the Carnival. It was just a year from my leaving Paris. I did not think, as I looked with such disgust on the empire of sham he had established in France, and saw the soul of the people imprisoned and held fast as in an iron vice, that it would burst its chains so soon. Whatever be the result, France has done gloriously; she has declared that she will not be satisfied with pretexts while there are facts in the world, – that to stop her march is a vain attempt, though the onward path be dangerous and difficult. It is vain to cry, Peace! peace! when there is no peace. The news from France, in these days, sounds ominous, though still vague. It would appear that the political is being merged in the social struggle: it is well. Whatever blood is to be shed, whatever altars cast down, those tremendous problems *must* be solved, whatever be the cost! That cost cannot fail to break many a bank, many a heart, in Europe, before the good can bud again out of a mighty corruption. To you, people of America, it may perhaps be given to look on and learn in time for a preventive wisdom. You may learn the real meaning of the words *Fraternity, Equality*: you may, despite the apes of the past who strive to tutor you, learn the needs of a true democracy. You may in time learn to reverence, learn to guard, the true aristocracy of a nation, the only really nobles, – the *Laboring Classes*.

And Metternich, too, is crushed; the seed of the woman has had his foot on the serpent. I have seen the Austrian arms dragged through the streets of Rome and burned in the Piazza del Popolo. The Italians embraced one another, and cried, *Miracolo! Providenza!* the modern Tribune Ciceronacchio fed the flame with faggots; Adam Mickiewicz, the great poet of Poland, long exiled from his country or the hopes of a country, looked on, while Polish women, exiled too, or who perhaps, like one nun who is here, had been daily scourged by the orders of a tyrant, brought little pieces that had been scattered in the street and threw them into the flames, – an offering received by the Italians with loud plaudits. It was a transport of the people, who found no way to vent their joy, but the symbol, the poesy, natural to the Italian mind. The ever-too-wise "upper classes" regret it, and the Germans choose to resent it as an insult to Germany; but it was nothing of the kind; the insult was to the prisons of Spielberg, to those who commanded the massacres of Milan, – a base tyranny little congenial to the native German heart, as the true Germans of Germany are at this moment showing by their resolves, by their struggles.

When the double-headed eagle was pulled down from above the lofty portal of the Palazzo di Venezia, the people placed there in its stead one of white and gold, inscribed with the name *Alta Italia*, and quick upon the emblem followed the news that Milan was fighting against her tyrants, – that Venice had driven them out and freed from their prisons the courageous Protestants in favor of truth, Tommaso and Manin, – that Manin, descendant of the last Doge, had raised the republican banner on the Place St. Mark, – and that Modena, that Parma, were driving out the unfeeling and imbecile creatures who had mocked Heaven and man by the pretence of government there.

With indescribable rapture these tidings were received in Rome. Men were seen dancing, women weeping with joy along the street. The youth rushed to enroll themselves in regiments to go to the frontier. In the Colosseum their names were received. Father Gavazzi, a truly patriotic monk, gave them the cross to carry on a new, a better, because defensive, crusade. Sterbini, long exiled, addressed them. He said: "Romans, do you wish to go; do you wish to go with all your hearts? If so, you *may*, and those who do not wish to go themselves may give money. To those who will go, the government gives bread and fifteen baiocchi a day." The people cried: "We wish to go, but we do not wish so much; the government is very poor; we can live on a paul a day." The princes answered by giving, one sixty thousand, others twenty, fifteen, ten thousand dollars. The people responded by giving at the benches which are opened in the piazzas literally everything; street-pedlers gave the gains of each day; women gave every ornament, – from the splendid necklace and bracelet down to the poorest bit of coral; servant-girls gave five pauls, two pauls, even half a paul, if they had no more. A man all in rags gave two pauls. "It is," said he, "all I have." "Then," said Torlonia, "take from me this dollar." The man of rags thanked him warmly, and handed that also to the bench, which refused to receive it. "No! *that* must stay with you," shouted all present. These are the people whom the traveller accuses of being unable to rise above selfish considerations; – a nation rich and glorious by nature, capable, like all nations, all men, of being degraded by slavery, capable, as are few nations, few men, of kindling into pure flame at the touch of a ray from the Sun of Truth, of Life.

The two or three days that followed, the troops were marching about by detachments, followed always by the people, to the Ponte Molle, often farther. The women wept; for the habits of the Romans are so domestic, that it seemed a great thing to have their sons and lovers gone even for a few months. The English – or at least those of the illiberal, bristling nature too often met here, which casts out its porcupine quills against everything like enthusiasm (of the more generous Saxon blood I know some noble examples) – laughed at all this. They have said that this people would not fight; when the

Sicilians, men and women, did so nobly, they said: "O, the Sicilians are quite unlike the Italians; you will see, when the struggle comes on in Lombardy, they cannot resist the Austrian force a moment." I said: "That force is only physical; do not you think a sentiment can sustain them?" They replied: "All stuff and poetry; it will fade the moment their blood flows." When the news came that the Milanese, men and women, fight as the Sicilians did, they said: "Well, the Lombards are a better race, but these Romans are good for nothing. It is a farce for a Roman to try to walk even; they never walk a mile; they will not be able to support the first day's march of thirty miles, and not have their usual *minéstra* to eat either." Now the troops were not willing to wait for the government to make the necessary arrangements for their march, so at the first night's station – Monterosi – they did *not* find food or bedding; yet the second night, at Civita Castellana, they were so well alive as to remain dancing and vivaing Pio Nono in the piazza till after midnight. No, Gentlemen, soul is not quite nothing, if matter be a clog upon its transports.

The Americans show a better, warmer feeling than they did; the meeting in New York was of use in instructing the Americans abroad! [*At Home and Abroad*, pp. 305-308]

26. To William Henry Channing, March 22, 1848

To Channing she wrote how the European revolutions fulfilled her personally and first hinted that she contemplated writing their history.

I have been engrossed, stunned almost, by the public events that have succeeded one another with such rapidity and grandeur. It is a time such as I always dreamed of, and for long secretly hoped to see. I rejoice to be in Europe at this time, and shall return possessed of a great history. Perhaps I shall be called to act. At present, I know not where to go, what to do. War is everywhere. I cannot leave Rome, and the men of Rome are marching out every day into Lombardy. The citadel of Milan is in the hands of my friends, Guerriere, &c., but there may be need to spill much blood yet in Italy. France and Germany are not in such a state that I can go there now. A glorious flame burns higher and higher in the heart of the nations. [*Memoirs*, II, 235]

27. On Mazzini's return from exile, April 19, 1848

In the *Tribune*, Fuller celebrated Mazzini's return to Milan
after the "Five Glorious Days." Weeping at the sight of two
thousand deserters from the Austrian army, Mazzini found
the people sublime and far beyond the warring workers of
Paris. But Fuller, in the flush of her unelaborated socialism,
found Mazzini lacking.

It is a glorious time too for the exiles who return, and reap even a
momentary fruit of their long sorrows. Mazzini has been able to return
from his seventeen years' exile, during which there was no hour, night
or day, that the thought of Italy was banished from his heart, – no
possible effort that he did not make to achieve the emancipation of his
people, and with it the progress of mankind. He returns, like
Wordsworth's great man, "to see what he foresaw." He will see his
predictions accomplishing yet for a long time, for Mazzini has a mind
far in advance of his times in general, and his nation in particular, – a
mind that will be best revered and understood when the "illustrious
Gioberti" shall be remembered as a pompous verbose charlatan, with
just talent enough to catch the echo from the advancing wave of his
day, but without any true sight of the wants of man at this epoch. And
yet Mazzini sees not all: he aims at political emancipation; but he sees
not, perhaps would deny, the bearing of some events, which even now
began to work their way. Of this, more anon; but not to-day, nor in the
small print of the Tribune. Suffice it to say, I allude to that of which
the cry of Communism, the systems of Fourier, &c., are but
forerunners. Mazzini sees much already, – at Milan, where he is, he has
probably this day received the intelligence of the accomplishment of his
foresight, implied in his letter to the Pope, which angered Italy by what
was thought its tone of irreverence and doubt, some six months since.
[*At Home and Abroad*, p. 320]

28. On the Pope's retreat from revolution,
May 7 and 13, 1848

Resuming her *Tribune* dispatch in May, Fuller summarized
the Pope's career of equivocation, which reached crisis

proportions after the Roman troops had left for Milan and
culminated in his infamous Allocution of April 29. From his
surrender of leadership she derived hope for a new order. Her
last dispatch for six months—written just before leaving
Rome to bear her child in the hills—she ended it on a note of
tender anticipation.

Thus affairs went on from day to day, – the Pope kissing the foot of
the brazen Jupiter and blessing palms of straw at St. Peter's; the *Circolo
Romano* erecting itself into a kind of Jacobin Club, dictating
programmes for an Italian Diet-General, and choosing committees to
provide for the expenses of the war; the Civic Guard arresting people
who tried to make mobs as if famishing, and, being searched, were
found well provided both with arms and money; the ministry at their
wits' end, with their trunks packed up ready to be off at a moment's
warning, – when the report, it is not yet known whether true or false,
that one of the Roman Civic Guard, a well-known artist engaged in the
war of Lombardy, had been taken and hung by the Austrians as a
brigand, roused the people to a sense of the position of their friends,
and they went to the Pope to demand that he should take a decisive
stand, and declare war against the Austrians.

The Pope summoned, a consistory; the people waited anxiously,
for expressions of his were reported, as if the troops ought not to have
thought of leaving the frontier, while every man, woman, and child in
Rome knew, and every letter and bulletin declared, that all their
thought was to render active aid to the cause of Italian independence.
This anxious doubt, however, had not prepared at all for the excess to
which they were to be disappointed.

The speech of the Pope declared, that he had never any thought of
the great results which had followed his actions; that he had only
intended local reforms, such as had previously been suggested by the
potentates of Europe; that he regretted the *mis*use which had been
made of his name; and wound up by lamenting over the war, – dear to
every Italian heart as the best and holiest cause in which for ages they
had been called to embark their hopes, – as if it was something
offensive to the spirit of religion, and which he would fain see hushed
up, and its motives smoothed out and ironed over.

A momentary stupefaction followed this astounding performance,
succeeded by a passion of indignation, in which the words *traitor* and

imbecile were associated with the name that had been so dear to his people. This again yielded to a settled grief: they felt that he was betrayed, but no traitor; timid and weak, but still a sovereign whom they had adored, and a man who had brought them much good, which could not be quite destroyed by his wishing to disown it. Even of this fact they had no time to stop and think; the necessity was too imminent of obviating the worst consequences of this ill; and the first thought was to prevent the news leaving Rome, to dishearten the provinces and army, before they had tried to persuade the Pontiff to wiser resolves, or, if this could not be, to supersede his power.

I cannot repress my admiration at the gentleness, clearness, and good sense with which the Roman people acted under these most difficult circumstances. It was astonishing to see the clear understanding which animated the crowd as one man, and the decision with which they acted to effect their purpose. Wonderfully has this people been developed within a year!

The Pope, besieged by deputations, who mildly but firmly showed him that, if he persisted, the temporal power must be placed in other hands, his ears filled with reports of Cardinals, "such venerable persons," as he pathetically styles them, would not yield in spirit, though compelled to in act. After two days' struggle, he was obliged to place the power in the hands of the persons most opposed to him, and nominally acquiesce in their proceedings, while in his second proclamation, very touching from the sweetness of its tone, he shows a fixed misunderstanding of the cause at issue, which leaves no hope of his ever again being more than a name or an effigy in their affairs. . . .

These events make indeed a crisis. The work begun by Napoleon is finished. There will never more be really a Pope, but only the effigy or simulacrum of one.

The loss of Pius IX. is for the moment a great one. His name had real moral weight, — was a trumpet appeal to sentiment. It is not the same with any man that is left. There is not one that can be truly a leader in the Roman dominion, not one who has even great intellectual weight.

The responsibility of events now lies wholly with the people, and that wave of thought which has begun to pervade them. Sovereigns and statesmen will go where they are carried; it is probable power will be changed continually from hand to hand, and government become, to all intents and purposes, representative. Italy needs now quite to throw aside her stupid king of Naples, who hangs like a dead weight on her movements. The king of Sardinia and the Grand Duke of Tuscany will be trusted while they keep their present course; but who can feel sure of any sovereign, now that Louis Philippe has shown himself so mad and Pius IX. so blind? It seems as if fate was at work to bewilder and cast down the dignities of the world and democratize society at a blow. . . .

. . . While all that was lovely and generous in his life is prized and reverenced, deep instruction may be drawn from his errors as to the inevitable dangers of a priestly or a princely environment, and a higher knowledge may elevate a nobler commonwealth than the world has yet known.

Hoping this era, I remain at present here. Should my hopes be dashed to the ground, it will not change my faith, but the struggle for its manifestation is to me of vital interest. My friends write to urge my return; they talk of our country as the land of the future. It is so, but that spirit which made it all it is of value in my eyes, which gave all of hope with which I can sympathize for that future, is more alive here at present than in America. My country is at present spoiled by prosperity, stupid with the lust of gain, soiled by crime in its willing perpetuation of slavery, shamed by an unjust war, noble sentiment much forgotten even by individuals, the aims of politicians selfish or petty, the literature frivolous and venal. In Europe, amid the teachings of adversity, a nobler spirit is struggling, – a spirit which cheers and animates mine. I hear earnest words of pure faith and love. I see deeds of brotherhood. This is what makes *my* America. I do not deeply distrust my country. She is not dead, but in my time she sleepeth, and the spirit of our fathers flames no more, but lies hid beneath the ashes. It will not be so long; bodies cannot live when the soul gets too overgrown with gluttony and falsehood. But it is not the making a President out of the Mexican war that would make me wish to come back. Here things are before my eyes worth recording, and, if I cannot help this work, I would gladly be its historian.

May 13.

Returning from a little tour in the Alban Mount, where everything looks so glorious this glorious spring, I find a temporary quiet. The Pope's brothers have come to sympathize with him; the crowd sighs over what he has done, presents him with great bouquets of flowers, and reads anxiously the news from the north and the proclamations of the new ministry. Meanwhile the nightingales sing; every tree and plant is in flower, and the sun and moon shine as if paradise were already re-established on earth. I go to one of the villas to dream it is so, beneath the pale light of the stars. *[At Home and Abroad, pp. 323-27]*

29. To Ralph Waldo Emerson, May 19, 1848

In December, Mazzini had written Fuller that he planned to visit Emerson, who was lecturing in Great Britain at the time. Mazzini admitted he was fearful that Emerson "will lead man too much to contemplation," which, however necessary for America, was wrong for "our own old World" where a Peter the Hermit was wanted "to appeal to the *collective* influences" (Emma Detti, *Margaret Fuller Ossoli e i suoi Corrispondenti*, p. 273). While in Europe, Emerson wrote three times offering Fuller escort home ("How much your letter made me wish to say, come live with me at Concord" [Rusk, *Letters*, IV, 28]). For Fuller such a reunion was improbable in the extreme; even as she wrote this reply she was packing to flee the inquisitive eyes of her Roman neighbors.

I should like to return with you, but I have much to do and learn in Europe yet. I am deeply interested in this public drama, and wish to see it *played out*. Methinks I have *my part* therein, either as actor or historian.

I cannot marvel at your readiness to close the book of European society. The shifting scenes entertain poorly. The flux of thought and feeling leaves some fertilizing soil; but for me, few indeed are the persons I should wish to see again; nor do I care to push the inquiry further. The simplest and most retired life would now please me, only I would not like to be confined to it, in case I grew weary, and now and then craved variety, for exhilaration. I want some scenes of natural beauty, and, imperfect as love is, I want human beings to love, as I suffocate without. For intellectual stimulus, books would mainly supply it, when wanted.

Why did you not try to be in Paris at the opening of the Assembly? There were elements worth scanning. *[Memoirs, II, 239]*

30. To Constanza Arconati Visconti, May 27, 1848

Even her last side trips to the lovely towns outside Rome fed
Fuller's political preoccupations; in her letter to Arconati she
risks offense, predicting the defeat of Orioli, an editor of a
moderate journal, and Mamiani (Pius' minister since he
reversed himself), who hoped to keep the republicans at bay
by shaping a truly constitutional monarchy.

This is my last day at Rome. I have been passing several days at Subiaco
and Tivoli, and return again to the country to-morrow. These scenes of
natural beauty have filled my heart, and increased, if possible,
my desire that the people who have this rich inheritance may no longer
be deprived of its benefits by bad institutions.

The people of Subiaco are poor, though very industrious, and
cultivating every inch of ground, with even English care and
neatness; – so ignorant and uncultivated, while so finely and strongly
made by Nature. May God grant now, to this people, what they need!

An illumination took place last night, in honor of the "Illustrious
Gioberti." He is received here with great triumph, his carriage followed
with shouts of *"Viva Gioberti, morte ai Jesuiti!"* which must be pain to
the many Jesuits, who, it is said, still linger here in disguise. His
triumphs are shared by Mamiani and Orioli, self-trumpeted celebrities,
self-constituted rulers of the Roman states, – men of straw, to my
mind, whom the fire already kindled will burn into a handful of ashes.

I sit in my obscure corner, and watch the progress of events. It is
the position that pleases me best, and, I believe, the most favorable one.
Everything confirms me in my radicalism; and, without any desire to
hasten matters, indeed with surprise to see them rush so like a torrent, I
seem to see them all tending to realize my own hopes.

My health and spirits now much restored, I am beginning to set
down some of my impressions. I am going into the mountains, hoping
there to find pure, strengthening air, and tranquillity for so many days
as to allow me to do something. *[Memoirs, II, 240-41]*

31. To Giovanni Angelo Ossoli, August 22, 1848

While Ossoli and the Civic Guard were waiting in Rome for a
sign (which never came) from the Pope to march north and

deliver the Bolognesi from the invading Austrians, Fuller was waiting in Rieti to deliver her child. Writing after false labor, she begged Ossoli to visit the *caffè* frequented by republicans to seek news of the young leaders of fallen Milan. (Fuller's Italian, like Ossoli's, is ridden with errors.)

I am a little better, dear, but if I can spend the day like this, suffering less, it annoys me though that it seems to mean I must wait still longer.

Wait!! How boring always. But − if I were sure of being all right, I would much prefer to go through this ordeal before your arrival, but when I think that I could die alone without being able to touch a dear hand, I want to wait some more. So I hope for your presence Saturday morning.

I see by the papers that the Pope is holding up the departure of the troops, he is acting as I expected, and I am very glad that you are not joining up yet. Soon these matters will be more certain; you will be able to make decisions more advantageously than now.

See if you hear any details of Milan, wouldn't it be possible in the Caffè degli Belle Arti. I'm very unhappy about the fate of these friends, how they must be suffering now.

I'm also thinking so much of you, I hope that you are less tormented, if we were together it would be a consolation. Now everything is going badly, but it's not possible that it can go this way always, always. Goodbye, my love. I am sorry that so many days must pass before you come, so many, so many. I am glad that I now have the little portrait, I look at it often. May God protect you. *[Houghton MS in Italian; my translation]*

32. To Giovanni Angelo Ossoli, October 15, 1848

Six weeks after the birth of Angelino, as his parents called him, news of Mary Rotch's death heightened Fuller's anxiety about everything: money; her landlord, Giovanni, in Rieti who was "trying *to corrupt* Chiara," the nurse; the legal snarl over baptizing her baby, the anguishing thought of leaving him to resume work in Rome. Twelve days after writing the letter below, she felt the need and capacity for suspending maternal happiness, telling Ossoli: "I also need to be with

you and to go another time into the world from which I have
been absent five months now."

My love,

One of the letters you sent me informs me of the death of the old lady
my friend of whom I have spoken to you so often. I have wept so much
it had made me ill, but I could not help it. There was not in the world a
person more good, more affectionate to me. I have lost a very good
friend. The other letters are important, I will tell you of them when
you come.

Think always, in seeking a house for me, not to pledge me to stay
in Rome. It seems to me often that I cannot stay long without seeing
the baby. He is so dear and life seems to me so uncertain; I do not
know how to leave my dear ones. Take the apartments for a short time.
I need to be in Rome at least a month to write and also to be near you,
but I want to be free to return here, if I feel too anxious for him, too
miserable.

O love, how difficult is life! But you, you are good, if it were only
possible for me to make you happy!

The banker has given me receipts in his letter. Also he wishes to
receive the enclosed immediately, will you see that he has it right away;
and as to my signature for a bill of exchange in Paris, he says the sooner
I send it the better he can do for me.

Do not think for a moment of Giovanni as godfather. It would be,
I think, to trust him too far. I do not think him worthy. It is better for
you to trust in some one your equal who, like a gentleman will keep
your secret. More another time from your M.

Write immediately that you have received this yesterday the baby
seemed to suffer and was troublesome but today he is well and so
beautiful.

I have something curious to tell you of Giovanni when you come.

[Houghton MS in Italian; my translation]

*33. On defeat in the north and
Charles Albert, December 2, 1848*

In picking up her pen for the *Tribune* in December, Fuller
swiftly recapitulated the collapse, beginning in May, of the

war with Austria. She shrewdly foresaw the dangers of the antagonism developed between the troops of Naples and the people of the Papal States and in her harsh analysis of Charles Albert, king of Piedmont, foreshadows his second defeat in the spring of 1849.

... The Roman volunteers received the astounding news that they were not to expect protection or countenance from their prince; all the army stood aghast, that they were no longer to fight in the name of Pio. It had been so dear, so sweet, to love and really reverence the head of their Church, so inspiring to find their religion for once in accordance with the aspirations of the soul! They were to be deprived, too, of the aid of the disciplined Neapolitan troops and their artillery, on which they had counted. How cunningly all this was contrived to cause dissension and dismay may easily be seen.

The Neapolitan General Pepe nobly refused to obey, and called on the troops to remain with him. They wavered; but they are a pampered army, personally much attached to the king, who pays them well and indulges them at the expense of his people, that they may be his support against that people when in a throe of nature it rises and strives for its rights. For the same reason, the sentiment of patriotism was little diffused among them in comparison with the other troops. And the alternative presented was one in which it required a very clear sense of higher duty to act against habit. Generally, after wavering awhile, they obeyed and returned. The Roman States, which had received them with so many testimonials of affection and honor, on their retreat were not slack to show a correspondent aversion and contempt. The towns would not suffer their passage; the hamlets were unwilling to serve them even with fire and water. They were filled at once with shame and rage; one officer killed himself, unable to bear it; in the unreflecting minds of the soldiers, hate sprung up for the rest of Italy, and especially Rome, which will make them admirable tools of tyranny in case of civil war.

This was the first great calamity of the war. But apart from the treachery of the king of Naples and the dereliction of the Pope, it was impossible it should end thoroughly well. ... [Charles Albert] fought and planned, not for Italy, but the house of Savoy, which his Balbis and Giobertis had so long been prophesying was to reign supreme in the new great era of Italy. These prophecies he more than half believed, because they chimed with his amitious wishes; but he had not soul enough to realize them; he trusted only in his disciplined troops; he had not nobleness enough to believe he might rely at all on the sentiment of the people. For his troops he dared not have good generals; conscious of meanness and timidity, he shrank from the approach of able and earnest men; he was only afraid they would, in helping Italy, take her and themselves out of his guardianship. Antonini was insulted, Garibaldi rejected; other experienced leaders, who had rushed to Italy at the first trumpet-sound, could never get employment from him. As to his generalship, it was entirely inadequate, even if he had made use of the first favorable moments. But his first thought was not to strike a blow at the Austrians before they recovered from the discomfiture of Milan, but to use the panic and need of his assistance to induce Lombardy and Venice to annex themselves to his kingdom. He did not even wish seriously to get the better till this was done, and when this was done, it was too late. The Austrian army was recruited, the generals had recovered their spirits, and were burning to retrieve and avenge their past defeat. The conduct of Charles Albert had been shamefully evasive in the first months. . . .

It is said Charles Albert feels bitterly the imputations on his courage, and says they are most ungrateful, since he has exposed the lives of himself and his sons in the combat. Indeed, there ought to be made a distinction between personal and mental courage. The former Charles Albert may possess, may have too much of what this still aristocratic world calls "the feelings of a gentleman" to shun exposing himself to a chance shot now and then. An entire want of mental courage he has shown. The battle, decisive against him, was made so by his giving up the moment fortune turned against him. It is shameful to hear so many say this result was inevitable, just because the material advantages were in favor of the Austrians. Pray, was never a battle won against material odds? It is precisely such that a good leader, a noble man, may expect to win. Were the Austrians driven out of Milan because the Milanese had that advantage? The Austrians would again have suffered repulse from them, but for the baseness of this man, on whom they had been cajoled into relying, – a baseness that deserves the pillory; and on a pillory will the "Magnanimous," as he was meanly called in face of the crimes of his youth and the timid seifishness of his middle age, stand in the sight of posterity. He made use of his power only to betray Milan; he took from the citizens all means of defence, and then gave them up to the spoiler; he promised to defend them "to the last drop of his blood," and sold them the next minute; even the paltry terms he made, he has not seen maintained. Had the people slain him in their rage, he well deserved it at their hands; and all his conduct since show how righteous would have been that sudden verdict of passion.

Of all this great drama I have much to write, but elsewhere, in a more full form, and where I can duly sketch the portraits of actors little known in America. The materials are over-rich. I have bought my right in them by much sympathetic suffering; yet, amid the blood and tears of Italy, 't is joy to see some glorious new births. The Italians are getting cured of mean adulation and hasty boasts; they are learning to prize and seek realities; the effigies of straw are getting knocked down, and living, growing men take their places. Italy is being educated for the future, her leaders are learning that the time is past for trust in princes and precedents, – that there is no hope except in truth and God; her lower people are learning to shout less and think more. [At Home and Abroad, pp. 330-34]

34. To her mother, November 16, 1848

As soon as she returned to Rome, Fuller wrote a long letter to her mother. So used now to the anomalous combinations of her life, she passed easily from heavy hints at her own motherhood to the pleasures of revenge, from the cruelty of her struggle for bread to the new gentleness of her disposition. (Fuller mistakes the name of the Pope's confessor here; it was Palma, not Parma.)

* * * Of other circumstances which complicate my position I cannot write. Were you here, I would confide in you fully, and have more than once, in the silence of the night, recited to you those most strange and romantic chapters in the story of my sad life. At one time when I thought I might die, I empowered a person, who has given me, as far as possible to him, the aid and sympathy of a brother, to communicate them to you, on his return to the United States. But now I think we shall meet again, and I am sure you will always love your daughter, and will know gladly that in all events she has tried to aid and striven never to injure her fellows. In earlier days, I dreamed of doing and being

much, but now am content with the Magdalen to rest my plea hereon,
"*She has loved much.*"

You, loved mother, keep me informed, as you have, of important
facts, *especially the worst.* The thought of you, the knowledge of your
angelic nature, is always one of my greatest supports. Happy those who
have such a mother! Myriad instances of selfishness and corruption of
heart cannot destroy the confidence in human nature.

I am again in Rome, situated for the first time entirely to my mind.
I have but one room, but large; and everything about the bed so
gracefully and adroitly disposed that it makes a beautiful parlor, and of
course I pay much less. I have the sun all day, and an excellent
chimney. It is very high and has pure air, and the most beautiful view
all around imaginable. Add, that I am with the dearest, delightful old
couple one can imagine, quick, prompt, and kind, sensible and
contented. Having no children, they like to regard me and the Prussian
sculptor, my neighbor, as such; yet are too delicate ever to intrude. In
the attic, dwells a priest, who insists on making my fire when Antonia is
away. To be sure, he pays himself for his trouble, by asking a great
many questions. The stories below are occupied by a frightful Russian
princess with moustaches, and a footman who ties her bonnet for her;
and a fat English lady, with a fine carriage, who gives all her money to
the church, and has made for the house a terrace of flowers that would
delight you. Antonia has her flowers in a humble balcony, her birds,
and an immense black cat; always addressed by both husband and wife
as "Amoretto," (little love!)

The house looks out on the Piazza Barberini, and I see both that
palace and the Pope's. The scene to-day has been one of terrible
interest. The poor, weak Pope has fallen more and more under the
dominion of the cardinals, till at last all truth was hidden from his eyes.
He had suffered the minister, Rossi, to go on, tightening the reins, and,
because the people preserved a sullen silence, he thought they would
bear it. Yesterday, the Chamber of Deputies, illegally prorogued, was
opened anew. Rossi, after two or three most unpopular measures, had
the imprudence to call the troops of the line to defend him, instead of
the National Guard. On the 14th, the Pope had invested him with the
privileges of a Roman citizen: (he had renounced his country when an
exile, and returned to it as ambassador of Louis Philippe.) This position
he enjoyed but one day. Yesterday, as he descended from his carriage,
to enter the Chamber, the crowd howled and hissed; then pushed him,

and, as he turned his head in consequence, a sure hand stabbed him in the back. He said no word, but died almost instantly in the arms of a cardinal. The act was undoubtedly the result of the combination of many, from the dexterity with which it was accomplished, and the silence which ensued. Those who had not abetted beforehand seemed entirely to approve when done. The troops of the line, on whom he had relied, remained at their posts, and looked coolly on. In the evening, they walked the streets with the people, singing, "Happy the hand which rids the world of a tyrant!" Had Rossi lived to enter the Chamber, he would have seen the most terrible and imposing mark of denunciation known in the history of nations, – the whole house, without a single exception, seated on the benches of opposition. The news of his death was received by the deputies with the same cold silence as by the people. For me, I never thought to have heard of a violent death with satisfaction, but this act affected me as one of terrible justice.

To-day, all the troops and the people united and went to the Quirinal to demand a change of measures. They found the Swiss Guard drawn out, and the Pope dared not show himself. They attempted to force the door of his palace, to enter his presence, and the guard fired. I saw a man borne by wounded. The drum beat to call out the National Guard. The carriage of Prince Barberini has returned with its frightened inmates and liveried retinue, and they have suddenly barred up the court-yard gate. Antonia, seeing it, observes, "Thank Heaven, we are poor, we have nothing to fear!" This is the echo of a sentiment which will soon be universal in Europe.

Never feel any apprehensions for my safety from such causes. There are those who will protect me, if necessary, and, besides, I am on the conquering side. These events have, to me, the deepest interest. These days are what I always longed for, – were I only free from private care! But, when the best and noblest want bread to give to the cause of liberty, I can just not demand *that* of them; their blood they would give me.

You cannot conceive the enchantment of this place. So much I suffered here last January and February, I thought myself a little weaned; but, returning, my heart swelled even to tears with the cry of the poet: –

"O, Rome, *my* country, city of the soul!"

Those have not lived who have not seen Rome. . . .

Is it not cruel that I cannot earn six hundred dollars a year, living here? I could live on that well, now I know Italy. Where I have been, this summer, a great basket of grapes sells for one cent! — delicious salad, enough for three or four persons, one cent, — a pair of chickens, fifteen cents. Foreigners cannot live so but I could, now that I speak the language fluently, and know the price of everything. Everybody loves, and wants to serve me, and I cannot earn this pitiful sum to learn and do what I want.

Of course, I wish to see America again; but in my own time, when I am ready, and not to weep over hopes destroyed and projects unfulfilled.

My dear friend, Madame Arconati, has shown me generous love; — a *contadina*, whom I have known this summer, hardly less. Every Sunday, she came in her holiday dress — beautiful corset of red silk richly embroidered, rich petticoat, nice shoes and stockings, and handsome coral necklace, on one arm an immense basket of grapes, in the other a pair of live chickens, to be eaten by me for her sake, (*"per amore mio,"*) and wanted no present, no reward; it was, as she said, "for the honor and pleasure of her acquaintance." The old father of the family never met me but he took off his hat, and said, "Madame, it is to me a *consolation* to see you." Are there not sweet flowers of affection in life, glorious moments, great thoughts? — why must they be so dearly paid for?

Many Americans have shown me great and thoughtful kindness, and none more so than W. S——— and his wife. They are now in Florence, but may return. I do not know whether I shall stay here or not; shall be guided much by the state of my health.

All is quieted now in Rome. Late at night the Pope had to yield, but not till the door of his palace was half burnt, and his confessor killed. This man, Parma, provoked his fate by firing on the people from a window. It seems the Pope never gave order to fire; his guard acted from a sudden impulse of their own. The new ministry chosen are little inclined to accept. It is almost impossible for any one to act, unless the Pope is stripped of his temporal power, and the hour for that is not yet quite ripe; though they talk more and more of proclaiming the Republic, and even of calling my friend Mazzini.

If I came home at this moment, I should feel as if forced to leave my own house, my own people, and the hour which I had always longed for. If I do come in this way, all I can promise is to plague other people as little as possible. My own plans and desires will be postponed to another world.

Do not feel anxious about me. Some higher power leads me through strange, dark, thorny paths, broken at times by glades opening down into prospects of sunny beauty, into which I am not permitted to enter. If God disposes for us, it is not for nothing. This I can say, my heart is in some respects better, it is kinder and more humble. Also, my mental acquisitions have certainly been great, however inadequate to my desires. [*Memoirs, II, 245-48, 250-52*]

35. On the Pope's flight and the condition of women, December 2, 1848

From Fuller's account of Rossi's murder in a December dispatch, I include only her careful detailing of the determining circumstances. With barely concealed triumph, she also cited the judgment of "a philosopher": "I cannot sympathize under any circumstances with so immoral a deed; but surely the manner of doing it was great." The Romans, she concluded, "took a very pagan view of this act, and the piece presented on the occasion at the theatres was 'The Death of Nero.'" In all the turmoil, the condition of woman is not forgotten.

I found Rome empty of foreigners. Most of the English have fled in affright, – the Germans and French are wanted at home, – the Czar has recalled many of his younger subjects; he does not like the schooling they get here. That large part of the population which lives by the visits of foreigners was suffering very much, – trade, industry, for every reason, stagnant. The people were every moment becoming more exasperated by the impudent measures of the Minister Rossi, and their mortification at seeing Rome represented and betrayed by a foreigner. And what foreigner? A pupil of Guizot and Louis Philippe. The news of the bombardment and storm of Vienna had just reached Rome. Zucchi, the Minister of War, at once left the city to put down over-free manifestations in the provinces, and impede the entrance of the troops of the patriot chief, Garibaldi, into Bologna. From the provinces came soldiery, called by Rossi to keep order at the opening of the Chamber of Deputies. He reviewed them in the face of the Civic Guard; the press began to be restrained; men were arbitrarily seized and sent out of the kingdom. The public indignation rose to its height; the cup overflowed.

. . . I believe [Pius IX] really thinks now the Progress movement tends to anarchy, blood, and all that looked worst in the first French revolution. However that may be, I cannot forgive him some of the circumstances of this flight. To fly to Naples; to throw himself in the arms of the bombarding monarch, blessing him and thanking his soldiery for preserving that part of Italy from anarchy; to protest that all his promises at Rome were null and void, when he thought himself in safety to choose a commission for governing in his absence, composed of men of princely blood, but as to character so null that everybody laughed, and said he chose those who could best be spared if they were killed; (but they all ran away directly;) when Rome was thus left without any government, to refuse to see any deputation, even the Senator of Rome, whom he had so gladly sanctioned, – these are the acts either of a fool or a foe. They are not his acts, to be sure, but he is responsible; he lets them stand as such in the face of the world, and weeps and prays for their success.

No more of him! His day is over. He has been made, it seems unconsciously, an instrument of good his regrets cannot destroy. Nor can he be made so important an instrument of ill. These acts have not had the effect the foes of freedom hoped. Rome remained quite cool and composed; all felt that they had not demanded more than was their duty to demand, and were willing to accept what might follow. In a few days all began to say: "Well, who would have thought it? The Pope, the Cardinals, the Princes are gone, and Rome is perfectly tranquil, and one does not miss anything, except that there are not so many rich carriages and liveries."

The Pope may regret too late that he ever gave the people a chance to make this reflection. . . .

Pray send here a good Ambassador, – one that has experience of foreign life, that he may act with good judgment, and, if possible, a man that has knowledge and views which extend beyond the cause of party politics in the United States, – a man of unity in principles, but capable of understanding variety in forms. And send a man capable of prizing the luxury of living in, or knowing Rome; the office of Ambassador is one that should not be thrown away on a person who cannot prize or use it. Another century, and I might ask to be made Ambassador myself, ('t is true, like other Ambassadors, I would employ clerks to do the most of the duty,) but woman's day has not come yet. They hold their clubs in Paris, but even George Sand will not act with women as they are. They say she pleads they are too mean, too treacherous. She should not abandon them for that, which is not nature, but misfortune. How much I shall have to say on that subject if I live, which I desire not, for I am very tired of the battle with giant wrongs, and would like to have some one younger and stronger arise to say what ought to be said, still more to do what ought to be done. Enough! if I felt these things in privileged America, the cries of mothers and wives beaten at night by sons and husbands for their diversion after drinking, as I have repeatedly heard them these past months, – the excuse for falsehood, "I *dare not* tell my husband, he would be ready to kill me," – have sharpened my perception as to the ills of woman's condition and the remedies that must be applied. Had I but genius, had I but energy, to tell what I know as it ought to be told! God grant them me, or some other more worthy woman, I pray. [*At Home and Abroad* pp. 337-38, 343-45]

36. On the people's response to the Pope's absence, January 6 and February 20, 1849

"The unreality of relation between the people and the hierarchy was obvious instantly upon the flight of Pius," Fuller wrote in the *Tribune*. The emerging reality now absorbed her in the aftermath of the Pope's flight. The first passage below is from Fuller's Roman journal for 1849, the only writing of hers to survive the wreck; the second is from the *Tribune*.

a. . . . Instead of the Pope comes from him an excommunication against those engaged in the movements of the 15th and 16th of November and in the changes to which they led and are leading *in somma*, against the major part of Romans in this city or in the provinces. I have not yet seen the document, but it is said to be worded in all the most foolish phrases of ancient superstition. The people received it with jeers, tore it at once from the walls, and yesterday (Saturday) evening carried it in procession through the Corso round a candle's end, the only light in the procession. They ran along giggling and mumbling in imitation of priestly chants, detachments occasionally digressing to throw copies into some privy. Such is the finale of St. Peterdom. . . . *[Houghton MS]*

b. The revolution, like all genuine ones, has been instinctive, its results unexpected and surprising to the greater part of those who achieved them. The waters, which had flowed so secretly beneath the crust of habit that many never heard their murmur, unless in dreams, have suddenly burst to light in full and beautiful jets; all rush to drink the pure and living draught.

As in the time of Jesus, the multitude had been long enslaved beneath a cumbrous ritual, their minds designedly darkened by those who should have enlightened them, brutified, corrupted, amid monstrous contradictions and abuses; yet the moment they hear a word correspondent to the original nature, "Yes, it is true," they cry. "It is spoken with authority. Yes, it ought to be so. Priests ought to be better and wiser than other men; if they were, they would not need pomp and temporal power to command respect. Yes, it is true; we ought not to lie; we should not try to impose upon one another. We ought rather to prefer that our children should work honestly for their bread, than get it by cheating, begging, or the prostitution of their mothers. It would be better to act worthily and kindly, probably would please God more than the kissing of relics. We have long darkly felt that these things were so; *now* we know it." [*At Home and Abroad*, p. 349]

37. On the birth of the Roman Republic, February 20, 1849

In her twenty-eighth dispatch to the *Tribune* (also sent February 20), Fuller described the opening of the Constitutional Assembly and the proclamation of the Republic on February 9.

Early next morning I rose and went forth to observe the Republic. Over the Quirinal I went, through the Forum, to the Capitol. There was nothing to be seen except the magnificent calm emperor, the tamers of horses, the fountain, the trophies, the lions, as usual; among the marbles, for living figures, a few dirty, bold women, and Murillo boys in

the sun just as usual. I passed into the Corso; there were men in the
liberty cap, – of course the lowest and vilest had been the first to
assume it; all the horrible beggars persecuting as impudently as usual. I
met some English; all their comfort was, "It would not last a month."
"They hoped to see all these fellows shot yet." The English clergyman,
more mild and legal, only hopes to see them (i.e. the ministry, deputies,
&c.) *hung.*

Mr. Carlyle would be delighted with his countrymen. They are
entirely ready and anxious to see a Cromwell for Italy. They, too,
think, when the people starve, "It is no matter what happens in the
back parlor." What signifies that, if there is "order" in the front? How
dare the people make a noise to disturb us yawning at billiards!

I met an American. He "had no confidence in the Republic." Why?
Because he "had no confidence in the people." Why? Because "they
were not like *our* people." Ah! Jonathan and John, – excuse me, but I
must say the Italian has a decided advantage over you in the power of
quickly feeling generous sympathy, as well as some other things which I
have not time now to particularize. I have memoranda from you both
in my notebook.

At last the procession mounts the Campidoglio. It is all dressed
with banners. The tricolor surmounts the palace of the senator; the
senator himself has fled. The deputies mount the steps, and one of
them reads, in a clear, friendly voice, the following words: –

"Fundamental Decree of the
Constitutional Assembly of Rome.

Art. I. – The Papacy has fallen in fact and in right from the
temporal government of the Roman State.

Art. II. – The Roman Pontiff shall have all the necessary
guarantees for independence in the exercise of his spiritual power.

Art. III. – The form of government of the Roman State shall be a
pure democracy, and will take the glorious name of Roman Republic.

Art. IV. – The Roman Republic shall have with the rest of Italy
the relations exacted by a common nationality."

Between each of these expressive sentences the speaker paused; the
great bell of the Capitol gave forth its solemn melodies; the cannon
answered; while the crowd shouted, *Viva la Republica! Viva Italia!*

The imposing grandeur of the spectacle to me gave new force to

the emotion that already swelled my heart; my nerves thrilled, and I
longed to see in some answering glance a spark of Rienzi, a little of that
soul which made my country what she is. The American at my side
remained impassive. Receiving all his birthright from a triumph of
democracy, he was quite indifferent to this manifestation on this
consecrated spot. Passing the winter in Rome to study art, he was
insensible to the artistic beauty of the scene, — insensible to this new
life of that spirit from which all the forms he gazes at in galleries
emanated. He "did not see the use of these popular demonstrations."

Again I must mention a remark of his, as a specimen of the
ignorance in which Americans usually remain during their flighty visits
to these scenes, where they associate only with one another. And I do it
the rather as this seemed a really thoughtful, intelligent man; no vain,
vulgar trifler. He said, "The people seem only to be looking on; they
take no part."

What people? said I.

"Why, these around us; there is no other people."

There are a few beggars, errand-boys, and nurse-maids.

"The others are only soldiers."

Soldiers! The Civic Guard! all the decent men in Rome. . . .

[*At Home and Abroad*, pp. 358-59]

38. To Giuseppe Mazzini, March 3, 1849

This letter to Mazzini probably reached Florence just as he
was quietly entering Rome—on foot at night—on March 5.
His visit three days later filled her with foreboding. To her
mother she wrote, "His life has known one hour of pure joy,
but I fear, I fear the entrance into Jerusalem may be followed
by the sacrifice" (Houghton MS). And with the Springs she
shared her fear that "it is in reserve for him to survive defeat"
(*Memoirs*, II, 263). (Mazzini's words in the following letter
may be translated, "the long exile just begun again, life
without comfort except for distant and conflicting
affections, and hope long protracted and the desire that
begins to become overwhelming finally to sleep in peace since
I have not been able to live in my land.")

Dear Mazzini,

Though knowing you occupied by the most important affairs, I again feel impelled to write a few lines.

What emboldens me is the persuasion that the best friends, – in point of perfect sympathy and intelligence, the only friends, – of a man of ideas and of marked character, must be women. You have your mother; no doubt you have others, perhaps many. Of that I know nothing; only I like to offer also my tribute of affection.

When I think that only two years ago, you thought of coming into Italy with us in disguise, it seems very glorious, that you are about to enter Republican Rome as a Roman Citizen. It seemed almost the most sublime and poetical fact of history. Yet, even in the first thrill of joy, I felt, "He will think his work but beginning now."

When I read from your hand these words "il lungo esilio testè ricominciato, la vita non confortato fuorchè d'affetti lontani e contesi, e la speranza lungamente protratta e il desiderio che comincia a farmi si supremo di dormire finalmente in pace, da chè non ho potuto vivere in terra mia."

When I read these words they made me weep bitterly and I thought of them always with a great pang at the heart. But it is not so, dear Mazzini. You do not return to sleep under the sod of Italy, but to see your thought springing up all over her soil. The gardeners seem to me, in point of instinctive wisdom or deep thought, mostly incompetent to the care of the garden, but an idea like this will be able to make use of any implements, [and,] it is to be hoped, will educate the men by making them work. It is not this, I believe, which still keeps your heart so melancholy, for I seem to read the same melancholy in your answer to the Roman assembly. You speak of "few and late years," but some full ones still remain; a century is not needed, nor ought the same man, in the same form of thought, to work too long on an age. He would mould and bend it too much to himself, better for him to die and return incarnated to give the same truth aid on yet another side. Jesus of Nazareth died young; but had he not spoken and acted as much truth as the world could bear in his time? A frailty, a perpetual shortcoming, motion in a curve line, seems the destiny of this earth. The excuse awaits us elsewhere: there must be one, for it is true, as said Goethe, that "*Care is taken* that the trees grow not up into heaven." Men like you, appointed ministers, must not be the less earnest in their

work, yet to the greatest, the day, the moment, is all their kingdom.
God takes care of the increase. Farewell! For your sake I would wish at
this moment to be an Italian and a man of action. But *though an
American*, I am not even a *woman of action*; so the best I can do is to
pray with the whole heart. Heaven bless dear Mazzini, cheer his heart
and give him worthy helpers to carry out its holy purposes! *[Houghton
MS]*

39. To Caroline Sturgis Tappan, March 16, 1849

Fuller's first account of Ossoli and her son, lost like most of
her later confessions to others, was written to Caroline
Sturgis. Sturgis' sister, Ellen Hooper—a beloved poet whose
self-repression and misery in marriage had always pained
Fuller—had recently died; perhaps Fuller's sisterly grief
inspired this confidence. Sturgis' natural interest was whetted
because she was then pregnant with her own first child, and
in her reply she evidently compared Angelino's rustic birth to
Jesus'. On March 16, Fuller wrote again, describing her visit
to the baby in December, and attached an engraving of the
Christ child in heavy swaddling, and apparently a picture now
lost of the holy family traveling to Egypt. (In the *Memoirs*,
[II, 266-67], the last paragraph below is presented as part of
a letter to Emerson.)

... After I wrote to you I went to Rieti. The weather was mild when I
set out, but by the fatality that has attended me throughout, in the
night changed to a cold, unknown in Italy and remained so all the time
I staid. There was, as is common in Italy, no fireplace except in the
kitchen. I suffered much in my room with its brick floor, and windows
through which came the cold wind freely. My darling did not suffer,
because he was a little swaddled child like this and robed in wool
besides, but I did very much. When I first took him in my arms he made
no sound but leaned his head against my bosom, and staid so, he
seemed to say how could you abandon me. What I felt you will know
only when you have your own. A little girl who lived in the house told
me all the day of my departure he could not be comforted, always
refusing the breast and looking at the door; he has been a strangely

precocious infant; I think it was through sympathy with me, and that in that regard it may be a happiness for him to be with these more plebeian, instinctive, joyous natures. I saw he was more serene, that he was not sensitive as when with me, and slept a great deal more. You speak of my being happy, all the solid happiness I have known has been at times when he went to sleep in my arms. You say when Ellen's beautiful life had been so wasted, it hardly seemed worth while to begin another. I had all those feelings too. I do not look forward to his career and his manly life: it is *now* I want to be with him, before passion, care, and bafflings begin. If I had a little money I should go with him into strict retirement for a year or two and live for him alone. This I cannot do: all life that has been or could be natural to me is invariably denied. God knows why, I suppose.

I receive with profound gratitude your thought of taking him, if any thing should happen to us. Should I live, I don't know whether I should wish him to be an Italian or American citizen; it depends on the course events take here politically, but should we die, the person to whom he would naturally fall is a sister of his father a person of great elegance and sweetness but entirely limited in mind. I should not like that. I shall think about it. Before he was born I did a great deal having the idea I might die and all my spirit remain incarnated in him, but now I think I shall live and carry him round myself, as I ride on my ass into Egypt. We shant go so mildly as this set.

You talk about your mangers, Carrie, but that was only for a little, presently came kings with gold cups and all sorts of things. Joseph pawned them; with part of the money he bought this nice donkey for the journey; and they lived on the rest till Joseph could work at his trade, we have no donkey and it costs a great deal to travel in diligences and steamers, and being a nobleman is a poor trade in a ruined despotism just turning into a Republic. I often think of Dickens's marchioness playing whist in the kitchen. So I play whist every where.

Speaking of the republic, you say, do I not wish Italy had a great man. Mazzini is a great man; in mind a great poetic statesman, in heart a lover, in action decisive and full of resource as Cesar. Dearly I love Mazzini, who also loves me. He came in just as I had finished the first letter to you. His soft radiant look makes melancholy music in my soul; it consecrates my present life that like the Magdalen I may at the important hour shed all the consecrated ointment on his head. There is one, Mazzini, who understands thee well, who knew thee no less when

an object of popular fear than now of idolatry, and who, if the pen be
not held too feebly, will make that posterity shall know thee too. . . .
[Houghton MS]

40. To Giovanni Angelo Ossoli, April 4, 1849

With her longing for her child sharpened by the letter to
Sturgis, Fuller left Rome at the end of March for a
three-week visit to her baby. The household where he lived
had become violently unstable, two brothers, Niccolò and
Pietro, were given to raging, knife-brandishing fights which
she could mediate only temporarily. And everyone in town
was in terror of the Garibaldini, who were at this time using
Rieti as their headquarters. Committed to Garibaldi and his
cause, his legionnaires were actually strictly disciplined and
their crimes limited generally to looting monastery kitchens,
but in the popular mind they were brigands and killers.
Although two weeks later—through the adventures related by
Emelyn Story (VI:2d)—Fuller came to admire the legionnaires, at first maternal fear made her accept their
exaggerated reputation, as in this letter. This document too
led Madeleine Stern to believe that April 4 was Fuller's and
Ossoli's wedding anniversary. (Fuller's allusion at the end is
to a new paper published by Mazzini, who had just been
made one of Rome's Triumvirs; *La Speranza dell' Epoca* was
the paper of the moderate Mamiani.)

My dear,

How strange it is that we cannot pass this day together. We must pray
to be happier another year. Yesterday I had bought small birds for our
dinner and I very much hoped to see you; since you didn't come, I
didn't eat. But today I am not sorry you didn't come because it's
raining hard again, and Angelino, who was so happy before, so
charming that I was wishing every minute for you to see him, today is
not well. He was in pain all night with his teeth, and today, poor little
thing, he can get no peace. Let's hope he will be well when you are able
to come.

It seems to me that I was sent by God to protect him in these terrible days! Niccola was crazy for more than forty hours, Chiara always crying, desperate. Last night Niccola slept and today is reasonable again.

Garibaldi has not passed the border. More Neapolitan troops have arrived in Aquila, and now here come more Roman troops from Terni to reinforce Garibaldi. But here they don't think that the Neapolitans will enter, but that they're making a show of force to draw away part of the Roman forces from Terracina, that probably they will invade from Terracina.

Garibaldi has no control over these desperadoes in his band. On Sunday they killed a priest, two citizens and perhaps nine, they say. Two bodies were found in the river. The presence of the regular troops could prevent these excesses. But certainly I don't now have courage to go out alone. Near here is a little garden where I go with Angelino on nice days, I never go out in the road.

Ask Antonia if anyone has been looking for me and please put this note immediately in the post for Florence.

How sorry I am that you had this terrible guard duty through the night. It will be the ruin of your health and how foolishly and thoughtlessly it's done like everything in Rome as if they were trying to put you off. Get for me right away the paper of Mazzini if you have money for a ⟨number⟩ . . . I am perfectly disgusted with this Epoca, it has become a reactionary paper. Goodbye, my own, God bless and keep you this April 4th, your Margaret. *[Houghton MS in Italian; my translation]*

41. On war in Rome, May 27, 1849

"The work is done," Fuller wrote for the *Tribune* during the May lull in the battle for Rome; "the revolution in Italy is now radical, nor can it stop till Italy becomes independent and united as a republic." Beginning with her doubts that the revolutionary impulse would prevail in France's relation to Rome, she ended this thirtieth dispatch by assailing the offensive expediency of the United States in sending a consul to observe the strength of the Roman Republic before recognizing it.

The people of Rome have burnt the Cardinals' carriages. They took the confessionals out of the churches, and made mock confessions in the piazzas, the scope of which was, "I have sinned, father, so and so." "Well, my son, how much will you *pay* to the Church for absolution?" Afterward the people thought of burning the confessionals, or using them for barricades; but at the request of the Triumvirate they desisted, and even put them back into the churches. But it was from no reaction of feeling that they stopped short, only from respect for the government. . . .

I do not dare to trust that people [the French]. The peasant is yet very ignorant. The suffering workman is frightened as he thinks of the punishments that ensued on the insurrections of May and June. The man of property is full of horror at the brotherly scope of Socialism. The aristocrat dreams of the guillotine always when he hears men speak of the people. The influence of the Jesuits is still immense in France. Both in France and England the grossest falsehoods have been circulated with unwearied diligence about the state of things in Italy. An amusing specimen of what is still done in this line I find just now in a foreign journal, where it says there are red flags on all the houses of Rome; meaning to imply that the Romans are athirst for blood. Now, the fact is, that these flags are put up at the entrance of those houses where there is no barricade, as a signal to coachmen and horsemen that they can pass freely. There is one on the house where I am, in which is no person but myself, who thirst for peace, and the Padrone, who thirsts for money. . . .

War near at hand seems to me even more dreadful than I had fancied it. True, it tries men's souls, lays bare selfishness in undeniable deformity. Here it has produced much fruit of noble sentiment, noble act; but still it breeds vice too, drunkenness, mental dissipation, tears asunder the tenderest ties, lavishes the productions of Earth, for which her starving poor stretch out their hands in vain, in the most unprofitable manner. And the ruin that ensues, how terrible! Let those who have ever passed happy days in Rome grieve to hear that the beautiful plantations of Villa Borghese — that chief delight and refreshment of citizens, foreigners, and little children — are laid low, as far as the obelisk. The fountain, singing alone amid the fallen groves, cannot be seen and heard without tears; it seems like some innocent infant calling and crowing amid dead bodies on a field which battle has strewn with the bodies of those who once cherished it. The plantations of Villa Salvage on the Tiber, also, the beautiful trees on the way from

St. John Lateran to La Maria Maggiore, the trees of the Forum, are
fallen. Rome is shorn of the locks which lent grace to her venerable
brow. She looks desolate, profaned. I feel what I never expected
to, – as if I might by and by be willing to leave Rome.

Then I have, for the first time, seen what wounded men suffer. The
night of the 30th of April I passed in the hospital, and saw the terrible
agonies of those dying or who needed amputation, felt their mental
pains and longing for the loved ones who were away; for many of these
were Lombards, who had come from the field of Novarra to fight with
a fairer chance, – many were students of the University, who had
enlisted and thrown themselves into the front of the engagement. The
impudent falsehoods of the French general's despatches are incredible.
The French were never decoyed on in any way. They were received
with every possible mark of hostility. They were defeated in open field,
the Garibaldi legion rushing out to meet them; and though they
suffered much from the walls, they sustained themselves nowhere. The
vanity that strives to cover over these facts is unworthy of men. . . .

I have been out on the balcony to look over the city. All sleeps
with that peculiar air of serene majesty known to this city only; – this
city that has grown, not out of the necessities of commerce nor the
luxuries of wealth, but first out of heroism, then out of faith. Swelling
domes, roofs softly tinted with yellow moss! what deep meaning, what
deep repose, in your faintly seen outline!

The young moon climbs among clouds, – the clouds of a departing
thunderstorm. Tender, smiling moon! can it be that thy full orb may
look down on a smoking, smouldering Rome, and see her best blood
run along the stones, without one nation in the world to defend, one to
aid, – scarce one to cry out a tardy "Shame"? We will wait, whisper the
nations, and see if they can bear it. Rack them well to see if they are
brave. *If they can do without us*, we will help them. Is it thus ye would
be served in your turn? Beware! [*At Home and Abroad*, pp. 381-84,
389]

42. To Ralph Waldo Emerson, June 10, 1849

The false peace, pending false negotiations, ended June 3,
when the French, who had announced that they would enter
Rome the next day, sprang their attack. (When this letter to
Emerson was published in the *Memoirs*, it gladdened the

hearts of French reviewers because the French had argued that their intervention was to expel foreign mercenaries. We note, however, that Fuller said that *Romans* were few, and elsewhere stressed the presence of men from other Italian states.)

I received your letter amid the round of cannonade and musketry. It was a terrible battle fought here from the first till the last light of day. I could see all its progress from my balcony. The Italians fought like lions. It is a truly heroic spirit that animates them. They make a stand here for honor and their rights, with little ground for hope that they can resist, now they are betrayed by France.

Since the 30th April, I go almost daily to the hospitals, and, though I have suffered, – for I had no idea before, how terrible gunshot-wounds and wound-fever are, – yet I have taken pleasure, and great pleasure, in being with the men; there is scarcely one who is not moved by a noble spirit. Many, especially among the Lombards, are the flower of the Italian youth. When they begin to get better, I carry them books and flowers; they read, and we talk.

The palace of the Pope, on the Quirinal, is now used for convalescents. In those beautiful gardens, I walk with them, – one with his sling, another with his crutch. The gardener plays off all his water-works for the defenders of the country, and gathers flowers for me, their friend.

A day or two since, we sat in the Pope's little pavilion, where he used to give private audience. The sun was going gloriously down over Monte Mario, where gleamed the white tents of the French light-horse among the trees. The cannonade was heard at intervals. Two bright-eyed boys sat at our feet, and gathered up eagerly every word said by the heroes of the day. It was a beautiful hour, stolen from the midst of ruin and sorrow; and tales were told as full of grace and pathos as in the gardens of Boccaccio, only in a very different spirit, – with noble hope for man, with reverence for woman.

The young ladies of the family, very young girls, were filled with enthusiasm for the suffering, wounded patriots, and they wished to go to the hosptial to give their services. Excepting the three superintendents, none but married ladies were permitted to serve there, but their services were accepted. Their governess then wished to go too, and, as she could speak several languages, she was admitted to the rooms of the wounded soldiers, to interpret for them, as the nurses knew nothing but Italian, and many of these poor men were suffering, because they could not make their wishes known. Some are French, some German, and many Poles. Indeed, I am afraid it is too true that there were comparatively but few Romans among them. This young lady passed several nights there.

Should I never return, — and sometimes I despair of doing so, it seems so far off, so difficult, I am caught in such a net of ties here, — if ever you know of my life here, I think you will only wonder at the constancy with which I have sustained myself; the degree of profit to which, amid great difficulties, I have put the time, at least in the way of observation. Meanwhile, love me all you can; let me feel, that, amid the fearful agitations of the world, there are pure hands, with healthful, even pulse, stretched out toward me, if I claim their grasp. *[Memoirs, II, 264-66]*

43. On the siege of Rome, June 21 and 23, 1849

By June 21, when Fuller began this dispatch, her identification with the Roman struggle was so complete that in the first paragraph below she unconsciously refers to the Italian side as "ours." Her grief over the loss of life, of Rome, and of the dream of a vindicated and noble people culminated in her despairing death wish.

On the eve of the bombardment one or two officers went round with a fine band. It played on the piazzas the Marseillaise and Roman marches; and when the people were thus assembled, they were told of the proclamation, and asked how they felt. Many shouted loudly, *Guerra! Viva la Republica Romana!* Afterward, bands of young men went round singing the chorus,

> "Vogliamo sempre quella,
> Vogliamo Liberta."

("We want always one thing; we want liberty.") Guitars played, and some danced. When the bombs began to come, one of the Trasteverini, those noble images of the old Roman race, redeemed her claim to that descent by seizing a bomb and extinguishing the match. She received a medal and a reward in money. A soldier did the same thing at Palazza Spada, where is the statue of Pompey, at whose base great Caesar fell. He was promoted. Immediately the people were seized with emulation; armed with pans of wet clay, they ran wherever the bombs fell, to extinguish them. Women collect the balls from the hostile cannon, and carry them to ours. As thus very little injury has been done to life, the people cry, "Madonna protects us against the bombs; she wills not that Rome should be destroyed."

Meanwhile many poor people are driven from their homes, and provisions are growing very dear. The heats are now terrible for us, and must be far more so for the French. It is said a vast number are ill of fever; indeed, it cannot be otherwise. Oudinot [the French general] himself has it, and perhaps this is one explanation of the mixture of violence and weakness in his actions.

He must be deeply ashamed at the poor result of his bad acts, – that at the end of two weeks and so much bravado, he has done nothing to Rome, unless intercept provisions, kill some of her brave youth, and injure churches, which should be sacred to him as to us. St. Maria Trastevere, that ancient church, so full of precious remains, and which had an air of mild repose more beautiful than almost any other, is said to have suffered particularly.

As to the men who die, I share the impassioned sorrow of the Triumvirs. "O Frenchmen!" they wrote, "could you know what men you destroy! *They* are no mercenaries, like those who fill your ranks, but the flower of the Italian youth, and the noblest among the aged. When you shall know of what minds you have robbed the world, how ought you to repent and mourn!"

This is especially true of the Emigrant and Garibaldi legions. The misfortunes of Northern and Southern Italy, the conscription which compels to the service of tyranny those who remain, has driven from the kingdom of Naples and from Lombardy all the brave and noble youth. Many are in Venice or Rome, the forlorn hope of Italy. . . .

June 23

The liberal party in France does what it can to wash its hands of this offence, but it seems weak, and unlikely to render effectual service at this crisis. Venice, Rome, Ancona, are the last strong-holds of hope, and they cannot stand for ever thus unsustained. Night before last, a tremendous cannonade left no moment to sleep, even had the anxious hearts of mothers and wives been able to crave it. At morning a little detachment of French had entered by the breach of St. Pancrazio, and intrenched itself in a vineyard. Another has possession of Villa Poniatowski, close to the Porta del Popolo, and attacks and alarms are hourly to be expected. I long to see the final one, dreadful as that hour may be, since now there seems no hope from delay. Men are daily slain, and this state of suspense is agonizing.

In the evening 't is pretty, though terrible, to see the bombs, fiery meteors, springing from the horizon line upon their bright path, to do their wicked message. 'T would not be so bad, methinks, to die by one of these, as wait to have every drop of pure blood, every childlike radiant hope, drained and driven from the heart by the betrayals of nations and of individuals, till at last the sickened eyes refuse more to open to that light which shines daily on such pits of iniquity. [*At Home and Abroad*, pp. 406-407, 409]

44. On Garibaldi's retreat and the entry of the French, July 6 and 10, 1849

In her last dispatch to the *Tribune*, written on July 6, two days after the French entered Rome, Fuller investigated the sources of the Italian failure. The glory of resistance and the horror of war both inform her final plea to Americans: "I pray you *do something*; let it not end in a mere cry of sentiment." She began by richly compensating for her early mistrust of Garibaldi, who was no longer able to withstand the French cannon and was marching with his men to the aid of Venice.

. . . We followed them to the piazza of St. John Lateran. Never have I seen a sight so beautiful, so romantic, and so sad. Whoever knows Rome knows the peculiar solemn grandeur of that piazza, scene of the first triumph of Rienzi, and whence may be seen the magnificence of the "mother of all churches," the baptistery with its porphyry columns, the Santa Scala with its glittering mosaics of the early ages, the obelisk standing fairest of any of those most imposing monuments of Rome, the view through the gates of the Campagna, on that side so richly strewn with ruins. The sun was setting, the crescent moon rising, the flower of the Italian youth were marshalling in that solemn place. They had been driven from every other spot where they had offered their hearts as bulwarks of Italian independence; in this last strong-hold they had sacrificed hecatombs of their best and bravest in that cause; they must now go or remain prisoners and slaves. *Where* go, they knew not; for except distant Hungary there is not now a spot which would receive them, or where they can act as honor commands. They had all put on the beautiful dress of the Garibaldi legion, the tunic of bright red cloth, the Greek cap, or else round hat with Puritan plume. Their long hair was blown back from resolute faces; all looked full of courage. They had counted the cost before they entered on this perilous struggle; they had weighed life and all its material advantages against liberty, and made their election; they turned not back, nor flinched, at this bitter crisis. I saw the wounded, all that could go, laden upon their baggage cars; some were already pale and fainting, still they wished to go. I saw many youths, born to rich inheritance, carrying in a handkerchief all their worldly goods. The women were ready; their eyes too were resolved, if sad. The wife of Garibaldi followed him on horseback. He himself was distinguished by the white tunic; his look was entirely that of a hero of the Middle Ages, – his face still young, for the excitements of his life, though so many, have all been youthful, and there is no fatigue upon his brow or cheek. Fall or stand, one sees in him a man engaged in the career for which he is adapted by nature. He went upon the parapet, and looked upon the road with a spy-glass, and, no obstruction being in sight, he turned his face for a moment back upon Rome, then led the way through the gate. Hard was the heart, stony and seared the eye, that had no tear for that moment. Go, fated, gallant band! and if God care not indeed for men as for the sparrows, most of ye go forth to perish. . . .

I know that many a respectable gentleman would be surprised to hear me speak in this way. Gentlemen who perform their "duties to society" by buying for themselves handsome clothes and furniture with the interest of their money, speak of Garibaldi and his men as "brigands" and "vagabonds." Such are they, doubtless, in the same sense as Jesus, Moses, and Eneas were. To me, men who can throw so lightly aside the ease of wealth, the joys of affection, for the sake of what they deem honor, in whatsoever form, are the "respectable." No doubt there are in these bands a number of men of lawless minds, and who follow this banner only because there is for them no other path. But the greater part are the noble youths who have fled from the

Austrian conscription, or fly now from the renewal of the Papal suffocation, darkened by French protection.

As for the protectors, they entirely threw aside the mask, as it was always supposed they would, the moment they had possession of Rome. I do not know whether they were really so bewildered by their priestly counsellors as to imagine they would be well received in a city which they had bombarded, and where twelve hundred men were lying wounded by their assault. To say nothing of the justice or injustice of the matter, it could not be supposed that the Roman people, if it had any sense of dignity, would welcome them. I did not appear in the street, as I would not give any countenance to such a wrong; but an English lady, my friend, told me they seemed to look expectingly for the strong party of friends they had always pretended to have within the walls. The French officers looked up to the windows for ladies, and, she being the only one they saw, saluted her. She made no reply. They then passed into the Corso. Many were assembled, the softer Romans being unable to control a curiosity the Milanese would have disclaimed, but preserving an icy silence. In an evil hour, a foolish priest dared to break it by the cry of *Viva Pio Nono*! The populace, roused to fury, rushed on him with their knives. He was much wounded; one or two others were killed in the rush. The people howled then, and hissed at the French, who, advancing their bayonets, and clearing the way before them, fortified themselves in the piazzas. Next day the French troops were marched to and fro through Rome, to inspire awe in the people; but it has only created a disgust amounting to loathing, to see that, with such an imposing force, and in great part fresh, the French were not ashamed to use bombs also, and kill women and children in their beds. Oudinot then, seeing the feeling of the people, and finding they pursued as a spy any man who so much as showed the way to his soldiers, – that the Italians went out of the cafés if Frenchmen entered, – in short, that the people regarded him and his followers in the same light as the Austrians, – has declared martial law in Rome; the press is stifled; everybody is to be in the house at half past nine o'clock in the evening, and whoever in any way insults his men, or puts any obstacle in their way, is to be shot.

The fruits of all this will be the same as elsewhere; temporary repression will sow the seeds of perpetual resistance; and never was Rome in so fair a way to be educated for a republican form of government as now. . . .

July 10

Yesterday I went over the scene of conflict. It was fearful even to *see* the Casinos Quattro Venti and Vascello, where the French and Romans had been several days so near one another, all shattered to pieces, with fragments of rich stucco and painting stilll sticking to rafters between the great holes made by the cannonade, and think that men had stayed and fought in them when only a mass of ruins. The French, indeed, were entirely sheltered the last days; to my unpractised eyes, the extent and thoroughness of their works seemed miraculous, and gave me the first clear idea of the incompetency of the Italians to resist organized armies. I saw their commanders had not even known enough of the art of war to understand how the French were conducting the siege. It is true, their resources were at any rate inadequate to resistance; only continual sorties would have arrested the progress of the foe, and to make them and man the wall their forces were inadequate. I was struck more than ever by the heroic valor of *our* people, – let me so call them now as ever; for go where I may, a large part of my heart will ever remain in Italy. I hope her children will always acknowledge me as a sister, though I drew not my first breath here. A Contadini showed me where thirty-seven braves are buried beneath a heap of wall that fell upon them in the shock of one cannonade. A marble nymph, with broken arm, looked sadly that way from her sun-dried fountain; some roses were blooming still, some red oleanders, amid the ruin. The sun was casting its last light on the mountains on the tranquil, sad Campagna, that sees one leaf more turned in the book of woe. This was in the Vascello. I then entered the French ground, all mapped and hollowed like a honeycomb. A pair of skeleton legs protruded from a bank of one barricade; lower, a dog had scratched away its light covering of earth from the body of a man, and discovered it lying face upward all dressed; the dog stood gazing on it with an air of stupid amazement. . . .   *[At Home and Abroad, pp. 412-15, 420]*

45. To William Henry Channing, August 28, 1849

Even in the hospitals of Rome, the soldiers' dedication prepared the martyr myths for the next wave of revolution. The memory of "these true priests of a higher hope," Fuller wrote in the *Tribune*, "will console amid the spectacles of meanness, selfishness, and faithlessness which life may yet have in store for the pilgrim" (*At Home and Abroad*, p. 408). But looking back from Rieti, where her starving baby was fighting for his life, she felt overwhelmed by the struggle.

You say, you are glad I have had this great opportunity for carrying out my principles. Would it were so! I found myself inferior in courage and fortitude to the occasion. I knew not how to bear the havoc and anguish incident to the struggle for these principles. I rejoiced that it lay not with me to cut down the trees, to destroy the Elysian gardens, for the defence of Rome; I do not know that I could have done it. And the sight of these far nobler growths, the beautiful young men, mown down in their stately prime, became too much for me. I forget the great ideas, to sympathize with the poor mothers, who had nursed their precious forms, only to see them all lopped and gashed. You say, I sustained them; often have they sustained my courage: one, kissing the pieces of bone that were so painfully extracted from his arm, hanging them round his neck to be worn as the true relics of to-day; mementoes that he also had done and borne something for his country and the hopes of humanity. One fair young man, who is made a cripple for life, clasped my hand as he saw me crying over the spasms I could not relieve, and faintly cried, "Viva l'Italia." "Think only, *cara bona donna*," said a poor wounded soldier, "that I can always wear my uniform on *festas*, just as it is now, with the holes where the balls went through, for a memory." "God is good; God knows," they often said to me, when I had not a word to cheer them. [*Memoirs*, II, 269-70]

46. To her mother [summer 1849] and November 7, 1849

After fleeing to Rieti, Fuller was further crushed by a letter from Greeley beginning, "Ah, Margaret, the world grows dark with us! You grieve, for Rome is fallen;—I mourn, for Pickie is dead." Writing her mother of this and of her grief gave her the opening she needed to reveal her own story. The second excerpt below is from her next letter to her mother, thanking her for the unqualified support which gave her courage to face others.

a. . . . This brings me to the main object of my present letter, – a piece of intelligence about myself, which I had hoped I might be able to communicate in such a way as to give you *pleasure*. That I cannot, – after suffering much in silence with that hope, – is like the rest of my earthly destiny.

The first moment, it may cause you a pang to know that your eldest child might long ago have been addressed by another name than yours, and has a little son a year old.

But, beloved mother, do not feel this long. I do assure you, that it was only great love for you that kept me silent. I have abstained a hundred times, when your sympathy, your counsel, would have been most precious, from a wish not to harass you with anxiety. Even now I would abstain, but it has become necessary, on account of the child, for us to live publicly and permanently together; and we have no hope, in the present state of Italian affairs, that we can do it at any better advantage, for several years, than now. . . .

He is not in any respect such a person as people in general would expect to find with me. He had no instructor except an old priest, who entirely neglected his education; and of all that is contained in books he is absolutely ignorant, and he has no enthusiasm of character. On the other hand, he has excellent practical sense; has been a judicious observer of all that passed before his eyes; has a nice sense of duty, which, in its unfailing, minute activity, may put most enthusiasts to shame; a very sweet temper, and great native refinement. His love for me has been unswerving and most tender. I have never suffered a pain that he could relieve. His devotion, when I am ill, is to be compared only with yours. His delicacy in trifles, his sweet domestic graces, remind me of E[ugene]. In him I have found a home, and one that interferes with no tie. Amid many ills and cares, we have had much joy together, in the sympathy with natural beauty, – with our child, – with all that is innocent and sweet.

I do not know whether he will always love me so well, for I am the elder, and the difference will become, in a few years, more perceptible than now. But life is so uncertain, and it is so necessary to take good things with their limitations, that I have not thought it worth while to calculate too curiously.

However my other friends may feel, I am sure that *you* will love him very much, and that he will love you no less. Could we all live together, on a moderate income, you would find peace with us. Heaven grant, that, on returning, I may gain means to effect this object. He, of course, can do nothing, while we are in the United States, but perhaps I can; and now that my health is better, I shall be able to exert myself, if sure that my child is watched by those who love him, and who are good and pure. . . . [*Memoirs, II, 273-75*]

b. Dearest Mother,

Of all your endless acts and words of love, never was any so dear to me as your last letter so generous, so sweet, so holy What on earth is so precious as a mother's love; and who has a mother like mine! . . .

Ossoli wishes you were here, almost as much as I. When there is anything really lovely and tranquil, he often says, "Would not '*La Madre*' like that?" He wept when he heard your letter. I never saw him weep at any other time, except when his father died, and when the French entered Rome. He has, I think, even a more holy feeling about a mother, from having lost his own, when very small. It has been a life-long want with him. He often shows me a little scar on his face, made by a jealous dog, when his mother was caressing him as an infant. He prizes that blemish much. [*Houghton MS copy and Memoirs, II, 307*]

47. To Costanza Arconati Visconti [autumn 1849]

Fearing that Arconati might not like her friends "to be running about in these blind alleys," as she strikingly characterized her behavior later, Fuller wrote her, as soon as she had settled in Florence, with all the candor she could summon and a new clarity about the directness required in friendship.

Reading a book called "The Last Days of the Republic in Rome," I see that my letter, giving my impressions of that period, may well have seemed to you strangely partial. If we can meet as once we did, and compare notes in the same spirit of candor, while making mutual allowance for our different points of view, your testimony and opinions would be invaluable to me. But will you have patience with my democracy, – my revolutionary spirit? Believe that in thought I am more radical than ever. The heart of Margaret you know, – it is always the same. Mazinni is immortally dear to me – a thousand times dearer for all the trial I saw made of him in Rome; – dearer for all he suffered. Many of his brave friends perished there. We who, less worthy, survive, would fain make up for the loss, by our increased devotion to him, the purest, the most disinterested of patriots, the most affectionate of brothers. You will not love me less that I am true to him.

Then, again, how will it affect you to know that I have united my destiny with that of an obscure young man,– younger than myself; a person of no intellectual culture, and in whom, in short, you will see no reason for my choosing; yet more, that this union is of long standing; that we have with us our child, of a year old, and that it is only lately I acquainted my family with the fact?

If you decide to meet with me as before, and wish to say something about the matter to your friends, it will be true to declare that there have been pecuniary reasons for this concealment. But *to you*, in confidence, I add, this is only half the truth; and I cannot explain, or satisfy my dear friend farther. I should wish to meet her independent of all relations, but, as we live in the midst of "society," she would have to inquire for me now as Margaret Ossoli. That being done, I should like to say nothing more on the subject.

However you may feel about all this, dear Madame Arconati, you will always be the same in my eyes. I earnestly wish you may not feel estranged; but, if you do, I would prefer that you should act upon it. Let us meet as friends, or not at all. In all events, I remain

> ever yours,
> Margaret [Memoirs, II, 314-15]

48. To Ellen Channing, December 11, 1849

Whatever their relations were earlier, there is evidence in 1849 of great tenderness between Fuller and her sister, both sorely tried mothers. In the month after she wrote this letter from Florence, Fuller was pained to learn that Ellen was to have another child by Ellery, who had fled during her last delivery. "Her courage in sustaining the consequences of her mistaken choice is truly admirable" (Houghton MS), she wrote to Arthur.

. . . You are anxious, my dear Ellen, to know some details of my past history and I should like to gratify you, but I hardly know how. There are some reasons which I cannot explain further than by the remark that Ossoli is still a member of the Roman Catholic church, why I do not go into all the matter of past history. I cannot, at least at present, tell exactly the facts, so I choose to say nothing. I should be glad if he disengaged himself entirely from the Roman ritual, but I doubt he ever will; his habitual attachment to it is strong, and I do not trouble myself about it as no priest has any influence over his mind.

About him, I do not like to say much, as he is an exceedingly delicate person. He is not precisely reserved, but it is not natural to him to *talk* about the objects of strong affection. I am sure he would not try to describe me to his sister, but would rather she would take her own impression of me, and, as much as possible, I wish to do the same by him. I expect that, to many of my friends Mr. Emerson for one, he will be nothing, and they will not understand that I should have life in common with him. But I do not think he will care; he has not the slightest tinge of self-love; he has, throughout our intercourse, been used to my having many such ties; he has no wish to be anything to persons with whom he does not feel spontaneously bound, and when I am occupied is happy in himself. But some of my friends and my family, who will see him in the details of practical life, cannot fail to prize the purity and simple strength of his character, and should he continue to love me as he has done, to consider his companionship will be an inestimable blessing to me. I say *if* because all human affections are frail, and I have experienced too great revulsions in my own not to know it, yet I feel great confidence in the permanence of his love. It has been unblemished so far, under many trials, especially as I have been more sick, desponding and unreasonable in many ways than I ever was before and more so, I hope, than I ever shall be again. But at all such times, he never had a thought except to sustain and cheer me; he is capable of the sacred love, the love passing that of women, he showed it to his father, to Rome, to me, now he loves his child in the same way. I think he will be an excellent father, though he could not speculate about it, or, in fact about anything.

Our meeting was singular, fateful I may say. Very soon he offered me his hand through life, but I never dreamed I should take it. I loved him and felt very unhappy to leave, but the connexion seemed so every way unfit, I did not hesitate a moment. He, however, thought I should return to him, as I did. I acted upon a strong impulse. I could not analyze at all what passed in my mind. I neither rejoice nor grieve, for bad or for good, I acted out my character. Had I never connected myself with any one my path was clear, now it is all hid, but in that case, my development must have been partial! As to marriage, I think the intercourse of heart and mind may be fully enjoyed without entering into this partnership of daily life, still I do not find it burdensome. We get along very well and I find have our better intercourse as much as if we did not buy (unhappily we have nothing to sell) together. The friction that I have seen mar so much the domestic happiness of others does not occur with us, or at least has not. Then there is the pleasure of always being at hand to help one another.

Still all this I had felt before in some degree. The great novelty, the immense gain to me is my relation with my child. I thought the mother's heart lived in me before, but it did not. I knew nothing about it. Yet before his birth I dreaded it. I thought I should not survive, but if I did and my child did, was I not cruel to bring another into this terrible world. I could not at that time get any other view. When he was born that deep melancholy changed at once into rapture, but it did not last long. Then came the prudential motherhood, then came Mrs. Edgworth, Mrs. Smith. I became a coward, a caretaker not only for the morrow but impiously faithless twenty or thirty years ahead. It seemed wicked to have brought the tender little thing into the midst of cares and perplexities we had not feared in the least for ourselves. I imagined everything: he was to be in danger of every enormity the Croats were then committing upon the babies of Lombardy. The house would be burned over his head, but if he escaped, how were we to get money to buy his bibs and primers. Then his father was to be killed in the fighting, and I to die of my cough. Your hazarding the opinion dear Ellen [tha]t it would have been best to tell Mother any part of [paper torn] till I arrived at some "clearing" however fruitless, and waterless, only shows the impossibility of judging for others in their great trials. I have borne Mother much love, and shown her some, and never more than by standing quite alone, in those strangely darkening days. I grieve she should have suffered now, but that is nothing in comparison with anxiety she might have been made to feel.

During the siege of Rome, I could not see my little boy. What I endured at that time in various ways not many would survive. In the burning sun, I went every day, to wait, in the crowd, for letters about him. Often they did not come. I saw blood that streamed on the wall where Ossoli was. I have a piece of bomb that burst close to him. I sought solace in tending the suffering men; but when I beheld the beautiful fair young men bleeding to death, or mutilated for life, I felt the wo of all the mothers who had nursed each to that full flower, to see it thus cut down. I felt the consolation, too for those youths died worthily. I was a Mater Dolorosa, and I remembered that the midwife who helped Angelino into the world came from the sign of the Mater Dolorosa. I thought, even if he lives, if he comes into the world at this great troubled time, terrible with perplexed duties, it may be to die thus at twenty years, one of a glorious hecatomb indeed, but still a sacrifice. It seemed then I was willing he should die. But when I really saw him lingering as he did all July and August between life and death, I could not let him go unless I could go with him.

When I saw his first smile, his poor wan feeble smile and more than four weeks we watched him night and day before we saw it, new resolution dawned in my heart. I resolved to live day by day and hour by hour for his dear sake and feed on ashes when offered. So if he is only treasure lent, if he must go as sweet Waldo did, as my little Pickie, as my children do, I shall at least have these days and hours with him. Now he is in the highest health and so gay — we cannot but feel happy in him, though the want of money is so serious a thing. . . .

. . . My love to dear Eliz[abet]h I wish she and Mr Emerson would write to me, but I suppose they dont know what to say. Tell them there is no need to say anything about these affairs if they dont want to. I am just the same for them I was before yr affec sister M. *[Houghton MS]*

49. To Marcus and Rebecca Spring, December 12, 1849

In a long letter she wrote in Florence to her Quaker friends, the Springs, Fuller tried to sort out her political ideas, to measure how far she had come from their pacifism and how close she could move toward American Fourierism. She also congratulated Marcus on initiating at home a public laundry like the one they had seen in London. At the end of this excerpt, she refers to a loan she had made impetuously in New York to Harro Harring, which even her fear of "the dragon of poverty" could not make her regret. She went on to refuse Marcus' offer of money, though she begged him to

"go to Wiley & Putnam and ask if all that stuff published as
my miscellanies is forever to be unprofitable as well as flat
and stale."

Dear Marcus & Rebecca,

. . . I have become a enthusiastic Socialist; elsewhere is no comfort, no
solution for the problems of the times. I rejoice in what you tell of
some successful practical study at the N[orth]. A[merican]. Phalanx. I
wish you had told more explicitly why you return to business in the
common way. Was it because you needed more money? or because a
truly congenial course was not yet clearly marked out for you? It is an
excellent thing you have done about that washing house. Blessed be he
who gets one such good thing done while the rest of us are only
blundering, observing, perhaps learning something. What you say is
deeply true about the peace way being the best. If any one see clearly
how to work in that way, let him in God's name. Only if he abstain
from fighting against giant wrongs let him be sure he is really once
ardently at work undermining them, or, better still sustaining the rights
that are to supplant them. Meanwhile I am not sure that I can keep my
hands free from blood. I doubt I have not the strength. Cobden is good,
but if he had stood in Kossuth's place, would he have not drawn his
sword against the Austrian? You, Marcus, could you let a Croat insult
Rebecca, carry off Eddie to be an Austrian serf; and leave little Marcus
bleeding in the dust? Yet it is true that while Moses slew the Egyptian,
Christ stood to be spit upon and that Death to man could do no harm.
You have the truth – you have the right – but could you act it,
Marcus, in all circumstances? Stifled under the Roman priesthood
would you not have thrown it off with all your force? Would you have
waited unknown centuries hoping the moment when you could use
another method? If so, you are a Christian; you know I never pretended
to be except in dabs and sparkles here and there. Yet the agonies of
that baptism of blood I felt, Oh how deeply in the golden June days of
Rome. Consistent no way, I felt I should have shrunk back, I could not
have had it shed. Christ did not have to see his dear ones pass the dark
river; he could go alone; however, in prophetic spirit no doubt, he
foresaw the crusades.

In answer to what you say of Harro, I wish indeed the little effort I
made for him had been wiselier applied. Yet these are not the things

one regrets. It does not do to calculate too closely with the affectionate human impulse; we must be content to make many mistakes, or we should move too slowly to help our brothers much. . . . *[Houghton MS copy]*

50. *To Caroline Sturgis Tappan, December 30, 1849*

Later that month, while gathering the force to face the future, Fuller wrote another long letter, now badly torn, to Carolyn Sturgis. She itemized the many kinds of division life held for her then: motherly pride and fear of spies, literary accomplishment and self-doubt, family outings and curses on the unsuspecting Austrians.

. . . I do not know what to write about [Angelino]: he changes so much, has so many characters. He is like me in that, his father's character is simple and uniform, though not monotonous, more than are the flowers of spring, flowers of the valley. He is now in the most perfect rosy health, a very gay, impetuous, ardent, but sweet tempered child. He seems to me to have nothing in common with the first baby with its ecstatic smiles, its exquisite sensitiveness, and a distinction in gesture and attitudes that struck everybody. His temperament seems changed by taking the milk of these robust women. His form is robust. . . .

I feel so refreshed by his young life. Ossoli diffuses such a power and sweetness over every day that I cannot endure to think yet of our future. Too much have we suffered already trying to command it. I do not feel force to make any effort yet. I suppose that very soon now I must do something. I hope I shall feel able when the time comes. I do not yet. My constitution seems making an effort to rally, by dint of much sleep. I had slept so little for a year and a half during the last months in pregnancy never an hour in peace after the baby's birth, such anxiety and anguish, when separated from him, I was consumed as by nightly fever. I constantly started up seeming to hear him call me. The last two months at Rome would have destroyed almost any woman. Then, when I went to him, he was so ill and I was constantly up with him at night, carrying him about, feeding him. At Perugia he began to get better. Then when we arrived here the Police [wanted] to send us away. It was as [much] as three weeks before we could [get] permis-

sion to stay. Now for two months we have been tranquil; we have
resolved to repose and enjoy being together as much as we can, in this
brief interval, perhaps all we shall ever know of peace. It is very sad we
have no money, we could be so quietly happy a while. I rejoice in all
Ossoli did but the results, in this our earthly state are disastrous,
especially as my strength is now so much impaired. This much I do
hope, in life or death, to be no more separated from Angelino.

Last winter I made the most vehement efforts at least to redeem
the time, hoping thus good for the future. But, of at least two volumes
written at that time, no line seems of any worth. I had suffered much
constraint, much that was uncongenial, harassing, even agonizing, but
this kind of pain found me unprepared. The position of a mother
separated from her only child is too frightfully unnatural. . . .

The Christmas holidays . . . interest me now through my child as
they never did for myself. I like to go out and watch the rising
generation who will be his contemporaries. On Sunday I went with the
Italian friend I mentioned [Arconati] in her carriage to the Cascine.
After we had taken the drive, we sat down on a stone seat in the sunny
walk to see the people pass; the Grand Duke and his children; the
elegant Austrian officers who will be driven out of Italy when Angelino
is a man; Princess Demidoff with her hussars; Harry Lorrequer and his
absurd brood; M. de Coaveilles who helped betray Rome; many lovely
children; many little frisking dogs with their bells. The sun shone
brightly on the Arno; a bark moved gently by. All seemed good to the
baby. He laid himself back in my arms, smiling, singing to himself,
dancing his feet. I hope he will retain some trace in his mind of the
perpetual exhilarating picture of Italy. . . .

Christmas day I was just up, and Nino all naked on his sofa, when
came some beautiful large toys that had been sent him: a bird, a horse,
a cat that could be moved to express different things. It almost made
me cry to see the kind of fearful rapture with which he regarded
them – legs and arms extended, fingers and toes quivering, mouth made
up to a little round O, eyes dilated. For a long time he did not even
wish to touch them. After he began to, he was different with all the
three: loving the bird; very wild and shouting with the horse; with the
cat, putting her face close to his, staring in her eyes, and then throwing
her away. Afterwards I drew him in a lottery, at a child's party given by
Mrs. Greenough, a toy of a child asleep on the neck of a tiger. The tiger
is stretching up to look at the child. This he likes best of any of his
toys. It is sweet to see him when he gets used to them and plays by

himself, whispering to them and seeming to contrive stories. You would laugh to know how much remorse I feel that I never gave children more toys in the course of my life. I regret all the money I ever spent on myself in little presents for grown people, hardened sinners. I did not know what pure delight could be bestowed. . . . *[Houghton MS]*

51. To William Henry Channing (?) [July 1849]

Although the passages below exist only in copies by another hand, the case for their authenticity is strong, as no one else in Fuller's circle would have voiced these views; only a few phrases from them have ever been published. No recipient is indicated, but the "dear William" was doubtless Channing. It appears that his candid inquiries about her marriage prompted the sharing of her most intimate thoughts. She expresses in the enigmatic second sentence her abandonment of her old ideal of perfect, even mystical, union and presents a new realistic commitment to a gratifying, if limited, relation. (The letter is postdated in still another hand, "July, 1849.")

a. What shall I say to you of his father? If earthly union be meant for the beginning of one permanent and full we ought not to be united, for the time was gone when I could more than *prefer* any man. Yet I shall never regret the step which has given me the experience of a mother and satisfied domestic wants in a most sincere and sweet companion.

Once you said to me in speaking of your two natures "Sometimes I feel as if would fain have been a violet, stilly growing in the precincts of the ancient forest." That is exactly true of him, my gentle friend, ignorant of great ideas, ignorant of books, enlightened as to his duties by pure sentiment and an unspoiled nature, but never failing in the degree that his nature has once promised.

The tie leaves me mentally free, as I wish him also to remain. I trust in the midst of a false world, we may be able to sustain some degree of truth, though indeed children involve one too deeply in this corrupt social contract and truth is easier to those who have not them. I however pined too much and was too suffocated without a child of my own. I say again I am not strong as we thought.

b. My love for Ossoli is most pure and tender, nor has anyone, except little children or mother, ever loved me as genuinely as he does. To you, dear William I was obliged to make myself known; others have loved me with a mixture of fancy and enthusiasm excited by my talent at embellishing subjects. He loves me from simple affinity; he loves to be with me, and serve and soothe me. Our relation covers only a part of my life, but I do not perceive that it interferes with anything I ought to have or be; I do not feel anyway constrained or limited or that I have made any sacrifice. Younger I might, because I should have been exposed to love some other in a way that might give him pain, but I do not feel apprehensive of that. There is more danger for him, as he is younger than I; if he should, I shall do all that this false state of society permits to give him what freedom he may need. I have thought a great deal about this; there are things I do not wish to put on paper. I daresay I shall tell them to you when we meet. You speak as if I might return to America without him. I thought of it at one time, knowing it would be very trying for him to go with me, that when I first am with my former friends, he may have many lonely hours. Beside he had then an employment in Rome and we needed the money. I thought I would go and either write for him to come for me, or return to Italy. But now that cannot be. He could not at present re-enter Rome without danger; he is separated from his employment and his natural friends, nor is any career open for him in Italy at present. Then I could not think of taking away the child for several months; his heart is fixed on the child as fervently as mine. Then it would not only be very strange and sad to me to be without his love and care for weeks and months, but I should feel very anxious about him under present circumstances. I trust we shall find means to make the voyage together and remain together. In our country he will have for resources, his walks and quiet communings with nature, which is always so great a part of his life; he will have the child, and I think my family, especially my mother, will love him very dearly and he will be learning the language with them. (I suppose I must myself be engaged in the old unhealthy [approximately three lines of manuscript are here cut out] she will not live to hear a great deal; and (it may be merely from a habit of feeling, formed in these past years of ill health) I cannot realize that I shall be here long either, though I feel perfectly willing now to stay my threescore years, if it be thought I need so much tuition from this planet. *[BPL MS copies]*

52. To Emelyn and William Story,
April 16 and May 10, 1850

On May 2, 1850, Fuller was making plans for leaving Italy. "I could have lived here always, full of bright visions, and expanding in my faculties, had destiny permitted," she wrote Lewis Cass, Jr., the U.S. Chargé d'Affaires in Rome (*Kindred Papers*, pp. 384-85). Realistic pessimism sets the tone of these letters to the Storys.

a. . . . There is a bark at Leghorn highly spoken of, which sails at the end of this month, we shall very likely take that. You ask me to pass the next year with you in Paris, how much I should have liked it, but I find it imperatively necessary to go to the U.S. if I want to have my arrangements made that may free me from care. Will I be more fortunate if I go in person? I do not know. I am ill adapted to push my claims and my pretensions; but, at least, it will not be such slow work passing from disappointment to disappointment as here, where I wait upon the post-office — wait two or three months to know the fate of any proposition. Enough! . . .

I go home prepared to expect all that is painful and difficult. It will be a consolation to see mother and my dear brother Eugene whom I have not seen for ten years hopes to come to New England this summer and on that account I wish to go *this* year. I had already heard from many quarters, dear E., of your letter to the Lowells, it had a very happy effect, & I was pleased that they particularly should take pains to show it as they did. I am glad to have people favorably impressed, because I feel lazy & weak, unlike the trouble of friction or the pain of conquest. Still I feel a good deal of contempt for those so easily disconcerted or reassured. I was not a child. I had lived in the midst of that blessed society in a way that entitled me to esteem and a favorable interpretation, where there was doubt about my motives or actions. I pity those who are inclined to think ill, when they might as well have inclined the other way. However let them go: there are many in the world who stand the test; enough to keep us from shivering to death. . . . *[Houghton MS]*

b. We are upon the move and my head full of boxes, bundles, pots of jelly and phials of medicine. I never thought much about a journey for

myself, except to try to return all the things, books especially, which I
had been borrowing but about my child I feel anxious lest I should not
take what is necessary for his health and comfort on this long a voyage,
where omissions are irreparable. The unpropitious (for after our
Siberian winter we have rain all the spring rain from 4th April up to this
10th May.) rainy weather delays us now from day to day, as our ship,
the "Elizabeth," (look out for news of shipwreck!) cannot finish taking
in her cargo till come one or two good days. . . .

I leave Italy with most sad and unsatisfied heart, hoping indeed, to
return, but fearing that may not in my "cross-biassed" life be permitted
till strength of feeling and keenness of perception be less than during
these bygone rich, if troubled, years. . . .

I reread the letter with shame, but really I cannot write to those
whom I prize most. I am so sad and weary, leaving Italy, that I seem
paralyzed. . . . To you may every Fate be propitious as you merit &
may we meet some day in more peace & amid as generous influences as
those of Rome. . . . *[Houghton MS copy]*

53. *To Marcus and Rebecca Spring, June 3, 1850*

In her farewell note to her close friend, Arconati, Fuller said
she should embark composedly, "praying, indeed fervently,
that it may not be my lot to lose my babe at sea, either by
unsolaced sickness, or amid the howling waves; or that, if I
should, it may be brief anguish, and Ossoli, he, and I go
together" (Emerson, Notebook on MFO). It was the sickness
that struck first after the little family set sail on May 17,
1850. Fuller's last letter, written on shipboard to the Springs,
who had brought her to Europe, was mailed at Gibraltar after
the death of the captain, Seth Hasty. Like most of her letters
of 1850, this was a conscious farewell.

Ship Elizabeth, off Gibraltar
. . . I had taken passage with Captain Hasty, one who seemed to me one
of the best and most high-minded of our American men. He showed the
kindest interest in me, his wife, an excellent woman, was with him – I
thought, during the voyage, if safe, and my child well, to have as much
respite from care and pain as sea-sickness would permit. But scarcely

was that enemy in some measure quelled, when the captain fell sick. At first his disease presented the appearance of nervous fever. I was with him a great deal; indeed, whenever I could relieve his wife from a ministry softened by great love and the courage of womanly heroism. The last days were truly terrible with disgusts and fatigues; for he died, we suppose (no physician has been allowed to come on board to see the body) of confluent small-pox. I have seen since we parted great suffering but nothing physical to be compared to this, where the once fair and expressive mould of man is thus lost in corruption before life has fled. He died yesterday morning, and was buried in deep water, the American Consul's barge towing out one from this ship which bore the body, about six o'clock. It was Sunday a divinely calm, soft, glowing afternoon had succeeded a morning of bleak, cold wind. You cannot think how beautiful the whole thing was – the decent array and sad reverence of the sailors; the many ships with their banners flying the stern pillar of Hercules all bathed in roseate vapor; the little angelwhite sails diving into the blue depths with that solemn spoil of the poor good man so still who had been so agonized and gasping as the last sun stooped. – Yes! it was beautiful but how dear a price we pay for the poems of this world! We shall now be in Quarantine a week, no person permitted to come on board till it is seen whether disease may break out in other cases. I have no good reason to think it will *not*; yet do not feel afraid. Ossoli has had it, so he is safe: the baby is of course subject to injury. In the earlier days before I suspected small-pox I carried him twice into the sick-room, at request of the captain, who was becoming fond of him. He laughed and pointed. He did not discern danger, but only thought it odd to see the old friend there in bed. It is vain by prudence to seek to evade the stern assaults of destiny. I submit. Should all end well, you see we shall be in New York later than we expected but keep a look-out. Should we arrive safe I should like to see a friendly face. Commend me to dear William and other of my dear friends; and Marcus, Rebeca, Eddie with most affectionate wishes that joy and peace may continue to dwell in your house adieu and love as you can

> your friend
> Margaret *[Houghton MS copy]*

CHRONOLOGY

1810 May 23, Sarah Margaret Fuller born at Cambridgeport, Massachusetts.

1818 Met Ellen Kilshaw, British visitor.

1824-25 Attended the Prescotts' school at Groton, Massachusetts.

1825-33 Lived in Cambridge; knew members of Harvard College class of 1829: William Henry Channing, James Freeman Clarke, George Davis; also Frederick Henry Hedge, Eliza Farrar, Anna Barker.

1833 Moved with family to farm at Groton; taught four youngest children: Ellen, Arthur, Richard, Lloyd; prepared to write life of Goethe.

1835 Summer, traveled with Farrars and Samuel Gray Ward to Trenton Falls, New York, and met Harriet Martineau; autumn, serious illness in Groton, may have caused spinal curvature; October 1, death of Timothy Fuller.

1836 First visited Emersons at Concord; began teaching at Bronson Alcott's Temple School.

1837 Joined Transcendental Club; became friendly with Caroline Sturgis; began two years of teaching at Greene Street School, Providence.

1839 Sold farm and moved to Jamaica Plain; published translation of *Eckermann's Conversations with Goethe* (Boston: Hilliard, Gray); initiated Conversation classes in Boston and Cambridge, which continued until 1844.

1840 July, began editing *The Dial* and continued until July 1842.

1841 April, Brook Farm opened.

1842 Published translation of *Correspondence of Fraulein Günderode with Bettina von Arnim* (Boston: Burnham).

1843 Traveled west with James and Sarah Clarke.

1844   Published *Summer on the Lakes in 1843* (Boston: Little and Brown); completed *Woman in the Nineteenth Century* at Fishkill, New York; December, moved to the Greeleys' home in New York and became literary critic and social reporter for *New York Tribune* continuing as journalist until 1849.

1845   Published *Woman in the Nineteenth Century* (New York: Tribune Press); met James Nathan.

1846   Published *Papers on Literature and Art* (New York: Wiley and Putnam); Spring, moved to Brooklyn Heights; August, sailed for Europe with Marcus and Rebecca Spring; traveled in England and Scotland; met Mazzini; autumn, went to Paris.

1847   Met Mickiewicz and Sand in Paris; visited Genoa and Naples before first stay in Rome in spring; met Angelo Ossoli and Costanza Arconati; summer, traveled in northern Italy and Switzerland; October, took rooms in Via del Corso, Rome, and became Ossoli's lover.

1848   January and March, uprisings in Italy; summer in Aquila and Rieti; September 5, Angelo Eugenio Filippo Ossoli born; November, took rooms on Piazza Barberini, Rome.

1849   February, Roman Republic proclaimed; March, visited son in Rieti; April through June, during seige of Rome by French, directed Hospital of the Fate Bene Fratelli; July, returned to Rieti; September, moved to Florence.

1850   May 17, sailed for America; July 19, died in shipwreck at Fire Island with Ossoli and child.

About The Feminist Press

The Feminist Press offers alternatives in education and in literature. Founded in 1970, this nonprofit, tax-exempt educational and publishing organization works to eliminate sexual stereotypes in books and schools, providing instead a new (or neglected) literature with a broader vision of human potential.

Our books—high quality paperbacks—include reprints of important works by women writers, feminist biographies of women, and nonsexist children's books.

The Clearinghouse on Women's Studies publishes resource guides, curricular materials, bibliographies, directories, and a newsletter, designed to provide information and support for women's studies at every educational level.

The Curriculum and Inservice Projects research sexism in the schools and explore ways to counter the effects of sex-role stereotyping. They develop supplementary materials for high school English and social studies classrooms, and work with teachers on new methods to help students become their best and freest selves.

Through this work we can begin to recreate the forgotten history of women, begin to create a more humane and eouitable society for the future. For a catalogue of all our publications, write to us. We hope that you will.

Reprints from The Feminist Press

The Woman and the Myth: Margaret Fuller's Life and Writings by Bell Gale Chevigny.

Portraits of Chinese Women in Revolution by Agnes Smedley. Edited with an introduction by Jan MacKinnon and Steve MacKinnon. With an afterword by Florence Howe.

The Yellow Wallpaper by Charlotte Perkins Gilman. With an afterword by Elaine Hedges.

Life in the Iron Mills by Rebecca Harding Davis. With a biographical inrpretation by Tillie Olsen.

Daughter of Earth by Agnes Smedley. With an afterword by Paul Lauter.

The Revolt of Mother and Other Stories by Mary E. Wilkins Freeman. With an afterword by Michele Clark.

The Storm and Other Stories (with *The Awakening*) by Kate Chopin. Edited with an introduction by Per Seyersted.